Anthony E. Henry · **Understanding Strategic Management**

Fourth Edition

D0861810

UNDERSTANDING STRATEGIC MANAGEMENT

Fourth Edition

Anthony E. Henry

Great Clarendon Street, Oxford, OX2 6DP,
United Kingdom

Oxford University Press is a department of the University of Oxford.
It furthers the University's objective of excellence in research, scholarship,
and education by publishing worldwide. Oxford is a registered trade mark of
Oxford University Press in the UK and in certain other countries

© Anthony E. Henry 2021

The moral rights of the author have been asserted

First edition 2007
Second edition 2011
Third edition 2018

Impression: 1

All rights reserved. No part of this publication may be reproduced, stored in
a retrieval system, or transmitted, in any form or by any means, without the
prior permission in writing of Oxford University Press, or as expressly permitted
by law, by licence or under terms agreed with the appropriate reprographics
rights organization. Enquiries concerning reproduction outside the scope of the
above should be sent to the Rights Department, Oxford University Press, at the
address above

You must not circulate this work in any other form
and you must impose this same condition on any acquirer

Published in the United States of America by Oxford University Press
198 Madison Avenue, New York, NY 10016, United States of America

British Library Cataloguing in Publication Data

Data available

Library of Congress Control Number: 2021932604

ISBN 978–0–19–885983–3

Printed in Great Britain by
Bell & Bain Ltd., Glasgow

Links to third party websites are provided by Oxford in good faith and
for information only. Oxford disclaims any responsibility for the materials
contained in any third party website referenced in this work.

'In all labour there is profit, but mere talk leads only to poverty.'
Proverbs 14:23

Brief Contents

Detailed Contents

PART ONE WHAT IS STRATEGY?

PART TWO STRATEGIC ANALYSIS

PART THREE STRATEGY FORMULATION

PART FOUR STRATEGY IMPLEMENTATION

List of Cases

Acknowledgements

First, I would like to thank my wife, Sue, for her patience and support, and for putting up with my long absences as I wrote another edition of this book. At Oxford University Press, I would like to thank my editor Elena So and all those involved with the publication of this book, as well as the reviewers who provided constructive comments.

About the Author

Anthony Henry worked as a Market Analyst for HSBC in central London before joining the university sector. He has experience working for public and private sector organizations, including Arthur Andersen. He has also counted traffic for a firm of transport consultants, worked in a soap factory, and delivered strategy workshops in the UK and Germany to managers in a FTSE-100 organization. He has worked as a Senior Lecturer in Strategic Management. Anthony currently delivers strategy to MBA and undergraduate students at Aston University's Business School. He also delivers consultancy workshops in strategy.

About the Book

The fourth edition of *Understanding Strategic Management* continues to help students understand strategy by clearly explaining strategy concepts, before analyzing and evaluating them to show how these are applied in the business world. This approach encourages students to think critically rather than simply describing strategic concepts, models, and frameworks. We continue the pursuit of *competitive advantage* as a key theme throughout the book. That said, there is a recognition that disruptive markets may ensure that any competitive advantage achieved by an organization is only temporary.

Each chapter provides clearly written and practical discussions of the strategy concepts students encounter. The use of analysis, formulation, and implementation provides students with a structure to understand the subject of strategic management while making it clear the business world has a tendency to differ from neat, academic theories. Each chapter includes relevant business examples to facilitate student understanding. Chapter 2 updates include a discussion of digital strategy including big data, artificial intelligence, the Internet of Things, and cloud computing. Chapter 4 has been revised to include an evaluation of whether organizations should be run for the benefit of shareholders or meet the needs of stakeholders. Chapter 6 includes a more comprehensive discussion and application of blue ocean strategy, while Chapter 7 updates corporate parenting. Organizational culture is updated in Chapter 10. And Chapter 11 includes a discussion of corporate social responsibility (CSR) and its benefit to organizations.

The majority of Case Study and Strategy in Focus features are written by the author to provide students with a seamless transition from discussion to application. Additional questions have been added to many case studies to help student learning and understanding. The lengths of some case studies have been extended to help students understand concepts covered in the main text. The Strategy in Focus business examples have been updated to help the reader further apply theory to practice. At the end of each chapter many of the review questions have been changed to facilitate student learning. In addition, Research Topics and Discussion Questions have been updated. This fourth edition is comprehensive enough to allow a detailed study of strategic management while its eleven chapters facilitate shorter courses without sacrificing important strategy content. Guidance on how to use this book and online resources is available to students in the next section.

Anthony E. Henry
May 2021

How to Use this Book

Learning objectives

Clear, concise learning objectives outline the main concepts and themes to be covered within the chapter. These lists will help you review your learning and effectively plan revision, ensuring you have considered all key areas.

Learning Objectives

After completing this chapter you should be able to:

- Explain the trade-off between specialization and coordination
- Discuss the advantages and disadvantages of different organizational structure
- Discuss organizational processes
- Explain the purpose of strategic control systems for organizations
- Evaluate different types of strategic change

Strategy in Focus boxes

Learn from real-life situations in the business world with these short illustrations taken from a range of contemporary news sources, demonstrating how vital effective strategic management is to any business.

STRATEGY IN FOCUS 3.1 The Threat of New Entrants: Amazon

Amazon will offer free grocery deliveries to Prime members across the UK by the end of the year, threatening efforts by supermarkets to profit from the boom in online shopping during the pandemic. Amazon's Fresh service was previously available to Prime members for an additional monthly charge and was limited to roughly 300 postcodes in mostly affluent areas of London and the south-east.

But the company said on Tuesday it would scrap the extra charge and expand Amazon Fresh 'to millions of Prime members across the UK before the end of the year'. That would pose a far more serious challenge to incumbents, Tesco, Sainsbury's, Asda, and Morrisons. Nick Carroll, associate director at market researcher Mintel, said Amazon currently had just 3 per cent of the UK online grocery market, compared with Ocado's 14 per cent and Tesco's more than 30 per cent. 'But they could become a significant player given their scale, and they could put a lot of pressure on pricing,' he said. 'For them, it will be market share first and profit later.'

Natalie Berg, founder of consultancy NBK Retail said the company was 'hitting the nuclear button'. 'It is one of the boldest moves they have ever made, the Covid pandemic has presented them with an opportunity to tighten their grip on ecommerce,' she added. 'They are using the

Case Studies

Applying the theoretical ideas from the chapter to a variety of business situations, these extensive Case Studies, with accompanying questions, encourage you to identify how strategy works in a variety of international, wide-ranging, and relevant business situations.

CASE STUDY Ryanair: How to Compete in the Airline Industry

Background

It may surprise many people to know that Ryanair is Europe's favourite airline. The low cost airline carries 149 million passengers every year on more than 2,500 daily flights. It flies from seventy-nine bases, connecting more than 240 destinations, in forty countries. It has more than 17,000 employees and an industry-leading thirty-five year safety record. Ryanair was founded in Ireland in 1985, initially operating daily from Waterford in the southeast of Ireland to London Gatwick. By 1990 the

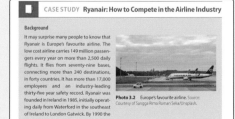

Photo 3.2 Europe's favourite airline. Source: Courtesy of Sangga Rima Roman Selia/Unsplash.

Extension Material signposts

If your course goes into extra depth on a specific topic or you want more examples and discussion to aid your understanding, follow the relevant signposts to Extension Material available online for additional coverage that builds seamlessly on the book.

For more examples and discussion to aid your understanding of this chapter, please visit the online resources and see the Extension Material for this chapter.

Working through Strategy signposts

To help you get a firmer handle on the essential tools of analysis, the Working through Strategy resources, available online, are signposted wherever additional coverage and examples of analytical tools and techniques are provided to further your understanding.

www.oup.com/he/henry4e
Visit the online resources that accompany this book for activities and more information on strategy.
Test your knowledge and understanding of this chapter further by trying the multiple-choice questions online.

Review and discussion questions

Reinforce your learning, aid your revision, and share ideas with these end-of-chapter review and discussion questions covering the main themes and issues raised in the chapter.

Review Questions

1. What are the five forces and how are they used to analyse an industry?
2. Explain how the value net and complementors help organizations understand how to add value for customers.
3. How does strategic group analysis enable a company to understand its competitors?

Discussion Question

'The effect of government policy on industry structure is too pervasive to consider government as a *sixth* competitive force.' *Discuss*.

Research topics

Take your learning further and practise your researching skills with these stimulating starting points for focused research on a specific topic or issue related to the chapter.

Research Topic

Use strategic groups to analyse the financial services industry, paying particular attention to what mobility barriers exist, and the trends that are changing this industry.

Recommended Reading

For a discussion of the five forces framework and strategic groups see:

- **M. E. Porter**, *Competitive Strategy: Techniques for Analysing Industries and Competitors*, Free Press, 1980.

For an insight into the need for organizations to cooperate as well as compete with players in their competitive environment, see:

- **A. Brandenburger** and **B. J. Nalebuff**, *Co-opetition*, Currency Doubleday, 1996.

An informative read on the use of game theory for strategy formulation is:

- **A. Brandenburger** and **B. J. Nalebuff**, 'The right game: use game theory to shape strategy', *Harvard Business Review*, vol. 73, no. 4 (1995), pp. 57–71.

For a discussion of hypercompetition, see:

- **R. A.D'Aveni**, *Hypercompetition: Managing the Dynamics of Strategic Manoeuvring*, Free Press, 1994.

Recommended reading

Seminal books and journal articles that have contributed to the field of strategic management are provided in an annotated list at the end of chapters, offering the opportunity to read around a particular topic, broaden your understanding, or provide useful leads for coursework and assignments.

Glossary

A

Acceptability – relates to the response of stakeholders to the proposed strategy.

Acquisition – when one organization seeks to acquire another, often smaller, organization.

Adaptive learning – the ability to cope with changes in one's environment.

Agency costs – the costs resulting from managers abusing their position as agent, and the associated costs of monitoring them to try to prevent this abuse.

Benchmarking – a continuous process of measuring products, services, and business practices against those companies recognized [as] industry leaders.

BHAGs – big hairy audacious goals: goals that stretch the organization and are readily communicated to all its members.

Big bang disruption – a change in industry dynamics in which not only the least profitable customers are lured away, but consumers in ev[ery] segment defect simultaneously.

Big data – extremely large data sets that may [be]

Glossary

A comprehensive glossary is provided at the end of the book to check your understanding of key terms.

How to Use the Online Resources

This book is accompanied by a bespoke package of online resources that are carefully integrated with the text to assist the learning and teaching of the subject. Students can benefit from extension material, multiple-choice questions, web links, and exercises, while lecturers can make use of a question test bank, suggested answers to questions in the book, and PowerPoint lecture slides.

Go to www.oup.com/he/henry4e to find out more.

OUP would like to thank Dr Omar F. Al-Tabbaa, Senior Lecturer in Strategy and International Business and Programme Director for M.Sc. International Business & Management at the University of Kent, for his contribution in updating and providing new material for the online resources.

PART ONE
WHAT IS
STRATEGY?

CHAPTER 1
WHAT IS STRATEGY?

 Learning Objectives

After completing this chapter, you should be able to:

- Explain what is meant by strategy
- Discuss the role of values, vision, and mission statements in facilitating strategy
- Discuss the development of strategic management
- Critically evaluate different perspectives on strategy formulation
- Develop and explain a strategic management framework

Introduction

What is **strategy**? How is strategy formulated and implemented? Are values important in determining which **markets** organizations seek to compete in? These are some of the questions that will be discussed in this first chapter. We start the chapter with a discussion of what is strategy. There is general agreement that the role of strategy is to help organizations achieve a **competitive advantage**. Where this consensus begins to break down is when we discuss *how* competitive advantage is achieved. In order to define strategy, we need to review different perspectives and the views of their adherents.

This chapter also looks at the co-dependent relationship between strategy analysis, formulation, and implementation. We note that separating these elements may be useful for exposition but has limitations when seeking to explain strategy in practice. The role of an organization's **values**, **vision**, and **mission** is explained as we discuss their importance in setting strategic goals. We also consider an organization's assumptions about its competitive environment—what Peter Drucker refers to as the **theory of the business**—and discuss how this can lead to organizational failure.[1] We conclude the chapter by developing a strategic management framework, which is a useful process in the search for competitive advantage. The framework is also helpful for navigating subsequent chapters.

1.1 **What Is Strategy?**

The use of strategy has existed for many centuries, although its use in **management** has a more recent history, dating back about sixty years. Strategy was born out of military conflicts and the use of a superior strategy enabled one warring party to defeat another. **Carl von Clausewitz**, writing in the nineteenth century, states that the decision to wage war ought to be *rational*—that is, based on estimates of what can be gained and the costs incurred by the war.[2] War should also be *instrumental*—that is, waged to achieve some specific goal, never for its own sake—and strategy should be directed to achieve one end: victory. While policy makers may be unsure about what they expect from modern military engagements, military personnel from commanders down to foot soldiers have only one question: what is our objective in committing to a particular course of action? If the objective is unclear, they can expect the formulation of strategy to be confused and its implementation to be unsuccessful.

In *The Art of War*, the Chinese philosopher and military strategist **Sun Tzu** wrote: '*the one who figures on victory at headquarters before even doing battle is the one who has the most strategic factors on his side. The one who figures on inability to prevail at headquarters before doing battle is the one with the least strategic factors on his side ... Observing the matter in this way I can see who will win and who will lose*'. Sun Tzu believed strategic advantage was on the side of the leader who believed he could win before he even left headquarters.[3] A good strategy can defeat overwhelming obstacles. When Admiral Nelson engaged the French and Spanish fleet off the coast of Spain in 1805, he was outnumbered by their thirty-three ships to his twenty-seven.[4] The standard rules of engagement at that time was for opposing ships to do battle in parallel formation. Each ship would fire broadsides at its opposite number. However, Nelson had other ideas. He divided the British fleet into two columns and sailed them at the line formed by the Franco-Spanish fleet, in order to engage them at right angles. Nelson surmised that the inexperience of the Franco-Spanish gunners would prevent them from being able to deal with the great swell, while the experience of his own captains would enable them to take advantage of the situation. The Franco-Spanish fleet lost twenty-two ships; the British lost none. Nelson correctly identified the crucial issues in this particular battle which allowed the actions of his fleet to be multiplied. The Battle of Trafalgar was Britain's greatest naval battle.

We need to exercise caution in drawing military analogies. Unlike war, in the modern business arena organizations are increasingly aware of the benefits of cooperation as well as competition. There is agreement that the role of strategy is to achieve *competitive advantage* for an organization. **Competitive advantage** is the configuration of an organization's activities which enable it to meet consumer needs better than its rivals. It derives from the discrete activities that a company performs when it designs, produces, markets, delivers, and supports its product or service. If a competitive advantage is to be sustainable, however, the advantage must be difficult for competitors to imitate. As **Bruce Henderson** points out, '*Your most dangerous competitors are those that are most like you.*' Why? Because '*the differences between you and your competitors are the basis of your advantage*'.[5]

The use of strategy is the primary way in which managers take account of a constantly changing environment. An effective strategy allows managers to use the organization's capabilities to exploit opportunities and limit threats in the environment. A debate arises when we try to pin down *what is strategy* and, importantly, *how is strategy formulated*. This discussion has continued unabated for decades and is rooted in a desire for managers to undertake better strategic thinking and therefore better strategic decisions. Strategy can be defined in a number of different ways. However, we should be aware that any definition is likely to be rooted within the different perspectives adopted by its adherents. For this reason, a definition of strategy which is accepted by everyone is not as straightforward as might first appear. That said, we offer a definition below before considering some different perspectives.

1.2 **Defining Strategy**

Strategy is '*the taking of decisions which allow an organisation to achieve a sustainable competitive advantage over the long term*'. The '*taking of decisions*' implies an intent, a desire to undertake some purposeful action in order to achieve a stated objective. In this case, we can see that the objective is to meet customer needs better than our competitors—that is, achieve a '*competitive advantage*'. And, unlike managerial or operational decisions, which focus on short-term horizons, strategy is concerned with the '*long term*'. Of course, 'long term' is relative to the industry we're competing in: for the fashion industry it may be three to six months, while for the oil industry it may be more than ten years. Finally, we might also add that if a strategy is to have any value to the company we would expect the customer benefits to exist over time and not be easily imitated by our competitors, hence '*sustainable*'.

Having defined strategy, we can now highlight and explain some of the different perspectives that exist among different strategists. In an article entitled 'What is strategy?', Harvard professor, **Michael Porter**, asserts that '*competitive strategy is about being different. It means deliberately choosing a different set of activities to deliver a unique mix of value*.'[6] All companies incur costs as a result of the many activities they undertake in order to be able to design, manufacture, market, and distribute their products or services to consumers. It is these activities which form the basis of competitive advantage.[7] A company can only outperform its competitors when the value it provides to the consumer is difficult for them to imitate. This occurs when: **(1)** the company provides a differentiated product or service which is more highly valued by customers, enabling it to charge a premium price; or **(2)** the company provides products or services with the same quality as a competitor offering, but charges a lower price. In other words, it acquires a cost advantage by undertaking certain activities more efficiently than its competitors. This, in turn, allows the company to charge a lower price. In this way, a company can achieve success by choosing a strategic position which differs from the competitors in its **industry**. Porter's competitive strategy is discussed in detail in **Chapters 3** and **6**.

Constantinos Markides argues that the essence of strategy is for an organization to select one strategic position that it can claim as its own.[8] A strategic position represents a company's answers to the following questions:

- *Who* should the company target as customers?
- *What* products or services should the company offer the targeted customers?
- *How* can the company do this efficiently?

John Kay views the strategy of an organization as '*the match between its internal capabilities and its external relationships*'. That is, a company's strategy describes the match between what it is particularly good at doing and its relationship with its customers, suppliers, and competitors.[9] This is because organizations are part of a network of relationships. To succeed, they must deal with customers and suppliers, with their competitors and potential competitors. These relationships may be contractual—based on precise, legal documentation—or they may be relational—that is, based on the need the parties have to continue doing business together. It is the unique structure of these relationships, which Kay refers to as architecture, which can be a source of a company's competitive advantage. We discuss the links between an organization's internal capabilities and its external environment in **Chapter 5**, when we evaluate the resource-based view of strategy.

If strategy is construed as the relationship between an organization and its environment, then it can be disaggregated from operational management issues. For example, strategy is not primarily concerned with every aspect of business behaviour such as employee motivation, accounting, and inventory control. That's not to say these cannot influence the strategy or be influenced by the strategy. It is the difference between these elements of management and strategy which helps explain the nature of strategy. Many organizations in an industry may possess good quality human resources, effective accounting practices, and technology suited to their needs. But this is not a strategy. When one organization succeeds in these endeavours it is not detrimental to others. Other organizations can simply copy best practice in the industry. In contrast to strategic management, operational management is about performing *similar activities* better than your competitors. It includes tools such as total quality management, benchmarking, outsourcing, and business process re-engineering. It is primarily a search for efficiency, but includes any practice that allows a company to utilize its inputs more effectively. For example, this might be developing better products faster than your competitors.

However, when we seek to understand strategy, we see it is different. For example, the success of BMW and Honda is based on their ability to recognize their **distinctive capabilities**, what each company can do better than other organizations, and compete in the markets which exploit these capabilities. They do not build on the best practice of their competitors. In fact, when they tried to copy their competitors they failed. Therefore, successful strategy is based on doing well what your competitors cannot do or cannot easily do. It is seldom based on what your competitors can do or are already doing. An effective strategy will be adaptive and opportunistic; this is not to imply anything vague and unfocused. On the contrary, strategy is about a company using analytical techniques to help it understand, and therefore influence, its position in the market.

1.2.1 Using Strategy to Overcome Challenges

Richard Rumelt argues that, over time, strategy has become confused by researchers, consultants, chief executive officers (CEOs), and just about anybody, equating it to mean whatever they want. The concept 'strategy' is erroneously equated with success, determination, ambition, inspirational **leadership**, and innovation. Rumelt believes strategy is more than just urging an organization forward towards a goal or vision. A strategy should honestly acknowledge the challenges being faced by an organization. A strategy should also provide an approach to overcome these challenges. As such, strategy is about discovering the critical factors in a situation and providing a way to coordinate and focus action to deal with these factors. In his book, *Good Strategy Bad Strategy*, he describes a good strategy as having an essential logical structure, which he calls a *kernel*.[10] The kernel of a strategy contains three elements: a *diagnosis*, a *guiding policy*, and a *coherent set of actions* (see **Table 1.1**).

1. Diagnosis

A diagnosis defines or explains the nature of the challenge which faces the organization. The purpose of a diagnosis is to simplify the complexity of the situation facing the organization. This is done by identifying which aspects of the situation are critical. An insightful diagnosis can transform a manager's view of the situation. It might classify the situation according to a certain pattern; this then guides managers to think how a similar pattern was handled by the organization in the past.

2. Guiding Policy

This outlines an overall approach for dealing with the obstacles identified in the diagnosis. It is a guiding policy because it directs management action in certain directions, but does not tell them exactly what they should do. Good guiding policies define a method by which managers can grapple with the situation and rule out numerous other possible actions.

3. Coherent Action

Strategy is about action; in order to be effective, it must be achieving something. Therefore, a set of coherent actions is necessary to carry out the guiding policy. It is not necessary to know all the actions that are to be undertaken as the events unfold. What is needed is sufficient clarity on what actions are required to focus the organization's attention. These actions are the steps which are coordinated to work together to accomplish the guiding policy. In reality, many organizations try to avoid making the difficult choices that emanate from strategy, but this only results in inaction.

Table 1.1 How to tackle the challenges faced by organizations.

When people in an organization engage in diagnosis, what initially appears as an overwhelming complex reality is replaced by a simpler story. This simplified reality allows you to make sense of the challenges and draws your attention to the crucial aspects that need to be dealt with. The end result is a *good strategy* which helps leaders to define what type of action is required.

An organization is faced with a constantly changing environment and needs to ensure that its internal resources and capabilities are more than sufficient to meet the needs of the environment. Organizations do not exist simply to survive in the marketplace; they want to grow and prosper in a competitive environment. In order to make sense of what is going on around them, managers must analyse the capabilities that reside inside their organization, and analyse the needs of the external environment. An organization's environment comprises the **macro-environment** and the **competitive environment**. The macro-environment consists of factors which may *not* have an immediate impact on the organization, but have the capacity to change the industry in which it competes, and even to create new industries. The competitive environment deals with the industry in which the organization competes. The changes taking place within an organization's competitive environment, such as an increase in the number of competitors, will have a far more immediate impact on the organization.

We cover tools for analysing the macro-environment and the competitive environment in detail in **Chapters 2** and **3**. In **Chapters 4** and **5**, we consider different ways of analysing the organization.

1.3 **Types of Strategy**

There are three basic forms of strategy which interest organizations: corporate strategy, business strategy, and functional or operational strategy. In reality, most organizations are concerned with business strategy and corporate strategy.

1.3.1 **Corporate Strategy**

Corporate strategy is concerned with the broader issue of which industries the organization wants to compete in. Corporate strategy deals with **mergers** and **acquisitions** and the allocation of resources between the organization's **strategic business units** (SBUs). A strategic business unit is a distinct part of an organization, which focuses upon a particular market or markets for its products and services. Unilever's takeover of Dollar Shave Club is part of its corporate strategy of moving into the market for razor blades, where it had no presence. Intel's move away from memory chips and into microprocessors was corporate strategy. Corporate strategy is often the responsibility of the most senior management within an organization, and is dealt with in **Chapter 7**.

1.3.2 **Business Strategy**

Business strategy, sometimes called competitive strategy, deals with how an organization is going to compete within a particular industry or market. It is concerned with how the organization will achieve a competitive advantage over its rivals. In contrast to corporate strategies, managers of SBUs are usually given substantial autonomy to formulate business strategies. Business strategy is dealt with in **Chapter 3**, when we assess industry analysis, and **Chapter 6**.

1.3.3 **Functional or Operational Strategy**

This deals with decisions according to functional lines such as research and development (R&D), marketing, and finance. These functions will be involved in the support of the business strategy. Sometimes this is referred to as operational strategy. Porter argues that operational strategy is a misnomer because it simply means managers taking decisions to implement business strategy. A more appropriate term would be operational management. Therefore, we will subsume this within business strategy in our discussions.

Figure 1.1 The different types of strategy

1.4 **Strategic Management**

A strategy allows an organization to configure its resources and capabilities to meet the needs of the environment to achieve competitive advantage. The process of undertaking a strategy is strategic management. All organizations set objectives or goals they want to achieve. Strategic management is about analysing the situation facing the organization. This analysis will allow managers to formulate strategies for dealing with the situation or challenge facing the company. The analysis will invariably produce more than one strategy that can be adopted. Therefore, managers are faced with

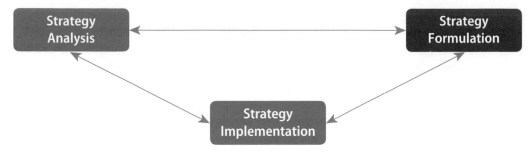

Figure 1.2   The interdependent relationship of analysis, formulation, and implementation.

a choice of which strategy they decide to implement. The end result is for the organization to achieve competitive advantage over its rivals in the industry.

A point worth noting is that these elements are co-dependent; that is, in formulating a strategy an organization must also consider how that strategy will be implemented. Failure to consider the co-ordination of strategy will decrease the likelihood of success. We might also note that a neat sequential pattern may not resemble how a given organization might undertake strategic management. **Figure 1.2** illustrates the interdependent relationship between analysis, formulation, and implementation. It is often said that analysis is easy; implementation is the difficult part. However, such thinking fails to realize the importance of analysis in understanding the challenges facing the organization. Analysis, formulation, and implementation all need to be considered if the organization's strategy is to meet the needs of its environment effectively. And, as we shall see later, a strategy must also meet the needs of its stakeholders.

1.4.1 **Strategy Analysis**

While bearing in mind that the strategic management process is co-dependent, the undertaking of strategy analysis by the organization is a useful starting point. Strategic analysis deals with the organization; it allows managers to evaluate how well the company is positioned to exploit opportunities and mitigate threats. As we shall see in **Chapters 2** and **3**, this also involves an analysis of the macro-environment and the industry.

Some organizations might actually implement a strategy without fully analysing their current situation. This may be because events in their hypercompetitive industry are changing so fast that they feel they simply do not have the luxury of undertaking detailed analysis. An organization's leader might take a series of decisions based on experience or intuition. In reality, without the use of some analysis, managers will never know why a strategy succeeds and what they can learn from this. They will not fully understand how it meets the industry's *key success factors*. **Key success factors** are the elements in the industry that keep customers loyal and allow the organization to compete successfully. By analysing what consumers want and the basis of competition in the industry, an organization is able to ascertain the key success factors for its industry. For instance, it might ask: which elements of its resources and capabilities brought it success? What was the role played by its internal structure and **organizational culture**? What factors drive competition in this industry? In short, without analysis, its success will likely be short-lived and difficult to repeat. See **Case Study: Intel's Theory of the Business** at the end of this chapter.

1.4.2 **Strategy Formulation**

A careful analysis of the organization and the needs of the environment will allow managers to assess where they can best achieve a strategic fit between the two. Without some form of analysis, decisions can only be based on experience. Experience alone may have been fine in the stable industries of the past, but in today's dynamic environments, managers cannot expect to follow today's patterns tomorrow. Analysis and strategic intent are all well and good, but **Henry Mintzberg** reminds us that strategy formulation also occurs as a creative and, at times, subconscious act which synthesizes experiences to form a novel strategy.[11] We will allude to more of Mintzberg's research later in this chapter. Similarly, **Kenichi Ohmae** accepts that strategic thinking starts with analysis, but stresses creative insight in the formulating of great strategies. For Ohmae, such insight does not form part of any conscious analysis.[12]

Markides argues that effective strategy formulation is a process of continuously asking questions. In this process, how a question is formulated can be more important than finding a solution.[13] Ohmae makes a similar point. He states that a vital part of strategic thinking is to formulate questions in a way that will help find a solution. A key part of strategy formulation is strategy evaluation which recognizes that an organization is seldom faced with one strategy, but requires a criterion to judge competing strategies.[14] Rumelt contends that the essential difficulty in creating strategy is 'choice'. This is because strategy does not eliminate scarcity, and a consequence of scarcity is you have to make a choice.[15] A common reason for poor strategy is that leaders are unwilling, or unable, to make the necessary choices between competing groups in their organizations and the different solutions on offer.

Strategy formulation primarily takes place at two different levels within the organization: the *business level* and the *corporate level*. Business and corporate strategies are addressed in detail in **Chapters 6** and **7**. For now, we can say that **corporate strategy** deals with the fundamental question of *what* markets the company wants to compete in, whereas **business strategy** deals with *how* a company competes in its chosen markets.

1.4.3 **Strategy Implementation**

The best-formulated strategy will amount to nothing if it is poorly communicated and coordinated throughout the organization. Effective implementation of strategies requires the organization to be sufficiently flexible in its **organizational structure** and design. Strategies need to be communicated, understood, and properly coordinated with stakeholders inside and outside the organization. **Stakeholders** are those individuals and groups upon whom the organization depends to achieve its objectives. Stakeholders, in turn, have an interest in and can influence the success of the organization. They include customers, suppliers, shareholders, employees, the local community, etc. In an age of collaboration, this may involve discussions with key suppliers and partners. Although the leader of an organization will ultimately be responsible for a strategy's success or failure, their role should be to encourage and create an organizational culture which empowers managers to respond to opportunities. In this way, each employee will be confident to try out new ideas and innovate without fear of reprisals. The values of an organization will be important here. We discuss culture in **Chapter 8**.

At a fundamental level we can ask: what is the purpose or mission of any organization? Why does it exist? These questions are relevant irrespective of whether an organization operates in the private, public, or voluntary sector. This is because all organizations must have a clear sense of direction if managers are to understand what they are seeking to achieve. For example, organizations in the private sector may seek to maximize returns to **shareholders**, or some form of sustainable investment, and organizations in the public sector may want to utilize their resources in a sustainable manner. Often the words *purpose* and *goals* are used interchangeably, but this misses an important distinction between the two: the goals or objectives that leaders set derive from a company's **purpose**. The purpose is the reason an organization exists. This will become more clear as we look at the purpose of organizations and how this guides their strategy.

1.5 Values, Vision, and Mission

The formulation of strategy does not occur in a vacuum but relies upon the values, vision and mission of the organization. These are the foundations on which a strategy is built. We can address each of these in turn.

1.5.1 Values

One of the most important drivers of an organization's strategy is its values. The values of an organization will determine the kind of industries and markets it will and will not compete in. The type of products and services it wants to produce, the goals it sets for itself, how it treats its stakeholders, and, importantly, how it will respond in a crisis. The values of the organization are also helpful in signposting to potential employees whether or not this is the sort of company they would want to work for.

In their quest for what makes a visionary organization, **Jim Collins** and **Jerry Porras** refer to *core values* and *purpose*.[16] The **core values** are an organization's essential and enduring beliefs, which will not be compromised for financial expediency and short-term gains. An organization's purpose (or mission) represents the reasons an organization exists beyond making a profit. The values of an organization do not shift as competitive conditions change, but remain largely inviolate. They are what members are expected to endorse and internalize as part of working for such organizations. More than that, they are what attracts individuals to these types of organizations in the first place. IBM's former chief executive officer, Thomas J. Watson Jr, stated that for any organization to survive and achieve success, it must have a set of beliefs on which all its policies and actions are based. '*The most important, single factor in corporate success is faithful adherence to those beliefs.*'[17]

A similar point was made by the founder of Johnson & Johnson, Robert Wood Johnson, when he wrote the organization's *credo* or set of beliefs in 1943. Unusually for this time, Johnson explicitly recognized the importance of meeting stakeholder needs. Stakeholders, as we noted, are those individuals and groups upon whom the organization depends to achieve its objectives. Johnson believed that service to customers should always come first, service to the organization's employees and management should be second, the local community third, and last should be service to shareholders. Johnson recognized that shareholders will receive a *fair return* only when the preceding elements are aligned. See **Strategy in Focus 1.1**, which illustrates how Johnson & Johnson's values guided their executive management decisions some forty years later when they were faced with a crisis.

Johnson & Johnson provides a classic example of how an organization's values guide its behaviour. This example demonstrates the importance of values in guiding how an organization decides and

STRATEGY IN FOCUS 1.1 Organizational Values at Johnson & Johnson: How their *Credo* Guides Strategy

General Robert Wood Johnson guided Johnson & Johnson from a small, family-owned business to a worldwide enterprise. In doing so he had an enlightened view of a corporation's responsibilities beyond the manufacturing and marketing of products. In 1935, in a pamphlet titled *Try Reality*, he urged his fellow industrialists to embrace 'a new industrial philosophy'. Johnson defined this as the corporation's responsibility to customers, employees, the community, and stockholders.

Eight years later, in 1943, Johnson wrote and first published the Johnson & Johnson *Credo*, a one-page document outlining these responsibilities in greater detail. Putting customers first and stockholders last was a refreshing approach to the management of a business. However, Johnson was a practical businessman. He believed that by putting the customer first the business would be well served, and it was. Johnson saw to it that his company embraced the *Credo*, and he urged his management to apply it as part of their everyday business philosophy.

In 1982, Johnson & Johnson faced a crisis. A drug, Tylenol, from one of its operating companies, was altered and cyanide placed in the capsule form of the product. This resulted in seven deaths. Johnson & Johnson's strategic response was inspired by the philosophy embodied in the *Credo*. The product was voluntarily recalled and destroyed, even though testing found the remaining capsules to be safe. Johnson & Johnson took a $100 million charge against earnings.

General Robert Wood Johnson: the man who guided Johnson & Johnson from a small, family-owned business to a worldwide enterprise.
Source: © Kesäperuna/Wikimedia Commons.

In 1986, as a result of a second tampering incident and another fatality, Johnson & Johnson took the decision to discontinue the sale of Tylenol in capsule form. The operating company reintroduced Tylenol in tamper-proof packaging and regained its leading share of the analgesic market. Faced with the loss of millions of dollars, the values that are embodied in Johnson & Johnson's *Credo* guided its strategic response and ensured that its quick and honest handling of the crisis preserved the company's reputation.

When Robert Wood Johnson wrote and then institutionalized the *Credo* within Johnson & Johnson, he never suggested that it guaranteed perfection. But its principles have become a constant goal, as well as a source of inspiration, for all who are part of the Johnson & Johnson Family of Companies.

Source: Adapted from http://www.johnson&johnson.com

implements its strategy. It is the values of an organization which form and shape the corporate culture over time. This, in turn, provides a signpost for what is acceptable behaviour. For example, as organizations continue to outsource activities overseas in search of cheaper manufacturing, they must ensure that employee conditions conform to their own organizational values. The use of child labour in some countries has forced organizations to face up to a credibility gap between their rhetoric and their deeds. The more robust the values in an organization are, the greater the clarity this provides for setting goals and therefore strategic direction and action. The more ambiguous the values within an organization are, the greater the opportunity for conflicting goals and for decisions to go unchallenged. It is interesting to reflect on the type of values which existed within financial institutions, such as Royal Bank of Scotland, and Lehman Brothers, which contributed to the global financial crisis. A discussion of values is dealt with in detail in **Chapter 9** when we look at visionary organizations.

1.5.2 **Vision**

A vision is an ambitious and imaginative goal which the organization would like to achieve at some point in the future. It is often associated with the founder or CEO of an organization. The prerequisite for producing a vision is not great intellect, but imagination, intuition, and an ability to synthesize disparate information. The length and complexity of vision statements differ between organizations, but clearly, they must be easy to understand and remember.[18] A vision must tap into the personal goals and values of the organization's employees if it is to be internalized by them. When it bears little resemblance to reality, disregards the capabilities of the organization and the problems of the organization, it will be rejected by employees. Employees will also reject a vision where they see a credibility gap between managers' rhetoric and their actions. In other words, leaders must be 'authentic'.[19]

If we look at a selection of vision statements from around the world, we can see that they are relatively short, express where the company expects to be in the future, and have some emotional connection with employees and stakeholders. The Indian telecoms company Reliance Jio has a vision '*to transform India with the power of digital revolution—to connect everyone and everything, everywhere—always at the highest quality and the most affordable price*'. The South African multinational enterprise, MTN Group, states that its vision '*is to lead the delivery of a bold, new digital world to our customers*'. The Irish airline company, Ryanair, has a vision where passengers will receive free fares. As chief executive, Michael O'Leary explains, '*the (free) flights will be full, and we will be making our money out of sharing the airport revenues of all the people who will be running through airports, and getting a share of the shopping and the retail revenues*.'[20]

The Hungarian airliner, Wizz Air, declares its vision statement as: '*our aim is to make flying affordable for the citizens of the CEE (Central and Eastern European region), as well as to provide a new travel experience to all travelers in the EU*.' The Saudi oil company, Saudi Aramco, has a vision to be '*the world's leading integrated energy and chemicals company, focused on maximizing income, facilitating the sustainable and diversified expansion of the Kingdom's economy, and enabling a globally competitive and vibrant Saudi energy sector*'. And the US car manufacturer, Tesla, says its vision is '*to create the most compelling car company of the 21st century by driving the world's transition to electric vehicles*'.

We stated that an organization's vision must derive from its organizational values if it is to be accepted by its employees. But how does a company ensure its vision is sufficiently stretching and ambitious? How can it ensure its vision will tap into the value system of its employees and motivate them? The challenge for organizations is how to preserve what is their very essence but still respond to a changing competitive environment. Collins and Porras suggest the use of *BHAGs* to stimulate progress. **BHAGs** are **Big Hairy Audacious Goals**: goals which stretch the organization and are easily communicated to all its members.[21]

A BHAG is clear and compelling, and it serves as a rallying cry to all employees as to where their energies should be focused. It has a finite time span so that everyone knows when the goal is achieved. Such goals include President John F. Kennedy's commitment to landing a man on the moon and returning him safely to earth before the decade was out; Ratan Tata, chairman of Tata Motors, promise of making a car for sale in India at INR 100,000 (Rs 1 lakh) in 2008, equivalent to $2,500.[22] BHAGs are easy to understand, and no matter how many different ways they may be put, they are still understood by everyone. BHAGs provide a way for organizations to communicate ambitious goals.

In 1907, Henry Ford proclaimed that he wanted to democratize the automobile and *'build a car for the great multitude . . . so low in price that no man making a good salary will be unable to own one'*.[23] At that time Ford was one of more than thirty car companies competing in this emerging market. It succeeded, but its success was short-lived. This highlights a couple of important points to bear in mind with BHAGs. First, they must fit with an organization's core values; this was the case with Ford. Second, once achieved, they need to be replaced. Ford achieved its BHAG, but did not set another. This allowed General Motors to supplant Ford's dominant position in the automobile industry by producing cars which reflected the American consumer's changing lifestyles.

The use of a vision is not without its problems. Rumelt is critical of what he calls 'template style strategy', where organizations simply fill in their unique vision of what the business will be like in the future.[24] Such popular visions include being 'the best' or 'the leading' organization in the industry. Enron, the giant US utility company and darling of Wall Street, which collapsed amidst allegations of fraud, possessed a vision *'to become the world's leading energy company'*. Similar template-style strategies are often applied to the mission and the values of the organization. A company will describe its values, making sure they are noncontroversial. For example, Enron's values were *'integrity, respect, communication and excellence'*.

1.5.3 Mission

An organization's mission seeks to answer the question: *'Why does the organization exist*?' A **mission statement** can be defined as the way in which an organization communicates the business it is in to the outside world. **Peter Drucker** argues that a mission statement is the same as asking the question: 'What business are we in?'[25] Because a mission statement answers the question 'Why do we exist?' or 'What business are we competing in?', it builds upon the values of the organization. And, unlike vision statements which focus on an aspirational future, it is more flexible to changes in the external environment. A mission statement needs to appeal to a broad spectrum of stakeholders if all stakeholders are to accept it.[26] In this respect, a mission statement which simply emphasizes the need to maximize shareholder value will be unlikely to motivate employees. The mission statement will be devised by the CEO and the board of directors but, given their remoteness from the customers, they may consult widely throughout the organization to ensure their mission accurately reflects the business they are in.

The following mission statements are from some of the organizations we used for the vision statements. These should be addressing the question: 'What business are we competing in?' If we can identify the business the company competes in from its mission statement, then we can conclude it meets the requirement of a mission statement. If not, it is likely to be what Rumelt calls 'template style' and, therefore, of less use. Ryanair's mission statement is *'To offer low fares that generate increased passenger traffic while maintaining a continuous focus on cost containment and efficiency operation'*.

Reliance Jio's mission '*promises to shape the future of India by providing end-to-end digital solutions for businesses, institutions and households and seamlessly bridging the rural-urban divide*'.

Tesla's mission '*is to accelerate the world's transition to sustainable energy. Tesla builds not only all-electric vehicles but also infinitely scalable clean energy generation and storage products.*' Aramco's mission is '*reliably supplying energy to the Kingdom and the world, and continue to progress towards becoming the world's leading integrated energy and chemicals enterprise, a top refiner and a creator of energy technologies*'. MTN Group's response is '*Our mission is to make our customers' lives a whole lot brighter*'. And, for Wizz Air, their business is built around the mission: '*offering more affordable travel opportunities to discover Europe and beyond. We challenge ourselves daily to be the most loved low cost airline.*'

It is not unusual, particularly in the public sector, for organizations to have mission statements at different levels ranging from a department all the way down to individual teams. If these statements are to guide employee behaviour, then it would seem that two conditions are necessary: **(1)** such statements are communicated clearly to all employees; **(2)** those employees internalize these statements and use them to direct their behaviour. The use of these statements may constitute a necessary, but not sufficient condition for organizational success. At some point, like Rumelt, we might ask what actually is being accomplished as a result of vision and mission statements.

Andrew Campbell, Marion Devine and **David Young** make a distinction between *mission* and a *sense of mission*.[27] They see a mission as an intellectual concept that can be used to guide the policies of an organization. However, a sense of mission is an emotional commitment that employees feel towards the organization. It occurs when employees feel that there is a match between the values of an organization and those of the individual. The key point is that individuals with a sense of mission are emotionally committed to the organization, what it stands for, and what it is trying to achieve. In summary, an organization's strategy will be built upon, and reflect, its values, its mission, and its vision. Together, these determine the type of strategies an organization will pursue and how these strategies will be implemented. **Figure 1.3** show the foundation of values on which organizations are built. This is followed by the reasons why they exist, their vision, and finally their strategy. One might argue there is a case for putting mission before values, or even putting them both on the same level, which would also be acceptable.

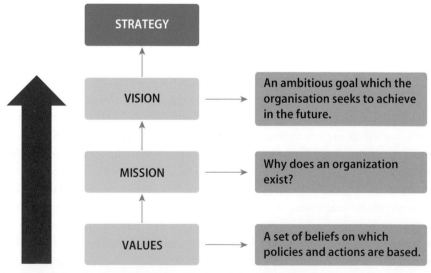

Figure 1.3   The relationship between values, mission, vision, and strategy.

1.6 **The Theory of the Business**

Peter Drucker contends that organizations encounter difficulties when the assumptions on which they are built and the basis on which they are being run no longer fit reality. These assumptions affect management behaviour and their decisions about what and what not to do. They also determine what managers believe are meaningful results. They include assumptions about markets, customers, competitors, and the organization's capabilities and weaknesses. Drucker refers to this as a company's theory of the business.[28]

Every organization has a theory of the business, regardless of whether it operates in the public, private, or not-for-profit sector. The reason many large corporations are no longer successful is that their theory of the business no longer works. For example, when the computer was in its infancy IBM's theory of the business suggested that the future of computing was in mainframes. Around this time the first personal computer was developed by enthusiasts. At the same time as *serious* computer makers were *reminding* themselves that there was absolutely no reason for personal computers, the Apple and the Macintosh went on sale, starting the PC revolution.

1.6.1 **Four Characteristics of an Organization's Theory of the Business**

(1) The assumptions an organization holds about the environment, mission, and its core **competencies** must fit reality. Simon Marks, the co-founder of Marks & Spencer, realized that continued success in his business meant that he as merchant should develop new core competencies. He would design products based on his customer knowledge, and find manufacturers to make them to his costs. This went against the established practice of manufacturers producing products *they* thought the consumer might buy.

(2) The assumptions in all three areas of environment, mission, and core competences have to fit one another.

(3) The theory of the business must be known and understood throughout the organization. This is relatively easy when an organization is founded, but as it grows it must be reinforced if the organization is not to pursue what is expedient rather than what is right.

(4) The theory of the business has to be continually tested.

In effect, the mental model a manager holds about an organization must be subject to change if the organization is to meet changing market conditions and survive. This was the challenge facing Intel chairman Gordon Moore and his senior manager, Andy Grove. The rivalry from Japanese competitors willing to compete aggressively on price threatened Intel's core memory chip business. Grove and Moore were faced with difficult choices about the company's future. See **Case Study: Intel's Theory of the Business** the end of this chapter.

Drucker argues that every theory of the business will eventually become obsolete and no longer meet the needs of the organization. However, there are two preventive measures. The first is *abandonment*: every three years a company can look at its markets, products, and policies and ask itself: if we were not already in these markets, producing these products, and following these policies, would we still want to be in them now? This was the question which the CEO of Intel, Andy Grove, put to his chairman, Gordon Moore before they exited the market for memory chips.[29] Of course, given the nature of dynamic environments, a more realistic timescale might be every year. Nonetheless, this forces managers in organizations to question the assumptions on which their business is based—their theory of the business.

The second preventive measure is to study what is happening outside the business, especially with noncustomers. This is because fundamental change rarely happens within your own industry or with your own customers. For example, satellite navigation equipment manufacturers did not perceive mobile phones as a competitor. However, the inclusion of free satellite navigation apps on mobile phones had a devastating effect on the market for satellite navigation equipment. This type of change invariably first manifests itself with your noncustomers. We will say much more about detecting changes that might impact the competitive environment in **Chapter 2**.

A theory of the business becomes obsolete when an organization has achieved its original objectives. As with the example earlier of Ford democratizing the automobile, the achievement of the objective may point to the need for new thinking, rather than be a cause for celebration. As Sam Walton, the founder of the American retailer Walmart, which previously owned the UK retailer Asda, noted: *'You can't just keep doing what works one time, because everything around you is always changing. To succeed you have to stay out in front of that change.'*[30]

1.7 Business Models

The concept of a **business model** is actually captured by Drucker in 'the theory of the business', discussed in **Section 1.6**. This is because a business model will include assumptions about markets, customers, and the organization's capabilities and weaknesses. **Joan Magretta** defines a business model as *'a story which explains how an organization works'*.[31] It answers questions posed by Drucker, such as: who is the customer? And what does the customer value? It also answers a crucial question for managers, concerned with how to make money from the business: what is the economic logic which explains how we can deliver value to customers, at an appropriate cost and price, which allows us to make an acceptable profit?

A good business model remains essential to every organization, whether it's a start-up or an established company. Although every viable organization is built on a sound business model, a business model isn't a strategy, even though the terms are often used interchangeably. A business model describes how the activities of a business fit together; its **value chain**. This includes all the activities associated with making a product—for instance, design, manufacturing, and purchasing. It also includes the activities associated with selling a product or service, such as transactions, distribution, and delivery. A business model describes how the organization operates, whereas a business strategy explains how an organization can compete better than its rivals. Therefore, a business model should complement a clear **competitive strategy**.

If a business model is to remain relevant, managers must be open to innovations.[32] Organizations are being encouraged to take an interest in business model innovation for three reasons. First, **product life cycles** are getting shorter, and this faster pace of change is leading managers to look for the next big thing. Second, competition can come from unexpected sources; we saw earlier that satellite navigation equipment manufacturers did not perceive mobile phones as a competitor.

Third, **disruptions** from a competitor's business model can offer the consumer better experiences and products more suited to their needs. It is crucial that managers are able to perceive when their business model may be becoming obsolete. But how can they know this? A business model will likely require change when each successive innovation offers smaller and smaller improvements to the product or service. And also, when your customers are conveying to you that competitor offerings are increasingly acceptable to them.

1.8 **The Development of Strategic Management**

We have seen that strategic management is concerned with how organizations achieve and sustain competitive advantage. However, major disagreements start to emerge when we look at *how* competitive advantage is achieved by the firm. The true test of how organizations achieve and sustain competitive advantage is ultimately decided in the marketplace. Therefore, one might expect research to provide an answer. But, even here, there is disagreement, as research findings are both accepted and contested.

The changes in strategic management as a discipline reflect the changing dynamics of modern economies. It began in the 1960s when organizations could rely on stable and expanding market conditions with a customer emphasis on price. Under such conditions it was natural that strategy was largely equated with corporate planning. It was not unusual for major corporations to have a corporate planning function or department which annually developed long-term plans for the next five years, and even longer in some instances. These were primarily finance-based budgetary control systems, giving the assurance that there was some scientific basis to this kind of planning. In times of relative stability, which in turn provides for some degree of predictability, this type of corporate planning was to be expected.

In the 1970s the corporate landscape was focused on **diversification**, in particular how to increase market share by capturing new markets. **Igor Ansoff's** growth vector matrix explained how organizations can engage in related and unrelated diversification to increase their market shares.[33] The hugely successful British conglomerate, Hanson plc, led by Lords Hanson and White, dominated the 1970s and 1980s corporate landscape with their simple business model of: buy asset-rich companies with good cash flows and run them better, managing for cash and return on capital.[34] Diversification works well as long as synergies ensue, resulting in increased profitability and an increase in the capital value of the firm. It also presupposes that management have sufficient skills and capabilities to run businesses operating in markets of which they may have little or no knowledge. We will say more about this in **Chapter 8**.

In the 1980s, the work of Michael Porter on industry analysis shifted the emphasis to firms analysing the competitive forces inherent within their industry as a means of gaining competitive advantage. Porter argues that firms should position themselves favourably against adversarial forces within their industry and adopt a strategy that would enable them to compete effectively.[35] In the 1980s corporations had also begun to focus on the core elements of their businesses. This was a period in corporate history in which managers were encouraged to '*stick to the knitting*', as exemplified in **Peters and Waterman's** best-selling book *In Search of Excellence*.[36] At the same time, Mintzberg was proposing that strategy not only involves intention, but can also develop as part of an emerging process (see **Figure 1.4**). In other words, an organization may have achieved success without going through the process of analysis, formulation, and implementation.

Different perspectives on strategy continued throughout the 1990s as new management techniques taught corporate leaders about downsizing, outsourcing, delayering, total quality management, economic value analysis, benchmarking, and re-engineering. Organizations were outsourcing all but the essential elements, or the core competences, of the organization. In contrast with Porter's work, the resource-based view (RBV) of the firm—exemplified by the likes of **Robert Grant**,[37] **Jay Barney**,[38] **John Kay**,[39] and **C. K. Prahalad and Gary Hamel**,[40]—exhorts the organization to look within itself at its resources and competences as the basis for competitive advantage. The RBV approach contends that market positioning will only provide temporary competitive advantage, since any successful position will be copied. Despite the disagreement between Porter's positioning approach and the resource-based view of strategy, **Raphael Amit** and **Paul Schoemaker** see RBV as a complement to industry analysis.[41] This is because industry analysis views the sources of profitability to be the characteristics of the industry and the firm's position within the industry, while the resource-based view sees the determinants of profitability as the firm's resources and capabilities.

Richard D'Aveni coined the term hypercompetition to describe a new competitive situation where firms must continually innovate, developing new products or services for the customer. For D'Aveni, sustainable competitive advantage now requires firms to constantly develop new products to provide customers with increased functionality and performance.[42] Gillette is an example of a hypercompetitive firm, which is forced to cannibalize its existing product each time it introduces a new razor. See **Chapter 3** for a discussion of hypercompetition. However, not everyone is convinced that hypercompetition represents a new framework for understanding competition. For example, Porter argues that hypercompetition can be seen as an excuse for a lack of managerial ability and poor strategic thinking.[43] Furthermore, Mintzberg argues that turbulence, inasmuch as it exists at all, is an opportunity for organizations to learn from a changing environment, as the Japanese have done.[44] Mintzberg is not denying turbulence per se; he is simply pointing out that there is a tendency in strategic management to characterize the previous decades as stable, and our current decade as turbulent. Research by Gerry McNamara and his colleagues seems to support Mintzberg, as they suggest that 'hypercompetition perspectives are important but no more so now than they were in recent years'.[45]

In the 1990s, organizations began to see the benefits of collaboration, cooperation, and joint alliances. '*Networking*' between corporations became the new buzzword. Supplier relationships were seen as a source of competitive advantage, and not as one of competition. **Adam Brandenburger** and **Barry Nalebuff** refer to this détente as co-opetition, that is, a blend of competition and cooperation existing simultaneously. In effect, a non-zero-sum game.[46] This is discussed in detail in **Chapter 3**. In the twenty-first century, the ascendency of the resource-based view and development of **dynamic capabilities** continue.[47] Dynamic capabilities imply an ability for an organization to develop new capabilities as old ones become less effective and no longer unique. If the capabilities of the organization co-evolve with the market, this maintains a dynamic fit between internal and external conditions.[48] As such, dynamic capabilities may allow an organization to sustain competitive advantage rather than rely on market barriers for advantage. This is discussed in detail in **Chapter 5**.

Another approach to strategic management is **chaos** and **complexity theory**, which argues against the standard, linear approaches. Drawing upon the natural sciences, organizations are seen as non-linear feedback loops which link to other organizations (or families) by similar loops. Organizations operate far from the equilibrium state of neoclassical economics, between the borders of stability and instability. This implies that in the short term some control is possible, but over time, linear, rational approaches to decision-making may be insufficient to meet the context in which organizations operate.[49]

In the 2000s, we saw the significance of **strategy as practice**, which views strategy as something which people 'do', rather than something companies 'have'. Strategy as practice is not intended to replace the established frameworks of Porter or Ansoff, but rather to complement them by asking questions about how organizations *actually* use these frameworks. It seeks to portray a dynamic picture of strategies in organizations in which people, their daily activities, and the strategies which they think about collectively matter to how strategy is put into practice. The implication of strategy as practice is that a clearer understanding of strategic management requires the learning of key concepts in strategy, as well as an awareness that strategy is a social and ongoing process in organizations. The role of the strategists and their practices became the research focus. As **Gunter Muller-Stewens** points out: 'it was about the innovative craftsperson, how exactly they execute their craft, and which tools they use.'[50]

1.9 **Different Perspectives on Strategy Formulation**

The issue of how strategy is actually formulated has led to claims and counterclaims about the merits of different schools of thought within strategic management. This ongoing debate has been largely implicit in strategic management books, but waged more explicitly in the various strategic management journals.[51] There are numerous perspectives on strategy formulation which in many respects overlap and branch off from each other. For example, Henry Mintzberg and Joseph Lampel identify ten different schools of strategic thought; the question is whether these are fundamentally different ways of making strategy or different parts of the same process.[52] We can identify two broad perspectives of strategic management which at first reading may appear to be polar opposites: the *rationalist or design school* and the *learning school*.

1.9.1 **The Rationalist School**

The rationalist or design school is associated with the work of **Kenneth Andrews** and **Igor Ansoff**.[53] According to Andrews, an organization needs to match its strengths and weaknesses, which derive from its resources and competences, with the needs of its business environment. The business environment comprises both threats and opportunities. This provides the familiar **SWOT** analysis of strengths, weaknesses, opportunities, and threats. An external analysis is used to identify the opportunities and threats facing the firm, while an internal analysis of the organization identifies its strengths and weaknesses.

For the rationalist school, the match between these elements will lead to the creation of a number of different strategies, each of which can be evaluated and the best strategy then implemented. In the past, organizations had planning departments which created strategies for managers to implement. The role of top management was to choose the most appropriate strategy. However, planning is not the same as strategy. The organizations which used planning to describe the future in great detail were disappointed to find that the future did not turn out as they expected.[54] These elaborate corporate plans were seldom consulted by managers, who continued to make the decisions they would have made had the plan never existed.

Over time, planning began to move away from forecasting, to become a basis for strategic choice. The oil company Shell developed **scenario planning**. Scenario planning allows managers to produce different, internally consistent views of what the future might turn out to be. This allows companies to organize their thinking about their environment and formulate strategic alternatives. The use of models also became prevalent as companies tried to forecast the future of the business and how it might be influenced by internal and external developments. Models are useful for assembling and analysing data, but can only provide a background for strategic decisions. The sophisticated econometric models simply cannot represent the real world because it is too complex to be adequately described.

A response was to develop ever more complicated mathematical models in an attempt to capture more of the complex reality. The problem is, the model does not forecast reality in a way which users find credible, nor can they understand the relationships described by the model. Not surprisingly, these formal approaches to analyse the environment were not accepted by managers. Another response was to simply reject analytical models altogether and rely on intuition and judgement. However, even a manager's intuition will be based on an implicit model. It will be the product of previous experience in dealing with an analogous situation. The benefit of the formal model is that these assumptions are explicit, which should help facilitate a better understanding of the issue.

The need began to develop for more qualitative ways of organizing data. Management tools, such as the product portfolio and the product life cycle, were developed. Many of these tools were developed by consultants with an emphasis on the characteristics of industry or market. The role of competitors and competitive behaviour in influencing outcomes was not dominant—that is, not until Michael Porter placed competitor analysis at the heart of strategy with his five forces framework. For the past four decades Porter, more than anyone else, has exemplified the rationalist approach to strategy formulation using his *generic* strategies. Porter's work is discussed in detail in **Chapters 3**, **4**, and **6**.

1.9.2   The Learning School

Successful firms can pursue strategies that are opportunistic and adaptive rather than being planned. The American political scientist, **Charles Lindblom**, wrote an article called 'The science of muddling through'.[55] He contrasted the *root* method and the *branch* method of decision-making.

The root method requires a comprehensive evaluation of all options based upon the objectives. The branch method involves managers building outwards in small steps from their current situation. For Lindblom, the root method was not useful for complex policy questions. Instead, managers should follow the branch approach, the *science of muddling through*.

Other researchers, such as **Richard Cyert** and **James March**, argue that organizations should not be viewed as entities with personalities and goals like individuals.[56] Rather, they are more appropriately viewed as shifting coalitions, in which conflicting demands and objectives are imperfectly reconciled. With this approach, change takes place incrementally. For Cyert and March, a rationalist approach in which senior managers determine and impose a pattern of behaviour on the organization, fails to take account of the reality of organizational dynamics.

In contrast with the rationalist school, Mintzberg argues that a rational approach to strategy fails to take account of how strategy making occurs in reality.[57] **Mintzberg and Waters** suggest three approaches to strategy formulation: *intended*, *realized*, and *emergent strategies*.[58] (1) An **intended strategy** is one which the organization has deliberately chosen to pursue and will therefore have been worked out in detail. (2) A **realized strategy** is the strategy that the organization actually carries out. For a variety of reasons—for example, a change in consumer tastes—the intended strategy may no longer be relevant for the market conditions and therefore is not implemented. Mintzberg and Waters refer to this as an unrealized strategy. (3) In such a case, managers will have to use their experience and learning to develop an **emergent strategy** which meets the needs of the changing environment. When this emergent strategy is implemented it becomes the realized strategy. Mintzberg and Waters argue that strategy formulation is far more likely to be as a result of emergent strategies than to be based on any detailed intentions. This process is shown in **Figure 1.4**.

For Mintzberg, strategy is an immensely complex process, '*which involves the most sophisticated, subtle, and, at times subconscious elements of human thinking*'. That is, strategies can develop inadvertently, quite apart from the desired strategic intention of senior managers. Strategy comes about as a result of a process of learning.[59] However, Mintzberg does concede that all viable strategies will have emergent and deliberate qualities. This is because a viable strategy requires both flexible learning and some degree of deliberate intention. See **Strategy in Focus 1.2**, which shows two competing perspectives on Honda's success and ultimate domination of the US motorcycle industry. The rationalist school views Honda's success as part of a deliberate strategy. Mintzberg, in contrast, argues that it results from an emergent strategy.

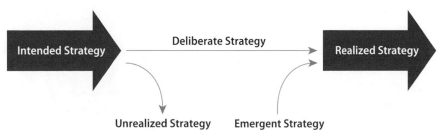

Figure 1.4   Deliberate and emergent strategies: Source H. Mintzberg and J. A. Waters, 'Of strategies, deliberate and emergent', Strategic Management Journal, vol. 6, no. 3 (1985), pp. 257–72. © John Wiley & Sons Ltd. Reproduced with permission

STRATEGY IN FOCUS 1.2 Honda's Dominance of the US Motorcycle Industry: Deliberate or Emergent Strategies?

Honda and the Super Cub is probably the best known and most debated case in business strategy. In the 1950s, motorcycles were sold through specialist outlets welcoming only testosterone-loaded young men. Bikes were powerful and noisy, and the riders' leather clothes smelt of leaking oil. Honda entered the US market in 1959 and changed everything. Five years later the company made one in two bikes sold in the US. Their best-selling machine was the 50cc Super Cub. The company's advertising slogan was: 'You meet the nicest people on a Honda.'

The story benefits from deconstruction. One school of explanation derives from the original Harvard Business School case study. That case is based on a 1975 report by the Boston Consulting Group for the British government, which described these events as the archetype of an orchestrated attack on Western markets by Japanese manufacturers of consumer goods. Having established large **economies of scale** in the domestic market, Honda was able to exploit its cost advantage globally.

Quite a different history was given by Richard Pascale, who went to Tokyo to interview the elderly Japanese who had managed Honda's first steps in the US. These executives explained that Honda had never imagined that small bikes, popular in Japan, would find a market in the wide-open spaces of the US. They had focused on large machines, planning to compete with US manufacturers. Mr Honda, they said, was especially confident of success with these products because the shape of the handlebars looked like the eyebrows of Buddha.

But the eyebrows of Buddha were not appealing in the world of Marlon Brando and James Dean. The Japanese hawked their wares around the western US, to dealers 'who treated us discourteously and gave the impression of being motorcycle enthusiasts who, secondarily, were in business'. The few machines they sold, ridden more aggressively than was possible in Japan, leaked even more oil than their US counterparts.

Dispirited and short of foreign currency, the Honda executives imported some Super Cubs to ease their own progress around the asphalt jungle of Los Angeles. Passers-by expressed interest, and eventually a Sears buyer approached them.

An old Honda Super Cub motorcycle. Source: © Zoi Op/Shutterstock.com.

And the 'nicest people' slogan? That was invented by a University of California undergraduate on summer assignment. Only the naive will believe either account.

Successful business strategy is a mixture of luck and judgement, opportunism and design, and even with hindsight the relative contributions of each cannot be disentangled. Mr Honda was an irascible genius who made inspired, intuitive decisions—with assistance from the meticulous market analysis of his colleagues and the intense discipline of Honda's production line operations. It is a mistake to believe that the ultimate truth about Honda can be established through diligent research and debate. The Harvard account, although paranoid, is right to emphasize Honda's operational capabilities. Mr Pascale correctly stresses the human factors, but his interviewees must have laughed as he wrote down the story of the eyebrows of Buddha.

The Boston Consulting Group naturally saw the **experience curve** at work and later, when peddling a different panacea, realized it was an example of time-based competition. Gary Hamel and C. K. Prahalad perceived the development of Honda's 'core competence' in engine manufacture. Henry Mintzberg seized on Mr Pascale's account as an instance of emergent strategy. But there is no true story and no point in debating what it might be.

The lesson of Honda is that a business with a distinctive capability that develops innovative products to exploit that capability and recognizes the appropriate distribution channels for such innovations can take the world by storm. And that lesson is valid whether Honda's achievement was the result of careful planning or serendipity.

Source: John Kay, 'Driving through the spin on Honda's big success', *Financial Times*, 16 November 2004. Used under licence from the *Financial Times*. All rights reserved.

We argued at the start of this section on different perspectives that the truth often lies somewhere between competing positions and drawn battle lines. The question is not whether some approaches to strategic management are overly rational and analytical, failing to take account of more complex processes within strategy-making. The real question is how strategic management as a discipline moves forward and ultimately benefits the performance of organizations, and in so doing increases society's net benefit. There is a danger which emanates from having battle lines and positions too demarcated; common ground can often be overlooked. However, as is often the case, the truth lies somewhere between these two perspectives. Successful strategy formulation will inevitably involve both analytical techniques and a creative process: '*it's a complicated world out there. We all know we shall get nowhere without emergent learning alongside deliberate planning.*'[60]

1.10 A Strategic Management Framework

A framework is useful to help us to structure our thoughts and navigate around the different aspects of strategic management. If the use of strategy is to enable an organization to achieve a sustainable competitive advantage, then a framework needs to address the process necessary for this. In **Figure 1.5** we outline a framework which provides an understanding of the organization and its environment. However, all managers need a clear sense of direction, and this is provided by a company's values. These values will determine the objectives managers set and, therefore, the strategy necessary to achieve them. It is in this respect that strategy can be seen as the lynchpin between the organization and its environment.

Figure 1.5 shows the importance of values in the strategy making process. This is shown by the arrow emanating from *values*, which determine the *strategic objectives* the organization sets. The objectives, in turn, will determine the *resources and capabilities* the company requires to achieve them. Some capabilities it may already have; others it will need to acquire, or develop itself. Objectives need to be clearly defined, as they provide direction and motivation for individuals in the firm. The more clearly the objectives are stated and imbued within the organization, the greater the understanding by the organization's participants of their role in achieving them. An organization's objectives will reflect its *strengths and weaknesses*, and the *opportunities and threats* within its environment. They will also determine the types of resources an organization accumulates. All organizations will require appropriate *structures and processes* in order to coordinate and implement action to achieve their chosen strategy. How the organization is structured and the processes it utilizes will again reflect the organization's objectives.

An organization's values will also determine the relationship with its stakeholders. Stakeholders reside within the organization and the environment. For example, managers and employees are internal stakeholders, while suppliers, shareholders, and the local community are external stakeholders. The distinction between internal and external stakeholders is not always this simple, since a shareholder may also be an employee.

Figure 1.5 links strategy with the organization, its external environment, and its stakeholders. This is because a strategy reflects the organization's values, its mission (why it exists), and its stated vision, but it must also be feasible. We might ask: does the organization have the resources and capabilities to carry it out? Is the organization's culture, its structures, and processes helpful

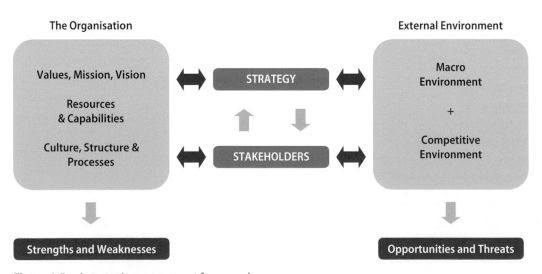

Figure 1.5   A strategic management framework.

or a hindrance to the strategy? The links between strategy, the organization and its external environment are shown because there must be a strategic fit between the internal capabilities of the organization and the needs of its external environment in terms of the markets and industries it serves, or is seeking to serve. The two-way arrows positioned between strategy, the organization, and its environment provide feedback on the appropriateness of the strategy. Importantly, we must ask ourselves: how will our stakeholders respond to the strategy? As we have seen, an intended strategy may not always be implemented, often because of a change in market conditions. We also need to be aware that changes in the macro-environment may have their greatest impact on the competitive environment.

Do managers analyse their environment and then develop a strategy based on this analysis to position themselves against that environment? Or, do managers develop a strategy based on the experience and capabilities contained within their organization and then seek to leverage this in their environment? These are interesting questions which have provoked much debate within strategic management. On the one hand is the positioning school, which is characterized by the work of Porter.[61] This is often referred to as strategic fit or an 'outside-in' approach to strategic management. On the other hand is the resource-based view, referred to as an 'inside-out' approach to strategy, which has come to be associated with Grant, Barney, Hamel, and Prahalad. This debate will be addressed in detail in **Chapters 3** and **5**.

Another question we might consider is: can any of these approaches deal with a rapidly changing environment? The work of **David Teece, Constance Helfat,** and **Sidney Winter** on dynamic capabilities suggest neither approach can adequately deal with the dynamic environments of the twenty-first century. We will say considerably more on this in **Chapter 5**.

Summary

This chapter has introduced the reader to some of the complexities that emanate from a study of strategic management. There are conflicting and competing definitions. There is disagreement over how strategy is formulated, which gives rise to competing perspectives. This should not be seen as an insurmountable issue, since any discipline as young as strategic management will inevitably be concerned with the exactitude of its terminology and the rigour of its modus operandi. What we have tried to show is that, in and among all this ambiguity, there is common ground and clarity of thought and expression. The fact that different perspectives exist at all is simply part of the dynamic nature of strategic management.

We have identified a number of different perspectives which deal with strategy. These different perspectives will be evaluated more fully as we assess differential firm performance in later chapters. The rationalist approach covers strategy analysis, formulation, and implementation. However, we again reiterate that this linear approach, although highly useful in explaining the discipline of strategy, does not always fully capture how strategy works in reality. This is not to demean its usefulness, since all organizations need to undertake analysis before they are ready to take decisions; it is more to open up thinking about the different ways in which strategy formulation occurs.

CASE STUDY Intel's Theory of the Business

Andy Grove: Intel's First Employee

Andy Grove was born Andras Istvan Grof in Hungary, where he lived under both Nazi and later Communist occupation. He arrived in the United States in January 1957 and shortly after changed his name to Andrew Stephen Grove. He acquired a PhD in chemical engineering at the University of California at Berkeley before joining Fairchild Semiconductor. In 1968, Gordon Moore, along with another executive, Robert Noyce, left Fairchild Semiconductor to found Intel. When Andy Grove heard they were leaving, he decided to go with them. As Grove recalls, 'I never got an invitation'; he just went. At this time, there were many companies already making chips to help companies manage their payroll and accounting. What Moore envisaged was an opportunity in a relatively new area; Intel could put memory or data storage on microchips. These chips would allow computers to be faster. By 1970, through innovation, hard work, and sheer determination, Intel produced the industry's first blockbuster: a low-cost memory on a chip.

The Memory Chip Market

By 1993, Andy Grove was president of Intel, a high-growth corporation with revenues in excess of $1 billion a year. The CEO was co-founder, Gordon Moore, who developed Moore's Law. This stated that the number of transistors you could place onto a memory chip tended to double every eighteen months. In reality, Intel had come to expect that Moore's Law applied only to them. In the early 1980s, there were competitors in the memory chip market, but as far as the executives at Intel were concerned, this was a market they had created. The market was booming and Intel was defined by memory chips. Unfortunately, someone had forgotten to tell this to their Japanese competitors. The company began to get undercut by Japanese manufacturers capable of mass-producing high-quality, low-priced chips. Between 1978 and 1988, the market share held by Japanese companies doubled from thirty per cent to sixty per cent.

Intel® Core™ i5 Processor Source: © Badar ul islam Majid / Unsplash.com.

Initially, because the company was so successful, it simply continued as before. Its success in memory chips brought with it a belief that it could innovate itself out of the situation by developing a better chip. This would reassert its dominance and it could again charge a premium price. In the 'Icarus Paradox', Danny Miller states the very capabilities that create a company's success can also be its downfall. Unless the executives at Intel were able to correctly diagnose the situation the company was facing and take action, Intel's success would be short-lived.

Intel's microprocessors were in many of the products of the new emerging market for personal computers, but this was in its infancy. There was still a stalwart belief that memory chips had a viable future.

Although there was some research being undertaken on microprocessors, the company's resources and capabilities remained primarily focused on memory chips. Most people at Intel had so much emotional capital invested in memory chips, it was difficult to accept the reality that Japanese firms had turned their specialty into a commodity product. The quality attributed to the Japanese memory chips was higher than Grove and others had thought was possible. Not surprisingly, their first reaction was one of denial, before they came to the realization that they were behind. There was a great deal of debate and discussion at Intel about what to do, but no real discussion about their core product, memory chips. Intel was desperately trying to earn a premium price for its product. They began to think if they could earn 2X (twice) the price of Japanese memories they would be fine, but began to realize that there was no point in this if 'X' got smaller and smaller. This was despite the company losing more and more money on its memory business.

At the time, R&D was spread between different technologies. The majority was spent on memory chips. A smaller team worked on another technology Intel had invented: microprocessors. Microprocessors are the brains of the computer; they calculate, while memory chips merely store. However, because business had been so good, Intel just kept on doing the same thing. As Andy Grove was to say, later, 'we persevered because we could afford to'. In 1985, their denial came face to face with reality. Profits fell from $198 million in 1984 to less than $2 million in 1985.

Time for a Change

Months of meetings, bickering, and arguments had produced nothing but conflicting proposals. In the middle of 1985, Grove was discussing the problem in his office with Intel Chairman and CEO, Gordon Moore. In his book, *Only the Paranoid Survive*, Grove said: 'Intel equals memories in all our minds. How could we give up our identity? How could we exist as a company that was not in the memory business? It was close to being inconceivable.' Nonetheless, he looked out of the window at the Ferris wheel of the Great American amusement park revolving in the distance, turned to Moore and asked this question.

'If we got kicked out and the board brought in a new CEO, what do you think he would do?' Without hesitating, Moore answered, 'He would get us out of memories.' Grove stared at his CEO, numb, before suggesting, 'Why shouldn't you and I walk out the door, come back and do it ourselves?'

Even though Grove was now able to say to his senior manager in charge of the memory business, 'Get us out of memories!', he still allowed R&D expenditure on a product he and the manager knew they had no plans to sell. Grove rationalized that such a major change had to take place via a number of smaller steps. However, after a few months, he realized that this halfway decision was untenable and found the determination to make a painful choice. Intel was getting out of the memory business once and for all. This meant firing more than 7,000 people—one-third of the workforce—and closing seven factories. Grove was to take away an important lesson from this: 'People who do not have an emotional stake in a decision can see what needs to be done sooner.'

Grove came to realize that when faced with difficult choices, you have to make painful decisions, and you can't hedge your commitments to them. If you do, individuals in the company will be confused and not only will you lose direction, but you will sap the energy of your organization as well. Intel faced what Grove called a 'strategic inflection point'. This is a time in the life of the business when its fundamentals are about to change. Strategic inflection points are major changes in the way a company competes, such that simply adopting a new technology or competing in the same old way will be insufficient. It does not have to lead to disaster, since it creates opportunities for those who can compete in the new way. This includes both incumbents and newcomers.

While Grove and Moore made their historic decision to exit memory chips, unbeknown to them, their middle managers were directing their manufacturing resources to the emerging microprocessor business. In performing their roles as managers, they were simply allocating resources from less profitable to more profitable lines of production: microprocessors. The decision to exit memory chips was less drastic as a result of the actions of Intel's middle managers. The problem for Grove was not a lack of strategic choice or information on which to base decisions; his emotional commitment to memory chips clouded his judgement and obscured the urgent need to take a difficult decision.

When Intel decided to manufacture only microprocessors in 1985, its biggest customer and also its biggest shareholder was IBM. IBM had bought shares in Intel in order to protect its supplies of microprocessors. It was sixty times the size of Intel. It wanted Intel to license its 386 microprocessor designs to other manufacturers in order for IBM to be assured of its supply of processors. This meant Intel would be relegated to the uncertain role of a parts supplier to a giant corporation. When Intel launched the 386, Grove made it clear that the technology would not be licensed to other producers. Grove was simply not prepared to give away Intel's advantage to IBM.

Back to Growth

The growth of the personal computer market was to drive Intel's massive success. If an individual had invested $1,000 in Intel in 1985, by 2012 the investment would be worth $47,000. During the same period, the S&P 500 would have returned $7,600. During Grove's eleven years as CEO, Intel grew at a compound annual growth rate of nearly thirty per cent. Grove relinquished his role as CEO in 1998 and became Intel's chairman.

In 1990, the marketing director launched a marketing campaign with the slogan 'Intel inside'. The successful marketing campaign turned Intel into a globally recognized brand. In 1994, a mathematician found inconsistencies in the way that Intel's Pentium chip performed complex, scientific calculations. Intel engineers worked out that a spreadsheet user would only encounter a problem once every 27,000 years of spreadsheet use. When the mathematician's findings were posted on the Internet there was a public outcry; IBM announced it was suspending sales of its Pentium chip-based computers. Grove should have recognized a strategic inflection point, but instead could only see the issue from an engineer's perspective and not the consumer's. In the end, he had to recall the product (which cost Intel $475 million) and apologize to consumers. He had failed to realize that a brand is developed with the customer and, as such, a customer's subjective reality becomes the company's objective reality. Or, to put this more simply, 'the customer is king'.

More Change?

Grove remained as Intel's chairman until 2005. The culture he engendered at Intel was that knowledge power overrules position power. In other words, anyone's ideas can be challenged as long as you are prepared to make your point using data. His notion of 'constructive confrontation' meant that decisions were debated loudly and fiercely. He relied upon what he called helpful *Cassandras*. These are 'people who are quick to recognize impending change and cry out an early warning'. Grove was to learn early on that 'the more successful you are, the more people want a chunk of your business and then another chunk and then another until there is nothing left'. As CEO, Grove believed that his primary responsibility was to guard against competitor attacks and develop this attitude throughout the organization.

By 2016, Intel CEO Brian Krzanich had entered into a technology alliance with Arm Holdings, as the company sought to move away from the personal computer as a core computing platform, and embraced the 'Internet of things': the spread of smart and connected devices. Krzanich's view was to offer Intel's core strength of making chips to other chip companies working with Arm designs. This allows it to hedge against the Internet of things, in which Intel's own chip architecture is barely making an impression. In a major change for Intel, outright competition was giving way to collaboration.

As it continued its move away from its core market of PC processors, Intel focused on the new computing landscape taking shape around artificial intelligence. It acquired Nervana, an artificial intelligence (AI) start-up, to help extend its reach into software as well as chips. Nervana was founded to design a complete system to handle *deep learning*, an approach to AI that emulates the working of neural networks in the brain. The purchase complements the range of technologies Intel has been developing to deal with the computing tasks required by AI. These include the machine learning techniques used to train AI systems, as well as processing the large amounts of data such systems work with. This was important because Intel failed to catch the mobile computing wave, losing out to a generation of chips based on designs from the UK's Arm Holdings. However, it did succeed in extending its dominance of PC processors into the server market, making today's cloud data centres a key revenue generator for the company.

Intel rival Nvidia has taken an early lead in neural networks with its graphics processing units, or GPUs. GPUs were originally designed to generate images in computing games, but these have proved well-suited to handling deep learning. By adding the acquisition of Nervana's technology, alongside its organic development of Xeon processors, Intel reduced the need to develop GPUs itself. This also helped to reduce Intel's dependence on revenues from the shrinking PC market, down to 55 per cent of revenues in 2016, from 64 per cent in 2013 and 72 per cent in 2010. By 2018, sales from newer markets such as AI and driverless cars had grown to 49 per cent of Intel's revenues and were on the point of eclipsing its sales from PCs for the first time.

Brian Krzanich, chief executive, said the figures confirmed his confidence in Intel's strategy, which has relied on rapid diversification into new markets. The jump in revenue also appeared to validate Mr Krzanich's break with Intel's past to mount big acquisitions such as the $16.7 billion purchase of Altera, whose products are used in AI, and the $15.3 billion acquisition of driverless car technology company Mobileye. Mr Krzanich resigned in 2018 for not disclosing a consensual affair with another employee; Intel's policy bars affairs between managers and anyone who reports to them, either directly or indirectly. Intel appointed Robert Swan as its chief executive seven months after he stepped in to lead the company on an interim basis following Brian Krzanich's resignation. Mr Swan had previously served as

Intel's chief financial officer (CFO) since 2016. He will be only the company's seventh CEO in its fifty-year history.

Intel continues to transform its business to capture more of a large and expanding opportunity that includes the data centre, artificial intelligence, and autonomous driving, while continuing to get value from the PC business. In a letter to employees posted to Intel's website, Mr Swan said the company's strategy of focusing on data, rather than its historic focus on PCs, 'is not changing'. However, he added: 'Our execution must improve . . . we need to continue to evolve.' Unlike his six predecessors, who had all been engineers and semiconductor specialists, Mr Swan has spent most of his career in finance departments in companies such as General Electric, Electronic Data Systems, and, recently, eBay. In 2020, its data centre chips business was hurt by a slowdown in China and pause in capital spending by cloud computing companies.

Its shift to making chips based on 10-nanometre technology, a reduction in the size of the features on its processors, has not gone well. It started development late, a previously unheard-of position for Intel, which normally leads the industry in each generation of technology. This has left it facing stiffer competition from companies that were more agile, such as AMD and the Taiwanese producer, TSMC. Intel believes it won't get back on to the leading edge of the technology until 2021. Falling behind has also put the company under more pressure to boost its capital spending in an attempt to reach the subsequent 7-nanometre era quicker. But funding overlapping generations of technology like this adds to a company's financial strain.

By July 2020, the company was twelve months behind schedule in developing the process technology needed to make its next generation of chips, based on 7-nanometre technology. The setback threatens to leave it well behind TSMC in the global race to make the most efficient and fastest microprocessors.

Sources: A. Grove, *Only the Paranoid Survive*, Profile Books, 1996; Laura Sydell, 'Intel legends Moore and Grove: making it last', http://www.npr.com, 6 April 2012; C. Heath and D. Heath, 'Decisive: how to make better decisions in life and work', *Random House Business*, 2014; Richard S. Tedlow, 'Fortune classic: the education of Andy Grove', fortune.com, 21 March 2016; Phil Rosenthal, 'What the late Intel boss Andrew Grove can teach about managing change', *Chicago Tribune*, 22 March 2016; Herminia Ibarra, 'Andy Grove and the line between good and bad fear', *The Financial Times*, 12 April 2016; Richard Waters, 'Intel chief fights to end dependence on the shrinking PC business', *The Financial Times*, 9 September 2016; Richard Waters, 'Intel acquires artificial intelligence start-up in tech expansion', *The Financial Times*, 10 August 2016; Richard Waters, 'Intel's move beyond PC chips boosts revenues', *The Financial Times*, 26 April 2018; Richard Waters, 'Intel chief forced to step down for non-disclosure of employee affair', *The Financial Times*, 21 June April 2018; Mamta Badkar and Tim Bradshaw, 'US chipmaker Intel appoints Robert Swan as chief executive', *The Financial Times*, 31 January 2019; 'How Intel found itself "in a little bit of a bathtub"', *The Financial Times*, 9 May 2019; Chris Nuttall, 'Intel chipper on chips for 2020', *The Financial Times*, 24 January 2020; Richard Waters, 'Intel engineering executive leaves in leadership shake-up', *The Financial Times*, 28 July 2020.

Questions

1. How would you describe Intel's theory of the business?

2. Given that Intel's culture was one of open discussion based on data and not opinion, why did it take so long for Gordon Moore and Andy Grove to change direction?

3. How did 'helpful Cassandras' enable Intel's CEO and Chairman to change their business model?

4. Why is Intel concentrating its efforts on data centres and AI?

+ For more examples and discussion to aid your understanding of this chapter, please visit the online resources and see the Extension Material for this chapter.

Review Questions

1. What is strategy?
2. Explain the key differences between the design school and the learning school.

Discussion Question

'Values are irrelevant to an organization; what's important is that an company makes increasing profits.' **Discuss**.

Research Topic

1. Identify organizations where their stated values have not matched their actions, and show what, if any, the consequences of this were for the company's reputation and their revenues.
2. Select a combination of public and private sector organizations and identify the extent to which their vision and mission statements:
   i) are what Rumelt calls 'template-style strategy' (see Rumelt 2011, pp. 64–70), or
   ii) provide aspiration for the company's future (vision) and clearly state what business the organization is in (it's mission).

Recommended Reading

- **M. E. Porter**, 'What is strategy?', *Harvard Business Review*, vol. 74, no. 6 (1996), pp. 61–78.
- **R. P. Rumelt**, *Good Strategy Bad Strategy*, Crown Business, 2011.

For an insight into the debate on deliberate and emergent strategies, see:

- **R. T. Pascale**, 'Perspectives on strategy: the real story behind Honda's success', *California Management Review*, vol. 26, no. 3 (1984), pp. 47–72.
- **H. Mintzberg**, 'The design school: reconsidering the basic premises of strategic management', *Strategic Management Journal*, vol. 11, no. 3 (1990), pp. 171–95.
- **H. I. Ansoff**, 'Critique of Henry Mintzberg's "The design school: reconsidering the basic premises of strategic management"', *Strategic Management Journal*, vol. 12, no. 6 (1991), pp. 449–61.
- **R. T. Pascale**, 'Reflections on Honda', *California Management Review*, vol. 38, no. 4 (1996), pp. 112–17.

- **H. Mintzberg**, 'Learning 1, Planning 0', *California Management Review*, vol. 38, no. 4 (1996), pp. 92–3.

For a comprehensive discussion of the history of strategy, see:

- **L. Freedman**, *Strategy*, Oxford University Press, 2013.

www.oup.com/he/henry4e

Visit the online resources that accompany this book for activities and more information on strategy.

Test your knowledge and understanding of this chapter further by trying the multiple-choice questions online.

References and Notes

1   **P. F. Drucker**, *Managing in a Time of Great Change*, Butterworth Heinemann, 1995, chapter 1.
2   **Carl von Clausewitz**, *On War*, edited by A. Rapaport. Penguin, 1982.
3   **D. E. Hawkins** and **S. Rajagopal**, *Sun Tzu and the Project Battleground*, Palgrave Macmillan, 2005.
4   **R. P. Rumelt**, *Good Strategy Bad Strategy*, Crown Business, 2011.
5   **B. D. Henderson**, 'The origin of strategy', *Harvard Business Review*, vol. 67, no. 6 (1989), pp. 139–43.
6   **M. E. Porter**, 'What is strategy?', *Harvard Business Review*, vol. 74, no. 6 (1996), pp. 61–78.
7   **Porter**, see n. 6 above.
8   **C. C. Markides**, 'A dynamic view of strategy', *Sloan Management Review*, vol. 40, no. 3 (1999), pp. 55–63.
9   **J. Kay**, *Foundations of Corporate Success*, Oxford University Press, 1993.
10 **R. P. Rumelt**, *Good Strategy Bad Strategy*, 2nd edn, Crown Business, 2013.
11 **H. Mintzberg**, 'The fall and rise of strategic planning', *Harvard Business Review*, vol. 72, no. 1 (1994), pp. 107–14.
12 **K. Ohmae**, *The Mind of the Strategist: The Art of Japanese Business*, McGraw-Hill, 1984.
13 **C. C. Markides**, 'In search of strategy', *Sloan Management Review*, vol. 40, no. 3 (1999), pp. 6–7.
14 **Ohmae**, see n. 12 above.
15 **Rumelt**, see n. 4 above.
16 **J. C. Collins** and **J. I. Porras**, *Built to Last: Successful Habit of Visionary Companies*, Harper, 1994.
17 **Collins** and **Porras**, see n. 16 above, p. 74.
18 **M. Lipton**, 'Demystifying the development of an organizational vision', *Sloan Management Review*, vol. 37, no. 4 (1996), pp. 83–92.
19 For a discussion of authentic leadership, see **P. Northouse**, *Leadership: Theory and Practice*, Sage, 2016.
20 **G. Topham**, 'From low-fare to no-fare: will travel really become free?', *The Guardian*, 26 November 2016.
21 **Collins and Porras**, see n. 16 above.
22 https://punemirror.indiatimes.com/news/india/i-am-still-proud-of-the-car-ratan-tata-on-tata-nano-life-after-retirement-and-a-piece-of-advice/articleshow/74470416.cms. Accessed 2 April 2020.
23 **Collins** and **Porras**, see n. 16 above, p. 97.

24 **Rumelt**, see n. 4 above.

25 **P. F. Drucker**, *Managing in a Time of Great Change*, Butterworth Heinemann, 1995.

26 **R. E. Freeman**, *Strategic Management: A Stakeholder Approach*, Pitman, 1984, p. 46.

27 **A. Campbell**, **M. Devine**, and **D. Young**, *A Sense of Mission*, Economist Publications/Hutchinson, 1990.

28 **Drucker**, see n. 25 above.

29 **A. S. Grove**, *Only the Paranoid Survive*, Random House, 1996.

30 **Collins** and **Porras**, see n. 16 above, p. 81.

31 **J. Magretta**, 'Why business models matter', *Harvard Business Review*, vol. 80, no. 5 (2002), pp. 86–92; **A. Ovans**, 'What is a business model?', *Harvard Business Review*, January (2015), pp. 2–7.

32 **S. Cliffe**, 'When your business model is in trouble: an interview with Rita Gunther McGrath', *Harvard Business Review*, vol. 89 (2011), pp. 96–8.

33 **I. Ansoff**, *Corporate Strategy*, chapter 6, McGraw-Hill, 1965.

34 **N. Pratley**, 'Legacy of the lord with the Midas touch', *The Guardian*, 3 November 2004.

35 **M. E. Porter**, *Competitive Strategy: Techniques for Analysing Industries and Competitors*, Free Press, 1980; **M. E. Porter**, *Competitive Advantage*, Free Press, 1985.

36 **T. J. Peters** and **R. H. Waterman**, *In Search of Excellence*, Harper & Row, 1982.

37 **R. M. Grant**, 'The resource-based theory of competitive advantage: implications for strategy formulation', *California Management Review*, vol. 33, Spring (1991), pp. 114–35.

38 **J. Barney**, 'Firm resources and sustained competitive advantage', *Journal of Management*, vol. 17, no. 1 (1991), pp. 99–120; **J. B. Barney**, 'Resource-based theories of competitive advantage: a ten-year retrospective on the resource-based view', *Journal of Management*, vol. 27 (2001), pp. 643–50.

39 **Kay**, see n. 9 above.

40 **C. K. Prahalad** and **G. Hamel**, 'The core competence of the organization', *Harvard Business Review*, vol. 68, no. 3 (1990), pp. 79–91; **G. Hamel** and **C. K. Prahalad**, *Competing for the Future*, Harvard Business School Press, 1994.

41 **R. Amit** and **P. J. H. Schoemaker**, 'Strategic assets and organisational rents', *Strategic Management Journal*, vol. 14, no. 1 (1993), pp. 33–46.

42 **R. A. D'Aveni**, *Hypercompetition: Managing the Dynamics of Strategic Manoeuvring*, Free Press, 1994.

43 **Porter**, see n. 6 above.

44 **Mintzberg**, see n. 11 above.

45 **G. McNamara**, **P. M. Vaaler**, and **C. Devers**, 'Same as it ever was: the search for evidence of increasing hypercompetition', *Strategic Management Journal*, vol. 24, no. 3 (2003), pp. 261–78.

46 **A. Brandenburger** and **B. J. Nalebuff**, *Co-opetition*, Currency Doubleday, 1996.

47 **D. J. Teece**, **G. Pisano**, and **A. Shuen**, 'Dynamic capabilities and strategic management', *Strategic Management Journal*, vol. 18, no. 7 (1997), pp. 509–33; **D. J. Teece**, 'The foundations of enterprise performance: dynamic and ordinary capabilities in an (economic) theory of firms', *Academy of Management*, vol. 28, no. 4 (2014), pp. 328–52.

48 **S. Tallman**, 'Dynamic capabilities' in *The Oxford Handbook of Strategy*, edited by A. Campbell and D. Faulkner, Oxford University Press, 2006, 378–409.

49 **R. D. Stacy** and **C. Mowles**, *Strategic Management and Organisational Dynamics*, Pearson, 2016.

50 **G. Muller-Stewens**, '*The New Strategist*', Kogan Page, 2020.

51 **H. Mintzberg**, 'The design school: reconsidering the basic premises of strategic management', *Strategic Management Journal*, vol. 11, no 3 (1990), pp. 171–95; **H. I. Ansoff**, 'Critique of Henry Mintzberg's "The design school: reconsidering the basic premises of strategic management"' *Strategic Management Journal*, vol. 12, no. 6 (1991), pp. 449–61.

[52] **H. Mintzberg** and **J. Lampel**, 'Reflecting on the strategy process', *Sloan Management Review*, vol. 40, no. 3 (1999), pp. 21–30.

[53] **K. R. Andrews**, *The Concept of Corporate Strategy*, Irwin, 1971; **I. Ansoff**, *Corporate Strategy*, chapter 6, McGraw-Hill, 1965.

[54] This section draws heavily upon **J. Kay**, **P. McKiernan**, and **D. O. Faulkner**, 'The history of strategy and some thoughts about the future' in *The Oxford Handbook of Strategy*, edited by A. Campbell and D. Faulkner, Oxford University Press, 2006, pp. 27–52.

[55] **J. Kay**, 'History vindicates the science of muddling through', *The Financial Times*, 14 April 2009.

[56] **Kay et al.**, see n. 55 above.

[57] **Mintzberg**, see n. 53 above.

[58] **H. Mintzberg** and **J. A. Waters**, 'Of strategies, deliberate and emergent', *Strategic Management Journal*, vol. 6, no. 3 (1985), pp. 257–72.

[59] **Mintzberg**, see n. 11 above.

[60] **H. Mintzberg**, 'Learning 1, Planning 0', *California Management Review*, vol. 38, no. 4 (1996), pp. 92–3.

[61] **Henderson**, see n. 5 above.

PART TWO
STRATEGIC ANALYSIS

CHAPTER 2
EVALUATING THE MACRO-ENVIRONMENT

 Learning Objectives

After completing this chapter you should be able to:

- Define the macro-environment
- Discuss the role of scanning and monitoring in detecting environmental trends
- Evaluate PESTLE as a framework for analysing the macro-environment
- Use scenario planning to deal with uncertainty
- Explain SWOT analysis
- Evaluate the relationship between the macro and the competitive environment

Introduction

What happens in the macro-environment is important to an organization. This is because changes that take place in the macro-environment may point to trends that can substantially impact an organization's competitive environment. These changes are referred to as **disruptions**, *discontinuities*, or **tipping points**. In this chapter, we will evaluate the tools of analysis an organization can use to discern changes in its macro-environment. This includes scenario planning, which is used to help managers make better decisions under conditions of uncertainty. The benefits and limitations of a PESTLE framework. A SWOT analysis, and its links with scenario planning and PESTLE analysis is also briefly discussed, before being taken up in detail in **Chapter 4**. The aim of this chapter is not merely to apply these techniques but, importantly, to understand their limitations. The chapter ends with a discussion of the links between the macro and competitive environment.

2.1 The Macro-environment

The external environment facing the organization consists of both a macro-environment and a competitive environment. The **competitive environment** consists of the industry and markets in which organizations compete, and is analysed in detail in **Chapter 3**. The **macro-environment**, in contrast, is often referred to as the general environment. This is because changes that occur here will have an effect that transcends organizations and specific industries. **Figure 2.1** shows the relationship between the macro-environment, the competitive environment, and the organization. It should be noted that, other things being equal, it is changes in the competitive environment that have the most direct and immediate impact on the organization.

That said, organizations must continually scan and monitor their macro-environment for *signals*, often weak or barely perceptible, which might indicate a structural change in their competitive environment. For example, Blockbuster was unwise not to scan the macro-environment for signs of change—in this case, technological change. The possibility of changing technologies was a clear threat to its bricks and mortar-based business, ushering in as it did an era of streaming entertainment content. Similarly, traditional booksellers with their high fixed costs bound up in expensive properties, were not scanning their macro-environment for evidence of change. Instead, they continued to compete with each other in the same industry, with the same tired business models—until Amazon came along and fundamentally changed the business model for selling books, with its online bookstore.

In order to scan and monitor their environment, organizations require tools of analysis or models that will allow them to factor in the changes in the macro-environment and evaluate their impact. One such approach involves *scanning* the environment to detect signals that will act as a signpost for future changes in the organization's industry. In addition, an organization must *monitor* its environment to discern patterns and trends that are beginning to form and try to *forecast* the future direction of these trends. **Peter Ginter and Jack Duncan**[1] argue that macro-environmental analysis can act as

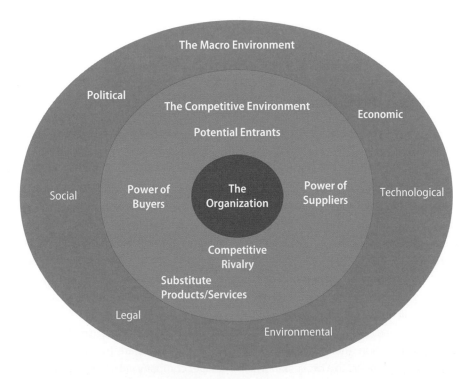

Figure 2.1   The organization and its external environment.

an early-warning system by giving organizations time to anticipate opportunities and threats and develop appropriate responses.

Therefore, the aim of macro-environmental analysis is to aid the organization in discerning trends in the macro-environment that might impact upon its industry and markets. The organization is then able to formulate a strategy and use its internal resources and capabilities to position itself to exploit opportunities as they arise. At the same time, the strategy will be acting to mitigate the effects of any threats. However, as we shall see in **Chapter 3**, there is a belief that the rate of change in the competitive environment is increasing, and becoming more turbulent and unpredictable. This uncertainty effectively shortens the lead time an organization has to anticipate and respond to changes in its competitive environment.

2.2 Scanning, Monitoring, and Forecasting Changes in the Environment

The purpose of scanning and monitoring the macro-environment is to try to discern changes, however small, that have the potential to disrupt an organization's competitive environment. Once these changes are discerned, it is up to the organization to monitor them, and to find out if they might become a trend that can affect its industry. Clearly, experience and intuition will be involved in trying to forecast where these changes will eventually manifest themselves, or indeed if they will have any impact at all. In reality, the problem with trying to predict changes in any environment is that there are *known knowns, known unknowns, and unknown unknowns.*[2] In other words, there are things that we know that we know, there are things that we know we don't know, and there are things we don't even know that we don't know. We look at scanning, monitoring, and forecasting changes in the macro-environment with this caveat in mind.

2.2.1 Scanning the Environment

It is often said that there are two certainties in life: death and taxes. However, a third certainty can be added: change. If the external environment facing organizations was stable and simple to understand, then they would be faced with an enviable situation of having relatively little change or, if change occurred, it would be easy to forecast based on historic trends. Some commodity markets exhibit a relative degree of stability, making predictions or extrapolations based on past data quite reliable. However, most environmental conditions facing organizations are complex, uncertain, and prone to change. They are complex because of the sheer volume of data that exists in the environment. Therefore, any analytical tool or framework can only extract and simplify a tiny proportion of this data. At the same time, any given source of data, for example economic data on the well-being of the economy, is ambiguous, as it can be interpreted in a number of different ways. Lastly, the world does not stand still but is continually changing.

If past performance is no guarantee of what will occur in the future because of uneven changes and disruptive innovation, then attempts at forecasting the future are fraught with uncertainty. **Disruptive innovation** refers to a process in which a smaller company with fewer resources is able to successfully challenge established, incumbent businesses.[3] It was popularized by Harvard professor,

Clayton Christensen, who differentiated between what he called *sustaining* and *disruptive innova-tions*.[4] A **sustaining innovation** allows an organization to enhance the performance of its existing technology. This sustaining innovation is usually adopted by incumbent firms in the industry which will have invested substantial financial and emotional capital in their current technology. As a result, they seek to 'sustain' or continue using the current technology in the industry. In contrast, a disruptive technology creates a new performance trajectory for consumers based on different attributes than those of the existing technology used by the incumbent firms.

Throughout history these discontinuities have often manifested themselves in disruptive tech-nologies, from the replacement of the horse and carriage by motorcars to IBM mainframes being disrupted by the PC revolution. The key to exploiting disruptive technologies is first to recognize their existence, irrespective of the capital already invested in the current technologies. Next, to make a corporate-wide decision to embrace the disruptive technology. This will mean being prepared to change the business model on which your organization is based. We will say much more about disruptive innovation in **Chapters 3** and **7**. Examples of disruptive innovators include Amazon and Netflix, which have both taken advantage of the Internet to change the way established products are customized and delivered to end consumers.

Fahey and Narayanan suggest three goals for an analysis of the macro-environment.[5] First, the analysis should provide an understanding of current and potential changes taking place in the en-vironment. Second, it should provide important intelligence for strategic decision makers. Third, environmental analysis should facilitate and foster strategic thinking in organizations. Scanning may reveal 'actual or imminent environmental change because it explicitly focuses on areas that the organization may have previously neglected'.[6] Scanning the environment has been made far more cost-effective with the advent of the Internet. Prior to the Internet, the view was that scanning was a costly activity, which could only take account of a fraction of the information that existed in an organization's environment. By redefining search costs, the Internet has changed the economics of undertaking scanning. At the same time, it has provided access to a wealth of data which requires time and effort to structure properly.

Scanning, therefore, is an opportunity for the organization to detect **weak signals** in the macro-environment before they begin to coalesce into a discernible pattern which might affect its com-petitive environment. Weak signals refer to minor changes in the external environment that an organization's scanning of the environment may barely register. This is because their impact has yet to be felt. The key for organizations is to be able to read these signals correctly and monitor them until they coalesce into a more clearly discernible pattern. However, there are errors that can follow when looking for patterns. The first is that the organization may fail to identify these signals. The second is that the organization may discern a pattern that is not there, but is based on the assumptions and mental models that managers carry in their heads.

This is referred to as **cognitive bias**. Cognitive bias takes place as we think about different courses of action. It leads managers to rely heavily upon their own intuition and judgements which are based on past experiences. In effect, managers assign too much, or not enough, significance to informa-tion which leads them to make inappropriate decisions.[7] This is because we view our experience through filters which have the effect of distorting reality. As a result, our experience betrays us, in-stead of making us wiser, because it introduces systematic errors into our decision-making process.[8] As the Russian novelist, **Leo Tolstoy** said, 'everyone thinks of changing the world, but no one thinks of changing himself'.

We saw in **Chapter 1** how a manager's reliance on his or her existing theory of the business can affect the success of the organization, by blindsiding them to changes taking place in their environment. Ansoff[9] makes the point that the detection of weak signals requires senior management commitment and sensitivity on the part of the observers. This means that the organization must be diligent in continually scanning its macro-environment for weak signals. When it believes that it has discerned something significant occurring in its macro-environment, this broad scanning can turn into a more focused monitoring. Of course, managers must first be aware of, and then deal with, their cognitive bias if the weak signals are not to be misinterpreted.

2.2.2 Monitoring the Environment

While scanning the environment may make organizations aware of weak signals, unless these are carefully monitored the resulting patterns will be missed. Monitoring can be seen as the activity that follows these initially disparate signals and tracks them as they grow into more clearly discernible patterns. Monitoring allows an organization to see how these macro-environment trends will impact on its competitive environment. Whereas scanning is a more broad-brush approach, monitoring uses a finer brush stroke. However, the two are inseparable, since without an identification of weak signals in the macro-environment there is no focus for an organization's monitoring activities. One way in which an organization might monitor weak signals is to set thresholds such that any activity which occurs above the threshold will be monitored. This might include, for example, when an interest is shown by a major competitor in a particular social or technological change. This interest then becomes the threshold at which the organization itself starts to take an interest.

2.2.3 Forecasting Changes in the Environment

The purpose of scanning and monitoring the macro-environment is to aid the organization in developing viable forecasts of future trends before they become an unmitigated threat. This is particularly useful when dealing with disruptions which themselves will usually evolve from weak signals that exist in the environment. The objective is to use this information to develop robust strategies that ensure a degree of competitive advantage. To accomplish this requires some understanding of the nature of uncertainty which we will address when we look at scenario planning.

2.3 PESTLE Analysis

A useful tool when scanning the macro-environment is **PESTLE analysis**. This refers to political, economic, social, technological, legal, and environmental factors. It is worth noting that some commentators exclude legal and environmental factors, preferring to limit the acronym to PEST. It is not important whether we use PESTLE or PEST, but to understand how this framework can be used, and to be aware of its limitations. As long as the choice of acronym is clearly defined we have a consistent approach.

PESTLE analysis is simply another tool to help the organization detect and monitor those weak signals in the hope of recognizing, and responding, to changes taking place in the macro-environment.

It is used to help detect trends in the macro-environment that will ultimately find their way into the industry in which the organization competes. It provides a link between the macro-environment and competitive environment, because weak signals in the macro-environment may become a key force for change in the industry conditions. Although we will deal with each factor in turn, it should be noted that interrelationships between the factors exist.

2.3.1 Political Factors

The political factor of PESTLE deals with the effects of government policy, and other political institutions. This includes items such as government stability, taxation policy, and government regulation. Government stability is seldom a major issue in Western economies. However, where multinational corporations operate across international borders, political factors to take into account include the stability of governments and political systems in those countries. For example, will there be any sudden and detrimental legislative changes that might jeopardize the substantial investments they will have made? What are the effects of a change in government policy on the safety of their personnel operating in these countries? How will a change in policy affect the organization's infrastructure which allows the efficient transfer of goods and services, as well as financial assets?

A change in government policy in favour of deregulation has the effect of opening up markets to competition. Organizations within the industry are forced to innovate and achieve efficiencies to remain competitive. This is because new entrants will often enter a market with lower cost curves and more innovative products and services owing to a better use of technology, and a clearer understanding of consumer needs. Firms therefore need to be scanning their macro-environment for signs of change in government policy which may impact their industry.

Car manufacturers around the world are having to deal with political issues, environmental issues, as well as a technological shift towards electric vehicles. In the EU, an agreement was reached to reduce carbon dioxide emissions from new cars by 37.5 per cent by 2030, compared with 2021; emissions from new vans will have to be 31 per cent lower. The European Automobile Manufacturers' Association (ACEA), which represents companies such as Renault and BMW, said the targets 'will be extremely demanding on Europe's auto industry'.[10] The EU decision is driven by its signing of the Paris Agreement. The central aim of this agreement is to strengthen the global response to the threat of climate change by keeping a global temperature rise in check.[11] Under the Paris Agreement countries, including EU member states, have committed to keeping a global temperature rise this century to well below 2°C (35.6°F) and pursue efforts to limit it to 1.5C. Cars are responsible for around 12 per cent of total EU emissions of carbon dioxide (CO_2), the main greenhouse gas.[12]

That said, the EU decision has faced opposition from different stakeholders. Europe's car industry sees it as being 'unrealistic', while environmental groups criticize it for being insufficient to achieve climate change targets. In the USA, California sets tougher environmental regulations than the rest of the country. The combined market share for electric vehicles and plug-in hybrids in the 'Golden State' has continued to grow. But is the increase moving at a quick enough pace to reach the goal set by state policymakers for 5 million zero-carbon emission vehicles on California's roads by 2030?[13] The discussion of PESTLE analysis, and how these macro-environmental factors affect the car industry, highlights the interrelationships between different PESTLE factors. And, the dangers of simply viewing each factor as a discrete element.

Porter and van der Linde[14] suggest that environmental regulations, such as reducing pollution, may act to spur competitive companies on to innovate and reduce costs to counter the increased costs of regulation. While US carmakers fought new fuel consumption standards in the vain hope that they would go away, Japanese and German car makers developed lighter and more fuel-efficient cars. The companies that reap the competitive benefits will be the early movers: *'the companies that see the opportunity first and embrace innovation-based solutions'.* To do this, managers need to develop a new mindset which recognizes sustainable improvement as a competitive opportunity rather than as a threat.

2.3.2 Economic Factors

The changes in economic activity manifest themselves through changes in interest rates, disposable income, unemployment rates, retail price index (inflation), gross domestic product (GDP), and exchange rates. However, economic data can be notoriously fickle and ambiguous. In addition, an economic indicator can never provide a complete picture (even of the subset of data it purports to track), but rather provides a snapshot and simplification of complex economic phenomena. This makes scanning and monitoring the macro-environment for signs of economic shifts very difficult.

The strengthening of an economy will generally benefit industries, but the extent of its effect will vary according to which economic factors are most affected. For example, the construction industry and manufacturing are most susceptible to increases in the rate of interest. Manufacturing organizations that export goods abroad will be scanning the macro-environment for signs of an appreciation in exchange rates, the effect of which will be to make it harder for them to sell their goods abroad, but relatively easier for competing importers to sell their goods in the domestic market.

Since the financial crisis in 2008, there have been many political and economic signals aimed at the financial services industry. For example, the bailout of US and European banks by taxpayers led to government proposals to ensure that banks were not undercapitalized. Further regulation has been proposed to safeguard consumers, along with proposals that banks separate their investment activities from their retail activities.

2.3.3 Social Factors

Social factors include changes in demographics such as changes in incomes, the age and size of populations, and culture. In many Western economies, a trend exists towards an ageing population. The question arises: how should organizations respond? Products and services aimed at a younger market segment will need to be refined if they are to meet the **critical success factors** required by a changing industry. Critical success factors are those factors in an industry which keep customers loyal and allow the organization to compete successfully. Retail organizations in Europe and the USA have responded to this changing demographic by employing older personnel. They recognize that retired individuals often possess a wealth of experience that can add value when serving customers.

In China, decades of the one-child policy have changed its demographics into the shape of an hourglass, with the elderly at the top and the youngest at the bottom. The policy has created a challenge in which an only child will be relied on to support their two ageing parents, and four grandparents. The so-called 4-2-1 challenge is the future facing the 'BAT generation'. A generation so named because it has grown up in a world with tech giants Baidu, Alibaba, and Tencent.[15] The majority of them are in China's 430 million-strong middle-class, which is projected to grow to 659 million by 2030. The changing tastes of this generation will have a huge impact not only on China, but also on the rest of the world. These millennials have disposable income and enjoy spending it. In the past, much of this expenditure has been spent on Western luxury retail goods, such as Apple laptops and Gucci handbags, but that is changing.

Research by McKinsey found that Chinese consumers now rank local products higher than foreign ones in nine out of seventeen categories, including beer, electronics, and even fashion. This is driven by a pride in China's cultural identity and its economic success. The spending power of this demographic group means that new products and technological breakthroughs will increasingly be based on the desires and needs of China's BAT generation. For example, a number of companies operating in China have begun to target the rapidly growing ACGN (anime, comics, games, novels) subculture of Chinese millennials. Fast forward to 2030, and as the BAT generation gets older, their expenditure habits will start to change. By 2030, they will represent about 40 per cent of China's population. They will also be in charge of making purchasing decisions for their families: perhaps 100 million elderly people and 224 million children.

The BAT generation start to reach their peak earning power between the ages of thirty and fifty, and now have to juggle supporting their parents with providing for their own children, thus necessitating a change in their spending habits. The 4-2-1 challenge changes to 1-2-4. They have lower disposable incomes, which means less money spent on luxury brands and more on health care, insurance and education for their children.

2.3.4 Technological Factors

Some of the major disruptions taking place in the macro-environment are technological. Think about how Amazon, Alibaba, and Reliance Industries have used the Internet to challenge traditional retailing. Technological factors include the speed with which new technological discoveries supersede established technologies. The rate of change of technology and innovation has the effect of causing new industries to emerge and changes the ways in which existing industries compete. For instance, the rapid rate of change of technology has changed the dynamics in industries such as retail, newspaper publishing, banking, financial services, and insurance.

This has allowed new entrants to enter the market at a lower cost base than incumbents, offering more competitively priced products and services and gaining market share in the process. For example, Blockbuster's mail order business model was no match for Netflix's use of digital technology to stream films online 'on demand' and via 'subscription' (see **Case Study: Disruptive Innovation from Netflix** at the end of this chapter). Organizations may not be able to predict all technological events, but using PESTLE and scenario planning they may be in a stronger competitive position to respond to these events once they have occurred.

Technological factors affecting corporations include big data. **Big data** refers to extremely large data sets that may be analysed computationally by the use of algorithms. Given the size of data involved, it is particularly useful for large corporations such as Google, Facebook, and Alibaba. It enables Amazon, for example, to reveal patterns, trends and associations that relate to consumer behaviour.[16] This enables Amazon to provide targeted offerings based on an analysis of customers and their preferences, the types of purchases they make, their demographics and their willingness to make a purchase.

Another technological factor is artificial intelligence. **Artificial intelligence** (AI) is any technology that aims to emulate cognitive human behaviour such as learning and problem solving. The aim is to create intelligent machines that can perform tasks and react like human beings. This is different from 'machine learning' which is a learning algorithm based on data, such as Amazon's 'Alexa'. Witness Ant Group, an affiliate of Alibaba, which uses AI and data from Alipay, its core mobile payments platform, to service more than ten times as many customers as the largest US banks, but with less than one-tenth the number of employees.[17]

A much discussed technological trend is the 'Internet of Things'. **The Internet of Things** (IoT) refers to a network of physical objects—'things'—that are embedded with sensors, software, and other technologies which allow these things to connect, interact and exchange data with other devices and systems over the Internet. It includes 'dumb' or non-Internet enabled devices. As long as the different devices all have sensors and technology embedded within them, they can be monitored and controlled remotely.

A technological factor which continues to grow and impact businesses is cloud computing. **Cloud computing** refers to the practice of using a network of remote servers hosted on the Internet to store, manage, and process data, rather than a local server or a personal computer. Some of the world's largest corporations including Alibaba, Tencent, Microsoft and Amazon have developed successful cloud computing businesses in which they sell analytics, computing power and storage to companies, including giving them access to AI. For an understanding of the importance with which technology companies place on cloud computing in India, see **Strategy in Focus 2.1: Bharti Airtel and Amazon Team Up in the Cloud**.

2.3.5 Legal Factors

Legal factors include legislative changes or constraints. These include factors such as health and safety legislation, changes to mergers and acquisitions policy, and employment regulations. An awareness of legal changes which impact an organization's industry will help an organization to see how its industry is changing, and what steps it needs to take to stay ahead of those changes. For example, the imposition of minimum wage legislation imposes an additional cost on businesses which companies can choose to absorb by increasing their productivity, pass the cost on to the consumer, or reduce their headcount.

2.3.6 Environmental Factors

It is often said that 'consumers are becoming more green'. That is, their primary focus is a concern for the environment. This includes how waste is recycled, the amount of plastic packaging being used to store and distribute products, animal welfare, and the effects of climate change. For example, the global impact of the coronavirus has highlighted the need to ensure the highest standards of hygiene and safety when trading different livestock which have the potential to cross-contaminate and affect humans. Many organizations also make a point of stressing their corporate social responsibility credentials on their website and product packaging.

Irrespective of the industry a company competes in, now more than ever, it has to be aware of environmental issues and the impact of its activities on different stakeholders. (See **Strategy in Focus 2.2**, which highlights BP's intent to move away from fossil fuels.) The Germany utility company,

STRATEGY IN FOCUS 2.1   Bharti Airtel and Amazon Team Up in the Cloud

Bharti Airtel has struck a deal with Amazon to fend off Mukesh Ambani's Reliance Jio and Microsoft in the battle for India's cloud computing market. The strategic alliance between the mobile operator and Amazon Web Services, the cloud business of Jeff Bezos, is the latest big bet taken by US tech giants on the rapidly digitizing country of 1.4 billion people, where Facebook, Google and Microsoft have all made recent investments. 'We've decided to go really deep with Amazon Web Services,' said Harmeen Mehta, head of Airtel's cloud division, in a press briefing. 'This makes a partnership to be reckoned with.'

The deal will see Airtel, India's second-largest mobile operator with 300 million subscribers, offer its customers a range of cloud services spanning from data migration to analytics. Puneet Chandok, president of Amazon's commercial business in India and South Asia, called the alliance a 'massive opportunity', adding that the coronavirus pandemic has shown that 'digital transformation is not optional any more'. The deal comes almost exactly a year after rival telecoms group Reliance Jio announced a ten-year partnership with Microsoft's cloud platform Azure. Mr Ambani said Jio would provide free connectivity and cloud services to start-ups, throwing down the gauntlet in an intensifying scramble for market share.

Thomas Kurian, chief executive of Google Cloud, said he was 'bullish' on India and would start up a new cloud region in Delhi after launching one in Mumbai three years ago. Chinese titans Alibaba and Tencent are also starting to deepen their cloud presence in India and southeast Asia, a region that has emerged as a key battleground in the tech war between Washington and Beijing.

India's public cloud market is expected to be worth $7 billion by 2024, reports International Data Corporation, the US market research group. 'We're seeing massive adoption for cloud as a result of COVID-19, this only helps the customer in the current environment,' said Rishu Sharma, cloud analyst at IDC based in Gurgaon. 'This partnership is most likely going to start a price war,' she said. 'The focus is now going to be on guaranteeing better contracts, pricing and an optimal customer service.'

According to market research firm Canalys, Amazon Web Services holds 32.4 per cent of the global cloud services market, Microsoft Azure 17.6 per cent and Google Cloud is tied with Alibaba Cloud at 6 per cent.

Source: Stephanie Findlay 'Bharti Airtel and Amazon team up for India cloud market push', *Financial Times*, 5 August 2020.

RWE, which is Europe's biggest producer of carbon dioxide emissions, has signalled its intention to become carbon neutral by 2040. RWE operates some of the largest coal power stations on the continent. It plans to lower carbon emissions by 70 per cent compared with its 2012 levels. RWE has long been a prime target of climate activists. Many companies are adopting performance measures which include environmental and social factors, as well as financial measures. These include a 'balanced scorecard' and 'triple bottom line' approach, both of which are covered in detail in **Chapter 4**.

STRATEGY IN FOCUS 2.2 BP Moves Away from Fossil Fuels

BP has won guarded praise from climate emergency campaigners and a hefty share price bounce by unveiling new plans to shift away from fossil fuels and towards low carbon energy within the next decade. BP revealed the energy transition strategy alongside its first dividend cut since its Deepwater Horizon oil spill in 2010. Despite reporting one of its worst quarterly results on record in 2020, BP shares closed up as the company set out new plans to shift away from fossil fuels and towards clean energy. BP's new chief executive, Bernard Looney, promised to grow low-carbon investments eightfold by 2025, and tenfold by 2030, while cutting its fossil fuel output by 40 per cent from 2019 levels as part of his plan to reinvent BP as a 'net zero carbon' company by 2050.

The plan has won the cautious approval of green groups and climate action campaigners, which welcomed the near-term targets and ambitious spending plans. Mel Evans, a senior climate campaigner for Greenpeace UK, said BP had 'woken up to the immediate need to cut carbon emissions this decade'. Mark van Baal, of the green shareholder group Follow This, said BP was 'the first oil major that walks the walk instead of just offering ambitions for 2050, like its peers'. 'BP shows a sense of urgency and imagination beyond oil and gas. It seems that other oil majors want to stay oil and gas companies, only not look like one,' he added.

The plan to transform BP from an oil major to an integrated energy company is set to increase the budget for low-carbon technologies from $500 million, or 3 per cent of its total spending, to $5 billion or almost a third of its budget within the next ten years. The spending would increase its renewable energy capacity twentyfold and include investments in carbon capture, bioenergy and hydrogen production too. BP also plans to shrink its oil and gas production by more than 1 million barrels of oil a day, to about 1.5 million barrels a day by the end of the decade, and rule out oil exploration in new geographies. CEO Looney said the next decade would be 'a critical one in the fight against climate change' and promised a 'decade of delivery for BP' to help drive a transition in the energy industry.

The decision to rein in BP's shareholder dividends was part of a new financial framework to deliver investment in the energy transition 'at scale', while reducing debts and remaining an attractive investment proposition for shareholders, he added. BP was the FTSE 100's biggest dividend distributor, with payouts in 2020 set to reach £6.7 billion for its shareholders, which include thousands of individual investors. The oil company will save over £3 billion every year by paying out 5.25 cents per share, down from 10.5 cents. BP's decision to cut its dividend for the first time in a decade comes just months after Royal Dutch Shell slashed its shareholder dividend for the first time since the Second World War. Shell cut its payout by two-thirds due to a 'crisis of uncertainty' triggered by the collapse in global oil demand caused by the coronavirus, which has forced oil companies to revise their forecasts for oil market prices and slash the value of their oil and gas reserves.

Source: Gillian Ambrose, 'BP enjoys share bounce after unveiling plans to shift away from fossil fuels'. *The Guardian*, 4 August 2020.

2.3.7 How to Undertake PESTLE Analysis

As you undertake PESTLE analysis, it becomes apparent these are not discrete categories but often have a great degree of overlap between them. Hence, there is no need to be concerned if you find yourself making similar points in the different PESTLE categories. For instance, there might be some similarity between 'Economic' and 'Social' or 'Political' and 'Legal' categories. A key point of the PESTLE analysis is to surface some broad trends taking place in the macro-environment.

As we have seen, it may initially be difficult to determine with any degree of certainty the sort of patterns which may be developing in the macro-environment. However, once these trends are identified another key point of PESTLE analysis is to determine whether these trends will have a potential impact on a company's competitive environment. And how should the company respond to these impacts? Given the broad nature of PESTLE analysis it is quite straightforward for use at a corporate level. **Table 2.1** shows a PESTLE analysis for the German auto manufacturer, Volkswagen. Note that the same points are made in some of the different PESTLE categories which illustrates the interdependence within the PESTLE framework. We might also note that PESTLE requires an evaluation and assessment of the points being raised, rather than simply describing them.

Political	Paris Agreement—countries are actively pursuing efforts to slow the global temperature increases in the 21st century. Cars are responsible for around 12% of total EU emissions of carbon dioxide (CO_2). Impact for VW: How will it comply with regulation to reduce carbon dioxide emissions for all new cars by 37.5 per cent by 2030, compared with 2021?
Economic	What is happening to exchange rates, GDP, disposable incomes, and interest rates? Impact for VW: VW sells more cars than any other car manufacturer, including Toyota. If German exchange rates increase this has an impact of the cost of its cars for customers based abroad. If German wages are rising (without matching productivity increases) VW may need to consider further outsourcing of its supply chain.
Social	How will social factors, such as changes in buyer habits, the age and size of populations, and culture impact VW? How will global shocks, such as the COVID-19 global pandemic affect social behaviour? Impact for VW: we might consider how the growth of the Chinese BAT generation might impact VW sales in China in the future. VW needs to ensure its massive investment in electric vehicles will appeal to a wider market, including women, who only purchased 15 per cent of their all-new electric VW Golf car sold in 2020. The coronavirus pandemic left customers needing to travel less and hence less reliant on their cars. What can VW do to mitigate the falls in auto sales?
Technological	What is happening to the trend for electric vehicles among consumers? How quickly will current automobile technology become obsolete? Impact for VW: to what extent is VW embracing and investing in the new technology? How will this affect its manufacturing processes? Is it developing strategic alliances and partnerships which will help secure its future?
Legal	Paris Agreement Impact for VW: How will it comply with regulation to reduce carbon dioxide emissions for all new cars by 37.5 per cent by 2030, compared with 2021?
Environmental	Concerns about global warming—consumer groups are increasingly environmentally aware and environmental groups continue to apply pressure for tighter environmental regulations. Impact for VW: more stringent environmental regulations usually means an increase in the cost of manufacturing cars. Can VW pass this cost on to the consumer? Can they absorb it themselves via more efficient manufacturing processes? Can they innovate and move away from their existing business model?

Table 2.1   PESTLE Analysis for Volkswagen Group (VW)

2.3.8 Limitations of PESTLE Analysis

PESTLE analysis is not simply writing a 'shopping list', the use of disparate bullet points without any consideration of their interactions, or wider ramifications. In listing PESTLE factors, one must clearly exercise judgement to draw out the implications of each factor on the organization's industry, and ultimately on the organization itself. Importantly, it requires management time and resources to filter all this information, and an awareness of management bias, if the information is to be interpreted objectively. Furthermore, the rate of change of PESTLE factors in the macro-environment and their increasing unpredictability may act to limit the use of PESTLE analysis. Porter, we noted, argues that the industry is the only true arena for the organization to analyse, since it is the industry which has the greatest impact on a firm's markets and products.[18] While there is agreement that the industry in which an organization competes has the greatest effect on its ability to achieve competitive advantage, it would be unwise to refrain from analysing the macro-environment for early warning signs of changes to industry conditions.

Kees van der Heijden,[19] a former head of scenario planning at Shell, identifies three main types of uncertainty.

1. **Risks.** This is where past performance of similar events allows us to estimate the probabilities of future outcomes.
2. **Structural uncertainties.** This is where an event is unique, and therefore does not offer evidence to estimate the probabilities of future outcomes.
3. **Unknowables.** This is where we cannot even imagine the event.

Most managers are capable of dealing with the type of uncertainty that appears in the form of *risks*. Also, what is *unknowable* cannot, by definition, be forecast and therefore the organization must wait for the event to occur before it can react to it. This leaves **structural uncertainties**, where no probable pattern of outcomes can be derived from previous experience. In such a situation, van der Heijden suggests scenario planning as a useful tool of analysis to help the organization make sense of an uncertain and dynamic environment that has little in the way of clear road maps.

2.4 Scenario Planning

Paul Schoemaker[20] states scenario planning may be defined as *'a disciplined method for imagining possible futures'*. For **Michael Porter**, scenario planning is *'an internally consistent view of what the future might turn out to be'*.[21] The oil multinational Royal Dutch Shell has used scenario planning since the 1970s to help it generate and evaluate its strategic options. Scenario planning has given Shell a better success rate in its oil forecasts than its competitors, and it was the first oil company to see overcapacity in the tanker business and Europe's petrochemicals.[22] As **Adam Kahane** reminds us:

> In the oil industry, experts have sometimes been able to suggest, but rarely to predict, the key turning points in crude oil prices. . . . The Shell approach to strategic planning is, instead of forecasts, to use scenarios, a set of stories about alternative futures.[23]

These *stories* promote a discussion of possibilities, beyond the most likely one, and encourage the organization to consider 'what if' questions. Therefore, a **scenario** can be seen as a challenging, plausible, and internally consistent view of what the future might turn out to be. It is not a forecast in the sense that one is able to extrapolate, using past data. But, it does deal with the future, and provides a useful tool of analysis for the organization to structure the abundance of information that is contained in the present. In particular, scenarios help organizations to recognize the weak signals that signpost changes in its macro-environment. And it is these weak signals which precede environmental discontinuities and disruptions, or what former CEO of Intel, Andy Grove, refers to as 'strategic inflection points', which help shape the competitive environment.[24] If an organization is to remain proactive in its competitive environment it must not allow the rules of the game to be changed to its detriment; that is, it must be capable of dealing with a **tipping point**. A phrase popularized by journalist, **Malcolm Gladwell**, a tipping point refers to a moment in time when consumer demand for a product crosses a threshold and tips, causing demand to increase exponentially.[25]

Strategic decisions are almost always fraught with ambiguity and uncertainty, which create complexity for decision makers. As human beings, we are subject to biases and imperfect reasoning about uncertainty. We will tend to misread events that are unlikely, and either ignore or overemphasize unlikely but significant events. In an attempt to resolve these shortcomings, most companies will use some form of discounted cash flow coupled with sensitivity analysis when analysing risky strategic decisions. The problem with these quantitative approaches is that they imbue the decision-making with a false sense of objectivity and can be misleading. For example, sensitivity analysis is overly simplistic in that by varying one parameter at a time it fails to incorporate any links or correlations between them. In contrast, scenario planning helps to overcome many of the shortcomings of traditional decision-making methods by allowing organizations to change several variables at the same time, without keeping other variables constant. Crucially, scenario planning helps to overcome some of the *biases* and *imperfect reasoning* that human beings make under conditions of uncertainty.[26]

Scenarios are a tool of analysis to help improve the decision-making process set against the background of a number of possible future environments. They benefit the organization by readily helping managers think in a more systematic way. This allows individuals to recognize change more readily in their business environment, instead of ignoring or rejecting it. Van der Heijden outlines the benefits of scenario planning for Shell:

- More robust strategic decisions
- Better thinking about the future by a 'stretching mental model'
- Enhancing corporate perception and recognizing events as a pattern
- Improving communication throughout the company by providing a context for decisions
- A means to provide leadership to the organization.

The process of scenario planning should have the objective of positively influencing the strategy of the organization. This requires that the scenarios devised should stretch the imagination of management while also remaining plausible. In order to achieve this, organizations must be prepared to invest resources in educating managers to help them make the best use of scenarios. They need to recognize that developing scenarios takes time and is most effective when managers from different parts of the business interact. By constructing multiple scenarios, an organization can explore the consequences of uncertainty for its choice of strategies. Furthermore, an organization can formulate strategies knowing that the assumptions on which it competes are surfaced and adequately assessed.

2.4.1 **How to Build Scenarios**

Scenario planning is relevant to almost any situation in which a decision maker needs to understand how the future of his or her industry or **strategic business unit** might develop.[27] It divides our knowledge into two areas: **(1)** things we think we know something about; and **(2)** things we consider uncertain or unknowable. The first area is based on the past and continuity. For example, an organization can make fairly safe assumptions about the direction of a country's demographic profile. The uncertain elements include such things as future oil prices, interest rates, the outcomes of political elections, and when a pandemic might occur. Even here it is not necessary to account for every possible outcome, since simplifying the outcome is fine for scenario planning. Therefore, an organization might simply categorize future interest rates as high, medium, or low, rather than trying to work out every possible permutation. Scenario planning is also useful to help an organization which might be considering a major capital outlay. It is important to note that, as scenarios highlight possible futures but not specific strategy formulations, a wide range of viewpoints, such as those of consultants and policy analysts, can also be included in the process. This also highlights that scenarios are best undertaken in teams.

A Process for Scenario Planning

1. **Define the scope**. This involves setting the scope of analysis and the time frame. The scope refers to a key issue or challenge that concerns the organization. The scope of analysis may include its products, markets, and geographical areas. The time frame can be a few years, much less for hypercompetitive industries, but considerably more, upwards of fifteen to twenty years, for oil exploration. The time frame can be determined by factors such as an organization's product life cycles, and the rate of technological change in the industry. Once the time frame is set, the question becomes: what knowledge would the organization benefit most from in that timescale?

2. **Identify the major stakeholders**. Stakeholders are individuals and groups who can affect and are affected by the organization's decisions. The organization needs to know their current levels of interests and power, and how these have changed over time.

3. **Identify basic trends**. Which PESTLE and industry factors will have the most impact on the issues identified in Step 1? At this point, we are trying to determine the key drivers, or reasons, for change. This will be based on assumptions we have made about why certain factors are drivers, and it will be helpful to surface these assumptions. The impact of these basic trends on our current strategy can then be listed as *positive*, *negative*, or *uncertain*.

4. **Identify key uncertainties**. Now we ask: which events that have an uncertain outcome will most affect the issues with which the organization is concerned? Here again the organization might consider PESTLE factors, in addition to industry factors. For example, what trends in consumer behaviour are likely to characterize future consumer demand? These key uncertainties should be limited to keep the analysis simple.

5. **Construct initial scenario themes**. Once the basic trends and key uncertainties are developed, the organization has the basic building blocks for scenario planning. It can then identify disruptive changes in market conditions by placing all positive elements in one scenario, and placing the negative elements in another broad scenario.

6. **Check for consistency and plausibility**. This involves checking to see if the trends identified are compatible with the chosen time frame. If they are not, then remove all the trends that do not fit the time frame. Do the scenarios combine outcomes of uncertainty that actually go together? In other words, ensure that inconsistent outcomes are not put in a scenario, such as having full employment and zero inflation together. Finally, have major stakeholders been placed in a position they will not tolerate or cannot change? In this case, the scenario described will probably change into another one. The key then is to identify this ultimate scenario.

7. **Develop learning scenarios**. Here the role is to develop relevant themes for the organization around which possible outcomes and trends can be organized. The scenarios can be given a name or title to reflect that they tell a story. This also helps individuals to remember the scenarios. At this stage, the scenarios are useful for research and further learning within the organization rather than decision-making.

8. **Identify research needs**. Further research may be required to understand uncertainties and trends more fully. This is because organizations are knowledgeable about their own competitive environment, but less knowledgeable about other industries. Therefore, the organization may need to study changes (in disruptive technology, for instance) which have yet to impact its industry, but may ultimately do so.

9. **Develop quantitative models**. Once further research has been gained, the organization may wish to revisit the internal consistency of the scenarios and decide whether it might benefit from formalizing some interactions in a quantitative model. For example, scenarios can use a range of statistical techniques but the best scenarios are simple to understand. As such, we can use a scale of 0 and 1, where 0 represents a minimal impact on the organization, and 1 represents a maximum impact.

10. **Evolve towards decision scenarios**. The ultimate aim of the scenario building process is to move the organization towards scenarios that can be used to test its strategy formulations and help it generate new ideas. At this point it is helpful to double check Steps 1–8 to see if the scenarios take account of the issues facing the organization. We might expect to build two or three different scenarios to test our strategy options.

If the scenarios are useful to the organization, they might have the following characteristics:

(1) they address the challenges facing individuals in the organization;

(2) the scenarios are based on drivers for change, and internally consistent;

(3) they describe different futures which differ radically from an existing trend and, therefore, take account of disruptions; as opposed to being variations on a particular theme; and

(4) each scenario describes an equilibrium state that can exist for a considerable period of time as opposed to being merely short-lived.

As Schoemaker states: '*scenario planning attempts to capture the richness and range of possibilities, stimulating decision makers to consider changes they would otherwise ignore ... organizing ... into narratives that are easier to grasp and use than great volumes of data. Above all ... scenarios are aimed at challenging the prevailing mind-set.*'[28]

It is worth reiterating that scenarios are not intended to predict the future. They are designed to help managers deal with a highly uncertain and dynamic environment. They may be utilized at the

2

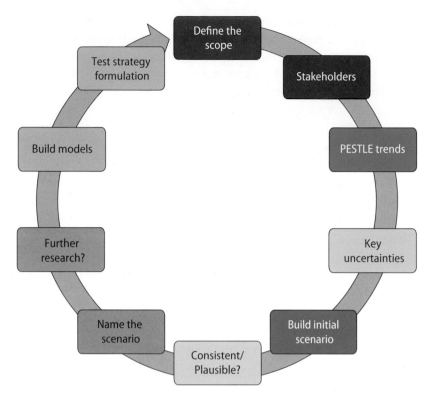

Figure 2.2   How to undertake scenario planning.

macro or competitive environment. Porter, while recognizing the value of multiple scenarios for an organization's choice of strategy, argues that '*Macro scenarios, despite their relevance, are too general to be sufficient for developing strategy in a particular industry*'.[29] Given the success of Shell with scenario planning, whether this statement is accepted may depend more on the industry being addressed rather than scenario planning, per se.

In summary, scenarios encourage management to '*think the unthinkable*', to question and surface assumptions they hold about the environment, and to be prepared to view events from a radically different perspective. Scenarios are a tool of analysis that examines the impact of uncertainty on organizations and industries by explicitly identifying some of the key uncertainties—the scenario variables. For scenarios to be effective, they must encourage the creation of robust strategies that match the organization's limited resources with the endless challenges in its external environment. To achieve this, they must identify and address as many as possible of the long-term opportunities and threats facing the organization.

2.5 **An Introduction to SWOT Analysis**

SWOT analysis refers to strengths, weaknesses, opportunities, and threats. Strengths and weaknesses refer to the organization's internal environment over which the organization has control. Strengths are areas where the organization excels or has a competitive advantage in comparison with its competitors, while weaknesses are areas where the organization is at a competitive disadvantage. Opportunities and threats manifest themselves in the organization's external environment, over which it has less control. SWOT may be used in the macro-environment and at the industry level. However, the unpredictable nature of events in the macro-environment tends to make the use of SWOT analysis more problematic.

Taken together, scenario planning and PESTLE analysis can help managers identify the external opportunities and threats (OT) facing an organization. The firm's internal strengths and weaknesses (SW) can best be determined following an appraisal of its own resources and capabilities. SWOT analysis allows an organization to assess the relevance of its current strategy in light of changes to industry conditions. It is readily understood within organizations as managers seek to turn potential threats into opportunities and weaknesses into strengths. There is some debate as to whether it is the external analysis which precedes the internal analysis of a firm's resources and capabilities, or vice versa. We discuss this in detail when we look at the resource-based view of strategy in **Chapter 5**. We can say that SWOT analysis is best undertaken once an audit of the macro-environment and the organization's own internal resources and capabilities has been completed. We will revisit SWOT analysis in detail in **Chapter 4**, and also explain how to use the TOWS matrix.

2.6 The Macro-environment and Industry Analysis

By making the links between the macro-environment and industry analysis explicit, an organization can conduct its analyses in more depth. It allows the organization to assess its ability to deal with the impact of macro-environmental trends on its industries, and markets. To be of benefit, these macro-environment factors require constant and structured monitoring. They allow an organization to detect important weak signals that coalesce into discernible patterns and point to structural changes in an industry. In this respect, both scenario planning and PESTLE have an important role to play in identifying the disruptions that will have the greatest impact on an organization's competitive environment. Although the macro-environment and industry analysis are discussed in separate chapters, it may be helpful to think of them as part of the same continuum. Seen in this way, the analysis undertaken simply moves an organization further along this continuum.

Summary

All organizations need to be aware of the events taking place in their macro-environment and understand what impact these might have on their industry conditions. Changes in the macro-environment can affect the way existing organizations compete and cause new industries to emerge. Therefore, it becomes important for organizations to scan and monitor their macro-environment in order to detect signs of change. We have seen that weak signals, which are often difficult to detect, may act as a precursor of disruptions. These disruptions may arise as a result of step changes in technology, for example, and represent structural changes that will impact an organization's industry.

The use of scenario planning is relevant here to help the organization develop different ways of thinking about its environment. Scenario planning involves developing a challenging, plausible, and internally consistent view of what the future might turn out to be. A major benefit of scenarios is to help organizations recognize the weak signals that signpost change in the environment, and to enable managers to question the assumptions they hold about the nature of competition.

PESTLE analysis is used for making sense of an organization's macro-environment. By monitoring changes in PESTLE factors, an organization is better able to position itself to take advantage of opportunities and mitigate threats. SWOT analysis deals with the strengths and weaknesses in the internal environment of the organization, and the opportunities and threats in its external environment. It can be applied when an organization has undertaken an analysis of its macro-environment using PESTLE analysis, to identify opportunities and threats. It can also be used after an appraisal of its internal capabilities to determine its strengths and weaknesses, and therefore its ability to handle external threats and opportunities.

We have seen that a relationship exists between the macro-environment and the competitive or industry environment. Events taking place in the macro-environment will eventually find their way into an organization's industry. Therefore, scanning and monitoring the macro-environment using scenario planning and PESTLE will benefit an organization in its competitive environment. It allows managers to periodically test the mental business models they hold. Finally, disruptive technological trends can be detected and acted upon, before they rewrite how an organization competes in its industry.

CASE STUDY **Disruptive Innovation from Netflix**

Introduction

Netflix was co-founded in 1997 by Reed Hastings and Mark Randolph. At that time, they were offering customers the opportunity to rent movies delivered by mail for a flat fee. The story goes that Hastings got the idea for Netflix only after he received a large late fee for a film he rented from his video store in California. Hastings had lost the film and after searching for six weeks had to pay up $40. Later, on his way to the gym, he reflected on the gym's business model; you pay a set fee and work out as little or as much as you want. This became Netflix's offering: customers can rent a DVD for as long as they like and no late fees are ever charged.

Netflix is the world's leading Internet television network, with more than 100 million members in over 190 countries. Source: © Diabluses/Shutterstock.com.

Netflix has gone through a number of changes since it began in 1997 as a DVD mail order service. The company has navigated the change from DVDs to streaming to becoming a global TV network. The dominant competitor during its inception, Blockbuster, has long since gone bankrupt. Today, Netflix is the world's leading internet television network, with more than 100 million members in over 190 countries enjoying more than 125 million hours of TV shows and movies per day. This includes original series, documentaries, and feature films. Netflix members pay a subscription to watch as much as they want, any time, anywhere, on nearly any Internet-connected screen. Members can play, pause, and resume watching, all without commercials or commitments.

Was it inevitable that Netflix's way of doing business would succeed over Blockbuster's and its use of streaming technology become the dominant format? Were there any signals which might have warned Blockbuster of a potentially disruptive technology? The truth is, something always exists which might point to a change in competitive conditions. However, senior managers need to open their eyes to perceive the change.

Competitors in the Same Market

In 2000, Netflix was little more than a failing start-up. Far from making any money, the company was incurring increasing losses. The CEO, Reed Hastings, flew to Dallas to propose a partnership with Blockbuster CEO, John Antioco as Blockbuster was the established competitor in the market. A year earlier, Netflix had revised its business model from customers paying for each DVD they rented to a subscription service, which worked better for consumers. Hastings' proposal to Blockbuster was simple. He was offering to sell Netflix to Blockbuster for $50 million. As part of the deal, Netflix would run the Blockbuster brand online and Antioco would promote Netflix in its store. On the face of it, the idea made sense; Netflix was an online retailer, while Blockbuster had a bricks-and-mortar presence. Why not try to expand the DVD market by helping each other? However, given Netflix's loss-making business, Hastings and his team were laughed out of the office. Within ten years Hastings would have the last laugh.

Back in 2000, Blockbuster was the dominant player within the video rental industry. It had access to more than 9,000 retail stores across America and 528 stores, at its peak, in the UK. It had millions of customers, a massive marketing budget, and efficient operations. Viewed from this perspective, the approach from Hastings seemed to be asking Mr Antioco to hand over the brand they had worked hard to build. The trouble with Blockbuster's business model wasn't entirely clear at that time, but it could be seen if you looked hard enough. The company's profits were heavily dependent on the late fees it charges its customers. Netflix, in contrast, had no retail locations, which reduced its costs. And, as it charged customers a subscription for its DVDs, this made late fees redundant. Once a customer paid their subscription, it was up to the customer to decide how long they wanted to keep the DVD. At the same time, they could return their DVDs and cancel their subscription.

Competing in Different Ways

A major advantage of Blockbuster was that the customer could walk into a store and immediately rent a DVD. With Netflix, customers received their DVDs by post which was slow in comparison to Blockbuster. Also, the Netflix brand was not as developed as Blockbuster's, making it more difficult for consumers to find. However, as resistance to the Netflix model for renting DVDs was overcome, it would reach a tipping point. This occurred as existing customers shared their enthusiasm for the Netflix service with their friends and family. If Blockbuster was to compete effectively with Netflix, it would have to change its business model. It's easy to think, 'Why do this, why incur a fall in profit just because a small, niche

2

player is operating in the market?'
Nevertheless, Blockbuster had an
opportunity to recognize that
Netflix's customer offering might
cause the video rental industry to
evolve in a manner which put it at
a disadvantage.

They were faced with a choice
of monitoring the changes taking place around them or simply continuing with business as
usual—blindly believing what
has worked in the past will continue to work in the future. Un-

By 2013, both US and UK Blockbuster businesses had
been placed in administration. Source: © JLRphotography/
Shutterstock.com.

fortunately for Blockbuster this was not to be the case. Blockbuster's US parent company
filed for Chapter 11 bankruptcy protection in 2010. It was subsequently acquired by Dish
Network through a bankruptcy auction in 2011. By 2013, both US and UK Blockbuster businesses were placed in administration. Was this inevitable? Perhaps not. There were signals
there to detect if Blockbuster had been scanning its environment and monitoring for signs
of change or disruption.

Blockbuster is not the only competitor to underrate Netflix and other streaming providers. In 2007 Netflix introduced streaming, which allows members to instantly watch TV shows
and films on their personal computers. By 2010 it had partnered with consumer electronics companies to stream on the Xbox 360, PS3, Internet-connected TVs, and other Internet-
connected devices, including Apple devices. In the same year, executives from the cable and
entertainment industry predicted that the early success of Netflix's streaming service would
be short-lived. Their argument was that Netflix's supply of content from film studios and TV
networks would soon slow down to a trickle. Around 2013, Netflix executives began to wonder if the days of licensing a back catalogue of great TV shows cheaply might be coming to
an end. TV and film companies were starting to realize how valuable streaming rights were,
which meant that getting them would become increasingly difficult for Netflix. Netflix made
the decision to start making its own shows and movies, starting with the hugely successful
'House of Cards' and more recently, 'Stranger Things', and hits like true crime documentary
'Tiger King'.

The huge investment Netflix has made in its 'originals' over the past few years has paid
off in a string of hits which has won consumer loyalty and industry accolades, including a
Golden Globe. In 2017, Netflix's market capitalization was a huge $64 billion (£49 billion).
By 2020 it had risen to a staggering $194 billion, having increased its market value by more
than $50 billion in the first few months of 2020. With its share price hitting a record high of
around $427, it was now worth more than its rival, Disney. Unlike Disney, Netflix is entirely
dependent on paid subscriptions for revenue. Disney is much more varied, being as reliant
on tourism and merchandise sales as it is on the content it puts out for streaming. While
that diversity has traditionally been Disney's strength, it became a liability in 2020 when
the pandemic forced Disney to shut down its theme parks and delay its film releases. For

Blockbuster, it was a case of the 'innovator's dilemma'; you end up competing with a business which you initially ignored. Unfortunately for Blockbuster, this realization came too late for their executive team to make a difference.

Sources: Greg Sandoval, 'Blockbuster laughed at Netflix partnership offer', http://www.cnet.com, 9 December 2010; Brian Stelter, 'Internet kills the video store', http://www.nytimes.com, 6 November 2013; 'Blockbuster to shut a quarter of UK stores', *The Guardian*, 14 November 2013; Greg Satell, 'A look back at why Blockbuster really failed and why he didn't have to', *Forbes*, 5 September 2014; Nathan McAlone, 'Netflix's website in 1999 looked nothing like it does today', http://ukbusinessinsider.com, 25 April 2016; 'Netflix's content chief said something about its "originals" that should make investors optimistic about the future', http://ukbusinessinsider.com, 23 April 2017; http://www.wikipedia.org; http://www.netflix.com; Ariel Shapiro, 'Netflix Stock Hits Record High, Is Now Worth More Than Disney', Forbes, 16 April 2020.

Questions

1. Use PESTLE analysis to identify the weak signals which were starting to impact Blockbuster's rental business before it went bankrupt.
2. What are the main reasons for Netflix's continued growth and profitability?
3. How sustainable is Netflix's subscription-based business model?

 For more examples and discussion to aid your understanding of this chapter, please visit the online resources and see the Extension Material for this chapter.

  ## Review Questions

1. Explain the role that *weak signals* play in helping managers to understand potential changes in their macro-environment.
2. Why might PESTLE analysis be particularly appropriate for companies in the oil industry?

 ## Discussion Question

'Scenario planning is little more than an educated guess and therefore irrelevant for companies.' **Discuss**.

Research Topics

1. Develop two plausible scenarios for the UK fast fashion retailer, Boohoo.
2. Describe the theory of the business on which Blockbuster and Netflix was based. Explain how this resulted in Blockbuster going bankrupt and Netflix dominating film and TV streaming.

Recommended Reading

Two books that deal with the use of scenario planning in the macro-environment and the competitive environment are:

- **M. E. Porter**, *Competitive Advantage*, chapter 13, Free Press, 1985.
- **K. van der Heijden**, *Scenarios: The Art of Strategic Conversation*, Wiley, 1996.

For a discussion of how to undertake scenario planning and its benefits, see:

- **P. J. H. Schoemaker**, 'Scenario planning: a tool for strategic thinking', *Sloan Management Review*, vol. 36, no. 2 (1995), pp. 25–40.

For an interesting read on the effects of weak signals, see:

- **M. Gladwell**, *The Tipping Point*, Abacus, 2000.

 www.oup.com/he/henry4e
Visit the online resources that accompany this book for activities and more information on strategy.

Test your knowledge and understanding of this chapter further by trying the multiple-choice questions online.

 ## References and Notes

1   **P. Ginter** and **J. Duncan**, 'Macroenvironmental analysis for strategic management', *Long Range Planning*, vol. 23, no. 6 (1990), pp. 91–100.
2   Remarks made by Donald Rumsfeld, former US Secretary of Defense at a Department of Defense news briefing on 12 February 2002.
3   **C. M. Christensen**, **M. E. Raynor**, and **R. MacDonald**, 'What is disruptive innovation?', *Harvard Business Review*, vol. 93, no. 12 (2015), pp. 44–53.
4   **J. Bower** and **C. M. Christensen**, 'Disruptive technologies: catching the wave', *Harvard Business Review*, January–February (1995), pp. 43–53.
5   Quoted in **D. Mercer**, *Marketing Strategy: The Challenge of the External Environment*, Open University, 1998.
6   Quoted in **Mercer**, see n. 5 above.
7   **J. B. Soll**, **K. L. Milkman**, and **J. W. Payne**, 'Outsmart your own biases', *Harvard Business Review*, May (2015), pp. 65–71.
8   **J. Beshears** and **F. Gino**, 'Leaders as decision architects', *Harvard Business Review*, May (2015), pp.52–62.
9   **H. I. Ansoff**, *Implementing Strategic Management*, Prentice Hall, 1984.
10 See https://www.theguardian.com/business/2018/dec/18/carmakers-criticise-unrealistic-eu-plan-slash-vehicle-emissions.
11 See https://unfccc.int/process-and-meetings/the-paris-agreement/what-is-the-paris-agreement.
12 See https://ec.europa.eu/clima/policies/transport/vehicles/cars_en.

13 See https://www.latimes.com/business/story/2019-12-01/electric-vehicle-sales-in-california-on-the-rise-but-is-it-enough-to-reach-the-5-million-goal-by-2030.

14 **M. E. Porter** and **C. van der Linde**, 'Green and competitive: ending the stalemate', *Harvard Business Review*, vol. 73, no. 5 (1995), pp. 120–33.

15 See https://www.wired.co.uk/article/china-one-child-policy-economics. Accessed April 2020.

16 **N. Walton** and **N. Piper**, *Technology Strategy*, Red Globe Press, 2020; **P. Armstrong**, *Disruptive Technology*, Kogan Page, 2017.

17 **M. Iansiti** and **K. R. Lakhani**, 'Competing in the age of AI', *Harvard Business Review*, vol. 98, no. 1, (2020), pp. 61–7.

18 For a discussion on why Porter believes scenario planning is best applied at an industry level, see **M. E. Porter**, *Competitive Advantage*, Free Press, 1985, p. 447.

19 **K. van der Heijden**, *Scenarios: The Art of Strategic Conversation*, Wiley, 1996.

20 **P. J. H. Schoemaker**, 'Scenario planning: a tool for strategic thinking', *Sloan Management Review*, vol. 36, no. 2 (1995), pp. 25–40.

21 **Porter**, see n. 18 above, p. 446.

22 **Schoemaker**, see n. 20 above.

23 **A. Kahane**, 'Scenario for energy: a sustainable world vs. global mercantilism', *Long Range Planning*, vol. 25, no. 4 (1992), pp. 38–46. See also **A. Kahane**, *Transformative Scenario Planning: Working Together to Change the Future*, Berrett-Koehler, 2012.

24 See **G. Morgan**, *Riding the Cutting Edge*, Josey Base, 1988 and **A. Grove**, *Only the Paranoid Survive*, Random House, 1996.

25 **M. Gladwell**, *The Tipping Point*, Abacus, 2000. The tipping point is the moment of critical mass, the threshold, the boiling point at which an idea, trend, or other social phenomenon goes viral.

26 For a brief discussion of decision-making under conditions of uncertainty, see **R. Gertner**, 'Scenario analysis: telling a good story', in *Mastering Strategy*, Prentice Hall, 2000, pp. 245–50.

27 Section 2.3.1, 'How to Build Scenarios' is based on **Schoemaker**, see n. 20 above.

28 **Schoemaker**, see n. 20 above, p. 27.

29 For a discussion on why Porter believes scenario planning is best applied at an industry level, see **Porter**, see n. 21 above, p. 447.

CHAPTER 3
INDUSTRY ANALYSIS

 Learning Objectives

After completing this chapter you should be able to:

- Explain the importance of industry analysis
- Evaluate Porter's five forces framework as a tool of industry analysis
- Discuss the value net and the role of complementors in creating value for organizations
- Explain the industry life cycle
- Analyse strategic groups within an industry
- Explain the impact of hypercompetition and disruptive innovation on industry dynamics

Introduction

The external environment facing an organization consists of its macro-environment and competitive environment. Any changes that occur in the macro-environment have the potential to impact an organization's competitive environment. Therefore, it is important that organizations scan and monitor their macro-environment to discern *weak signal*s that may be able to affect or fundamentally change the industry within which they compete. The macro-environment was discussed in **Chapter 2**. In this chapter we assess the impact of the competitive environment and how an organization might achieve competitive advantage.

It is widely accepted that the nature of competition in an industry is more directly influenced by developments taking place in the competitive environment. This is not to suggest that the macro-environment is unimportant but its impact is often less obvious than events taking place in the competitive environment. In this chapter we look at some of the tools of analysis available to analyse industries. We discuss Michael Porter's approach to competitive strategy and focus on his structural analysis of industries: the *five forces framework*. The strategy formulations, or *generic strategies*, emanating from the five forces framework are discussed in detail in **Chapter 7**, when we consider business strategy.

3.1 The Background to Porter's Five Forces Framework

Michael Porter's ideas on competitive strategy include some of the most pervasive analytical tools used in strategic management.[1] In the 1970s Porter was working with two different disciplines—business policy (strategy) and industrial organization. Both disciplines involved evaluating industries and therefore had common issues but they remained very much separate subject areas. Porter recognized that an opportunity existed to bring thinking about industrial organization into strategy, and thinking about strategy into industrial organization. He sought to synthesize these two different disciplines—strategy (business policy) and industrial organization, which is a branch of microeconomics.

Porter was faced with a dilemma. The Harvard Business School tradition used studies to try to capture what was going on in an organization. This meant going out and collecting data from organizations, commonly referred to as field research. However, each organization is unique with different employees producing different products and operating in different markets. Thus, the data collected about one organization cannot be used to predict what might occur in another organization. Therefore, what was needed was to put all these individual case studies of firms together and see what common patterns emerged over time. In this way Porter hoped to make some generalizations that affect all organizations. His early work on business economics used models to try to represent what was occurring in the business world. Such economic models are a simplification of reality, as they can never fully replicate the complexity that exists in the real world. The use of models is an attempt to try to represent what goes on in the real world and to predict or derive useful outcomes.

In the end, Porter used neither case studies nor statistical modelling. Instead, he decided to use *frameworks*.[2] The benefit of using frameworks is that they can more readily capture the full richness of a phenomenon with a limited number of dimensions. In framework building, the skill is to use the smallest number of core elements that still capture the wide variation that takes place between organizations in competition. As Porter recognized, these dimensions have to be intuitive—that is, they must make sense to practitioners in the context of their own industry. Porter's contribution was to develop a framework for analysing industries that could be generalized from a few core elements, in this case five—hence the *five forces framework*. The five forces framework is an attempt to capture the variation of competition, while being pervasive and rigorous. Porter's insight is that organizations seeking above-average profits and therefore a competitive advantage, should not just react to their competitive environment but should actively seek to shape it. However, as we shall see, Porter's five forces framework is not without its critics.

3.2 Porter's Five Forces Framework

The **five forces framework** is undertaken from the perspective of an **incumbent firm**—that is, an organization already operating in the industry.[3] An industry is a group of organizations producing a similar product or service. The analysis is best used at the level of an organization's strategic business unit (SBU). Typically, a strategic business unit exists when a diversified corporation serves several different markets. Each SBU will be responsible for the business strategies necessary to compete in that market. And these business strategies must work towards achieving the overall corporate strategy. For example, Mukesh Ambani's Reliance Industries Ltd, includes Reliance Jio, its telecoms subsidiary which offers cheap smartphones and even cheaper data prices. Jio has more than 388 million mobile phone and data services subscribers. We could, therefore, conduct a five forces analysis for Reliance Jio. Although each organization in an industry is unique, the forces within the industry which affect its performance, and hence its profitability, will be common to all organizations in the industry. It is in this sense that Porter's contribution is pervasive—the ability to generalize these five forces to all organizations within the industry.

Although the five forces analysis is undertaken from the perspective of an incumbent firm, it can be used to determine whether a firm outside an industry should enter the industry. In this case the barriers to entry which may be protecting the incumbents constitute an additional cost that outsiders must factor into their analysis of whether to enter the industry. An organization thinking of entering an industry will need to know whether it can successfully compete with incumbents in the industry. This will require it to adopt a distinctive positioning. For example, Amazon entered book retailing by utilizing the Internet to create **support activities** which allowed it to alter the traditional bookselling business model.

The five forces framework is an analytical tool for assessing the competitive environment. The competitive environment is the industry or market in which an organization competes. It enables an organization to determine the attractiveness or profit potential of a particular industry by examining the interaction of five competitive forces. It is the combined strength of these five forces which will ultimately determine an organization's return on investment or the potential for profits within a given industry. The five forces are:

(1) *threat of new entrants;*

(2) *bargaining power of buyers;*

(3) *bargaining power of suppliers;*

(4) *threat of substitute products or services; and*

(5) *intensity of rivalry among firms in an industry.*

By examining all five competitive forces an organization is able to assess its ability to compete effectively in an industry. The five forces framework is based on an economic theory known as the **structure–conduct–performance** (SCP) model. This states that the *structure* of an industry determines an organization's competitive behaviour (*conduct*), which in turn, determines its profitability (*performance*).

The five forces framework is a rigorous approach to looking at industries and where organizations stand in relation to the structural forces prevalent in that industry.[4] In this respect it differs from SWOT analysis, which was introduced in **Chapter 2**, and is further explored in **Chapter 4**. SWOT analysis is company-specific, while Porter's five forces is industry-specific. The five forces framework allows an organization to make informed decisions, given its resources, about whether existing competition, bargaining power of suppliers, bargaining power of buyers, threat of new entrants, and threat of substitutes make this industry an attractive (profitable) one to compete in. Using Porter's five forces, an incumbent organization can, for example, decide that industry conditions suggest that it would be more beneficial to use its resources and capabilities in an alternative industry—that is, whether it should exit the industry, or at least decrease its resource commitment to that industry. The five forces framework also enables an organization to improve its competitive position in relation to industry trends. For example, an awareness of a trend towards consolidation among suppliers (leading to an increase in supplier power) might lead an organization to strengthen its relationships with its existing supplier to avoid downward pressures on its profit margins. Therefore, accurately estimating future trends in the five forces should also provide an organization with an indication of future profits in the industry.

Clearly, if the five forces do not have the same impact upon different industries then we would expect different industries to exhibit different levels of profit. Similarly, within an industry each of these five competitive forces will have a different impact on the industry structure. For Porter, the aim of competitive strategy is to find a position within the industry that an organization can effectively defend against the impact of the five forces, or to try to influence the five forces in its favour. In evaluating the five forces, managers need to be aware that each competitive force will have a different effect on their industry. Therefore, managers need to understand the relative impact of each of the five forces on their industry structure. They can then ascertain their ability to influence the forces with the greatest impact on their industry structure through their strategy formulation. Their ability to change the industry structure will be in direct proportion to their influence over the five forces.

The five forces framework of industry competition is shown in **Figure 3.1**. We can discuss each of the elements that make up the five forces to ascertain their potential impact on industry profitability.

3.2.1 What Determines the Threat of New Entrants

The threat of new entrants is the extent to which new competitors may decide to enter an industry and reduce the level of profits being earned by incumbent firms. Where organizations in an industry earn profits well in excess of their cost of capital, the industry is more likely to attract new entrants. The problem for many industries is that they are too easy to enter—and the easier it is for new organizations to enter the industry, the greater the excess capacity and the more intense the competition. The threat of entry will depend on the existence of *barriers to entry* and the reaction of existing competitors. If entry barriers are high, the threat of entry to the industry by new organizations will be low. Similarly, if a new entrant expects that existing firms in the industry will retaliate, for example by lowering their prices, this will act to deter the organization from entering the market. See **Strategy in Focus 3.1**.

The main **barriers to entry** include economies of scale, capital requirement, product differentiation, access to distribution channels, and cost advantages independent of size.

Economies of Scale

Economies of scale occur when the cost of each individual unit produced falls as the total number of units produced increases. Economies of scale tend to be associated with manufacturing organizations, since the high capital costs of their plant need to be recovered over a high volume of output. In industries such as chemicals, automobiles, and aerospace large-scale production is essential to achieve efficiency. The effect of economies of scale is to deter new entrants because it forces them to choose between two undesirable options: (1) either they enter the industry at a high volume of output and risk a strong reaction (retaliation) from existing organizations; or (2) they enter the industry at a small scale, avoiding retaliation from existing firms, but operating at a cost disadvantage.

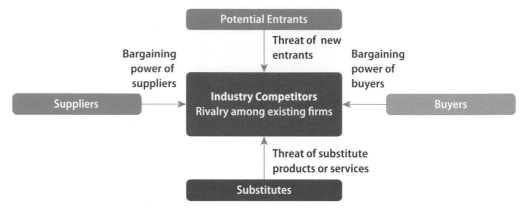

Figure 3.1   Porter's five forces framework of industry competition. Source: Reprinted with permission of Free Press, a Division of Simon & Schuster Inc., from Michael E. Porter, *Competitive Strategy: Techniques for Analyzing Industries and Competitors*, Free Press. Copyright © 1980, 1998 by Free Press. All rights reserved.

Photo 3.1   The car manufacturing industry is an example of economies of scale. Source: © xieyuliang/Shutterstock.com.

Capital Requirements

If organizations need to invest substantial financial resources to compete in an industry, this creates a barrier to entry. For example, organizations wishing to enter the oil industry would face huge capital costs involved in exploration and in specialist plant and machinery. This entry barrier is further strengthened because the major oil companies are vertically integrated. They compete in different stages of production and distribution—that is, both *upstream* (extraction of oil) and *downstream* (sale of products to the consumer).

Product Differentiation

Where an organization's products are already established in an industry, providing it with high brand awareness and generating customer loyalty, new entrants will have to spend disproportionately on advertising and promotion to establish their product. This acts as a barrier to entry. For example, consider the amount of promotional expenditure that would be required for an organization trying to compete with established brands Coca-Cola and Pepsi.

Access to Distribution Channels

A new entrant will need to have access to distribution for its product in order to compete successfully in the industry. For example, Häagen-Dazs tried to prevent Ben & Jerry's ice cream from successfully competing in the luxury segment of the ice cream market by having sole agreements with its distributors. Ben & Jerry's co-founders, Ben Cohen and Jerry Greenfield, successfully mounted a legal challenge against Häagen-Dazs's parent company, Pillsbury, in order to gain access to distribution channels to get its ice cream in retail stores.

Cost Advantages Independent of Size

Some competitors within an industry may possess advantages that are independent of size or economies of scale. They may benefit from early entry into the market and associated 'first-mover' advantages. The early experience that such firms acquire may make it difficult for new entrants to imitate their success. Other cost advantages include government policies that may favour incumbent firms, favourable low cost access to raw materials, and the use of patents to protect proprietary knowledge.[5]

3.2.2 What Determines the Bargaining Power of Buyers

Buyers can affect an industry through their ability to force down prices, bargain for higher quality or more services, and play competitors off against each other. This power of buyers will reflect the extent to which their purchase represents a sizeable proportion of the organization's overall sales. The power of buyers is increased in the following circumstances.

Concentration of Buyers and High Volumes

Where there is a concentration of buyers in relation to the number of suppliers, and the volume purchase of any one buyer is high, the importance of the buyer's business to the supplier increases. For example, Walmart, the world's largest retailer, is able to exert pressure on its suppliers' margins because of the size of the purchases it makes and the importance of these huge purchases to the suppliers. In the UK, suppliers of farm produce have long complained that the concentration of supermarket purchases allows them to drive down margins for their products.

Purchases are Standard or Undifferentiated

When they are dealing with a standard or undifferentiated product, buyers are confident that they can always find alternative suppliers. Because the product is standard, buyers exert pressure on price rather than product features as they play one competitor off against its rival. For example, the price of steel worldwide is subject to downward pressure, as buyers can simply purchase this commoditized product at the lowest price.

STRATEGY IN FOCUS 3.1 The Threat of New Entrants: Amazon

Amazon will offer free grocery deliveries to Prime members across the UK by the end of the year, threatening efforts by supermarkets to profit from the boom in online shopping during the pandemic. Amazon's Fresh service was previously available to Prime members for an additional monthly charge and was limited to roughly 300 postcodes in mostly affluent areas of London and the south-east.

But the company said on Tuesday it would scrap the extra charge and expand Amazon Fresh 'to millions of Prime members across the UK before the end of the year'. That would pose a far more serious challenge to incumbents, Tesco, Sainsbury's, Asda, and Morrisons. Nick Carroll, associate director at market researcher Mintel, said Amazon currently had just 3 per cent of the UK online grocery market, compared with Ocado's 14 per cent and Tesco's more than 30 per cent. 'But they could become a significant player given their scale, and they could put a lot of pressure on pricing,' he said. 'For them, it will be market share first and profit later.'

Natalie Berg, founder of consultancy NBK Retail said the company was 'hitting the nuclear button'. 'It is one of the boldest moves they have ever made, the Covid pandemic has presented them with an opportunity to tighten their grip on ecommerce,' she added. 'They are using the frequency aspect of food to bait people into their ecosystem.'

Amazon does not reveal how many Prime members it has in the UK but Mr Carroll estimates that roughly 15 million Britons have signed up to the £7.99 a month package. He said that while Amazon did not yet have the capacity to rival the likes of Tesco, which has been fulfilling more than 1 million orders a week during the pandemic, it would probably target the urban areas where online food shoppers are disproportionately located.

'There is already a significant amount of switching in online grocery,' he said. 'You are only as good as your last promotion.' Amazon does not offer own-label food ranges. Fresh and chilled products are instead sourced from Wm Morrison, which has substantial food manufacturing capacity, along with upmarket regional chain Booths as well as Whole Foods, which Amazon acquired in 2017. It also offers products from big food labels and independent suppliers. The company said its range extended to 'tens of thousands' of items, comprehensive enough for a weekly shop.

The offer of free delivery to Prime customers comes as conventional supermarkets try to rationalize the pricing of online grocery, usually their least profitable sales channel, amid a surge of interest in online shopping caused by the COVID-19 pandemic. At the start of 2020, online grocery accounted for roughly 7 per cent of total UK food retail sales. By May that had risen to about 13 per cent as wary shoppers opted to order online rather than visit supermarkets.

Amazon said it would be fulfilling orders from its own network of dedicated distribution centres around the country. 'We have retrofitted existing buildings and also expanded our fulfilment network in key locations in order to best meet customer demand,' it said, declining to give more details.

Ms Berg said few other companies could afford to swallow the cost of delivery this way. 'There is a question about how sustainable it is. There is a risk it becomes too popular. It's hard to offer free delivery and then take it away.'

Source: 'Amazon challenges UK supermarkets with free grocery delivery', *The Financial Times*, 28 July 2020.

Switching Costs are Low

Where the costs to the buyer of switching supplier is low or involves few risks, the buyer's bargaining power is enhanced. Clearly, undifferentiated products benefit buyers as the cost of switching is low.

There is a Threat of Backward Integration

When buyers have the ability to integrate backwards (that is, to supply the product or service themselves), they pose a threat to the supplier which will strengthen their bargaining position. For example, Coca-Cola and Pepsi Cola engage in tapered integration. They operate their own bottling subsidiaries while also using independent contractors to bottle and distribute their products. That way, both companies can threaten to use their own production capacity more intensively, thereby extracting favourable terms from their bottling suppliers.

3.2.3 What Determines the Bargaining Power of Suppliers

Suppliers can exert bargaining power over participants in an industry by raising prices or reducing the quality of purchased goods and services. The factors that increase supplier power are the mirror image of those that increase buyer power. The supplier is the producer of an organization's inputs for making goods and services. Suppliers are powerful under the following circumstances.

Concentration of Suppliers

The larger the supplier, and the more dominant it is, the more pressure it can place on organizations in the industry it sells to. This is especially the case where a supplier is selling to many fragmented buyers.

Suppliers are Faced with Few Substitutes

Where there are few or no substitute supplies available the supplier will be in a powerful position. TSMC faces few substitutes for its highly differentiated product allowing it to charge premium prices for its microprocessors.

Differentiated Products and High Switching Costs

If it is difficult and costly for organizations in the industry to switch to other suppliers, this prevents them playing one supplier off against another. This may arise because an organization's product specifications tie it to a particular supplier. This is often seen in the automobile sector where the requirement for specialist tooling may tie a car manufacturer to a particular supplier. Companies such as JLR are often linked with 'first tier' suppliers, and trying to source alternative supplies of the same quality and specification is difficult, expensive, and time-consuming.

Threat of Forward Integration

When suppliers have the ability to integrate forwards into the buyers' industry and compete with their buyers, this will act to reduce profitability in the buyers' industry. This threat reduces the organization's ability to negotiate lower prices from their suppliers.

3.2.4 What Determines the Threat of Substitute Products and Services

This is competition not from new entrants but from different products or services which can meet similar consumer needs. By placing a ceiling on the prices organizations in the industry can profitably charge, substitutes limit the potential returns of an industry. The existence of substitutes means that customers can switch to these substitutes in response to a price increase by firms in the industry. The threat of substitute is determined by the price–performance ratio.

The Price–Performance Ratio

The more attractive the **price–performance ratio** of substitute products, the greater the restraint on the prices that can be charged and therefore on an industry's profits. An attractive price–performance ratio could be a substitute product that is of a higher quality, even if it comes at a higher price. For example, the cost of travel to France via the Channel Tunnel is more expensive than a ferry crossing, but the convenience in time saved makes it a viable substitute. In trying to determine a substitute product, the organization will need to identify products which can perform the same function as the organization's own product.

3.2.5 What Determines the Intensity of Rivalry among Competitors in an Industry

A key determinant of the attractiveness of an industry is rivalry among incumbent or existing organizations in the industry. Where a high degree of rivalry exists, this causes industry profits to be reduced. Such rivalry may take the form of competing aggressively on price. Price cuts can easily be matched by rivals and ultimately lowers profits for all organizations in the industry. In contrast, advertising, product innovations, and improved customer service may act to expand overall demand in the industry. Rivalry can increase when competitors in an industry see an opportunity to improve their market position. However, this will invariably be met by retaliatory moves from other organizations in the industry. The following factors affect competitive rivalry.

Numerous or Equally Balanced Competitors

Where there are few competitors in an industry and they are of a similar size, there is likely to be intense competition as each competitor fights for market dominance. This is often seen in oligopolistic markets, where a few firms dominate the market. Examples include supermarket retailers, investment banks, and pharmaceuticals.

Industry Growth Rate

When an industry is characterized by slow growth, an organization can only increase its market share at the expense of competitors in that industry. This will be resisted by competitors, resulting in more intense competition.

High Fixed Costs

High fixed costs in an industry create pressure for organizations to increase their capacity to gain economies of scale. Where the demand conditions will allow only some firms in the industry to reach the volume of sales required to achieve scale economies, this will engender a fight for market share. The excess capacity in the industry usually results in a price war. An example is the airline industry.

Lack of Differentiation

Where products are undifferentiated, competition in the industry will be more intense, driven by customer choice based on price and service. Furthermore, a lack of switching costs implies that competitors are unable to prevent customers from going to their rivals.

High Exit Barriers

The existence of high exit barriers may hinder firms needing to exit the industry. For example, some plants are so specialized that they cannot easily be used to produce alternative goods. As demand conditions deteriorate, this creates excess capacity in the industry, which acts to reduce profitability.

3.2.6 How to Compete Using the Five Forces Framework

Porter's five forces framework can help organizations to understand the attractiveness or profit potential of their industry. This is achieved by analysing the relative impact of each of the five forces on their industry structure. Organizations can then formulate a strategy which defends their position in relation to the five forces. Furthermore, organizations should seek to devise a strategy that will actively influence these five competitive forces in their favour. As we noted earlier, Porter's five forces framework works best when used at the level of the strategic business unit.

We can take a particular industry, for example, the low cost European airline industry, and look at a specific company, such as the Irish airline Ryanair. We can use Porter's five forces framework to determine how attractive the industry is for that incumbent organization. As we know the drivers or determinants for each of the five forces, we can analyse each of these drivers in turn, which will allow us to determine their strength. For example, if we look at 'the threat of new entrants' we know this is determined by factors such as economies of scale and capital requirements. We can then analyse, for example, the capital requirements needed in the airline industry, and can relate this to Ryanair. Therefore, if the capital requirements are substantive then we know this acts as a barrier to entry for other organizations seeking to enter the industry. And the threat of entry to the industry will likely be low. Conversely, if the capital requirements necessary to compete in an industry are insignificant or low, this will not act to deter new entrants. In this case, we can say the threat of entry will likely be high. But this is only one determinant of the threat of entry.

To determine attractiveness of an industry based on the likelihood of threat of entry, we need to aggregate the scores for all the determinants of the threat of entry. For example, if the need for economies of scale and capital requirements are high, and product differentiation in the industry is high, and access to distribution channels and cost advantages independent of size are low, we might say overall the threat of entry is 'low'. Therefore in using Porter's five forces framework to analyse an industry, once we have assessed the determinants for each of the five forces, we can then give each of the five forces a rating such as *high*, *medium*, or *low*.

This is shown in **Figure 3.2**. Adding up the balance of each rating for each of the five forces gives a company an overall indicator of the attractiveness of that industry. For example, if the bargaining power of buyers is high, the threat of entry low, and the availability of substitute products or services high. If the power of suppliers is medium, and industry rivalry high. On balance, we can say this is unlikely to be an attractive industry to compete in. What existing firms in the industry need to do of course, is to try to influence each of the five forces in their favour, or at least try to mitigate any threats that these forces might pose.

To succeed, organizations need only to compete in industries with few competitors, low bargaining power of buyers and suppliers, and where the threat of new entrants and substitutes is minimal! This is unlikely to be achieved, particularly in today's global environment. In reality, organizations need to compete in industries where their resources and capabilities provide them with a strategic fit with their competitive environment. See **Case Study: Ryanair: How to Compete in the Airline Industry**. Porter's work on strategy formulation includes three *generic* strategies: *overall cost leadership*, *differentiation*,

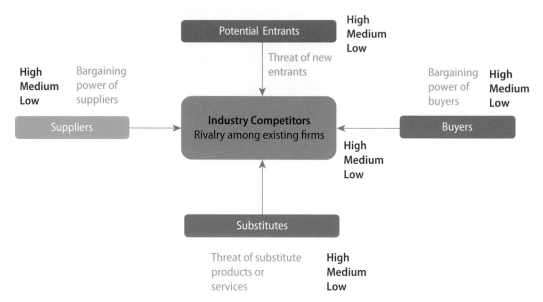

Figure 3.2   Rating the strength of each of the five forces.

and *focus*. These strategies enable an organization to position itself against the five forces.[6] These generic strategies are discussed in **Chapter 7**.

3.3 **The Limitations of Porter's Five Forces**

We can now address some of the criticisms of Porter's five forces. We might also observe that some of the criticisms, such as the use of complementors by **Adam Brandenburger and Barry Nalebuff**,[7] can be seen as an attempt to expand and improve the framework.

1. The five forces framework assumes a **zero-sum game**; that is, competitors can only succeed at the expense of other players in the industry. However, organizations are increasingly aware of the added value that other players, such as suppliers (and indeed competitors), can contribute. For example, in the automobile industry Toyota and Honda work closely with their suppliers to ensure that parts are available at the right price, of the exact quality, and only when needed in order to reduce inventory and associated costs.

2. The five forces framework is a static analysis which assumes relatively stable markets. It tells us little about how players in the industry interact with each other and the effects of actual and anticipated competitor moves on an organization's decision-making. **C. K. Prahalad**[8] states that organizations face significant and discontinuous change in their competitive environment.[9] He argues that the disruptive forces which have brought about this change are accelerating. For Prahalad, strategy is not about positioning the company in a given industry space, but influencing and actually creating industry space.

3. **Mintzberg and Waters**[10] argue that organizations may develop an intended or deliberate strategy, but unexpected changes in the environment may force them to abandon that strategy. A subsequent strategy emerges as a result of ad-hoc management decision-making. Furthermore,

in emerging industries you do not know who your rivals are, which makes the use of the five forces framework problematic.

4. Why are there only five forces? Some have argued that other forces, in addition to the five forces, are required. For example, the government has been put forward as one possible candidate.

5. A revision of the five forces is required which brings us closer to a dynamic theory of strategy. Brandenburger and Nalebuff[11] utilize game theory to show how organizations can collaborate as well as compete with their competitors to create a larger industry in which everyone gains. This is referred to as **co-opetition**, which we discuss later in this chapter.

Perhaps, not surprisingly, Porter tends to reject these criticisms, particularly the notion that his framework is static.[12] He does, however, accept that there may be a role for Brandenburger and Nalebuff's work in the five forces.[13]

3.4 **The Value Net**

In an extension of Porter's five forces, **Brandenburger and Nalebuff**[14] use game theory to capture the dynamic nature of markets in their analysis. They developed the **value net**, which more closely represents the complexity in an industry. The value net represents a map of the industry, the players in the industry, and their relationship to each other. This is illustrated in **Figure 3.3**. In seeing business as a game, they do not mean traditional games, such as chess, where there are winners and losers. For Brandenburger and Nalebuff, success for one player can also mean success for another player. In other words, the pay-off from the game can be a *win-win* solution. They also recognize that in business the rules of the game are not fixed, as in most games, but that the game itself can be changed. The players in the game are the customers, suppliers, and competitors (where competitors include rivals, threat of new entrants, and substitute products or services). Brandenburger and Nalebuff enhance Porter's five forces by introducing a new player called a **complementor**.[15]

An organization is your complementor if customers value your product more when they have that organization's product than when they have your product alone. An organization is a competitor if customers value your product less when they have that organization's product than when they have your product alone.[16] For example, Microsoft's Windows software and Intel's microprocessors

Figure 3.3   **The value net.** Source: Reprinted with permission of *Harvard Business Review*. A. Brandenburger and B. J. Nalebuff, 'The value net from the right game: use game theory to shape strategy', *Harvard Business Review*, vol. 73, no. 4 (1995). Copyright © 1995 by the Harvard Business School Publishing Corporation. All rights reserved.

are complements. Without Intel's innovative microprocessors, Microsoft's upgraded software which requires faster processing speeds, becomes less valuable to the consumer. By making products more valuable to the consumer, complementors create greater value for the industry. At the same time, complementors may use their market position to affect the industry dynamics and the distribution of profits within the industry.

Nintendo's domination of the video games industry in the 1990s is a useful example of how an organization can successfully add and appropriate value from an industry. Nintendo reduced the bargaining power of its buyers by keeping its games cartridge in short supply. Although buyers were highly concentrated, Nintendo's strategy of deliberately restricting its games cartridge ensured that retailers lost added value. Nintendo's complementors were the games developers. To reduce the value accruing to games developers Nintendo developed software in-house. They put security in the hardware and licensed the right to develop games for their system to outside programmers. Therefore, Nintendo controlled its complementors, reducing their added value, but increasing its own added value through royalties on each game cartridge sold. By utilizing chip technology that was not cutting-edge, Nintendo ensured that its suppliers produced a commoditized product from which they would derive little added value. This allowed Nintendo to keep the cost of their games console down, which enhanced their market share.

The Irish low cost airline, Ryanair, and Stansted airport are complements. Stansted airport is Ryanair's biggest UK base. Around 80 per cent of the passengers who pass through the airport fly via Ryanair. In order to get to their flight, passengers travel through the airport invariably spending at the numerous retail outlets, which provide substantial revenues for Stansted airport. The more passengers who fly with Ryanair, the greater the opportunity for Stansted to capture that revenue. The challenge is to find an acceptable way in which this extra revenue is shared.

Brandenburger and Nalebuff use the concept of added value to help determine how the profits will be divided. They argue that in trying to increase your organization's own complement's added value, you must also be thinking of ways in which you can limit the added value of another organization's complement. A strategy to achieve this is to create a shortage of your organization's differentiated product, which builds up its market dominance. At the same time, you encourage more suppliers of a complementary product into the industry, which has the effect of commoditizing that product. The reduction in value of the complementary product will thereby ensure that greater profit is appropriated by your product. In essence, an organization needs to try to create value and a larger market, which is best undertaken by cooperating with customers and suppliers. At the same time, an organization is concerned with how this larger market is to be divided—that is, its competitive position. As Brandenburger and Nalebuff suggest, 'a company has to keep its eye on both balls, creating and capturing, at the same time'. They call this *co-opetition* because 'it combines competition and cooperation'.[17]

3.4.1 A Complementary Sixth Force

Some critics of Porter's five forces have suggested that his framework would benefit from the inclusion of government as a sixth force. This is difficult to assess accurately given the wide-ranging role that governments occupy in economic life. Clearly, the government has the potential to influence different aspects of industry structure. Government policy and regulations can set limits on the behaviour of organizations as suppliers or buyers. Government safety and pollution standards, as seen

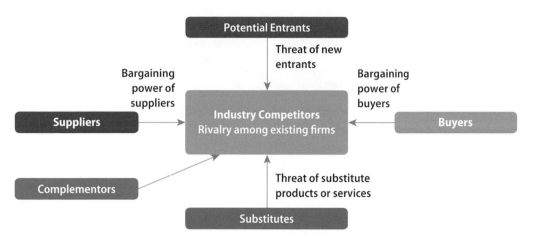

Figure 3.4 The inclusion of complementors within Porter's five forces. Source: Adapted with permission of Free Press, a Division of Simon & Schuster Inc., from Michael E. Porter, *Competitive Strategy: Techniques for Analyzing Industries and Competitors*, Free Press. Copyright © 1980, 1998 by Free Press. All rights reserved.

by the desire to eliminate petrol, diesel, and hybrid engines by 2035 in the UK,[18] can influence industry growth and alter its cost structure. The use of government subsidies or taxation will influence competition in an industry. Given this wide-ranging role of government, Porter argues it is 'usually more illuminating to consider how Government affects competition *through* the five forces than to consider it as a force in and of itself'.[19]

Porter recognizes that complements have a role to play in competitive analysis. If we extend Porter's five forces framework to take account of complements, it evolves as shown in **Figure 3.4**. The inclusion of complementors into Porter's five forces makes the framework more defensible because it adds a dynamic element to the analysis. This allows organizations in the industry to be more aware of their interdependencies. Instead of win-lose, there now exists an explicit recognition that a sustainable strategy can involve both cooperation and competition. There is *cooperation* among suppliers, organizations, and customers to create value, and *competition* in how this value is divided up. The same holds true for complementors and substitutes. Instead of viewing substitutes as inherently adversarial and complements as friendly, an organization can have elements of cooperation in its interactions with its substitutes and competitive elements with complementors.

3.5 **The Industry Life Cycle**

The **industry life cycle** suggests that industries go through four stages of development: *introduction*, *growth*, *maturity*, and *decline* (see **Figure 3.5**). There will clearly be variations between different industries as to the length of each life cycle. **McGahan** points out that even within an industry different **strategic groups** may be experiencing different stages of the life cycle.[20] The life cycle is frequently applied to product markets where a product life cycle can be discerned which follows the same stages as the industry life cycle. The product life cycle allows an organization to vary its **marketing mix** to produce an appropriate response according to each stage in a product's development. The industry life cycle is the supply-side equivalent of the product life cycle.

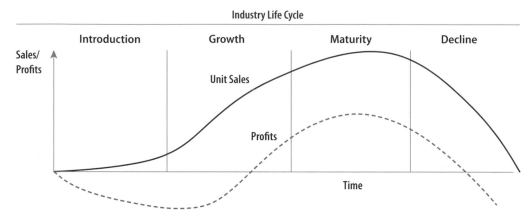

Figure 3.5   Industry life cycle.

The industry life cycle helps an organization to see how it is positioned in terms of the development of its markets. The different stages of the industry life cycle will have an impact upon competitive conditions facing the organization. For example, one would expect the level of competitive rivalry during the introduction stage, when a market is being opened up, to be different from that in the maturity stage, when the market is saturated and market share comes at the expense of your competitors. Therefore, an organization can benefit from an understanding of the industry life cycle and formulate its strategy to match the needs of each stage more closely.

3.5.1 Introduction Stage

The introduction stage of the industry life cycle (**Figure 3.5**) is characterized by slow growth in sales and high costs as a result of limited production. Organizations invest in research and development (R&D) to produce new products. This commands a premium price and confers upon the organization a first-mover advantage.[21] During this stage profits will be negative, as sales are insufficient to cover the capital outlay on R&D. An advantage of being the first mover is that an organization may set the industry standard even in the face of a superior technology.[22] Consider the VHS standard set by Matsushita for video recording in the face of a superior product, Betamax, developed by Sony. However, the tendency is for product life cycles to be compressed, as each stage is cut short by rapid change, which means that any first-mover advantage is quickly eroded. This also means that the timescale for a firm to recoup its capital expenditure is shortened, which brings a greater risk for the first mover.

3.5.2 Growth Stage

In the growth stage, sales increase rapidly as the market grows, allowing organizations to reap the benefits of economies of scale. The increase in product sales brings greater profits, which in turn attracts new entrants to the market. As consumer awareness of the product grows, so organizations vie to have their brands adopted and increase spending on marketing activities. A goal for the firm is not merely to attract new customers, but to ensure that customers repeat their purchases.

3.5.3 **Maturity Stage**

The maturity stage of the life cycle sees a slowing in sales growth and profits as the market becomes saturated. Firms will begin to exit the industry, and low cost competition based on efficient production and technically proficient processes becomes more important. As market share can only be achieved at the expense of competitors, rivalry becomes more intense within the industry. With exit barriers, the rivalry will be more intense still as marginal firms find it difficult to exit the industry. During the maturity stage of the life cycle it is conceivable that a product may benefit from innovation or finding new consumer markets. It may become *rejuvenated*. For example, Johnson & Johnson have successfully targeted their baby-oil products at female consumers and thereby created a new market. Somewhat controversially, the pharmaceutical industry has found that drugs which are deemed unacceptable on health grounds in Western economies can be marketed to developing nations where regulatory requirements are less stringent.

3.5.4 **Decline Stage**

In the decline stage organizations experience a fall in sales and profitability. Consumer loyalty shifts to new products based on newer technologies. For example, fewer consumers bother to write cheques, preferring instead to use debit and credit cards, and mobile payment apps. Streaming video content supersedes renting and buying DVDs. Competition within the industry will be based on price as consumers shun the old products. Some organizations will continue to exit the industry and consolidation may occur as a strategy for the remaining firms to achieve acceptable profits. A knowledge of the industry life cycle enables managers to understand how each stage can affect their competitive environment. In line with their competitors, they must ensure that their strategy formulation is sufficiently robust to meet the needs of each stage of the cycle.

3.6 **Strategic Group Analysis**

The analysis so far has been at the level of the entire industry. In addition to analysis at an industry level, it is also possible to undertake structural analysis *within* an industry. A closer analysis of the industry shows that strategic groups or clusters of organizations tend to exist. According to Porter, 'a **strategic group** is the group of firms in an industry following the same or a similar strategy'.[23] **Strategic group analysis** is about identifying organizations within an industry that possess similar resource capabilities and are pursuing similar strategies. If we recognize the capabilities and strategies of organizations that are most like our organization, we have a greater understanding of our competitors. Why? Because in any industry, an organization's greatest competitors are going to be the companies that are most like it.

Strategic groups within an industry constitute a cluster of companies and inform us that just because organizations occupy the same industry this does not make them competitors. In the volume market for cars, Ford, Toyota, and Volkswagen occupy the same strategic group within the car industry. They are clearly in competition for the same customers. Aston Martin and Ford are in the same industry but they do not compete with each other. Aston Martin produce a limited number of expensive cars and each car is scrutinized before it moves along the 200-hour build process in order to pass final inspection, sometimes conducted by the CEO himself. Therefore, Ford and Aston Martin would occupy different strategic groups. Companies in the same strategic groups tend to have similar market shares, albeit that one of them may be the clear market leader. They also respond in similar ways to external trends or competitor moves within the industry. Strategic group analysis falls between analysing each organization individually and looking at the industry as a whole.

3.6.1 Strategic Maps

A **strategic map** is a useful tool for comparing the strategies of organizations in an industry. An organization selects two characteristics that can differentiate competitors within the industry and draws them on the vertical and horizontal axes. A starting point might be to look at the most profitable and least profitable companies in the industry, and the characteristics that separate them. A certain amount of judgement is required when deciding the two-dimensional axes on which strategic groups are mapped. For example, the two axes might include characteristics such as price, product range, geographical coverage, reliability, extent of **vertical integration**, and marketing expenditure. **Figure 3.6** represents a simplified illustration of the world automobile industry. The two characteristics chosen are price and product range to map the strategic groups.

3.6.2 Mobility Barriers

In the same way that an organization may be prevented from entering an industry by barriers to entry, **mobility barriers** inhibit movement between strategic groups. Porter defines mobility barriers as 'factors that deter movement of firms from one strategic position to another'.[24] **McGee and Thomas**

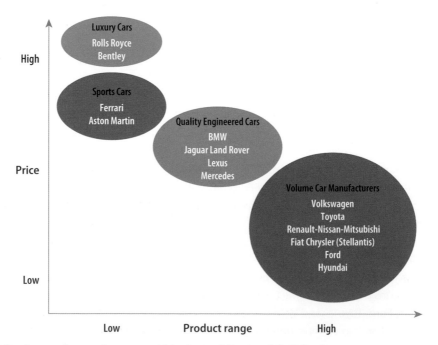

Figure 3.6   A map of strategic groups within the world automobile industry.

view mobility barriers as 'factors which deter or inhibit movement of a firm from one strategic position to another'. Therefore a mobility barrier is essentially a limitation on **replicability** or imitation.'[25] For example, if barriers which derive from economies of scale exist, they will be more likely to protect a strategic group which includes organizations that have large plants. If the factors that prevent mobility result from an organization's strategy, it simply increases the cost to other organizations of adopting that strategy. Porter suggests that organizations in strategic groups with high mobility barriers will achieve greater profits than those in groups with lower mobility barriers. However, there is conflicting evidence on this point.[26] The changing trends within an industry may point to the existence of viable strategic space between groups which could be exploited by an organization if it possesses the resource capabilities.

Mobility barriers may be changed by an organization's strategy. For example, where an industry exists that has a commoditized product, an organization may try to create a new strategic group. It might do this by spending on promotion and advertising to try to establish differentiation and brand loyalty. In the same way, external trends such as changes in buyers' behaviour or a change in technology can impact strategic groups by creating new groups and making others obsolete. Organizations will face different hurdles in overcoming mobility barriers which will depend on their existing strategic positions and their resources and capabilities. For example, Toyota has successfully managed to overcome mobility barriers to entering the luxury car market. Its Lexus brand now competes with BMW and Mercedes.

In **Figure 3.6** we see a representation of the world automobile industry with its strategic groups. At the luxury end of the market are cars such as Rolls-Royce and Bentley, with limited, often bespoke, product ranges and high prices; such cars are often bought as status symbols. Also, at the luxury end of the market, with comparable prices in some cases, are the sports models of Ferrari and Lamborghini. At the other end of the market are those companies with the broadest product range, which compete on design, as well as price and reliability. These are companies such as Toyota, Volkswagen, and Fiat Chrysler. The strategic group with Mercedes, BMW, JLR, and Lexus produce a lower product range but a higher quality of engineering and price than the volume manufacturers.

There has been movement in the industry as manufacturers such as BMW and Audi introduced lower priced, compact saloons to draw customers away from volume manufacturers. However, this strategy carries a risk of alienating existing customers loyal to your brand, who may perceive the introduction of compact cars as denigrating the brand. There is also movement between different groups as witnessed by BMW and Porsche who have introduced sports utility vehicles in an attempt to capture a share of the lucrative sport utility vehicle (SUV) market.

By drawing arrows from each strategic group to show in which direction the groups may be moving, it becomes possible to assess the extent of structural changes. For instance, if strategic groups are moving farther apart, this may mean that strategic 'spaces' exist which can be exploited without increasing competition. If strategic groups are converging, this implies greater volatility. In undertaking strategic group analysis, an organization can better understand its industry structure, and how it might evolve over time.

By mapping competitors following similar strategies into strategic groups, an organization can ascertain its most direct competitors. By understanding competitor capabilities, an organization can assess the viability of mobility barriers in preventing competitors from gaining market share. And, by forecasting the impact of industry trends, an organization is better able to assess the sustainability of strategic groups and the viability of strategic space. That said, there are critics who question the existence of strategic groups and whether studying intra-industry groups provides information that cannot be acquired by looking at industries and individual firms.[27]

It is important to realize that the relevance of strategic group analysis depends upon the characteristics or dimensions used to map these organizations. The aim should be to establish which characteristics can clearly differentiate one group of companies from another. We've seen that such characteristics might include price, product portfolio and geographical coverage, extent of vertical integration, and marketing expenditure. In reality, some strategic groups might overlap as issues such as globalization force many companies to compete on converging characteristics. It is worth noting that industry dynamics will alter strategic groups over time.

To summarize, strategic group analysis enables an organization to better understand competitive positions in its industry. By mapping competitors following similar strategies into strategic groups, an organization can:

- identify who its direct competitors are and the extent of competitive rivalry within the organization's strategic group;
- identify the viability of mobility barriers which prevent organizations moving from one strategic group to another;
- track the direction in which competitor organizations are moving; and
- assess structural changes and identify strategic spaces which may be exploited.

Taken together, these changes may help an organization predict a change in industry evolution.

3.7 Hypercompetition and Disruptive Innovation

3.7.1 Hypercompetition

The term hypercompetition was introduced by **Richard D'Aveni** to explain a relentless mode of competitive behaviour that aims to force competitors out of the industry. Hypercompetition is defined as 'an environment characterized by intense and rapid competitive moves, in which competitors must move quickly to build advantage and erode the advantage of their rivals'.[28] This fierce competition is often seen in the video games and software industry. For example, Apple's closed systems prevent competitors from gaining access to their software code. Their huge financial reserves have allowed them to compete aggressively by buying up potential threats while they are still emerging companies. More important, Apple's constant upgrading of new product offerings has the effect of destabilizing the consumer electronics industry and forcing competitors to react. D'Aveni argues that organizations can no longer build a *sustainable* competitive advantage as this advantage is eventually eroded. In fact, he argues that organizations must consciously disrupt their own competitive advantages as well as the advantages of competitors.

Hypercompetition is characterized by competitors creating constant disequilibrium, which causes the industry to 'escalate towards higher and higher levels of uncertainty, dynamisms, heterogeneity of players, and hostility'.[29] The driving force of competition is the pursuit of profit, which is obtained by achieving competitive advantage. However, competitive advantage will only be transitory as rival organizations look for ways to undermine it or make it obsolete. Therefore, under conditions of hypercompetition managers must continually recreate their competitive advantage if they are to gain market dominance.[30] There is empirical support that managers do not respond to a hyper-competitive environment with a single sustainable competitive advantage. Instead, they create multiple short-term advantages, which are linked together to create competitive advantage over time. This also supports the view that hypercompetition is widespread among organizations rather than being limited to high-technology industries.[31] **Clayton Christensen** argues that the existence of competitive advantage will set in motion creative innovations that cause the advantage to be eroded as competitors try to catch up.[32] For Christensen, the pursuit of competitive advantage is not futile, but the real issue for strategists is to understand the processes of competition and how competitive advantage comes about.

We saw in Porter's five forces framework that where an organization incurs huge fixed costs in set-ting up a plant, competition for market share will be intense. Networks of consumers and the rapid rate of technological change exacerbate the effects of extreme-scale economies. Networks of con-sumers simply means that unless others are using the same technology our use of that technology becomes redundant. This forces convergence around a single technical standard such as Microsoft Windows. At the same time, the rate of technological change continues to accelerate as organizations such as Apple continually shorten the lifespan of technologies and products; this further intensifies competition. Taken together, these factors produce intense competition, particularly in emerging markets for new technologies. They create high-stakes industries where the successful competitor has the opportunity for complete domination.

In hypercompetitive industries such as consumer electronics, competitive advantage requires an organization to risk a current advantage for the promise of a new advantage. Organizations aggres-sively position themselves against each other to create new competitive advantages which make opponents' advantages obsolete. At best, only a temporary competitive advantage can be achieved until your competitors catch up or outmanoeuvre your last competitive move. As D'Aveni states, 'the frequency, boldness, and aggressiveness of dynamic movements by players accelerate to create a condition of constant disequilibrium and change'.[33] In effect, hypercompetition requires an organiza-tion to replace successful products before its competitors do and thereby sustain market dominance by constantly recreating its competitive advantage.

3.7.2 Disruptive Innovation

Clayton Christensen's work on disruptive innovation, first introduced in 1995,[34] has resonance with Richard D'Aveni's insights. Christensen uses the term 'disruption' to describe a process in which a smaller company with fewer resources can successfully challenge established incumbent busi-nesses.[35] It is able to do this because incumbent businesses are focused on improving products for their most demanding customers at the high end of the market, which provides them with the great-est profit. In so doing, incumbents exceed the needs of many mainstream customer segments whilst ignoring less profitable consumer segments. This provides an opportunity for new entrants to target these neglected segments by offering them products with more suitable functionality, invariably at a lower price. As a result, new entrants thereby gain a foothold in the market.

Incumbent firms, focused on the pursuit of higher profits in the more demanding segments, will invariably not respond strenuously to the loss of a less profitable segment. However, over time, new entrants start to move upmarket and improve the quality and performance of their product offerings

STRATEGY IN FOCUS 3.2 Disruptive Innovation from Microsoft and Tesla

The term 'disruptive innovation', coined by Clayton Christensen of Harvard Business School, has been much misused in the tech world. Every start-up likes to style itself a disrupter. But Christensen would have appreciated the shockwaves from two truly disruptive technologies that have reverberated through Wall Street in recent days. It can take years for the kind of ground-shaking new ideas that he had in mind to take hold. When they do, the shifts in value can be dramatic, as investors scramble to reposition themselves for a new era.

Exhibit A is the public cloud—the name given to the storage and processing of corporate information in centralized data centres. For years, this was deemed inferior to established practice in corporate IT. Though the cloud was cheaper, the demands of security, reliability and responsiveness all made it imperative to keep important computing workloads in a company's own facilities. This makes the cloud a model of Christensen-style disruptive technology. The IT industry's incumbents felt they were selling a better technology and could always make the switch to the cloud when needed. But responding effectively to a new way of operating that eats into a company's existing business from below is never easy.

When a market like this tips, the effects are dramatic. Microsoft reported that the cloud now makes up a third of its business and is seeing annual growth of nearly 40 per cent—an almost unimaginable spurt for a company with annual revenue of $125 billion that spent the first decade and a half of this century in the doldrums. By lowering prices and opening up access to new customers, technologies like this create new markets that are much larger than the ones they replace. According to Satya Nadella, Microsoft's chief executive, tech spending as a percentage of global GDP is expected to double over the next decade as digitization spreads. As the platform for much of that new activity, the cloud has become the centre of the action.

Microsoft itself has beaten what Christensen called the 'innovator's dilemma'—the difficulty incumbents have in shifting to a new technology that threatens to erode their existing, more profitable business model. But many of the old powers of the IT industry, like HP and IBM, are still struggling to find an answer. When Mr Nadella took over in 2014, Microsoft was worth 70 per cent more than IBM. Now, at $1.32 trillion, it is worth eleven times as much as its erstwhile rival.

Exhibit B in disruptive innovation centres on electric cars. Even after a huge jump in his company's stock market value in recent months, Elon Musk, head of Tesla, was able to deliver another jolt to Wall Street with the latest earnings this week. By most performance measures, electric drivetrains have long been inferior to internal combustion engines. They were also deemed to represent much less of an engineering challenge, a commodity that the reigning powers of the industry would be able to switch to easily. There seemed little advantage in being first. But this is starting to look like it might be another of Christensen's disruptive technologies.

Despite the big carmakers' confidence, they have yet to produce electric vehicles that can match Tesla's in terms of energy efficiency—or performance per dollar. The complacency in senior auto ranks is starting to turn to panic. The head of Volkswagen resorted to reading the riot act to his senior managers for not moving fast enough to counter the threat, warning that the carmaker risked being disrupted in much the way Nokia had been by the launch of the iPhone.

How long will it take for the incumbents to catch up? Gene Berdichevsky, one of Tesla's first employees and now head of battery company Sila Nanotechnologies, says carmakers have seriously underestimated the many different innovations that go into the batteries and other design aspects that enhance performance in electric cars. In summer 2020, it will be three years since the launch of Tesla's mass-market Model 3. Despite squandering a year or more of this lead as he struggled to tame his company's manufacturing operations, Mr Musk still has a significant edge: Mr Berdichevsky predicts it will take until the middle of the decade for other carmakers to start to close the performance gap.

Many other factors besides energy efficiency will determine which electric car customers pick. But having a clear head start in the core technology gives Mr Musk an important performance and cost advantage. How far he can ride that lead will make this one of the most significant disruptive technology stories of the decade.

Source: 'Why Microsoft and Tesla are the decade's big disrupters', *The Financial Times*, 31 January 2020.

to attract the incumbents' mainstream customers. They do this because moving upmarket also provides them with greater profitability. But new entrants are aware that without an improvement in quality to match the standards of mainstream customers, they simply will not accept the new entrants' products, even at a lower price. However, once the quality rises enough to satisfy them, they gladly adopt the new product with its lower price. When mainstream customers start adopting the entrants' offerings in volume, Christensen argues that disruption has occurred.

Larry Downs and Paul Nunes[36] argue that the strategic model of disruptive innovation has a blind spot. We have seen that disrupters offer cheap substitutes to incumbents' products and capture low-end customers before moving upmarket to capture higher-value customers. However, as they point out, the disruption described by Christensen allows incumbent businesses some time to develop their own new products as they see their market being eroded. This is all well and good when new entrants display a similar business model to that already used in the industry. But what happens when the disruption does not come from competitors within the same industry or organizations with vaguely similar business models?

What if organizations do not enter at the bottom of a mature market and continue to more through profitable segments? For example, consider the fate of in-car satellite navigation product makers such as TomTom and Garmin. What devastated TomTom and Garmin's market was the ubiquitous use of smartphones with free navigation apps, preloaded on every smartphone. Eighteen months after the debut of navigation apps, leading global positioning system (GPS) manufacturers had lost 85 per cent of their market value. Mobile phone manufacturers were not seeking to compete with GPS manufacturers, the latter were simply collateral damage. This was '**big bang disruption**', a term Downes and Nunes use[37] to capture a change in industry dynamics in which not only the least profitable customers are lured away, but consumers in every segment defect simultaneously.

Therefore, to understand industry dynamics, incumbent businesses now need to be aware that the stages of the industry life cycle, alluded to earlier in the chapter, effectively become compressed. In addition, the traditional bell shape of the industry life cycle curve now more resembles a shark's fin, with an almost vertical rise and corresponding steep fall. And all this occurs within a much shorter period of time. The question thus arises: how can incumbent organizations survive such big bang disruptions? We look at this question in **Chapter 7**, within the context of strategy formulation.

Summary

It is clear that the business environment has a more direct impact on an organization's performance. Porter's five forces framework enables an incumbent organization to assess the attractiveness of its industry based on the relative strength of the five forces. An organization should position itself against, and seek to influence, the five forces. Critics of the five forces framework argue that a major limitation of the framework is its static nature; a charge contested by Porter.

Brandenburger and Nalebuff introduce the concept of the value net in the business environment. The value net represents a map of the industry, the customers, suppliers, and competitors in the industry, and their relationship to each other. They also introduce the role of complementor. The five forces can be extended and made more dynamic by adding complementors as an additional force. A strategic group is a cluster of firms in an industry following the same or a similar strategy. A strategic map is useful for identifying mobility barriers which prevent organizations moving from one strategic group to another. By analysing the effects of industry trends on strategic groups, it may help organizations to predict a change in industry dynamics.

In hypercompetitive environments organizations must consciously disrupt their own competitive advantages as well as those of opponents. Competitive advantage is seen as temporary, and lasts only as long as it takes for competitors to catch up or outmanoeuvre your last competitive move. Hypercompetition is characterized by intense and rapid competitive moves. It is more likely to be seen in industries characterized by rapid technology innovation.

Disruptive innovation occurs when an incumbent organization focuses on its most profitable upmarket segment leaving a new entrant free to nibble away at its lower value customers, unchallenged. The entrant gradually moves upmarket to acquire the incumbent's higher-end customers. With big bang disruptions, the disruption of consumers is fast and total, leaving the incumbent little or no time to react.

CASE STUDY Ryanair: How to Compete in the Airline Industry

Background

It may surprise many people to know that Ryanair is Europe's favourite airline. The low cost airline carries 149 million passengers every year on more than 2,500 daily flights. It flies from seventy-nine bases, connecting more than 240 destinations, in forty countries. It has more than 17,000 employees and an industry-leading thirty-five year safety record. Ryanair was founded in Ireland in 1985, initially operating daily from Waterford in the southeast of Ireland to London Gatwick. By 1990 the

Photo 3.2   Europe's favourite airline. Source: Courtesy of Sangga Rima Roman Selia/Unsplash.

airline had accumulated £20 million in losses and went through a process of restructuring. As part of this restructuring, a new CEO, Michael O'Leary, was hired and dispatched to the USA to understand what makes low cost Southwest Airlines so successful. The intention was to copy Southwest Airlines' US business model and adapt it for use in Europe. In 1991, despite the Gulf War, Ryanair made a profit for the first time.

Southwest Airlines

Southwest Airlines is the world's first successful low cost airline. It pioneered a model for reducing operating costs which is now used all over the world. To reduce costs Southwest fills its planes with more seats, makes sure each flight is packed, and flies its aircraft more often than full-service airlines. In addition, it only purchases one type of aircraft, Boeing 737-800s. The advantage of this is that they only need to train mechanics to service one type of airplane. Supply parts and inventory for aircraft maintenance are streamlined. If they have to take a plane out of service at the last minute for maintenance, the fleet is totally interchangeable; both on-board crews and ground crews are already familiar with it. And it faces few challenges in how and where it can park its planes on the ground, since they're all the same shape and size.

Moreover, Southwest does not assign seat numbers. This means that if one plane is substituted for another, and the new plane has a different seat configuration, there's no need to adjust the entire seating arrangement and issue new boarding passes. Passengers simply board and sit where they like. To lure customers from other airlines, Southwest Airlines does not charge for the first and second checked baggage. It also recognizes that consumers have different travel needs; some are content to book weeks in advance, while others have a need for more immediate flights. The use of yield-management systems allows Southwest to raise ticket prices when demand is high and reduce them during quiet periods, which also increases efficiency. Its flights are usually point-to-point; that is, the plane lands, is turned around, and often heads back to where it came from.

How Ryanair Competes

Michael O'Leary was to take careful note of Southwest Airline's low cost structure and how it competes in the airline industry. However, Mr O'Leary is a pragmatist and understood that Southwest's business model would not work in the regulated European airline industry. In 1997, the so-called 'Open Skies' policy of the European Union was implemented, which effectively deregulated the scheduled airline business in Europe. This enables airlines to compete freely throughout Europe. At the same time, Ryanair became a public limited company, offering its shares on the Dublin and New York (NASDAQ) Stock Exchange. This provided further capital for the purchase of aircraft.

Since deregulation, Mr O'Leary has taken the no-frills concept pioneered by Southwest Airlines and substantially extended it. The airline is not known for its glamorous waiting rooms, nor for having an empathetic customer service. Under Mr O'Leary's leadership, Ryanair has used punitive fees to manage passenger behaviour more than other airlines. For example, to reduce ground-staff numbers, it is now prohibitively expensive to check in at the airport or to store luggage in the hold when travelling with Ryanair. When it flies to a city, it utilizes that city's secondary and even tertiary airports, where the costs of operating are cheaper than flying to the main airport. As a result, there's less delay in turning around the aircraft to get it back in the sky.

The airline has often made provocative announcements; for example, it made headlines with a suggestion that it might charge passengers to use aircraft toilets. No doubt it believes that 'all publicity is good publicity', since such outbursts keep its advertising budget to a minimum.

In common with Southwest Airlines, Ryanair flies only Boeing 737-800s. In 2006, it flew 42.5 million passengers in the year and took delivery of its hundredth Boeing 737-800. It also launched its Web check-in service, giving passengers the opportunity to check-in online. In order to generate further revenue, Ryanair introduced on-board mobile phone use across its entire fleet which lets customers gamble and play bingo during the flight. The year before, to celebrate its twentieth anniversary, it offered 100,000 flights at only ninety-nine pence each. At the same time, it reminded passengers that its competitors add a fuel surcharge to top up the price of their tickets.

Growth in passenger numbers continue as it strips out non-essential services and introduces yield-management systems which allow it to vary ticket prices according to demand. For Ryanair's CEO, pricing is not complex; it is all about what the market will bear. In 2010, traffic grew to 72.1 million passengers with an average fare of only €39 and no fuel surcharges, despite a sharp increase in fuel costs. Their business model is 'load factor-active, yield-passive'. Ryanair takes whatever ticket prices it can get in order to ensure the aircraft is as full as possible; in other words, it achieves a high load factor.

In the past, Mr O'Leary has suggested a load factor of between 82 and 83 per cent throughout the year would be fine; Ryanair's actual load factor is often in excess of 90 per cent. What this allows it to do is to capitalize on the prevailing low-fare trend. It creates a virtuous cycle in which low fares encourage greater passenger traffic. As more passengers fly, so this continues to drive both the cost reduction it achieves from using airports, and lowers its unit cost per employee and per aircraft. Crucially, high passenger numbers also drive the demand for ancillary services. It actively supports its load factor by offering a range of lower fares and aggressive seat sales. By 2015, traffic passed the 100 million customer mark; 106.4 million customers are flown, at an average fare of €46 and a 93 per cent load factor.

Customer Service

In 2013, Ryanair was considered to have the worst customer service out of Britain's 100 biggest brands in a survey by a consumer magazine. In the same year, two quarterly profit warnings showed Ryanair failing to keep up with its rivals, including easyJet, whose friendlier image had attracted flyers. The usually belligerent Mr O'Leary was forced to make a conscious effort to improve Ryanair's corporate reputation and avoid losing sales to competitors. In a bid to show how Ryanair is undergoing 'revolutionary' customer change, the boss of Europe's biggest low cost airline was presented to the world cuddling a puppy. The chief executive revealed his new image at an event to launch the airline's new, updated website and app. Mr O'Leary said the airline had an 'Always Getting Better' plan, starting with 'fixing the things our customers don't like'.

By 2014 it had relaxed its hard-line cabin baggage allowance, reduced penalties for failing to print out boarding passes, and introduced allocated seating. For example, an unpopular €70 fee for re-issuing boarding passes at the airport was lowered to €10. Mr O'Leary also promised that flyers will no longer pay disproportionate charges for small transgressions in hand-luggage size: he blamed local agents in some airports for applying his rules with excess zeal. 'There's no more conflict,' he said. The new website drastically reduces the number of steps required to book a flight, and allows regular travellers to store information about their travel documents and payment card. The moves were a response to easyJet filling its planes more successfully than any other European airline and making healthy profits. To placate customers, Ryanair also followed its arch-rival into primary hubs such as Rome Fiumicino and Brussels, and began moving away from 'secondary' airports. The effect of this 'nicer guy' approach was a leap in profits to €867 million.

Lowest Cost Competitor

Ryanair has always been efficient at making money from its ancillary services. In 2016 ancillary services accounted for 27 per cent of its revenue. For example, consumers can expect to pay for eve-

Photo 3.3 Michael O'Leary, CEO of Ryanair. Source: Courtesy of World Travel & Tourism Council.

rything else after paying for their flight. This includes seat reservations, booking hotels through Ryanair's website, snacks on the plane, and water to drink; just about everything comes at a cost. This constant cost cutting has allowed Ryanair to make a profit even when consumer demand falls. Customers keep coming back, not least because the cost reductions are passed on to them in the form of lower fares (**Figure 3.7**).

The threat of substitutes refers to products and services which can meet similar needs. Therefore, the question becomes: if one chooses not to fly with the low cost airline industry, what alternatives are available? Here the price–performance ratio comes into play. The more attractive the price–performance ratio of substitute products, the greater is the restraint on an industry's profits. Therefore, the price–performance ratio of the low cost airline industry vis-à-vis their substitutes will determine profitability levels within the industry. Given Ryanair's low fares, and the convenience and speed of flying to one's destination, can ferry, train, or coach substitutes offer viable alternatives?

Other full-service airlines such as Air France and Lufthansa have struggled to cut their wage costs to compete. British Airways, which is part of the International Airlines Group, has tried to copy Ryanair by squeezing extra seats onto their planes and selling supermarket sandwiches on board to generate extra revenue. However, unlike Ryanair, British Airways has always been concerned to protect its brand image. That said, Ryanair became Europe's favourite airline in 2016 in terms of the number of passengers it carries, taking the mantle from Germany's Lufthansa.

Aircraft are the single largest capital cost in any airline, so getting fleet costs right is a key objective. Another major cost is fuel, which is determined by the price of oil, and falling oil prices which resulted from the global pandemic in 2020, benefitted all airlines. Unfortunately, the same global pandemic also massively reduced passenger numbers in 2020 forcing European airlines, such as Germany's Lufthansa, to seek a massive €9 billion government bailout. In 2013, Ryanair acquired 180 new Boeing 737-800s with a list price of $15 billion. This was negotiated at a time when Boeing was launching its all-new Boeing 737 MAX aircraft with extra seats. With this deal Ryanair had the capacity to grow the fleet by 50 per cent without compromising on flight cost per passenger. It since expanded that order even further to add 110 units of the 737 MAX aircraft, with options on another 100. These planes provide extra seats and new, efficient engines that will cut unit costs even more and further improve the carrier's competitiveness.

However, by 2020 Ryanair was expressing deep regret over the delivery delays to their first Boeing MAX-200 aircraft order, which was expected in spring 2019. Delivery of the 210 aircrafts would now not take place until the end of 2020, at the earliest. That said, they remain committed supporters of the Boeing 737 aircraft, in particular the new MAX series, as this air-craft will deliver 4 per cent more seats, but at 16 per cent lower fuel consumption, and 40 per cent lower noise emissions per passenger. The expectation is that these new aircraft will enable Ryanair Group Airlines to grow to more than 200 million passengers annually over the next five or six years, while at the same time they will help cut their operating costs and significantly lower their environmental footprint.

Ryanair is a massive customer for Boeing, which allows it to negotiate the best prices for its fleet of aircraft. Also, aircraft manufacture is dominated by two players, Boeing and Airbus, and Ryanair has said in the past that it will buy from Airbus if it doesn't receive the deal it needs from Boeing. For now, they continue their discussions with Boeing around compensation for the pro-longed delay in these aircraft deliveries, which they argue has materially damaged their traffic and cost base over 2019/20. They would hope to reach agreement with Boeing on a package of measures which will be reflected in modestly lower pricing on these aircraft when they are eventually delivered from late 2020 onwards. Ryanair also remained hopeful that Boeing might deliver up to forty of these aircraft in time for summer 2021.

Mr O'Leary is all too aware that, given Ryanair's low cost base, it can still make profits even when its ticket prices are cheaper than any of its rivals. Cheaper tickets also ensure the airline achieves consistent load factors of 95 per cent, or more. He predicts that as fares continue to fall, his airline will fly more than 200 million passengers a year by 2024. O'Leary also shared a dream: 'I have this vision that in the next five to ten years fares on Ryanair will be free; in which case the flights will be full, and we will be making our money out of sharing the airport revenues of all the people who will be running through airports, and getting a share of the shopping and the retail revenues.'

In 2017, the Irish airline made a profit after tax of €1.3 billion (£1.1 billion), even though it slashed ticket prices. Michael O'Leary said fares had fallen by 13 per cent, but profitability has

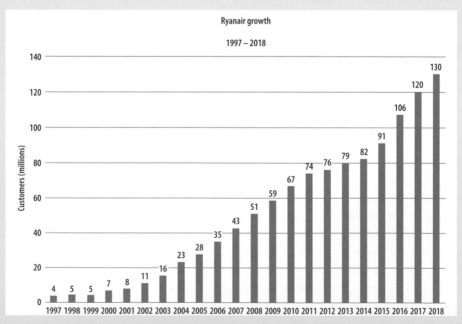

Figure 3.7   Ryanair passenger numbers (in millions) from 1997 to 2018.
Source: Data from Ryanair.com

doubled over three years. He added, 'Frankly I see no reason why that trend won't continue.' In 2018 profit after tax rose to €1.45 billion in 2018, before falling back to €885 million in 2019, and €649 million to March 2020, impacted by the falling passenger numbers due to coronavirus. For example, in July 2019 Ryanair carried 14.4 million passengers; a year later, in July 2020, the coronavirus pandemic had reduced this to 4.4 million passengers. Fortunately, the airline has substantial cash reserves but it will still be relieved when business returns to normal.

Sources: Seth Stevenson, 'The Southwest secret—how the airline manages to turn a profit, year after year', *Slate*, 12 June 2012; 'Why are no-frills airlines so cheap', *The Economist*, 18 October 2013; 'Oh really, O'Leary', *The Economist*, 19 October 2013; Simon Calder, 'Michael O'Leary launches Ryanair's "always getting better" plan', *The Independent*, 26 March 2014; 'Ryanair close to paying $10 billion Boeing order', http://reuter.co.uk, 5 September 2014; 'Ryanair wants to control even more of Europe's aviation market', *The Economist*, 7 November 2016; Joe Gill, 'Nice and profitable: how Ryanair revamped itself', *The Irish Times*, 21 May 2016; Stuart Jeffries, 'Nice is more than a destination: what Ryanair can teach United Airlines', *The Guardian*, 11 April 2017; 'Ryanair makes £1.1bn pound profit despite cutting fares', *The Guardian*, 13 May 2017; 'Ryanair: restricted leg room', *Financial Times*, 30 May 2017; Gwyn Topham, 'From low-fare to no-fare: will travel really become free?', *The Guardian*, 26 November 2016; Joe Miller and Peggy Hollinger, 'Lufthansa chief says €9 bn bailout larger than needed for survival', *The Financial Times*, 3 June 2020; http://ryanair.com (accessed August 2020).

Questions

1. Conduct a five forces analysis to determine how attractive the low cost airline industry is. You might label each competitive force as high, medium, or low, depending on their relative strength and potential impact on Ryanair's profitability.

2. Why haven't other airlines imitated Ryanair's success?

3. What are the advantages and disadvantages of Ryanair being reliant on one aircraft manufacturer; Boeing?

 For more examples and discussion to aid your understanding of this chapter, please visit the online resources and see the Extension Material for this chapter.

 ## Review Questions

1. What are the five forces and how are they used to analyse an industry?
2. Explain how the value net and complementors help organizations understand how to add value for customers.
3. How does strategic group analysis enable a company to understand its competitors?

 ## Discussion Question

'The effect of government policy on industry structure is too pervasive to consider government as a *sixth* competitive force.' **Discuss**.

Research Topic

Use strategic groups to analyse the financial services industry, paying particular attention to what mobility barriers exist, and the trends that are changing this industry.

Recommended Reading

For a discussion of the five forces framework and strategic groups see:

- **M. E. Porter**, *Competitive Strategy: Techniques for Analysing Industries and Competitors*, Free Press, 1980.

For an insight into the need for organizations to cooperate as well as compete with players in their competitive environment, see:

- **A. Brandenburger** and **B. J. Nalebuff**, *Co-opetition*, Currency Doubleday, 1996.

An informative read on the use of game theory for strategy formulation is:

- **A. Brandenburger** and **B. J. Nalebuff**, 'The right game: use game theory to shape strategy', *Harvard Business Review*, vol. 73, no. 4 (1995), pp. 57–71.

For a discussion of hypercompetition, see:

- **R. A. D'Aveni**, *Hypercompetition: Managing the Dynamics of Strategic Manoeuvring*, Free Press, 1994.

www.oup.com/he/henry4e

Visit the online resources that accompany this book for activities and more information on strategy.

Test your knowledge and understanding of this chapter further by trying the multiple-choice questions online.

References and Notes

1. See **M. E. Porter**, *Competitive Strategy: Techniques for Analysing Industries and Competitors*, Free Press, 1980.
2. For a discussion of the background to Porter's five forces, see **Argyres** and **McGahan**, 'An interview with Michael Porter', *Academy of Management Executive*, vol. 16, no. 2 (2002), pp. 43–52.
3. For a more recent discussion, see **M. E. Porter**, 'The five forces that shape strategy', *Harvard Business Review*, vol. 86, no. 1 (2008), pp. 78–93.
4. For a discussion of the structural analysis of industries, **Porter**, see n. 1 above.
5. **Porter**, see n. 1 above, chapter 1, for a full discussion of cost advantages independent of size.
6. **Porter**, see n. 1 above, chapter 2, for a discussion of strategy formulation.
7. For an introduction to the role of complements, see **A. Brandenburger** and **B. J. Nalebuff**, 'The right game: use game theory to shape strategy', *Harvard Business Review*, vol. 73, no. 4 (1995), pp. 57–71.
8. For a discussion of the static nature of Porter's five forces, see **C. K. Prahalad**, 'Changes in the competitive battlefield', in *Mastering Strategy*, edited by T. Dickson, Prentice Hall, 2000, pp. 75–80.
9. For an insight into how industry players with relatively few resources but big ambitions can take on industry giants and win, see **G. Hamel** and **C. K. Prahalad**, 'Strategy as stretch and leverage',

Harvard Business Review, no. 71, vol. 2 (1993), pp. 75–84; and **G. Hamel** and **C. K. Prahalad**, *Competing for the Future*, Harvard Business School Press, 1994.

10 **H. Mintzberg** and **J. A. Waters**, 'Of strategies deliberate and emergent', *Strategic Management Journal*, vol. 6, no. 3 (1985), pp. 257–72.

11 **A. Brandenburger** and **B. J. Nalebuff**, *Co-opetition*, Currency Doubleday, 1996.

12 For a more detailed discussion of Porter's response to his critics, see **N. Argyres** and **A. M. McGahan**, 'An interview with Michael Porter', *Academy of Management Executive*, vol. 16, no. 2 (2002), pp. 43–52.

13 For a wider discussion of Michael Porter's ideas on strategy, see **M. E. Porter**, 'What is strategy?', *Harvard Business Review*, vol. 74, no. 6 (1996), pp. 61–78.

14 **Brandenburger** and **Nalebuff**, see n. 11 above.

15 **Brandenburger** and **Nalebuff**, see n. 11 above.

16 **A. Brandenburger** and **B. J. Nalebuff**, 'Co-opetition: competitive and cooperative business strategies for the digital economy', *Strategy and Leadership*, vol. 25, no. 6 (1997), pp. 28–33.

17 **Brandenburger** and **Nalebuff**, see n. 16 above.

18 See https://www.bbc.co.uk/news/uk-40726868. Accessed 23 April 2020.

19 **Porter**, see n. 1 above, pp. 28–9.

20 See **A. McGahan**, 'How industries evolve', *Business Strategy Review*, vol. 11, no. 3 (2000), pp. 1–16.

21 **M. B. Lieberman** and **D. G. Montgomery**, 'First mover advantages', *Strategic Management Journal*, vol. 9, no. 5 (1988), pp. 41–58.

22 **C. Shapiro** and **H. R. Varian**, 'Standard wars', *California Management Review*, vol. 41, no. 2 (1999), pp. 8–32.

23 **Porter**, see n. 1 above, p. 29.

24 **Porter**, see n. 1 above, p. 135.

25 **J. McGee** and **H. Thomas**, 'Strategic groups: theory, research and taxonomy', *Strategic Management Journal*, vol. 7, no. 2 (1986), p. 153.

26 **R. M. Grant**, *Contemporary Strategy Analysis*, Blackwell, 2005, chapter 4.

27 **D. Dranove**, **M. Peteraf**, and **M. Shanley**, 'Do strategic groups exist? An economic framework of analysis', *Strategic Management Journal*, vol. 19, no. 11 (1998), pp. 1029–44.

28 **R. A. D'Aveni**, *Hypercompetition: Managing the Dynamics of Strategic Manoeuvring*, Free Press, 1994, pp. 217–18.

29 **R. A. D'Aveni**, 'Coping with hypercompetition: utilising the new 7S's framework', *Academy of Management Executive*, vol. 9, no. 3 (1995), p. 46.

30 See **R. A. D'Aveni**, **G. B. Dagnino**, and **K. G. Smith**, 'The age of temporary advantage', *Strategic Management Journal*, vol. 31, no. 13 (2010), pp. 1371–85, for speculation on what strategic management would look like if sustainable advantages did not exist.

31 **R. R. Wiggins** and **T. Ruefli**, 'Schumpeter's ghost: is hypercompetition making the best of times shorter?', *Strategic Management Journal*, vol. 26, no. 10 (2005), pp. 887–911.

32 **C. M. Christensen**, 'The past and future of competitive advantage', *Sloan Management Review*, vol. 42, no. 2 (2001), pp. 105–9.

33 **R. A. D'Aveni**, see n. 29 above, p. 46.

34 **J. Bower** and **C. M. Christensen**, 'Disruptive technologies: catching the wave', *Harvard Business Review*, vol. 73, no. 1 (1995), pp. 43–53.

35 For a discussion of disruptive innovation and the misunderstandings surrounding its use, see **C. M. Christensen**, **M. E. Raynor**, and **R. McDonald**, 'What is disruptive innovation?', *Harvard Business Review*, vol. 93, no. 12 (2015), pp. 44–53.

36 **L. Downs** and **P. Nunes**, 'Big bang disruption: a new kind of innovator can wipe out incumbents in a flash', *Harvard Business Review*, vol. 91, no. 3 (2013), pp. 44–56.

37 **L. Downs** and **P. Nunes**, see n. 36 above, pp. 44–56.

CHAPTER 4
THE ORGANIZATION: VALUE-CREATING ACTIVITIES

 Learning Objectives

After completing this chapter you should be able to:

- Explain differential firm performance
- Analyse an organization's value-chain activities
- Evaluate how linkages in the value chain can create competitive advantage
- Undertake SWOT and TOWS matrix analysis
- Evaluate shareholder primacy vs. meeting the needs of stakeholders
- Identify the benefits of using a Balanced Scorecard and Triple Bottom Line when assessing the performance of an organization

Introduction

In this chapter, we turn our attention to how an organization can analyse its value-creating activities. We also consider some of the different ways in which an organization can assess its performance. It is important to realize that, as with strategy formulation, a debate exists about what constitutes differential firm performance. **Differential firm performance** refers to the observation that organizations which possess similar resources and operate within the same industry experience different levels of profitability. A common criticism made about industry analysis is that it fails to adequately answer this question. Indeed, many contributors within the field of strategic management would argue that a focus on industry analysis has diverted attention away from this question. The views of these individuals are discussed in detail in **Chapter 5**.

4.1 Background to Differential Firm Performance

Since **Michael Porter's** seminal work on industry and competitor analysis,[1] a debate continues about what drives an organization's performance. Is the industry context in which the organization finds itself the main determinant of its performance? Or are there factors contained within each individual organization which may more readily account for how well that organization performs?[2] Put another way, in devising strategy, should a company's main focus be the characteristics of its industry or the characteristics of its own organization?

For Porter,[3] as we saw in our discussion of the competitive environment, industry characteristics are paramount. His approach is often referred to as the 'positioning school.' That is, the organization is viewed as capable of adopting a strategy which allows it to *position* itself within the industry to take advantage of the prevailing industry structure. Thus, for Porter, the attractiveness or profitability of an industry is determined by his five forces framework. As we see when we come to look at strategy formulation in **Chapter 7**, if we adopt this view the corollary is that an organization is faced with a limited number of strategies on which to compete.

Richard Rumelt[4] argues that, contrary to the assertions of the positioning school, the defining factor in differential firm performance is not the industry structure in which the organization finds itself. Instead, it is more to do with factors that reside inside each organization such as its resources, and the strategy being adopted. This is contested by **Hawawini et al.**[5] who argue that the organization's external environment (or industry effects) are more important than organization-specific factors. If Rumelt is correct, it has implications for exactly what the organization should be focusing its strategic attention on and provides a broader canvas for strategy formulation. Therefore, it is not surprising to find that strategic management as a discipline has become increasingly concerned with the internal environment of the organization. This approach is characterized by the *resource-based view of strategy*, associated with the work of **C. K. Prahalad, Gary Hamel, Jay Barney, and Robert Grant**,[6] which we consider in **Chapter 5**.

4.2 Value Chain Analysis

Value chain analysis looks at the activities that go to make up a product or service with a view to ascertaining how much value each activity adds. It was devised by Porter as a technique to help an organization assess its internal resources.[7] The value or margin of a product is calculated by the amount of revenue it earns, in this case total revenue, which is calculated by the price of the product (or service) multiplied by the quantity consumed. If we know the total cost of each product, then the difference between the total revenue and total cost is the profit margin for the organization. Thus, the greater the difference between the organization's revenue and its costs, the greater the value it is adding.[8]

If we want to increase the value an organization adds for the consumers of its products, we need to know where this occurs and how much value each activity adds. We need to know how an organization might enhance this value added further by reconfiguring parts (or all) of the value-added process. However, it is increasingly recognized that organizations can also add value through co-operation with their suppliers, customers, and distributors. This process is referred to as the **value chain system** and recognizes that an organization's own value chain will interact with the value chain prevalent in other organizations. For example, a supplier's value chain, referred to as *upstream value*, will influence an organization's performance. Similarly, an organization's product will ultimately become part of a buyer's value chain, providing *downstream value*. How an organization manages the linkages between itself and other organizations will have an impact on how value is created within the supply chain system. If this is done carefully, it can result in a *non-zero-sum game* in which all parties within the supply chain system benefit and may provide the organization with competitive advantage.

Competitive advantage may derive from specific activities within the organization, how these activities relate to each other, and how they relate to supplier and customer activities. Where competitive advantage is a result of the configuration of many different activities, clearly it will be more difficult to imitate and therefore more sustainable. Strategy, then, can be seen to be about how an organization configures its range of activities vis-à-vis its competitors. Therefore, if an organization wishes to pursue a **low cost strategy**, this implies that it engages in a particular configuration of its activities. If an organization wishes to pursue a **differentiation strategy**, it would need a different configuration of its value-chain activities. A detailed discussion of strategy formulation for an organization is provided in **Chapter 7**.

4.2.1 **Primary Activities**

We can see that an organization is a collection of activities which aid it in the design, production, marketing, and support of its product.[9] All these activities can be captured using value chain analysis. In assessing an organization's activities it is important to analyse these at the level of the strategic business unit (SBU). The activities contained within the value chain are classified by Porter as *primary activities* and *support activities*[10] (see **Figure 4.1**). **Primary activities** are activities that are directly involved in the creation of a product or service. **Support activities** are activities that ensure that the primary activities are carried out efficiently and effectively. These primary and support activities provide the link between an organization's strategy and its implementation. This is because once the organization is seen as a collection of activities, and every employee is involved in an activity, it becomes apparent that everyone has a role to play in strategy implementation. Therefore, it is

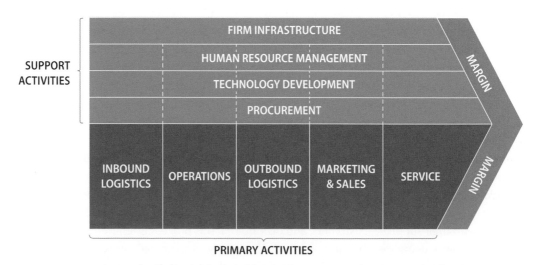

Figure 4.1   The value chain. Source: Modified with permission of the Free Press, a Division of Simon & Schuster Inc., from Michael E. Porter, *Competitive Advantage: Creating and Sustaining Superior Performance*, Free Press. Copyright © 1985, 1988, Free Press. All rights reserved.

Inbound logistics	These activities cover receiving, storing, and distributing inputs to the product. They include material handling, warehousing, inventory control, vehicle scheduling, and returns to suppliers.
Operations	These activities deal with transforming an organization's inputs into final products such as machining, packaging, assembly, testing, printing, and facility operations.
Outbound logistics	These activities are associated with collecting, storing, and distributing the product or service to buyers. Outbound logistics include warehousing, material handling, delivery, order processing, and scheduling.
Marketing and sales	This includes activities that make a product available for buyers to purchase and induces them to buy. It includes advertising, promotion, sales force, quoting, channel selection, channel relations, and pricing.
Service	These activities enhance or maintain the value of products, such as installation, repair, training, parts supply, and product adjustment.

Table 4.1 Primary activities within the value chain.

crucial that an organization's strategy is clearly communicated throughout the organization so that all employees understand why they are involved in particular activities, and how this relates to the activities of others.

Primary activities are those activities that are directly involved in the creation and sale of a product or service. They include the following five generic categories: *inbound logistics*, *operations*, *outbound logistics*, *marketing and sales*, and *service*. These are explained in **Table 4.1**. Each primary activity can be subdivided into a number of distinct activities to reflect a particular industry and the organization's strategy. Depending on the industry within which the organization competes, each of these primary activities can have an impact on its competitive advantage. For example, a distribution company such as UPS will clearly be more concerned about its inbound and outbound logistics—how it receives and stores products and gets them to the end user. The fact that UPS can accurately track the whereabouts of any of its parcels using sophisticated satellite technology and convey this to its customers is a means of adding value.

4.2.2 Support Activities

Support activities are there to ensure that the primary activities are carried out efficiently and effectively. The four generic support activities are *procurement*, *technology development*, *human resource management*, and *firm infrastructure* (see **Table 4.2**). The first three support activities may be associated with specific primary activities, while firm infrastructure supports the entire value chain. As we saw with primary activities, each support activity can be divided into a number of distinct activities to reflect a particular industry. Each category of primary and support activities includes a further three activities which impact on competitive advantage. These are *direct* and *indirect activities*, and *quality assurance*. Direct activities involve creating value for the buyer, for example through product design. Indirect activities allow direct activities to take place, such as regular maintenance. Quality assurance ensures that the appropriate quality of the other activities is maintained, for example through monitoring and testing.

Procurement	This activity deals with the process of purchasing resource inputs to support any of the primary activities. Inputs to the organization's productive process include such things as raw materials, office supplies, and buildings.
Technology development	This activity covers an organization's 'know-how', its procedures, and any use of its technology that has an impact upon product, process, and resource developments.
Human resource management	These activities include selection, recruitment, training, development, and remuneration of employees. They may support individual primary and support activities, as occurs when an organization hires particular individuals such as economists. They may also support the entire value chain, as occurs when an organization engages in company-wide pay negotiations.
Firm infrastructure	This consists of activities that usually support the entire value chain, such as general management, planning, finance, accounting, and quality management. An organization's infrastructure is usually used to support the entire value chain.

Table 4.2 Support activities.

4.3 Evaluating the Value Chain

In deciding which activities to include in the categories that make up its value chain, an organization needs to be aware of the activities' contribution to its competitive advantage. The value activities included will involve an element of judgement and subjectivity. Value chain analysis is much more than an evaluation of the discrete activities within the value chain. To be effective, value chain analysis needs to recognize and understand the relationship or linkages between these activities. **Linkages** are the relationships between the way one value activity is performed and the cost or performance of another activity.[11] The linkages between activities will not always be apparent. However, if the organization is to add value it must appreciate how the manner in which one activity is performed impacts upon the cost and performance of other activities.[12] The aim is to see if a given activity can be undertaken differently and thereby improved, providing competitive advantage. In addition, an organization must understand the relationship between its own value activities and the activities of suppliers, distributors, and customers; that is, it needs to appreciate its value chain system.

The Japanese car producers Honda and Toyota are well-known examples of organizations that add value by working with suppliers and distributors to identify ways in which their value chains can be reconfigured to reduce lead times and cut costs. The use of just-in-time (JIT) and lean production methods allows parts to be delivered only when they are ready for assembly, thereby reducing lead times and cutting inventory costs.

4.3.1 The Importance of Linkages within the Value Chain

An organization's value-chain activities represent the cornerstone of competitive advantage. However, its value chain should be seen not as a series of independent activities, but rather as a system of *interdependent activities*; that is, each value-chain activity is related to the others by way of linkages in the value chain. For example, Toyota's JIT methods are part of the Toyota Production System (TPS). The TPS imbues all aspects of production in pursuit of the most efficient methods

Photo 4.1   Toyota's use of just-in-time production methods add value to the company.
Source: © BjoernWylezich/Shutterstock.com.

of producing products. The TPS has evolved through years of trial and error to improve efficiency based on the JIT concept. By eliminating both defective products and the associated wasteful practices, Toyota has succeeded in improving both productivity and work efficiency.[13] Therefore, competitive advantage can derive from the linkages between its different activities as well as from the activities themselves.

Porter suggests that linkages can lead to competitive advantage in two ways: *optimization* and *coordination*. This is a recognition that linkages will often involve trade-offs. For example, an organization may spend more on product design and the quality of its materials in order to avoid greater maintenance costs during the product's use. By optimizing these linkages between its activities an organization can achieve competitive advantage. Similarly, an organization can reduce its costs, or improve its ability to differentiate, by better coordinating activities in its value chain. An understanding of linkages helps an organization to achieve competitive advantage by focusing on the relationship between interdependent activities as well as individual activities. While the linkages between primary and support activities are apparent, the linkages between primary activities may be more difficult to discern. For instance, better servicing and maintenance of machinery will lead to a reduction in its downtime. The key to deriving benefit from linkages is to understand how each value-chain activity impacts on, and is impacted by, other activities.

Today, many organizations outsource what they consider to be non-core activities in their value chain to third party companies. This is because other organizations will have developed expertise in these non-core activities and be capable of undertaking them at a lower cost. This allows your organization to focus on activities in their value chain where they can add the greatest value. However, there are risks with outsourcing activities which, if undertaken incorrectly, can damage the organization's reputation and reduce its revenue (see **Strategy in Focus 4.1**). This illustrates how important it is for an organization to identify all the linkages within its value chain if it is to mitigate the associated risks of outsourcing.

4

STRATEGY IN FOCUS 4.1 Can Supply Chains be Made More Resilient?

Is it as simple as politicians say for companies to diversify their supply chains to build resilience against pandemics and global shocks? One thing a lot of policymakers are keen on is making supply chains 'resilient' to shocks. But how? The standard view seems to be diversification and in particular not sourcing all your supplier contracts from China.

We can have a look at whether diversification is remotely as easy for business people to do as for politicians to say. John Neill, chairman and chief executive of the UK-headquartered logistics and supply chain business Unipart, has a great deal of experience here. In the car industry, which is where Unipart started out and still does a lot of work, a sourcing procedure for a new component involves doing a substantial amount of work. If we take the product like fuel tanks, which Unipart supplies to the UK car industry, it takes months or years to find a supplier, discuss specifications, assess production quality, and make sure their procedures are reliable and repeatable.

'Let's say we wanted to re-shore one of those components for fuel tanks to the UK,' Neill suggests. 'We would have to put them through a whole range of quality and safety tests to prove to our customers that they meet all their safety requirements. They are rightly incredibly risk averse on a safety-critical product like this.' By all means build in geographical diversification and spare capacity to be resilient against the next pandemic. But you will probably go bust before it arrives. Why? Imagine that you've decided to have three suppliers for a component. John Neill argues, 'This would require three sets of tooling, three teams that need to go in and work with them and support them. The costs would be astronomical and those would make you uncompetitive. So you might have a more robust supply chain than the other guys but no one's going to buy your cars because they're too expensive.'

Another thing: what, exactly, is supplier diversification taking out insurance against? Sure, there have been country or region-specific shocks in the past, like the Fukushima earthquake in Japan in 2011, when many companies woke up to how much of the world's silicon wafer manufacture was located in the area. There was also the rare earths episode a year earlier, when China, a big producer of the minerals essential to manufacture many electronics, whacked on export restrictions to divert them to its own industry. The rest of the world, faced with shortages and rocketing prices, scrambled to reopen old rare earths mines and dig new ones.

But the pandemic is a global shock. As Unipart's CEO says: 'I can't think of a single thing that we could have done if we'd known coronavirus was coming that would have protected us. Factories and operations all over the world have stopped. Let's say we were sourcing all our requirements in the UK. The government shut down various parts of the UK anyway. So we'd still be in the same position.' Car supply chains are notoriously complex, with very low tolerance for engineering and logistical errors. It's obviously easier to diversify supply of something cheaper and simpler than cars, such as clinical masks.

The difficulty of re-engineering value chains is an important point. There are going to have to be some seriously incentives to get a lot of manufacturing companies to diversify. And if it's really going to be done across the board it will end up with products being much more expensive, or much less sophisticated, than before. And possibly not achieve resilience anyway. Careful what you wish for.

Source: Alan Beattie, 'Why supply chain diversification isn't all that easy', *The Financial Times*, 11 May 2020.

4.3.2 Managing Linkages within the Value Chain System

The extent to which an organization can manage the linkages between the value chains of others within the value-chain system may become an important competence and competitive advantage. Porter argues that in addition to analysing its own activities, an organization should also seek to assess the benefits to be accrued from better links with the value chain of its suppliers, distributors, and consumers. These linkages are similar to the linkages within an organization's own value chain in that the manner in which they are undertaken impacts upon the cost or performance of an organization's activities. For example, Japanese automobile manufacturers manage external value chains in order to facilitate JIT deliveries of parts that can be put to immediate use rather than being tied up in expensive and unproductive inventory. The American retailer Walmart manages the value-chain linkages between itself and its suppliers. This enables Walmart to leverage its massive buying power, while at the same time providing suppliers with scale economies for their products through Walmart stores.

How an organization manages the linkages between its own and other value chains will have an impact on how value is created within the value chain system. For example, if an organization can change the configuration of a supplier's value chain to optimize the performance of their respective activities, it will benefit itself and the supplier, leading to a win-win solution. In the same way, by improving the coordination between its own value chain and a supplier's value chain, both benefit. The extent to which an organization can appropriate some of these benefits will reflect the bargaining power of its suppliers. Therefore, an organization should be prepared to influence the coordination of its suppliers' value chains and be prepared to negotiate to appropriate some of the rewards. The organization needs to undertake the same analysis with its distributors if it is to lower its costs or improve its differentiation.

The consumer also has a value chain, and an organization's product is an input into the buyer's value chain. For buyers, an organization needs to construct a value chain for them based on the activities that are relevant to how they use the product. This is important because the consumers of an organization's product will assess that organization on the benefits they derive from it. An organization's ability to differentiate its offering will be a product of how its value chain relates to the buyer's value chain. Value for the consumer is created when an organization is able to lower the buyer's costs or improve differentiation for the buyer. The buyer's perception of the value to be derived from a product will determine an organization's ability to charge a premium price.

4.3.3 Transaction Costs—'Make or Buy' Decision

In seeking to influence the value chain of its suppliers, distributors, and consumers, an organization needs also to address transaction costs, or what is often referred to as the '*make or buy*' decision. That is, does the organization want to undertake all the activities involved with the product or service itself, or might it prefer to outsource some of these activities in its value chain? This evaluation should be integral to the analysis it undertakes as part of its assessment of its own value chain. Many organizations in both the public and private sectors make a conscious choice as to the value activities they perform internally and those value activities that they are prepared to purchase. There is a recognition here of transaction cost economics—that some organizations may be able to provide certain value-chain activities at a lower cost. Clearly, where these activities constitute a core competence, organizations may prefer to keep them in-house. We look at **transaction cost analysis** in **Chapter 8**.

An organization's own value chain analysis will help it to understand where it can add value in its activities and where its costs in some activities may exceed its value. Financial considerations are important, but so too is an organization's strategic capability. If an activity underpins an organization's strategic capability, that is, its ability to compete successfully in the marketplace, it will want to retain that activity. The decision an organization faces as to whether to continue with an activity or outsource it to a lower-cost producer will depend on the extent to which that activity is of strategic importance to it. Most organizations would be unlikely to outsource what may constitute the source of their competitive advantage, but instead would seek to outsource lower-value activities to organizations that specialize in these activities.

Campbell and Goold[14] note that identifying the extent of value-chain overlaps between different businesses can also be a source of synergy opportunity. For example, if two businesses within the same corporation purchase similar components, economies of scale may result by combining these purchases. Or if two businesses have overseas offices in the same country, they could reap synergies by sharing premises, sales forces, and management.

4.4 SWOT Analysis

We briefly introduced SWOT analysis in **Chapter 2** when we discussed the macro-environment. Those within the *positioning school* argue that external analysis should precede the internal analysis of an organization's resources and capabilities. Others, who adopt a resource-based view, argue that it is the capabilities inside the organization which should be the start point for analysis. That said, SWOT analysis can be usefully undertaken once an audit of the external environment and the organization's internal environment has been completed. Moreover, an understanding of an organization's value chain will help signpost where its strengths and any weaknesses may reside.

4.4.1 How to Undertake a SWOT Analysis

SWOT analysis[15] refers to strengths, weaknesses, opportunities, and threats. Strengths and weaknesses refer to the organization's internal environment over which the organization has control. Strengths are areas where the organization excels in comparison with its competitors. Weaknesses are areas where the organization may be at a comparative disadvantage. Opportunities and threats refer to the organization's external environment, over which the organization has much less control. We noted that a SWOT analysis may prove useful in both the macro-environment and the competitive environment. However, the unpredictable nature of events in the macro-environment tends to make the use of SWOT analysis more problematic.

A SWOT analysis allows an organization to determine the extent of the strategic fit between its capabilities and the needs of its external environment. This implies that the organization has some understanding of the value-chain activities that underpin its strengths and weaknesses. In addition, its analysis of the markets and industries in which it competes needs to be sufficiently robust if it is to be aware of real opportunities and threats that exist. SWOT analysis becomes more complicated when existing strengths can quickly become a weakness. For example, such things as changes in consumer tastes, disruptive technologies, and new competitors will cause markets to change, thereby eroding an organization's current strengths and the source of its competitive advantage. A problem occurs when competitors are so busy investing in the capabilities that provide them with their current strengths that they fail to recognize threats in their external environment which will turn these strengths into a weakness. This is particularly the case where these threats emanate from outside their industry.

This analytical audit provides the organization with a better understanding of how it might best serve its markets. It illuminates the strategic choices which best match the organization's capabilities with the needs of its external environment. Yet, as we have noted, there can be a contradiction inherent in pursuing a strategic fit between an organization's strengths and the needs of its markets. As a result, SWOT analysis should not simply be about matching an organization's existing strengths to the needs of the external environment, but also about being aware of how the external environment may evolve. Over time these can move in different directions, making strategy formulation problematic.

A SWOT analysis for Indian conglomerate Tata Group is shown in **Figure 4.2**. Its strengths include its geographical scope of operations, financial resources, and corporate reputation. Weaknesses include the timings of its international acquisitions, and it has allowed itself to lag behind Reliance Industries and Amazon in its consumer Internet offerings. Its conglomerate structure makes restructuring its businesses difficult. Opportunities include focusing on the growing Indian market with its widespread adoption of smartphones and Internet users. There is an opportunity to build a 'super app' which would bring together its many different consumer services, from jewellery and groceries to

Internal Factors

Strength (S)	Weaknesses (W)
• Geographical scope of operations • Competes in diversified markets; IT , steel, retail, airlines • Financial resources, over $110 bn in revenues • Tata Consultancy Services • Corporate reputation built by Ratan Tata • Ability to attract investment funds	• Many international acquisitions made before the financial crisis are struggling to achieve profits; in UK Tata Steel • Falling behind Reliance Industries Ltd and Amazon in its consumer Internet offerings • Conglomerate structure • Acrimonious public dispute with former chairman Cyrus Mistry
Opportunities (O)	**Threats (T)**
• Focus on growing Indian market 1.4 bn population, rising incomes , consumption and smartphone use • Build a 'super app' to combine a suite of digital services in one place • Simplify Tata Group's structure of more than 30 companies • Joint ventures	• Economic downtown in the global economy due to coronavirus • Extra tariffs or customs checks for UK businesses • Powerful competitors; Reliance Jio, Amazon, Alibaba and Tencent • Geopolitical tensions between India and China • Indian court rulings might be unfavourable to Tata

External Factors

Figure 4.2 SWOT analysis for Tata Group.

financial services and satellite television, for the first time. Also, an opportunity exists to simplify Tata Group's structure of more than thirty companies enabling it to revive underperforming businesses.

Tata faces threats from the economic downturn which threatens its flagship Tata Consultancy Services, an IT outsourcing company with more than $20 billion in annual revenue. It faces relentless competitors in Amazon, Reliance Jio, and Alibaba, which are seeking to dominate the massive e-commerce market in India. With the majority of its international investments in the UK, extra tariffs or customs checks for UK businesses from the EU could make Tata's businesses in UK markets uncompetitive. This analysis provides some clear insights at a corporate level. If we disaggregate Tata Group into its strategic business units, such as Tata Steel, Tata Consultancy Services, and Tata Motors, this provides a finer grain of analysis to assess its strategic choices.

We can amalgamate the tools of analysis drawn from the macro-environment, the competitive environment, and an internal analysis of the organization to produce a SWOT analysis. We can use scenario planning and PESTLE analysis to identify the external opportunities and threats (OT) facing an organization. The organization's internal strengths and weaknesses (SW) can best be determined following an appraisal of its resources and capabilities, which reside within the activities of its value chain. Why use this analysis? SWOT analysis allows an organization to assess the fit of its current strategy to its changing environment, and to help turn potential threats into opportunities, and weaknesses into strengths. It can help an organization to identify its resources and capabilities more clearly, and to assess whether these are a benefit or a constraint to exploiting opportunities in the marketplace. Ultimately it can be used to help formulate an organization's strategy.

4.4.2 Limitations of SWOT Analysis

Although SWOT analysis is widely used in organizations and can be a useful tool if used correctly, it also suffers from some drawbacks. One of these is that it is not an end in itself but is simply an organizing framework.[16] It can provide useful signposts for the organization but it will not tell managers what they should do. Some common criticisms of SWOT are given below.

- It often produces lengthy lists which are each accorded the same weighting. The reality is that not all threats facing the organization will be weighted the same. For example, the impact of disruptive innovations will seriously undermine the competitive advantage of an organization, while other threats will have a less detrimental effect.

- Strengths and weaknesses may not be readily translated into opportunities and threats. For instance, an organization's strength embodied in its resources and capabilities may be moving in the opposite direction to how its market is developing.

- Ambiguity: the same factor can simultaneously be characterized as both a strength and a weakness. For example, the UK stationer and bookseller W. H. Smith has a store on most high streets. This makes it readily accessible for consumers. At the same time, the fixed costs of its premises make it increasingly difficult to compete with online retailers not encumbered with the same cost structure.

- The same factor can also be an opportunity and a threat. For example, consumers can subscribe and download newspapers on tablets, which benefits the newspaper publishing industry. At the same time, the reduction in print readership is a threat to an industry with high fixed costs.

- The analysis may be too focused within the industry boundary and miss the *weak signals*, *tipping points*, or *disruptive innovations* which can restructure the organization's industry.[17]

4.5 The TOWS Matrix

As a result of the limitations of SWOT, the **TOWS matrix** or situational analysis was introduced. The TOWS matrix provides a conceptual framework for identifying and analysing the threats (T) and opportunities (O) in the external environment and assessing the organization's weaknesses (W) and strengths (S).[18] The variables in the TOWS matrix are the same as SWOT. What is different is that these variables are now matched in a systematic fashion. This allows managers to make strategy formulation clearer by combining internal strengths and weaknesses to external opportunities and threats. In contrast, SWOT analysis is a technique for audit and analysis. Therefore, a manager would utilize SWOT at the beginning of the analysis, and TOWS afterwards to build upon the SWOT analysis.

The four TOWS strategies are Strength/Opportunity (SO), where an organization seeks to maximize both its strengths and its opportunities, and Weakness/Opportunity (WO), where an organization seeks to minimize its weaknesses and maximize the opportunities it faces. An organization may identify an opportunity in its external environment but be unable to take advantage of it due to weaknesses in the organization. Strength/Threat (ST) deals with the strength of the organization which is used to counteract the threats in the external environment. Weakness/Threat (WT) is where the aim of the organization is to minimize both its internal weaknesses and its external threats. The benefit of combining the internal and external analysis is to provide clarity and more robust decision-making. This is shown in **Figure 4.3**.

If we continue with the Tata Group example, for SO we can say a viable option might be for Tata to use its substantial financial resources to invest in the growing and prosperous Indian market to build market share. For WO, it might take a decision to focus primarily on e-commerce and build its own digital platform to rival Amazon and Reliance Jio. In developing options for ST, Tata can use its ability to attract investment funds to engage in new ventures to enable it to challenge its powerful competitors. Lastly, with WT, Tata might negotiate with its former chairman, Cyrus Mistry, to reach an amicable solution which allows Tata to continue business as usual and prevents further resources and time used to fight legal cases. This is shown in **Figure 4.4**. As with all tools of analysis, TOWS is not a substitute for managerial judgement but a useful tool to aid the decision-making process.

Internal Factors

		Strength (S)	Weaknesses (W)
External Factors	**Opportunities (O)**	**SO** The organization makes use of its strengths to exploit opportunities	**WO** Managers develop options that overcome weaknesses, to be able to take advantage of opportunities that exist
	Threats (T)	**ST** Managers develop options which exploit strengths to overcome threats	**WT** This is minimizing your weaknesses to help you minimize threats

Figure 4.3   A TOWS analysis.

Internal Factors

	Strength (S)	Weaknesses (W)
Opportunities (O)	**SO** Use financial resources to invest in growing e-commerce Indian market. Leverage existing market knowledge of competing in Indian.	**WO** Build its own digital platform to match competitors Amazon and Reliance Jio. Enter into a joint-venture to rapidly acquire capabilities for e-commerce in India.
Threats (T)	**ST** Use ability to attract funds to develop capabilities to challenge competitors.	**WT** Reach an amicable solution with former chairman to avoid further legal proceedings. Consolidate acquisitions to conserve resources during the global slowdown.

External Factors (vertical axis label on the left)

Figure 4.4   A TOWS analysis for Tata Group.

4.6 **Organizational Performance**

How can an organization assess its performance and keep its attention on its strategic aims? The choice of performance measures is a challenge because these play a key role in strategy formulation, evaluating whether an organization's objectives have been achieved, and in compensating managers. Therefore, the purpose of assessing organizational performance is to help the organization ascertain whether the strategies being implemented are actually adding value. To address performance, we must first address the fundamental question: *why do businesses exist?*[19] With this in mind, we can evaluate the two main perspectives based on shareholders and stakeholders.

4.6.1 **Maximizing Shareholder Value**

In the USA and the UK there exists a predominant belief that the role of corporations is to serve the owners of the business: the shareholders. This is referred to as 'shareholder primacy'. In a much quoted passage, the Nobel prize-winning economist **Milton Friedman** argued '*there is one and only one social responsibility of business—to use its resources and engage in activities designed to increase its profits so long as it stays within the rules of the game which is to say, engages in open and free competition without deception or fraud*'.[20]

Friedman's contention is that corporate executives act as agents and, therefore, to engage in forms of corporate social responsibility is using their position to spend someone else's money for a general social interest.[21] The effect of which is to impose a tax on the owners by ensuring that they receive lower returns from their investment than they otherwise would. If the effect of such actions by corporate executives raises prices for consumers, then this places a tax on consumers. The fact that managers may be involved in the pursuit of socially responsible aims does not mitigate their actions and still amounts to a misallocation of shareholders' wealth.

As such, Friedman does not recognize a social role for the corporations that would encompass the needs of stakeholders; his concern is for the shareholders. However, he does argue against the violation of accepted legal business practices. In this respect Friedman would have perceived the fraudulent use of corporate funds as a gross misallocation of resources which ultimately leads to less money for shareholders. It's worth noting that Friedman's role for the corporation is rooted in his belief in the market mechanism and political economy. He states: 'in a free enterprise, private property system, a corporate executive is an employee of the owners of the business. He has direct responsibility to his employers.'

Friedman's concern is that the blurring of corporate executives' boundaries of responsibilities resulting from intrusions into social responsibilities would ultimately lead to an erosion of free enterprise and the onset of a socialist state. The very act of executives being involved in decisions that are in the domain of the political arena turns such executives into public employees and civil servants, though they remain employees of a private enterprise. And if they are public servants they must be elected through a political process and not chosen by shareholders. Friedman does concede that actions he terms 'social responsibility' may be in a corporation's self-interest and, therefore, justified to some limited extent.

In their seminal work, **Berle and Means**[22] cast doubt on profit-maximizing theories. They were not questioning whether the objective of organizations should be to maximize profits for the shareholders but whether this actually occurs. Indeed, in an article in the *Harvard Law Review*, Berle states *'you cannot abandon emphasis on the view that business corporations exist for the sole purpose of making profits for their shareholders until . . . you are prepared to offer a clear and reasonably enforceable scheme of responsibilities to someone else'*. Their concerns were around the **principal–agent problem**. This problem has occupied economists since the time of the Scottish economist **Adam Smith**.[23] In the eighteenth century, Smith documented what is now known as the agency problem. The agency problem arises because of the separation between ownership of an organization and its control. It is inherent in the relationship between the providers of capital, referred to as the principal, and those who employ that capital, referred to as the agents. Smith's concern was that any given person will simply not watch over another person's money in the same way as they would watch over their own money.

Michael Jensen and William Meckling state that an agency relationship exists when one party, the principal, contracts work from another party, the agent, to perform on their behalf. However, this agency relationship can give rise to a number of agency problems.[24] These occur because no contract, however precisely drawn, can possibly take account of every conceivable action in which an agent may engage. The question arises as to how to ensure that the agent will always act in the best interest of the principal. **Agency costs** occur when there is a divergence between these interests. Thus, agency costs can be seen to be the costs associated with monitoring agents to prevent them acting in their own interests.

The profit-maximizing assumption is contested by behavioural psychologists, **Cyert and March**, who claim that organizations consist of shifting coalitions.[25] This approach argues that organizational behaviour is determined by the interests and beliefs of the dominant coalition(s). Some economists have moved away from profit maximization and argued instead for market share or sales maximization. Others suggest that managers actually run companies based upon utility functions which include profit, but also include other elements. This idea of coalitions within and around organizations has found its expression in **stakeholder theory**. However, whether the objective of shareholder interest can be subordinated to a multiplicity of stakeholders' interests is an ongoing debate. See the **Case Study: The Pursuit of Shareholder Value at Boohoo** which considers the ramifications of shareholder maximization.

CASE STUDY   The Pursuit of Shareholder Value at Boohoo

Boohoo, the UK 'fast fashion' company which is targeted at young women, was co-founded in 2006 by Mahmud Kamani and Carol Kane. The company was floated on the alternative investment market (AIM) in 2014. Since its flotation in March 2014, it have grown from a single brand, generating £140 million of sales in 2015, to seven brands, generating in excess of £1 billion of sales annually, while delivering consistent growth. Boohoo's nimble pivot from party frocks to loungewear—'made for staying in, chilling out and taking some much needed "you" time'—tapped the mood of young consumers during the coronavirus lockdown.

The joy of shopping.
Source: © freestocks / Unsplash.com.

As the share prices of most UK retailers suffered big falls, Boohoo's reached an all-time high in June 2020, giving the company a £5.2 billion market value market valuation. While established UK high street stores such as Next and Marks & Spencer experienced sharp falls in sales during the pandemic, Boohoo experienced sales growth of 45 per cent to the three months ending 31 May 2020, and expected a 25 per cent increase for the year ending February 2021. Even brands that appeal to the same customers as Boohoo, such as Primark, suffered sales falls during the pandemic in 2020.

About 40 per cent of Boohoo's cut-price clothing ranges, mostly targeted at 16- to 24-year-old women, are made in the UK. It makes small batches initially and does larger runs if they sell well, so it avoids the need to drop prices to clear stock. 'Our suppliers are experts at our test and repeat model and our need to turn things around quickly,' the company said.

It achieves strong profit margins because it is an own-label business, unlike Asos, which sells other people's products as well as its own brand. A further reason for its solid profit margins is that it has chosen to outsource much of its information technology (IT), rather than develop this in-house.

The German online fashion platform, Zalando, and increasingly Next, sell brands from Topshop to Ted Baker alongside their own label. In contrast, Boohoo has preferred to buy brands. It acquired Karen Millen in 2019, and Oasis and Warehouse in 2020. It has made no secret of its willingness to acquire more, and has a substantial war chest to do so. There have also been questions about its treatment of suppliers, its promotions, and its executive pay levels. That said, both the co-founders agreed to bring in outside help. In 2019, as the company grew rapidly in size, they relinquished their co-chief executive roles and brought in an experienced CEO from outside the company.

In July 2020, the month following its all-time high share price, the company saw more than £2 billion wiped from its market valuation. Why the dramatic fall? Well, as so often happens with high growth companies, the working conditions of its suppliers came under scrutiny. The company came under fire for allegedly risking the spread of coronavirus after claims that factories in Leicester, supplying the online retailer, told staff to come into work during lockdown, despite being sick. The city of Leicester is the UK's largest clothing manufacturing hub and has attracted the attention of workers' rights groups for a number of years, with some workers having been shown to receive as little as £3.50 an hour. This is considerably below the minimum wage.

Meg Lewis, campaign manager for Labour behind the Wheel, added that many Leicester factories had faced pressure to continue operating during lockdown. Kate Hills, the founder of garment industry group Make it British, said she had heard of manufacturers in Leicester flouting rules to keep up with heavy demand from online retailers, such as Boohoo. Boohoo refused to comment on virus cases among garment workers or claims that it had ramped up production during lockdown. It did, however, say it had 'closely followed and adhered to all aspects of the guidance provided by government'. Boohoo said it was able to keep prices low as it did not have any bricks and mortar stores and used social media rather than expensive TV advertising to reach customers.

As a result of the allegations, the share price plunged 23 per cent after the retailer admitted it did not know the identity of a supplier alleged to be paying workers illegally low wages to make clothes for it. A *Sunday Times* newspaper investigation found workers making garments for Boohoo's Nasty Gal Brand were paid £3.50 an hour at a factory. Boohoo's response was to take 'immediate action to thoroughly investigate how our garments were in their hands'. In the meantime, shareholder groups and pay campaigners pointed out a plan for Boohoo to pay bonuses of up £150 million to its two founders and other executives, just days before it was accused of sourcing clothes from cramped factories that were fuelling the spread of coronavirus.

Tom Powdrill, the head of stewardship at Pirc, the shareholder advisory service, said the reports into Boohoo's supply chains and their links to coronavirus outbreaks, combined with the bonus award, were 'reputationally awful'. It sends exactly the wrong message at a time when everyone is struggling with the health crisis. Standard Life Aberdeen, Boohoo's third largest independent shareholder, sold its shares in the fashion group after describing the company's response to allegations of worker abuse at suppliers' factories as 'inadequate'. Rival fashion platforms including Next, Asos, Very.co.uk, and Zalando said they would temporarily drop Boohoo products from their websites, pending greater transparency into the UK brand's supply chain.

Boohoo's own investigation had not discovered 'evidence of suppliers paying workers £3.50 per hour' but did find 'evidence of non-compliance with our code of conduct' by the suppliers involved in the Nasty Gal order. It said it had terminated its contracts with them and would launch an independent review of its UK supply chain to calm growing concerns from investors and customers about the treatment of workers who make its clothes. Both Next and Zalando refused to resume selling Boohoo labels until they saw more tangible signs of actions with their suppliers. Boohoo responded to the allegations by appointing a senior QC to investigate its supply chain and promising to improve its compliance. In addition, the company earmarked £10 million to improve conditions in Leicester.

Carry Somers, founder of the industry campaign group, Fashion Revolution, said her main concerns about Boohoo's supply chain were that she could not learn anything about it. 'They say [the factory allegedly paying low wages] is not one of their authorised suppliers, but how do shareholders know that if they don't publish a list of suppliers?' Boohoo ranks near the bottom of Fashion Revolution's supply chain transparency index of the world's 250 largest fashion brands. It still fared better than some, but Ms Somers said most of the retailer's points came from having published the policies that its suppliers needed to abide by. 'Policies are one thing, but what's really important is how these are carried out,' she said.

A longstanding problem for Boohoo is that production of its clothes may be outsourced from trusted suppliers into a network of more than 1,000 tiny outfits, that typically employ fewer than ten staff each and move around the city. There have been suggestions that social media influencers, a key portal between Boohoo and its young customer base, might now become more wary of the brand. 'If you are an influencer and you were to promote Boohoo right now you would lose a huge number of followers,' said Sara McCorquodale, founder of Corq, an analysis agency. 'The influencer business is about popularity . . . influencers ignore this at their peril.' That said, there is little evidence that unsavoury conduct revelations have a significant impact on consumers, especially at the budget end of the industry. 'Values tend to wash out at the till,' was the wry observation of one prominent fashion industry executive.

Even the removal of Boohoo brands from third-party platforms including Asos, Next, Zalando, and Very.co.uk is also unlikely to be costly in financial terms. Boohoo said that revenue from these platforms accounted for less than 4 per cent of its total revenue. In the longer term, Boohoo's growth and diversification should lessen the influence of factories in a single UK city, which produce only simple designs. It has already fallen from 71 per cent of Boohoo's production in 2014, to about 40 per cent in 2020. In October 2020, PwC, auditor since before the company went public in 2014, signalled its intention to resign as auditor of the fashion retailer.

A review by QC, Alison Levitt, found that although the company did not intentionally profit from the abuses, it certainly knew about them and had not acted quickly enough. She was satisfied that Boohoo did not deliberately allow poor conditions and low pay within its supply chain, and did not break any laws. However, Boohoo's oversight of its supply chain had been 'inadequate for many years' and its internal processes were 'well below the standard which would be expected of a company of its size and status', she said. Her findings included 'serious' and 'endemic' issues in the company's supply chain including poor working conditions, low pay, and a neglect for workers' rights. Boohoo's bosses had been aware of problems since at least the end of 2019, Ms Levitt said. 'Boohoo has not felt any real sense of responsibility for the factory workers in Leicester and the reason is a very human one: it is because they are largely invisible to them.'

Boohoo may be seen as a disruptive innovator with low-priced products that have quickly acquired a mainstream customer base. It may be seen as entrepreneurial. But as investors such as Standard Life Aberdeen sell their shares in Boohoo, and other fund managers demand closer engagement with the company over its employment issues, CEO John Lyttle faces the challenge of not just growing the company, but helping it to grow up.

Sources: 'Boohoo's agile model catches investors' eye', *The Financial Times*, 19 June 2020; 'Boohoo accused of fuelling virus spread in Leicester production push', *The Financial Times*, 1 July 2020; 'Boohoo shares tumbled on concerns over factory conditions', *The Financial Times*, 6 July 2020; 'Boohoo launches independent investigation into supply chain', *The Financial Times*, 8 July 2020; 'Boohoo comes out fighting after market tears it to shreds', *The Financial Times*, 9 July 2020; 'Major investor drops boohoo after inadequate response to malpractice claims', *The Financial Times*, 13 July 2020; 'Boohoo shares tumble as auditor PwC quits in wake of worker exploitation allegations', *The Independent*, 19 October 2020; 'PwC to quit as auditor to Boohoo on reputation concerns', *The Financial Times*, 16 October 2020.

Questions

1. Why do you think Boohoo has been able to grow so rapidly in the highly competitive fast fashion market?

2. Evaluate the extent to which Boohoo is pursuing shareholder primacy, or meeting the needs of stakeholders.

3. How were different stakeholders able to influence how Boohoo dealt with its UK supply chain?

4.6.2 Meeting the Needs of Stakeholders

We have seen that when the focus is on owners there is a presumption that shareholder value is the dominant objective of the organization. An alternative approach is a view of the organization that serves the interest of stakeholders. **R. Edward Freeman**[26] defines stakeholders as those individuals or groups who affect or are affected by the achievement of an organization's objectives. These include customers, suppliers, employees, government, competitors, the local community, and, of course, shareholders. Those who advocate a stakeholder model dispute that the primary role of organizations should be to create shareholder value.

Stakeholder proponents argue many different groups are affected by an organization's decisions. They argue that the role of management is to balance these stakeholder needs, rather than simply to focus on shareholders. Indeed, multinational corporations require executives to recognize that their actions can have effects beyond their nation's borders as a result of the globalized economy. The collapse of the US corporation Lehman Bros. is a case in point; its impact was felt far beyond the loss to shareholders. The problem is that stakeholders have conflicting needs. As a result, the task of management in balancing these different interests becomes more fraught. This is because stakeholders have different objectives which leave managers trying to balance multiple objectives.

How Should an Organization Respond to Different Stakeholders?

One way of trying to prioritize the different interests of stakeholders is to assess the influence they exert on an organization's objectives. **Mendelow**[27] proposed a model which ranks stakeholders according to their *power* and *interest*. This is shown in **Figure 4.5**, which categorizes stakeholders according to how much power they possess and the level of interest they show in what the organization does. The organization is then faced with different approaches to stakeholders, depending on where they reside in the stakeholder power–interest matrix.

High Power and High Interest Stakeholders

Power refers to a stakeholder's *ability* to influence an organization's objectives. Interest refers to their *willingness* to influence the organization's objectives. If a stakeholder exhibits both high power and high interest how should an organization interact with them? Such a stakeholder might be a regulatory body concerned with competition and consumer affairs. Consider, for example, the role of the Prudential Regulation Authority (PRA), the supervisory arm of the Bank of England. In 2020, it advised the six largest banks in the UK—Lloyds, RBS, Barclays, HSBC, Santander, and Standard Chartered—to halt their dividend payments after they were warned against paying out billions of pounds to shareholders during the coronavirus pandemic.[28]

The regulator also said it 'expects' the banks to refrain from paying any cash bonuses to senior staff. The regulator's concern was that the banks needed to 'serve the needs of businesses and households' during the coronavirus shutdown. In letters to each of the chief executives of the six banks, the Bank of England warned it was 'ready to consider use of our supervisory powers' if they did not comply with its recommendations on dividends and bonuses. By bowing to the regulator's wishes on dividends, the banks have avoided being subjected to formal action.

Where a stakeholder exhibits high power and high interest in the activities of a corporation, it is in the interest of the organization to engage and consult with them before taking any major strategic decisions. This is because these stakeholders possess the ability to force a change in strategy if it does not meet with their expectations. Prior to the PRA decision, the European Central Bank had also ordered Eurozone banks to freeze dividend payments and share buybacks.

High Power and Low Interest Stakeholders

Other stakeholders may exhibit high power but a relatively low level of interest in what an organization does. Institutional shareholders are routinely placed within this sector. However, there is a trend for institutional investors to become increasingly interested in the activities, especially corporate social responsibility (CSR) activities, of organizations in which they choose to invest. Furthermore, there is a growing interest in what is termed environmental, social, and governance (ESG) activities. This interest is as a result of the concerns of individuals whose funds institutional shareholders manage. For example, a major investment company, Standard Life Aberdeen, sold its shares in fashion retailer Boohoo after describing the company's response to allegations of worker abuse at its factories as 'inadequate'. Rival fashion platforms including Next, Asos, Very.co.uk, and Berlin-based Zalando also temporarily dropped Boohoo products from their websites, pending greater transparency into the UK brand's supply chain.[29] Therefore, even where a stakeholder exhibits high power but a low interest, organizations still need to keep these stakeholders satisfied that they are following the law and behaving in an ethical manner.

Low Power and High Interest Stakeholders

Stakeholders who have low power but a high level of interest in an organization's activities should be kept informed by the organization. This is because these stakeholders can form coalitions. These coalitions often temporarily coalesce around a single social issue and can be a powerful force for change. This is often seen during environmental disasters, or concern for the environment. For instance, Greenpeace activists protested peacefully inside and outside the headquarters of RWE, the German energy giant, calling for the company to immediately suspend its coal mining operations. They argue RWE is Europe's biggest corporate emitter of CO_2. Greenpeace Germany have been calling for RWE's CEO, Rolf Martin Schmitz, to sign a moratorium preventing further coal mining by the company while the German government's coal phase out plan is being fixed.

During such times environmental pressure groups benefit from a groundswell of public opinion which, for a time, may increase their power when negotiating with corporations. A recent survey published by Greenpeace Germany showed that a clear majority of Germans want RWE to halt

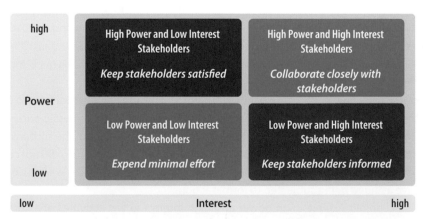

Figure 4.5   The stakeholder power–interest matrix (adapted from Mendelow, 1991).[30]

further destruction of the Hambach Forest and villages by its open-pit mines.[31] In order to avoid the creation of coalitions which may garner public support against your company, it is essential to keep such stakeholders informed about your current activities, and how these might need to change.

Low Power and Low Interest Stakeholders

Where stakeholders have low power and a low level of interest in the organization's activities they are unlikely to affect the strategic direction of a corporation. As a result, the organization can expend minimal efforts in its interactions with such stakeholders. That said, a company might still want to communicate to these stakeholders any proposed activities which might impact them.

We can see that without each stakeholder the corporation cannot function efficiently or cannot function at all. Without capital and shareholders there is no corporate entity. Without banks and other debt investors, the corporation cannot maximize its ability to earn a return on its capital. Without customers there will be no business for the corporation to do. Similarly, without employees, the corporation will be unable to do business. And if the community loses confidence in a corporation it may quickly lose its business legitimacy, resulting in collapse. It is only by aligning and attending to the needs of different stakeholders that the corporation fulfils its duty to society—to promote prosperity in a sustainable manner. Stakeholder theory asserts a corporation has duties and responsibilities to different stakeholders. However, this presents a number of problems.

Elaine Sternberg maintains that trying to balance stakeholder needs or benefits is unworkable.[32] This is because Freeman's definition of stakeholders leads to an infinite number of stakeholder needs. Furthermore, stakeholder analysis cannot offer guidance as to which stakeholders should be selected. And even if it could, it does not explain what counts as a legitimate need. Also, no guidance is provided as to what weighting each stakeholder group should have in relation to other stakeholders. Nonetheless, modern corporations realize that even when an organization's priority is to create value for its shareholders, it cannot afford to do so without some understanding of the expectations of stakeholders. As such, their criteria for successful performance may differ markedly from purely shareholder maximization. As we saw in **Chapter 1**, some organizations make a point of including stakeholder interest in their core values and vision. See **Strategy in Focus 4.2**, which illustrates the issues surrounding a focus on corporate social responsibility (CSR).

STRATEGY IN FOCUS 4.2 **Is a Focus on CSR Good for Business?**

Companies that rank highly on corporate social responsibility (CSR) measures are more likely to be the target of hedge fund activism, academic research has found. This is because some activist investors view CSR as a sign that a company is wasting money rather than focusing on shareholder returns, according to research published in Academy of Management. That is particularly the case if hedge funds activists, which tend to target and call for a shake-up at inefficient companies, view a company's efforts to do good as little more than superficial greenwashing.

The research looked at 506 US-based activist campaigns between 2000 and 2016 and found that companies whose CSR ratings were above the industry average had a 5 per cent chance of being subject to hedge fund activism. That compares with a 3 per cent likelihood for the industry average. In industries with poorer CSR ratings on average, companies that put greater emphasis on such issues are more likely to be targeted, the research also found.

This is because 'activist hedge funds look at CSR as a signal of relative misalignment' with delivering shareholder returns, says Prof. Durand. A focus on ethically oriented practices was seen as a sign of wasteful spending, which 'prevent firms from maximising shareholder value in the short term', wrote the academics, who also interviewed a range of hedge fund managers for their research. The findings coincide with a surge of interest in environmental, social, and governance (ESG) investing in recent years, which is helping persuade companies to improve their reputations for ethical behaviour in order to attract investors. For example, global sustainable investing assets totalled more than $30 trillion in 2018, according to the Global Sustainable Investment Alliance, up from $22.8 trillion in 2016.

While the coronavirus crisis, which started in 2020, diverted some investors' focus away from ethical investing, many in the industry believe demand for this type of investing will continue to grow. Paul Polman, Unilever's former chief executive, is among business leaders who have stuck to their guns in defending broader ESG mandates when challenged by outside investors. After he fended off an unsolicited $143 billion takeover approach from Kraft Heinz and its private equity investors in 2017, he described the abortive bid for Unilever as 'a clash between people who think about billions of people in the world and some people that think about a few billionaires'.

Prof. Durand says he believes that conclusions from the research, which goes only up to 2016, are still valid despite a recent pick-up in ESG investing. He says that activist hedge funds are not fundamentally opposed to a company focusing on CSR, but rather concerned that it was an indicator of greater waste. Signalling credentials in corporate social responsibility 'can be a cosmetic signal sent to customers' without any clear proof that it generates value for shareholders, he says.

But there have been signs that parts of the hedge fund industry, known for its focus on profits, have started to view a focus on environmental, social and governance characteristics as being in line with shareholder returns. Strong CSR performance creates shareholder value and is 'fully aligned with shareholders' interest', says Quentin Dumortier, founder of hedge fund firm Atlas Global Investors. 'An activist today should actually aim at pushing companies toward best-in-class and authentic CSR strategies as a powerful driver to create shareholder value.' Some commentators argue however that the idea that better ESG ratings will lead to better returns is false and instead see unnecessary costs incurred through ethical behaviour in many areas. The researchers also note that unintended attention from activist hedge funds concerned by CSR distractions can create additional costs for targeted businesses. These could include hiring lawyers or a public relations specialist, or the loss of focus as top management respond to the activist attack. Countering a hostile activist can cost tens of millions of dollars or more.

Prof. Durand adds that the impact of hedge funds on companies' ethical efforts is not straightforward. Nor is it always negative if clearly communicated. Explaining how CSR meshes into the business model reduces the chances of becoming an activist target, he says. Hedge funds targeting such companies 'are not anti-CSR, per se', Prof. Durand argues. But their scepticism over the benefits of ESG commitments made by companies is 'because they prefer shorter-term rather than longer-term returns'.

Source: Laurence Fletcher, 'Ethical CSR focus triggers hostile investor activism, study finds', *The Financial Times*, 3 August 2020.

We return to these issues in **Chapter 11**, when we evaluate shareholder and stakeholder perspectives in more detail.

4.6.3 Performance Measurement

A view of the role of organizations as simply to create value for shareholders is increasingly contested as companies seek to assess the impact of their decisions on wider society. As result, their corporate performance measurements will go beyond financial measurements. Nevertheless, an organization needs to be able to assess the performance of its managers. Companies based on what is referred to as the Anglo-American model have tended to adopt performance measurements which reflect shareholder value.[33] The overriding concern in many quoted companies continues to reflect shareholder value.

Measuring an organization's performance is necessary to understand whether the strategies being implemented actually add value to the organization.[34] Let us accept for the moment that the role of organizations is to create value for its owners. Then, the use of performance measurements acts as a control on management to ensure they fulfil their fiduciary duty to shareholders. All organizations undertake investment decisions where returns will only be known with certainty at some point in the future. This necessitates some form of calculation to approximate what the present value of future income is worth. The problem is that as future cash flows are uncertain, this makes any calculation based upon them fraught with difficulties. Therefore, management tends to rely upon more traditional accounting measures.

The result of using traditional financial measures is that the emphasis is upon past financial performance. In addition, the financial measures often used by corporations tend to draw attention to short-term performance only. It is important to remember that traditional accounting measures require comparison if they are to be useful. The fact that an organization makes a return on investment of 15 per cent may sound great, until you discover that the industry average is 23 per cent. Similarly, comparison with key competitors can draw attention to where an organization might need to benchmark its performance. This is discussed later in the chapter.

4.7 **The Balanced Scorecard**

The balanced scorecard was developed by **Robert Kaplan and David Norton**[35] as a means for organizations to measure their performance from a wider perspective than traditional financial measures. Kaplan and Norton's research identified two major problems with corporate strategies.

The first was that most companies measure their performance using financial ratios. But these financial measures are lag indicators which only report how a company performed in the past. What they do not do is show how well an organization might perform in the future. Furthermore, exclusive reliance on financial indicators could promote behaviour that sacrifices long-term value creation for short-term performance.[36] When Kaplan and Norton tried to find out which factors determine an organization's success, they uncovered a number of factors. These were customer satisfaction and loyalty, employee commitment, and the speed at which organizations learn and adapt. The second problem identified was a gap between an organization's strategy and its implementation by employees. This was because many organizations simply issued strategic statements that their employees failed to understand. Kaplan and Norton found that strategy was rarely translated into action because it was simply not translated into measures that employees could make sense of in their everyday work.

The balanced scorecard is an attempt to overcome these two weaknesses. It is not about formulating strategy, but an aid to understand and check what you have to do throughout the organization, to make your strategy work. Financial measures are important, but they reflect the results of actions that have already been taken. The balanced scorecard retains measures of financial performance but supplements them with operational measures which more clearly highlight an organization's future performance. As they state, 'the scorecard wasn't a replacement for financial measures; it was their complement'. The balanced scorecard then provides managers with a more comprehensive assessment of the state of their organization. It enables managers to provide consistency between the aims of the organization and the strategies undertaken to achieve those aims.

The balanced scorecard allows an organization to evaluate its respective strengths and weaknesses from four different perspectives: financial, customer, internal business, and learning and growth. The idea is that an organization's perspective of how it sees itself and how the outside world views it can be shown by integrating these four perspectives into a single balanced view. Assume, for example, that an organization wants to improve its market share. Using a balanced scorecard approach the organization would need to translate what this actually means. For instance, what are the measures that it needs to undertake to increase its customers? This then leads management to assess what changes it needs to make to its internal business processes to accomplish this. Once the need for internal change is understood, it is then possible to assess what new skills and competencies the organization needs to acquire to improve its performance. Norton and Kaplan outline a set of measures that organizations can use for each of these steps.

The balanced scorecard approach looks at an organization from four perspectives.[37]

We can show this diagrammatically to highlight the linkages and interdependence of each of the balance scorecard perspectives. **Figure 4.6** shows an organization's vision and strategy in the centre of the diagram. In order for the vision and strategy to be realized, we can link them to the four operational measures listed below: *financial*, *customer*, *internal business*, and *learning and growth*. We can allocate each of these four perspectives with their own specific objectives and how we might measure these objectives. We can now see that the balanced scorecard approach provides management

1. Financial Perspective—How do we look to shareholders? This financial perspective would include traditional financial measures such as cash flow, increase in sales, and return on capital employed (ROCE).

2. Customer Perspective—How do customers view us? The customer perspective measures include how an organization is creating value and differentiating its products and services in relation to competitor products. It might also include the extent to which customers are prepared to endorse new product offerings from the company.

3. Internal Business Perspective—What must we excel at? The internal business perspective measures will reflect such things as employee motivation, productivity, and quality—the different business processes that create customer and shareholder satisfaction.

4. Learning and Growth Perspective—Can we continue to improve and create value? The learning and growth perspective includes measures that take account of the speed and efficiency of new product development. It embodies a climate that supports organizational change, innovation, and growth.

Table 4.3 The four perspectives of the balanced scorecard.

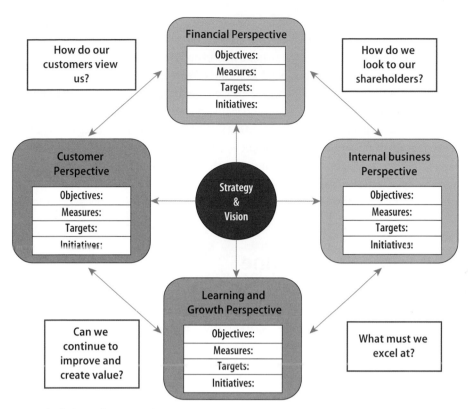

Figure 4.6 The balanced scorecard.

with a comprehensive assessment of their organization. It also provides employees with measures which they fully understand thereby enabling them to implement the organization's strategy.

In the anniversary edition of the *Harvard Business Review*, the balanced scorecard was listed as one of the fifteen most important management concepts to be introduced within its pages. However, when assessed in terms of satisfaction by organizations, the balanced scorecard rated below average. The list of companies that have used this approach include the Royal Bank of Scotland, Exxon Mobil, Ericsson, the Swedish insurance company Skandia, BP Chemicals, and Xerox. In addition, the balanced scorecard is also popular with public sector organizations.

Criticisms of the Balanced Scorecard

Criticisms of the balanced scorecard concern the measurements it leaves out, such as employee satisfaction and supplier performance. However, this might be because what an organization chooses to measure is often what it finds easy to measure. Another problem is that many organizations suffer from information overload as they go from measuring a few factors to measuring too many factors. One of the greatest failings is that organizations do not use the measurements to motivate people because managers do not sufficiently link measures to a programme of actions. In this respect, identifying the right things to measure is merely the starting point. If organizations are to achieve a sustainable competitive advantage, they need to understand better the role of intangibles, such as brands, as well as their own people.

The balanced scorecard may provide a bridge between the needs of shareholders and the needs of stakeholders. Concern about the impact of their activities on the environment is forcing many companies to think hard about ways in which they can reduce their carbon footprint. For example, by 2021, the Swedish car manufacturer, Volvo, plans to introduce five 100 per cent electric models, and ensure the rest of its petrol and diesel range has a hybrid engine of some form.[38]

In summary, Kaplan and Norton's balanced scorecard takes traditional financial performance measures and complements these with criteria which measure performance from three additional perspectives: customers, internal business processes, and learning and growth. The balanced scorecard helps prevent the underachievement of strategic goals that result from an overemphasis on short-term financial measures. By adopting a more balanced approach, the organization can actively pursue strategies that achieve its aims by setting performance measures that have some correlation with these strategies. In addition, this approach also takes account of the different expectations of stakeholders, recognizing perhaps that maximizing shareholder value is not a prime motivator for employees or customers.

4.8 The Triple Bottom Line

The **triple bottom line (TBL)** is a sustainability framework that examines a company's responsibilities in terms of its economic, environmental, and social impact.[39] The term 'triple bottom line' was coined by **John Elkington** in 1994. The triple bottom line is a recognition that success or failure on sustainability goals cannot be measured only in financial terms. For companies who want to follow a sustainability agenda TBL allows them to consider: what are the implications for how they measure their performance, and what do they measure? In order to do this companies need to undertake an audit against the TBL.

If we look at **economic bottom line**, the concern for organizations is how this can be assessed and what long-term indicators of sustainability can be added. Traditionally, there was little overlap between a company's financial needs to serve its shareholders and the interests of other stakeholders in terms of the environmental and social bottom lines. However, if a company wants to include a wider economic sustainability, it might also consider the long-term sustainability of: the demand for its products and services, the company's costs, and its innovation programmes and business ecosystem.

Environmental bottom line probably receives the greatest media and activist interest. This is concerned with 'natural capital'. Natural capital refers to the elements of the natural environment which provide valuable goods and services to people. For example, a woodland can be regarded as a natural capital asset, from which flows valuable benefits, or ecosystem services, such as flood risk reduction and carbon capture.[40] There are many different types of natural capital. The questions organizations need to ask themselves are: how is natural capital affected by our current operations, and how will it be affected by our future operations? Can it be quantified and, therefore, taken account of? And, given the company's activities, is the natural capital sustainable?

Social bottom line not only refers to public health, skills, and education, but seeks to embrace wider measures of a society's health. It is a measure of 'the ability of people to work together for common purposes in groups and organisations'.[41] The inexorable march of globalization has made the interface between economic and social bottom lines increasingly problematic. For example, how can organizations in the face of intense international competition, square the circle between increasing competitiveness and the inevitable job losses this often entails? A social bottom line must also be measured in terms of the well-being of the billions of people who inhabit the planet and how it impacts the planet.[42] **Figure 4.7** shows how the economy, the environment, and society are interlinked.

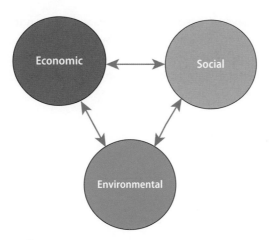

Figure 4.7 The triple bottom line.

The Danish pharmaceutical multinational Novo Nordisk measures its results using a triple bottom line. Novo Nordisk, based in Copenhagen, was founded in 1923 to make insulin. The company now controls more than half the market for insulin. It relies upon its treatment of diabetes for 80 per cent of its revenue. But instead of simply selling expensive, differentiated insulin products to maximize its profits, it adopts a dual approach. It also sells high-quality generic products, human insulin, for countries and populations that can't afford the advanced products that the more affluent patients want. By adopting this enlightened approach, Novo Nordisk has considerably enhanced its corporate reputation.

Novo Nordisk believes that a healthy economy, environment, and society are fundamental to long-term business success. The company's business philosophy is one of balancing financial, social, and environmental considerations.[43] As such, Novo Nordisk manages its business in accordance with the triple bottom line (TBL) business principle and pursues business solutions that maximize value to its stakeholders as well as its shareholders. This is because in the long term, social and environmental issues become financial issues. Novo Nordisk's board believes that if companies keep polluting then they will face stricter environmental regulations, and energy consumption will therefore become more costly.[44] Similarly, if companies don't treat employees well, don't behave as good corporate citizens in their local communities, and don't provide inexpensive products for poorer countries, governments will impose regulations on such companies that will end up being very costly.

Limitation of the Triple Bottom Line

Since his original work on TBL, Elkington has come to the opinion his ideas as currently practised by many corporations may be due for a 'product recall'. This is because many companies assume the aim of a TBL is to measure the financial, social, and environmental performance of the company over a period of time. And that a company that produces a TBL is taking account of the true cost of doing business. Yet for Elkington the TBL was never designed to be an accounting tool which simply sought to balance and trade off different outcomes. It was actually envisaged as a framework which might encourage a debate about the transformation of capitalism. It was intended as a genetic code, a blueprint, for how capitalism might improve over time.

While some companies have adopted a TBL as envisaged by Elkington, such as Novo Nordisk, Unilever, and Germany's Covestro, without a more 'radical intent' it appears unlikely that more corporations will embrace the framework for value creation in tomorrow's capitalism. The limitations can be seen to apply to *how* the triple bottom line is being implemented rather than a criticism of the sustainability framework itself.

4.9 Benchmarking

Why do some organizations excel at some practices and activities while others do not? Can something be learned from the way in which successful companies carry out their practices that will improve your own company's performance? This is the essence of benchmarking. Benchmarking involves comparisons between different organizations with a view to improving performance by imitating or, indeed, improving upon the most efficient practices. This should not be limited to competitors within the same industry, but instead be measured against *any* organization that has a reputation for being the best in its class.

In Japan benchmarking is practised through what is called *Shukko*.[45] This is where employees work with other organizations and acquire new practices which will benefit their organization. *Shukko* may lead to the transfer of technology between employees and/or organizations, and also provide for management development. However, its key advantage is the acquisition of specific knowledge which is lacking in the organization. In the USA, the Xerox Corporation, widely credited with developing benchmarking, defines it as 'a continuous process of measuring our products, services, and business practices against the toughest competitors and those companies recognized as industry leaders'. A key to successful benchmarking will be the open learning that is allowed to take place between organizations. Clearly, organizations that are not competitors will be less concerned about sharing best practice.

For example, in order to improve the service on its frequent-flyer programme, British Airways visited the Oriental Hotel in Bangkok. The Oriental Hotel has a reputation for looking after and pampering its guests. Thus, British Airways was able to improve upon its practices on how to record details of its customer preferences. The Xerox approach to benchmarking is included in **Table 4.4** and involves ten sequential steps. The starting point is for an organization to identify

Planning	1 Identify what is to be benchmarked. 2 Identify comparable companies. 3 Determine data collection method and collect data.
Analysis	4 Determine current performance 'gap'. 5 Project future performance levels.
Integration	6 Communicate benchmark findings and gain acceptance. 7 Establish functional goals.
Action	8 Develop action plans. 9 Implement specific actions and monitor progress. 10 Recalculate benchmarks.

Table 4.4   The Xerox approach to benchmarking. Source: M. Zairi, *Benchmarking for Best Practice—Continuous Learning through Sustainable Innovation*, Butterworth Heinemann, 1996.

what it wants to benchmark in order for it to identify suitable companies to benchmark against. Benchmarking should not be confined to your own industry; the net should be spread widely to truly capture best practice. The end goal is for the organization to reach a level of maturity in which it attains a leadership position by having benchmarked practices fully integrated into its own processes.

Benchmarking exposes organizations to state-of-the-art practices and, by inculcating a continuous learning process, can help engender an organizational culture that actively pursues change and innovation. In this respect, it can be a vehicle for empowering employees and optimizing their creative potentials. The downside is that some organizations may harbour unrealistic expectations about what benchmarking can achieve. The choice of companies to benchmark against will require managerial skill and time to ensure that an appropriate match is obtained. Even where benchmarking practices can be formulated into organizational objectives, unless managers can facilitate a cultural environment that embraces change and innovation, these 'best practices' will simply fail at the implementation stage.

Summary

In this chapter, we introduced an important debate within strategic management; whether the industry context in which an organization finds itself is the main determinant of its performance, or whether there are internal factors within an organization which may more readily account for how well that organization performs. The former approach is characteristic of the positioning school and the work of Michael Porter. The latter is associated with the resource-based view of strategy, and is addressed in **Chapter 5**. We assessed value chain analysis as a tool to assess an organization's activities by showing where these activities add value. Organizations add value through the configuration of their value-chain activities and the linkages between these activities. Organizations also add value through the linkages with their suppliers, distributors, and consumers; this process is referred to as the value chain system.

We revisited SWOT analysis, pointing out that to be of benefit it should include a prior analysis of the macro and competitive environment. SWOT is a much-used tool of analysis primarily because it is relatively easy to use. That said, it has limitations: for example, the analysis may be too focused within an organization's industry boundary and some factors can be seen as both a strength and a weakness. We noted that the choice of performance measure must first address a more fundamental issue: *why do businesses exist?* We evaluated the balanced scorecard as an attempt to actively link strategy to an organization's objectives. We also evaluated the triple bottom line which is a sustainability framework that examines a company's social, environment, and economic impact. We concluded the chapter with a discussion of benchmarking. We noted that benchmarking should not be limited solely to direct competitors or those within the same industry. An organization should be willing to compare itself against competitors outside its industry.

╬   **For more examples and discussion to aid your understanding of this chapter, please visit the online resources and see the Extension Material for this chapter.**

Review Questions

1. Why is an organization's understanding of its value chain important?
2. How can an organization balance its responsibilities to both shareholders and stakeholders?
3. Explain why a company might prefer to use a balanced scorecard approach to assess its performance.

Discussion Question

'Shareholder primacy is the only objective a company should be pursuing.' **Discuss**.

Research Topic

What are the value-chain activities for the Spanish retailer Zara? How is Zara able to successfully manage the linkages in its value chain system?

Recommended Reading

There are many books dealing with the responsibilities of organizations. One that benefits from being written by a practitioner who has influenced the corporate governance debate is:

- **A. Cadbury**, *Corporate Governance and Chairmanship—A Personal View*, Oxford University Press, 2002.

A key reading to understand value chain analysis is the work of Michael Porter. It was Porter who developed value chain analysis and remains the best expositor:

- **M. E. Porter**, *Competitive Advantage*, chapter 2, Free Press, 1985.

For a discussion of qualitative as well as quantitative measures of performance, see:

- **R. S. Kaplan** and **D. P. Norton**, 'The balanced scorecard—measures that drive performance', *Harvard Business Review*, vol. 69, no.1 (1992), pp. 71–9.

www.oup.com/he/henry4e
Visit the online resources that accompany this book for activities and more information on strategy.

Test your knowledge and understanding of this chapter further by trying the multiple-choice questions online.

References and Notes

1   **M. E. Porter**, *Competitive Strategy*, Free Press, 1980.

2   For a collection of articles that deal with differential firm performance, see **S. Segal-Horn** (ed.), *The Strategy Reader*, 2nd edn, Oxford University Press, 2004.

3   **Porter**, see n. 1 above.

4   **R. P. Rumelt**, 'How much does industry matter?', *Strategic Management Journal*, vol. 12, no. 3 (1991), pp. 167–85.

5   **G. Hawawini**, **V. Subramanian**, and **P. Verdin**, 'Is performance driven by industry or by firm-specific factors? A new look at the evidence', *Strategic Management Journal*, vol. 24, no. 1 (2003), pp. 1–16.

6   For an introduction to the resource-based view of strategy, see **C. K. Prahalad** and **G. Hamel**, 'The core competence of the corporation', *Harvard Business Review*, vol. 68, no. 3 (1990), pp. 79–91; **G. Hamel** and **C. K. Prahalad**, 'Strategy as stretch and leverage', *Harvard Business Review*, vol. 71, no. 2 (1993), pp. 75–84; **J. Barney**, 'Firm resources and sustained competitive advantage', *Journal of Management*, vol. 17, no. 1 (1991), pp. 99–120; and **R. Grant**, 'The resource-based theory of competitive advantage: implications for strategy formulation', *California Management Review*, vol. 33, no. 3 (1991), pp. 114–35.

7   **Porter**, see n. 1 above, chapter 2.

8   For a discussion of the role of activity systems within strategy, see **M. E. Porter**, 'What is strategy?', *Harvard Business Review*, vol. 74, no. 6 (1996), pp. 61–78.

9   This section draws heavily upon **Porter**, see n. 1 above, especially chapter 2, which contains a discussion of value chain analysis and competitive advantage.

10 **Porter**, see n. 1 above.

11 **Porter**, see n. 1 above, p. 48.

12 Where an organization's activities are embedded within its routines and form part of its culture, it is often difficult to identify clearly where value is derived. Hence, this may form the basis of competitive advantage.

13 See http://www.toyota-global.com/company/vision_philosophy/toyota_production_system/origin_of_the_toyota_production_system.html.

14 **A. Campbell** and **M. Goold**, *Synergy: Why Links between Business Units often Fail and How to Make Them Work*, Capstone, 1998.

15 The introduction of SWOT analysis is widely associated with Kenneth Andrews; see **K. R. Andrews**, *The Concept of Corporate Strategy*, Irwin, 1971.

16 **J. Kay, P. McKiernan,** and **D. O. Faulkner**, 'The history strategy and some thoughts about the future', *The Oxford Handbook of Strategy*, Oxford University Press, 2006.

17 For a discussion of tipping points, see **M. Gladwell**, *The Tipping Point—How Little Things Can Make a Big Difference*, Little Brown, 2000; for disruptive innovations, see **J. Bower** and **C. M. Christensen**, 'Disruptive technologies: catching the wave', *Harvard Business Review*, vol. 73, no. 1 (1995), pp. 43–53.

18 **H. Weihrich**, 'The TOWS matrix – a tool for situation analysis', *Long Range Planning*, vol.15, no. 2 (1982), pp. 54–66.

19 For a discussion of this fundamental question, see the **Caux Round Table**, an organization of business leaders which seeks to include moral responsibility within business decisions: http://www.cauxroundtable.org.

20 **M. Friedman,** *Capitalism and Freedom*, University of Chicago Press, 1962, p. 133.

21 **M. Friedman**, 'The social responsibility of business is to increase its profits', *New York Times Magazine*, 13 September 1970.

22   **A. A. Berle** and **G. C. Means**, *The Modern Corporation and Private Property*, Macmillan, 1932.

23   **A. Smith**, *The Wealth of Nations*, 1776.

24   **M. C. Jensen** and **W. H. Meckling**, 'The theory of the firm: managerial behaviour, agency costs and ownership structure', *Journal of Financial Economics*, vol. 3, no. 3 (1976), pp. 305–60; **E. F. Fama** and **M. C. Jensen**, 'The separation of ownership and control', *Journal of Law and Economics*, vol. 88, no. 2 (1983), pp. 301–25.

25   **R. M. Cyert** and **J. G. March,** *A Behavioural Theory of the Firm*, Prentice-Hall, 1963.

26   **R. E. Freeman**, *Strategic Management: A Stakeholder Approach*, Pitman, 1984.

27   Adapted from **A. Mendelow**, *Proceedings of Second International Conference on Information Systems*, Cambridge, 1991.

28   **S. Morris**, **D. Crow**, and **C. Giles**, 'British lenders suspend dividends after BoE pressure', *The Financial Times*, 1 April 2020.

29   **S. Austin**, 'Major investor drops Boohoo after inadequate response to malpractice claims', *The Financial Times*, 13 July 2020; **P. Nilsson**, 'Boohoo launches independent investigation into supply chain', *The Financial Times*, 8 July 2020.

30   **A. Mendelow**, *Proceedings of 2nd International Conference on Information Systems*, Cambridge, MA, 1991.

31   Greenpeace.org. https://www.greenpeace.org/international/press-release/22536/greenpeace-activists-crash-energy-giant-rwe-with-urgent-call-to-quit-coal.

32   **E. Sternberg**, 'The defects of stakeholder theory', *Corporate Governance: International Review*, vol. 5, no. 1 (1997), pp. 3–10.

33   **E. Sternberg**, *Corporate Governance: Accountability in the Marketplace*, 2nd edn, IEA, 2004.

34   **R. D. Buzzell** and **B. T. Gale**, *The PIMS Principles: Linking Strategy to Performance*, Free Press, 1987.

35   **R. S. Kaplan** and **D. P. Norton**, 'The balanced scorecard—measures that drive performance', *Harvard Business Review*, vol. 69, no. 1 (1992), pp. 71–9.

36   **R. S. Kaplan** and **D. P. Norton**, 'Transforming the balanced scorecard from performance measurement to strategic management: part 1', *Accounting Horizons*, vol. 15, no. 1 (2001), pp. 87–104.

37   See **R. S. Kaplan** and **D. P. Norton**, 'Using the balanced scorecard as a strategic management system', *Harvard Business Review*, vol. 74, no. 1 (1996), pp. 75–85.

38   **A. Vaughan**, 'Volvo signals carmakers' growing confidence in an electric future', *The Guardian*, 5 July 2017.

39   **J. Elkington**, 'Accounting for the triple bottom line', *Measuring Business Excellence*, vol. 2, no. 3 (1998), pp. 18–22.

40   **https://ecosystemsknowledge.net/resources/resources-theme/natural-capital-introduction** (accessed 30 November 2020).

41   **J. Elkington**, see n. 39 above, p. 21.

42   **J. Elkington**, '25 years ago I coined the phrase triple bottom line. Here's why it's time to rethink it', *Harvard Business Review*, 25 June 2018.

43   Novonordisk.co.uk (accessed 14 November 2020).

44   'The best performing CEOs in the world', *Harvard Business Review*, November 2015.

45   See **M. Zairi**, *Benchmarking for Best Practice—Continuous Learning through Sustainable Innovation*, Butterworth Heinemann, 1996.

CHAPTER 5
THE INTERNAL ENVIRONMENT: A RESOURCE-BASED VIEW OF STRATEGY

 Learning Objectives

After completing this chapter you should be able to:

- Explain and discuss differential firm performance from a resource-based view
- Explain the role of capabilities in helping an organization achieve competitive advantage
- Evaluate the VRIO framework as a means of achieving *sustainable* competitive advantage
- Explain a knowledge-based view of the organization
- Discuss dynamic capabilities as a way of dealing with the limitations of the resource-based view of strategy

Introduction

Chapter 4 was devoted to an analysis of the internal environment and how an organization might usefully analyse its value-creating activities. In order to assess the importance of the organization's internal environment we placed our discussion in the context of the factors which account for an organization's performance. In **Chapter 3** we saw that the answer to the question 'What drives an organization's performance?' was based on an understanding of an organization's markets and industry. This 'positioning approach' accepts the importance of an organization's resources, but argues that in formulating strategy an analysis of the competitive environment is a more appropriate starting point.

We will continue to ask the question 'Why do organizations which possess similar resources and compete in the same industry, experience different levels of profitability?' as we evaluate an alternative approach to this question. We have already noted that a criticism made about the positioning approach is that it fails to answer this question adequately. In this chapter, we explore a different perspective, which suggests that relative firm performance and therefore profitability, is determined by an organization's resources and capabilities. This has been termed the *resource-based view*.

5.1 **The Resource-Based View of Strategy**

The resource-based view of strategy has a long antecedent, with links stretching back to Edith Penrose in the 1950s.[1] However, it is more commonly associated with the work of **C. K. Prahalad and Gary Hamel, Richard Rumelt, Jay Barney, Robert Grant, and Birger Wernerfelt**.[2] As we will see later, advocates such as David Teece, have sought to introduce a dynamic element to the theory to overcome some of the inherent criticisms of this framework. The resource-based view also deals with the competitive environment facing the organization, but takes an 'inside-out' approach; its starting point is the organization's *internal* environment. As such, it is often seen as a competing perspective to Porter's five forces framework, evaluated in **Chapter 3**, which takes the industry structure as its starting point, hence 'outside-in'.

The resource-based view emphasizes the internal capabilities of the organization in formulating strategy to achieve a sustainable competitive advantage in its markets and industries. If we see the organization as made of resources and capabilities which can be configured (and reconfigured) to provide it with competitive advantage, then this perspective does indeed become inside-out. In other words, a company's internal capabilities determine the strategic choices it makes in competing in its external environment. In some cases, an organization's capabilities may actually allow it to create new markets and add value for the consumer, such as Apple's various i products and Tesla's electric cars. Clearly, where an organization's capabilities are seen to be paramount in the creation of competitive advantage it will pay attention to the configuration of its value-chain activities. This is because it will need to identify the capabilities within its value-chain activities which provide it with competitive advantage.

If we look at Toyota's much-admired manufacturing system, we see it manages *inbound logistics* in the form of excellent material and inventory control systems. This ensures that inventory levels are sufficient to meet customer demand by having parts delivered prior to their assembly. If we look at other primary activities in the value chain, such as *operations*, we find automated and efficient plants with embedded quality control systems. This is backed by *marketing and sales* through advertising and dealership networks, and *service* through the use of guarantees and warranties. Toyota's value-chain activities, its linkages across them, and its linkages with the value chain of its suppliers are configured in such a way that they provide the Japanese competitor with a core competence or distinctive capability. It is this capability which provides it with competitive advantage and which its competitors have found difficult to match. Toyota is also able to appropriate the added value that is derived from these activities. For instance, Toyota makes more profit than the three largest automobile companies in the US combined.

If organizations in an industry face similar industry conditions we might expect them, other things being equal, to exhibit some degree of similarity with respect to profitability. However, if we compare the profitability of Toyota with its rivals in the automobile industry, we see a divergence in profitability between organizations that compete in the same industry. Porter[3] argues that it is the industry structure within which organizations compete, and how they position themselves against competitive forces in that structure, which determines how profitable individual companies will be. In contrast, the resource-based view points not to industry structure, but to the unique cluster of resources and capabilities that each organization possesses.[4] Therefore, for proponents of the resource-based view, the answer to why firms within the same industry experience different levels of performance is found by looking *inside* the organization.

The resource-based view of strategy is based on two assumptions about the resources and capabilities that each organization possesses. The first assumption is **resource heterogeneity**; this implies that different organizations competing in the same industry may possess different resources and capabilities. As a result, a company competing in a given industry may be able to undertake activities better than its rivals in the same industry. For example, Toyota's lean manufacturing and just-in-time (JIT) delivery of supply parts has enabled it to reduce costs in the production of automobiles. The second assumption is **resource immobility**. This implies that the resource and capability differences that exist between organizations may continue over time. The reason for this is, it is assumed to be too costly for organizations who do not possess these resources and capabilities to develop or acquire them. This helps to explain why some organizations consistently outperform other organizations—differential firm performance.[5]

As is so often the case, the differences between competing perspectives can be overdone. For example, **Raphael Amit and Paul Schoemaker** argue that the resource-based view can be seen as a complement to the positioning school.[6] **Gary Hamel and C. K. Prahalad** concede that Porter's approach, which embodies the notion of **strategic fit**, matching an organization's resources to the needs of the external environment, is not so much wrong, but more what they refer to as *unbalanced*. For many managers, the concept of strategy simply implies pursuing opportunities that *fit* the company's resources. Hamel and Prahalad suggest this approach is not wrong, but tends to obscure an approach in which **strategic stretch** supplements strategic fit.[7] They argue being strategic means creating a chasm between ambition and resources. In other words, an organization with a relatively small amount of resources, but with big ambitions can leverage its resources to achieve a greater output for its smaller inputs.

5.1.1 **Resources**

The resource-based view of competition draws upon the resources and capabilities that reside within an organization, or that an organization might want to develop, in order to achieve a sustainable competitive advantage. **Resources** may be thought of as inputs that enable an organization to carry out its activities. Where organizations in the same industry have similar resources, but differing performance, we might deduce that they vary in the extent to which they utilize their resources. Resources in and of themselves confer no value to organizations. It is only when they are put to some productive use that value follows. Resources can be categorized as tangible or intangible.

Tangible Resources

Tangible resources refer to the physical assets that an organization possesses and can be categorized as physical resources, financial resources, and human resources. Physical resources include the current state of buildings, technology, materials, and productive capacity. To add value, these physical resources must be capable of responding flexibly to changes in the marketplace. Clearly, organizations with the most up-to-date technology and processes which possess the knowledge to exploit their potential will be at an advantage. Its financial resources will include its cash balances, debtors and creditors, and gearing (debt-to-equity ratio). The extent to which an organization can achieve an acceptable return on its capital employed will determine the extent to which it can attract outside capital or financial resources. This will be linked to expectations about its future growth.

The total workforce employed and their productive capacity form a tangible human resource. This is often measured by criteria such as profit or sales per employee. In reality, measurement of employee productivity is difficult and problematic. Human resource processes such as annual reviews rarely capture the full extent of employee endeavour. This is because the ability to perform well in a role is a function of attitude and motivation rather than formal qualifications. Indeed, research by **Daniel Goleman** to determine the personal capabilities that drive outstanding performance suggest that emotional intelligence is more important than technical ability and IQ.[8] In assessing resources, the concept of opportunity cost is helpful to determine whether existing resources can provide further value. In other words, can an organization's resources be used more effectively in a different capacity? In addition, can these assets be sweated i.e. ensuring that the value derived from existing assets is maximized?

Intangible Resources

Intangible resources comprise brand names, patents and copyrights, an organization's ability to innovate, and reputation. Given intangible resources are more difficult for competitors to identify, it is not surprising that their value to the organization tends to exceed tangible resources. For example, an intangible resource for the marketing group WPP was the creative insight of its founder, Sir Martin Sorrell. His ability to make major acquisitions, taking over some of the oldest and most prestigious advertising companies in the world, and integrating them profitably into WPP is a capability few competitors can imitate. Organizations with valuable *tacit knowledge* built up through their culture, processes, and employees over time possess an intangible resource which cannot readily be transferred. This is referred to as **path dependency**. It is the combination of unique experiences an organization has acquired to date as a result of its tenure in business.

The reputation or 'goodwill' of an organization is increasingly recognized as a valuable intangible asset, which can easily be damaged by ill-thought-out strategies and marketing campaigns. In recent years, the low cost airline, Ryanair, has moved away from controversial statements about customers, focusing instead on improving its website and customer service.[9] Johnson & Johnson's response to malicious tampering with their Tylenol product (see **Chapter 1**) ensures that it consistently remains top of organizations ranked according to their reputation.[10]

5.1.2 **Organizational Capabilities**

While the existence of resources is important, resources per se do not confer any benefit on an organization. These assets need to be deployed in a way that allows them to work together effectively. It is an organization's *capability* that allows it to deploy these resources towards a desired task. **Robert Grant** distinguishes between resources and capabilities.[11] He sees resources as inputs into the production process. These include items such as capital equipment, the skills of individual employees, patents, brands, and finance. On their own these resources are not productive; they only become productive when they are configured and coordinated for some specific use. A capability is the capacity for a team of resources to perform some task or activity. Therefore, resources are the source of an organization's capability. For example, just because a company possesses resources such as access to finance, a purpose-built plant, and trained employees does not mean it will automatically achieve success in manufacturing. These resources still need to be configured together and deployed as a capability towards some desired end.

We can distinguish between *threshold capabilities* and *distinctive capabilities*. A **threshold capability** is necessary for an organization to be able to compete in the marketplace. In this respect, all competing organizations possess threshold capabilities; it is a prerequisite for competing in the industry. For example, in order to be able to compete in the automobile industry an organization must possess knowledge about design, engine, and body manufacture. Without this base knowledge, a company would simply be unable to compete at all in that industry, irrespective of their resources. Capabilities, in and of themselves, do not confer any competitive advantage for the organization. To achieve competitive advantage an organization must possess **distinctive capabilities**. A prerequisite for a distinctive capability is that it must be highly valued by the consumer and difficult for your competitors to imitate. As we will see, where a company's distinctive capability resides within the nexus of its value chain—its own interdependent activities and the linkages within its value chain system—this can be a powerful source of competitive advantage.

There can be a degree of confusion with the different terms that circulate around the resource-based view of strategy. When examining the literature, we should bear in mind that the terms *capability* and *competence* are often used interchangeably, as are *distinctive capability* and *core competence*.

Prahalad and Hamel[12] argue that the critical task of management is to create an organization capable of creating products that customers need, but have not yet even imagined. To achieve this, management must successfully operate across organizational boundaries rather than focusing on discrete individual strategic business units (SBUs). They developed the term **core competencies** to describe the collective learning of individual members within an organization and their ability to work across organizational boundaries.[13] They point out that many major corporations have had the potential to build up core competencies, but senior management lacked the vision to see the company other than as a portfolio of discrete businesses. This is what Prahalad and Hamel refer to as the **tyranny of the SBU**.[14] As they state:

> The skills that together constitute core competence must coalesce around individuals whose efforts are not so narrowly focused that they cannot recognize the opportunities for blending their functional expertise with those of others in new and interesting ways.[15]

A core competence is enhanced as it is applied and shared across the organization. For Prahalad and Hamel, competencies are the glue that binds businesses together and spurs new business development. For example, Toyota's core competencies derive from its ability to blend core competencies across the whole organization. It may simply be that the organization has deployed its collection of resources in such a way that allows it to compete more successfully. In fast fashion, Zara is the classic example of a company which has achieved core competence in the way it configures its value chain. As a vertically integrated company that controls design, manufacture, and sales, Zara is able to respond rapidly to changes in fashions. Many organizations have tried to emulate Zara's success, but found their business model less easy to imitate than they might have first thought. That said, these distinctive capabilities or core competencies still need to be protected if the organization is to appropriate the rewards that derive from their use.

The US motor manufacturer Tesla has achieved a distinctive capability in the production of batteries and all electric cars. This in no small measure results from their **first-mover advantages**. This refers to organizations that benefit from the learning and experience they acquire as a result of being first in the marketplace. Other motor manufacturers are placed in the unenviable position of playing 'catch-up'. Prahalad and Hamel provide three tests that can be applied to core competencies in an organization which are listed in **Table 5.1**.

John Kay argues it is the *distinctive capabilities* of an organization which provide it with competitive advantage.[16] An organization's capabilities are only distinctive when they emanate from a characteristic which other organizations do not have. Furthermore, possessing a distinctive characteristic is a necessary but not sufficient criterion for success; it must also be *sustainable* and *appropriable*. For a distinctive capability to be sustainable it needs to persist over time. To be appropriable, a distinctive capability needs to benefit the organization which holds it rather than its employees, its customers, or its competitors. These distinctive capabilities derive from three areas: *architecture*, *reputation*, and *innovation*.[17] These in turn are linked to relationships between an organization and its stakeholders: its employees, customers, shareholders, and suppliers, as well as a group of collaborating companies to which it may network. It is these relationships that allow an organization's resources to provide it with distinctive capabilities through the conduit of its architecture, reputation, and innovation.

Architecture

An organization's architecture comprises the system of relational contracts that exist inside and outside the organization. Internal architecture refers to an organization's relationship with its employees, and the relationship that exists between employees. External architecture refers to its relationships with its customers and suppliers. In addition, an organization may engage in relationships with other companies working in related activities; this form of architecture is referred to as networks. There is a myth about great leaders of organizations which detracts from the reality of organizational behaviour. Organizations depend far less on individual leaders and groups than they do on their *organizational routines*.

Organizational capabilities require that the knowledge of individuals is integrated with a company's resources, such as its capital equipment and technology. This is accomplished by organizational routines.[18] **Organizational routines** are regular, predictable, and sequential patterns of work activity undertaken by members of an organization. Therefore, an organization's capabilities comprise a number of interacting routines. For a company's capabilities to operate effectively it must achieve cooperation and coordination between routines. It is these organizational routines which develop over time and are continually used in changing competitive conditions, which allow the organization to get the best out of their ordinary employees. As Kay states, '*Architecture does not create extraordinary organizations by collecting extraordinary people. It does so by enabling very ordinary people to perform in extraordinary ways*.'[19] For example, Amazon uses its capability in web development aligned

---

1. A core competence should provide access to a wide variety of markets. For example, Honda's distinctive capabilities in engine design and production have enabled it to compete in markets such as cars, lawnmowers, and powerboats.

2. A core competence should make a significant contribution to the perceived customer benefits of the end products. For example, BMW has distinctive capabilities in engineering, which allow it to produce high quality cars that sell at a premium.

3. A core competence should be difficult for competitors to imitate. For example, in the USA, Southwest Airlines' competitors have found that having similar resources have not enabled them to replicate what makes the airline so successful. In the UK, competitors of Ryanair have been unable to deconstruct the airline's success.

Table 5.1   How to test for a core competence.

to efficient logistics in warehousing, distribution, and buyer relationships to produce a vast array of consumer goods at low prices. The resulting convenience for the consumer has enabled Amazon to achieve superior growth.

Where a distinctive architecture is based upon the output of all employees rather than a few individuals, it allows the added value created to be more readily appropriated by the organization. For a distinctive architecture to be sustainable, the relational contracts that an organization enters into must be difficult for its competitors to identify and imitate. The relationships will inevitably be implicit, complex, and subtle, based in and around the organization. This lack of formalization inhibits imitation and ensures that architecture remains a source of competitive advantage. Architecture, then, refers to the ability of the organization to create organizational knowledge which is more than just the sum of individual employees. It includes an organization's ability to respond effectively to changes taking place in its external environment, as well as its exchange of information both within and outside the company.

Reputation

Reputation as a source of distinctive capability is important in those markets where consumers can only ascertain the quality of a product from their long-term experience. An example would include the use of a firm of architects. A company's reputation is built up through its reliable relationships, which take time to nurture and develop. A reputation for providing high-quality products and services can be used to secure repeat business and charge premium prices. In addition, reputation can be leveraged when entering related markets. For example, Apple uses its brand image to compete across the consumer electronics industry. Reputation can also be used to help facilitate a more successful entry into unrelated markets. Richard Branson's Virgin Group leverages the Virgin brand that has consumer acceptance to operate in diverse markets from financial services to health clubs.

Innovation

An organization's ability to innovate successfully is also a source of distinctive capability that is sustainable and appropriable (see **Strategy in Focus 5.1**). For example, it may produce innovative products such as Apple with its iTunes, iPad, and iPhones. In a survey of senior executives around the world to find the fifty most innovative companies, Apple came top for the third year running.[20] Apple's innovation in product design and development is difficult for competitors to imitate. Apple entered the mobile phone market in 2007 with the introduction of its iPhone, and in 2010 introduced the iPad—its touch-screen computer. Apple continues to update the design and specification of its most successful product ever, the iPhone, and launched the iPhone 8 in 2017 to mark its tenth anniversary. In 2020, Apple introduced its flagship iPhones, the iPhone 12 and iPhone 12 mini, which were sold alongside the more expensive iPhone 12 Pro and iPhone 12 Pro Max. This constant innovation and new product development has proved to be a source of sustainable competitive advantage as competitors struggle to imitate Apple's success.

The competitive advantage that appears to emanate from innovation may actually derive from an organization's architecture. An organization may develop innovative processes which are embedded within the routines of the organization and are therefore difficult for competitors to copy. By seeking patents and copyrights, organizations can protect innovative products and ensure that they appropriate the value deriving from their use. In hypercompetitive markets, as we saw in **Chapter 3**, **D'Aveni**[21] argues for continuous new product development which allows an organization to stay one

STRATEGY IN FOCUS 5.1 Innovation at Netflix

The best way to stay innovative, many bosses will tell you, is to hire the best people and let them get on with it. Few take this as literally as Reed Hastings of Netflix. The video-streamer's employees can take as much holiday as they fancy and put anything on the company's tab so long as, to cite the entirety of its corporate expense policy, they 'act in Netflix's best interest'. Anyone may access sensitive information like a running tally of subscribers, which Wall Street would kill for. Executives seal multimillion-dollar deals without sign-off from top brass. High-achievers are rewarded with the plushest salaries in the business—whether their business is writing computer code or film scripts. Underperformers are unceremoniously cut loose.

It sounds like a recipe for expensive anarchy. But managing 'on the edge of chaos', as Mr Hastings mischievously puts it, has served Netflix well. Most of its 7,900 full-time workers seem happy being treated like professional athletes, paid handsomely as long as no one can do their job better. Each generates $2.6 million in annual revenue on average, nine times more than Disney employees, and $26.5 million in shareholder value, three times more than a Googler does. Investors lap it up as hungrily as Netflix binge-watchers, who now number 193 million worldwide. Since going public in 2002 the firm's share price has risen 500-fold (see **Figure 5.1**), in the top ten eighteen-year runs in America Inc.'s history, as Mr Hastings points out with a hint of pride in his voice. In 2020, it briefly overtook Disney to become the world's most valuable entertainment company.

The 125 reasons why

This track record has earned Mr Hastings kudos. A PowerPoint 'culture deck' outlining his management philosophy has been viewed 20 million times since he posted it online eleven years ago. Sheryl Sandberg, Mark Zuckerberg's right-hand woman at Facebook, has called it the most important document ever to emerge from Silicon Valley. A new book in which Mr Hastings fleshes out those 125 slides is destined for the bestseller list. But it raises a question: are the 'No Rules Rules' of the title the right set as Netflix metamorphoses from California start-up into global show-business colossus?

It is easy to put too much stock in corporate culture, which can be a story triumphant companies tell themselves after the fact. GE's rise in the 1990s had more to do with financial engineering than with the much-aped habit introduced by Jack Welch, the conglomerate's CEO at the time, of ranking employees and 'yanking' the bottom 10 per cent. Netflix would not

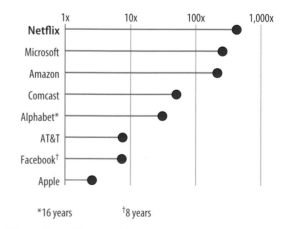

Figure 5.1   The Reed Run.

be where it is without its boss's uncanny foresight to bet on streaming in the late 2000s, or the uncannily flat-footed response from Hollywood incumbents, which took a decade to grasp the threat. Investors have displayed deep reserves of cheap capital, and deeper ones of patience. Over the past year the firm's prodigious revenue-generators each burned through $123,000 of cash (see **Figure 5.2**); this year quarterly cashflow turned positive for only the first time since 2014. Luck played a role, as when cut-price DVD players debuted just in time for Christmas in 2001, months after the dot.com crash forced Mr Hastings to lay off a third of his 120-odd workers, from what was then a DVD-by-mail rental service.

Still, as Michael Nathanson of MoffattNathanson, a consultancy, observes, 'Every time that Netflix faced a roadblock it found a clever way to work around it and emerge stronger.' Most notably, when TV networks and studios at last woke up to the reality of streaming and began to hog content licences, Netflix started producing its own shows, and later feature films. The swivel might have taken longer with employees bogged down in chains of approvals. 'Radical candour', whereby everyone's ideas, from Mr Hastings down, can be challenged by all-comers, helps weed out bad ones. 'Sunshining', the stomach-churning spectacle of publicly explaining choices, helps not to repeat mistakes. Senior Netflixers' 'ability to swallow their pride is truly exceptional', says Willy Shih of Harvard Business School, who has written two case studies on the firm.

Now this innovation-friendly culture is under fire on three fronts. The first two—the firm's growing size and scope—are internal to Netflix. The third source of pressure comes from the outside.

Start with size. The flat hierarchy and frankness that works in Silicon Valley, with its narrow range of temperaments and socioeconomic backgrounds, is harder to sustain in a global workforce that has swelled nearly fourfold in five years (more if you include temporary contractors, who now number more than 2,200, up from fewer than 400 in 2015). Asians, Europeans, and Latin Americans can find visitors from headquarters 'exotic', in Mr Hastings's words. Negotiating 'context', as Netflix managers and their subordinates do constantly in the absence of explicit rules, offers useful flexibility. But it takes time that could be spent perfecting a product—ever more of it as tacit cultural understanding is diluted by international expansion. Revenue per worker is down by 7 per cent from 2015.

Many countries grant workers more protections than America does. This is a problem for the 'keeper test', which requires managers constantly to question if they would fight to stop their underlings from leaving—and, if the answer is 'no', immediately send the individual on their way with generous severance. These golden handshakes, which range from four months'

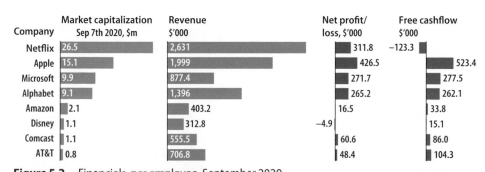

Figure 5.2   Financials, per employee, September 2020.

salary in America to more than six months in the Netherlands, are 'too generous' to reject, says Mr Hastings. Netflix has not been sued even in Brazil, where employee lawsuits are a national sport to rival football. The bonhomie may not last.

A larger workforce poses a separate risk to internal transparency. Even while the attrition rate hovers at around 10 per cent, the number of ex-Netflixers with knowledge of the firm's finances and strategic bets is now growing by hundreds each year. Unwanted disclosures have been rare and, says Mr Hastings, immaterial. But, he concedes, serious leaks may be 'a matter of time'.

The second challenge has to do with Netflix's sectoral girth. In its first decade it was primarily a firm of technologists like Mr Hastings, whom his co-founder, Marc Randolph (who left the firm in 2003), likened to the hyper-rational, emotionless Mr Spock in 'Star Trek'. That was never entirely fair—Netflix products are data-driven but Mr Hastings attaches as much weight to judgement in managing people as Captain Kirk ever did. Still, by the standards of Tinseltown, where Hastings now spends a couple of days most weeks amid studio intrigues and moody showrunners, he and his firm can come across as robotic.

One producer who has worked with Netflix detects hints of its horizontal hierarchy permeating Hollywood 'by osmosis'. This can speed things along. But, she grouses, 'sometimes you need a production assistant to assist, not commission scripts'. At the same time, Netflix missed a chance to revolutionize other old studio ways. The $150 million five-year deal it signed in 2018 with Shonda Rhimes, a star TV producer, may be more generous than most networks could afford. But it is Hollywoodian in its structure, says a former executive—and antithetical to the keeper test.

Moreover, Netflix may have no choice but to expand into new industries. This would be a departure from its laser focus on its core product: quality streamed entertainment. But show business is increasingly the preserve of conglomerates. Disney has theme parks, merchandising and TV networks. Comcast (the cable giant that owns NBCUniversal) and AT&T (the telecoms group which controls HBO and WarnerMedia) possess the pipes along which content flows. Apple's and Amazon's Hollywood ambitions are tethered to their powerful technology platforms.

Disrupting sluggish behemoths is one thing. Competing with them head-on may require a different trade-off between flexibility and efficiency. It may also mean takeovers. Mr Hastings has no shopping plans. But a strong culture, he admits, 'is a material weakness if you are going to make big acquisitions'. Cultural sparks could fly when you integrate more than a few dozen people, as they flew when his first firm, Pure Software, bought rivals in the 1990s.

The third set of challenges is external. COVID-19 has muted the exchange of ideas. It is also harder to evaluate—and dismiss—people by Zoom; Netflix's twelve-month rolling attrition rate has declined by a third, to 7 per cent. In September 2020 Mr Hastings said he did not see 'any positives' to home-working.

Dear white people

Then there is public pressure for corporate America to care more about diversity. Mr Hastings added inclusion to Netflix values in 2016 but it barely features in his investor letters or annual reports. He acknowledges a tension between the desire for diversity and Netflix's arch-meritocratic ideals (the firm eschews quotas, as it does all management metrics, in favour of that Kirkian judgment). Its corporate temperament screams 'hypermasculine', as Erin Meyer, Mr Hastings's co-author and professor at INSEAD business school in France, has herself noted. And one person's radical candour is another's microaggression.

Netflix shareholders and their representatives on the board have confidence that Mr Hastings can reconcile these strains. He has given them plenty of reasons to trust his own judgment. But he is fully aware that his position is safe only as long as he can keep the magic going. The keeper test applies to him, as well.

Source: 'Can Reed Hastings preserve Netflix's culture of innovation as it grows?', *The Economist*, 12 September 2020.

step ahead of competitors. The deliberate cannibalization of a successful product by its successor ensures that the organization is able to appropriate the rewards from its innovations.

In fact, Apple's iconoclastic co-founder and former CEO, Steve Jobs, was doing both: constantly developing new products while also seeking to appropriate more of the value from these products. Apple developed its first in-house microprocessor, the A4, to power their iPad. This, along with its battery technology, allows Apple to control what components go into its products and reduces its dependence on third-party manufacturers. At the same time, Apple also has its own software—its iWork suite of programmes that are similar to Microsoft Office. This combination of in-house hardware and software has the advantage of making Apple's technology more proprietary, difficult to imitate, and importantly, allows Apple to appropriate more of the value from its activities. It also allows Apple to blend all these technologies in a way that no other competitor can. To increase the adoption of Apple's products, complementary products such as Microsoft Office, are integrated seamlessly, which enlarges the overall market.

In an article entitled 'Strategy and the delusion of grand design', Kay[22] summarizes *distinctive capability* as the characteristics of a company that either cannot be copied by competitors or can only be copied with great difficulty. As we have seen, these will include such things as patents and copyrights, a strong brand image, patterns of supplier or customer relationships, and skills, knowledge, and routines that are often embedded within the organization and are difficult for a competitor to unravel. It is these distinctive capabilities that are the basis of sustainable competitive advantage. The task then is to identify and match these distinctive capabilities with the needs of the marketplace.

Kay points out a contradiction inherent in the question, 'How do organizations create distinctive capabilities?', since if distinctive capabilities can be replicated they fail to be distinctive capabilities. What is truly irreproducible has three sources: (1) a market structure that limits entry; (2) a company's history which by definition will require time to replicate; and (3) tacitness in relationships. Tacitness refers to the routines and behaviours which take place within an organization which cannot be copied, since the participants themselves are unsure how they work. **Tacit knowledge** is defined as knowledge which is highly personal, hard to formalize and, therefore, difficult to communicate to others. Therefore, organizations would do well to identify what distinctive capabilities they already possess rather than what distinctive capabilities they would like to have.

The key success factors (KSFs), identified in **Chapter 2**, can be used to identify resources and capabilities. Key success factors are those factors that keep customers loyal and allow the organization to compete successfully in the industry. If we know what the key success factors in an industry are, we can work backwards to determine which resources and capabilities allow the

organization to meet these success factors. In reality, the capabilities we seek to identify are embedded in an organization's value chain. Therefore, value chain analysis, discussed in **Chapter 4**, is
best used to identify these capabilities.

5.2 The VRIO Framework and Sustainable Competitive Advantage

In order to assess the extent to which a capability may provide an organization with a sustainable
competitive advantage, we can make use of the **VRIO framework** developed by **Jay Barney**.[23] The
VRIO framework asks four questions with reference to a capability's *Value, Rarity, Imitability*, and
Organization. The answer to these questions also provide managers with a capability analysis of their
organization's internal strengths and weaknesses. The four questions are shown in **Table 5.2**.

5.2.1 Valuable Capabilities

Organizational capabilities can only be a source of competitive advantage or sustainable competitive advantage when they are *valuable*. Capabilities are valuable when they enable a company to exploit an external opportunity and/or neutralize an external threat. The question then arises as to how
an organization might assess this. The answer is to identify any change in the organization's revenues
and costs as a result of using its capabilities. If there is an increase in its revenues or a decrease in its
costs compared to when the capabilities were not being deployed, then the capability is valuable.
For example, when the Swedish furniture company IKEA develop products with designers, this is usually based on a price for the end consumer. By utilizing wood that grows quickly and in abundance,
cheaper manufacturing methods, and producing in high volumes, IKEA is able to reduce its costs.

A competing organization seeking to build or acquire these capabilities would need to ensure
the cost of doing so does not outweigh the expected revenue. Where a competitor does not possess valuable capabilities it will be at a *competitive disadvantage* to organizations which do. Environmental models such as *Porter's five forces* (discussed in **Chapter 3**) and *SWOT analysis* (discussed
in **Chapter 4**) seek to identify the organization's resources which can exploit opportunities and/or
neutralize threats. The resource-based view goes further in suggesting the additional characteristics
these capabilities must possess if they are to provide sustainable competitive advantage. Clearly,

V—Value	Do an organization's capabilities allow it to exploit environmental opportunities and neutralize environmental threats?
R—Rarity	Are capabilities possessed by only a few competitors?
I—Imitability	Are capabilities costly for other organizations to acquire or imitate?
O—Organization	Is the company organized to allow it to exploit the valuable, rare, and difficult to imitate capabilities it possesses?

Table 5.2   Questions for the VRIO framework.

there are links between the work of Porter and the resource-based view, and differences between the two approaches can be overstated.

Value chain analysis (discussed in **Chapter 4**), can be used to look at the activities that go to make up a product or service with a view to ascertaining how much value each activity adds. A company can look at the interdependent linkages between activities within the value chain. This helps it to understand the relationship between the way one value activity is performed and the cost or performance of another activity.[24] Furthermore, within its value chain system (see **Chapter 4**), a company can identify activities which create value within its own value chain as well as the value chain of its consumers, suppliers, and distributors. Clearly, if the capability adds no value to consumers the company will not increase its revenue. This also explains why companies with similar resources experience different levels of profitability. Thus, by understanding the linkages within its value chain a company is able to deploy its resources into a capability, while a competing organization might lack this insight.

Managers seeking to develop capabilities should be aware that the value of their capabilities can be market dependent. For example, the ability of a company to achieve competitive advantage through its flexibility in responding to a rapidly changing market will no longer be valuable if the market suddenly becomes stable and unchanging. As the market context changes, what were once valuable capabilities may no longer be valuable.[25]

5.2.2 **Rarity**

If valuable organizational capabilities reside within a large number of competitors or potential competitors then they cannot be a source of sustainable competitive advantage. The reason is that each competitor would have the potential to exploit those capabilities in the same way.[26] For example, once Amazon demonstrated the value of e-books to readers other publishers quickly followed suit. A valuable capability for implementing a strategy is visionary leadership that provides insight into how markets and products may develop. If this capability is not rare then many organizations will also be able to formulate and implement the same strategies. The visionary leadership of Jeff Bezos in founding and guiding Amazon is based on his understanding of the Internet, price leadership, and consumer convenience to achieve market dominance. That capabilities are **valuable and rare** is a necessary but not sufficient condition for sustainable competitive advantage. Where an organization's capabilities are valuable but not rare, they provide *competitive parity*, not competitive advantage.

5.2.3 **Imitability**

Valuable and rare capabilities provide a means of *temporary* competitive advantage. If the organization is to achieve *sustainable* competitive advantage it is necessary that competing organizations cannot copy these capabilities. Where valuable and rare capabilities can easily be imitated, competitors will simply compete away an organization's ability to generate above-average returns. An example is the dot.com of the 1990s; some of these companies had innovative ideas and gained a temporary competitive advantage largely by first-mover advantages into the market. Unfortunately, others quickly followed, acquiring the capabilities to imitate their strategies and eroding any lasting value. Valuable and rare capabilities can provide a source of sustainable competitive advantage when an organization that does not possess them can only acquire or develop them, at cost disadvantage compared to organizations that do possess them.

Consider the British manufacturing company, Dyson, which is famous for its vacuum cleaners.[27] Its founder, the inventor Sir James Dyson, spends heavily on R&D of new products. He continually innovates across the product range. For example, 80 per cent of the fifteen million vacuum cleaners it sells worldwide are now battery-powered cordless models. Dyson uses the technology he developed for its vacuum cleaners across different products. The company created the Dyson Institute of Technology to address the shortage of engineers and now recruits and trains engineers in-house. It has taken on this responsibility in order to grow and drive the business forward (see **Strategy in Focus 5.2**).

STRATEGY IN FOCUS 5.2   Sir James Dyson: a Difficult Man to Imitate

Inventor Sir James Dyson has no plans to step back from his namesake business as it reported record sales and profit. Dyson, who founded the firm famed for its vacuum cleaners, said he has no plans to move on in the near future.

'I have no retirement plan. I'm fully committed to the business,' said Sir James. 'There may be a time they kick me out but I'm very happy designing and building new products and technology.'

His vow to remain at the helm of the business came as it posted annual sales up 45 per cent to £2.5 billion and profits of £631 million, a 41 per cent rise on the previous year (see **Figure 5.3**). The jump in profits came despite the business,

Photo 5.1   Eighty per cent of the vacuum cleaners Dyson sells are cordless, like this Dyson v6 absolute cordless vacuum cleaner. Source: © KeithHoman/Shutterstock.com.

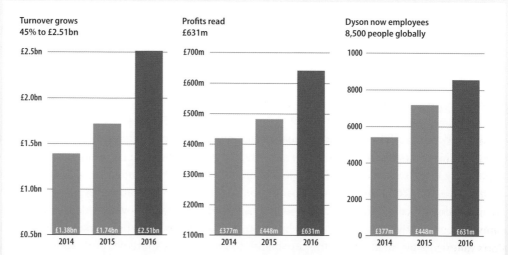

Figure 5.3   Turnover, profit, and employee numbers at Dyson. Source: Reproduced with permission of *The Telegraph*.

which has delivered Sir James a fortune estimated at £5 billion, investing heavily in R&D of new products.

Over the past couple of years Dyson has revamped its range, particularly in vacuum cleaners, and in 2016, 80 per cent of the fifteen million it sold worldwide were battery-powered cordless models. 'Considering we were not making them two years ago that's a huge turnaround,' said Sir James.

Also helping drive growth was the launch of Dyson's Supersonic hair dryer, which uses high-speed motor technology developed for the company's vacuum cleaners, and was a step into a new sector for the business. Profits leapt despite Dyson spending about £7 million a week on new products and technology and Sir James said the company plans to move into new sectors where its expertise can be leveraged—but only when the time is right.

'We're looking at more non-domestic products but we are not rushing to do lots of different things,' he said. 'We are a private company so we can do it when we are ready.'

The company is the UK's biggest investor in robotics and AI research, which it sees as massive growth areas. However, Sir James downplayed recent reports that one-third of UK jobs could be taken over by robots. 'I hope that robotics means that we need a lot less human cleaners but to design and make robots you need an army of highly skilled engineers,' he said.

He is a passionate supporter of developing the UK's engineering base, which is struggling to turn out enough people with the skills the sector needs. Sir James announced he was starting his own university at the company's Wiltshire base to generate the engineers, spending £15 million in the first year of the four-year course which will initially have twenty-five students, a number he expects to grow rapidly. Dyson also bought a 500-acre ex-RAF base to allow it to expand its UK operations, having outgrown its current site.

Source: Alan Tovery, 'Sir James Dyson to remain at controls as Dyson reports record results', *The Telegraph*, 27 March 2017. © Telegraph Media Group Limited. Reproduced with permission.

An organization's capabilities will be difficult to imitate if it embodies *unique organizational conditions*, *causal ambiguity*, and **social complexity**.

Unique Organizational Conditions

An organization may have acquired its capabilities as a result of being in a unique location which enables it to add value to consumers, which allows it to generate superior returns. The unique location it possesses is a capability that is difficult to imitate. French wines have long experienced a competitive advantage through the uniqueness of their climate, soil, terrain, and expertise handed down through generations; this is referred to as terroir. Similarly, a Scottish whisky distiller which is located beside a loch with qualities of water which enhances its blend of whisky has a capability which is difficult to imitate. These are examples of first-mover advantages.

In addition to first-mover advantages, competitors will find it extremely difficult to replicate capabilities that an organization possesses as a result of the path it has followed to arrive at its current position. As we noted previously, this refers to path dependency which embodies the unique experiences an organization has acquired to date as a result of its tenure in business. Competitors simply cannot acquire these capabilities on the open market and therefore cannot imitate that organization's value-creating strategy.

Causal Ambiguity

Causal ambiguity exists when the link between the capabilities of an organization and its competitive advantage is not understood, or is only partially understood by competitors. As a result, competitors are unsure as to which capabilities to acquire and, if acquired, how to integrate them within their own value chain system. The capabilities are more likely to be a source of sustainable competitive advantage when the organization itself is unsure of the exact source of its competitive advantage. For example, W. L. Gore and Associates (makers of Gore-Tex fabric) has a culture based on devolved management, which precludes the need for hierarchy, which in turn successfully facilitates innovation among the company's employees. Even managers within W. L. Gore would experience great difficulty in trying to explain exactly how these disparate activities enable the company to compete successfully. This is because, over time, the way managers work together becomes 'taken for granted' as opposed to being written in a HR company manual.

Social Complexity

Another reason why an organization's capabilities may be difficult for competitors to imitate is because they may be based on complex social interactions. These may exist between managers in an organization, in an organization's culture, and in its reputation with its suppliers and customers. John Kay refers to this social complexity as an organization's *architecture*.[28] When it is known how these socially complex resources add value to the organization, there is no causal ambiguity between the capabilities and competitive advantage of the organization. However, the fact that competitors may know, for example, that the culture within an organization improves efficiency does not mean that they can readily imitate that culture.

5.2.4 **Organization**

So far, we have seen that providing a positive answer to questions of value, rarity, and inimitability progressively moves an organization towards a potential for competitive advantage. We therefore have the necessary but not quite sufficient conditions for sustainable competitive advantage. In order to exploit being in possession of valuable, rare, and inimitable capabilities a company must also be sufficiently organized. This requires the use of appropriate formal and informal management control systems, procedures, and policies. (See **Case Study: The Dynamic Capabilities of Warren Buffett**.) When this organizational support is lacking, any exploitation of the company's valuable, rare, and inimitable capabilities will be sub-optimal. **Barney and Hesterly** argue where there is a conflict between a company's capabilities and its ability to organize these capabilities, the latter should be changed. However, once control systems, procedures, and policies are in place they tend to be quite inflexible. When that happens the company is unlikely to fully exploit its available capabilities.[29]

The VRIO framework is summarized in **Figure 5.4**. This illustrates the four capabilities of valuable, rare, inimitable, and organization. The figure demonstrates the competitive implication of each capability. As can be seen, it is the accumulation of these capabilities which carry the organization closer to sustained competitive advantage. As the organization passes through each capability stage starting with whether it is valuable, so it achieves a necessary but not sufficient condition for sustainable competitive advantage. It is only when the VRI capabilities are fully met and these are supported by the organization's structure and formal and informal management control systems that the capabilities can be exploited.

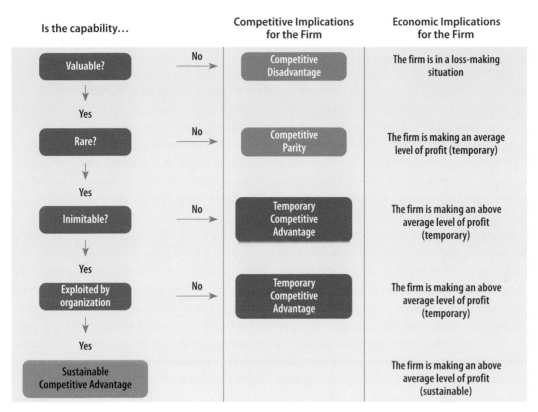

Figure 5.4   The VRIO framework.

The use of the term *sustainability* here does not refer to permanence. Rather, it implies that a competitive advantage will not be competed away because competitors are unable to imitate it. The competitive advantage may indeed be eroded by structural changes within the industry such that what was once a competitive advantage in one industry setting may not transcend industry changes. It then becomes a weakness or an irrelevance. This has resonance with the concept of *creative destruction*, highlighted by economist **Joseph Schumpeter**, which causes economies to advance through transformational changes.[30]

5.2.5 Make-or-Buy Decision

The recognition of an organization's core competence or activities which it performs exceptionally well can be the basis for its decision to provide a product or service itself, or to outsource it. If the organization is to focus on its core competencies as the basis of its sustainable competitive advantage, then the corollary of this is that activities which do not constitute a core competence for the organization can be given to outside companies who can provide these at a lower cost. This decision is intrinsically linked with an understanding of the activities contained within the organization's value chain. And, the extent to which a company wants to be vertically integrated. For example, British Airways recognizes that the provision of in-flight meals and snacks adds little value to its activities and can be produced cheaper by the market. The make-or-buy decision, or what is more appropriately termed *transaction cost*s, is discussed in **Chapter 8**.

5.3 Criticisms of the Resource-Based View

Most would agree that the resource-based view of the organization represents a leap forward in strategic management. There are clear links and complementarity with the work of **Michael Porter** and the positioning school, and equally sharp departures. Whether one would go so far as to classify the resource-based view as a new paradigm within strategic management is a matter of debate. Furthermore, although the resource-based view encourages managers to focus on strategies for exploiting organization-specific assets, it is not clear how organizations might create sustainable competitive advantage. A common criticism made of the resource-based view is that it says very little on the important issues of how existing resources and capabilities can develop and change over time, and how *new capabilities* might be created.

Danny Miller et al. introduced the term *asymmetries* to try to explain *how* an organization might develop its capabilities.[31] **Asymmetries** are hard-to-copy ways in which a company differs from its rivals, and which may ultimately provide competitive advantage. Asymmetries within an organization might include, for example, its unique experiences, its value-chain relationships, or its processes and procedures. The idea is that managers identify and build upon these asymmetries within their organization rather than trying to copy the capabilities of other companies. In doing so, a company can use its organizational skills to leverage these asymmetries and exploit opportunities in its market environment. However, this requires that organizations understand the differences between themselves and their rivals, and which of their identified asymmetries are relevant to the marketplace.

A similar criticism is that the role played by managers within organizations is often assumed to be self-evident and therefore seldom addressed. In response to this criticism, the VRIO framework was formulated which explicitly recognizes that capabilities need to be exploited by the organization rather than simply being possessed by them. Another criticism is that the resource-based view does not explain how and why certain organizations achieve competitive advantage in rapidly changing environments, such as semiconductors and software.[32] It fails to answer how a company might modify its existing capabilities, or create new capabilities to deal with rapid change. The introduction of *dynamic capabilities*, as we shall see in **Section 5.4**, has helped mitigate concerns about the limitations of the resource-based view in rapidly changing markets.

Priem and Butler argue that the resource-based view of strategy lacks detail and is therefore difficult for organizations to implement.[33] Furthermore, the resource-based theory is tautological and cannot be tested empirically. In other words, the valuable, rare, and inimitable capabilities that generate sustained competitive advantage are defined by their ability to generate sustained competitive advantage, producing a circular argument which cannot be falsified.[34] As such, a more detailed road map is required if it is to prove useful to organizations. Finally, we are back in the realm of deliberate strategies (see **Chapter 1**) with no formal recognition of emergent strategies and the role that these might play.

5.4 A Knowledge-Based View of the Organization

The **knowledge-based view of the organization** views the organization as a knowledge-creating entity. This approach argues that the most important source of a company's sustainable competitive advantage is knowledge, and the capability to create and utilize such knowledge.[35] This is because the use of knowledge allows a company to provide new products and processes. In addition, it also enables a company to make existing products and services more efficient and effective. The knowledge-based view of the organization is widely associated with **Ikujiro Nonaka and Robert Grant**.[36]

Grant argues that much current thinking about resources and capabilities has been shaped by an interest in **knowledge management**.[37] Much of the literature has been dominated by organizational learning. It has exhorted companies to become learning organizations and offered remedies for teaching smart people how to learn. We say more on these issues in **Chapters 10** and **11**. Grant suggests that the single most important contribution of knowledge management is the recognition that different types of knowledge have different characteristics. We might also add that, unlike other resources, knowledge tends not to be depleted with use. Furthermore, the leveraging of knowledge across organizational boundaries is an active pursuit of most corporations in their search for sustainable competitive advantage. This search can also be achieved by the organization entering into **strategic alliances** (see **Chapter 8**).

Ikujiro Nonaka argues that the creation of new knowledge always begins with an individual's personal knowledge, which is then transformed into organizational knowledge valuable to the company.[38] The task of the knowledge-creating company is to make this personal knowledge available to individuals throughout the organization. For example, a number of years ago the Japanese corporation, Matsushita Electric Company based in Osaka, was engaged in trying to develop a bread-making machine. Despite their best efforts they could not get the machine to knead the dough correctly; the resulting bread had an overbaked crust, while the inside was hardly baked. The product development team analysed the problem, including comparing X-rays of dough kneaded by the machine and dough kneaded by a professional baker, but could find no solution.

In the end a software developer, Ikuko Tanaka, came up with a creative solution. The Osaka International Hotel had a reputation for making the best bread in Osaka. Therefore, Tanaka trained with the hotel's head baker to study his kneading technique. She observed that the baker had a distinctive way of stretching the dough. It took a year of trial and error, working closely with the project's engineers, before Tanaka came up with product specifications. This included the addition of special ribs inside the machine which successfully reproduced the baker's stretching technique and the quality of the bread she had learned to make at the hotel. The result was Matsushita developing a product that in its first year set a record for sales of a new kitchen appliance.

Nonaka uses this example to illustrate two very different types of knowledge. There is **explicit knowledge**, which is the product specifications for the bread-making machine. Explicit knowledge is objective and rational and can be easily communicated and shared, for example, in product specifications, scientific formulas, and manuals. This was the end product of the bread-making example. The starting point embodies what Nonaka calls **tacit knowledge**. We noted earlier that tacit knowledge is highly personal, hard to formalize, and therefore difficult to communicate to others. This was the knowledge possessed by the chief baker at the Osaka International Hotel. In contrast with explicit knowledge, tacit knowledge is deeply rooted in an individual's commitment to a specific context, for example, a craft or profession.

At the same time, tacit knowledge has an important cognitive dimension. It consists of mental models, beliefs, and perspectives that are so ingrained we take them for granted and therefore cannot easily articulate them. These implicit models profoundly shape how we perceive the world around us. And it is because tacit knowledge includes mental models and beliefs, in addition to know-how, that moving from the tacit to the explicit is really a process of articulating one's vision of the world—what it is and what it ought to be. Therefore, when employees invent new knowledge, they are also reinventing themselves and their company.

Nonaka and Takeuchi[39] argue it is precisely because explicit knowledge is so readily transferred that it requires some form of protection, such as copyright or patent, if it is to remain within the organization. Tacit knowledge or 'know-how', in contrast, cannot be codified. It is highly personal, and difficult to formalize and disseminate to others. It is revealed through its application and acquired through practice. Transfer of tacit knowledge can be slow, costly, and uncertain. As we have seen, tacit knowledge will require individuals to coalesce around the provider of that knowledge if it is to be *eventually* acquired.

In their discussion of the organization as a knowledge-creating entity, **Nonaka, Toyama, and Nagata** take issue with Grant's assertion that knowledge creation is an individual activity, with the organization merely focused on applying its existing knowledge.[40] They see this view of knowledge and human beings as 'static and inhuman'. They argue instead that knowledge is created through dynamic interactions between and among individuals and their environments, in contrast to an individual acting alone. For Nonaka et al., sustainable competitive advantage is achieved via an organization's capability to exploit existing knowledge, and to create new knowledge out of existing knowledge, rather than simply exploiting existing technologies or knowledge. In their dynamic process of knowledge creation, knowledge is created through interactions among and between individuals. And in the knowledge-creating organization, these interactions cannot be owned, even by the participants of the interactions.

What does this discussion of knowledge management mean for an organization? For the organization, managing knowledge will require an understanding of its characteristics. If organizations are to learn and grow they need to be able to share tacit knowledge effectively. However, managing this tacit knowledge throughout all areas of the organization is a daunting task. If an organization is to learn in ways that benefit its performance, individuals and groups within the organization must be willing to modify their behaviour accordingly. Therefore, the question for organizations is not *should we?* but *how do we?*

5.5 Dynamic Capabilities

In order to survive and grow all organizations must adapt to and exploit changes in their business environment. At the same time, organizations also need to grasp opportunities and create change. In order to understand why some companies are better at this than others we need to assess dynamic capabilities within organizations.

5.5.1 What are Dynamic Capabilities?

The dynamic capabilities framework was initially introduced by **David Teece and Gary Pisano**.[41] Subsequent work by Teece, Pisano, and Amy Shuen further developed this framework to address the limitations of the resource-based view of strategy.[42] **Teece, Pisano, and Shuen** originally defined **dynamic capabilities** as 'the firm's ability to integrate, build, and reconfigure internal and external competences to address rapidly changing environments'.[43] In this early definition, the authors use the term *dynamic* to denote a capacity for organizations to renew their capabilities in order to achieve a level of *fit* with their changing business environment. In fact, Teece and his colleagues assert that dynamic capabilities are important to sustain firm-level competitive advantage, particularly in high velocity markets. **Kathleen Eisenhardt and Jeffrey Martin** refined the original definition of dynamic capabilities, suggesting it involves 'the firm's processes that use resources . . . to match and even create market change'.[44] But they also note that dynamic capabilities can operate in moderate environments as well as rapidly changing ones.

Constance Helfat et al. define dynamic capabilities as 'the capacity of an organisation to purposefully create, extend, and modify its resource base'.[45] This definition states that, irrespective of its ultimate effect, the action of dynamic capabilities is first and foremost on a company's resource base. When an organization has a *capacity*, this implies that the organization is able to *perform a particular activity in a reliable and minimally satisfactory manner*.[46] Indeed, the use of the term *purposefully* in this definition is to convey some degree of *intent*, even if these intentions are not fully explicit. This is to differentiate dynamic capabilities from organizational routines which consist of rote activities that lack intent. For example, if we refer to the capability to manufacture a car, we mean the specific and intended purpose to make a functioning automobile.[47] It also differentiates dynamic capabilities from an accidental outcome or chance.

We can make a distinction between *operational capabilities* and *dynamic capabilities*.[48] Operational capabilities allow an organization to make a living in the present. In other words, an operational capability maintains the status quo within the company. The company undertakes activities on an ongoing basis, using the same techniques to support its existing products and services for the same consumers. Operational capabilities are also referred to as zero-order capabilities.[49]

Dynamic capabilities, in contrast, are concerned with change, and enable an organization to extend or modify how it currently makes a living. Dynamic capabilities come in many forms; some allow an organization to develop new products and production processes. Other dynamic capabilities allow an organization to undertake acquisitions and strategic alliances. Still others make use of the capabilities of managers to deliver profitable growth and change. In addition, there is the management and organizational processes which are an integral part of dynamic capabilities and help an organization to identify and respond to the need for change. Teece refers to this as the capability to sense and shape opportunities and threats.[50]

Sidney Winter contends that the value of dynamic capabilities is not accepted by all strategy scholars.[51] While some may view dynamic capabilities as a source of competitive advantage, others remain sceptical about their existence. Others argue that they have merit, but not necessarily to confer competitive advantage, while others doubt the efforts to strengthen such capabilities are a genuine option for managers in industry.

5.5.2 Dynamic Capabilities vs Operational Capabilities

In reality, the distinction between dynamic and operational capabilities is actually difficult to define for three reasons.[52]

1) **Change is always occurring to some extent.**

It is often said there are only two certainties in life: death and taxes. However, it would be more accurate to also include a third certainty: *change*. A conundrum is that if everything is always changing then how can we discuss or even consider things that don't change? Clearly, if we cannot make a distinction between things that change and those that do not change then any distinction between dynamic and operational capabilities become problematic. A possible solution is to view change in the context of one's own perspective. For instance, when you view something close up you are more likely to observe change than when you view from a distance. In the same way, an organization viewed at a high level of abstraction may appear to exhibit no change in its capabilities. But a detailed look inside the organization may reveal changes in the features of a capability which are not visible from a distance.

Another solution to the dilemma of constant change is the time period over which one assesses change. This is because incremental change is difficult to perceive whereas the summation of such change is readily observable. For example, the development of wireless telephony took many years before it eventually became a new communication technology. A view of wireless telephony at any one moment in time would not review the magnitude of the change taking place.

2) **The blurring of the boundary between radical and non-radical change.**

There is a presumption that unless a capability causes a radical change in how a company makes a living, it is not dynamic. However, because a radical change can be difficult to define, this may not be a particularly helpful definition for a dynamic capability. For example, in the oil industry, oil reserves start to diminish as soon as production begins which means new oil reserves have to continually be found. This oil replenishment capability when viewed from a distance may appear as more of the same activity the organization has always undertaken and therefore an operational capability. In reality, the capability is dynamic since it allows the organization to repeatedly augment its assets by discovering new and different geological formations that contain oil. Therefore, just because a capability may not generate a perceived radical shift short term does not preclude it from being dynamic, since large amounts of change may be apparent when viewed over the long run.

3) **Some capabilities can be used for both operational and dynamic purposes.**

It can be difficult to draw a distinction between dynamic and operational capabilities, particularly when a given capability can be used for both dynamic and operational purposes. For example, in the consumer group Procter & Gamble, a brand manager may have responsibility for promoting established as well as new brands. Yet the manager will utilize the same organization routines and processes for new and existing products. This implies brand management can be both an operational and a dynamic capability.

5.5.3 Dynamic Capabilities and Competitive Advantage

To sustain their competitive advantage, organizations need to renew their valuable resources as their external environment changes. It is the use of dynamic capabilities which allow organizations to do this. Dynamic capabilities not only enable organizations to have a sustainable competitive advantage, but also help companies to avoid developing **core rigidities**, which prevent development and stifle innovation. Core rigidities refer to resources that used to be valuable, but over time have become obsolete and now act to constrain the development of the organization. Dynamic capabilities are developed inside a company rather than bought in the market. They are path dependent, and embedded in the company. If they could be readily acquired, they would cease to be dynamic capabilities. However, it may be that an organization possesses a dynamic capability in mergers and acquisitions, which allows it to acquire a company that already possesses dynamic capabilities.

A dynamic capability should not be confused with the capability we discussed in the resource based view of strategy (VRIO framework). A dynamic capability is a *process* which allows you to change your resource base. It is future orientated, whereas VRIO capabilities are concerned with competing today, and remain 'static' if no dynamic capabilities are deployed to change them. The impact of dynamic capabilities is on an organization's resource base and allows a new configuration of resources to be created so the company can sustain its competitive advantage.[53]

5.5.4 Challenges for Dynamic Capabilities

One reason for the confusion that exists within the dynamic capabilities framework is that key participants remain divided on crucial conceptual issues. There appears to be a divide between the two seminal papers in this field on how dynamic capabilities can help organizations to achieve and sustain competitive advantage. This refers to the original work by Teece et al.[54] and subsequent revisions by Eisenhardt and Martin.[55] **Margaret Peteraf et al**. refer to this difference as 'the elephant in the room of research on dynamic capabilities'.[56] That we have two contradictory positions for the dynamic capabilities framework's core elements is not seen as a cause for concern, but only because the framework is still developing. What these authors suggest is that by using a contingency-based approach it may be possible to unify the research on dynamic capabilities while also maintaining the assumptions that led to their differences.

Teece is less positive on this matter, arguing that Eisenhardt and Martin's work represents a re-conceptualization of dynamic capabilities.[57] The effect of this is to compromise crucial elements in Teece's original formulation of dynamic capabilities. Furthermore, when you look at rapidly changing or high-velocity markets, conceptual differences between the key approaches are apparent. For example, Teece et al. consider dynamic capabilities important for sustainable firm-level competitive advantage, especially in rapidly changing markets. In contrast, Eisenhardt and Martin argue that dynamic capabilities are unsuited to creating sustainable competitive advantage and are likely to break down in high-velocity markets. They point to the emotional inability of managers to cope with uncertainty in rapidly changing environments.

They view dynamic capabilities as *organizational processes*, such as product development routines, alliance and acquisition capabilities, and resource allocation routines. These processes of dynamic capabilities are limited to simple rules that are less stable than fixed routines and likely to collapse in rapidly changing environments. Their claim that all dynamic capabilities can be captured as best practice is problematic, since if dynamic capabilities can be captured as best practice, they can be imitated by rivals and cannot, therefore, be a source of competitive advantage.

For Teece, the issue may simply be that Eisenhardt and Martin are dealing with a different class of capability: an ordinary capability. Such capabilities can be captured as best practice and would be subject to imitation. Whereas for Teece, what constitutes replicable best practice within an organization is not likely to constitute a dynamic capability. Another point of departure between these two approaches to dynamic capabilities is the role of managers. Within the Teecian framework managerial action complements organizational routines, since dynamic capabilities involve a combination of organizational routines and entrepreneurial leadership.[58]

Although there is confusion over terminology and conceptualization, the dynamic capabilities framework does offer a relevant perspective for assessing differential firm performance. There is still more work to do on research if a conceptual framework is to be unified and accepted by proponents. Much of the research is often disconnected and pointing in different directions. What is required is a consolidation of the main principles and to capitalize on past research in a more focused way.[59] That said, the proliferation of recent journal articles on the resource-based view and dynamic capabilities is testimony to their enduring appeal.

Summary

The resource-based view has shaken up strategic management by questioning industry selection and positioning which results in organizations pursuing similar strategies. Instead, this approach emphasizes the organization's own set of resources and capabilities as a determinant of competitive advantage.

In this chapter, we have explored resources and capabilities in order to identify how competitive advantage might be achieved. We have also addressed the issue of sustainable competitive advantage. There is slight confusion among the terms used by different adherents to the resource-based view but, as we have seen, this is readily overcome. Where Prahalad and Hamel discuss core competence, Kay uses the term distinctive capabilities, while Grant distinguishes between resources and capabilities. Each term refers to a means of achieving sustainable competitive advantage although the generic term *capabilities* now seems to proliferate within the literature. We examined Barney's VRIO framework which evaluates four attributes that an organization's capabilities must possess in order to provide it with the potential for sustainable competitive advantage: (1) it must be valuable; (2) it must be rare; (3) it must be difficult to imitate; and (4) the organization should possess the structure and management systems to support the capabilities in a manner which facilitates their exploitation.

We discussed criticisms of the resource-based view as a static and equilibrium-based model which provides challenges for organizations trying to implement this approach in changing environments. A knowledge-based view of the organization was considered as a possible source of competitive advantage. The dynamic capabilities framework was evaluated as a means of dealing with the static limitations of the resource-based view. While there is *movement* towards a unified framework, until this is accomplished it is likely to impede progress both conceptually and empirically.

We end by arguing that Porter's industry analysis remains important and the choice should not be seen as one of *either/or*, but rather one of complementarity. Organizations cannot neglect the industries within which they operate but neither can they afford to focus slavishly upon them at the expense of their internal resources and capabilities, and miss opportunities to establish sustainable competitive advantage.

 CASE STUDY The Dynamic Capabilities of Warren Buffett

Warren Buffett is CEO and chairman of Berkshire Hathaway, a diversified conglomerate which he runs with **Charlie Munger**, his long-time associate and friend. Munger serves as vice chairman, and is six years Buffett's senior. Berkshire, as the conglomerate is commonly called, is based in Omaha, Nebraska. There the similarity with any other company ends.

In his office in Omaha, Buffett displays only one certificate of his education. Despite having a degree in economics from Columbia Business School it is a certificate for something more mundane, for

Photo 5.2   Warren Buffett, Chairman/CEO of Berkshire Hathaway.
Source: © KristaKennell/Shutterstock.com.

completing the 'Dale Carnegie Course in Effective Speaking, Leadership Training, and the Art of Winning Friends and Influencing People'. It is dated 23 January 1952.

More than fifty years ago, Warren Buffett began investing the money of residents in his home town of Omaha. Few could have imagined back in 1956 that this scruffy young man would make them fabulously wealthy. Over time, he would gradually shift from a company obtaining most of its gains from investment activities to one that grows in value by owning businesses. One of these businesses was a worthless textile mill called Berkshire Hathaway, which was eventually closed. Nowadays, the company's annual meeting attracts around 40,000 shareholders. Buffett and Munger spend five hours answering questions from shareholders, journalists, and analysts.

In an age when diversified conglomerates are out of fashion, Berkshire's gain in net worth during 2016 was a phenomenal $27.5 billion. Berkshire owns more than sixty companies, including GEICO insurance, BSNF, a rail group, and Mid-American Energy, a utility company. Berkshire acquired Kraft Heinz, which it co-owns with 3G, a buyout fund. Its portfolio of investments includes large shareholdings in mainly American companies such as Coca-Cola, Wells Fargo, IBM, American Express, and recently Apple. Buffett first bought Apple stock in early 2016. The purchase marked a shift in strategy for the investor, who has steered clear of technology stocks; he doesn't even own a smartphone.

His insurance businesses, with premiums paid up front and claims paid later, provide a 'float' for which to fund his investments. Assuming the risks are priced correctly when an insurance policy is written, the revenue generated is free cash. Buffett is keen to perpetuate the culture and character that Hathaway embodies. A fellow board member is Bill Gates. In 2006, Buffett donated Berkshire Hathaway shares worth more than $30 billion to the Bill & Melinda Gates Foundation, the biggest single charitable donation in history. The charitable Foundation has only three trustees: Bill and Melinda Gates, and Warren Buffett.

After Buffett's death, he intends his vast wealth to be given away. That said, he purports to be in excellent health on his regular diet of Cherry Coke and hamburgers. He plays the ukulele and bridge. The one exception to his humble lifestyle is a corporate jet, which is second-hand and named 'The Indefensible'. This brings up the often-avoided question of succession.

In 2017, Warren Buffett and Charlie Munger were aged eighty-six and ninety-three, respectively. The partnership between the two men is one of mutual respect and admiration. As Munger puts it, they 'don't agree totally on everything, and yet we're quite respectful of one another'. Buffett points out that whenever they do disagree, Charlie says, 'Well, you'll end up agreeing with me because you're smart and I'm right.'

Buffett's role is to deliver significant growth to shareholders over time. He has only two jobs: 'to attract and keep outstanding managers to run our various operations. The other is capital allocation.' Over the past fifty-two years Berkshire's per-share book value has grown from $19 to $172,108, a rate of 19 per cent compounded annually. In contrast to other companies, Berkshire directors retain all earnings, paying no dividends. This reflects the belief that they can earn a greater return on capital by investing shareholder funds.

Photo 5.3   Charlie Munger, vice president of Berkshire Hathaway.
Source: © KentSievers/Shutterstock.com.

The Sage of Omaha, as Buffett is commonly called, is renowned for taking the right financial decisions. In the late 1990s Buffett warned against the excesses of the dot.com boom. While financial analysts were busy talking of a new investment paradigm he quietly avoided all the new start-up companies he did not understand. From 1998 to 2000 Berkshire Hathaway's share price fell by 44 per cent; at the same time the stock market rose by 32 per cent. When these 'new economy' companies went bankrupt after the bubble burst, sticking to his principles paid off.

Prior to the financial collapse of 2007–08, he described derivatives as 'financial weapons of mass destruction', the very derivatives on which Lehman Brothers and investment banks depended to turbo-charge their profitability prior to their collapse. It was Warren Buffett's reputation which allowed him to take a shareholding in Goldman Sachs and GE on advantageous terms during the financial crisis, which proved hugely profitable. In 2019 he had an estimated net worth at $80.8 billion, making him one of richest men in the world after Bill Gates and Jeff Bezos.

Berkshire's portfolio of shares and bonds has continued to grow and to deliver substantive capital gains, interest, and dividends. If he can acquire a company's shares when they are cheap, as he did with Coca-Cola after the 'new Coke' fiasco, he will. But as Buffett puts it, 'it's far better to buy a wonderful company at a fair price than a fair company at a wonderful price'. The portfolio earnings have provided major support in financing the purchase of businesses.

There has occurred a gradual shift from a company obtaining most of its gains from investment activities to one that grows in value by owning businesses. By the early 1990s, the focus was changing from financial investments to the outright ownership of businesses. Buffett believes his unconventional, two-pronged approach to capital allocation provides him with a real edge. By 2016, investment in shares comprised only one-fifth of Berkshire's assets.

Berkshire Hathaway is a closed-end fund, where shares can be redeemed by selling to another investor, unlike the open-ended funds, favoured by the European Union, which tends to constrain long-term investments. Buffett avoids the financial engineering and creative accounting prevalent among other conglomerates whose professed strength is transferable management capabilities.

His successful formula is to buy quality companies he understands with good defences against competitors. He trusts managers to run them as before, and retains them for the long term. His continued success is contrary to the *efficient market hypothesis*. This states that, over the long term, the current market price always reflects all available and relevant information about a company. This implies that over the long term you cannot outperform the market, which Buffett consistently does. His choice of acquisitions includes companies with advantage over their competitors that are hard to replicate. This might be a popular brand or companies with some degree of monopoly power, often in mature industries. He admires companies with a strong ethical culture, with managers whose focus is performing a good job rather than making money.

As for Berkshire, a major problem it faces is that its prospective returns fall as its assets increase. That said, Berkshire Hathaway trades at around 40 per cent over its book value, evidence that conglomerates can add rather than destroy the value of the companies they own. As **Andrew Campbell**, co-author of *Strategy for the Corporate Level* states, '*no other firm in the past 100 years has been able to do consistently what Berkshire Hathaway has done*'.

Sources: 'Playing out the last time', *The Economist*, 1 May 2014; 'Life after Warren', *The Economist*, 26 April 2014; 'A sage that knows his onions', *The Economist*, 16 October 2008; 'Warren Buffett', *The Economist*, 18 December 2008; '$1 billion stakes on the menu', *The Economist*, 21 May 2016; Berkshire Hathaway http://www.berkshirehathaway.com; Forbes Media https://www.forbes.com; John Kay, 'Berkshire's business model is simple and effective, yet rarely copied', *The Financial Times*, 4 May 2016.

Questions

1. What are the dynamic capabilities which Warren Buffett possesses?

2. Why do you think no organization has copied Berkshire Hathaway's relatively simple business model?

3. How will Berkshire Hathaway survive the loss of Warren Buffett and Charlie Munger?

 For more examples and discussion to aid your understanding of this chapter, please visit the online resources and see the Extension Material for this chapter.

 ## Review Questions

1. Evaluate the key differences between Porter's five forces framework and the resource-based view of strategy.
2. Explain how an understanding of knowledge as a capability might help an organization to achieve competitive advantage.
3. How does the dynamic capabilities framework improve upon the resource-based view of strategy?

 ## Discussion Question

1. 'First-mover advantages are more important than a company's capabilities.' *Discuss*.
2. 'It always better to make a product or deliver a service in-house rather than leave it to the market.' *Discuss*.

 ## Research Topic

Identify the capabilities that reside inside the Tata Group. To what extent do these capabilities provide Tata with a competitive advantage?

 ## Recommended Reading

A good introduction to the resource-based view of strategy is:

- **J. Barney**, 'Firm resources and sustained competitive advantage', *Journal of Management*, vol. 17, no. 1 (1991), pp. 99–120.

An article that is widely credited with popularizing the views of the resource-based approach is:

- **C. K. Prahalad** and **G. Hamel**, 'The core competence of the organization', *Harvard Business Review*, vol. 68, no. 3 (1990), pp. 79–91.

For a seminal introduction to dynamic capabilities, see:

- **D. J. Teece**, **G. Pisano**, and **A. Shuen**, 'Dynamic capabilities and strategic management', *Strategic Management Journal*, vol. 18, no. 7 (1997), pp. 509–33.

For an informative discussion of distinctive capabilities, see:

- **J. Kay**, *Foundations of Corporate Success*, Oxford University Press, 1993.

www.oup.com/he/henry4e
Visit the online resources that accompany this book for activities and more information on strategy.

Test your knowledge and understanding of this chapter further by trying the multiple-choice questions online.

References and Notes

1   **E. T. Penrose**, *The Theory of the Growth of the Firm*, John Wiley & Sons, 1959.

2   **C. K. Prahalad** and **G. Hamel**, 'The core competence of the corporation', *Harvard Business Review*, vol. 68, no. 3 (1990), pp. 79–91; **R. P. Rumelt**, 'How much does industry matter?', *Strategic Management Journal*, vol. 12, no. 3 (1991), pp. 167–85; **J. Barney**, 'Firm resources and sustained competitive advantage', *Journal of Management*, vol. 17, no. 1 (1991), pp. 99–120; **R. Grant**, 'The resource-based theory of competitive advantage: implications for strategy formulation', *California Management Review*, vol. 33, no. 3 (1991), pp. 114–35; **B. Wernerfelt**, 'A resource-based view of the firm', *Strategic Management Journal*, vol. 5 (1984), pp. 171–80.

3   **M. E. Porter**, *Competitive Strategy*, Free Press, 1980.

4   **D. J. Collis** and **C. A. Montgomery**, 'Competing on resources: strategy in the 1990s', *Harvard Business Review*, vol. 73, no. 4 (1995), pp. 118–28; **G. Stalk**, **P. Evans**, and **L. E. Schulman**, 'Competing on capabilities: the new rules of corporate strategy', *Harvard Business Review*, vol. 70, no. 2 (1992), pp. 57–69.

5   See **J. B. Barney**, 'Resource-based theories of competitive advantage: a ten-year retrospective on the resource-based view', *Journal of Management*, vol. 27 (2001), pp. 643–50.

6   **R. Amit** and **P. J. H. Schoemaker**, 'Strategic assets and organizational rents', *Strategic Management Journal*, vol. 14, no. 1 (1993), pp. 33–46.

7   **G. Hamel** and **C. K. Prahalad**, 'Strategy as stretch and leverage', *Harvard Business Review*, vol. 71, no. 2 (1993), pp. 75–84.

8   **D. Goleman**, 'What makes a leader?', *Harvard Business Review*, vol. 76, no. 6 (1998), pp. 93–102.

9   **Gwyn Topham**, 'Fewer rules, less hassle, more profit—how being nice paid off at Ryanair', *The Guardian*, 30 May 2015.

10   See http://www.harrisinteractive.com for a list of companies and their reputation quotient (the Reputation Index).

11   **Grant**, n. 2.

12   **Prahalad** and **Hamel**, see n. 2 above.

13   **Prahalad** and **Hamel's** use of the term *core competence* is nowadays used less in the literature, as *capability* has become the dominant term.

14   **Prahalad** and **Hamel**, see n. 2 above.

[15] **C. K. Prahalad** and **G. Hamel**, 'The core competence of the corporation', *Harvard Business Review*, vol. 68, no. 3 (1990), pp. 82.

[16] **J. Kay**, *Foundations of Corporate Success*, Oxford University Press, 1993.

[17] For a detailed discussion of the role architecture, reputation, and innovation in achieving distinctive capability, see **Kay**, see n. 16 above, chapters 5, 6, and 7.

[18] **R. R. Nelson** and **S. G. Winter**, *An Evolutionary Theory of Economic Change*, Harvard University Press, 1982.

[19] **Kay**, see n. 16 above, p. 69.

[20] See 'The 50 most innovative companies', *Business Week*, 3 May 2007 (available online at: http://www.businessweek.com).

[21] **R. A. D'Aveni**, 'Strategic supremacy through disruption and dominance', *Sloan Management Review*, vol. 40, no. 3 (1999), pp. 117–35.

[22] **J. Kay**, 'Strategy and the delusion of grand design', in *Mastering Strategy*, Pearson Education, 2000, pp. 5–10.

[23] In Barney's initial article, **Barney** (see n. 2 above), the framework for assessing capabilities was VRIN, where N stood for no strategic substitute. This has evolved into VRIO where O represents organization. The question now becomes to what extent the firm is organized to exploit the capabilities of value, rarity, and imitability. See **J. B. Barney**, *Gaining and Sustaining Competitive Advantage*, Addison-Wesley, 1997.

[24] **M. E. Porter**, *Competitive Advantage*, Free Press, 1985.

[25] See **J. B. Barney**, **M. Wright**, and **D. Ketchen Jr**, 'The resource based view of the firm: ten years after 1991', *Journal of Management*, vol. 27 (2001), pp. 625–41.

[26] For a discussion of the conditions that make a resource valuable to a firm before a decision is actually made on whether to acquire or build it, see **J. Schmidt** and **T. Keil**, 'What makes a resource valuable? Identifying the drivers of firm-idiosyncratic resource value', *Academy of Management Review*, vol. 38, no. 2 (2013), pp. 206–28.

[27] **A. Tovey**, 'Sir James Dyson to remain at controls as Dyson reports record results', *The Telegraph*, 27 March 2017.

[28] For a discussion of architecture, see **Kay**, see n. 16 above, chapter 5.

[29] See **J. B. Barney** and **W. S. Hesterly**, *Strategic Management and Competitive Advantage*, Pearson, 2015.

[30] The term *creative destruction* was coined by Austrian economist, Joseph Schumpeter. In his discussion of the opening up of new markets and organizational development, Schumpeter refers to a process 'that incessantly revolutionizes the economic structure from within, incessantly destroying the old one, incessantly creating a new one. This process of Creative Destruction is the essential fact about capitalism.' **J. A. Schumpeter**, *Capitalism, Socialism, and Democracy*, Harper and Row, 1942, p. 83.

[31] **D. Miller**, **R. Eisenstat**, and **N. Foote**, 'Strategy from the inside out: building capability creating organisations', *California Management Review*, vol. 44, no. 3 (2002), pp. 37–54.

[32] See **D. J. Teece**, **G. Pisano,** and **A. Shuen**, 'Dynamic capabilities and strategic management', *Strategic Management Journal*, vol. 18, no. 7 (1997), pp. 509–33; **E. Cavusgil**, **S. H. Seggie**, and **M. B. Talay**, 'Dynamic capabilities view: foundations and research agenda', *Journal of Marketing Theory and Practice*, vol. 15, no. 2 (2007), pp. 159–66.

[33] **R. Priem** and **J. Butler**, 'Is the resource based view a useful perspective for strategic management research?', *Academy of Management Review*, vol. 26, no. 1 (2001a), pp. 22–40.

[34] **R. Priem** and **J. Butler**, 'Tautology in the resource-based view and the implications of externally determined resource value: further comments', *Academy of Management Review*, vol. 26, no. 1 (2001b), pp. 57–66; **I. V. Kozlenkova**, **S. A. Samaha**, and **R. W. Palmatier**, 'Resource-based theory in marketing', *Journal of the Academy of Marketing Science*, vol. 42 (2014), pp. 1–21.

[35]　See **I. Nonaka**, **R. Toyama**, and **A. Nagata**, 'A firm as a knowledge-creating entity: a new perspective on the theory of the firm', *Industrial and Corporate Change*, vol. 9, no. 1 (2000), pp. 1–20.

[36]　**I. Nonaka**, 'The knowledge creating company', *Harvard Business Review*, November–December, vol. 69, (1991), pp. 96–104. See also **I. Nonaka** and **H. Takeuchi**, *The Knowledge-creating Company*, Oxford University Press, 1995; **R. M. Grant**, 'Towards a knowledge-based theory of the firm', *Strategic Management Journal*, vol. 17 (Winter Special Issue, 1996), pp. 109–22.

[37]　**R. M. Grant**, *Contemporary Strategy Analysis*, 5th edn, Blackwell, 2005.

[38]　**Nonaka**, see n. 36 above.

[39]　**Nonaka** and **Takeuchi**, see n. 36 above.

[40]　**Nonaka**, **Toyama**, and **Nagata**, see n. 35 above.

[41]　**D. J. Teece** and **G. Pisano**, 'The dynamic capabilities of firms: an introduction', *Industrial and Corporate Change*, vol. 3, no. 3 (1994), pp. 537–56.

[42]　**Teece**, **Pisano**, and **Shuen**, see n. 31 above.

[43]　**Teece**, **Pisano**, and **Shuen**, see n. 31 above, p. 516.

[44]　**K. M. Eisenhardt** and **J. A. Martin**, 'Dynamic capabilities: what are they?', *Strategic Management Journal*, vol. 21, no. 5 (2000), pp. 1105–21.

[45]　**C. E. Helfat**, **S. Finklestein**, **W. Mitchell**, **M. A. Peteraf**, **H. Singh**, **D. J. Teece**, and **S. Winter**, *Dynamic Capabilities*, Blackwell, 2007.

[46]　**Helfat et al.**, see n. 45 above.

[47]　For a discussion of the different terms surrounding dynamic capabilities and the confusion this may cause, see **C. E. Helfat** and **S. Winter**, 'Untangling dynamic and operational capabilities: strategy for the (n)ever-changing world', *Strategic Management Journal*, vol. 32, no. 11 (2011), pp. 1243–50.

[48]　**Helfat et al.**, see n. 45 above; also **Helfat** and **Winter**, see n. 47 above.

[49]　**Helfat** and **Winter**, see n. 47 above.

[50]　**D. J. Teece**, 'Explicating dynamic capabilities: the nature and microfoundations of (sustainable) enterprise performance', *Strategic Management Journal*, vol. 28, no.13 (2007), pp. 1319–50.

[51]　**S. Winter**, 'Understanding dynamic capabilities', *Strategic Management Journal*, vol. 24, no. 10 (2003), pp. 991–5.

[52]　**Helfat** and **Winter**, see n. 47 above.

[53]　**V. Ambrosini** and **C. Bowman**, 'What are dynamic capabilities and are they a useful construct in strategic management?', *International Journal of Management Reviews*, vol. 11, no 1 (2009), pp. 29–49.

[54]　**Teece**, **Pisano**, and **Shuen**, see n. 32 above, pp. 509–33.

[55]　**Eisenhardt** and **Martin**, see n. 44 above.

[56]　**M. Peteraf**, **G. Stefano**, and **G. Verona**, 'The elephant in the room of dynamic capabilities: bringing two diverging conversations together', *Strategic Management Journal*, vol. 34, no. 12 (2013), pp. 1389–410.

[57]　**D. J. Teece**, 'The foundations of enterprise performance: dynamic and ordinary capabilities in an (economic) theory of firms', *Academy of Management*, vol. 28, no. 4 (2014), pp. 328–52.

[58]　**Teece**, see n. 57 above.

[59]　**I. Barreto**, 'Dynamic capabilities: a review of past research and an agenda for the future', *Journal of Management*, vol. 36, no. 1 (2010), pp. 256–80.

PART THREE
STRATEGY FORMULATION

CHAPTER 6
BUSINESS STRATEGY

 Learning Objectives

After completing this chapter you should be able to:

- Discuss the role of business strategy
- Evaluate Michael Porter's generic strategies
- Discuss a resource-based approach to strategy formulation
- Identify and explain how blue ocean strategy seeks to make competition irrelevant
- Analyse strategy formulation in turbulent markets
- Evaluate disruptive innovation as a means of capturing market share

Introduction

In exploring strategy analysis, we discussed different analytical tools to help organizations evaluate their macro and competitive environment. Analytical tools and frameworks which can be used to better understand the macro environment include PESTLE analysis and scenario planning. A key task for the strategist is to identify the *weak signals* in the macro-environment that have the potential to disrupt an industry's structure (see **Chapter 2**). In **Chapter 3** we evaluated the industry using Porter's five forces framework and the industry life cycle. **Chapter 4** was devoted to an analysis of the internal environment, how an organization might usefully analyse its value-creating activities, and ways in which an organization can assess its performance. **Chapter 5** explored a different perspective of competitive advantage, which suggests that differences in organizational performance are determined by an organization's resources and capabilities. This is the resource-based view and dynamic capabilities.

Although the chapters on strategy formulation are separate from those on implementation for ease of exposition, in reality an organization must be mindful of its ability to implement strategy. Strategy is best viewed as a non-linear, incremental process in which persuasion is as important as rationally formulated plans.[1] Strategy formulation implies a deliberate form of decision-making, but the strategy actually being pursued may be as a result of deliberate and emergent factors.[2] In reality, strategy formulation will derive from the objectives and mission that the organization has set itself. This was discussed in detail in **Chapter 1**.

In this and subsequent chapters we address strategy formulation at the *business*, *corporate*, and *global* levels.

6.1 What is Business Strategy?

Any given organization may comprise a number of different businesses, each operating in distinct markets and serving different customers. A market is defined by demand conditions and based on an organization's customers and potential customers. The industry in which it competes is determined by supply conditions such as a common technology or distribution channels. In choosing which markets to serve, an organization will de facto determine the industry in which it competes. For example, white goods such as refrigerators and washing machines are distributed through the same channels, yet only refrigerators chill food and washing machines clean clothes. The markets, based on consumer demand, are for chilled food storage and laundry services. Therefore, we can see that although a domestic appliance industry exists based on a common technology (white boxes with motors in them), a domestic appliance market does not.[3]

Business strategy is a means of separating out and formulating a competitive strategy at the level of the individual business unit. This is sometimes referred to as a strategic business unit (SBU). An SBU is a distinct part of an organization which focuses upon a particular market or markets for its products and services. It should be remembered that a parent company sets the overall or corporate strategy. The role of the business unit is to devise a strategy that allows it to compete successfully in the marketplace and to contribute to the corporate strategy. In this respect, the managers of a business unit may have considerable autonomy to devise their business strategy. This reflects their knowledge of local markets, customers, and competitors. However, this cannot be decided in isolation from the corporate strategy being pursued. The business unit managers must ultimately show that their business strategy contributes to the corporate strategy.

Corporate strategy focuses upon the fundamental question 'What business (or businesses) do we want to be in?', and is discussed in **Chapter 7**. If corporate strategy answers the question 'What business should we be in?', or more accurately 'Which markets do we want to serve?', it remains for competitive or business strategy to answer the question 'How are we going to compete in our chosen markets?'[4] The key to bear in mind with business strategy is that it is always in pursuit of a sustainable competitive advantage. The question is *how* it achieves this. To answer this, we will start by evaluating Porter's generic competitive strategies.

6.2 Generic Competitive Strategies

A competitive advantage is about performing different activities or performing similar activities but in different ways. In other words, a company must be capable of producing value for the consumer that is recognized as being superior to that of its competitors. It is precisely because competitive advantage is determined vis-à-vis your competitors that Porter's analysis is concerned with the competitive environment of industry structure and the five competitive forces. **Porter** argues that competitive strategy is about developing a defendable position in an industry that enables you to deal effectively with the five competitive forces and, thus, generate a superior return on investment for the company.[5] To achieve superior value that is recognized by the consumer an organization can do one of two things.

First, it can offer its products or services at a lower price than rivals, but without sacrificing the quality of the product. Second, it can produce a differentiated product that consumers perceive to be of better value than the product offerings of rival companies, and hence charge a premium price for its goods. In addition, an organization must choose which market segments it wants its products to compete within. For example, does it want to try to cover all or most market segments and adopt a broad-based approach? Or would it be content to compete within a particular market niche which may require a different set of resources and capabilities, and which may be overlooked by rivals too busy seeking to gain dominant market shares?

While recognizing that the best strategy for an organization will actually be unique and reflect its individual circumstances, Porter developed three generic strategies to help an organization outperform rivals within an industry, and so successfully position itself against the five forces we discussed in **Chapter 3**. These business strategies are referred to as *generic* because they apply to different types of organizations in different industries. They are *overall cost leadership*, *differentiation*, and *focus strategies*.

1. *Overall cost leadership*

   A cost-leadership strategy involves a company being the lowest-cost producer within the industry while maintaining the industry standard. This allows the organization to outperform rivals within the industry because it can charge lower prices and its lowest-cost base still allows it to earn a profit. In effect, this company can charge the *lowest* price within the industry, which rivals simply cannot match. Therefore, a cost-leadership strategy allows the company to make superior profits. Reliance Jio, the Indian mobile company, is the overall cost leader in the telecoms industry with its no-frills service and highly focused cost reductions, which allow it to charge lower prices while generating profits.

2. *Differentiation strategy*

   A differentiation strategy is based on an organization producing products or services which are perceived by customers as unique or superior to competitor offerings. It presents an opportunity to create greater value by meeting customer needs more closely than rivals. It is this perceived added value that is the basis on which customers are prepared to pay a premium price. Clearly, the cost of producing the differentiation must not outweigh the price being charged. Or, put another way, customers should be prepared to pay a price which exceeds the cost of the differentiation, thereby allowing the organization to earn superior profits. Apple follows a differentiation strategy with its innovative product design for which consumers are prepared to pay a premium price.

3. *Focus strategy*

   A focus business strategy allows an organization to target a segment or niche within the market. The segment may be based on a particular customer group, geographical market, or specific product line. Unlike overall cost leadership and differentiation strategies, which are industry-wide, a focus strategy is aimed at serving a particular target market efficiently. A focus strategy is adopted by companies selling high-end jewellery and fashion brands, for example, Burberry. These generic strategies are shown in **Figure 6.1**.

High-end fashion stores, such as Burberry, adopt a focus strategy. Source: © ArsenieKrasnevsky/Shutterstock.com.

Figure 6.1 illustrates Porter's generic strategies and shows how an organization can choose to adopt a broad-based approach that seeks to cover most (or all) markets within the industry—that is, engage in a broad target. Alternatively, the company may choose to focus upon a narrow strategic target (segment) of the industry. Whichever strategic target—broad-based or narrow segment—the organization chooses to concentrate its resources and capabilities on, it must then adopt either a cost-leadership strategy or a differentiation strategy. As we shall see later, Porter warns organizations about the dangers of attempting to pursue these three strategies simultaneously.

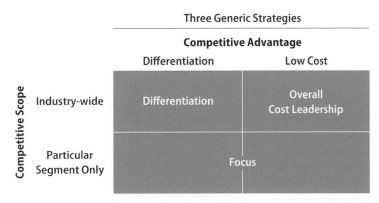

Figure 6.1   Three generic strategies. Source: Reprinted with permission of Free Press, a Division of Simon & Schuster Inc., from *Competitive Strategy: Techniques for Analyzing Industries and Competitors*, by Michael E. Porter. Copyright © 1980, 1998 Free Press. All rights reserved.

6.2.1 **Overall Cost-Leadership Strategies**

We should note that implementing each of the three generic strategies will involve organizations in utilizing different resources and capabilities. For example, the capabilities required to be a low cost producer will often differ markedly from the capabilities required to produce a differentiated product. A cost-leadership strategy is adopted when an organization seeks to achieve the lowest costs within an industry and targets its products or services at a broad market. A cost-leadership strategy requires an organization to pursue:[6]

- aggressive construction of efficient-scale facilities
- vigorous pursuit of cost reductions from experience
- tight cost and overhead control
- avoidance of marginal customer accounts
- cost minimization in areas like research and development (R&D), service, sales force, and advertising.

In reality, the organization must concentrate on all the activities that occur within its value chain and ensure that the costs associated with each activity are sufficiently pared down. At the same time, it must also ensure that all these activities are also properly coordinated across its value chain. Value chain analysis was discussed in **Chapter 4**.[7]

An overall cost-leadership strategy implies a high market share and standardized products that utilize common components. This allows the organization to achieve economies of scale and reduce costs. Therefore, the organization may have to invest in the latest technology to reduce manufacturing costs and production processes. Such a decision will only be undertaken if it allows the organization to achieve its lower-cost strategy. A low cost position within the industry can create a virtuous cycle in which the higher margins achieved by the low cost company allow it to continually reinvest and update plant and equipment, which in turn further reduces costs, which increases margins, and so on.

For some time now car manufacturers have ensured that new models, which are expensive to develop, share common platforms with existing cars, thereby reducing their manufacturing cost. Toyota has achieved a low cost position within the automobile industry and earns more revenue in a year than the three largest US auto producers, General Motors, Ford, and Fiat Chrysler, combined. When average earnings per vehicle are calculated, the Japanese automaker makes more than four times per car than General Motors.[8] Toyota continues to perpetuate this position by utilizing lean manufacturing processes within and across its value chain. In Toyota's case this low cost production has achieved above-average quality standards. Notice also that any differentiation that does occur within the industry is matched by, or more accurately driven by, Toyota.

The Experience Curve

The concept of the experience curve was developed by the Boston Consulting Group in 1968 and helps an organization identify a relationship between its costs of production and its accumulated experience. The experience curve suggests that as output doubles the unit cost of production falls by between 20 and 30 per cent. The actual percentage reduction in costs will vary between different industries. However, as a general rule, we can say that if a product costs £10 per unit to produce, for

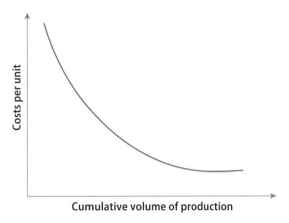

Figure 6.2   The experience curve.

example, and a firm produces 100 units, if the organization doubles its output to 200 units, the cost will fall to between £7 and £8 per unit. The experience curve is shown in **Figure 6.2**.

If we apply this concept to the overall cost leader, we can see that a result of its dominant market share is that it will have accumulated the greatest experience, and it is this experience (or learning) which allows it to reduce its costs. And as we saw in **Chapter 5**, the ability to learn is recognized as a dynamic capability. As its market share continues to grow so its costs differential with rivals within the industry widens as it moves further down the experience curve. The corollary of this is that an organization should pursue a strategy of growth which enhances its accumulative experience and further lowers its costs. The experience curve allows an organization to anticipate cost reductions based upon future growth in sales because each doubling of sales reduces cost by between 20 and 30 per cent. The idea then is to price its current products on this anticipated cost reduction. The effect is to undercut competitors, increase market share, and thereby benefit from cost reductions, which increase profit margins. In theory, cost savings due to accumulated experience can continue ad infinitum although, in reality, you might expect the rate of reduction to decrease over time. Where cumulative experience is less important within an industry, one would expect other factors to out-weigh the experience curve.

Economies and Diseconomies of Scale

Another source of cost advantage for an organization derives from *economies of scale*. This occurs as a company grows in size and increases its volume of production, so its average cost of production falls. In effect, a company is able to benefit from specialization of labour and management, and bet-ter utilization of its capital assets. This increase in production results in a lowering in its cost structure over time.[9] Economies of scale tend to be associated with industries that have high fixed costs, such as aircraft manufacture and breweries. This is shown as a falling 'U-shaped' curve in **Figure 6.3**. Given the huge research and development costs involved in aircraft production, it is necessary that suffi-cient aircraft be sold to commercial buyers to offset these costs.

Although these high fixed costs act as a barrier to entry for other organizations, it also ensures intense rivalry between aircraft manufacturers Boeing and Airbus. Economies of scale derive from larger companies being able to purchase big, specialized capital equipment that a smaller company would simply not be able to afford. This expensive equipment requires large production runs in order

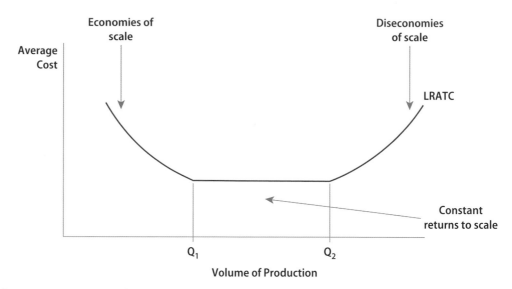

Figure 6.3   Economies of scale.

to be efficient. Smaller companies are simply unable to achieve the volume of production necessary to offset the cost of purchasing such equipment.

Although economies of scale provide a cost advantage to large organizations with high fixed costs, there does comes a point when average total costs will start to rise. At this point, companies begin to experience **diseconomies of scale**. **Diseconomies of scale** can occur when an organization gets so large that management is unable to cope efficiently with the complexity and coordination of its operations. Furthermore, with the increased specialization of roles necessary for mass produc-tion can come a degree of worker alienation and de-motivation. This may result in less efficient pro-duction and potential quality issues. Diseconomies of scale occur when an increase in a company's output causes a more than proportionate increase in its cost and is shown as Q_2 in **Figure 6.3**. As diseconomies of scale begin to set in, the LRATC curve starts to rise.

Between economies and diseconomies of scale lie constant returns to scale. This is where an in-crease in a company's output causes a proportionate increase in its cost. The company can expand its production without adversely affecting its costs; this is shown as the horizontal line in **Figure 6.3**.

Advantages of Cost-Leadership Strategies

A major benefit of being the lowest-cost competitor within an industry is that it allows an organiza-tion to generate above-average profitability even where intense competition exists. For example, Re-liance Jio's lower cost base allows it to still earn a return after the other (higher-cost) competitors have competed away their profit through *rivalry* (see **Strategy in Focus 6.1**). Similarly, its low cost position allows the company to defend itself against *buyers* who can only drive prices down to the level of the next most efficient competitor. Even in this unlikely situation, the overall cost leader can still gener-ate positive returns. When faced with the bargaining power of *suppliers*, being a low cost producer provides a hedge against any increases in their input prices. Should there be a *threat of entry* from companies outside the industry, Reliance Jio is in an advantageous position to compete on price which effectively acts as a barrier to entry. Finally, as the low-price competitor Reliance Jio will be in

STRATEGY IN FOCUS 6.1 Reliance Jio: India's Wireless Wonder

There's a new king of telecom in India: Reliance Jio Infocomm, the wireless carrier created by multibillionaire Mukesh Ambani, which ranked No. 1 on last year's Change the World list. The network had 331 million subscribers at the end of June, exceeding Vodafone Idea (320 million customers) for the first time. Owned by Ambani's energy and retailing giant, Reliance Industries Ltd. (RIL), the telecom company could become the foundation of an online and e-commerce platform in India that rivals Alibaba in China and Amazon in the USA, analysts at UBS predict.

It's an amazing feat for the carrier, which started offering mobile service for free just three years ago before converting subscribers to still-cheap data plans in 2017. Currently, one Jio plan charges just three rupees per gigabyte of data used, equal to 5¢, and is ranked as the cheapest rate in the world.

To create the low cost carrier, Ambani spent billions to build a thoroughly modern wireless network that supports only 4G standards, bypassing older 2G and 3G technology, and relies on the kind of routers and equipment used to build the Internet instead of on more specialized— and expensive—telecommunications switching gear.

Ambani's wireless price war is eating his competitors. While Jio said net profit in the quarter ending June 30 jumped 46 per cent, to $130 million, Vodafone Idea lost $690 million and third-ranked Airtel lost $410 million. Both had been profitable a year earlier.

Reliance has been expanding its offerings into e-commerce and cloud services, leading UBS analysts to make the comparison to top Internet companies. 'Can RIL evolve into India's Amazon/Alibaba/Walmart? Yes,' the analysts concluded. With Ambani's deep pockets and willingness to cost cut his way to industry domination, it's certainly plausible.

Source: 'How Reliance Jio became India's Wireless Wonder', Fortune.com, 25 August 2019, https://fortune.com/2019/08/25/reliance-jio-india-mobile-wireless-service (accessed 11 June 2020).

a better position than its competitors to counter *substitutes* given its superior price–performance ratio. Porter argues that 'fundamentally, the risks in pursuing the generic strategies are twofold: first, failing to attain or sustain the strategy; second, for the value of the strategic advantage provided by the strategy to erode within industry evolution'.[10]

The Risks of Following an Overall Cost-Leadership Strategy

A low cost position protects the organization against all of the five forces. However, there are risks associated with this strategy.

- A cost-leadership strategy can prove expensive, as the organization continually updates its capital equipment.
- There is also the ease with which competitors may be able to imitate the activities of the cost leader.

- A change in technology may invalidate the cost leader's past investments in capital equipment and allow competitors to take market share.

- Customer tastes may change, which results in them being less price sensitive and more willing to pay a higher price for a differentiated product. An organization following an overall cost-leadership strategy may not be able to adjust readily to these market changes.

6.2.2 Differentiation Strategies

A differentiation strategy is aimed at a broad market and involves the organization competing on the basis of a product or service that is recognized by consumers as unique. This difference must be sufficiently valued by consumers that they are willing to pay a premium price for it. A major benefit of producing a differentiated product is that rivals will find it difficult to imitate. We might add that the choice of a differentiation strategy by an organization will involve different resources, capabilities, and organizational arrangements from a strategy based on cost leadership. It is for this reason that Porter believes an organization which seeks to follow more than one of the generic strategies is confused, or is what he refers to as 'stuck in the middle'.[11]

Organizations may differentiate their product offerings in a variety of ways. These include:

- product design or brand image (e.g. BMW, Apple)
- customizing products to suit consumers' specific requirements (e.g. Apple)
- state-of-the-art technology (e.g. Foxconn, Tesla, Amazon)
- marketing abilities (e.g. Unilever, S4 Capital, WPP)
- reliability (e.g. Toyota, BMW)
- customer service (e.g. Amazon).

In reality, we would expect the organization to use a number of dimensions on which it can differentiate its product. Hence companies will occupy more than one dimension. When evaluating its value chain, the organization would then be able to point to different activities where it is clearly differentiated from its competitors. Although the aim of a differentiation strategy is not to focus primarily on costs, it is clearly important that the organization has some knowledge of its cost structure. Then any differentiation achieved can be set at a price which customers will be prepared to pay and that easily covers the cost of the differentiation.

Advantages of Differentiation Strategy

A differentiation strategy allows an organization to achieve above-average profits in an industry by creating a defensible position for coping with the five forces. For instance, differentiation provides a defence against competitive *rivalry* because it creates brand loyalty that helps protect the organization from price competition. This brand loyalty and unique product offering have to be overcome by entrants thinking of entering the market, which acts as a *barrier to entry*. The power of *buyers* is constrained as they lack a comparable alternative. A differentiation strategy provides the organization with higher margins that enables it to deal more easily with cost pressures from *suppliers*. In addition, suppliers may value the benefits that derive from being associated with a successful product or service. Finally, a successfully differentiated product has customer loyalty that protects the organization from the use of *substitutes*. The more difficult it is for competitors to imitate the differentiation, the more likely it will be for the organization to achieve a sustainable competitive advantage. This implies that the basis of the differentiation is not readily identifiable, and even when known, is far from easy to replicate.

Risks of Following a Differentiation Strategy

As with an overall cost-leadership strategy, a differentiation strategy has inherent risks.

- The organization must ensure that the high price charged for differentiation is not so far above competitors that consumers perceive the difference as not worth paying, and it results in reduced brand loyalty.

- Buyers may decide that their need for a differentiated product has declined. For example, the use of the Internet has greatly reduced the search costs involved in comparing products.

- Competitors may narrow the attributes of differentiation which results in consumers being faced with a viable competitor offering.

6.2.3 Focus Strategies

Whereas the low cost and differentiation strategies we have discussed are aimed at the entire industry, a **focus strategy** is aimed at serving one or only a few segments of the market. This might be a particular group of consumers or a specific geographical market—in effect, any viable segment of the market. For example, the German automotive manufacturer Mercedes-Benz continues to provide the comfort, performance, and safety which consumers have come to expect from the brand, while also offering dramatic styling and innovative new features. Porter argues that by focusing on a narrow segment or niche of the market, the organization may be better placed to meet the needs of buyers than competitors who are trying to compete across the whole industry. By focusing on the needs of particular segments that exist within the industry, an organization can achieve competitive advantage through either lower costs or differentiation.

Cost-Focus Strategy

With a cost-focus strategy, an organization seeks to become the cost leader, but only within a particular segment of the market. Similarly, with a differentiation-focus strategy, the organization seeks to differentiate its products or services to effectively meet the needs of a particular segment of the market. A focus strategy is based upon the company being able to exploit only some of the differences within the industry. For example, the company may target segments that it believes it can more readily defend from competition. A cost-focus strategy may be possible because larger competitors within the industry have cost advantages that derive from economies of scale, but may be unable to produce cost-effective small production runs. The same logic applies to custom-built orders that do not allow larger competitors to exploit their economies of scale based upon standardization.

For example, the German retailer Aldi continues to thrive in the discount segment of retailing. A typical Aldi store is relatively small (around 15,000 square feet) and has about 700 products, 95 per cent of which are store brands. This compares with the 25,000 plus products that a more traditional supermarket carries. As with a cost-leadership strategy, quality cannot be sacrificed for cost savings. For instance, in taste tests many of Aldi's own-label products have beaten branded products. Aldi stores its

Since the financial crisis budget supermarkets like Aldi have seen success with a cost-focus strategy.
Source: © JoeSeer/Shutterstock.com.

products on pallets rather than shelves to cut the time it takes to restock and therefore to cut costs. It is difficult to see traditional supermarket retailers wanting to imitate this practice or, indeed, having the capability to manage costs in this niche market. Since the financial crisis, many consumers have flocked to Aldi's lower prices and unbranded goods, allowing both Aldi and Lidl to take market share from the big players in the supermarket industry. This would imply that the market for Aldi and Lidl's products has changed providing them with an opportunity to compete across the supermarket industry.

Differentiation-Focus Strategy

A differentiation-focus strategy offers a unique product that is highly valued within a segment of the market. The special needs within that segment are perceived to be more effectively met by the niche player than by rivals who compete across the market. This in turn helps to develop brand loyalty which makes entry by other competitors more difficult. As with broad based cost leadership and differentiation, the extent to which a focus strategy achieves a sustainable competitive advantage will depend upon the organization's resources and distinctive capabilities and the ease with which these can be imitated. In addition, the durability of the segment may be an issue, as it may be less durable than the industry as a whole.

Advantages of Focus Strategies

The same factors that apply to overall cost-leadership and differentiation strategies discussed above also apply to a focus strategy. As with low cost and differentiation strategies, a focus strategy can provide a defence against competitive forces.

The Risks of Following a Focus Strategy

The risks of a focus strategy are:

- the segment may not be durable; for instance, customer preferences may change and the niche player may be unable to respond

- broad-based competitors believe the segment represents an attractive submarket and out-focuses the focuser

- the difference between the segment and the main market narrows, leaving focus-based competitors at a disadvantage.

6.2.4 Stuck in the Middle

Michael Porter's generic strategies represent different approaches for dealing with competitive forces within an industry. In contrast, an organization that tries to pursue more than one of these generic strategies is referred to as *stuck in the middle*. An organization stuck in the middle lacks the market share and capital investment to be a low cost producer. It does not possess the industrywide differentiation which would preclude the need to be a low cost producer. Nor does it have the focus capabilities to create differentiation or a low cost position in a few segments.[12] It is, therefore, unwise for an organization to try to pursue both a low cost strategy and a differentiation strategy. While the actual choice of generic strategy will be dictated by the organization's resources and capabilities, it should seek to make a definitive choice as each generic strategy is mutually inconsistent. However, the empirical evidence is less clear cut.

Criticisms of Generic Strategies

While many organizations may choose to adopt a low cost strategy or differentiation strategy, it may not be true to suggest that these are inconsistent. Organizations are increasingly finding that a route to competitive advantage is being able to combine being a low cost producer with some form of differentiation; this is referred to as a **hybrid strategy**. Such a strategy is adopted by the Swedish furniture manufacturer IKEA, which provides low cost manufacture with a differentiated product. Often the two are complementary, so that being a cost leader allows an organization to invest in differentiation required by the market. Eva Pertusa-Ortega, Molina-Azorin, and Claver-Corte undertook a sample of 164 Spanish companies in different sectors and found a large number of organizations use hybrid strategies.[13] They also found that such strategies tend to be associated with higher levels of organizational performance than a company which simply pursues one generic strategy, such as cost leadership.

Let us consider, for example, the Japanese car manufacturer Toyota. It has an enviable record on cost reductions while at the same time its cars are differentiated from other major players such as Ford and General Motors. Therefore, it occupies a position in which it is the *overall cost leader* in the auto industry, but its products are also renowned for reliability providing them with *differentiation* and brand loyalty. Far from being 'stuck in the middle', Toyota's approach of differentiation and low cost manufacturing has proved to be the most profitable strategy.

In the UK supermarket retailers selling similar foodstuffs have sought to differentiate themselves through selling clothing, consumer electronics, savings products, and garden furniture, in the process turning themselves into department stores selling food! For example, Tesco, the market leader, continues to expand its range of non-food items as it moves into higher-margin goods and services. The problem for all supermarkets is that such products are easily imitated by rivals. There is some evidence (albeit ambiguous) that organizations trying to pursue more than one generic strategy may end up stuck in the middle. For example, Sainsbury's was stuck in the middle trying to sell higher-priced foods, but with the slogan 'Good food costs less at Sainsbury's'. Its foodstuffs were not perceived by consumers to be sufficiently differentiated to warrant a premium price when compared with other supermarkets. Nor were its operations sufficiently low cost to be able to compete on price. In trying to be simultaneously a low cost producer and a differentiator, it conceded market leadership to Tesco.

In the same way, the British retailer Marks & Spencer found that its clothes were no longer perceived by consumers to be differentiated on the basis of outstanding value for money. Instead, the retailer saw its fortunes decline as it grappled with tired clothing lines, loss of identity, incoherent objectives, and no clear vision. It was unable to compete effectively with competitor retailers such as Next. Moreover, it struggles to compete effectively with the logistics of a fast fashion outfit such as Zara, which is able to rapidly change its store inventory based on real-time consumer purchasers. M&S, which historically prided itself on its quality British-made goods, was forced to source its supplies from low cost economies. Its famous customer service and no-quibble money-back guarantee was no match for poor product lines.

6.3 A Resource-Based Approach to Strategy Formulation

The resource-based view of strategy (discussed in **Chapter 5**) argues there are two fundamental reasons for making the resources and capabilities of an organization, the foundation for its strategy. First, internal resources and capabilities provide the basic direction for an organization's strategy. And second, resources and capabilities are the primary source of profit for the organization. **Robert Grant** distinguishes between resources and capabilities.[14] He sees resources as inputs into the production process. A capability is the capacity for a team of resources to perform some task or activity. Therefore, resources are the source of an organization's capability. And it is capabilities that are the main source of its competitive advantage.

In a constantly changing world Grant argues that a focus solely upon the external environment may not provide a sufficient foundation for a long-term strategy. This is because when the external environment is constantly changing, '*the firm's own resources and capabilities may be a much more stable basis on which to define its identity. Hence, a definition of a business in terms of what it is capable of doing may offer a more durable basis for strategy.*'[15] A focus on which markets the organization competes in and, therefore, which customer needs it seeks to satisfy may be inappropriate when faced with a rapidly changing environment. Given this type of environment, the focus instead should be on internal factors. The resource-based view argues that even the choices articulated by Porter, competing on cost or differentiation within a broad or narrow market, are themselves predicated upon the capabilities within the organization. Since no organization can hope to follow an overall cost-leadership strategy if it does not possess economies of scale and technically proficient plant and machinery.

The aim of the resource-based approach to strategy formulation is to maximize **Ricardian rents**. Ricardian rents are the surplus that is left over when the inputs to a productive process, which includes the cost of capital being employed, have been covered. As resources depreciate or are imitated by competitors, so the rents they generate also begin to diminish. To appreciate rents fully we need to understand the relationship between resources and capabilities. While resources that reside within an organization may be largely transparent and, therefore, easy to identify, an organization may be less capable of assessing its capabilities objectively. This is because some features of an organization's capabilities will be unique and not easily captured as part of its value chain analysis. What is essential is that an organization can assess its capabilities relative to those of its competitors, as this allows it to exploit any differential advantage it may possess.

Organizational capabilities require that the knowledge of individuals is integrated with an organization's resources such as its capital equipment and technology. This is accomplished by what Nelson and Winter refer to as *organizational routines*.[16] We saw in **Chapter 5** that organizational routines are regular, predictable, and sequential patterns of work activity undertaken by members of an organization. Therefore, an organization's capabilities comprise a number of interacting routines. For resources and capabilities to operate efficiently the organization must achieve cooperation and coordination between routines. Therefore, the type of management style within the organization, its vision, and its values are all crucial ingredients to achieve the efficient operation of routines. An organization's capability is *path dependent*; it is the result of everything that has happened to it since its inception. The danger with this is that an organization's core capability can easily become a core rigidity, stifling the need to change when its environment changes.[17]

6.3.1 **Appraising Capabilities**

The profits that accrue to an organization's capabilities depend upon three factors: (1) establishing a competitive advantage; (2) sustaining a competitive advantage which the capabilities confer; and (3) the ability of the organization to appropriate the profits (or rents) earned from its capabilities.[18] We can look at each of these factors in turn.

1. **Establishing a competitive advantage**

   In order for a capability to establish a competitive advantage it must be *scarce*—that is, not widely available within the industry. When an organization possesses capabilities which few other organizations possess, such as Foxconn's capability in manufacturing, it provides a source of competitive advantage. In addition, a capability must also be *relevant*. Relevance implies that the capability meets the key or **critical success factors** for superior performance in an industry, those factors in an industry which keep customers loyal and allow the organization to compete successfully.

2. **Sustaining a competitive advantage**

   The characteristics of capabilities that provide for the sustainability of a competitive advantage are *durability*, *transferability*, and *replicability*.

   Durability refers to the rate at which an organization's resources and capabilities depreciate or become obsolete. While resources such as capital equipment may be quickly depreciated by technological changes, other resources such as an organization's brand tend to depreciate far slower. In contrast with most resources, an organization's capabilities tend to be more durable. This is because the organization may be able to replace the resources on which the capabilities are based more readily as they wear out. An organization's culture may also play a part in sustaining competitive advantage, by ensuring the continuity of capabilities through its socialization of employees.[19]

Transferability refers to how easily a competitor can buy the resources and capabilities necessary to duplicate a competing organization's strategy. If a competitor organization can acquire resources and capabilities on similar terms to your own, then your competitive advantage will be unsustainable. However, we might expect a company which is the first to acquire such resources and capabilities may also acquire some advantage. This is because it will gain experience and knowledge of these resources which competitors will lack: **first-mover advantages**.[20] Similarly, capabilities may be less transferable if they represent a collection of interactive resources. In that case, it may be that the only way to imitate the competitive advantage of a rival is to transfer capabilities in their entirety. For example, we might see an investment bank acquire a team of rival fund managers, rather than simply acquire the fund's 'star' leader. However, the dynamics present in one organization that allow a capability to flourish may not be present to the same extent in another organization.

Replicability is the use of a company's internal investments to build the resources and capabilities of its competitors. Where the capabilities are based upon complex organizational routines, this will be far more difficult. Even where an organization's routines seem relatively straightforward, they may be difficult for competitors to imitate successfully. Although Ryanair's business model is fairly transparent, no other competing airline is able to match its level of profitability.

3. **Appropriating the profits earned from capabilities**

The extent of profits which derive from an organization's capabilities will depend not only on its ability to sustain its competitive advantage, but also on its ability to appropriate or capture these profits for itself. This will depend upon the balance of power between the organization and its employees. Where an employee's contribution to the company is readily identifiable, their skills are scarce and easy to take from one company to another, we would expect the employee to be in a strong bargaining position for a share of the profits. But where the employee's contribution is not so clearly defined and is enhanced by organizational routines inside the company, we would expect the organization to appropriate a greater share of the profits.

6.3.2 Implications for Strategy Formulation

We have seen that an organization's most valuable capabilities are those that are durable, imperfectly transferable, difficult to replicate, and in which it has clear ownership. Given this, its strategy should be based upon exploiting these capabilities, which limit its activities to where it possesses a competitive advantage. For example, the British car manufacturer Morgan builds handmade sports cars for a specific segment of the market, playing to its strengths rather than trying to compete on price against mass-market players such as Ford. The dynamic of the marketplace necessitates that competitors constantly focus upon updating their capabilities rather than trying vainly to shore up their existing advantages, which will simply be imitated.

Figure 6.4 provides a four-stage model to guide organizations in their strategy formulation. The start point is to identify the resources and capabilities that already exist inside the organization.

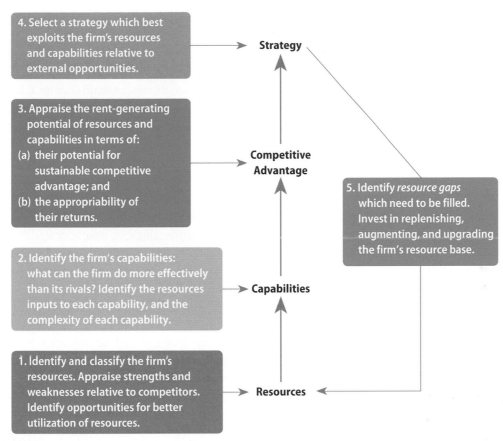

Figure 6.4   Strategy formulation: a resource-based approach. Source: Adapted from R. M. Grant and J. Jordan, *Foundations of Strategy*, Wiley (2015), p. 111.

Stage 2 requires the organization to understand the relationship between its resource inputs and how these provide it with a capability. This is a difficult challenge for managers since, as we saw in **Chapter 5**, this relationship is not always clear. **Stage 3** involves an appraisal of the organization's resources and capabilities. Some of these resources and capabilities will be necessary simply to compete in the market, while others provide a source of competitive advantage.

The organization needs to identify which capabilities provide it with competitive advantage and are of strategic importance. It also needs to know which of its capabilities are a strength—that is, what activities it can perform better than its competitors. In **Stage 4**, the organization uses the preceding analysis to formulate a strategy which allows it to exploit its strengths in relation to the opportunities that exist in the market. At the same time, the strategy should allow any competitive weakness in its activities to be outsourced, or acquire new resources and capabilities to try to turn these weaknesses into strengths. The overall objective is to analyse a company's resources and capabilities as a route to sustainable competitive advantage. This analysis then forms the basis of a company's strategy formulation.

To ensure sustainable competitive advantage, an organization needs to upgrade its resources and capabilities based on what it believes will be the basis of *future* competition. To do this, the organization needs to be able to analyse its competitive environment and to evaluate trends which may start within the macro-environment, but which have their greatest impact in the competitive environment. These trends will help determine the capabilities required to compete successfully in the future. As we mentioned in **Chapter 5**, **Prahalad and Hamel** refer to these capabilities as *core competencies*.[21] One approach to assess the external environment is to try to identify the *weak signals* we discussed in **Chapter 2**. Another is to produce a series of scenarios (also discussed in **Chapter 2**) based on what the organization believes may occur in the future. The goal is for an organization's strategy to go a little beyond its current resources and capabilities to ensure that the resources and capabilities necessary to address future competitive challenges are being built up.[22]

Porter's generic approach to business strategy is often characterized as static and incapable of dealing with a dynamic competitive landscape.[23] Others point to the use of hybrid strategies in which an organization might simultaneously pursue both a cost-leadership strategy and a differentiation strategy.[24] There is empirical support for and against Porter's generic strategies.[25] **Kay** tends to dismiss the concept of generic strategies, arguing instead that each organization is sufficiently different to make such generalizations of limited value.[26] He argues that, because the distinctive capabilities of organizations differ, any search for generic strategies will inevitably fail. This is because their general adoption by organizations would simply wipe out any competitive advantage that might have been derived. He reasons 'there can be no such recipes because their value would be destroyed by the very fact of their identification'.[27]

To summarize, the resource-based view shifts the discussion on competitive advantage from an emphasis on the competitive environment to the resources and capabilities inside the organization. The focus of attention becomes the configuration of resources to create capabilities. Moreover, as we saw in **Chapter 5**, an organization needs to acquire dynamic capabilities in order to compete in rapidly changing markets. A criticism made of the resource-based view is that it is unclear how resources and capabilities evolve over time.[28] That said, the purpose of strategy remains the same in each perspective; for the organization to exploit the opportunities within its business environment by playing to its strengths and transforming its weaknesses. It is *how* the organization gets to this position that generates contention. There is empirical support for both views, suggesting perhaps that they should not be seen so much as incompatible, but more as occupying different positions on the same continuum.[29]

6.4 **Blue Ocean Strategy**

W. Chan Kim and Renee Mauborgne suggest that companies need to create and capture blue oceans of uncontested market space.[30] They envisage the business world in terms of *red oceans* and *blue oceans*. **Red oceans** represent all the industries that currently exist today; the known market space. In red oceans, industry boundaries are clearly defined and accepted by competitors in the industry. The objective is to outperform your rivals and gain a greater share of existing demand. But as more companies compete for this finite demand, so the prospects for profits and growth rates reduce. As a result, trying to differentiate your product becomes harder, as products and services become commoditized, and intense competition turns the market into a blood-red ocean. In contrast, **blue oceans** represent all the industries not in existence today: the unknown market space. Blue oceans represent a strategic position unoccupied by competitors that has the potential for demand creation

Performers skipping rope at Cirque du Soleil's show 'Quidam'. Source: © VereridisVasilis/Shutterstock.com.

and highly profitable growth. Although a blue ocean can be created outside the existing industry boundaries, for example, eBay for online auctions, most blue oceans are created within red oceans by expanding existing industry boundaries.

Red oceans will always be important but with supply exceeding demand in many industries, competing for a share of shrinking markets is unlikely to lead to sustainable growth. As Kim and Mauborgne observe, 'the only way to beat the competition is to stop trying to beat the competition'. In other words, companies need to move beyond competing. To do this, they need to create new profit and growth opportunities, by creating blue oceans. In a study of the business launches of 108 companies, they found that 86 per cent of the launches were incremental improvements within a red ocean of existing market space. These accounted for 62 per cent of total revenues and 39 per cent of total profits. The other 14 per cent of the launches created a blue ocean, and these blue oceans generated 38 per cent of total revenues and 61 per cent of total profits. On the basis of these findings, the performance benefits of creating blue oceans appear to be self-evident.

Is the industry or the company the best unit of analysis to study if companies seek profitable growth? For example, a study of visionary companies highlighted companies such as Hewlett-Packard (HP) which outperformed the market over the long term.[31] But, at the same time, so did the entire computer hardware industry.[32] According to **Foster and Kaplan**, the success of these companies derived from industry sector performance rather than the companies themselves. As the saying goes, *a rising tide lifts all boats*! Furthermore, HP did not outperform competitors within its industry.[33] If these same companies can be highly profitable one moment and losing profit the next, it would suggest that the *company* is not the appropriate unit of analysis for exploring high performance and blue oceans. And if industry conditions and boundaries are not given, but can be influenced by play-ers in the industry, then companies do not necessarily have to compete in a given industry space. This leads Kim and Mauborgne to the conclusion that neither the company nor the industry is the best unit of analysis if we wish to study profitable growth.

To create blue oceans and sustained high performance requires an analysis of the *strategic move* rather than an analysis of the company or the industry. A **strategic move** is defined as 'the set of managerial actions and decisions involved in making a major market-creating business offering'.[34] The strategic move allows a company to deliver products and services that open up and capture new market space, resulting in a substantial increase in demand. Kim and Mauborgne's research suggests that companies which create blue oceans focus on *value innovation*.

6.4.1 Value Innovation

Value innovation occurs when organizations shift their focus from beating the competition to making the competition irrelevant by placing equal emphasis on *both* value and innovation. A focus on im-proving value without innovation tends to lead to an incremental improvement in value. Such a small improvement is unlikely to differentiate a company in the industry. Similarly, innovation without value tends to be technology driven, and may go beyond what consumers are prepared to pay for.

Value innovation occurs when companies align innovation with customer utility, price, and cost. Value innovation goes against Porter's assertion that an organization can pursue either differentia-tion *or* a low cost strategy. That is, *either* create greater value to customers at a higher cost *or* create reasonable value at a lower cost. It implies that companies which seek to create and capture blue oceans can pursue differentiation *and* low cost at the same time. A key feature of value innovation is that market boundaries and industry structure are not given, but they can be reconstructed by the actions and beliefs of industry players.[35]

An example is Cirque du Soleil, a Canadian company, which pursues both differentiation and low cost simultaneously. When Cirque du Soleil was founded in 1984, competitors in the circus industry would benchmark against each other and try to gain market share by improving their traditional cir-cus acts. They would hire famous clowns and lion tamers which increased their cost structure but did not really improve the customer experience of visiting the circus. The result was an increase in cost but without any increase in revenue, as demand continued to fall as the industry matured. Cirque du Soleil's approach was to re-define the problem. It did this by looking across the market boundaries that define the circus, and the theatre. It acquired a better understanding not only of circus custom-ers but also of circus noncustomers. Kim and Mauborgne categorize **noncustomers** as buyers who only minimally purchase an industry's offering, buyers who refuse to use the industry's offerings, and buyers who have never even thought of the industry's offering as an option for them.[36] Such noncustomers might include theatre or ballet audiences, who would seldom or never visit the circus.

How did Cirque du Soleil break the value-cost trade off? How did it simultaneously increase the value it provides to customers and lower its cost structure? It looked at the factors on which circuses compete such as animal acts, star performers, and the venue of three separate rings for performances. These factors were taken for granted by competitors in the industry. Yet on closer examination it was clear the public were increasingly uncomfortable with the use of animals in acts. Furthermore, animal acts were expensive to maintain with their high insurance and medical costs. The use of star perform-ers in the circus could not compete with the attraction of movie stars, but added high cost, without adding much value to consumers. Finally, the classic three-ring circus confounded audiences, as they wondered which venue they should be watching. This also increased the cost as each of these venues had to be filled with performers. The solution was to eliminate or reduce all these factors which the traditional circus took for granted, and hence reduce their cost.

As a result, Cirque du Soleil kept the clowns but changed their act from slapstick to a style more suited to a sophisticated audience. It did away with the three-ring circus and replaced it with a single tent which offered much greater comfort for consumers. In doing so, Cirque du Soleil recognized that the tent was a symbol associated with the circus. By looking across the market boundary of theatre, and borrowing ideas from Broadway shows, it was able to offer factors not associated with the circus. It had multiple productions, with each show having its own storyline and original music scores. It drew on complex dance routines drawn from the ballet. The introduction of all these new factors led to a substantial increase in demand.

In **Figure 6.5**, cost savings are made by eliminating and reducing the factors an industry competes on. By eliminating many of the costly elements of the circus Cirque du Soleil was able to dramatically reduce its cost structure, and achieve both differentiation and low cost. Buyer value occurs by raising and creating elements the industry has never offered before. For example, the use of multiple productions, original scores, and artistic theatre and dance. Over time, costs are reduced further creating a virtuous cycle, as economies of scale occur from a superior consumer offering which generates high sales volumes. **Blue ocean strategy** allows a company to achieve a leap in value for both the company and its buyers, by driving costs down while simultaneously driving value up for buyers.

If we accept that buyer value comes from the utility and price that the company offers to buyers, and the value to the company is obtained from the price charged and its cost structure, then we can see that value innovation is achieved only when a company's utility, price, and cost activities are all properly aligned. As such, Kim and Mauborgne argue that value innovation is more than innovation; it requires a company to orientate its entire activity system in order to achieve a leap in value for both

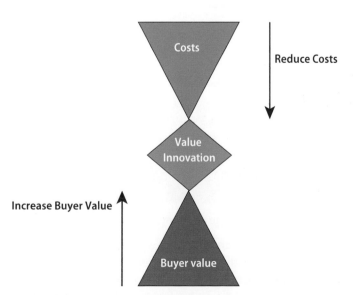

Figure 6.5   Value innovation.

Red Ocean Strategy	Blue Ocean Strategy
Compete in existing market space	Create uncontested market space
Try to beat the competition	Make the competition irrelevant
Exploit existing market demand	Create and capture new demand
Move the value-cost trade off	Break the value-cost trade off
Compete by differentiation *or* low cost	Pursue both differentiation and low cost

Figure 6.6   Red ocean versus blue ocean strategy.

 STRATEGY IN FOCUS 6.2 Amazon's Blue Ocean Strategy

Could delivery drones be a common sight in the future? Source: © SanitFuangnakhon/Shutterstock.com.

The Internet retail giant has secured an agreement with UK authorities to develop the technology to deliver products by drone within thirty minutes of receiving an order via its Prime Air service. Amazon is taking advantage of the UK's willingness to embrace a burgeoning interest in the unmanned aerial vehicle sector. The UK, which wants to establish itself as a world leader in unmanned vehicles of all types, has extended that cooperation, with the Civil Aviation Authority relaxing normal rules requiring drones to stay within 'line of sight' of their operators—taken to be about 1,500 ft—and not to fly above 400 ft to avoid other air traffic.

However, Amazon is determined to make Prime Air a reality, with chief executive Jeff Bezos personally supporting the programme. But putting aside technological challenges, is there really a market for deliveries by drone? Amazon says almost 90 per cent of its current orders weigh below 2.25 kg, meaning they will be able to be delivered by drone. Human nature is also set to drive demand for drone delivery services, especially as Amazon does not see a major extra cost once the technology is perfected, and analysts think it could add just $1 (77p) to an order.

'One should never underestimate the seductive power of instant gratification,' says an independent retail analyst. 'Delivery by drone will allow Amazon to add value in the way that going into a shop and being helped by assistants adds value. It's allowing Amazon to not just level the playing field, but to create one of its own and disconnect itself from rivals who will be unable to keep up.'

Some critics argue that customers will never feel they so urgently need to have, say, a certain book, within thirty minutes to justify a drone service, but Amazon sees airborne delivery as being economic enough that everyday sundries will be arriving by drone. Paul Misener, Amazon's vice president of global innovation policy and communications, says: 'If a customer runs out of coffee or toothpaste, two-day shipping may not be the right choice. We're developing shipping options so they can choose what works best for them.' The company imagines scenarios such as having forgotten to bring a corkscrew to a picnic and ordering one to be delivered by air, or running out of milk and deciding it is easier to use Prime Air than go to the supermarket.

Questions have also been asked about the security of drones packed with potentially high value goods, which could prove tempting targets for the criminally inclined. Amazon does not believe this will be an issue, pointing out that delivery trucks, which carry far more products than a single drone can, are not routinely victims of crime. Whether the economics stack up or not—and Amazon clearly believes they do—how drones will work in the existing aviation environment is the biggest challenge to their development.

'Integration is the number one, two and three biggest problem for drones,' says a member of the Royal Aeronautical Society's unmanned aerial vehicle group. 'Think of them like bikes on the road. It would be lovely to have cycle lanes everywhere but it's just not practical, they have to fit in with the cars and lorries.'

Perhaps more difficult will be working out how drones will operate in a complex urban environment, where buildings can rise above the 400 ft ceiling, and hard-to-detect obstacles such as telephone wires are common. The Internet retailer is confident it can overcome such worries, but there is a host of other factors to consider. Weather is one: wind and rain can have a huge impact on such small aircraft, making them hard to fly. Range is another: although the drones' current range of ten miles is expected to increase, Amazon would need to expand its distribution network massively to hit the target of deliveries within thirty minutes. Physically getting the packages into customers' hands also raises questions.

These problems are all to be solved, but with Amazon's might behind the project, there's a good chance solutions can be found.

Source: Alan Tovey, 'Can Amazon's drones deliver the *Back to the Future* world?', *The Telegraph*, 31 July 2016.
© Telegraph Media Group Limited.

buyers and company. This is more readily achieved when market boundaries and industry structure are not seen as a given but can be reconstructed by the industry players.

6.4.2 The Strategy Canvas

In order to create a blue ocean of uncontested market space we use an analytical framework called the *strategy canvas*. The **strategy canvas** allows you to see where competitors are investing, the factors on which the industry competes, and what value customers receive from the current offerings on the market. This allows you to capture what is happening in the known market space. The horizontal axis of the strategy canvas captures the factors the industry competes on and invests in. On the vertical axis, we show the value a company offers the buyers in terms of each of these factors. A high score on the vertical axis means a company offers buyers more, and therefore invests more, in that factor. We can then plot the current offering of a particular industry against all these factors on our strategy canvas to derive a **value curve**. The value curve is a graphic representation of a company's relative performance across its industry's factors of competition.

Kim and Mauborgne maintain the traditional competitor behaviour of benchmarking against competitors won't work. This may incrementally improve sales, but it won't open up uncontested market space. To open up a blue ocean, you need to shift your strategic focus from current competition to alternatives, and noncustomers. This re-orientation of your strategic focus allows you to redefine the problems in the industry, and create buyer value elements that reside across industry boundaries. As such, it represents a move away from traditional competitive analysis which suggests offering better solutions to current problems within your industry.

The Four Actions Framework

In order for a company to create a new value curve, it becomes necessary to challenge the industry's strategic logic and existing business model. To achieve that, we can use an analytical tool called the *Four Actions Framework*. We ask four questions:

The Four Actions Framework

1. Which of the factors that the industry takes for granted should be *eliminated*?

2. Which factors should be *reduced* well below the industry's standard?

3. Which factors should be *raised* well above the industry's standard?

4. Which factors should be *created* that the industry has never offered?

The first question forces you to consider eliminating factors on which companies in the industry have always competed. Such factors may add little or no value to the consumer. The second question encourages you to consider whether products have been over-designed as you try to match or beat the competition. In answering the first two questions you begin to understand which factors you can eliminate and reduce, and thereby reduce your cost structure. The third question allows you to eliminate the compromises your industry forces customers to make. The fourth question enables you to discover new sources of value for buyers and to create new demand. This, in turn, allows you to increase the price of your product or service offering. Taken together, these four factors allow you

ELIMINATE	RAISE
Star performers Animal acts Multiple venues Selling confectionery in the aisles	Unique venue
REDUCE	CREATE
Slapstick humour Thrill and danger	Theme Refined environment Multiple productions Artistic music and dance routines

Figure 6.7   ERRC grid for Cirque du Soleil.

to reconstruct buyer value elements and offer buyers an entirely new experience. By eliminating and creating new factors of competition, companies change the factors on which they compete. As a result, they make the existing rules of competition irrelevant.

The Eliminate-Raise-Reduce-Create Grid

The Four Actions Framework is used with an analytical tool called the *eliminate-raise-reduce-create grid*. The ERRC grid enables a company to consider the above four questions, and fill in the grid, to produce a new value curve. If we take Cirque du Soleil as an example, we can see how the ERRC grid works. By reassessing the factors on which the circus has always competed, Cirque du Soleil was able to identify which factors could be eliminated and reduced from the industry. It eliminated the animal acts, so-called star performers, and multiple venues. It reduced the slapstick humour and thrill seeking. It increased the use of more luxurious venues, and created entirely new productions by drawing across industry boundaries. See **Figure 6.7**.

   A key benefit of the ERRC grid is it is readily understood by managers in the company which is likely to create a high level of engagement in its application. It also forces companies to evaluate the factors on which an industry competes. In doing so, it allows them to make explicit any unconscious assumptions or cognitive bias they may be unaware of when competing. When seen through the lens of a value curve, a blue ocean strategy should also exhibit *focus*, *divergence* and a *compelling tagline*. It needs focus to avoid wasting its resources by trying to compete across all the key factors of competition. As it is no longer benchmarking against competitors in the industry, we would expect its value curve to diverge from that of other players in the industry. Finally, a good tagline delivers a clear message to consumers about the company's offering.

6.4.3 **The Blue Ocean**

The strategy canvas for Cirque du Soleil shows the existing factors on which competition in the industry is based. It also highlights new factors which they have introduced allowing the company to create new market space. We can see the value curve of Cirque du Soleil is markedly different from the existing players in the industry. See **Figure 6.8**. Its strategic profile meets the three criteria Kim

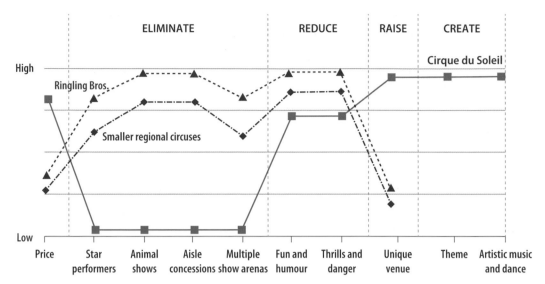

Figure 6.8   The strategy canvas of Cirque du Soleil. Source: W. C. Kim and R. Mauborgne, *Blue Ocean Strategy*, Harvard Business Press (2005), p. 40.

and Mauborgne utilize to define blue ocean strategy: focus, divergence, and a compelling tagline. Furthermore, the strategy canvas allows the company to compare its strategic profile with that of competitors in the industry. Finally, the canvas allows us to see how comprehensively Cirque du Soleil has departed from the existing strategic logic of how players are expected to compete in the circus industry.

Blue Ocean Idea (BOI) Index

In formulating a blue ocean strategy, we start with buyer utility. Does a company's product or service offering provide buyers with exceptional utility? Would this offering appeal to the three tiers of non-customers we discussed earlier? If the answer to these questions is 'no' then the company can either scrap the idea, or try to reconfigure it until the answer becomes 'yes'. The next step in the process is to consider the price of the product offering. Can a company set a price which will attract a majority of buyers? These two steps allow a company to create a leap in net buyer value, or the difference between the price consumers pay for a product minus the utility they receive from the product. The next step is the target cost of the offering. Or is it possible to make an acceptable level of profit at the company's stated price? The Tata Nano is an example of how a product met its target cost by streamlining operations and introducing cost innovation in manufacture, in order to achieve its stated price.

This is important because a company's price minus its cost will determine its profit. If we put all these factors together, we can see it is a combination of providing exceptional buyer utility, strategic pricing, and target costing that allows a company to achieve value innovation. And value innovation produces an increase in value for both the buyers and the company. A final step in the blue ocean strategy formulation process is to ensure there are no hurdles to adoption. Resistance to a blue ocean strategy might be forthcoming because managers are used to competing in red oceans, and a blue ocean strategy represents a significant departure from existing ways of competing. **Figure 6.9** shows the blue ocean idea index.

Utility	Is there exceptional utility in your product or service offering?
	Are there compelling reasons for consumers to want to buy your offering?
Price	Is the target price accessible to a majority of buyers?
Cost	Does your cost structure meet the target cost?
Adoption	Have you being able to address constraints to adopting the blue ocean idea?

Figure 6.9   Blue ocean idea index.

In summary, 'the focus of blue ocean strategy is not on restricting output at a higher price but rather on creating new aggregate demand through a leap in value at an accessible price'.[37] This provides an incentive for companies to reduce costs as low as possible at the very start.

6.5 Strategy Formulation in Turbulent Markets

If markets are becoming increasing turbulent and hypercompetitive, how can organizations formulate successful strategies to achieve sustainable competitive advantage?[38] The answer lies in a clearer understanding of the competitive conditions that operate in the marketplace, and the relationship between an environment's turbulence and the choice of strategy.

Clayton Christensen argues that the practices and business models that constitute advantages for today's most successful companies only do so because of particular factors at work under particular conditions at this particular point in time.[39] He asserts that strategists need to get to grips with *why* and under what conditions certain practices lead to competitive advantage. Christensen contends that even tacit knowledge that is difficult to imitate confers only a temporary advantage. This is because scientific progress that results in better understanding has a tendency to transform knowledge that once resided within an organization's proprietary routines into explicit and replicable knowledge. The task for organizations then is to be sufficiently aware of the factors which underpin their competitive advantage such that they will know when old competitive advantages are due to disappear and how new ones can be built.

There is an understanding that more attention needs to be paid to the differences between the strategies of dominant incumbent players and those of challengers who are seeking to disrupt the current environment. By better understanding the interaction between strategy and the environment, managers can better tailor their strategies to the environment, or better still, attempt to change the environment to their benefit. **Richard D'Aveni** argues that the firm with strategic supremacy shapes the basis of competition for its rivals. It determines the rules on which rivals will compete within the industry.[40] For example, Gillette's heavy investment in R&D initially put it at a disadvantage in a market increasingly dominated by its competitor Bic's disposable razors.

But, instead of trying to compete according to industry rules that suited Bic, Gillette redefined the rules of the game for razors. To achieve this, Gillette introduced its Sensor razor, which defined winning in terms of brand image and shaving quality. This disruption of the competitive environment by Gillette continued with the introduction of Mach3 razors. Gillette successfully changed the rules of the game, which in turn changed the competitive environment. The new competitive environment is characterized by periods of stability punctuated by **disruptions**. Gillette deliberately disrupts the market with a new product offering for example, its Fusion razors with flexball technology, and consolidates its gains around the new standard. The lesson to be acquired in these hypercompetitive markets is that strategic paradigms that work well in one environment may not operate at all in another.

D'Aveni argues market turbulence occurs within an industry as a result of competence-enhancing or competence-destroying disruptions. Competence-destroying disruptions occur through events such as changes in customer tastes, technological substitution, or obsolescence of a competence. In contrast, competence-enhancing disruptions make a market leader's competencies more valuable. These competence disruptions can occur infrequently or constantly. They result in four different competitive environments: *equilibrium*, *fluctuating equilibrium*, *punctuated equilibrium*, and *disequilibrium*.[41]

- **Equilibrium**. This environment is characterized by long periods of little or no competence-destroying turbulence. Incumbent leaders exercise control through barriers to entry. A challenger must make these barriers to entry irrelevant.

- **Fluctuating equilibrium**. The environment is characterized by rapid turbulence based on frequent competence-enhancing disruptions. Challengers try to destroy the underlying core competencies of the leader and move the environment to punctuated equilibrium or disequilibrium.

- **Punctuated equilibrium**. This is characterized by brief dynamic periods based on discontinuous change or competence-destroying revolutions. This is particularly so in industries which experience fast technological change followed by a dominant standard. The leader has to decide when and how to respond to the next revolution. The challenger seeks to disrupt the stability sought by the leader.

- **Disequilibrium**. This is the most challenging of the hypercompetitive environments, characterized by frequent and discontinuous disruptions. The leaders will constantly be creating new competencies, and deliberately disrupting themselves before their rivals do. Examples include Apple's introduction of new iproducts, which intentionally cannibalizes their existing product. The challengers have to disrupt this environment in ways that cannot easily be matched or change the environment to become less disruptive.

By understanding the pattern of turbulence in their competitive environment, managers can develop better strategies to ensure strategic supremacy.

6.6 Disruptive Innovation and Strategy Formulation

Joseph Bower and Clayton Christensen's work on **disruptive innovations** has resonance with Richard D'Aveni's insights.[42] **Disruption** describes a process in which a smaller company with fewer resources is able to successfully challenge established incumbent businesses.[43] The smaller company is able to do this because incumbent businesses are focused on improving products for their most demanding customers, which provides them with the greatest profit. These improvements in products by incumbent firms exceed the product performance needs of mainstream customers while ignoring the performance needs of others. This provides an opportunity for entrants to target these neglected segments by offering them products with more suitable functionality, invariably at a lower price. These entrants thereby gain a foothold in the market.

In **Figure 6.10** we see product performance trajectories (the red lines which show how products or services improve over time) and customer demand trajectories (the green lines which show customers' willingness to pay for performance). The incumbent organization is focused on improving products for their most demanding customers at the high end of the market; this is shown as *Incumbent's sustaining trajectory*. In so doing, incumbents exceed the needs of the mainstream customer segments while ignoring less profitable consumer segments. This provides a new entrant with an opportunity to target these neglected segments. It offers customers at the low end of the market products with are simpler, more convenient, and invariably at a lower price, which initially may be inferior to the existing technology of the incumbent firm. Over time, the new entrant improves the performance attributes of its product offering and is able to compete with established products in their traditional markets. This is shown as *Entrant's disruptive trajectory* in **Figure 6.10**.

Incumbent organizations, focused on the pursuit of higher profits in the more demanding segments, will invariably not respond strenuously to the loss of a less profitable segment. Over time, however, new entrants start to move upmarket and improve the quality and performance of their product offerings to attract the incumbents' mainstream customers. They do this because moving upmarket also provides them with greater profitability. However, unless there is an improvement in quality to match the standards of mainstream customers, they simply will not accept the new entrant's products, even at a low price. Once the quality rises enough to satisfy them, they gladly adopt the new product with its lower price. When mainstream customers start adopting the new entrant's offerings in volume, disruption has occurred.

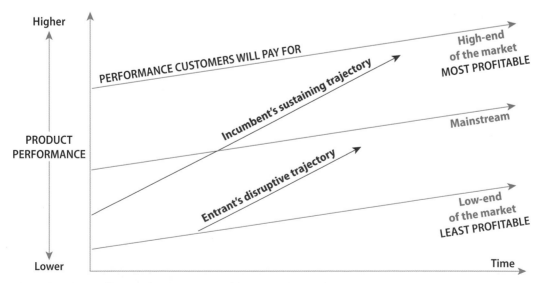

Figure 6.10   The disruptive innovation model. Source: C. M. Christensen, M. E. Raynor, and R. McDonald, 'What is disruptive innovation?', *Harvard Business Review*, vol. 93, no. 12 (2015), pp. 44–53.

Christensen, Raynor, and McDonald argue the incumbent organization has the capabilities to succeed, but fails to use them effectively to deal with potential disrupters.[44] This is because their resource allocations are designed to meet sustaining innovation needs. This makes them unprepared to respond to a different type of challenge. As we saw earlier, the entrants lull the incumbent into a false sense of security by not competing with them for their best customers, initially settling for low-end consumers. But, the trajectory of the disrupter will ultimately 'crush' the incumbent.

There is a great deal of confusion as to what constitutes disruptive innovation. The term is readily bandied about and often used inappropriately.[45] For example, Uber, the transportation company which uses mobile application to connect customers who require a taxi with taxi drivers, is often said to have disrupted the taxi business. Yet according to the criteria established by Christensen et al. for disruption, Uber is not a disruptive innovation. This is because Uber did not start by appealing to low-end or unserved consumers and then migrate to the mainstream market, which is the pattern for a disrupter. Instead, Uber initially built a position in the mainstream market and only then appealed to overlooked customer segments.

The disruptive theory differentiates disruptive innovation from sustaining innovations. Sustaining innovations make good products better; disruptive innovations are initially considered inferior by an incumbent's customers. Customers will not switch to the new offering simply because it offers a lower price, but wait until the product quality improves enough to satisfy their needs. When that happens, customers adopt the new product at a lower price, and disruption occurs. On this basis, it is clear that Uber's strategy is one of sustaining innovation rather than disruption. The reason it is important to define clearly disruption theory is to enable managers to understand the different types of threats that their business may encounter and respond accordingly. For example, small competitors on a disruptive trajectory may pose a major threat whereas other small competitors may be safely ignored. The **Case Study: Disrupting the Competition for One Dollar** at the end of the chapter shows how a small competitor disrupted the market for razor blades.

6.6.1 How to Respond to Disruptive Innovation

There are a number of approaches that may help incumbent companies deal with disruptive innovators. These are as follows:

1. **Identify the strengths of your disrupter's business model.**[46]
   This is necessary because all disruptive innovations derive from business model advantages that can increase as disruptive businesses move upmarket in search of more demanding customers. Identifying a disrupter's business model helps the incumbent identify what kinds of customers the disrupter might attract. The incumbent can then determine how many customers of each kind it has which might be susceptible to disruption.

2. **Identify your own relative advantages.**
   An incumbent organization will need to know what is it that people want its company to do for them and what is it that the disrupter could do better. This provides a clearer picture of the incumbent's relative advantages. Where a disruptive business offers a significant advantage and no disadvantages in performing the same activities as the incumbent, disruption will be swift and complete. This occurred with online music and CDs. When the advantages of a disrupter are less suited to performing the same activities as the incumbent and its disadvantages are considerable, disruption will likely be much slower and easier to defend.

3. **Identify the barriers a disrupter would need to overcome.**

   Identifying the barriers a disrupter needs to overcome will enable the incumbent firm to see which activities within their business are the most vulnerable to disruption and which parts they can defend. What the incumbent organization needs to look for is barriers which are significant and difficult for the potential disrupter to overcome. The reason for this is that such barriers would tend to undermine any advantages the disrupter may possess.

4. **Create a separate unit.**

   The incumbent company may pursue its own innovation within the existing organization or set up a new unit to achieve this. Where the existing culture and capabilities to undertake innovative change reside inside the company this can be undertaken internally. Where innovative change marks a step change in how the company operates, then it may be useful to set up a separate unit divorced from the existing culture. This business unit would then be given entrepreneurial autonomy to develop and test new ideas.

6.6.2 Limitations of Disruptive Innovation

Given the widespread discussion and pervasiveness of disruptive innovation, it is perhaps not surprising that it has attracted criticism. Harvard historian, **Jill Lepore**, wrote in *The New Yorker* that disruptive innovation is no more than a theory of why businesses fail.[47] It cannot explain change or continuity. It is simply an idea forged in time which is generalized from selected examples. **John Kay** concurs with Lepore, pointing out that the claims of Christensen and his followers are inflated and tautological.[48]

   Andrew King and Baljir Baatartogtokh argue that in explaining the success and failure across the seventy-seven cases cited by Christensen and Raynor,[49] other factors may be more appropriate than the theory of disruption.[50] Their research suggests the theory of disruption has little predictive power as to what may transpire in the market. They conclude it is no substitute for careful analysis and making difficult choices.

Summary

Business strategy is concerned with *how* an organization is going to compete in its chosen industry or market. It deals with individual business units that operate within an industry or distinct market segment. The aim of business strategy is to achieve a sustainable competitive advantage. In this chapter, we evaluated Michael Porter's generic competitive strategies of overall cost leadership, differentiation, and focus. We noted that each strategy provides the means for an organization to occupy a defendable position against the five competitive forces that determine industry profitability. Whether the organization pursues a low cost or differentiation strategy, it must choose which market segments it wants its products to compete within.

   The resource-based view (RBV) has its primary focus upon the resources and capabilities within the organization. Proponents argue an organization should seek to match its internal resources and capabilities to the needs of the external environment. The RBV sees profit deriving from two sources: first, the sustainability of the competitive advantage that resources and capabilities confer and, second, the ability of the organization to appropriate the profits (or rents) earned from its capabilities.

Blue ocean strategy was discussed as an opportunity to make existing competition irrelevant. To open up a blue ocean, requires a shift in focus from current competition to alternatives, and noncustomers. This re-orientation of your strategic focus allows you to redefine the problems in the industry, and to create buyer value elements that reside across industry boundaries.

We discussed the role of competitive strategies within turbulent and hypercompetitive markets. We noted that market turbulence can occur within an industry as a result of competence-enhancing or competence-destroying disruptions. We evaluated the role of disruptive innovations in which a smaller company with fewer resources can successfully challenge established incumbent businesses. Finally, we suggested strategies for incumbent organizations to avoid disruptive innovations.

CASE STUDY Disrupting the Competition for One Dollar

Over the past few years the male grooming market has continued to flourish as consumer product companies market everything from men's hair loss shampoo to skin creams. Male grooming is still massively outsold by female products, but what was essentially a niche product is now mainstream. Within the male grooming market, the sale of razors continues to decline, not least because of the increasing popularity of men growing beards. The US razor market has declined every year since 2013; in Western Europe sales of razors have fallen every year since 2014.

Razor blades kit from Dollar Shave Club.
Source: © Dollar Shave Club.

The undisputed leader in the men's razor market is Gillette, the world's largest maker of razors. Gillette has dominated this market for decades, with little interference. Its parent is the US multinational Procter & Gamble, which operates in five key business segments: grooming; healthcare; beauty; fabric and home care; and baby, feminine, and family care. In 2016, household brands such as Fairy washing up liquid, Ariel washing powder, Gillette razors, and Pampers nappies generated revenues worldwide of more than $60 billion. Almost half of all revenue is generated in the USA, around 23 per cent in Europe, and the rest is split between established and emerging markets.

In 2012, the male grooming market in the USA began to change. Prior to this, Gillette ruled supreme, with its constant innovations in blade technology. Its introduction of five-blade razors, Fusion Proglide razors with FlexBall technology, and lubricating razors are all aimed at winning more sales at higher prices. This is not unlike the situation with computer printers—the printer was relatively inexpensive, but the ink cartridges were expensive, and so it is with razors and their indispensable blades. Thus, in 2012 Michael Dubin, fed up with the paying high prices for disposable razors, founded Dollar Shave Club.

Dollar Shave Club offers its mostly male customers easy access to good-quality razors via its subscription service. Prior to Dollar Shave's launch, personal care subscription services existed, but they simply supplied consumers with a surprise box of items based on what they thought the customers' preferences were. What Dubin did was to provide the consumer with exactly what was ordered. To start with, customers receive a razor handle and a pack of razor blades. Thereafter, each month consumers receive replacement razor blades at their agreed price of $1, $6, or $9, plus packaging.

Although Gillette remains the leader in razor technology and market share, arguably it failed to capitalize on its position and scan the market for changes in consumer behaviour. That said, Gillette was thinking about a subscription service for its razors, but did not launch Gillette Shave Club until September 2015. The irony is Gillette had the idea before Dollar Shave Club launched, but its delay meant it was second to market. Clearly, it used to be the big company eating the small company; now, it's about the fast company stealing a march on the slow.

By 2015, Dollar Shave Club had gone from 0 to 54 per cent of the online shaving market. Despite its massive marketing and R&D expenditure, Gillette Shave Club trails with an estimated 21 per cent. At the same time, Gillette accused Dollar Shave Club of infringing its patented technology, as the competitive rivalry intensified. The success of Dollar Shave Club is a result of offering simpler and cheaper razors, as well as Dubin's irreverent use of social media to mock his competitors' products. He has tapped into a vein of consumer resentment of paying over the odds for razor blades while lampooning his competitors. A YouTube video which went viral with more than twenty-four million views reminds consumers that the high price they pay for razors from competitors goes to celebrities advertising the product.

Dollar Shave Club, along with a rival start-up called Harry's, is taking market share from Gillette despite the popularity of beards. But no competing subscription brand has managed to match Dollar Shave Club's rapid growth. In 2016, it had achieved more than three million subscribers, with estimated revenues of $200 million. This remarkable growth did not go unnoticed; it attracted both venture capitalists and Anglo-Dutch multinational, Unilever. Impressed with Dubin's business model of getting customers to pay for his razor blades in advance and his management of the corporation, Unilever acquired Dollar Shave Club for $1 billion.

Importantly, the acquisition has provided Unilever with a presence and capabilities it currently lacks in the razor market. At a multiple of five times 2016's expected earnings, it didn't come cheap, but then again, Dollar Shave Club has managed 5 per cent of the men's razor blade market since launching in 2012. Since 2010, Procter & Gamble, which shelled out $57 billion for Gillette in 2005, has seen its market share decline from 71 per cent to 58 per cent. Dollar Shave Club is gaining market share from what was always an intractable market, dominated by Gillette, with its closest competitor, Edgewell Personal Care, achieving less than half of Gillette's market share.

Before Dollar Shave Club entered the market, the business model was based around the introduction of new technologies to achieve a smoother and closer shave. This provided the justification for higher prices. As it attracts consumers from the leading brands, Dollar Shave Club has also started to move its product range upmarket, introducing premium brands. It offers shave butter and post-shave cream. It also offers One Wipe Charlies, for men's toilet needs, again using social media fronted by Michael Dubin in his trademark jocular style.

The global market for men's razors and blades is worth around $15 billion, according to Euromonitor, about one-fifth of which is in the USA. Unilever, no doubt, expects to leverage Dubin's capability of connecting directly with the customer. In effect, the subscription model provides Unilever with an opportunity to bypass leading retailers and perhaps even take on Amazon. With Unilever's global reach, Dollar Shave Club can progress into emerging economies such as India, whose male grooming market should be worth an estimated $1.2 billion by 2024.

What was once a market based on technological innovation is fast turning into a market based on customer need and value.

Sources: Lindsay Whipp, 'Made-up men reflect changing $50bn male grooming industry', *The Financial Times*, 4 February 2017; John Murray Brown and Arash Massoudi, 'Unilever buys Dollar Shave Club for $1bn', *The Financial Times*, 20 July 2016; Lindsay Whipp, 'Gillette sues Dollar Shave Club in cut throat battle', *The Financial Times*, 17 December 2015; Lex, 'Dollar Shave Club: smooth cut', *The Financial Times*, 20 July 2016; Lindsay Whipp, 'P&G: a plot twist in the soap opera', *The Financial Times*, 20 October 2015; Alan Livsey, 'Dollar Shave Club wins market share and customers with back-to-basics approach', *The Financial Times*, 17 March 2017.

Questions

1. How has Dollar Shave Club managed to disrupt the razor market?

2. Discuss whether Dollar Shave Club conforms to Clayton Christensen's model of disruptive innovation.

3. How safe is Dollar Shave Club from disruption?

+ **For more examples and discussion to aid your understanding of this chapter, please visit the online resources and see the Extension Material for this chapter.**

 ## Review Questions

1. Comment on Michael Porter's assertion that an organization trying to pursue more than one generic strategy will end up *stuck in the middle*.
2. How can pursuing a blue ocean strategy make the competition irrelevant?
3. Explain how an understanding of disruptive innovation can prevent an incumbent organization from losing its mainstream customers.

 ## Discussion Question

'If markets are hypercompetitive, this makes the use of any business strategy redundant.'
Discuss.

 ## Research Topic

How will Taiwanese company Hon Hai, better known as Foxconn Technology Group, which makes personal computers and smartphones for brands such as Apple, Dell, and Huawei, continue to prosper in the midst of a US–China trade war, and a decline in demand for smartphones?

Recommended Reading

For a discussion of generic strategies see:

- **M. E. Porter**, *Competitive Strategy: Techniques for Analysing Industries and Competitors*, Free Press, 1985.

For an understanding of disruptive innovations see:

- **J. Bower** and **C. M. Christensen**, 'Disruptive technologies: catching the wave', *Harvard Business Review*, vol. 73, no. 1 (1995), pp. 43–53.
- **C. M. Christensen**, **M. E. Raynor**, and **R. McDonald**, 'What is disruptive innovation?', *Harvard Business Review*, vol. 93, no. 12 (2015), pp. 44–53.

For a discussion of blue ocean strategies see:

- **W. C. Kim** and **R. Mauborgne**, *Blue Ocean Strategy*, Harvard Business Press, 2005.
- **W. C. Kim** and **R. Mauborgne**, *Blue Ocean Shift*, Hachette Book Group, 2017.

For an insight into strategies in turbulent markets see:

- **R. A. D'Aveni**, 'Strategic supremacy through disruption and dominance', *Sloan Management Review*, vol. 40, no. 3 (1991), pp. 127–35.

www.oup.com/he/henry4e
Visit the online resources that accompany this book for activities and more information on strategy.

Test your knowledge and understanding of this chapter further by trying the multiple-choice questions online.

References and Notes

[1] **J. B. Quinn**, *Strategies for Change: Logical Incrementalism*, Irwin, 1978.
[2] See **H. Mintzberg** and **J. A. Waters**, 'Of strategies, deliberate and emergent', *Strategic Management Journal*, vol. 6, no. 3 (1985), pp. 257–72; also **H. Mintzberg**, 'Learning 1, Planning 0', *California Management Review*, vol. 38, no. 4 (1996), pp. 92–3.
[3] The discussion of markets, industries, and strategic groups draws upon **John Kay's** definitions. For further explanation of what constitutes an industry and market, see *Foundations of Corporate Strategy*, Oxford University Press, 1993, chapter 9.
[4] The terms *competitive strategy* and *business strategy* can be used interchangeably.
[5] **M. E. Porter**, *Competitive Strategy: Techniques for Analysing Industries and Competitors*, Free Press, 1980.
[6] **Porter**, see n. 5 above, p. 35.
[7] For a discussion of value chains, see **M. E. Porter**, *Competitive Advantage*, Free Press, 1985.
[8] **Wayland, M.** (2015), 'Toyota's per-car profits lap Detroit's Big 3 automakers', http://www.detroitnews.com/story/business/autos/2015/02/22/toyota-per-car-profits-beat-ford-gm-chrysler/23852189/whatever.

9   The long-run average total cost (LRATC) curve represents the lowest unit cost at which any specific output can be produced in the long run, when a company is able to adjust the size of its plant.

10   **Porter**, see n. 5 above, p. 45.

11   **Porter**, see n. 5 above, p. 41.

12   **Porter**, see n. 5 above, p. 41.

13   **E. M. Pertusa-Ortega**, **J. F. Molina-Azorín**, and **E. Claver-Corte**, 'Competitive strategies and firm performance: a comparative analysis of pure, hybrid and "stuck-in-the-middle" strategies in Spanish firms', *British Journal of Management*, vol. 20, no. 4 (2009), pp. 508–23.

14   **R. M. Grant**, 'The resource-based theory of competitive advantage: implications for strategy formulation', *California Management Review*, vol. 33 (Spring 1991), pp. 114–35.

15   **Grant**, see n. 14 above, p. 116.

16   **R. R. Nelson** and **S. G. Winter**, *An Evolutionary Theory of Economic Change*, Harvard University Press, 1982.

17   **D. A. Leonard-Barton**, 'Core capabilities and core rigidities: a paradox in managing new product development', *Strategic Management Journal*, vol. 13 (Summer 1992), pp. 111–25.

18   **R. M. Grant** *Contemporary Strategy Analysis*, 9th edn, Wiley, 2016.

19   **J. Barney**, 'Organizational culture: can it be a source of sustained competitive advantage?', *Academy of Management Review*, vol. 11, no. 3 (1986), pp. 656–65; **J. Barney**, 'Looking inside for competitive advantage', *Academy of Management Executive*, vol. 9, no. 4 (1995), pp. 49–61.

20   **M. B. Lieberman** and **D. G. Montgomery**, 'First mover advantages', *Strategic Management Journal*, vol. 9, no. 5 (1988), pp. 41–58.

21   **C. Prahalad** and **G. Hamel**, 'The core competence of the organization', *Harvard Business Review*, vol. 36, no. 3 (1990), pp. 79–91.

22   **G. Hamel** and **C. K. Prahalad**, 'Strategy as stretch and leverage', *Harvard Business Review*, vol. 71, no. 2 (1993), pp. 75–84.

23   This notion of a static framework is rejected by Michael Porter; see **M. E. Porter**, 'What is strategy?', *Harvard Business Review*, vol. 74, no. 6 (1999), pp. 61–78.

24   **C. W. L. Hill**, 'Differentiation versus low cost or differentiation and low cost', *Academy of Management Review*, vol. 13, no. 3 (1988), pp. 401–12; **Pertusa-Ortega et al.**, see n. 13 above.

25   A critique of generic strategies is provided by **C. Campbell-Hunt**, 'What have we learned about generic strategy? A meta-analysis', *Strategic Management Journal*, vol. 21, no. 2 (2000), pp. 127–54.

26   **Kay**, see n. 3 above.

27   **Kay**, see n. 3 above, p. 368.

28   **M. E. Porter**, 'Towards a dynamic theory of strategy', *Strategic Management Journal*, vol. 12 (Special Issue) (1991), pp. 95–117.

29   Empirical support for the resource-based view can be found in **R. Henderson** and **I. Cockburn**, 'Measuring competence? Exploring firm effects in pharmaceutical research', *Strategic Management Journal*, vol. 15 (Special Issue) (1994), pp. 63–84.

30   This section draws upon **W. C. Kim** and **R. Mauborgne**, *Blue Ocean Strategy*, Harvard Business Press (2005).

31   **J. Collins** and **J. Porras**, *Built to Last*, Harper Business, 1994.

32   **R. Foster** and **S. Kaplan**, *Creative Destruction*, Doubleday, 2001.

33   **Foster** and **Kaplan**, see n. 32 above.

34   **Kim** and **Mauborgne**, see n. 30 above, p. 10.

35   **Kim** and **Mauborgne**, see n. 30 above, p. 17.

36   **Kim** and **Mauborgne**, see n. 30 above, pp. 103–4.

37   **Kim** and **Mauborgne**, see n. 30 above, p. 216.

[38] For a discussion of whether sustainable competitive advantage remains a viable aim, see **R. A. D'Aveni**, **G. B. Dagnino**, and **K. G. Smith**, 'The age of temporary advantage', *Strategic Management Journal*, vol. 31, no. 13 (2010), pp. 1371–85; **R. R. Wiggins** and **T. Ruefli**, 'Schumpeter's ghost: is hypercompetition making the best of times shorter?', *Strategic Management Journal*, vol. 26, no. 10 (2005), pp. 887–911; **R. McGrath**, 'Transient advantage', *Harvard Business Review*, vol. 91, no. 6 (2013), pp. 62–70.

[39] **C. M. Christensen**, 'The past and future of competitive advantage', *Sloan Management Review*, vol. 42, no. 2 (2001), pp. 105–9.

[40] **R. A. D'Aveni**, 'Strategic supremacy through disruption and dominance', *Sloan Management Review*, vol. 40, no. 3 (1999), pp. 127–35.

[41] **D'Aveni**, see n. 40 above.

[42] **J. Bower** and **C. M. Christensen**, 'Disruptive technologies: catching the wave', *Harvard Business Review*, vol. 73, no. 1 (1995), pp. 43–53. See also **C. M. Christensen**, *The Innovator's Dilemma: When New Technologies Cause Great Firms to Fail*, Harvard Business Press, 1997; **C. M. Christensen** and **M. Raynor**, *The Innovator's Solution: Creating and Sustaining Successful Growth*, Harvard Business Press, 2003.

[43] For a discussion of disruptive innovation and the misunderstandings surrounding its use, read **C. M. Christensen**, **M. E. Raynor**, and **R. McDonald**, 'What is disruptive innovation?', *Harvard Business Review*, vol. 93, no. 12 (2015), pp. 44–53.

[44] **C. M. Christensen**, **M. E. Raynor**, and **R. McDonald**, 'What is disruptive innovation?', *Harvard Business Review*, vol. 93, no. 12 (2015), pp. 44–53.

[45] **Christensen et al.**, see n. 43 above.

[46] **M. Wessel** and **C. M. Christensen**, 'Surviving disruptive: it's not enough to know that a threat is coming. You need to know whether it's coming right for you', *Harvard Business Review* (2012), pp. 56–64.

[47] **J. Lepore**, 'The disruption machine', *The New Yorker*, 23 June 2014.

[48] **J. Kay**, 'Innovation disrupted by warring gurus', *The Financial Times*, 19 August 2014.

[49] **Christensen** et al., see n. 42 above.

[50] **A. King** and **B. Baatartogtokh**, 'How useful is the theory of disruptive innovation?', *Sloan Management Review*, vol. 57, no. 1 (2015).

CHAPTER 7
CORPORATE STRATEGY

Learning Objectives

After completing this chapter you should be able to:

- Identify different growth strategies available to organizations
- Discuss related and unrelated diversification strategies
- Evaluate mergers and acquisitions, internal developments, joint ventures, and strategic alliances
- Discuss different types of portfolio analysis and explain how they benefit corporate decision-making
- Explain the role of corporate parenting in creating value for corporations
- Explain how a company can differentiate between different strategic options

Introduction

In **Chapter 6** we looked at business strategy and how an organization competes in its chosen markets. In this chapter we turn our attention to corporate strategy. Corporate strategy is concerned with the question: what businesses do we want to compete in? Where an organization is made up of multiple business units, a question arises as to how resources are to be allocated across these businesses. How an organization determines which businesses to invest in and which to divest is covered in this chapter. Clearly, the overall objectives of the organization will be paramount in guiding these decisions. These objectives and, therefore, the overall direction for the organization are determined by the corporate parent.

The role of a corporate parent is to add value across the business units. A measurement of the value being added by the corporate parent is whether it is greater than if the business units were managed independently of the parent, or managed by another corporate parent. Where a corporate parent adds greater value the organization is said to achieve synergy. In formulating a corporate strategy, executives must be mindful of the organization's internal resources and capabilities and how these meet the changing needs of the external environment. The impact of corporate strategy on stakeholders, such as major shareholders, customers, suppliers, local communities, and employees who possess sufficient power and influence to undermine the strategy, must also be considered.

7.1 Corporate Strategy

We noted in previous chapters that all organizations exist for a purpose. Once the purpose of the organization is determined, for instance to maximize shareholder value, the role of corporate strategy is to enable the organization to fulfil that purpose. Therefore, corporate strategy defines the scope of the industries and markets within which the organization competes in order to achieve its purpose. Business strategy, in contrast, determines *how* it will compete successfully in those markets and contribute to the corporate strategy. The managers of a business unit will have considerable autonomy to devise their business strategy. This reflects their knowledge of local markets, customers, and competitors. However, these managers must ultimately show that their business strategy contributes to the corporate strategy.

A corporate strategy sets the direction in which the organization will go. Even where the organization simply comprises a single business with only one or a few products, corporate strategy is relevant. The organization must still consider the fundamental question of why it exists. And once the why (purpose) is answered, a corporate strategy can be formulated that enables the organization to achieve its purpose. Where an organization is made up of many businesses operating in different markets, corporate strategy is also concerned with how resources are to be allocated across these business units. Clearly the objectives of the organization will be paramount in guiding these decisions. These objectives and the overall direction of the organization are determined by the corporate parent.

A question at the forefront of corporate strategy is: how does an organization add value across the businesses that make up the organization? This is the role of **corporate parenting**. A **corporate parent** exists where an organization is made up of multiple business units. It refers to all those levels of management that are not part of customer-facing and profit-run businesses within the multi-business organization. Corporate parents are often described as corporate headquarters and derided as simply *cost centres*. This is because a corporate parent has no external customers and as such it cannot generate any direct revenues. Given that it incurs corporate overhead costs, the corporate parent must demonstrate that these costs are offset by the tangible benefits it provides to the business units in the portfolio. The question then becomes: what is the corporate parent doing which allows these businesses to perform better collectively than they would as stand-alone units?[1]

Corporate parenting is of benefit if the corporate parent adds greater value by its management and coordination of these individual business units. The idea is that by effectively managing the related capabilities in each business unit, as well as leveraging its management skills across these units, a corporate parent can achieve synergy. **Synergy** occurs when the total output from combining businesses is greater than the output of the businesses operating individually. It is often described mathematically as '2 + 2 = 5'. For example, it can derive from economies of scale such as occur when two business units decide to combine their manufacturing facilities, which results in lower unit costs. As a result, the value of the combined businesses is greater than the value that can be derived from two separate businesses.

7.2 **Growth Strategies**

In order to grow, organizations can pursue a number of different strategies depending on the level of risk they are prepared to countenance, their capabilities, and their management expertise. The organization might choose to direct its energies to internal growth strategies or it may seek to diversify into other businesses. Igor Ansoff devised a matrix to analyse the different strategic directions organizations can pursue.[2]

There are four strategies that an organization might follow: *market penetration*, *product development*, *market development*, and *diversification*. These options are summarized below and shown in **Figure 7.1**:

● **Market penetration**: increasing market share in your existing markets using your existing products.

● **Market development**: entering new markets with your existing products.

● **Product development**: developing new products to sell in your existing markets.

● **Diversification**: developing new products to serve new markets.

The first three strategies are particularly relevant to organizations that operate within the boundaries of an individual business. However, an organization that seeks to broaden its scope of activities will be concerned with how it can best diversify into different businesses. This issue of the multi-business organization is addressed in detail when we look at diversification.

7.2.1 **Market Penetration**

An organization pursuing a strategy of market penetration seeks to increase the market share in its existing markets by using its existing products. Its aim is to attract new consumers and get existing consumers to increase their usage of the product or service. This strategy relies upon the organization's existing resources and capabilities and, therefore, is relatively low risk. To achieve market penetration, the organization will usually improve its product quality and levels of service, backed by promotional spend. Its knowledge of both products and the markets should enable it to respond more readily to changing

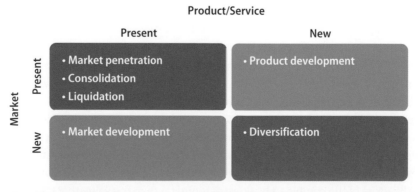

Figure 7.1   **Ansoff's growth matrix.** Source: I. H. Ansoff, 'Strategies for diversification', *Harvard Business Review*, vol. 35, no. 2 (1957), pp. 113–24. Reproduced with permission of *Harvard Business Review*.

consumer needs. When the market is growing, market penetration is relatively simple to achieve. However, in a mature market, a strategy of market penetration implies taking market share from your competitor which will invite retaliation. If demand conditions are insufficient to permit market penetration, the organization must decide whether it can still retain its existing market share, or whether it would be wiser to exit the industry. This strategy is shown in the first quadrant of **Figure 7.1**.

7.2.2 Product Development

This strategy involves developing new products for your existing markets. The ability to innovate is crucial in developing products for rapidly changing consumer markets. A strategy of product development is necessary where organizations are faced with shorter product life cycles. In industries such as consumer electronics organizations are forced to develop new products continually to maintain and grow their market share, and keep competitors on the defensive. The phenomenal growth of Apple's iPod, iTunes, and iPhone is testimony to the rewards that successful product development brings. A challenge is that new product development can be expensive and carries a greater risk of failure; witness the lacklustre performance of the Apple Watch. There is no guarantee that consumers will adopt the product. An organization that actively monitors consumers is more likely to develop products that meet customer needs. However, a more successful strategy is to develop products that *create* consumer need, as Apple has been able to do.

7.2.3 Market Development

Market development involves entering new markets with a company's existing products. This may be done by targeting new market segments and new geographical areas, or by devising new uses for its products. The existing product may undergo some slight modification to ensure that it fits these new markets better. This is often the case where certain social and cultural adjustments are made to ensure that the product more closely meets the needs of particular geographical market segments. Many retailing organizations follow this route to growth. For example, the US giant Walmart, French retailer Carrefour, and UK retailer Tesco have all sought to enter new geographical markets with only marginal changes to their product offerings. As with the previous strategies, market development builds on a company's existing resources and capabilities. Although the company will have extensive knowledge of its product, its experience of new markets will be less complete, thus increasing the level of risk.

7.2.4 Diversification

The fourth quadrant in the growth vector matrix is diversification. Here we are dealing with a company that seeks to broaden its scope of activities by moving away from its current products and markets and into new products and new markets. Although this will involve the greatest level of risk, it may be necessary where an organization's existing products and markets offer little opportunity for growth. However, this risk can be mitigated by the organization diversifying into related businesses—that is, businesses that have some links with its existing value chain. In addition, broadening the scope of the organization can help to spread risk by reducing the reliance on any one market or product. When the scope of an organization takes it into unrelated markets, there may still be a sound business logic for the decision. This is particularly true where a business is cyclical in nature. By diversifying into another business it may be possible to smooth these cycles so that a peak period in one market coincides with a downturn in another market. This issue of the multi-business organization is addressed in **Section 7.3**, when we discuss *related* and *unrelated* *diversification*.

7.3 Related Diversification

Related diversification refers to entry into a related industry in which there is still some link with the organization's value chain. Where an organization occupies a competitive advantage in an industry that is becoming increasingly unattractive, it may wish to diversify into a related industry or market. The aim is to enter a market where there is a close match with the capabilities that provide success in its current markets, and thereby generate synergy. For example, Honda possesses distinctive capabilities in engine design and manufacture. This allows Honda to leverage its capability in engine production into related markets such as motorcycles, lawnmowers, and outboard engines. Related diversification can be separated into **vertical integration** and **horizontal integration**. Vertical integration occurs when an organization goes *upstream*, towards its inputs, or *downstream*, closer to its ultimate consumer. The more control an organization has over the different stages of its value chain, the more vertically integrated it is. Horizontal integration takes place when an organization takes over a competitor or offers complementary products at the same stage within the value chain. We can look at each of these in greater detail.

7.3.1 Vertical Integration

We can differentiate between two kinds of vertical integration. **Vertical integration backwards** occurs when an organization moves upstream towards its inputs. A company may desire to have greater control over the inputs or raw materials that go to make up its products. For example, the British supermarket retailer Morrisons grows many of its own vegetables and is Britain's biggest abattoir owner. Vertical integration allows it to be nimble in delivering promotions on fresh food. Where the costs of inputs to its productive processes fluctuate, a company may decide that it is in its best interest to own these inputs. Similarly, an organization may feel it necessary to have control over the quality of its inputs or may want to gain access to new technologies. Clearly, an organization must decide if the value it derives from owning an asset is greater than the value to be derived from outsourcing it. In some instances, the input will simply be too important to the organization for it to allow it to be outsourced.

   Vertical integration forward occurs when an organization moves downstream towards its end consumers. In such a case, an organization might acquire transport and warehousing to ensure its control over the channels of distribution to the consumer. It may acquire retail outlets to ensure that it chooses where, when, how, and at what price its products are sold. Whether the organization adopts vertical integration forward or backward, the end result is the same: it moves along its value chain and secures greater control over its value-chain activities. Examples of vertically integrated companies occur in the oil industry. Companies such as ExxonMobil, Shell, and BP often adopt a vertically integrated structure allowing them to operate along the supply chain from crude oil explo-ration all the way to refined product sale. A downside of vertical integration is that the organization becomes increasingly dependent on a particular market and may be unable to respond quickly to market changes.

7.3.2 Horizontal Integration

Horizontal integration occurs when an organization takes over a competitor or offers complemen-tary products at the same stage within its value chain. HSBC was able to acquire market share in the UK when it took over Midland Bank. Walt Disney acquired Marvel Entertainment for $4 billion (£2.5 billion). Both companies promote popular characters around the world on media platform and through third-party licensing deals. Disney was also able to monetize Marvel's 5,000 characters across its entire ecosystem from television channels to theme parks, movies, consumer products and video games providing opportunities for long-term growth and value creation. A rationale for horizontal integration is efficiency savings through economies of scale. By combining two separate organizations, it is argued that economies of scale can be achieved far faster than through organic (internal) growth.

7.3.3 Transaction-Cost Analysis

To understand **transaction-cost analysis** it is helpful to appreciate why organizations exist. Organi-zations exist because they are capable of undertaking transactions more efficiently than individuals can in the marketplace. All transactions undertaken between individuals, between companies, or between individuals and companies involve **transaction costs**. These transaction costs include: the *search costs* involved in making a purchase, such as the time involved in collecting information about the quality or price of a product; the costs involved in *negotiating* and drawing up a contract that tries to cover as many eventualities as possible; and the costs of *monitoring* the other party to ensure their legal obligations are fulfilled. In the event of the agreement being reneged upon, there is the cost of *enforcement* through the courts.

According to **Oliver Williamson**, transaction-cost analysis implies that organizations should pro-duce goods and services internally where the transaction costs of doing so are less than purchasing these on the open market.[3] Therefore, transaction-cost analysis provides a rationale for organizations to assess whether to integrate vertically. For instance, when organizations integrate vertically and operate at different points along their value chain, there may be a tendency for them to be become too large and overly bureaucratic. Where the administrative costs of managing their internal transac-tions are greater than the transaction costs occurring within the market, outsourcing these activities to a third-party specialist is a more efficient option. Where this is the case, the imposition of contracts ensures that third-party producers supply products and services at an acceptable quality and price. However, where transaction costs are much greater than administrative costs, the organization may choose vertical integration.

Many organizations actively seek to outsource activities in which they add less value. The benefit is one of efficiency gains achieved through outsourcing to a specialist provider and flexibility in being able to respond more readily to market changes.

7.4 **Unrelated or Conglomerate Diversification**

Unrelated diversification refers to a situation where an organization moves into a totally un-related market. It is sometimes called **conglomerate diversification** to reflect that it involves managing a portfolio of companies. The lack of any link between existing markets and products and the diversified industry carries the greatest element of uncertainty and, therefore, risk. It may be that the organization's management skills are sufficiently robust to provide it with a ca-pability that can be leveraged across different business units. This was certainly the case with the British conglomerate Hanson and BTR, which experienced success in the twentieth century. As with all strategic decisions, the rationale for diversification needs to be clearly thought out. Man-agement complacency or poorly prepared analysis will simply multiply the likelihood of failure. A common reason for diversification is an organization's existing markets having been saturated or declining. In such a case, the organization will seek growth opportunities elsewhere. These opportunities may also more closely reflect the organization's development of its own capabili-ties. Another reason for conglomerate diversification might be that regulatory authorities view vertical and horizontal integration by the company as uncompetitive. A third reason for diversifi-cation is that management may believe that by not having all their eggs in one basket (focusing on one market or product range) they can diversify risk. If an organization operates across many different businesses, the failure of one business will not cause the company to collapse. By the turn of the century, organizations had internalized the mantra of Peters and Waterman of 'stick to the knitting' as they began to de-layer, downsize, and divest themselves of all non-core busi-ness activities.[4]

Michael Porter's study of the activities of large prestigious US companies between 1950 and 1986 found that the majority of them had divested more acquisitions than they had retained.[5] Porter sug-gests the reason for some acquisitions is more often the result of chief executives' ego than the exist-ence of a market opportunity. Constantinos Markides found that an organization's decision to focus upon its core business is the most useful form of restructuring.[6] Other research points to the increase in the share price of parent organizations that sell off unrelated activities.[7] This adds weight to sug-gestions that conglomerate diversification may be more in the interest of managers as agents rather than shareholders as principals. Hence the stock market rewards organizations that divest them-selves of unrelated diversification with a rise in share price, signalling that this strategy is viewed as more appropriate for adding value.

Diversification may have become less popular, but there still remain stellar examples of success-fully diversified companies such as Tata Group, Berkshire Hathaway, and GE. The US giant GE is lo-cated in more than 130 countries and operates nine unrelated businesses.[8] Under the leadership of chief executive and chairman Jack Welch, GE transformed itself throughout the 1980s and 1990s from a maker of electrical appliances to a giant conglomerate. With his 'number one, number two' objective, Welch only operated or acquired businesses which could be number one or number two in their market.[9] Any businesses that did not perform or could not be improved to meet that objective were closed or sold. Welch changed the company's focus away from products towards high-value services and turned it into a global corporation. GE continues to operate a series of diverse compa-nies from aviation to health care.

7.4.1 Can Conglomerate Diversification Succeed?

The Indian conglomerate, Tata Group, is a 152-year-old business empire spanning companies from manufacturing to airlines, retail, and consultancy services. At the turn of the millennium it embarked on an overseas acquisition programme. Tata acquired Jaguar Land Rover, Tetley, and Anglo-Dutch steelmaker Corus. Having started operations under British colonial rule, Tata became the UK's leading industrial employer in a proud symbol of the shifting balance of twenty-first-century economic power.[10] Founded by Jamsetji Tata in 1868, the group operates in more than 100 countries across six continents, with a mission 'To improve the quality of life of the communities we serve globally, through long-term stakeholder value creation based on Leadership with Trust'. (See **Strategy in Focus 7.1** for a discussion of organizations that continue to follow a diversification strategy.)

Warren Buffett is chairman of Berkshire Hathaway which he runs with his business partner, Charlie Munger, and is one of the richest men in the world.[11] Berkshire Hathaway is a diversified holding company and investment firm that includes diverse interests in insurance, soft drinks, confectionery, furniture, restaurants, carpets, and plane rentals. The billionaire investor spends his time as the head of Berkshire buying up troubled businesses and turning them around. Its subsidiaries include companies such as Duracell, Heinz, NetJets, and Fruit of the Loom. His strategy appears to have little to do with exploiting synergies across these businesses.

Berkshire Hathaway experienced a compound annual return of 20.5 per cent since it began trading in 1965, against 10 per cent for the S&P 500 index.[12] During the Internet boom of the 1990s, when fund managers talked of the new economy and a new investment paradigm, Buffett wisely sat out the fleeting dot.com era preferring instead to stick to his *old economy portfolio*. This became one more reason for his richly deserved accolade, the Oracle or Sage of Omaha. In 2019, Berkshire increased its per-share market value by 11 per cent; the S&P 500 index rose by 31.5 per cent over the same period.[13] This is one of a very few cases when the stock market has beaten Berkshire Hathaway's performance. Over time, however, the company has comfortably beaten the S&P 500 index.

 STRATEGY IN FOCUS 7.1 Conglomerate Diversification

In engaging in conglomerate diversification, business leaders adopt the rationale that a number of companies exist that are poorly managed and underperforming. The aim then is to incorporate these companies within the conglomerate with a view to restructuring them to release value. In the UK, Hanson Trust and BTR were industry giants that dominated the conglomerate game. In the 1980s Hanson regularly outperformed the FTSE 100 with its ever-growing revenues and profit. BTR was seen as one of the best-managed companies into the 1990s. However, by the mid-1990s market sentiment had moved against these conglomerates, as the environment in which both firms competed had begun to change beyond their theory of the business. Undoubtedly leadership succession also played a role, as the calibres of the original leaders were difficult to replicate.

Today successful diversified conglomerates, such as GE and Berkshire Hathaway in the USA, still exist. In India, the Tata Group has wide-ranging interests that include engineering, chemicals, consumer products, information technology and communications, and energy, among others. It has acquired many high-profile British companies such as Corus, the steel maker (now part of Tata Steel), Jaguar Land Rover, and the Tetley tea brand. Other examples include the French multinational conglomerate Louis Vuitton Moët Hennessy, commonly known as LVMH, which specializes in luxury goods. There is also Reliance Industries Limited (RIL) an Indian conglomerate headquartered in Mumbai, Maharashtra, India. Reliance owns businesses across India which include energy, petrochemicals, textiles, retail, and telecommunications. Its disruption of the telecoms sector using its Reliance Jio subsidiary is proving particularly successful. Western companies from Facebook to Google have flocked to India to invest in the burgeoning telecoms sector via an alliance with Reliance Jio.

Where a company is poorly managed and underperforming, restructuring it using cost controls and customer-focused measures to release value may be relatively straightforward. However, as we will see later in this chapter, a question that needs to be addressed is: can a parent company release more value from its acquisitions (related or unrelated) than can be released by a rival organization? Or, to adopt a resource-based view, can an acquirer deploy its distinctive capabilities effectively in an acquired business to release value? The value created by an acquisition must outweigh the cost of the acquisition. Where a substantial bid premium has been paid this becomes more difficult to achieve.

We might note that diversification is often rationalized by managers in terms of risk reduction. Yet if shareholders require a diversified portfolio of shares they can achieve this far more cheaply than an organization because the cost of buying shares in a company is cheaper than buying the company, which inevitably attracts a bid premium. This is the reason many commentators argue that diversification is often in the interests of the managers of diversifying companies, and not their shareholders.

Michael Goold and Kathleen Luchs point out that an assumption that the pursuit of synergy is the only rationale for having a group of companies tends to contradict the available evidence.[14] This suggests that not all corporations should focus their management effort on acquiring and managing a portfolio of interrelated businesses. They argue that the ultimate test of diversification is that the businesses in the portfolio are worth more under the management of the corporate parent than they would be under any other rival organization. These ideas are developed in detail when we discuss corporate parenting in **Section 7.7**. Research by Goold and Luchs indicates that conglomerate diversifications with a sound rationale and clear vision can achieve synergy. A body of research exists that shows that unrelated diversification tends not to be as successful as related diversification.[15] Nonetheless, this issue is not clear cut, as Goold and Luchs point out: '*despite extensive research, empirical evidence on the performance of companies pursuing more and less related diversification strategies is ambiguous and contradictory*'.[16] The examples of Tata Group, Alibaba, Tencent, and Berkshire Hathaway show that a carefully managed conglomerate can produce a sound growth strategy.

7.5 Implementing Growth Strategies

We have seen that in pursuing a strategy of growth the organization is faced with either concentrating on its existing markets or diversifying into new markets. We can now turn our attention to looking at how these different growth strategies can be implemented (see **Figure 7.2**). This includes *mergers* and *acquisitions*, *internal developments*, *joint ventures*, and *strategic alliances*.

7.5.1 Mergers and Acquisitions

A popular way for companies to grow is via mergers and acquisitions. A **merger** occurs when two organizations join together to share their combined resources. A merger implies that both organizations accept the logic of combining into a single organization and willingly agree to do so. Shareholders from each organization become shareholders in the new combined organization. An **acquisition** occurs when one organization seeks to acquire another (often smaller) organization. The acquisition may be in the interest of both organizations, particularly where the acquiring company has substantial financial resources and the company being acquired possesses proprietary technology, but needs funds to develop it further. The acquisition may be in the form of shares of the new organization, and perhaps a cash payment. Where payment is only in the form of cash, the acquired shareholders will no longer be owners. Clearly, where the shareholders feel the price being paid for their shareholding represents fair value they will be more likely to concede ownership.[17]

However, where the acquisition is unwelcome and contested it is referred to as a *takeover*, specifically a *hostile takeover*. In a hostile takeover, the board of directors of the takeover target is likely to say one of two things: first, that the offer being made undervalues the organization and, therefore, should be rejected; and second, that the strategies being proposed by the takeover organization are incoherent and will not allow the true value embedded within the target company to be released. The terms 'mergers' and 'acquisitions' are often used interchangeably, hence the term M&A, which is often seen in the financial press. If we look at the evidence on mergers and acquisitions, it tends not to support them as a way of achieving sustainable growth.

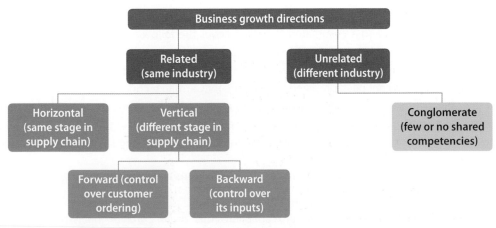

Figure 7.2   Growth strategies.

In 2013 Microsoft acquired the handset and services business of Nokia for $7.2 billion in an auda-cious effort to transform Microsoft's mobile business. The deal was brokered by former Microsoft CEO Steve Ballmer, stating that Microsoft and Nokia had not been as agile separately as they would be jointly, citing how development could be slowed down when intellectual property rights were held by two different companies. Clearly, Microsoft executives thought buying their way into the mobile market was faster and less expensive than building the business organically. By 2015 the deal had soured, resulting in staff lay-offs and massive restructuring charges for Microsoft.

In 2016 the UK supermarket Sainsbury's took over Home Retail Group, which includes Argos and Homebase, for £1.4 billion. The rationale behind the deal was access to Argos's home delivery and digital expertise. In addition, Sainsbury's expected cost savings of £500 million from relocating Argos stores into Sainsbury's supermarkets, and click and collect points within smaller convenience stores. In 2020, Sainsbury's continued to cut hundreds of management jobs as it looked to integrate its com-mercial, retail, finance, technology and HR teams across Sainsbury's and Argos, and make efficiencies. At the same time, it was also seeking to manage the onslaught from German discounters, Aldi and Lidl, which have taken market share from the largest 'big four' UK supermarkets.

The disastrous takeover of Dutch bank ABN Amro by The Royal Bank of Scotland (RBS), the Belgian–Dutch bank Fortis and Banco Santander of Spain is a salutary lesson. The consortium paid €71 billion ($98.5 billion; £49 billion) for part of the Dutch lender—three times the book value. By the time RBS, then led by its CEO Sir Fred Goodwin, had secured the ABN Amro deal, the Dutch bank had sold on to Bank of America the asset which was most prized by RBS—its Chicago-based LaSalle unit. The price RBS paid for a lack of due diligence is the toxic assets it acquired with ABN and a reliance on UK government bailouts. The Belgian–Dutch bank Fortis was nationalized by the Dutch government to avert a liquidity crisis. In 2020, the UK Treasury said it would 'fully dispose' of its 62 per cent stake in the bank by the end of March 2025, a year later than planned. The Office for Budget Responsibility estimated that UK taxpayers would make a loss of £32.1 billion on the £45 billion bailout of the bank during the financial crisis in 2008.[18]

An organization may seek to implement a mergers and acquisitions route to growth for a number of different reasons. For example, to enter new markets quickly or acquire capabilities it does not possess. A key issue with acquiring another organization's assets is whether value is being created or destroyed. Many mergers and acquisitions that appear to exhibit sound business logic often fail miserably to live up to the pre-merger hype and expectations. A case in point was the merger of Ger-many's luxury car maker Daimler Benz with US automobile maker Chrysler to form DaimlerChrysler. This was initially billed as a merger of equals. In fact, the merger with Chrysler cost Daimler Benz $36 billion (£18 billion) and an estimated $50 billion over the following ten years.[19] Chrysler was eventually sold to private equity group Cerberus in 2007. Daimler's chief executive, Dieter Zetsche, conceded that the expected synergies between the organizations had been over-estimated, arguing that US consumers had not been prepared to pay more for German technology.[20]

If the objective of a merger and acquisition is to increase market share, one would expect the organization to engage in a strategy of horizontal integration. Where the organization is concerned about its inputs, for example, we might expect it to go upstream and engage in vertical integration.

The major benefits to be derived from mergers and acquisitions are as follows:

(i) Access to capabilities

M&As are a much quicker way to acquire capabilities than *organic growth*, that is, trying to develop in capabilities which a company lacks in-house. R&D takes time and buying a company with proprietary knowledge is an effective way to gain access to capabilities which may take years to develop in-house. For example, in 2020 Facebook paid about $400 million to acquire Giphy, which hosts a search engine for animated images known as GIFs, with a view to integrating the company's image library into Instagram and other apps.

(ii) Market entry

M&As enable a company to gain entry to markets where it has limited or no presence. It can also provide a way to enter new geographical areas without the difficulty of having to build the supplier networks. For example, Microsoft, which has a limited presence in social media, was seeking to buy TikTok which would allow it to enter a market dominated by rivals such as Facebook and Twitter. TikTok is a social network that has taken the world by storm with its viral videos. It has exploded in popularity, particularly among teenagers, with its viral-friendly features, facilitated by a suite of editing and visual effects tools. The app is owned by China's ByteDance.

(iii) Market share

A company can increase its market share by taking over a rival organization and seeking to consolidate the market. Sainsbury's and Asda planned a £7.3 billion supermarket merger in 2019, which would have provided them with a market share greater than the market leader, Tesco. The merger was, however, blocked by the Competition and Markets Authority on competition grounds. The CMA argued the proposed merger was 'more likely to lead to price rises than price cuts'. In 2016, the £79 billion takeover of SABMiller by AB InBev, the makers of Budweiser and Stella Artois, gave AB InBev a dominant position in the brewing industry. The acquisition was intended to boost its position in Africa and Asia where SABMiller had a strong market presence.

(iv) Speed

M&As allow for opportunities in the market to be exploited more efficiently. Where the technology is advancing quickly and there is a need to develop new and improved products, developing products organically may be too slow. M&As provide an opportunity to acquire specific knowledge and expertise quickly, thus providing you with rapid access to markets and products.

The disadvantages of mergers and acquisitions include the following:

(i) Paying a premium price for the acquired company and increasing your financial risk

In 2016, Microsoft's CEO, Satya Nadella, placed the company's biggest ever bet on the acquisition of LinkedIn, a social network used by professionals to make contacts and change jobs. Although LinkedIn has in recent years lost money, Nadella is buying access to billions of data points created when LinkedIn's 433 million users interact.[21] In 2020, AB InBev's shares had lost more than 60 per of their pre-merger value following concerns about its debt burden, which stood at $87.4 billion. This, despite efforts to win back investor confidence, by halving its dividend, replacing its chairman, and promising to sell more assets.

The legendary US investor Warren Buffett publicly derided Kraft's takeover of Cadbury as 'a bad deal', stating that Kraft's use of its shares in the Cadbury deal was 'very expensive currency'. Buffett, Kraft's largest shareholder with more than 9 per cent of shares, argued that the $1.3 billion (£798 million) of reorganization costs and $390 million of deal fees would offset any added value.

(ii) The problems of post-merger integration

The issues of combining different cultures may not have been properly considered, such that any reorganization is slow to release value to stakeholders. The failed merger of DaimlerChrysler suffered from post-merger integration, as well as unrealized synergies, as the combined group struggled with a conflicting American and German culture.

Porter suggests three criteria for increasing shareholder value in acquisitions:

1. **Attractiveness**. An organization should be capable of achieving above-average returns in the target company's industry. This would imply the industry is attractive, with barriers to entry which prevent profits being competed away.

2. **Cost of entry**. This includes the capital sum paid for the acquisition, also costs such as the time it takes for management to integrate the organizations. The cost of entry should not be so expensive that it effectively prohibits the organization from recouping its initial investment. This is all too often the case where companies have paid a high premium for an acquisition.

3. **Competitive advantage or better-off**. The acquisition must present an opportunity for competitive advantage for the parent company, or the acquired business. An organization should only consider acquiring another business if substantial synergies can be achieved.

Kay argues that added value or synergy is *only* forthcoming when distinctive capabilities or strategic assets are exploited more effectively. As a result, a merger that results in the acquisition of distinctive capabilities that are already being exploited adds no value.

7.5.2 Internal Development

Another route to growth is internal development. This is sometimes referred to as organic growth (see **Case Study: Organic Growth at Aldi**). It involves the organization using its own resources and developing the capabilities it believes will be necessary to compete in the future. Many organizations start their growth trajectory using organic growth and consider mergers and acquisitions as their industry matures. In reality, organizations simultaneously pursue a strategy of internal development and simply capitalize on acquisition opportunities as they arise.

The benefits of internal development are:

(i)   the organization experiences less financial risk;

(ii) it grows at a rate that it is able to control;

(iii) the learning that takes place within the company is captured for its own benefit; and

(iv) the organization does not need to use valuable resources trying to manage different cultures.

The main disadvantages of internal development are:

(i)   the time it takes the organization to build up necessary strategic capabilities. Stalk reminds us that the ways in which leading companies manage time represent the most powerful source of competitive advantage;[22]

(ii) with product cycle times reducing, a company developing internally may not be able to exploit market opportunities; and

(iii) where barriers to entry exist, a strategy of mergers and acquisitions may be necessary to enter the industry.

CASE STUDY Organic Growth at Aldi

It's been over a decade since German discount supermarkets Aldi and Lidl began to compete fiercely against the established 'Big Four' British supermarkets. Both stores had been slowly growing in the UK for many years, but the over-optimistic expansion of Tesco, Sainsbury's, Asda, and Morrisons created a window of opportunity. Also, since the financial crash, many shoppers were happy to turn from frequenting supermarkets that offered a vast range of different products to discount supermarkets, which offered less product choice but good quality, and especially low prices. With their under-populated hypermarkets, Tesco and the major competitors were woefully unprepared for the price war that the German 'discounters' unleashed.

By 2017 Aldi had overtaken the Co-op to become Britain's fifth biggest supermarket by market share, according to data from the consulting company Kantar, while Lidl was closing in on Waitrose for seventh place (see **Figure 7.3**). In May 2017, Aldi commanded 7 per cent of the UK grocery market, and Lidl was on 5 per cent (see **Figure 7.4a**). By May 2019 Aldi had attained a new record high market share of 8 per cent. The German-headquartered discount grocer has seen its market share increase since it launched in the UK in 1990. In July 2019 Aldi was voted Britain's favourite supermarket at the Good Housekeeping Food Awards 2019, as well as being crowned favourite wine retailer.

Aldi was also named the UK's lowest priced supermarket by trade magazine *The Grocer* in the same year. When compared with its nearest-priced competitor, Asda, a customer could save £4.47 on a basket of thirty-three everyday items and £18.22 compared with its most expensive competitor Waitrose. Aldi's Managing Director of Buying said: 'We're continuing to work hard to keep prices low for our customers, as well as expanding our store network to reach even more shoppers.' Aldi operates more than 890 stores and employs around 35,000 people across the UK and is hoping to operate more than 1,200 by 2025. To put that in perspective, Morrisons has just under 500 stores (though the stores are much bigger), while Tesco has more than 6,000, including its Express con-

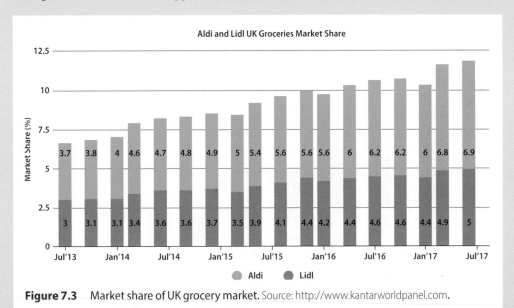

Figure 7.3   Market share of UK grocery market. Source: http://www.kantarworldpanel.com.

venience stores. By July 2020, Aldi was reportedly planning to recruit 1,200 new employees in the UK despite the widespread job loss in the retail industry due to the COVID-19 crisis.

Without a depreciating UK property portfolio Aldi and Lidl continue to expand into the gaps their rivals are leaving. Lidl plans to invest £500 million ramping up its presence in London, opening forty new stores over the next five years in a region where it has traditionally found it difficult to expand. In 2019, the chief executive of Lidl's UK business said 'It's coming up to twenty-five years since we first launched in London, and in that time we've grown to almost ninety stores, employing more than 5,000 people. London is at the heart of our growth plans across Great Britain.' Aldi, while expanding across the UK, plans expansion in London where their market share is just 3.4 per cent, compared to 8.1 per cent nationally. Aldi UK and Ireland chief executive officer added: 'For almost three decades we've proven that investment equals growth—investment in our infrastructure, our people and our prices. The commitment we have made to our customers to continue investing in the UK over the coming years remains as strong as ever.'

The coronavirus pandemic did provide relief for Tesco and Sainsbury's in 2020 as the UK's two biggest supermarkets increased sales at a faster rate than discounter Aldi for the first time in a decade, as the pandemic encouraged weekly shops and doing more online ordering. Since the lockdown began on March 2020, all supermarkets have been helped by a trend towards larger spend in each trip. Tesco and Sainsbury's have also been boosted by their ability to expand their home delivery and click-and-collect operations. Both have effectively doubled the number of orders they can dispatch in a week, to 1.2 million and 600,000 respectively, by hiring thousands of extra pickers and van drivers. Aside from higher transaction values, the main driver of growth at Aldi and Lidl continues to be new stores. Neither company offers online grocery ordering although Aldi did recently start a trial at a small number of stores.

Clearly, COVID-19 had been a massive boost to online grocery, and the discounters had no ready answer to online grocery orders. Online grocery tends to go against their entire corporate DNA, said an analyst, adding, 'They have done trials all over the world and none of them has really worked.'

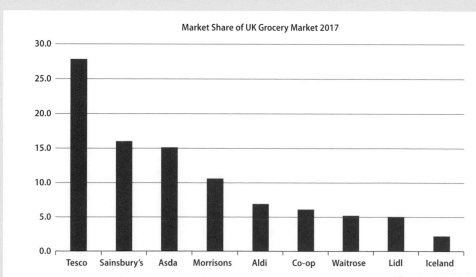

Figure 7.4a Aldi and Lidl UK groceries market share. Source: 'Why Aldi and Lidl will keep on growing', *Management Today*, 27 June 2017.

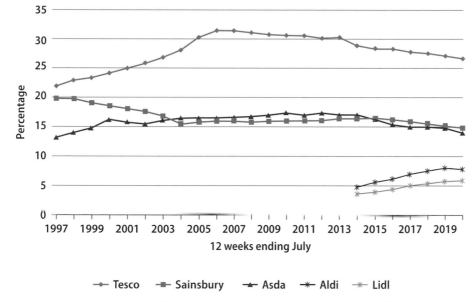

Figure 7.4b Market share of Tesco, Sainsbury's, Asda, Aldi, and Lidl since 1997.
Source: https://stirlingretail.com/2020/07/28/grocery-market-shares-in-the-uk-2020.

What state the UK economy will be in post COVID-19 will be key to which companies gain market share. A recession would help discounters, but gains in market share might be less than the one that followed the financial crisis because the 'Big Four' have improved their pricing competitiveness.

Those who would hope Aldi and Lidl are just going to go away will be disappointed. Aldi and Lidl have permanently changed the dynamics of the grocery market by forcing down margins, while the big supermarkets will need to continue shutting their less profitable stores to shore up their balance sheets. The discounters, on the other hand, have low prices built into their business models from the beginning, emphasizing bulk over brand and price over range. As Giles Hurley, Aldi chief executive stated, 'We have a unique business model and the critical advantage of private ownership means we can run the business for the long term.' He added. 'We've never focused on short-term profits. We focus on sales, stores, and customer numbers. We're not like other supermarkets.'

Source: Myles McCormick and Jonathan Eley, 'Lidl to ramp up London presence with £500m investment', *The Financial Times*, 12 June 2019; Adam Gale, 'Why Aldi and Lidl will keep on growing' *Management Today*, 27 June 2017; https://www.retail-insight-network.com/features/aldi-market-share-uk (accessed September 2020); https://www.retail-insight-network.com/news/aldi-double-uk-stores-portfolio (accessed September 2020); Jonathan Eley, 'Aldi profits dented by grocer's expansion in London', *The Financial Times*, 16 September 2019; Jonathan Eley, 'Tesco and Sainsbury's sales outpace Aldi for first time in a decade', *The Financial Times*, 27 May 2020.

Questions

1. How is Aldi able to continue gaining market share from the 'Big Four' UK supermarkets?

2. What are the benefits and disadvantages to Aldi of growing its business organically?

3. Discuss whether the UK supermarket sector will continue to grow organically or might consolidate via mergers and acquisitions.

7.5.3 Joint Ventures and Strategic Alliances

A company may decide that it is in its interest to collaborate with one or more organizations in order to achieve a specific objective. The agreement between such organizations may only be temporary, and can range from the establishment of a formal entity to a looser organizational arrangement. Collaboration continues to grow over time as companies recognize the benefits that cooperation may bring. A key reason for the expansion in cooperative ventures is the growth in international markets. A company that lacks the crucial market intelligence necessary to operate in overseas markets stands a greater chance of success if it collaborates with an established overseas competitor.

Joint Ventures

A joint venture exists when two organizations form a separate independent company in which they own shares equally. It is often formed when organizations feel it may be beneficial to:

(i)   combine their resources and capabilities to develop new technologies; or

(ii) gain access to new markets.

For example, the cost of developing a European long-haul airliner proved prohibitive for any one country. By entering into a collaborative alliance the UK, France, Germany, and Italy have formed the European Airbus consortium and successfully developed the A380, the world's largest passenger plane, at a greatly reduced risk. Each nation has contributed its own distinctive capabilities to ensure that they develop a product which will successfully compete with their US competitor, Boeing.

Organizations that are restricted from owning foreign assets outright may enter into a joint venture with a foreign partner as a means of gaining access to inputs or lucrative markets. For example, as China and India continue to globalize they seek to benefit from access to Western technology and funding by entering into joint ventures. At the same time, Western organizations gain access to massive consumer markets. However, the existence of a mass market does not automatically translate into profitability. For example, after gaining entry to the Chinese market, Tesco was forced to sell its joint venture in China for £275 million to its partner, China Resources Holdings.

Strategic Alliances

Strategic alliances take place when two or more separate organizations share some of their resources and capabilities, but stop short of forming a separate organization. The benefit is that each partner within the strategic alliance:

(i)   gains access to knowledge it would not otherwise possess;

(ii)   gains access to knowledge that would be expensive for it to develop; and

(iii) reduces competitive rivalry.

A useful alliance will involve complementary resources and capabilities which allow both organizations to grow and develop according to their strategic objectives. Gary Hamel and his colleagues argue that a strategic alliance may be useful to strengthen both companies against outside rivals, even if in the process it weakens one of them vis-à-vis the other.[23] Therefore, alliances may be viewed as competition in a different form. The ultimate aim of strategic alliances is to learn from your partners. The more focused companies view each alliance as an opportunity to view their partners' broad capabilities. They use the alliance to build new skills and systematically diffuse all new knowledge they acquire throughout their organizations.

Both joint venture and strategic alliances are less likely to succeed:

(i) when each partner's objectives are unclear and not agreed;

(ii) when the working relationship is not based on trust.

Where managerial differences exist these must be resolved prior to entering into the joint venture or strategic alliance. See **Strategy in Focus 7.2** which highlights the benefits of a strategic alliance between a Japanese biotechnology company and a Swiss pharmaceutical.

STRATEGY IN FOCUS 7.2 A Swiss-Japanese strategic alliance that thrived in the crisis

It was the start of one of the most unusual cross-cultural marriages when Roche bought a controlling stake in Chugai Pharmaceutical for $1.4 billion back in 2002, promising arm's length management. In the course of the eighteen months of negotiations it took to reach a deal, Chugai, a Japanese pioneer in biotechnology, presented a single sheet of paper with a list of conditions it would not budge on, the main ones being management autonomy and the continued listing of its shares in Tokyo.

If anyone described the deal as a merger, Chugai, with annual revenue less than a tenth of its Swiss parent, quietly corrected this to 'strategic alliance', but few took those words at face value. Nearly two decades later, the partnership has not only survived but has prospered during the coronavirus crisis, with the two companies now trialling their rheumatoid arthritis drug Actemra as a potential treatment for people who are critically ill with COVID-19.

With investors pinning their hopes on the drug, Chugai passed a new milestone in June 2020, replacing Sony as Japan's fifth most valuable company as its shares hit another all-time record. The stock has risen more than 70 per cent since the start of the year, adding $40 billion to its market capitalization. Roche has added nearly $30 billion. The success of the Roche-Chugai partnership stands out in an industry where deals at far bigger prices—such as Johnson & Johnson's $30 billion purchase of Swiss biotech group Actelion in 2017—have struggled to impress investors, but also because cross-border deals are particularly challenging in Japan. Companies can be resistant to foreign ownership and their natural instinct is to imagine themselves as buyer rather than bought.

Many alliances, even long-enduring ones such as that between Nissan and Renault, have faltered when faced with pressures such as a full merger, deeper technology transfer, or, naturally, testing times of flagging financial performance. Chugai says it had its own merger scare in August 2014. According to Tatsuro Kosaka, chief executive, that summer still brings back bitter memories of a panicked midnight call at a hot springs resort, informing him of media reports that Roche was set to offer $10 billion to take full control. Cutting his holiday short, he drove back to company headquarters in Tokyo the next day.

Regardless of Roche's intentions at the time, Mr Kosaka insists no talks about any such deal took place. He also rules out a full merger in the future. Instead, Roche has its 60 per cent stake and three executives on Chugai's nine-member board, but continues its hands-off approach. There is no one from the Swiss parent, for example, in the senior management team. This type of alliance is now being touted as a model for cross-border deals, but autonomy does have a cost. Chugai needs to keep on developing innovative drugs—not just to boost the financial performance of both companies but also to maintain trust within Roche that it can leave its Japanese business alone.

So far the relationship has worked well. Chugai has delivered three key drugs—Actemra, haemophilia blockbuster Hemlibra, and lung cancer drug Alecensa—that have made a meaningful contribution to Roche's global sales. At Chugai, sales have tripled and profits have increased more than ten-fold in the past eighteen years, thanks in large part to Roche's global sales network. Royalty fees from the Swiss parent have also allowed the Japanese company to focus on decades of costly research it would not have been able to afford if it had gone it alone. Actemra may be in the global spotlight now but Japan's first monoclonal antibody drug was created with Osaka University after twenty years of research dating back to the 1980s. When the drug was first approved by Japanese authorities in 2005, it was to treat the rare Castleman disease before it was launched a few years later to treat rheumatoid arthritis.

During the coronavirus pandemic crisis, the Roche-Chugai alliance will be able to make use of combined manufacturing resources to ensure it can meet global demand for Actemra, depending on trial results. In addition to Chugai's plant in Japan, special permission has been granted for Roche unit Genentech's site in Oregon to undertake part of the drug production process. The alliance has had a huge boost this year because of the hopes for Actemra, but investor enthusiasm is likely to wane without firm scientific proof of its effectiveness against COVID-19. And in the longer term, success will hinge more on whether Chugai can deliver another blockbuster.

The case of Nissan and Renault, although in a different industry, shows trust built over decades can abruptly collapse especially when a relationship is tied to certain individuals. But the Roche-Chugai alliance certainly provides useful lessons in these uncertain times for what it might take to keep a cross-border relationship intact.

Source: Kana Inagaki, 'A Swiss-Japanese alliance that has thrived in the crisis', *The Financial Times*, 24 June 2020.

7.6 Portfolio Analysis

Corporate strategy is concerned with the question: what businesses do we want to compete in? Or, more accurately, which markets have we identified in which we can effectively deploy our capabilities to provide competitive advantage? Where a company is made up of multiple business units, the question concerns how resources are to be allocated across these businesses. The subject of portfolio strategy is concerned with managing these strategic business units (SBUs) to decide which businesses to invest in and which to divest in order to maintain overall corporate performance. This was the key decision facing Jack Welch when he was CEO of GE.

A portfolio is simply the different business units that a company possesses. Portfolio analysis allows a company to assess the competitive position, and identify the rate of return it is receiving from its various business units. By disaggregating the company into its individual SBUs, the organization can devise appropriate strategies for each unit. The aim is to maximize the return on investment by allocating resources between SBUs to achieve a balanced portfolio. In effect, the parent company assumes the role of a proactive investor or banker which manages its investment to achieve the highest return based upon an acceptable level of risk. The two most widely used portfolio analyses are the **Boston Consulting Group (BCG) matrix** and the **General Electric–McKinsey matrix**. We can look at each of these in turn.

7.6.1 Boston Consulting Group Matrix

This matrix was developed by the Boston Consulting Group and was widely used in the 1970s and 1980s. Since then diversified organizations have largely fallen from favour as companies seek to focus upon their own capabilities. The BCG matrix plots an organization's business units according to (1) its *industry growth rate* and (2) its *relative market share* (**Figure 7.5**). Industry growth rate can be determined by reference to the growth rate of the overall economy. Therefore, if the industry is growing faster than the economy we can say it is a high growth industry. If the industry is growing slower than the economy it is characterized as a slow growth industry. A business unit's relative market share

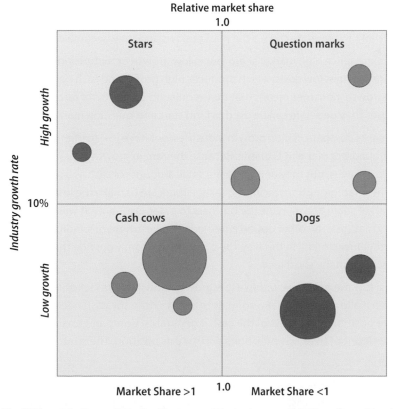

Figure 7.5 The BCG matrix. Source: B. Hedley, 'Strategy and the business portfolio', *Long Range Planning*, vol. 10, no. 1 (1977), p. 12. © 1977. Reproduced with permission from Elsevier.

(or competitive position) is defined as the ratio of its market share in relation to its largest competitor within the industry. A business unit that is the market leader will have a market share greater than 1.0.

A key element of the BCG matrix is market share. The matrix draws heavily upon the experience curve. This suggests that a high market share is a function of cost leadership achieved through economies of scale. This ability to reduce unit costs comes through the accumulated experience the business gains competing within the industry. In **Figure 7.5** each business unit (or product) is represented by a circle and plotted on the matrix according to its relative market share and industry growth rate. The size of the circle corresponds to the amount of revenue being generated by each business unit. The lines dividing the portfolio into four quadrants are somewhat arbitrary.[24] A high industry growth rate is put at 10 per cent, whereas the lines separating relative market share are set equal to the largest competitor, which is 1.0.

A business unit can fall within one of four strategic categories in which it will be characterized as a **star**, **cash cow**, **question mark**, or **dog**. These classifications can then be used to determine the strategic options for each business unit—that is, which business justifies further resource allocation, which generates cash for expansion, and which needs to be divested.

- **Stars** are characterized by high growth and high market share. They occupy the upper left quadrant of the matrix and are the business leaders, generating large amounts of cash. They represent the most favourable growth and investment opportunities to the company. As such, resources should be allocated to ensure that they maintain their competitive position. At times stars may require funding in excess of their ability to generate funds, but this will act as a deterrent to competitors. Over the long term, investment in stars will pay dividends, as their large market share will enable them to generate cash as the market slows and they become cash cows.

- **Cash cows** experience high market share, but in low growth or mature industries. Their high market share provides low costs, which produces high profits and cash generation. Their position in low growth industries means that they require little in terms of resource allocation. The cash surpluses they generate can be used to fund stars and question marks.

- **Question marks** compete in high growth industries, but have low market share. They occupy the upper right quadrant of the BCG matrix. Because they are in growth industries, question marks have high cash needs, but they only generate small amounts of cash as a result of their low market share. The strategic options facing a question mark are to make the investment necessary to increase market share and manage the business to a star. Over time, it will become a cash cow as the industry matures. The other option is immediate divestment or winding the business down with no further investment. In this way, the question mark may provide the company with some residual cash flow in the short term.

- **Dogs** have a low market share within a low growth industry. The lack of industry growth guards against allocating further resources to a dog. Often the cash needed to maintain its competitive position is in excess of the cash it generates. Companies need to ensure that only a minimal amount of their business units occupy this position. The strategic option is one of divestment.

According to **Barry Hedley**, the primary goal of a portfolio strategy should be to maintain the position of cash cows.[25] The cash from the cash cows can then be used to consolidate the position of stars which are not self-sustaining. Any surplus remaining can then be used to resource selected question marks to market dominance. An appropriate strategy for a multi-business company is to retain a balanced portfolio. The cash generated by cash cows and the liquidation of question marks and dogs should be sufficient to support the organization's stars and help selected question marks achieve market dominance.

What portfolio analysis shows us is that the strategy being formulated for each business unit should correspond to its position in the matrix. It should also align with the capabilities of the company's overall portfolio of businesses. For instance, managers of stars should be accorded more recognition for maintaining market share. In contrast with stars, managers of cash cows might be given a target of higher profit levels, as a more appropriate objective. This is because cash cows generate cash, but they operate in mature markets. Thus, setting an objective of maintaining market share would be unrealistic, and unlikely to motivate managers. The corporate parent must ensure that its overall performance is not suboptimal as a result of inappropriate business unit objectives, which will lead to poor resource allocation decisions, and demotivation of staff.

Criticisms of the BCG Matrix

The BCG matrix uses only industry growth rate and market share to assess a business unit's current performance. In particular, it overemphasizes the importance of market share and market dominance, which stems from its belief in the experience curve. Its simplicity of use and persuasive results ensured a wide following throughout the corporate world in the 1980s. However, the BCG matrix is a tool of analysis and, therefore, requires managers to use their judgement. It is not an excuse to suspend one's judgement.

Prahalad and Hamel note that '*major companies that have had the potential to build core competencies but failed to do so because top management was unable to conceive of the company as anything other than a collection of discrete businesses*'.[26] Hamel and Prahalad lament what they call 'the tyranny of the SBU', arguing instead for the modern company to be seen as a portfolio of competencies.[27] **Table 7.1** provides a comparison of the organization when viewed in terms of SBUs and core competencies.

	SBU	Core Competence
Basis for Competition	Competitiveness of today's products	Inter-firm competition to build competencies
Corporate Structure	Portfolio of businesses related in product-market terms	Portfolio of competencies, core products, and businesses
Status of the Business Unit	Autonomy is sacrosanct; the SBU 'owns' all resources other than cash	SBU is a potential reservoir of core competencies
Resource Allocation	Discrete businesses are the unit of analysis; capital is allocated business by business	Businesses and competencies are the unit of analysis; top management allocates capital and talent
Value Added of Top Management	Optimizing corporate returns through capital allocation trade-offs among businesses	Enunciating strategic architecture and building competencies to secure the future

Table 7.1   The organization: SBU and core competence. Source: Reprinted by permission of *Harvard Business Review*. Two concepts of the corporation, from C. K. Prahalad and G. Hamel, 'The core competence of the corporation', *Harvard Business Review*, vol. 68, no. 3 (1990). © 1990 by the Harvard Business School Publishing Corporation. All rights reserved.

7.6.2 The General Electric–McKinsey Matrix

General Electric and McKinsey & Company developed a more comprehensive measure of strategic success. In contrast with the BCG matrix's four quadrants, the General Electric (GE) matrix comprises a nine-cell matrix (**Figure 7.6**). The axes comprise (1) *industry attractiveness* and (2) *business strength/ competitive position*. Unlike the BCG matrix there is an attempt to broaden the analysis of a business unit's internal and external factors. For example, industry attractiveness includes factors such as industry profitability, market growth, and the number of competitors, among others. Similarly, business strength and competitive position go beyond market share to include a wider analysis of the organization's internal strengths and weaknesses. This includes factors such as technological capability, product quality, and management ability, as well as relative market share. These are the factors that managers believe will be important for achieving success.

As with the BCG matrix, each business unit is represented by a circle and plotted on the matrix. Each business unit (or product) is also identified by a letter. The size of the circles relates to the size of the industry and the shaded portion corresponds to the market share of each business unit. Each industry that a business unit operates within is graded on a scale of 1 (very unattractive) to 5 (very attractive). By mapping each business unit against the factors management believe to be important for success, each business unit can be assessed for its business strength and competitive position on a scale of 1 (very weak) to 5 (very strong).

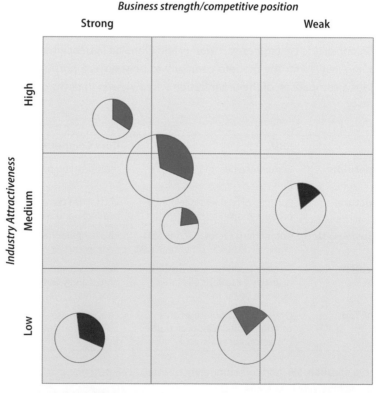

Figure 7.6   The General Electric–McKinsey matrix. Source: Adapted from 'Enduring ideas: the GE–McKinsey nine-box matrix', *McKinsey Quarterly*, September 2008.

The GE matrix overcomes some of the more simplistic analysis of the BCG matrix. The inclusion of a nine-cell matrix helps to broaden the criteria for assessing the performance of business units. Nonetheless, we should be aware that the analysis can become complex. It is also subjective. The different criteria which are used to measure industry attractiveness and competitive position are provided by the parent company. The parent company in turn uses these criteria to assess each business. In effect, the parent corporation is stating what it believes to be important and simply assessing its strategic business units according to this.

7.7 **Corporate Parenting**

In evaluating portfolio strategies,[28] the role of the corporate parent in **Section 7.6** is simply one of an investment manager; moving funds between businesses as it seeks to maximize its corporate returns. In contrast, **A**ndrew Campbell et al. seek to understand how, and under what conditions, corporate parents succeed in creating value. They argue that multi-business organizations create value by influencing or *parenting* the businesses they own. Sound corporate strategies create value through **parenting advantage**. This advantage occurs when an organization creates more value than any of its rivals could if they owned the same businesses. For example, Unilever adds value by sharing marketing and technological information across its business units in different countries. It also adds value by providing funds to its SBUs for R&D, to enable new product development. Left to its own devices the individual business unit would simply under-invest in this area.[29]

A parent company can be seen as an intermediary between the business divisions it owns and investors. Each parent company has costs, such as direct costs and the time it absorbs of the managers who are running the business divisions. Therefore, a parent company must generate some additional value that offsets these costs.[30] In this respect, a parent competes against other parent companies and also against other intermediaries, such as investment trusts. Therefore, the corporate strategies make sense as long as the parent company is able to create sufficient value to compete with other intermediaries.[31] If not, investors would gain more from making separate investments in each business division as an independent company. If there is a good fit between the corporate parent's skills and the needs and opportunities that exist for its businesses, the corporate parent is likely to create value. However, if there is not a good fit, the corporate parent is likely to destroy value. The concept of corporate parenting is useful in helping an organization to decide which new businesses it should acquire. This is because unless the corporate parent is creating greater value than its costs, the businesses would be better off as independent companies. In addition, it helps the corporate parent focus when deciding how each business should be managed.

In their influential book, subtitled *Creating Value in the Multibusiness Company*, **Michael Goold, Andrew Campbell, and Marcus Alexander** argue that successful parents create parenting advantage through their *value-creation insights*.[32] This is an essential feature of successful corporate parents. It states that corporate strategies should be based on *insights* into how corporate parents can create value in their portfolio of businesses. These insights tend to emanate from the corporate culture as well as the experience of the chief executive and his or her management team. Parenting advantage also involves creating a *fit* between how the parent operates—the *parent's distinctive characteristics*—and the *opportunities* that exist within the business units. The key is not simply to identify some level of fit, but rather to achieve a *closer fit* with its businesses than can be achieved by rival organizations. The idea of fit is a dynamic one, such that a fit in today's environment will not necessarily be a fit in tomorrow's environment. This means corporate strategists need to be aware of the trends occurring in their environment that will have an impact upon their business units. One way in which an organization might do this is via scenario planning, which was discussed in **Chapter 2**.

To understand fully the fit between a parent and its various businesses the organization needs to analyse its parenting opportunities and the critical success factors for each business.

7.7.1　Parenting Opportunities

Each business unit contains opportunities for the parent to create value. It may be that the business unit does not have a strong management team or lacks some specialized expertise, such as marketing. Each business will present the corporate parent with its own unique opportunities. Therefore, the issue is whether the business needs and opportunities identified can be exploited by the parent company. In other words, do the parent's capabilities fit with the needs and opportunities of the business?

Each type of business will have different critical success factors which determine its success in the market. In one business, it might be the ability to develop innovative solutions for consumers. In another, it might be product development and the speed to market. In order to create value the parent's characteristics must be compatible with the critical success factors needed for the business. This is crucial, since a misunderstanding of critical success factors may lead the parent company to destroy value.

Successful corporate strategy requires parents which possess value-creation insights and distinctive parenting characteristics, and which focus on businesses where they can create value. There are four ways in which the corporate parent can create value for their businesses: *stand-alone influence*, *linkage influence*, *functional and services influence*, and *corporate development activities*.

1. **Stand-alone influence**. This concerns the parent company's impact upon the strategies and performance of each business the parent owns. Stand-alone influence includes such things as the parent company setting performance targets and approving major capital expenditure for the business. There is an opportunity here for the parent to create substantial value. However, where the parent imposes inappropriate targets or fails to recognize the needs of the business for funds, it will destroy value.

2. **Linkage influence**. This occurs when parents seek to create value by enhancing the linkages that may be present between different businesses. For example, this might include transferring knowledge and capabilities across business units. The aim is to increase value through synergy.

3. **Functional and services influence**. The parent can provide functional leadership and cost-effective services for the businesses. The parent company creates value to the extent that they provide services which are more cost effective than the businesses can undertake themselves or purchase from external suppliers.

4. **Corporate development activities**. This involves the parent creating value by changing the composition of its portfolio of businesses. The parent actively seeks to add value through its activities in acquisitions, divestments, and strategic alliances. In reality, the parent company often destroys value through its acquisitions by paying a premium price which it fails to recover.[33]

Business strategy decisions are guided by their impact on competitive advantage. Similarly, corporate parenting proposes that the main criterion for corporate strategy decisions is their impact on *parenting advantage*. In this way, it aims to provide a measurement for corporate-level decisions which might improve corporate strategies. Parenting advantage—creating better value than one's rivals—should be used to guide corporate strategy development. As Campbell et al. state, 'parenting advantage is the only robust logic for a parent company to own a business . . . parenting advantage is the goal and criterion that should guide both the selection of businesses to include in the portfolio and the design of the parent organization'.[34]

7.7.2 The Heartland Matrix

The financial cost of the corporate headquarters is not the only reason a parent company needs to add value.[35] Corporate headquarters also subtract value. They do this by interference, bureaucracy, delays, and providing ineffective services. On one hand, added value may come from a parent company's wise guidance, technical expertise, and financial strength. On the other hand, subtracting value can come from inappropriate guidance, poor technical expertise, and insufficient financial strength of the parent company.[36] A point to remember is that the corporate parent can simultaneously be adding value in some areas while simultaneously subtracting value in other areas. We can now turn to the question of which businesses the corporate parent should include in its portfolio. Goold, Campbell, and Alexander suggest that businesses can be classified into five types: *heartland*, *edge of heartland*, *ballast*, *alien territory*, and *value trap*.[37]

To determine which of the above five types a business falls within, two questions can be asked.

1. Do the parenting opportunities in the business *fit* with value-creating insights of the parent, such that the parent can create a substantial amount of value?

2. Do the critical success factors in the business have any obvious *misfit* with the prospective parenting characteristics, such that the parent might influence the business in a way that destroys value?

The answer to the first question will range from a high fit, where the value-creation insights of the parent fit well with the opportunities in the business, to a low fit, where the value-creation insights of the parent company do not address the important opportunities that exist within the business. Clearly, where the value-creation insights address all the important opportunities in a business, there is no room for a rival to create superior value-creation insights. Where the degree of fit between parent and business units is low, it is likely that another corporate parent would add greater value.

The second question requires the corporate parent to understand the critical success factors in the business and compare these with its own parenting characteristics. A misfit is likely to occur when the parent does not understand the critical success factors of the business. It lacks a 'feel' for the business and, therefore, inadvertently influences the business in ways that destroy value. Those businesses that the parent does not understand well enough to ascertain the extent of misfit should be categorized as having a high misfit.

These business types are illustrated in the *heartland or parenting fit matrix* (**Figure 7.7**). This is divided into four quadrants. A business will occupy one of these quadrants according to how well there is a fit between its needs and opportunities and the skills of the corporate parent.

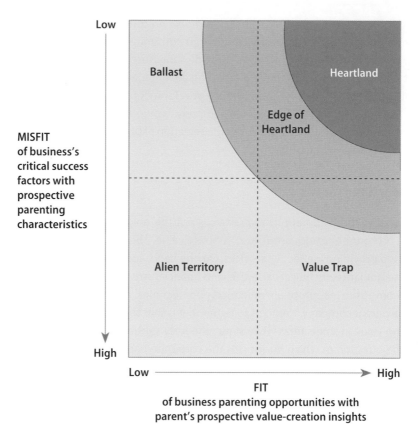

Figure 7.7   The heartland matrix. Source: Andrew Campbell, Jo Whitehead, Marcus Alexander, and Michael Goold, *Strategy for the Corporate Level*, Jossey-Bass, 2014.

Heartland Businesses

These are businesses with needs and opportunities that the parent company can address. The critical success factors of these businesses are clearly understood by the parent. Heartland businesses should be the main focus of the company's parenting. These are businesses the parent understands and can add the most value to. For example, the heartland of Procter & Gamble is fast-moving consumer goods, R&D, global distribution, and international brands which provide it with parenting advantage.[38] The heartland of LVMH is luxury brands in fashion, leather goods, perfumes, cosmetics, jewellery, wines, and spirits. These parent companies add a lot of value to businesses in their heartland while subtracting only a little value. As such, these parent companies help to increase profits of the businesses in their portfolio by 50 per cent, 100 per cent, or even more.

Edge-of-Heartland Businesses

Edge-of-heartland refers to a space in the matrix where the balance between added value and subtracted value of the parent company is unclear. If the parent company becomes good at added value and avoiding subtracting value, the business will become a heartland business. If not, it may become a ballast, alien territory, or value trap business. Edge-of-heartland businesses can come about when a parent company acquires a new business that meets the value-creation insights of the parent, but not all the heartland criteria. For example, the new business might be operating in markets with which the parent is unfamiliar. In such a case the parent should recognize that its feel for the business is less certain and this might require that it develop new parenting skills to deal with the business. The new business can be thought of as extending the boundaries around the heartland. The new business should be seen as an experiment in which the boundaries of the heartland business are tested. This will involve greater risk than a heartland business but offer the upside of substantial value creation.

For example, when British Airways launched the low-cost airline GO, it was expected to be in edge-of-heartland. Similarly, executives at Daimler, following the DaimlerChrysler merger, expected Chrysler to be in edge-of-heartland. HP expected its acquisition of Autonomy would also be edge-of-heartland. In each case, the acquiring company succeeded in subtracting more value than they created. British Airways sold GO to easyJet and Daimler sold Chrysler to a private equity group. Having bought Autonomy for $11.1 billion (£7.3 billion), HP was forced to book an $8.8 billion write-down on the company just one year later.

In contrast, examples of successful investments into edge-of-heartland are Intel into micropro-cessors and IBM into consulting. These companies made cautious investments into businesses which were different from their core business. However, over time, they were able to add value and avoid subtracting value, and the businesses became heartland. Other successful examples include Volks-wagen and General Motors moving into financial services, and PwC moving into consulting.

Ballast Businesses

Where the potential for added value is low and the potential for subtracting value is also likely to be low, the business is *ballast*. Ballast businesses are those businesses in which there are few opportuni-ties for the parent company to add value. Most portfolios will contain a number of ballast businesses which may have been part of the company for many years. Although the parent understands ballast businesses and they do not present any misfits, the issue is likely to be one of opportunity cost. That is, as there are few parenting opportunities in ballast businesses the parent's time would be better spent on other businesses, particularly heartland businesses.

Ballast businesses may be well run and offer the corporate parent a useful cash flow, but ultimately the issue is: what effect does retaining a ballast business have upon the rest of the portfolio? And is it worth more to the parent company than to its rivals? Ballast businesses are often found in diversified companies, for example, Louis Vuitton in LVMH. As Louis Vuitton does not seem to provide any ben-efits to the other brands in LVMH, it could perform just as well as an independent company.

Value Trap

Value trap businesses are businesses that appear attractive to the corporate parent on the surface but, in reality, there exist areas of misfit with the parent's skills and resources. They are called value trap because corporate executives are tempted by the potential for added value and underestimate the risk of subtracting value. Value-trap businesses should be avoided and kept out of the corporate portfolio unless the parent is capable of learning to reduce or eliminate the misfits, so the business can become edge-of-heartland. Examples include oil companies which acquired mineral companies believing their capabilities in exploration and project management would enable them to add value to such compa-nies. But, even as independent mineral companies were making profits, those owned by oil companies continued to make losses. Ultimately, the oil companies were forced to sell their mineral divisions.

Other examples of value trap businesses include the high-end perfume brand, Elizabeth Arden, which was bought by Unilever. Unilever's capabilities of dealing with mass-market products proved unsuitable for this exclusive perfume brand. It was eventually sold to a private equity company which was able to double the profits and increase its sales.

Alien Territory

If the subtracted value from the business is likely to be high and the potential for added value is low, the business unit is in *alien territory*. Businesses that lie within alien territory offer the parent little opportunity to create value. The parent company's value-creating insights are not relevant for such businesses and its parent characteristics do not fit the businesses. They may be in the portfolio as a result of being part of another company which was previously acquired. They are referred to as *alien* because their need is for a different corporate parent with a fundamentally different corporate strategy. Many companies entered new industries in the hope that they would provide growth potential. Examples include BP entering IT software, and BAT diversifying into financial services. Instead, they proved to be alien territory with little added value and lots of subtracted value, and were sold.

We should be aware that the heartland matrix has its limitations. The authors of the matrix describe it as 'conceptually strong but practically weak'.[39] This is because, if we revisit our description of *edge-of-heartland* business, we can see it is hard to assess in advance in which of the quadrants a business will lie. As a result, the framework may be more useful for describing what happened than it is for predicting what will happen. This can make its usefulness limited. In line with similar portfolio tools of analysis, it depends on the subjectivity of those making decisions as to what constitutes a good fit between the parent and business units. Also, corporate directors spend less time with each business than their own managers do. In such cases, their influence on these business units may be less soundly based than that of the managers who actually run them. Furthermore, corporate headquarters encourage managers of business units to compete with each other for resources. As a result, these managers will filter information going to the corporate parent in order to show their business in the best possible light. Where this occurs some value will be destroyed, as the information on which the corporate parent is making decisions is inevitably biased.[40]

To summarize, the best parents have *value-creation insights* about the most appropriate parenting opportunities and focus their activities on trying to create added value from these insights and avoid subtracting value. They possess distinctive parenting characteristics which enable them to create value. These characteristics will usually be superior to those of similar parents. Crucially, the best parents primarily focus their portfolios on those business units where their parenting skills can create substantial value—these are heartland businesses. They may make a conscious decision to invest time and resources in businesses that fall outside the heartland, such as ballast businesses. A point to bear in mind is that any such decision should be based on a clear understanding that ballast businesses are worth more to the corporate parent than to rival corporate parents. They should not be retained for emotional or historic reasons.

7.8 **Strategic Evaluation**

In this chapter and in **Chapter 6**, we have looked at a variety of different strategies that organizations can formulate. The question we now need to address is: how can a company differentiate between the strategic options that it faces? We might include a caveat here that it is unrealistic to expect any form of evaluation to identify a 'best' or optimal strategy. However, strategy evaluation can help to surface the implications of pursuing different strategic options before they are implemented. One method is to assess the strategy according to its *suitability*, *feasibility*, and *acceptability*.[41] We can assess each of these in turn.

7.8.1 Suitability

An organization will be concerned to evaluate how well the strategy matches the needs identified within its strategic analysis. There should be some consistency between the strategy, the opportunities within the external environment, the capabilities of the organization, and the organizational objectives. For example, is the strategy capable of overcoming a threat identified in the external environment and mitigating any weaknesses in the organization? The strategy should leverage the organization's capabilities to exploit external opportunities that may arise as a result of market changes. The strategy should also meet the organization's objectives and include some combination of qualitative and quantitative measures as suggested by the balanced scorecard (discussed in **Chapter 4**).

7.8.2 Feasibility

Feasibility concerns whether a strategy will work in practice. An organization must ensure that it possesses the necessary capabilities, such as finance, technological expertise, marketing, and other factors necessary to implement the strategy. Where capabilities are deficient, can the organization develop these and achieve competitive advantage? As we have seen, each industry has its own critical success factors. A strategy will not be tenable if it fails to meet these critical success factors. These will include factors such as quality levels, price, product development, innovation, and customer support.

7.8.3 Acceptability

The criterion of acceptability addresses the response of stakeholders to the proposed strategy. Clearly, if a strategic change is to be implemented, it must have the support of those who will be most affected by it. For example, managers of an SBU often understand their business far better than staff at head office. However, a proposed strategy from an SBU which takes into account local market conditions must also fit within the overall strategy set by the corporate parent. Similarly, stakeholders, such as institutional investors, will be particularly concerned about the impact of the strategy on profitability. Their attention will be drawn towards the return on capital employed, the cost–income ratio within the organization, and the perceived levels of risk that arise from the strategy. Other stakeholders, such as employees, customers, and key suppliers, will need to be assured that any changes will not negatively impact upon them. If the strategy is one of growth through mergers and acquisitions, the organization needs to consider if this will be acceptable to the competition authorities.

The criteria of suitability, feasibility, and acceptability help managers to be explicit about any assumptions that may underpin their strategies. In reality, it may be unlikely that an organization's strategy fulfils all three criteria. In that case, the organization must decide on the strategy that fits its stated aims and objectives more closely. Inevitably this will involve compromise.

Richard Rumelt proposes four tests of (1) *consistency*, (2) *consonance*, (3) *advantage*, and (4) *feasibility* to evaluate a strategy.[42] He argues that any strategy can be tested for four types of critical flaw. These are briefly discussed below.

1. **Consistency**. Any proposed strategy must not present mutually inconsistent goals and policies. For example, a high-technology organization might face a strategic choice between offering a customized high-cost product or a more standardized low cost product. Unless a choice is explicit throughout the organization, there may be conflict between the sales force, the design team, manufacturing, and marketing.

2. **Consonance**. The test of consonance allows the organization to evaluate the economic relationships that characterize the business. It also helps determine whether or not sufficient value is being created to sustain the need for the strategy over the long term. Consonance can include an assessment of why the organization exists, the economic foundation which supports the business, and the implications of changes.

3. **Advantage**. This addresses whether an organization can appropriate sufficient of the value that it creates. A strategy must create competitive advantage in one or more of the following three areas: superior skills, superior resources, and superior position.

4. **Feasibility**. Lastly, the criterion of feasibility is to ensure that any proposed strategy does not overtax an organization's available resources or create insoluble problems for it. It is pointless to formulate a *brilliant* strategy which the firm is simply incapable of implementing.

Summary

Corporate strategy is concerned with the question: what businesses do we want to compete in? Corporate strategy defines the scope of the industries and markets within which the company competes. Where a company is made up of multiple business units, a role arises as to how resources are to be allocated across these businesses. The purpose and objectives of the corporation are paramount in guiding these decisions. Once the objectives are determined, the role of corporate strategy is to enable the company to fulfil those objectives. The objectives and, therefore, the direction of the organization are determined by the corporate parent. The role of a corporate parent is to add value across its business units. Where a corporate parent adds greater value than a rival, the business is said to achieve synergy.

In order to grow, organizations can pursue a number of different strategies. Each strategy carries a different level of risk and is predicated upon an organization's capabilities. Where a company seeks to broaden its scope of activities it will be concerned with how it can best diversify into different businesses. This may take the form of related or conglomerate diversification. The methods by which an organization's corporate strategy can be implemented also differ. The organization's competitive position, cost implications, need for technology, speed, access to markets, and competitive threats will all help to guide the decision on which methods it chooses to implement its strategy. A popular method for assessing business performance is portfolio analysis: two approaches include the Boston Consulting Group matrix and the General Electric–McKinsey matrix.

The corporate parenting approach suggests that the parent company should use its value-creation insights and distinctive parenting characteristics to identify a heartland of businesses to which it can add substantial value. In evaluating strategies, executives must be aware of both the organization's internal resources and capabilities and how these meet the needs of the external environment. In addition, the opinions of stakeholders who have the power and influence to affect strategy must also be taken into account.

 For more examples and discussion to aid your understanding of this chapter, please visit the online resources and see the Extension Material for this chapter.

 ## Review Questions

1. Why do so many mergers and acquisitions destroy shareholder value?
2. Explain how the heartland matrix enables a parent company to allocate resources and expertise to the businesses it owns.
3. If an organization's portfolio of businesses includes some dogs, what are the options open to it according to the BCG matrix? Are there any circumstances in which a company might be prepared to tolerate dog businesses?

 ## Discussion Question

'Joint ventures are not an effective way to share capabilities between companies.' ***Discuss***.

 ## Research Topic

Choose a company following a conglomerate diversification corporate strategy, such as Berkshire Hathaway, Reliance Industries, or Alibaba. Identify the extent to which its diversification strategy has enabled it to achieve profitable growth, or led to losses and failure.

 ## Recommended Reading

- **C. C. Markides** and **P. J. Williamson**, 'Related diversification, core competencies and corporate performance', *Strategic Management Journal*, vol. 15 (Special Issue) (1994), pp. 149–65.
- **A. Seth**, 'Value creation in acquisitions: a re-examination of performance issues', *Strategic Management Journal*, vol. 11, no. 2 (1990), pp. 99–115.

For a discussion of portfolio analysis and the growth share (BCG) matrix, see:

- **B. Hedley**, 'Strategy and the business portfolio', *Long Range Planning*, vol. 10, no. 1 (1977), pp. 9–15.

For an understanding of the resource-based view and a critique of portfolio analysis with its focus upon strategic business units (SBUs), see the influential article:

- **C. K. Prahalad** and **G. Hamel**, 'The core competence of the corporation', *Harvard Business Review*, vol. 68, no. 3 (1990), pp. 79–91.

For a corporate parenting approach to corporate strategy that argues that a parent company should ensure that the value it creates from its businesses is more than could be achieved by a rival organization, see:

- **M. Goold**, **A. Campbell**, and **M. Alexander**, *Corporate Level Strategy: Creating Value in the Multibusiness Company*, John Wiley & Sons, 1994.

www.oup.com/he/henry4e

Visit the online resources that accompany this book for activities and more information on strategy.

Test your knowledge and understanding of this chapter further by trying the multiple-choice questions online.

References and Notes

1   **M. Goold**, **A. Campbell**, and **M. Alexander**, 'Corporate strategy and parenting theory', *Long Range Planning*, vol. 31, no. 2 (1994), pp. 308–14.

2   A version of this matrix is found in **H. I. Ansoff**, *The New Corporate Strategy*, John Wiley & Sons, 1998, shown in **Figure 7.1**.

3   **O. E. Williamson**, *Markets and Hierarchies: Analysis and Antitrust Implications*, Free Press, 1975.

4   **T. J. Peters** and **R. H. Waterman**, *In Search of Excellence*, Harper & Row, 1982.

5   **M. E. Porter**, 'From competitive advantage to corporate strategy', *Harvard Business Review*, vol. 65, no. 3 (1987), pp. 43–59.

6   **C. C. Markides**, 'Diversification, restructuring and economic performance', *Strategic Management Journal*, vol. 16, no. 2 (1995), pp. 101–18.

7   **M. Daley**, **V. Mehrotra**, and **R. Sivakumar**, 'Corporate focus and value creation: evidence from spin-offs', *Journal of Financial Economics*, vol. 45, no. 2 (1997), pp. 257–81.

8   For information on GE's business portfolio, see https://www.ge.com/about-us/fact-sheet.

9   **R. Slater**, 'The new GE: how Jack Welch revived an American institution', Irwin Professional Publishing, 1992.

10 Tata.com; 'Tata: transforming a conglomerate for India and the world', *The Financial Times*, 31 August 2020.

11 http://indianexpress.com/article/business/richest-people-in-the-world-bloomberg-bill-gates-warren-buffett-mark-zuckerberg-jeff-bezos-koch-brothers-2878601.

12 Figures from https://www.berkshirehathaway.com/letters/2019ltr.pdf.

13 See Berkshire Hathaway, https://www.berkshirehathaway.com/letters/2019ltr.pdf.

14 **M. Goold** and **K. Luchs**, 'Why diversify? Four decades of management thinking', *Academy of Management Executive*, vol. 7, no. 3 (1993), pp. 7–25.

15 **H. Singh** and **C. A. Montgomery,** 'Corporate acquisition strategies and economic performance', *Strategic Management Journal*, vol. 8, no. 4 (1987), pp. 377–86; and **C. C. Markides** and **P. J. Williamson**, 'Related diversification, core competencies and corporate performance', *Strategic Management Journal*, vol. 15 (Special Edition) (1994), pp. 149–65.

[16] **Goold** and **Luchs**, see n. 14 above, p. 15.

[17] See **A. Seth**, 'Value creation in acquisitions: a re-examination of performance issues', *Strategic Management Journal*, vol. 11, no. 2 (1990), pp. 99–115.

[18] **D. Crow**, 'Treasury puts back deadline for divestiture of RBS shares by one year', *The Financial Times*, 11 March 2020.

[19] 'Daimler offloads Chrysler for $7.4bn: private equity deal ends miserable decade for German engineer', *The Daily Telegraph*, 15 May 2007.

[20] 'Happily never after mergers, like marriages, fail without a meeting of minds', *The Financial Times*, 15 May 2007.

[21] **Porter**, see n. 5 above.

[22] **J. Kay**, *Foundations of Corporate Success*, Oxford University Press, 1993.

[23] **M. Murgia**, 'Social media is for grown-ups, not teeny-boppers, now', *The Daily Telegraph*, 15 June 2016.

[24] **B. Hedley**, 'Strategy and the business portfolio', *Long Range Planning*, vol. 10, no. 1 (1977), pp. 9–15.

[25] **Hedley**, see n. 24 above.

[26] **C. K. Prahalad** and **G. Hamel**, 'The core competence of the corporation', *Harvard Business Review*, vol. 68, no. 3 (1990), pp. 79–91.

[27] **G. Hamel** and **C. K. Prahalad**, *Competing for the Future*, Harvard Business School Press, 1994.

[28] **A. Campbell**, **M. Goold**, and **M. Alexander**, 'Corporate strategy: the quest for parenting advantage', *Harvard Business Review*, vol. 73, no. 2 (1995), pp. 120–32.

[29] **R. Buchanan** and **R. Sands**, 'Creating an effective corporate centre: the influence of strategy on head office role,' *European Business Journal*, vol. 6, no. 4 (1994), pp. 17–27.

[30] **A. Campbell**, **J. Whitehead**, **M. Alexander**, and **M. Goold**, *Strategy for the Corporate Level*, Jossey-Bass, 2014.

[31] **Campbell et al.**, see n. 30 above.

[32] **M. Goold**, **A. Campbell**, and **M. Alexander**, *Corporate Level Strategy: Creating Value in the Multibusiness Company*, John Wiley & Sons, 1994.

[33] **Porter**, see n. 5 above.

[34] **A. Campbell**, **M. Goold**, and **M. Alexander**, 'The value of the parent company', *California Management Review*, vol. 38, no. 1 (1995), p. 91.

[35] This section draws upon **A. Campbell**, **J. Whitehead**, **M. Alexander**, and **M. Goold**, *Strategy for the Corporate Level*, Jossey-Bass, 2014, especially chapter 4.

[36] **A. Campbell** et al., see n. 35 above, pp. 103–4.

[37] **Campbell et al.**, see n. 30 above.

[38] **A. Campbell** et al., see n. 35 above, p. 105.

[39] **A. Campbell** et al., see n. 35 above, p. 109.

[40] **M. Goold**, **A. Campbell**, and **M. Alexander**, 'Corporate strategy and parenting theory', *Long Range Planning*, vol. 31, no. 2 (1994), pp. 308–14.

[41] **G. Johnson** and **K. Scholes**, *Exploring Corporate Strategy*, Pearson, 2003.

[42] **R. Rumelt**, 'The evaluation of business strategy', in *The Strategy Process*, edited by **H. Mintzberg**, **B. Quinn**, and **S. Ghoshal**, Prentice-Hall, 1995.

CHAPTER 8
INTERNATIONAL STRATEGY

 Learning Objectives

After completing this chapter you should be able to:

- Discuss different perspectives on globalization
- Explain what motivates companies to expand internationally
- Evaluate the different types of international strategy
- Assess the entry mode strategies for entering international markets
- Evaluate Porter's diamond as an explanation for competitive advantage in different countries

Introduction

Why is it that so many companies are not content to simply compete in their domestic market but instead seek growth opportunities abroad? A crucial question for organizations that operate across international borders is: to what extent can they develop global brands and global products for all markets? Or, conversely, to what extent must their international strategy recognize and adapt to international differences based on, for instance, customer preferences? Central to these questions are the extent to which an organization believes globalization has led to a standardization of consumer tastes and preferences and, therefore, homogeneous markets. Or that important national differences still exist which necessitate that organizations provide different product offerings to different countries. Clearly, each company's understanding of the changes taking place in the international environment will have an impact on the type of strategy it pursues. In the same way, the level of risk an organization is prepared to accept and the amount of control it requires over its international operations will determine what entry mode strategy it adopts.

Another important issue to consider is how globalization affects the organizational structure and processes within a company—that is to say, whether its existing structure is sufficiently flexible to enable the rapid dispersal of knowledge and distinctive capabilities across its borders. This is important if the organization is to achieve synergies and more readily cope with external changes. In this chapter we discuss competitive advantage from an international perspective.

8.1 Globalization or Localization

Globalization refers to the linkages between markets that exist across national borders. These linkages may be economic, financial, social, or political—in effect, anything that leads to increased interdependence among nations. This implies that what happens in one country has an impact on occurrences in other countries. In contrast, localization implies that national differences between countries are important and that organizations must take account of these differences in their product offerings, distributions, and product promotions if they are to be successful.

Theodore Levitt, a proponent of globalization, argues that a major driving force for convergence between nations is technology.[1] Technology has created a world in which consumers worldwide desire standardized products. The national differences that existed have gone, and only corporations that realize this will be in a position to take advantage of the huge economies of scale in production, distribution, marketing, and management that globalization brings. For Levitt, this spells the end for multidomestic corporations—that is, corporations that operate in a number of countries and adjust their product offering to suit each country. It marks the ascendancy of the global corporation—one that sells the same products to all nations in the same way, thereby achieving low costs through economies of scale. As Levitt states, somewhat emphatically, *'the world's needs and desires have been irrevocably homogenized'*. Coca-Cola and Pepsi soft drinks are examples of globally standardized products that easily cross national borders.

Success in this globalized marketplace requires that organizations compete on price and quality, offering the same products sold at home to international markets. It requires organizations to search for similarities that exist in segments around the world in order to exploit economies of scale. Globalization and the resulting standardization of products both respond to homogenized markets and expand these markets by offering products at lower prices. In this respect, Levitt's global corporation is a result of globalization, but is also the cause of continuing convergence.

Contrary to Levitt's assertions, **Susan Douglas and Yoram Wind** argue that success requires standardized products and global brands; organizations can make greater profits by adapting products and marketing strategies to suit individual markets.[2] They point out that while there are global segments with similar needs, such as luxury goods, this is not a universal trend. For example, Nestlé's frozen food division, Findus, finds it necessary to market fish fingers to its UK consumers and *coq au vin* to the French, reflecting an understanding of the importance of national differences. For Douglas and Wind, *'The evidence suggests that the similarities in customer behaviour are restricted to a relatively limited number of target segments'* and 'substantial differences between countries' still exist.[3]

They also reject Levitt's assertion that consumers worldwide are becoming more price-sensitive, trading product features for a lower price. Instead, they point out that a strategy of offering low prices does not lead to a sustainable competitive advantage since it is readily imitated by competitors. In the same way, technological innovations may lower a competitor's cost structure and therefore its prices. As for economies of scale from supplying a global market, Douglas and Wind state that technological improvements have actually allowed scale efficiencies at lower levels of output. This means that organizations can service differences in national markets more efficiently. Even within the corporation, restrictions to globalization may arise from local managers of foreign subsidiaries who see standardization as demotivating. It deprives them of their autonomy to make decisions based on their local expertise.

Other impediments to globalization may also come from tariffs and import restrictions imposed by foreign governments. Therefore, Douglas and Wind argue that globalization is far from ubiquitous and that organizations would be unwise to ignore national differences. A similar point is made by **Pankaj Ghemawat** who states that geographic and other differences have not been superseded by globalization, but appear to be increasing in importance.[4] He argues that an understanding of regional strategies can help organizations boost their performance. **Geert Hofstede** argues that the national varieties that exist between countries are likely to survive for some time.[5] In contrast to the advocates of globalization, he sees a worldwide homogenization of people's attitudes 'under the influence of a presumed cultural melting-pot process' as very far off indeed. Hofstede reminds us that:

> Not all values and practices in a society, however, are affected by technology or its products. There is no evidence that the cultures of present-day generations from different countries are converging.[6]

Levitt, and Douglas and Wind, occupy opposite sides of the globalization debate. The debate is not academic, but pragmatic; the outcome affects corporations. For instance, if the world is becoming increasingly globalized, this impacts upon the strategic choices facing organizations. If the world is becoming increasingly localized, a different set of strategic responses are required. What is often lost sight of in the globalization debate is its effects on the lives of ordinary people. Clearly, one might take a utilitarian approach and argue that, on balance, a greater good is accomplished. However, this often masks local tragedies.

8.2 International Diversification

What motivates companies to pursue a strategy of international diversification? When a decision is made to expand abroad, what are the different types of market entry open to organizations? We will see that some of these market entry strategies coincide with the growth strategies we evaluated in **Chapter 7**. The motives for companies to expand internationally can be evaluated by looking at *organizational factors* and *environmental factors*. The organizational factors occur within the company while the environmental factors are exogenous, or outside the company's control.

8.2.1 Organizational Factors

The Role of the Management Team

The perception of the senior management team about the importance of international activities will play a role in the decision of the organization to internationalize. This may arise from a saturation of the domestic market; for example, the mobile phone giant Nokia was forced to expand beyond the confines of its domestic economy in Finland. Where an organization faces large fixed costs, such as can be seen with R&D within the pharmaceutical industry, expansion overseas allows it to achieve economies of scale by spreading its costs over greater units of output. Economies of scope can also be achieved by organizations—for example, Proctor & Gamble and Unilever have developed capabilities in managing and coordinating their marketing activities worldwide.

The extent to which managers possess knowledge and experience of overseas markets will have a bearing on their decision to expand abroad. Another factor will be the management perception of risks involved in overseas activities. In fact, the perceived level of risk can be correlated with the different types of market entry undertaken. We discuss entry mode strategies later in the chapter. An important consideration in deciding whether to internationalize will be the locational advantages that an organization might gain from its value chain. The various activities that go to make up an organization's value chain may be located in different countries to take account of differential costs and other locational advantages that a country may possess. We discussed the value chain in detail in **Chapter 4**. We will revisit locational advantages when we consider national differences as a source of competitive advantage.

Firm-Specific Factors

Firm-specific factors include the size of the company and the international appeal of its product. Other things being equal, the likelihood is that larger companies will internationalize more than smaller ones. This is not surprising given that larger companies possess greater resources, produce greater capacity, and are therefore likely to require wider market coverage to attain economies of scale. That said, some organizations may be relatively small, but the nature of their product offering may have an international appeal, such as software, in which case a small company could quickly internationalize. Products or services which possess an international brand image and, therefore, international appeal, may explain why some companies expand internationally, for example, Coca-Cola, Starbucks, and high-end fashion goods such as Armani.

8.2.2 **Environmental Factors**

Unsolicited Proposals

An unsolicited proposal may come about from an organization being approached by a foreign government, distributor, or customer. The widespread use of communication technology leads to many companies receiving unsolicited requests to expand abroad.

The 'Bandwagon' Effect

The bandwagon effect refers to organizations that follow competitors who have gone international. Clearly, organizations will not want to be seen to be missing out on new opportunities. In the same way, organizations may come to the conclusion that a presence in an overseas market is desirable.

Attractiveness of the Host Country

The market size of countries and a favourable government response towards foreign direct investment will be attractive to organizations. The rising per capita incomes of China and India, skilled labour and cheap manufacturing, coupled with populations that together make up more than a third of the world's population, are proving an irresistible lure for many organizations (see **Photo 8.1**).

8.3 **A Globalization Framework**

A **multinational enterprise** or **multinational corporation (MNE or MNC)**, refers to an organization that has productive activities in two or more countries. **Sumantra Ghoshal** proposes a framework which a multinational enterprise can benefit from when seeking to go global.[7] A global strategy

Photo 8.1   Modern Beijing: the rising per capita incomes and high population of China are proving an irresistible lure for many businesses. Source: © A.Aleksandravicius/Shutterstock.com.

implies that the organization is seeking to provide standardized products for all its international markets. As part of this framework, he states three strategic objectives inherent to all multinational enterprises:

1) The organization must **achieve efficiency** in its current activities.
2) It must **manage the risks** inherent in carrying out those activities.
3) It must **develop learning capabilities** that allow it to innovate and adapt to the future.

In order to gain competitive advantage the multinational will need to undertake actions that enable it to achieve these three objectives. These may involve trade-offs when multinational enterprises pursue goals that are conflicting. This is not a cause for concern, as Ghoshal's framework allows a multinational to differentiate between the benefits and costs of alternative strategies. An organization has three fundamental tools by which it can build competitive advantage.

1) It can exploit the differences in input and output markets that exist in different countries. For example, the cost of employing a software engineer in India is many times cheaper than in the USA, UK, or Europe.
2) It can benefit from economies of scale in its different activities.
3) It can take advantage of synergies or the economies of scope that derive from its diversity of activities.

Strategic Objectives of a Multinational Enterprise

1. **Achieving efficiency**

   The efficiency of an organization is the ratio of the value of its outputs to the costs of all its inputs.[8] In other words, the greater the ratio or the gap between an organization's costs and the value it generates, the more efficient it is. The differentiation of its products from competitor offerings allows an organization to set premium prices and, therefore, to maximize the value of its outputs. Similarly, by pursuing low-cost factors, such as wages or more efficient manufacturing processes, the organization will minimize the costs of its inputs.[9] In effect, this allows a multinational enterprise to configure its value chain to optimize the use of its resources.

2. **Managing risks**

   The multinational enterprise faces different types of risk. These include: *macro economic* risks that are outside its control, such as military conflicts; *political* risks, which emanate from decisions taken by national governments; *competitive* risks that deal with the uncertainty about how competitors will react to its strategies; and *resource* risks, which imply that the multinational enterprise may not have or be able to acquire the resources it needs to undertake its strategy. This might be because it lacks a particular technology. A key point to bear in mind is that risks change over time, necessitating an awareness and understanding of the external environment.

3. **Innovation, learning, and adaptation**

   Ghoshal argues that the multinational enterprise, by virtue of the different and varied environments within which it finds itself operating, is able to develop diverse capabilities and better learning opportunities than a domestic-based firm. Its diverse resource base may help the organization create innovations and exploit them in different locations. However, what is actually required for learning to take place is the existence of learning as an organizational objective that is actively supported and encouraged by senior management utilizing requisite systems and processes. In short, learning must pervade the organization's culture if it is to manifest itself in innovation.

Sources of Competitive Advantage for a Multinational Enterprise

We mentioned earlier that there are three tools for achieving global competitive advantage. These are *national differences*, *economies of scale*, and *economies of scope*. We can look at each of these in turn.

1. **National differences**

   This deals with what are sometimes called *locational advantages*. These derive from the observed fact that different countries have different factor endowments that provide these countries with different factor costs. For example, Russia has an abundant supply of natural gas, whereas Japan has very little. As a result of this factor endowment Russia is an exporter of natural gas whereas Japan is an importer. In the same way, the activities that go to make up a multinational enterprise's value chain have different factor costs. The aim of the multinational enterprise, then, is to configure its value chain in such a way that each of its activities is located in the country that has the lowest cost.

   National differences may also arise because of the clustering of key suppliers or technology companies around a particular location, for example, Silicon Valley in California. Other examples of supplier clusters include the city of Wuhan in China. Wuhan is the biggest transport hub in China and home to numerous supplier companies including Hon Hai, also known as Foxconn. Technology companies such as Apple, Chinese smartphone maker Xiaomi, and local electronic component maker BOE Technology rely on factories in Wuhan.[10] Supplies from Wuhan to the electronics and automotive industries were disrupted in 2020 as a result of COVID-19, leading many companies to consider on-shoring their supply chain.

2. Economies of scale

The concept of economies of scale states that as an organization increases the volume of its output so it is able to achieve a reduction in its unit costs. One reason for this is that as organizations produce ever larger outputs so their learning experience accumulates. This allows them to move down the experience curve, which in turn generates cost reductions. The organization should configure its value chain in order to ensure that it achieves economies of scale in each activity. This allows it to operate at the lowest point on its long-run average cost curve: its minimum efficient scale.

3. Economies of scope

Economies of scope arise from an understanding that the cost of undertaking two activities together is sometimes less than the cost of undertaking them separately. For example, car manufacturers use common platforms when making different types of cars. This allows them to achieve smaller production runs at a relatively low cost through economies of scope. This flexible manufacturing enables an organization to produce a customized offering for the consumer at relatively low unit costs. In managing its activities globally, the multinational enterprise needs to use all three sources of competitive advantage in order to simultaneously maximize its efficiency, risk, and learning. As Ghoshal states, 'The key to a successful global strategy is to manage the interactions between these different goals and means.'[11] **Table 8.1** provides a summary of the strategic objectives and sources of competitive advantage for multinational enterprises.

	Sources of competitive advantage		
Strategic objectives	**National differences**	**Scale economies**	**Scope economies**
Achieving efficiency in current operations	Benefiting from differences in factor costs—wages and cost of capital	Expanding and exploiting potential scale economies in each activity	Sharing of investments and costs across products, markets, and businesses
Managing risks	Managing different kinds of risks arising from market- or policy-induced changes in comparative advantages of different countries	Balancing scale with strategic and operational flexibility	Portfolio diversification of risks and creation of side-bets
Innovation, learning, and adaptation	Learning from societal differences in organizational and managerial processes and systems	Benefiting from experience—cost reduction and innovation	Shared learning across organizational components in different products, markets, or businesses

Table 8.1   Global strategy: strategic objectives and sources of competitive advantage.
Source: S. Ghoshal, 'Sources of competitive advantage', *Strategic Management Journal*, vol. 8, no. 5 (1987). © John Wiley & Sons Ltd. Reproduced with permission.

8.4 Types of International Strategy

When considering how to compete in international markets organizations are faced with a stark dilemma. On the one hand, to what extent should they produce standardized products for sale in different countries utilizing the locational advantages of low-cost countries? On the other hand, to what extent should they produce differentiated products that embody variations in local tastes and preferences, but incur greater costs? This is the debate between *globalization and localization*, which we discussed in detail in **Section 8.1**. We can say, other things being equal, globalization provides for greater efficiency through economies of scale brought about by standardization and locational advantages, while localization ensures that the organization's products are responsive to and meet the needs of local preferences.

The issue of globalization versus responsiveness to local needs highlights four basic strategies open to the organization seeking to diversify its activities overseas. These are: (1) multidomestic; (2) international; (3) global; and (4) transnational.

8.4.1 Multidomestic Strategy

A **multidomestic strategy** is aimed at adapting a product or service for use in national markets and thereby responding more effectively to the changes in local demand conditions. This assumes that each national market is unique and independent of the activities in other national markets. To this extent local managers are often given substantial autonomy to determine how a product will meet the needs of local consumers. A benefit of this decentralized multidomestic strategy is that value-chain activities can more closely reflect local market conditions. A disadvantage of a multidomestic strategy is that with increased variety come increased costs. Therefore, an important task for managers is to try to determine the point at which differentiation increases an organization's costs more than the value it adds for the consumer. At this point differentiation fails to be appreciated by the consumer. In addition, a multidomestic strategy tends to impede learning across country boundaries, as capabilities that reside within a given country are not automatically shared.

Walmart entered the German market with the acquisition of the Wertkauf and Interspar grocery chains. However, despite generating sales of $2.5 billion a year, it never posted a profit. Critics of the US giant said Walmart failed to understand the different culture that exists in Germany. For example, an attempt to introduce 'greeters' in stores, whose role was to smile at every customer, is thought to have been particularly unpopular. In addition, a lawsuit by employees forced Walmart to change part of an ethics manual that prevented romantic relationships between supervisors and employees. Although this practice was the norm in the USA, German workers saw it as a violation of their personal rights. Added to this, Walmart found that its position of being the cheapest retailer in its markets was already taken by Aldi. In an ironic twist, we now find Aldi investing in the USA, intensifying competition in the grocery sector.[12]

8.4.2 Global Strategy

With a **global strategy** the organization seeks to provide standardized products for its international markets. If a multidomestic strategy accepts cost increases as the price for local differentiation, a global strategy consciously embraces cost reductions as the benefit of manufacturing standardized products. An organization pursuing a global strategy will have their manufacturing, marketing, and

R&D centralized in a few locations. A combination of standardization with centralized facilities and functions enables them to reap substantial economies of scale. Industry examples include telecoms, consumer electronics, aerospace, pharmaceuticals, and semiconductors. Companies such as Huawei, Tata, Apple, and Boeing have developed global brands that cross national borders. A disadvantage of a global strategy is that it may overestimate the extent to which tastes are converging and fail to respond to important local differences. For example, the US retailer Walmart exited South Korea when it became clear that its hypermarket formula did not appeal to local tastes.

8.4.3 International Strategy

An **international strategy** is based upon an organization exploiting its core competencies and capabilities in foreign markets. Local managers may be provided with some degree of autonomy in adapting products to suit local markets, but this is likely to be at the margin only. The capabilities inherent within the organization will be centralized in the home country. For example, Apple has capabilities in design and product development. These value-chain activities are based in the USA, while other activities, such as manufacturing, take place in China. A disadvantage of this strategy is that its concentration of some activities in one country can leave it open to threats from currency appreciations. Also, the geographical distance and different cultures may make it difficult to control production and quality. Moreover, unforeseen events such as shutdowns in production following the global pandemic of coronavirus can substantially reduce the flow of vital parts and equipment. Finally, the lack of resources given to overseas subsidiaries can lead to a demotivation of local managers as their autonomy to make important decisions is eroded. **Table 8.2** shows the organizational characteristics that relate to these three international strategies.

8.4.4 Transnational Strategy

Christopher Bartlett and Sumantra Ghoshal argue that, until recently, most organizations in any given industry could obtain success by matching their resources and capabilities to achieve efficiency, or responsiveness, or knowledge transfer required by that industry.[13] Today the search for a match between an organization's capabilities and a single set of environment forces no longer holds. This has been replaced by a more complex set of environment demands. Organizations operating in global industries have to reconcile diverse and often conflicting strategic needs. In the past, companies could succeed with a unidimensional strategic capability that emphasized efficiency, or responsiveness, or transferring knowledge and core competencies. Now, however, more and more industries are driven by the realization that neither a multidomestic, nor an international or a global strategy, is sufficient. This is because industries are evolving towards what Bartlett and Ghoshal term *transnational industries*.

A **transnational strategy** is one in which an organization is confronted with multidimensional strategic requirements. It must simultaneously achieve global efficiency, national responsiveness, and a worldwide leveraging of its innovations and learning. However, organizations are somewhat constrained in responding to these environment changes by their internal capabilities. These, in turn, are contingent upon their *administrative heritage*. In seeking to adapt to the challenges of a changing international environment, an organization needs to understand what determines its administrative heritage. Administrative heritage includes a firm's configuration of its assets, its management style, and its organizational values. These are influenced by leadership, the home country's culture, and organizational history.

Organizational characteristic	Multidomestic	Global	International
Configuration of assets and capabilities	Decentralized and nationally self-sufficient	Centralized and globally scaled	Sources of core competencies centralized, others decentralized
Role of overseas operations	Sensing and exploiting local opportunities	Implementing parent company strategies	Adapting and leveraging parent company competencies
Development and diffusion of knowledge	Knowledge developed and retained within each unit	Knowledge developed and retained at the centre	Knowledge developed at the centre and transferred to overseas units

Table 8.2   Characteristics of multidomestic, global, and international companies.
Source: Reprinted by permission of Harvard Business School Press. From C. Bartlett and S. Ghoshal, *Managing across Borders: The Transnational Solution*, 2nd edn, 1998, p. 67. Copyright © 1989 by the Harvard Business School Publishing Corporation. All rights reserved.

The administrative heritage will influence a company's organizational form as well as its capabilities. Thus, if we map administrative heritage to the three strategies discussed above we see that a multidomestic company is structured to allow it to decentralize its assets and capabilities such that its foreign operations are able to respond to national differences between markets. An international company is structured in a way that allows it to transfer knowledge and capabilities to foreign operations that are less developed. Its foreign operations possess some autonomy to adapt new products and strategies, but they are more reliant on the parent company for these new products and ideas. This necessitates more coordination by the parent company than we see with a multidomestic company. A global organization's structure allows for a centralization of its assets, resources, and responsibilities. The role of its foreign subsidiaries is to build global scale. Unlike the multidomestic or international organization, the global organization has less autonomy to adapt new products or strategies.

A *transnational organization* seeks to maximize the trade-offs between efficiency and responsiveness to local need by redefining the problem. As Bartlett and Ghoshal state:

> It seeks efficiency not for its own sake, but as a means to achieve global competitiveness. It acknowledges the importance of local responsiveness, but as a tool for achieving flexibility in international operations.[14]

Therefore, a transnational strategy recognizes the benefits of efficiency that derive from the global company, the response to local needs of the multidomestic company, and the transfer of knowledge and capabilities across countries by the international company. However, where the transnational strategy differs from the other organizational forms is that it neither dogmatically centralizes nor decentralizes, but instead makes selective decisions. That is, it recognizes that some resources and capabilities are better centralized in the home country for economies of scale and protection of the capability. For example, R&D is a capability that most organizations agree is best kept in the home country. Other resources may be centralized, but not in the home country. For example, a production plant for labour-intensive products which service global operations may be built in a low-wage economy such as Mexico. Access to a particular technology may require centralization of activities in a specific country like the USA. In the same way, other resources may best be decentralized to create flexibility and avoid reliance on a single facility.

The managers of a transnational organization will centralize some resources in the home country and some abroad, and distribute others between the organization's various national operations. This leads to a far more complex configuration of resources and capabilities that are distributed, but also specialized. The dispersed resources are managed throughout the organization by creating inter-dependencies between the subsidiaries. This cannot be achieved through existing organizational forms, but requires an **integrated network**. This integrated network emphasizes '*significant flows of components, products, resources, people, and information that must be managed in the transnational*'.[15] In **Figure 8.1**, each of these four broad strategies are plotted according to the extent to which they reflect competitive pressures to reduce costs and the extent to which there exists a need to adapt to local market conditions.

For the transnational organization, each activity within the organization's value chain is undertaken in the location that provides for the lowest costs. Its resources and capabilities can be leveraged worldwide. However, accomplishment of this requires a move away from traditional organizational structures towards a different kind of corporate structure which allows the organization to manage these complex interactions through integrated networks. The discussion of the transnational organization, with its emphasis on internal resources and capabilities, has clear affinities with the resource-based view of strategy discussed in **Chapter 5**. For the transnational organization, the key capability for success is not a choice between efficiency, responsiveness, or learning. It is the simultaneous attainment of all three that allows the organization to remain competitive.

To summarize, a *global strategy* allows a multinational enterprise to achieve low costs through economies of scale and a coordinated strategy, but is unresponsive to the needs of local markets. The global organization is configured in a way that allows no slack resources for overseas subsidiaries. This effectively curtails its ability and, therefore, motivation to respond to local needs. This also prevents the global organization from accessing learning opportunities that exist outside its home country.

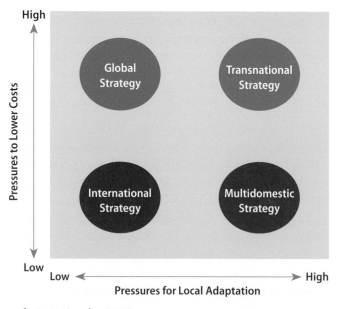

Figure 8.1   Types of international strategies.

A *multidomestic strategy* is the polar opposite of a global strategy. With a multidomestic strategy, the organization responds effectively to local market conditions and customer preferences in different countries. However, this level of differentiation means it is unable to achieve greater efficiency through low costs. Any local innovations may simply be the result of managers trying to protect their turf rather than working towards the corporate good.

An *international strategy* allows the parent company to transfer its knowledge and capabilities to other countries and the devolution of some autonomy to overseas managers. Its configuration of assets makes it less efficient than a global company and less responsive than a multidomestic company. Lastly, an organization following a *transnational strategy* seeks to achieve the efficiency and local responsiveness inherent in the previous three strategies, but also to leverage innovation and learning across countries. The idea is that its resources and capabilities can be leveraged worldwide. However, in order to accomplish this, a different kind of corporate structure is required which allows the organization to manage these complex interactions.

8.4.5 The Uppsala Model

The Uppsala model, developed by **Johanson and Vahlne**, seeks to explain the process by which organizations expand internationally.[16] According to the model, the international expansion of firms takes place gradually through a series of incremental decisions. As firms gain and accumulate more knowledge from foreign markets and operations, so they will gradually increase their market commitment to more foreign markets. Therefore, we would expect in the initial stages of the internationalization process, that firms are more likely to engage in export activities before the establishment of a foreign subsidiary.

Moreover, firms tend to expand first into neighbouring countries and then gradually commit to more geographically and psychically distant markets. **Psychic distance** refers to the differences in language, culture, legal and political systems etc. which may prevent or hinder the flows of information between a firm and a foreign market.[17] Hence, it can be argued that a lack of knowledge about the foreign market represents the main barrier to a company's internationalization. The Uppsala model suggests that countries with lower psychic distance are more likely to be selected for international expansion. This is because the more the organization knows about foreign markets the lower we would expect its level of risk to be.

The main factors of the model are *market knowledge* and *market commitment*. **Market knowledge** involves the general knowledge and specific structure of the foreign market—its language, rules, and regulations. **Market commitment** refers to the resources available to the company to commit to a particular foreign market. Aligned to this are factors that tend to affect the success of the entry to foreign markets. These are *commitment decisions* and *current activities*. Current activities refer to the level of commitment of the company in a specific market and it represents an important aspect which allows the company to accumulate the required knowledge and experience. Commitment decisions refers to the difficulty the company has in identifying market opportunities in new locations, given the level of knowledge and experiences it has accumulated.

Criticisms of the Uppsala Model

Although the Uppsala model has been widely used to describe the internationalization process of organizations, it is not without its critics. For instance, **Benito and Grisprud** argue that the internationalization process of organizations is the outcome of rational decisions rather than a learning process based on the gradual accumulation of knowledge about the new foreign market.[18] Others argue that the internationalization process of companies is primarily driven by economic opportunities in terms of the size of the foreign market.[19] The model is often considered outdated and therefore unable to explain the internationalization process of organizations over the past decades.[20] Moreover, if we argue that globalization has led to a more integrated world, the concept of psychic distance becomes less important in the internationalization process of firms. Furthermore, companies can now easily network with businesses which possess the required knowledge and experience to enter a new foreign market.

We saw that the Uppsala model was based on a key assumption of a company accumulating experiential knowledge as it expands abroad. In seeking to address criticisms of their model **Johanson and Vahlne** have had to recognize the role of **business networks**.[21] Instead of simply relying on their accumulated knowledge as they enter foreign markets, companies can acquire the knowledge of new foreign markets through their interactions with suppliers or strategic partners. As a result, Johanson and Vahlne concede that knowledge about a foreign market can often be acquired through networks, which provides a way of reducing the psychic distance between markets. That said, the Uppsala model may still have relevance for firms from emerging markets which tend to follow the psychic distance principle more closely.

8.5　Entry Mode Strategies

In this section, we address the different types of entry mode strategies that companies can use to enter international markets. **Keith Brouthers** states that in selecting an appropriate entry mode, organizations need to answer two questions:[22]

1) What levels of resource commitment are they prepared to make?

2) What level of control over their international operations do they require?

For instance, organizations may not be willing to commit resources in what they perceive to be high-risk countries. In contrast, where the perception of risk in countries is perceived to be low, organizations may want control over the operation. What is important is the organization's perception of international risk. This determines the answer to these two questions and drives the type of entry mode that an organization will choose.

Kent Miller views international risk as consisting of three integrated parts: (1) the general environment; (2) industry; and (3) firm-specific risks.[23] Although these risks are also faced by organizations which operate in the domestic environment, the difference is that for the international firm, some of these risks are far greater. **General environmental risks** refer to uncertainties that affect all industries within a given country in a similar way, such as political risk. **Industry risks** refer to input market uncertainties, such as labour or material supplies. **Firm-specific risks** include such things as uncertainties that arise as a result of employee disputes. These firm-specific uncertainties exist in the domestic market, but organizations operating abroad have the added responsibility of undertaking their activities in a different culture. Therefore, when considering an international entry mode strategy, managers need to be aware of the totality of risks, since if they consider only one type of international risk, this may lead to the adoption of an incorrect entry mode strategy. This is because the entry mode eventually adopted may result in unforeseen problems which arise because other international risk issues were not considered.

We can evaluate some of the different entry mode strategies in detail. These are exporting, licensing, international franchising, joint ventures and strategic alliances, and wholly owned subsidiaries.[24]

8.5.1 **Exporting**

Exporting is where an organization makes goods and services in the home country and sells them in other countries. Organizations are naturally a little tentative about committing resources to new markets about which they have varying degrees of knowledge. Under these conditions an organization may initially want to limit its resource commitments abroad until it builds up more local knowledge and develops its capabilities. It is attractive inasmuch as it provides an opportunity for an organization to acquire international experience while minimizing its risk exposure and resource commitments. At the same time, it also allows an organization to gain economies of scale through increased sales. A disadvantage of exporting is that it relies on local distributors, some of whom may be less than committed to marketing and promoting the international firm's products.

Figure 8.2 shows each entry mode strategy drawn against the degree of perceived risk and the amount of control acquired. What is apparent is that the level of risk increases as the organization seeks to maintain more control over its activities. Thus, exporting provides little perceived risk but little control, whereas a wholly owned subsidiary produces total control but comes with substantial risk.

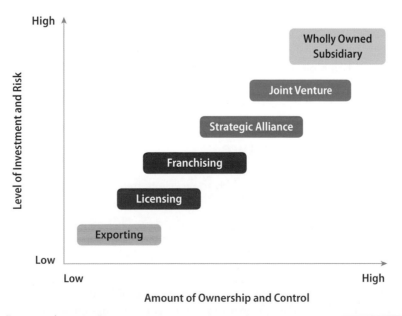

Figure 8.2   Entry mode strategies.

8.5.2 Licensing

Licensing can be seen as another way of gaining entry into overseas markets without large resource commitments. In return for a fee, the organization grants the right to use its patent, trademark, or intellectual property. The advantages of licensing are that it requires little capital and offers a relatively quick access to overseas markets. The disadvantages of licensing are that it requires an appropriate licensee who may in time be able to imitate your organization's product and become a competitor.

8.5.3 International Franchising

Franchising is a form of licensing that is employed by many international companies such as McDonald's, Benetton, and Pizza Hut. Its popularity has grown considerably since 1970. It is a system largely pioneered by US companies. The franchisor agrees to transfer a package of products, systems, and services that it has developed to a franchisee for a fee. The franchisee provides local market knowledge and entrepreneurship. The franchisor is responsible for improving the product, checking outlet quality, and promoting the brand. Unlike exporting, the host country may be more receptive to this form of market entry, as it involves local ownership and employment.

A number of disadvantages can stem from franchising. For instance, unless trust and understanding exist between both parties the franchise will underperform. As the franchisor is responsible for improving the product, the franchisee may *free ride* and so abdicate responsibility for success to the franchisor. Furthermore, should the franchisee provide a poor customer experience in one franchise this affects the reputation of the entire chain. To be successful, franchising needs to be seen by both franchisor and franchisee as mutually beneficial.

8.5.4 Joint Ventures and Strategic Alliances

Joint ventures and strategic alliances were covered in detail in **Chapter 7** when we discussed how organizations implement growth strategies. We can briefly restate that a joint venture exists when two organizations form a separate independent company in which they own shares equally (see **Strategy in Focus 8.1**). It is often formed when organizations feel it may be beneficial to combine

STRATEGY IN FOCUS 8.1 Northvolt and Norsk Hydro Recycling Joint Venture

Northvolt and Norsk Hydro are teaming up to recycle batteries from Norway's hundreds of thousands of electric cars as part of Europe's effort to build a green battery industry to take on Tesla and Asian rivals. The Swedish battery manufacturer—which last year raised more than €1 billion from the likes of Volkswagen, Goldman Sachs, and Ikea—and the Norwegian aluminium company will open a NKr100 million ($10 million) recycling hub in the south-eastern Norwegian town of Frederikstad next year.

'We believe we can be a frontrunner,' Arvid Moss, head of Hydro's energy business, told *The Financial Times*. Emma Nehrenheim, Northvolt chief environmental officer, said that with electric car sales set for 'hockey-stick growth' soon, 'there's going to be a similar trend in the recycling market a few years later'.

Northvolt is the leading business in a push to develop European battery makers to supply the continent's carmakers rather than Tesla or Panasonic. Founded by two former Tesla executives in 2017, Northvolt has one small battery factory close to Stockholm and is aiming to open a larger 'gigafactory' in northern Sweden next year.

It is aiming to obtain half of its raw materials from recycled batteries by 2030 and chose Norway because of the country's high number of electric cars, the result of generous government subsidies. Erna Solberg, Norway's centre-right prime minister, welcomed the news of the new recycling hub. 'Promoting the development of sustainable low-emission solutions, including electrification of the transport sector, has been one of the Norwegian government's priorities for many years,' she said.

Northvolt and Hydro, which is a small shareholder in the Swedish group, are setting up a joint venture called Hydro Volt. Hydro will receive aluminium from the recycling centre and Northvolt so-called 'black mass', which includes minerals such as cobalt, lithium, and manganese. The Frederikstad will initially be able to process about 8,000 tonnes of batteries a year, equivalent to at least 16,000 batteries. Mr Moss said it was important that the plant be 'scalable' but that it was too early to say if the joint venture might expand to other countries.

Northvolt is aiming to build a large recycling plant by 2022 next to its gigafactory in Skelleftea but needs a supply of material before it starts receiving its own batteries. Half of all new car sales in Norway are electric, with another 30 per cent hybrids as the country—Western Europe's largest oil producer—aims to phase out the sale of petrol vehicles by 2025. Ms Nehrenheim said recycling batteries had been challenging until now because of the purity of materials required. But she added: 'A circular raw material flow is mitigating a lot of risk. It's both securing raw materials, and ensuring these materials aren't entering nature through the risk of hazardous pollution.'

Source: Richard Milne, 'Northvolt and Norsk Hydro to build car battery recycling plant', *The Financial Times*, 1 June 2020.

their resources and capabilities to develop new technologies or gain access to new markets. Strategic alliances take place when two or more separate companies share some of their resources and capabilities, but stop short of forming a new company. The idea is that each partner within the strategic alliance gains access to knowledge that it would not otherwise possess and that would be expensive to develop. A useful alliance will involve complementary resources and capabilities that allow both organizations to grow and develop according to their strategic objectives. The ultimate aim of strategic alliances is to learn from your partners. Both joint ventures and strategic alliances work well when each partner's objectives are clear and agreed, and when the working relationship is one based on trust. The disadvantage occurs when managerial differences exist as these must be resolved prior to entering into a strategic alliance. Such problems are compounded when there is the potential for state interference. For example, the French food giant, Danone, and HSBC encountered state interference in their joint ventures in China.[25]

8.5.5 **Wholly Owned Subsidiaries**

A wholly owned subsidiary is where an organization seeks to have total control over its operations abroad. There are two types: a greenfield site, in which the organization sets up a new operation, or the organization can *acquire or merge* with an existing organization operating abroad. Both types of entry involve the greatest commitment of resources and, therefore, the most risk. The advantage is that this type of entry strategy also generates the greatest returns. The downside is that there is no one with whom to offset the costs. This type of strategy is also referred to as **foreign direct investment** (FDI). Organizations which use a direct investment strategy include Tesla, Nestlé, and Procter & Gamble.

Where an organization possesses unique resources and capabilities which provide for competitive advantage, it will be more inclined towards a wholly owned subsidiary. For example, Japanese auto makers like Toyota and Nissan tend to set up wholly owned subsidiaries abroad. Further, FDI may attract support from the host government in the form of favourable financing, interest rate holidays, and help with local regulations in return for generating local employment. The disadvantages are the financial risk and exposure involved in undertaking a new venture abroad. This is compounded when the organization fails to adequately recruit managers who are familiar with local market conditions.

We have seen that exporting provides an organization with relatively low international risks, but gives it little control over the marketing and distribution of its products. At the other extreme, a wholly owned subsidiary gives an organization total control over its operations and the ability to appropriate all its value, but at the expense of incurring substantial risk. The strategic choice becomes one of more control and higher risks, or low risk and low control. Licensing, international franchising, joint ventures, and strategic alliances provide varying degrees of control and exposure to international risks. When the perceived risk is high, the organization may choose to manage this by entering into a joint venture or franchise agreement as a means of sharing the risk.

8.6 **Porter's Diamond of National Advantage**

Why do some nations achieve competitive advantage in some industries while other countries achieve a similar advantage in other industries? **Michael Porter** argues that a nation's competitiveness derives from the capacity of its industry to innovate and upgrade.[26] This ability to innovate results from firms having to compete with strong domestic rivals, aggressive suppliers, and demanding local customers. A country's culture, national values, institutions, and economic structures all contribute to its competitive success. In this respect, a nation's competitive advantage results from a localized process. As Porter states: '*nations succeed in particular industries because their home environment is the most forward looking, dynamic, and challenging*'.[27] In effect, organizations that thrive in this sort of competitive environment are better placed to compete abroad.

Organizations that achieve competitive advantage in international markets do this through innovation. Innovation in its broadest sense refers to both new technology and new ways of doing things. It may often involve small changes that build up over time rather than a major technological leap. It does not have to represent new ideas, but can come about by pursuing established ideas more rigorously. Innovation does, however, involve investments in skills and knowledge. Sustainable competitive advantage in international markets requires an organization to engage in continuous improvements in its product offering. As competitors will eventually imitate any success, the key to sustainable competitive advantage is an ability to upgrade or continually increase the sophistication of product offerings. Innovation is based on an ability to embrace change. However, as **Danny Miller** points out in **The Icarus Paradox**, successful organizations have difficulty in seeing the need for change, let alone instituting change.[28] When an organization is content to sit back and enjoy its current success, a change in its environment or a new competitor will eventually overtake them.

8.6.1 The Diamond of National Advantage

Porter suggests that organizations are capable of consistent innovation because of four attributes that exist in their home market, which he refers to as the **diamond of national advantage**.[29] These are: (1) *factor conditions*; (2) *demand conditions*; (3) *related and supporting industries*; and (4) *firm strategy, structure, and rivalry*. Each point of the diamond contributes towards global success

1. **Factor conditions**

   Since the work of David Ricardo in the nineteenth century, it has been accepted that a country will tend to export goods that make the best use of the factors of production that it has in relative abundance. In other words, it will exploit its comparative advantage.[30] These factors of production include land, labour, and capital. For Porter, factor conditions refer to a country's use of its factors of production that enable it to compete in an industry, such as a skilled labour or a technological capability. In the modern economy, a country actively creates its most important factors of production, such as a skilled labour force for its industries. Therefore, a nation's natural stock of factors is far less important as a determinant of international competitive advantage than it was in the past. Natural factors of production such as labour or local resources, however abundant, are insufficient to provide for competitive advantage. What are required are factors of production that are specialized to an industry's needs.

   Today, much comparative advantage derives from human effort rather than natural conditions. Such factors will involve continuous investment to upgrade. For example, the concentration of computer companies around Silicon Valley resulted from Xerox's Palo Alto Research Centre, the proximity of Stanford University, and the work of two men, Hewlett and Packard. These dynamic factors could have occurred anywhere.[31] Factors such as these that are developed within a country are scarce and difficult for competitors to imitate. Therefore, nations are successful in industries where they are especially good at factor creation (see **Figure 8.3**).

2. **Demand conditions**

   Demand conditions that exist in the home country can have a positive impact on its industry and, therefore, on an organization's ability to compete abroad. This is particularly the case where consumers are both highly sophisticated and demanding. These consumers will be continuously pushing companies to innovate, and to improve and upgrade their products. One benefit of this is that the constant pressure to innovate and upgrade may provide an insight into future global trends that the organization will be in a better position to exploit. It is in meeting the challenge of this robust consumer demand that organizations gain advantages over foreign competitors which contributes to their success abroad. For example, Japanese companies developed a small, quiet, air-conditioning unit utilizing energy-efficient rotary compressors. This was to benefit Japanese consumers whose accommodation is small and tightly packed and who endure hot summers and high electrical costs.

Determinants of National Competitive Advantage

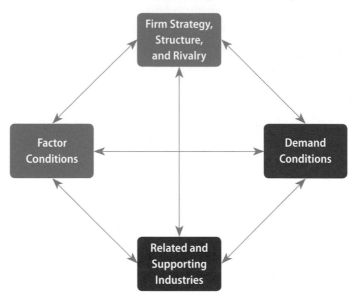

Figure 8.3   Determinants of national competitive advantage.
Source: M. E. Porter, *The Competitive Advantage of Nations*, Harvard Business School Publishing Corporation, 2001.
Copyright © 2001 by the Harvard Business School Publishing Corporation. Reprinted by permission of Harvard Business Review. All rights reserved.

3. Related and supporting industries

A third determinant of national advantage is the existence of related and supporting industries. For example, domestic suppliers that are capable of competing in international markets will be able to provide firms with the most cost-effective inputs. Companies that are located in close proximity to their suppliers can influence their technical efforts and thus increase their level of innovations. Close working relationships between related and supporting industries can produce mutually beneficial innovations. For example, a cluster of Italian footwear suppliers enables shoe companies to communicate readily with their leather suppliers and learn about new textures and colours that will help shape new styles. The suppliers benefit by receiving useful information about fashion trends that allows them to plan more effectively. This relationship benefits from proximity, but requires a conscious effort from both parties if it is to be effective.

4. Firm strategy, structure, and rivalry

The use of different management structures in different countries tends to reflect the dynamics of their particular industries. For instance, German management structures work well in technical industries, such as optics, which require precision manufacturing. This calls for a tightly disciplined management structure. The existence of strong domestic competitors is the most important factor for the creation of competitive advantage and international success. Domestic rivalry creates pressures for organizations to innovate, reduce costs, improve product quality, and design new products. It forces companies to update continually the sources of their competitive advantage. Intense domestic rivalry is a proving ground for domestic companies that acquire the necessary capabilities to compete successfully abroad. It is this rivalry that causes companies to seek out new markets abroad, confident that they have already been forged in the furnace of intense domestic competition.

In addition to these four country-specific determinants, there are also two external variables: (1) *the role of chance*; and (2) *the role of government*.

1. **The role of chance**

   This occurs as a result of unforeseen developments such as new inventions, political interventions by foreign governments, wars, major instabilities in financial markets, discontinuities in input costs such as the price of oil, and technological breakthroughs. A more useful term might be 'the role of unforeseen events'. These disruptions or tipping points were addressed in **Chapter 2**, when we evaluated the macro-environment.

2. **The role of government**

   Governments can influence all four aspects of the diamond through policies on subsidies, education and training, regulation of capital markets, establishment of local product standards, the purchase of goods and services, tax laws, and the regulation of competition.

8.6.2 Criticisms of Porter's Diamond

The main contention of Porter's diamond framework is that an organization builds on its home base to achieve international competitiveness. Competitive advantage for the organization depends upon four broad attributes which determine a nation's international competitiveness. An effective organization is able to leverage its resources, capabilities, and experience acquired through competing in a rigorous home country to compete successfully abroad.

Alan Rugman and Joseph D'Cruz agree that the single diamond framework works well for multinational enterprises based in the USA, Japan, and the European Union (EU)—the regional grouping referred to as the triad.[32] However, they argue that it is less effective when determining successful global competition in smaller open economies such as Canada and New Zealand.[33] In fact, they state that in order to help improve the international competitiveness of Canada, Porter's framework needs to be substantially revised. **Rugman and Alain Verbeke** also take issue with Porter's distinction between a country's home base, which Porter argues provides its firms with their source of competitive advantage, and other countries, which Porter argues can be selectively 'tapped into', but are much less important for competitive advantage than their home country.[34] As Rugman and Verbeke state:

> *this viewpoint does not adequately address the complexities of real world global strategic management ... small nations such as Canada and New Zealand ... may come to rely on a particular large host nation ... in such a way that the distinction between the home base and host nations as sources of global competitive advantage may become blurred.*[35]

According to **Rugman**, if we look at Canada, the implication of this for Canadian-owned multinational enterprises is that their managers should treat the US diamond as their home market.[36] This is because their competitive advantages derive from attributes that exist in the US diamond rather than the Canadian diamond. In effect, Canada and other smaller countries are simply too small to offer a basis for international competitive advantage on their own. Therefore, greater opportunities exist for small economies that treat a larger foreign diamond as their home diamond. To capture this, Rugman and D'Cruz suggest a **double diamond framework**. This allows managers of a Canadian multinational, for example, to address the determinants of competitiveness in Canada as well as in the USA when formulating their strategies.[37] **Richard Hodgetts** points out that the multinational enterprise Nestlé achieves around 95 per cent of its sales outside Switzerland.

> *Thus the Swiss diamond of competitive advantage is less relevant than that of foreign countries in shaping the contribution of Nestlé to the home economy. This is not only true for Switzerland but for 95 per cent of the world's nations.*[38]

When we look at smaller economies their home diamond may be important, but it is the larger diamonds of major trading partners that are of *paramount* importance. Therefore, any assessment of competitive advantage must take account of the relationship between the organization and its home and foreign diamond. As Hodgetts reminds us:

> *different diamonds need to be constructed and analysed for different countries, and these diamonds often require integration and linkage with the diamonds of other economically stronger countries thus creating a double diamond paradigm.*[39]

8.7 The Myths of Global Strategy

Subramanian Rangan argues[40] that there are seven common myths about companies considering a global strategy.[41]

1. **Any company with money can go global.**

   The reality is that companies that succeed abroad possess valuable intangible assets that help them beat competitors in their own home market. This can include a superior value proposition such as that developed by the Swedish furniture retailer IKEA, and a well-known brand name, e.g. Coca-Cola. For example, if an organization's exports are growing, this is evidence that it can offer better value than local competitors. This explains why companies often export before seeking to commit assets aboard.

2. **Internationalization in services is different.**

   Service companies are no different from product companies. A service company can only internationalize successfully if it also possesses valuable intangible assets that can be replicated abroad.

3. **Distance and national borders don't matter any more.**

   An argument often put forward is that national cultures are converging, and distance is less important because of developments in communication technology. The reality is that transport costs may be small, but they are still positive and increase with distance. Moreover, a country's culture shapes its institutions and its values. For example, US companies export to Canada first because of the common language. To be successful requires an organization to be local and global. For example, HSBC refers to itself as 'the world's local bank' and promotes its knowledge of local differences.

4. **Developing countries are where the action is.**

There is a belief that large markets are in developing countries like China, India, and Brazil. However, despite the economic convergence of China, it is the Western economies that currently dominate world trade. The implication is that any organization seeking to go global cannot ignore Western economies. This point is less valid given the reality of China as the world's second largest economy.

5. **Manufacture where labour costs are cheapest.**

Rangan argues that 'the only sounds that low wages should stir are loud yawns'. This is because, although important, labour costs are only part of the total delivered cost. An organization may find that low-wage economies impose tariffs and duties that increase the manufacturing cost. Furthermore, low wages may be associated with low productivity that actually increases unit costs.

6. **Globalization is here to stay.**

The drivers of globalization are technological changes and economic convergence between nations. As countries experience similar per capita incomes, so their consumer tastes begin to converge. However, if we were to see a re-emergence of sustained unemployment that has characterized market economies in the past, this might force governments to take unilateral actions that reverse the trend towards globalization. The argument here is that corporations may have to accept a more socially active role if they require globalization to continue. Therefore, organizations need to 'explore issues such as unemployment, employee retraining and equality of opportunity . . . if business does not become more sensitive to this possibility . . . expect to see governments reasserting themselves'.[42]

7. **Governments don't matter any more.**

Where organizations are believed to be pursuing their own self-interest, individuals will seek redress through their government. A global economy requires rules and these rules are set by governments. The implication for multinational corporations is that they need to work with governments to ensure an acceptable balance between the needs of companies and the needs of local people.

In discussing globalization and its drivers we have assumed, at least implicitly, that globalized companies exist. In fact, the idea of a globalized company may represent more wishful thinking than a state of reality. Rugman states that the largest 500 multinational enterprises (MNEs) account for around 90 per cent of foreign direct investment and about 50 per cent of world trade.[43] These impressive figures reveal an even more interesting fact. Rugman and Verbeke argue that most of these firms are not global companies, if 'global' means that they operate across innumerable foreign markets.[44] The evidence suggests there are few global firms with a global strategy, if by global we are referring to the ability to sell the same products and/or services around the world. They are 'regional multinationals', as the vast majority of their sales are in the home leg of their triad, which comprises North America, the EU, and Asia. It would appear the world of international business is in fact a regional one, not a global one.[45]

Thus, a US multinational enterprise would have the majority of its sales within the North American triad, a French multinational's sales would be predominantly in their home region, that is, the EU, and so forth. Therefore, what some refer to as globalization may more accurately be defined as regionalization.[46]

8.8 The Challenge of Globalization

In common with **Bartlett and Ghoshal**,[47] the former CEO of IBM, **Samuel Palmisano**, asserts that the traditional multinational enterprise is evolving into what he calls a **globally integrated enterprise**.[48] The goal of this enterprise is the integration of products and value delivery worldwide. The focus of these corporations is *how* to make things, rather than *what* to make, and *how* to deliver services, rather than *which* services to deliver. The backdrop to these changes is the continuing economic liberalization and information technology that has standardized technologies worldwide. For example, we see financial institutions and software companies building R&D and service centres in India to support employees, customers, and production worldwide. US radiologists send X-rays to Australia for interpretation. As organizations share business and technology standards, so integration into global production systems is facilitated.

The increase in outsourcing encourages organizations to see themselves in terms of components or activities. The globally integrated enterprise integrates value-chain activities such as procurement, research, and sales on a global basis in order to produce its goods and services for consumers. The choice for organizations is where they want the work for these activities to be done and whether they want them carried out in-house or outsourced. This should be seen as not merely a matter of outsourcing non-core activities, but is 'about actively managing different operations, expertise, and capabilities so as to open the enterprise up . . . allowing it to connect more intimately with partners, suppliers, and customers'.[49]

The globally integrated enterprise brings opportunities and a number of challenges. The opportunities include increases in living standards in developed and developing countries. Developing countries experience increased employment and prosperity as their workers become more integrated into global production systems. This is also helped by structural changes that allow small- and medium-sized organizations in developing countries to participate in the global economy. However, there are difficult challenges. The globally integrated enterprise requires a supply of high-value skills that requires nations to invest in education and training.

A key challenge in the global economy is how to prevent piracy of intellectual property rights without sacrificing collaboration. A possible solution is to shift the emphasis from protecting intellectual property, which limits its use, to maximizing intellectual capital based on shared ownership. How do companies maintain trust when their business models are dispersed globally? This will require shared values that transcend national borders. Finally, some of the changes that global corporate integration brings will require that capital markets and investors adjust their habits from short-term rewards to longer-term growth. Given the investment nature of Anglo-American economies, this is quite a challenge. Palmisano concludes:

> *The shift from MNCs to globally integrated enterprises provides an opportunity to advance both business growth and societal progress. But it raises issues that are too big . . . for business alone or government alone to solve.*[50]

There is some evidence which suggests that global firms, far from dominating the global landscape, are in retreat as multinationals' cross-border investment falls (see **Strategy in Focus 8.2**).

STRATEGY IN FOCUS 8.2 Globalization in Retreat

Between 1990 and 2005 Kentucky Fried Chicken (KFC) and McDonald's combined foreign sales soared by 400 per cent. McDonald's and KFC embodied an idea that would become incredibly powerful: global firms, run by global managers and owned by global shareholders, should sell global products to global customers. For a long time their planet-straddling model was as hot, crisp, and moreish as their fries. Today both companies have gone soggy. Their shares have lagged behind the American stock market over the past half-decade. Yum, which owns KFC, saw its foreign profits peak in 2012; they have fallen by 20 per cent since. Those of McDonald's are down by 29 per cent since 2013. In 2016, Yum threw in the towel in China and spun off its business there. In 2017, McDonald's sold a majority stake in its Chinese operation to a state-owned firm. The world is losing its taste for global businesses.

Their detractors and their champions both think of multinational firms—for the purposes of this article, firms that make more than 30 per cent of their sales outside their home region—as the apex predators of the global economy. They shape the ecosystems in which others seek their living. They direct the flows of goods, services, and capital that brought globalization to life. Though multinationals account for only 2 per cent of the world's jobs, they own or orchestrate the supply chains that account for more than 50 per cent of world trade; they make up 40 per cent of the value of the West's stock markets; and they own most of the world's intellectual property.

Although the idea of being at the top of the food chain makes these companies sound ruthless and all-conquering, rickety and overextended are often more fitting adjectives. And like jackals, politicians want to grab more of the spoils that multinational firms have come to control, including eighty million jobs on their payrolls and their profits of about $1 trillion. As multinational firms come to make ever more of their money from technology services they become yet more vulnerable to a backlash. The predators are increasingly coming to look like prey.

It all looked very different twenty-five years ago. With the Soviet Union collapsing and China opening up, a sense of destiny gripped Western firms; the 'end of history' announced by Francis Fukuyama, a scholar, in which all countries would converge towards democracy and capitalism seemed both a historical turning-point and a huge opportunity. There were already many multinationals, some long established. Shell, Coca-Cola, and Unilever had histories spanning the twentieth century. But they had been run, for the most part, as loose federations of national businesses. The new multinationals sought to be truly global.

Companies became obsessed with internationalizing their customers, production, capital, and management. Academics draw distinctions between going global 'vertically'—relocating production and the sourcing of raw materials—and 'horizontally'—selling into new markets. But in practice many firms went global every which way at once, enthusiastically buying rivals, courting customers, and opening factories wherever the opportunity arose. Though the trend started in the rich world, it soon caught on among large companies in developing economies, too. And it was huge: 85 per cent of the global stock of multinational investment was created after 1990, after adjusting for inflation.

By 2006 Sam Palmisano, the boss of IBM, was arguing that the 'globally integrated enterprise' would transcend all borders as it sought 'the integration of production and value delivery worldwide'. From the Seattle demonstrations of 1999 onwards, anti-globalization activists had been saying much the same, while drawing less solace from the prospect. The only business star to resist the orthodoxy was billionaire, Warren Buffett; he sought out monopolies at home instead. Such a spree could not last forever; an increasing body of evidence suggests that it has now ended. In 2016 multinationals' cross-border investment probably fell by 10–15 per cent. Impressive as the share of trade accounted for by cross-border supply chains is, it has stagnated since 2007. The proportion of sales that Western firms make outside their home region has shrunk. Multinationals' profits are falling and the flow of new multinational investment has been declining relative to GDP. The global firm is in retreat.

The Other End of the End of History

To understand why this is, consider the three parties that made the boom possible: investors; the 'headquarters countries' in which global firms are domiciled; and the 'host countries' that received multinational investment. For their different reasons, each thought that multinational firms would provide superior financial or economic performance.

Investors saw a huge potential for economies of scale. As China, India, and the Soviet Union opened up, and as Europe liberalized itself into a single market, firms could sell the same product to more people. And as the federation model was replaced by global integration, firms would be able to fine-tune the mix of inputs they got from around the world—a geographic arbitrage that would improve efficiency. From the rich world they could get management, capital, brands, and technology. From the emerging world they could get cheap workers and raw materials, as well as lighter rules on pollution. These advantages led investors to think global firms would grow faster and make higher profits. That was true for a while. But it is not true today. For the three countries which have, historically, hosted the most and biggest multinationals, the USA, the UK, and the Netherlands, return on equity (ROE) on foreign investment has shrunk to 4–8 per cent. The trend is similar across the Organisation for Economic Co-operation and Development (OECD).

What about the second constituency for multinationals, the 'headquarters countries'? In the 1990s and 2000s they wanted their national champions to go global in order to become bigger and brainier. The mood changed after the financial crisis. Multinational firms started to be seen as agents of inequality. They created jobs abroad, but not at home. Between 2009 and 2013, only 5 per cent, or 400,000, of the net jobs created in the USA were created by multinational firms domiciled there. The profits from their hoard of intellectual property were pocketed by a wealthy shareholder elite. Takeovers of Western firms now often come with strings attached by governments to safeguard local jobs and plants.

A typical multinational has over 500 legal entities, some based in tax havens. Using US figures, it pays a tax rate of about 10 per cent on its foreign profits. The European Union (EU) is trying to raise that figure. It has cracked down on Luxembourg, which offered generous deals to multinationals that parked profits there. US politicians also want Apple to shift more of its supply chain home. If these trends continue, global firms' tax and wage bills will rise, squeezing profits further.

Of all those involved in the spread of global businesses, the 'host countries' that receive investment by multinationals remain the most enthusiastic. China, where by 2010 30 per cent of industrial output and 50 per cent of exports were produced by the subsidiaries or joint ventures of multinational firms, is still attractive. India has a campaign called 'make in India' to attract multinational supply chains. But there are gathering clouds. China has been turning the screws on foreign firms in a push for 'indigenous innovation'. Bosses say that more products have to be sourced locally, and intellectual property often ends up handed over to local partners. Many fear that China's approach will be mimicked around the developing world, forcing multinational firms to invest more locally and create more jobs—a mirror image of the pressures placed on them at home.

Today multinationals need to rethink their competitive advantage. Roughly 50 per cent of the stock of foreign direct investment makes an ROE of less than 10 per cent. Ford and General Motors make 80 per cent or more of their profits in North America, suggesting that their foreign returns are abysmal. Retailers such as the UK's Tesco and France's Casino have abandoned many of their foreign adventures. LafargeHolcim, a cement maker, plans to sell, or has sold, businesses in India, South Korea, and Vietnam. P&G's foreign sales have dropped by almost one-third since 2012, as it has closed or sold weak businesses. Politicians will increasingly insist that companies buying foreign firms promise to preserve their national character, including jobs, R&D activity, and tax payments.

SoftBank, a Japanese firm that bought ARM, a British chip company, in 2016, agreed to such commitments. The new, prudent age of the multinational will have costs. The result will be a more fragmented and parochial kind of capitalism, and quite possibly a less efficient one—but also, perhaps, one with wider public support. And the infatuation with global companies will come to be seen as a passing episode in business history, rather than its end.

Source: 'The retreat of the global company', *The Economist*, 28 January 2017. Reproduced with permission.

Summary

We started this chapter with an evaluation of the views of Theodore Levitt on globalization. While globalization may indeed be increasing, the assertion that consumer preferences are *irrevocably homogenized* is considered by some to ignore the realities of important national differences. Douglas and Wind argue that while there exist global segments with similar needs, this is not a universal trend. This debate between globalization and localization is of crucial importance as it goes to the heart of the type of international strategy an organization adopts.

We saw that the motives for companies to expand internationally can be evaluated by looking at organizational and environmental factors. A global framework for guiding managers is provided by Ghoshal, who outlines three objectives and sources of competitive advantage for multinational enterprises. We assessed four types of international strategy: multidomestic, global, international, and transnational. The transnational organization, developed by Bartlett and Ghoshal, is a recognition that a search for a match between an organization's capabilities and a single set of environment forces no longer holds.

In selecting an appropriate entry mode strategy, organizations need to answer two questions: what levels of resource commitment are they prepared to make, and what level of control over their international operations do they require? The answer to these questions will be determined by an organization's perception of international risk. We saw that, according to Porter, organizations are capable of consistent innovation because of four attributes that exist in their home market, which he refers to as the *diamond of national advantage*. There are criticisms of Porter's diamond and some, such as Rugman and D'Cruz, argue that smaller nations' competitive advantage may actually derive from attributes that exist in their larger foreign diamond. To take account of this, Rugman suggests using a double diamond framework.

Lastly, we addressed some of the myths of globalization, and a globally integrated enterprise.

CASE STUDY Saudi Aramco—The Biggest Player in a Changing Oil Market

When Saudi Arabia, one of the most conservative of nations, promised to open the books of its state-owned oil company, Saudi Aramco, to the world and allow outside investors to take a stake in the company, there was always going to be a great deal of interest. The economy of Saudi Arabia is based around oil and the state-run Saudi Aramco—a fact not lost on its ruling elite who have observed a need to diversify beyond hydrocarbons. It also meant greater transparency for corporate governance, and a move towards relaxing existing social norms. After more than three years since the idea was first floated to list the company, Saudi Aramco shares began trading on Riyadh's Tadawul stock exchange in December 2019. The architect of this ground-breaking decision was Saudi Arabia's Crown Prince Mohammed bin Salman.

Saudi Aramco

Saudi Aramco, officially known as Saudi Arabian Oil Company, is the world's largest crude producer and most profitable company. In 2019 it made profits amounting to a staggering $88 billion. By comparison, the iPhone maker Apple (the world's most profitable publicly quoted company) made profits of $55 billion. A year earlier, in 2018, it made profits of $111 billion, more than a third greater than the combined net income of the five 'super majors' Exxon Mobil, Royal Dutch Shell, BP, Chevron, and Total. The company was founded in 1933 as a subsidiary of Standard Oil of California. It began producing commercial quantities of crude oil in 1938. In 1973, the Saudi Arabian government purchased a 25 per cent interest in Aramco, gradually increasing its stake to 100 per cent in the late 1970s. In 1988, the Saudi Arabian Oil Company (Saudi Aramco) was officially established and continues to supply oil to energy markets around the world.

Saudi Aramco had reserves equivalent to 260.2 billion barrels of oil in 2017, larger than the combined reserves of Exxon Mobil, Chevron, Shell, BP, and Total. This equates to fifty-two years of proven oil reserves. The company produced 10.3 million barrels per day (bpd) of crude oil in 2018, and extracts oil more cheaply than any

Photo 8.2   Mohammed bin Salman.
Source: © Wikimedia Commons.

Western major oil company. It has the lowest production cost in the world, at $2.80 a barrel, according to company documents. It also produced 1.1 million barrels of natural gas liquids and 8.9 billion standard cubic feet per day of natural gas.

And being the lowest-cost producer means that even when there is volatility in oil prices caused by a change in demand, global regulations, or even a global pandemic, it can still prosper. It is also very well managed, given the potential for corruption and insider dealing in a state monopoly. When production was crippled by a drone attack in September 2019, it restored its operations quickly. Saudi Aramco's drilling for oil and gas and refining fuels is about as solid and cash generative a business as any investor could want, even given the uncertain future for fossil fuels. The problem is that fifty-two years may be an inordinate amount of time for a company to change direction, but for a country it is an entirely different matter.

The chairmanship of the company has been held by the energy minister, Khalid al-Falih, since 2015, but in 2019 he was replaced with Yasir al-Rumayyan, head of the country's sovereign wealth fund, ahead of the planned stock market listing or initial public offering (IPO). The CEO is Amin Nasser. Mr Rumayyan, who was already on the board of Saudi Aramco, has consolidated his position in recent years as the head of the country's Public Investment Fund (PIF), the main vehicle through which Prince Mohammed has sought to diversify the kingdom's economy away from oil. The PIF funds Prince Mohammed's domestic reforms, with international investments that have included ride-hailing company Uber, electric car maker Tesla, and SoftBank's Vision Fund.

The Initial Public Offering (IPO)

Mr Rumayyan has seen his influence grow since his appointment as an adviser to the royal court in 2015, when King Salman took the throne and entrusted his son Prince Mohammed to embark on an ambitious transformation programme for the economy. The flotation of Saudi Aramco was at the heart of plans for economic reforms, with proceeds from the IPO expected to be ploughed into new sectors that will generate revenue when demand for oil weakens in the decades to come. Announcing plans for an Aramco IPO in 2016, Crown Prince Mohammed bin Salman said the kingdom must end its 'oil addiction' to ensure it was no longer at the mercy of commodity price volatility. He also made it clear that he expects the valuation of Saudi Aramco to be worth $2 trillion. A problem for the numerous Western banks, such as JP Morgan, Bank of America, Citigroup, Credit Suisse, Goldman Sachs, and Morgan Stanley, queueing up to get a piece of the fees from world's largest IPO is that this valuation is determined by the market and not royal decree. In the end, the Riyadh listing was led by HSBC, NCB, and Samba.

In December 2019, Saudi Aramco went public with its IPO, raising a record $25.6 billion by selling only 1.5 per cent of the company. This is the largest initial public offering in history, surpassing the $25 billion raised by China's Alibaba when it was floated on Wall Street in 2014. The amount being offered to the public was initially going to be up to 5 per cent of the company to raise $100 billion, but this was subsequently scaled back by Prince Mohammed. To put that in perspective, 1.5 per cent is significantly lower than what most companies distribute. For example, Apple, Alphabet, and Amazon all have more than 84 per cent of their shares held by the public. However, this allows Saudi Arabia to remain in control of the company and to use the money generated from the public offering to diversify away from oil.

On the first day of trading the company touched $1.9 trillion, but by day two it had hit the $2 trillion mark coveted by crown prince Mohammed bin Salman. At $2 trillion it was worth more than technology giants Apple and Microsoft. It was even bigger than the world's five largest oil companies—Exxon Mobil, Total, Shell, Chevron, and BP—combined. On closer inspection, it appears that the market may have been given a helping hand.

MbS—Crown Prince Mohammed bin Salman

Prince Mohammed, known also as 'MbS' is a man on a mission. Since he consolidated his power base, he has begun to shake up the kingdom on a scale not witnessed since his grandfather, Abdulaziz, founded the modern state eighty-eight years ago. As Deputy Prime Minister, he has overturned tradition by removing a ban on women drivers and part-privatized Saudi Aramco. In 2017, Prince Mohammed ordered the incarceration of hundreds of his relatives and business-men in an anti-corruption crackdown at Riyadh's Ritz-Carlton hotel, extracting $100 billion in settlements during an unprecedented purge of the kingdom's established elite. It was felt that many wealthy Saudi families were pressured to buy shares in the Saudi Aramco listing, and that banks were encouraged to make loans available to retail investors to purchase shares.

There is a tension between what international observers see of his reforms which contrasts with the positive viewpoint of people in Saudi Arabia, where the crown prince's headstrong ap-proach has pulled the society into the twenty-first century. Now young people can enjoy pop concerts and sporting events. One success that officials point to is the visible increase in women working, particularly in shopping malls as the government has pushed retailers to hire Saudis. However, the killing of critical journalist Jamal Khashoggi by Saudi agents in 2018 definitively cast a shadow over the prince's reformist credentials. Saudi officials acknowledge mistakes. But there is also frustration that Prince Mohammed is not, in their view, given sufficient credit for tak-ing on an unsustainable economic system built on petrodollars and patronage. 'There's no ques-tion we've had a tough time getting to where we are and it's been more difficult than we would have hoped,' says a senior Saudi official. But he adds, 'You can't underplay what we've managed to achieve. We are going through an evolution and everyone is judging us while it's happening.'

Prince Mohammed is clear about his prime objectives: reining in the domineering role of the state and creating private sector jobs for the youthful population. A National Transformation Plan, unveiled in 2016, was to cut unemployment from 11.6 per cent to 9 per cent, create more than 450,000 private sector jobs and increase non-oil revenues, while also lowering public sector wages from 45 per cent to 40 per cent of total government spending—all by 2020. But it became clear that many goals were unrealistic and the next year Riyadh revised the NTP, with targets removed or pushed out by five to ten years. This was exacerbated by the falling price of crude oil.

'Saudi Arabia does not have to sell a single Saudi Aramco share, but the idea itself reflects a different approach to state administration,' wrote Abdulrahman al-Rashed, a Saudi columnist. 'That is something that any visitor who knows Saudi Arabia will verify — the country is chang-ing in all aspects of life.' There is one issue that unites sceptics and optimists: with the IPO com-pleted, the ultimate test of Prince Mohammed's abilities will be delivering the next phase of building a strong economy. 'Urban, young Saudis are extremely happy and feel they owe the leadership a lot of credit,' says Steffen Hertog, a Gulf expert at the London School of Economics. But he warns that 'social reforms are low-hanging fruit'. Creating sufficient jobs to tackle 30 per cent youth unemployment is a bigger task.

The Future

In the oil and gas industry things are changing fast. Since becoming CEO of oil company BP in 2020, Bernard Looney has promoted the transformation of BP into a diversified energy producer fit for the twenty-first century, even as his US competitors such as ExxonMobil continue to pin their hopes on a future increase in the demand for oil. BP has set itself a target of net zero emissions by 2050, to write billions of pounds off the value of its oil and gas assets, and pledges to cut production by 40 per cent in the next decade. Looney's plans to increase investments in renewables ten-fold in the coming years and the move away from oil were even praised by Greenpeace, which has called for greater action against climate change.

In contrast, Exxon intends to increase its fossil fuel output by almost a third in the next four years. It sees things differently to other oil companies. It accepts that there will be a global energy transition, and that it must help tackle emissions, but believes oil will remain a pillar of the world's economy. It estimates that demand will reach 111 million barrels per day in 2040, compared with about 100 million in 2019. This means a production increase equivalent to adding another Saudi Arabia would be needed, just to try to meet this projected extra demand for oil.

The challenge facing Saudi Aramco and the rest of the oil and gas industry is record low oil demand brought about by the global pandemic as travel is curtailed. The benchmark for oil prices, Brent crude, fell below $20 a barrel for the first time in almost two decades in 2020 following the coronavirus outbreak, and averaged just $42 a barrel for the year compared to $64 a barrel in 2019 and $71 a barrel in 2018. Another cause for concern is the greater regulation aimed at reducing carbon emissions; and the transition to greener energy sources. That said, consumption could stay robust at tens of millions of barrels a day for decades to come even in the most dramatic shift to cleaner energy. Although low-cost producers will continue pumping for long as they can, it's starting to look like the beginning of the end. Clearly, trying to diversify Saudi Aramco and Saudi Arabia out of oil and gas makes strategic sense.

Sources: 'BP's Looney stakes future on producing less oil', *The Financial Times*, 13 September 2020; 'Oil prices hit highest level since March on vaccine hopes', *The Financial Times*, 24 November 2020; 'Why ExxonMobil is sticking with oil as rivals look to a greener future', *The Financial Times*, 28 October 2020; 'Saudi Arabia replaces Aramco chairman with MBS ally' *The Financial Times*, 2 September 2019; 'Saudi Aramco does not rule the world', *The Financial Times*, 20 November 2019; https://www.investopedia.com/what-is-saudi-aramco-4682590 (accessed 29 November 2020); 'What does the Aramco IPO tell us about Saudi reforms?', *The Financial Times*, 10 December 2019; https://www.reuters.com (accessed 29 November 2020); Aramco.com (accessed 29 November 2020); 'Q and A: Will the oil industry recover from Covid-19 crisis?', *The Financial Times*, 21 May 2020; 'Investors pull green leavers to reshape energy sector', *The Financial Times*, 15 July 2020; 'Mohammed bin Salman: a combustible royal blazes a trail', *The Financial Times*, 13 December 2019; 'Saudi Aramco public debut is a hollow victory', *The Financial Times*, 12 December 2019; 'Saudi Aramco touches $2 trillion on second day of trading', *The Financial Times*, 12 December 2019; 'The slow death of big oil', *The Financial Times*, 17 September 2020.

Questions

1. What has Saudi Arabia achieved by part privatizing Saudi Aramco?

2. Why is Saudi Aramco seeking to diversify away from oil and gas when it is the lowest cost producer in the industry?

3. Identify the trends taking place in the oil and gas industry and suggest how they might impact Saudi Aramco.

For more examples and discussion to aid your understanding of this chapter, please visit the online resources and see the Extension Material for this chapter.

Review Questions

1. What are the key arguments for globalization and localization?
2. What are the advantages and disadvantages of following a multidomestic strategy?
3. If a company wished to expand abroad, which entry mode strategy might it consider adopting, and why?

Discussion Question

'Companies with highly competitive domestic markets are more likely to be successful if they expand abroad.' ***Discuss***.

Research Topic

Are global companies expanding, or are they in retreat? What does the evidence show?

Recommended Reading

For opposing perspectives on globalization see:

- **S. Douglas** and **Y. Wind**, 'The myth of globalization', *Columbia Journal of World Business*, vol. 22, no. 4 (1987), pp. 19–29.
- **T. Levitt**, 'The globalization of markets', *Harvard Business Review*, vol. 61, no. 3 (1983), pp. 92–102.

For a discussion of a new organizational form, the transnational corporation, which is needed to deal with a dynamic business world, see:

- **C. A. Bartlett** and **S. Ghoshal**, *Managing Across Borders: The Transnational Solution*, Harvard Business School Press, 1989.

For an understanding of what it means to be a global company, see:

- **A. M. Rugman**, *The Regional Multinationals*, Cambridge University Press, 2005.

www.oup.com/he/henry4e

Visit the online resources that accompany this book for activities and more information on strategy.

Test your knowledge and understanding of this chapter further by trying the multiple-choice questions online.

References and Notes

1   **T. Levitt**, 'The globalization of markets', *Harvard Business Review*, vol. 61, no. 3 (1983), pp. 92–102.

2   **S. Douglas** and **Y. Wind**, 'The myth of globalization', *Columbia Journal of World Business*, vol. 22, no. 4 (1987), pp. 19–29.

3   **Douglas** and **Wind,** see n. 2 above.

4   **P. Ghemawat**, 'Regional strategies for global leadership', *Harvard Business Review*, vol. 83, no. 12 (2005), pp. 98–108.

5   **G. Hofstede**, *Cultures and Organizations: Software of the Mind*, McGraw-Hill, 1991.

6   **Hofstede**, see n. 5 above.

7   **S. Ghoshal**, 'Global strategy: an organizing framework', *Strategic Management Journal*, vol. 8, no. 5 (1987), pp. 425–40.

8   **Ghoshal**, see n. 7 above.

9   See **Porter's** generic strategies in **Chapter 7** for an explanation of the firm as a low-cost producer and differentiator.

10 'Coronavirus/China stocks: supply chain reaction', *The Financial Times*, 3 February 2020.

11 **Ghoshal**, see n. 7 above, p. 427.

12 'Wal-Mart quits Germany but insists ASDA is safe', *The Daily Telegraph*, 29 July 2006; 'Aldi to invest extra $1.6bn in US expansion', *The Financial Times*, 9 February 2017.

13 The discussion of transnational strategy draws upon the work of **C. Bartlett** and **S. Ghoshal**, *Managing across Borders: The Transnational Solution*, Harvard Business School Press, 1989.

14 **Bartlett** and **Ghoshal**, see n. 13 above, p. 59.

15 **Bartlett** and **Ghoshal**, see n. 13 above, p. 61.

16 **J. Johanson** and **J. E. Vahlne**, 'The internationalization process of the firm—a model of knowledge development and increasing foreign market commitments', *Journal of International Business Studies*, vol. 8, no. 1 (1977), pp. 23–32.

17 **J. Johanson** and **P. F. Wiedersheim**, 'The internationalization of the firm-four Swedish cases 1', *Journal of Management Studies*, vol. 12, no. 3 (1975), pp. 305–23.

18 **G. R. Benito** and **G. Gripsrud**, 'The expansion of foreign direct investments: discrete rational location choices or a cultural learning process?', *Journal of International Business Studies*, vol. 23, no. 3 (1992), pp. 461–76.

19 **P. D. Ellis**, 'Does psychic distance moderate the market size–entry sequence relationship?', *Journal of International Business Studies*, vol. 39, no. 3 (2008), pp. 351–69.

20 **M. Forsgren** and **P. Hagström**, 'Ignorant and impatient internationalization? The Uppsala model and internationalization patterns for Internet-related firms', *Critical Perspectives on International Business*, vol. 3, no. 4 (2007), pp. 291–305.

21 **J. Johanson** and **J. E. Vahlne**, 'The Uppsala internationalization process model revisited: from liability of foreignness to liability of outsidership', *Journal of International Business Studies*, vol. 40, no. 9 (2009), pp. 1411–31.

22 **K. D. Brouthers**, 'The influence of international risk on entry-mode strategy in the computer software industry', *Management International Review*, vol. 35 no. 1 (1995), pp. 7–28.

23 **K. D. Miller**, 'A framework for integrated risk management in international business', *Journal of International Business Studies*, vol. 23, no. 2 (1992), pp. 311–31.

24 For a discussion of different entry modes, see **J. G. Frynas** and **K. Mellahi**, *Global Strategic Management*, Oxford University Press, 2015.

25 'The lessons from Danone HSBC's troubled partnerships in China', *The Economist*, 19 April 2007.

26 **M. E. Porter**, *The Competitive Advantage of Nations*, Free Press, 1990, chapter 3.

27 **M. E. Porter**, 'The competitive advantage of nations', *Harvard Business Review*, vol. 68, no. 2 (1990), p. 74.

28 **D. Miller**, *The Icarus Paradox: How Excellent Companies Can Bring about Their Own Downfall*, Harper Business, 1990.

29 **Porter**, see n. 27 above.

30 **David Ricardo's** work on comparative advantage is contained in *On the Principles of Political Economy and Taxation*, which was published in 1817.

31 **A. S. Blinder**, 'Offshoring: the next industrial revolution', *Foreign Affairs*, vol. 85, no. 2 (2006), pp. 113–28.

32 **A. Rugman** and **J. R. D'Cruz**, 'The "double diamond" model of international competitiveness: the Canadian experience', *Management International Review*, vol. 33, no. 2 (1993), pp. 17–39.

33 For a discussion of the relevance of **Porter's** diamond for New Zealand, see **W. R. Cartwright**, 'Multiple linked "diamonds" and the international competitiveness of export-dependent industries: the New Zealand experience', *Management International Review*, vol. 33, no. 2 (1993), pp. 55–70.

34 **A. Rugman** and **A. Verbeke**, 'Foreign subsidiaries and multinational strategic management: an extension and correction of Porter's single diamond framework', *Management International Review*, 33, no. 2 (1993), pp. 71–84.

35 **Rugman** and **Verbeke**, see n. 34 above, p. 76.

36 **A. Rugman**, 'Porter takes the wrong turn', *Business Quarterly*, vol. 56, no. 3 (1992), pp. 59–64.

37 **A. Rugman** and **J. R. D'Cruz**, *Fast Forward: Improving Canada's International Competitiveness*, Kodak Canada, 1991.

38 **R. M. Hodgetts**, 'Porter's diamond framework in a Mexican context', *Management International Review*, vol. 33, no. 2 (1993), p. 45.

39 **Hodgetts**, see n. 38 above, p. 46.

40 **S. Rangan**, 'The seven myths regarding global strategy', in *Mastering Strategy*, Prentice Hall, 2000.

41 **S. Rangan** and **R. Z. Lawrence**, *A Prism on Globalization*, Brookings Institute, Washington, DC, 1999.

42 **Rangan**, see n. 40 above, p. 123.

43 **A. M. Rugman**, *The End of Globalization*, Random House, 2000.

44 **A. Rugman** and **A. Verbeke**, 'A perspective on regional and global strategies of multinational enterprise', *Journal of International Business Studies*, vol. 35, no. 1 (2004), pp. 3–18.

45 **A. Rugman**, *The Regional Multinationals*, Cambridge University Press, 2005.

46 **Ghemawat**, see n. 4 above.

47 **Bartlett** and **Ghoshal**, see n. 13 above, p. 21.

48 **S. J. Palmisano**, 'The globally integrated enterprise', *Foreign Affairs*, vol. 85, no. 3 (2006), pp. 127–36.

49 **Palmisano**, see n. 48 above, p. 131.

50 **Palmisano**, see n. 48 above, p. 136.

8

PART FOUR
STRATEGY IMPLEMENTATION

CHAPTER 9
ORGANIZATIONAL STRUCTURES AND STRATEGIC CHANGE

 Learning Objectives

After completing this chapter you should be able to:

- Explain the trade-off between specialization and coordination
- Discuss the advantages and disadvantages of different organizational structures
- Discuss organizational processes
- Explain the purpose of strategic control systems for organizations
- Evaluate different types of strategic change
- Identify the attributes of a visionary organization

Introduction

In **Part 3** we assessed the role that strategy formulation plays in the achievement of competitive advantage. In **Part 4** we turn our attention to strategy implementation. We might restate that although a linear approach aids the student of strategic management in getting to grips with the subject, in the fast-moving corporate world organizations are often faced with implementing a strategy without the luxury of comprehensive analysis. That is not to say that analysis is unimportant, since organizations neglect strategic analysis at their peril. It is to recognize that decisions often need to be made quickly, as competitors seldom wait for their rivals to undertake a complete analysis of the business environment.

It is often said that the best formulated strategy in the world will fail if it is poorly implemented. To implement strategies effectively requires the organization to be sufficiently flexible in its organizational design. Strategies need to be effectively communicated and properly resourced. The reason for change needs to be understood and properly coordinated with **stakeholders** inside and outside the organization. In an age of collaboration, this may involve discussions with customers, suppliers, communities, and strategic partners. Although the leader of an organization will ultimately be responsible for a strategy's success or failure, their role should be to encourage and create an organizational culture that empowers managers to respond to opportunities. In this way, each employee will be confident to try out new ideas and innovate without fear of reprisals.

Appropriate reward mechanisms need to be in place that help to guide employee behaviour and signpost the important goals of the organization. The **values** of an organization will be important here in specifying what a company stands for. There must also be sufficient control mechanisms in place to allow the strategy to be evaluated against its stated aims and if necessary, allow for changes.

Although **systems**, **procedures**, and **policies** may aid the implementation of a strategy, ultimately it is individuals who implement strategy. Unless individuals and groups, within and outside the organization, accept the rationale for strategic change, any proposed implementation will be unsuccessful. We address the role that leadership plays in managing strategic change in **Chapter 10**.

In this chapter, we address the role of **organizational structures**, **organizational processes**, **strategic control systems**, and **strategic change**. The backdrop to the chapter is the role these play in providing an organization with competitive advantage.

9.1 **Organizational Structures**

Organizational structure is concerned with the division of labour into specialized tasks and coordination between these tasks. Organizations exist because they are more efficient at undertaking economic activities than individuals are on their own. Therefore, organizations are a means by which human economic activity can be coordinated. **Henry Mintzberg** argues that all organized human activity gives rise to two opposing forces: the need to divide labour into separate tasks, and the coordination of these tasks to accomplish some goal.[1] **Adam Smith** first discussed specialization and the division of labour centuries earlier in 1776. Smith showed that if you specialize human activity such that individuals only undertake one or a few tasks, they then become proficient at that task.[2] If each task is part of some larger activity, such as building a car, then we find that more cars can be built when each individual specializes than if a person tried to build a car by themselves. This is what made Henry Ford's Model T automobile so successful—the division of labour along a moving conveyor belt. Yet, as Mintzberg points out, greater specialization requires greater coordination.

The use of rules, policies, and procedures to coordinate employees will be appropriate for organizations that operate in a relatively stable environment. This is especially the case where employees have little autonomy and are not expected to make complex decisions. Where individuals are part of an organization that operates in a dynamic environment and are afforded far greater autonomy, the effort required by management to coordinate their activities will be greater. Nevertheless, these different activities must still be coordinated if the organization is to achieve economies of scale and synergy.

There is widespread acceptance that a change in strategy will warrant a change in organizational structure to implement that strategy. **Alfred Chandler** wrote his famous dictum that 'structure follows strategy'.[3] He studied a number of large US corporations, including General Motors and DuPont, in the early part of the twentieth century. He found that as these organizations grew in size and complexity, so this brought about a need to change their organizational structure. For instance, Chandler found that as DuPont increased its product lines, so the ensuing complexity was too much for its centralized functional structure. An expansion of its activities produced 'new administrative needs' which required a new structure to meet these needs. In effect, the existing structure becomes no longer useful for supporting the strategic change, which in turn necessitates a change of structure.

The same was true of General Motors. DuPont decentralized its organization to what became known as a divisional structure. Under a divisional structure the parent company retains control of overall strategic direction, but the divisional managers have autonomy as to how the strategy will be implemented. This is discussed in detail later.

For Chandler, it is the formulation of a new strategy that brings about the need for a new structure. Hence his dictum 'structure follows strategy' (**Figure 9.1**). This is not to say that structure has no impact on strategy; for example, changes in the external environment may necessitate a change in an organization's structure. Therefore, there will be instances when Chandler's dictum may not hold, but as a general rule there is substantive support for this proposition. For example, a dynamic assessment of the contingent relationship between strategy and structure by **Terry Amburgey and Tina Dacin** found that a reciprocal relationship does exist.[4] In other words, strategy affects structure, but structure also affects strategy. However, they found that strategy was a more important determinant of structure than structure was of strategy. They conclude: '*our research supports the existence of a hierarchical relationship between strategy and structure*', but note that '*a change in strategy is more likely to produce a change in structure than a change in structure is to produce a change in strategy*'.[5]

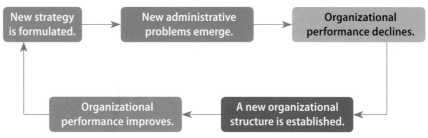

Figure 9.1   Strategy and structure.
Source: Adapted from Alfred D. Chandler, *Strategy and Structure: Chapters in the History of the American Industrial Enterprise*, MIT Press, 1962. © 1962 Massachusetts Institute of Technology, by permission of the MIT Press.

In many respects, whether structure follows strategy or strategy follows structure may be a bit of a red herring. The real issue may be more about organizing complementary practices that fit together in a dynamic manner. For example, an organization introducing flexible technology will be unlikely to obtain increases in performance when it fails to change related working practices. Therefore, to ensure a better organizational fit it becomes necessary to go beyond a discussion of strategy and structure to include processes. This idea of complementarities is discussed later in the chapter.

We can now evaluate different types of organizational structures in terms of how well they meet the trade-off between specialization and coordination.

9.1.1 The Entrepreneurial Structure

The entrepreneurial or simple structure revolves around the founder of the firm. This is a centralized structure in which the founder or entrepreneur takes all the major decisions. This is not unexpected, especially where the founder possesses some technical expertise or specific knowledge that is the basis for the organization's existence. In these small companies, staff members will often be expected to be flexible in their work roles, which may not be clearly drawn. The vision of the entrepreneur and flexible work patterns of staff are major strengths of this type of organization. But, as the organization grows, so the entrepreneur's ability to manage each facet of the business becomes stretched. Where the founder recognizes that his or her strength lies in formulating a strategic intent or purpose, but not necessarily in trying to manage functions such as marketing or finance, they will recruit specialists to run these activities. Steve Jobs, the co-founder of Apple, ran the company during its start-up. As Apple grew in size, his management style was perceived to be a liability. He was eventually replaced, not by an individual who possessed his visionary zeal or technical expertise, but by someone the financial markets believed could successfully manage a growing organization. In an ironic twist, Jobs was brought back to head up the computer firm. With Jobs as CEO, Apple went on to design and manufacture spectacularly successful consumer products making it one of the most successful corporations in the world—a legacy that Jobs' successor at Apple, Tim Cook, continues to emulate.

9.1.2 The Functional Structure

A functional structure is appropriate for an organization which produces one or a few related products or services. Tasks are grouped together according to functional specialisms such as finance, marketing, and R&D. A manager will be responsible for a department which comprises these functions. The use of a functional structure promotes efficiency through the specialized division of labour. It allows managers to learn from each other and may facilitate the development of capabilities. Under a functional structure, control systems, which are used to guide the behaviour of members of the organization, are straightforward and do not involve great complexity. There is a high degree of centralization, with each functional manager reporting to the CEO and board of directors (**Figure 9.2**).

The functional structure has a number of disadvantages. Each functional or departmental manager may begin to focus exclusively on their departmental goals at the expense of the organizational goals. This can lead to the development of a departmental subculture whose values may not fully align with those within the organization. As the organization grows and its range of products expands, coordination between functions becomes more difficult. This can lead to a decline in performance which, as Chandler argued, leads to a search for a new structure. This new structure will involve greater decentralization of decision-making to improve the efficiency of coordination.

Figure 9.2   A functional structure.

9.1.3 The Divisional Structure

As organizations grow and diversify into producing different products for different markets, a more effective and efficient structure is required. The **divisional structure** comprises individual business units that include their own functional specialisms and have direct responsibility for their own performance (**Figure 9.3**). This decentralization of decision-making is also necessary where the external environment is dynamic and exhibits some degree of uncertainty. It gives managers substantial

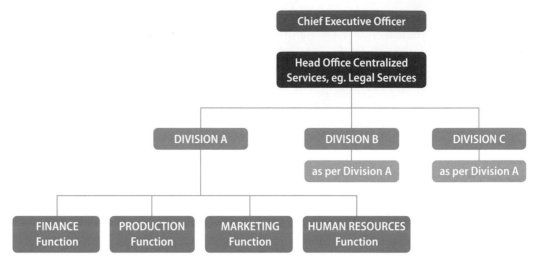

Figure 9.3   A divisional structure.

autonomy to respond to local market conditions. A divisional structure may be organized according to *product*, *market*, or *geographic* areas.

A structure based on product occurs when each product line is based in its own division, with a manager responsible for profitability within that division. The divisional manager will have autonomy to set a business-level strategy based on their understanding of the product and markets. Organizations that have adopted a divisional structure by product include DuPont, General Motors, and Procter & Gamble. A structure based on market occurs when an organization is concerned to meet the needs of different customer groups. For example, HSBC and Barclays Bank are organized according to the markets they serve: corporate customers, small business customers, and retail customers. Each division has responsibility for its own profits and can see its contribution to corporate profitability. A geographic structure occurs when the divisions are categorized according to geographic location. Breaking the organization's structure down into geographic locations facilitates better management decisions by allowing managers to take decisions based upon the needs and characteristics of customers within different areas.

The advantages of a divisional structure include the decentralized decision-making which allows divisional managers to respond effectively to the needs of their business unit. There is a more clearly defined career path for individuals within the division rather than the limited specialisms that exist under a functional structure. This leads to higher levels of motivation and a commitment to innovation. Under a divisional structure, employees are more likely to be aligned to the organization's objectives. A divisional structure allows the parent company to focus its attention on corporate strategy rather than being drawn into operational issues. In addition, the profit contribution of each division is transparent which helps the centre to make effective parenting decisions.

There are disadvantages with a divisional structure. Where the parent company allocates resources to divisions according to their profit contribution, this presupposes that each division has an equal opportunity to make the same level of profits. Markets, products, and geographic regions will differ, and some mechanism which takes account of these differences and allocates resources fairly needs to be devised by head office. The emphasis on, for example, quarterly profit target may force the division to focus its attention on short-term issues rather than on key business-level strategies.

The duplication of functions across many different divisions as well as at head office can be expensive and needs to be offset against improvements in performance. The use of divisional structures among large corporations is widespread, with many organizations adopting variations of the divisional form. However, where organizations face greater uncertainty and more rapid change in their environment a different kind of organizational structure is required.

9.1.4 The Matrix Structure

A **matrix structure** is an attempt to increase organizational flexibility to meet the needs of a rapidly changing environment. It aims simultaneously to maximize the benefits from functional specialisms that occur from the division of labour while increasing the efficiency of coordination across these functions. It involves learning new roles and modes of behaviour. In a matrix structure, an individual reports to two managers. This will include their functional head (for instance, the head of manufacturing) and also a project manager. Individuals are usually assigned to the project on a temporary basis (**Figure 9.4**). In theory, a matrix structure should increase the speed of decision-making, facilitate innovation, and enhance responsiveness to the external environment. In reality, matrix structures can be complex and difficult to implement effectively. They violate a fundamental principle of management, which is the *unity of command*.

Unless both managers have the same expectations from individuals reporting to them this can create role incompatibility and **role ambiguity**. Role incompatibility occurs when the different expectations of managers make it highly unlikely that individuals can meet the expectations of both managers. Role ambiguity implies that individuals are unclear as to what their role and responsibilities are. The need to meet the expectations of different managers may ultimately result in role overload, where an individual experiences difficulty in managing varied expectations. Christopher Bartlett and Sumantra Ghoshal argue that concentrating on a matrix structure to manage complex

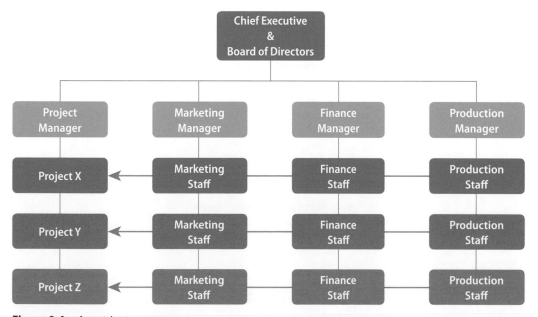

Figure 9.4   A matrix structure.

and dynamic environments does little to change the other important elements that make up an organization.[6] They distinguish between an organization's *anatomy*, its *physiology*, and *psychology*. Its anatomy refers to an organization's structure. Its physiology includes the systems that allow information to circulate throughout the organization. Its psychology is the shared beliefs, norms, and values that permeate the organization. As they state, simply 'reconfiguring the formal structure is a blunt and sometimes brutal instrument of change'.[7] What is required is first to alter the company's psychology—the beliefs and behaviours of individuals that are spread throughout the organization. These changes can then be reinforced by improving the organizational physiology, which involves improvements in communication and decision-making. Only then should senior managers realign the organizational anatomy by making changes to its formal structure.

9.1.5 The Network Structure

A network structure involves a configuration of outsourced activities that are controlled by a central hub. This is particularly useful in responding to fast-moving and unpredictable environments such as occurs in the fashion industry. The network structure allows the capabilities of the organization to be retained at the centre while non-core activities are outsourced to specialist firms, which allows for greater efficiency (**Figure 9.5**). The major advantage of the network structure is the flexibility it provides to organizations, enabling them to respond quickly to changes in the marketplace. Organizations such as Tesla and Apple both outsource manufacturing activities to specialist companies, while retaining tight control at the centre over their distinctive capabilities, such as R&D and design.

Where an organization operates across many countries a *transnational structure* may be more effective in helping a multinational corporation to respond to the needs of local markets and achieve efficiencies from globalization. The transnational structure differs from the other organizational forms in that it neither dogmatically centralizes nor decentralizes, but instead makes selective decisions. The transnational corporation was discussed in detail when we looked at international strategies in **Chapter 8**.

In recognition of the complex and fraught nature of organization design, **Michael Goold and Andrew Campbell** propose a framework to guide executive management.[8] Their *nine tests* of organization design are based on their observations of different size companies. The framework is an attempt to help top management to evaluate their existing structure or, indeed, a new structure objectively. The first four tests help executives to assess alternative structures by seeing whether a

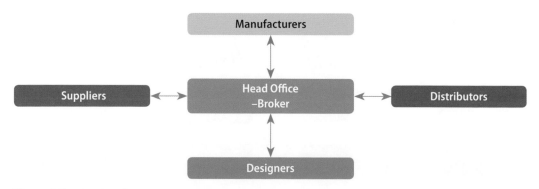

Figure 9.5   A network structure.

proposed structure can support the strategy being pursued. The remaining five tests are used to adjust potential organization designs by tackling problem areas, such as the problem of effective control that results from increased decentralization. This framework is not a panacea, which Goold and Campbell acknowledge. Rather, it is an attempt to de-politicize and depersonalize the process of organization design.

Organizational structures are invariably linked with the vision of the CEO who runs the company. When Jack Welch ran GE, it was his understanding of the markets the company faced which determined the structure he put in place. Questions about structure and strategy are invariably linked (see **Strategy in Focus 9.1**). For example, IKEA's CEO, Jesper Brodin, faces the challenge of changing the location of stores from large out-of-town sites to smaller city centre outlets with pick-up points to reflect changing consumer needs. At the same time, Internet purchases continue to make the need for out-of-town sites less compelling.

STRATEGY IN FOCUS 9.1 IKEA's Challenge over Strategy and Structure

Photo 9.1   IKEA's popular Ektorp three-seat sofa.
Source: Inter IKEA Systems B.V.

When IKEA introduced the Ektorp sofa two decades ago, it cost €599. The same product, largely looking the same, is still sold today. But thanks to clever tweaks—it can be flat-packed, with a hinged back and detachable arm rests—it costs only €299. Something similar is going on with IKEA CEOs. The furniture retailer, born in Sweden but now based in the Netherlands, is to have its sixth CEO in its seventy-four-year history. Jesper Brodin is also of a certain, familiar mould.

He is a former assistant to Ingvar Kamprad, IKEA's founder, comes from southern Sweden, wears a jumper and shirt combo, and sounds slightly subdued in interviews, much like most of his predecessors. Still, IKEA is a company in the midst of a great transformation. And Mr Brodin brings a valuable insight into the upheaval and the challenges that will bring, having worked across IKEA's complicated structure. IKEA has recently undergone as big a shake-up as it has ever been through. IKEA of Sweden, headed by Mr Brodin and responsible for product design, manufacturing, and supply chain, was sold last year by the retailer to its sister company Inter IKEA, which is responsible for the brand and concept. IKEA itself is now, formally, little more than the world's largest franchisee for the flat-pack furniture group. But what a franchisee: IKEA operates 340 stores, vastly outnumbering the roughly forty managed by other franchisees, and brings in €34 billion in annual revenues.

Mr Brodin says his new role will be about 'focusing on the customer meeting'. But the nature of that meeting is changing rapidly. From its first store in 1958 until recently, IKEA followed a tried-and-trusted recipe of placing its stores near 'the potato fields' as its managers like to say, in out-of-town sites with big car parks next to huge warehouses. Now IKEA is experimenting with other formats; smaller stores, city centre outlets, pick-up points, but it is unclear how well these will work. Some customers are already criticizing the cost and selection. Tougher still for IKEA is that many customers, such as millennials, no longer want to shop in store, but instead buy online. This threatens a key element of IKEA's success; its labyrinthine store layouts and infamous market hall are designed to maximize impulse purchases of everything from wine glasses and picture frames to plants and napkins.

IKEA plays down the risks. Peter Agnefjall, the outgoing CEO, says annual visits to ikea.com have doubled to two billion in his almost four years in charge. As with many retailers, IKEA's buzzword is 'multichannel', selling to customers through physical stores, the internet, and combinations of the two. It is also targeting huge growth: its aim is to have €50 billion of revenues by 2020, up from €34 billion in 2016, with even more stretching targets beyond that.

There are other big questions that IKEA will need to answer. One is whether the new division of labour between IKEA and Inter IKEA will work. A senior insider says Inter IKEA could now use other franchisees to enter South America and Africa. In any case, Inter IKEA, used to working in the shadows, now has an even bigger role in the IKEA system. No matter how identikit Jesper Brodin may seem to his predecessors, he is facing a much changed set of challenges. Another intriguing issue is IKEA's sheer size. A former CEO, Anders Dahlvig, once suggested that IKEA could break up into three separate companies covering North America, Europe, and Asia, each with their own product development and supply chain. Mr Dahlvig, chief executive from 1999 to 2009, is now the chairman of Inter IKEA. Holding together IKEA's rather special tight-knit culture as it expands into new countries such as India and Croatia could be tricky, as highlighted by scandals in its network of stores, including bribery allegations in Russia.

There are also concerns about the turnover in CEOs. Mr Dahlvig was only IKEA's third CEO. Two more have come and gone since. While Mr Agnefjall denies that the corporate shake-up played any role, the insider says that some people have reacted negatively to moving from being an integrated company to a pure retailer. 'Some people think it's less interesting', he adds. All this means that no matter how identikit Mr Brodin may seem to his predecessors, he is facing a much-changed set of challenges. He will need more than an Allen key and a sketchy set of instructions to succeed.

Source: Richard Milne, 'Ikea must break the mould to overcome challenges', *The Financial Times*, 7 June 2017. Used under licence from *The Financial Times*. All rights reserved.

9.2 **Organizational Processes**

The division of labour allows organizational activities to be separated out and common activities grouped together. However, this creates a dilemma. While the level of coordination improves within a homogeneous group, the level of coordination across different groups may decline. What is required is organizational integration which allows coordination to occur effectively across an organization's activities. This is not an easy task given that each specialized group will have a tendency to seek its own goals and adopt behaviour to support this. One answer may be to concentrate more on horizontal processes rather than organizational structure. **Ghoshal and Bartlett** argue that top management has continued to focus on structural solutions, despite evidence that such structures can become inflexible and unresponsive to change.[9] As organizations grew and their divisional structure struggled to cope with the increased complexity, management adopted a strategic business unit (SBU) approach. This was a variation on the divisional structure which allowed senior managers to concentrate on specific businesses. The problem was that this created business silos which impeded coordination across different business units. These and other structural solutions simply failed to help the organization create an entrepreneurial culture, build capabilities, and to discard outdated ideas. The consequence of failing hierarchical structures leads to downsizing as organizations seek to remove non-performing layers.

Ghoshal and Bartlett studied twenty organizations in the USA, Europe, and Japan which understood the importance of processes over structures. They identified three distinct processes: **entrepreneurial process, competence-building process,** and **renewal process**. Together they constitute what Ghoshal and Bartlett refer to as a company's 'core organizational processes'.

1. **The entrepreneurial process**

   This seeks to motivate employees to manage their operations as if they belonged to them. This requires a change in the current role of managers as simply implementers of strategy with only the most senior managers having the authority to initiate new ideas. To institute an entrepreneurial process requires a culture that recognizes the capabilities of individuals in the organization. Top management needs to understand that employees perform more effectively when they are trusted to work, utilizing their own self-discipline rather than a formal control system.

   A self-disciplined approach requires top management to adopt a supportive role. This does not mean that no control systems exist. For example, 3M uses small project teams to foster creativity and entrepreneurship. These project teams include someone with an innovative idea, and a few individuals who want to support it. If the idea takes off, the project team may eventually grow into a department or division. However, this entrepreneurial activity is set within the context of clear corporate targets, such as contributing to a twenty per cent return on equity. At Google, they use 10x, which stands for doing things ten times better instead of focusing on incremental change. This approach helps Google to improve its technology and deliver better products for users by giving employees permission to think big and not be afraid to come up with new solutions.

2. **The competence-building process**

   Large organizations need to be able to exploit the vast amount of employee knowledge that exists in their different businesses. This requires a competence-building process which coordinates the distinctive capabilities across those businesses. The employees within the individual businesses need to be given the task of creating these competencies. This recognizes their closeness to the customer and hence greater ability to exploit local opportunities. As with the entrepreneurial process, the role of senior management is to ensure that the competencies are coordinated across different business units.

Senior managers must also ensure that their control systems are fair and transparent to encourage risk-taking. Individual employees need to adopt the organization's values and goals to help build a sense of community. This type of culture can only exist if it is nurtured by top management. For example, throughout the Japanese organization Kao there are open meeting areas. This entitles every employee who has an interest in a subject being discussed to sit in on a meeting and contribute their ideas.

3. **The renewal process**

This process 'is designed to challenge a company's strategies and the assumptions behind them'. This requires senior management proactively to shake up the organization's status quo. Their role is then to mediate the resulting conflict that will inevitably arise. Intel's move away from memory chips and towards microprocessors represents a renewal process. The organization was founded on memory chips. The decision by co-founder Andy Grove to re-base the organization on microprocessors directly cut across entrenched views of what Intel stood for. A result of emphasizing process over structure is to create an organization in which individual employees are willing and able to innovate. They will share new ideas and knowledge, and work towards common organization-wide goals. This occurs without the constant intrusion of managerial control systems.

9.3 Strategic Control Systems

The design of all organizations must include control and reward systems, which ensure that members of an organization are actively working to achieve the corporate goals. Control systems are necessary for senior managers to be able to assess the performance of individual business units. A **strategic control system** will include agreed objectives between senior managers and managers of business units, and a mechanism for monitoring performance based on these objectives and for providing feedback to managers. It will also include a system of rewards and sanctions that motivate managers and make them aware of the consequences of not meeting agreed targets. Most organizations use budgetary controls which measure and monitor financial performance. However, as we saw in **Chapter 4**, financial controls need to be used with broader strategic controls if important competitive information is not to be overlooked.[10]

A well-designed reward system can be instrumental in successful strategy implementation. That said, a great deal of contention has arisen over rewarding executives for achieving lacklustre results and revising performance targets downwards to enable them to be more easily met. A reward system should recognize an individual's or group's achievement and motivate them to work towards the organization's goals. Where individuals are already highly paid, a reward system has to move beyond merely pecuniary factors to keep them motivated. A tension exists between the short-term quarterly targets on which managerial rewards are commonly based, and getting managers to adopt longer time horizons which exploit opportunities more effectively in their business environment. We saw in **Chapter 4** the use of a balanced scorecard is helpful in moving managerial attention away from purely financial concerns to consider other issues that impact upon the business, such as customer retention.

Strategic control systems include similar elements to budgetary control systems, but they involve longer-term objectives. This can create difficulties because managers will be more inclined to invest their time in achieving short-term targets than targets that are many years off. To overcome this, strategic control systems can include a series of short-term milestones that need to be achieved if a strategy is to be implemented. In this way, the management reward systems can be aligned with the implementation of the strategy. **Goold and Quinn** suggest three reasons for establishing control systems.[11]

1) **A strategic control system should coordinate the activities of employees.**

   Where the nature of strategic change is emergent and incremental rather than planned and precise, strategic control systems need to be designed to reflect this.[12] On the one hand, strategic control systems must be loose enough to deal with dynamic environments such as the software industry. On the other hand, they must be rigorous enough to allow effective control to take place.

2) **A strategic control system should motivate managers to achieve their objectives.**

   Research has shown that clearly defined goals result in improved performance. These goals should be objectively measured and involve a challenge for individuals. They should not be perceived as too easy, nor be insurmountable. Allowing participation in setting objectives for complex tasks also helps improve performance. When addressing the goals of business unit managers, the strategic controls should focus on a few results-orientated goals which help guide behaviour. These can be financial and non-financial.[13]

   However, this approach is less helpful in circumstances where the business output is difficult to measure and what constitutes results is unclear. In such a case organizations may choose not to use strategic control systems, but instead adopt what **William Ouchi** calls clan controls.[14] This is where individual members of a clan have shared values, which ensure that they pursue organizational goals without the overt need for a system of control. New members joining the organization are socialized into the values of the clan.

3) **A strategic control system helps senior managers know when to intervene in the decisions of unit managers.**

   In theory, a useful strategic control system needs to be able to assess continually the assumptions on which a strategy is based, as well as monitor management objectives. In reality, rather than undertake this kind of in-, analysis, senior managers prefer to use their intuition and business experience to help them decide when to intervene in businesses.

However a control system is designed, we might bear in mind that all control systems stand or fall according to the level of trust they embody. Trust is the key ingredient in all effective control systems.

Goold and Quinn suggest that managers may need to adapt strategic control systems to different business conditions. They point out that while in theory there are benefits to be derived from a strategic control system, in reality there are difficulties in trying to devise one. These difficulties are likely to be more pronounced in certain sorts of businesses. This implies strategic control processes may need to be designed to take account of the specific circumstances faced by each business.[15] Their solution is a framework for a contingency theory of strategic control, highlighting the conditions under which strategic control systems might be useful for an organization (**Figure 9.6**). It compares environmental turbulence with the ability of senior managers to state and measure strategic objectives.

The ideal use of strategic controls is when the environment faced by the organization exhibits low turbulence and it is easy to state and measure precise objectives. In this type of organization,

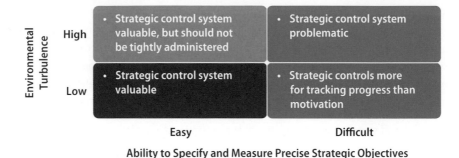

Figure 9.6   Approaches to strategic controls in different sorts of businesses.
Source: M. Goold and J. Quinn, 'The paradox of strategic controls', *Strategic Management Journal*,
11 January 1990. © John Wiley & Sons Ltd.

a formal strategic control system can be designed which will help monitor strategy implementation. In addition, because strategic objectives can be stated and readily measured, the strategic control system can be used to set goals and motivate managers. This is shown in the lower left-hand quadrant of **Figure 9.6**. In organizations where the environmental turbulence is high and the ability to specify objectives is easy, a strategic control system may still be of benefit, but needs to be more loosely exercised. This reflects the dynamic nature of the environment in which the organization operates.

Where the organization faces an environment in which turbulence is low, but there is difficulty in specifying and measuring objectives, strategic controls can act as a means of monitoring strategy. This might be done through the use of milestones or signposts. Finally, in organizations that exhibit high turbulence and a difficulty in measuring objectives, strategic control systems pose a real problem. The difficulty in measuring objectives precludes their use as a motivational vehicle for managers. In this case, a looser arrangement is required that emphasizes informal relationships between senior managers and unit managers. Therefore, a strategic control system may be best thought of as contingent upon the business environment the organization faces.

9.3.1 Single and Double-Loop Learning

In addressing control systems, **Chris Argyris** makes the point that organizations need to move beyond what he calls **single-loop learning**.[16] This occurs when firm performance is measured against agreed goals. Feedback is obtained only after seeing whether the goals have been met at the end of a specified period (e.g. a quarter). Until this time has elapsed, no action to change strategy or goals is taken. In a stable and relatively predictable environment a single-loop control system would not be a cause for concern. However, in an environment characterized by greater change and uncertainty, single-loop learning is inappropriate. Argyris argues instead for **double-loop learning** in which learning becomes a continuous process. As part of double-loop learning the assumptions on which strategies and goals are based are continually challenged and monitored. This allows the organization to detect and respond to changes in its environment more readily.

The more formal an organization's structure, the more constrained are its members, particularly in networking across functions to provide innovative solutions to business problems. The less prescribed an organization's structure, the more autonomy and flexibility its members have to cross boundary lines in pursuit of knowledge and capabilities. Therefore, the more likely it is that an innovative culture can be encouraged. However, a conflict arises as to how 'loose' an organization's structure should be before it impacts negatively on individual members' roles. One solution is a loose–tight structure: tight, in that there is an unflinching pursuit of the organization's objectives; loose, in that there is flexibility as to how these will be achieved.

9.3.2 Employee Commitment and Strategy Implementation

The former chairman and CEO of Google, Eric Schmidt, argues that as Google grows older so its capacity to innovate quickly may start to suffer. This is because there is a natural tendency to become more conservative as an organization grows older, leading to it becoming more risk averse, taking small steps instead of big strides. Schmidt argues that 'true innovation comes from doing things differently, often radically different, and that involves risk'. Google has what they call twenty per cent time, which allows its engineers to spend around one day a week working on things they find interesting. To date this has produced innovations such as Google Chrome, developed by the current CEO, Sundar Pichai.

It is often said by leaders of organizations that people are their most valuable assets. It is a truism that without the actions of individual members of an organization a strategy cannot be effectively implemented. The question thus arises: how much support do organizations provide to their employees? And what impact does an organization's commitment to its employees have on organizational performance? Jangwoo Lee and Danny Miller suggest that an organization's commitment to its employees can be seen in the way that it cares for employee welfare and satisfaction, the fairness of its rewards, and the investment it makes in their development and compensation.[17] Their study of the competitive strategies of Korean firms found that an organization's commitment to its employees provides only a small financial benefit to the organization. However, when an organization's commitment to its employees is aligned to a dedicated positioning strategy, its potential for achieving a competitive advantage improves. Not surprisingly, they found a 'strategy appears to be necessary to channel effort to achieve the maximum benefit'.

This suggests that a loyal and committed workforce implementing a dedicated strategy may be a basis for improved profitability. This is because a dedicated strategy is implemented more effectively by an organization that shows a commitment to its employees. While an organization's commitment to its employees has a positive impact on its return on assets in the context of an intensive positioning strategy. This study also suggests that the resource-based view and positioning approach to strategy both have their part to play. An asset-specific resource, such as a motivated workforce, can help in the implementation of a positioning strategy, while a positioning strategy is clearly necessary to channel the efforts of employees. However, a sense of trust that emanates from an organization's commitment to its employees and their commitment to the organization's success takes time to establish. The **Case Study: W. L. Gore's Unconventional Success** at the end of the chapter highlights the counter-intuitive approach of leading a company without traditional organizational structures and strategic control systems.

9.4 Strategic Change

Strategic change is about changing the way in which an organization interacts with its external environment. It is about creating new and innovative ways of doing business. It involves changing an organization's systems in order to adapt to external changes. Organizational systems may be divided into three elements: (1) structure; (2) processes; and (3) culture. Organizational structure is concerned with the division of labour into specialized tasks and coordination between these tasks. Organizational processes deal with the control systems to manage employees and guide their behaviour to ensure that the firm achieves its goals. This will include such things as budgeting and formal planning. **Organizational culture** can be thought of as the shared norms and values adopted by the members of an organization. In the absence of formal control mechanisms, values and culture can be a powerful force in motivating and guiding behaviour.[18]

Strategic change is necessary for an organization to ensure a fit between its internal resources and capabilities and the requirements of a changing environment. However, the organization should not be seen as passive, simply responding to changes in its environment. An organization may instead seek to actively influence its competitive environment. It may seek to drive the changes taking place in its industry. For example, Gillette constantly redefines the *rules of the game* by actively destabilizing existing competitive advantages in its industry. In implementing strategic change, organizations need to consider the *size* of any change and the *speed* with which that will be undertaken.

In a classic article, **Larry Greiner** argues that as organizations grow they go through five distinct phases of development.[19] These phases are characterized by relatively calm periods of growth that end in a management crisis. The extent to which these crises can be anticipated will depend upon how well management knows its own organizational history. This is because each phase is influenced by the preceding phase. As an organization grows, it proceeds through evolutionary change and revolutionary change. How managers tackle each revolutionary change will determine whether or not the organization will proceed to the next evolutionary change.

Revolutionary change describes 'those periods of substantial turmoil in organizational life'.[20] It involves a break with existing business practices which occurs over a short period of time. It is usually a response to changes in the external environment, such as a shift in the use of certain technologies. It may also occur as a result of internal changes in the organization. For instance, a new CEO often has a window of opportunity in which he or she can push through fundamental changes in the way the organization delivers its products or services. When this window closes organizational inertia often precludes radical change.

In contrast, evolutionary change describes 'prolonged periods of growth where no major upheaval occurs in organizational practices'.[21] It involves a series of small, gradual changes. However, the end result may be the same as for revolutionary change. This is because the accumulated effect of many small changes is similar to making one large change. The main difference is the timescale it requires to undertake the changes. The rationale for evolutionary change is best seen by addressing how individuals learn. Most individuals learn incrementally over a period of time. By definition an organization, which is fundamentally a collection of individuals, learns in the same way. If individuals are to internalize change for the benefit of organizations, they need time to learn.

Greiner contends how an organization develops is determined by the interactions between its age, its size, its stages of evolutionary and revolutionary change, and the growth rate of its industry. The task of managers during each revolutionary change is to develop a new set of practices that will help them to manage in the next evolutionary growth period. However, each new management practice will eventually become obsolete for managing change in the next growth period. As Greiner states, '*managers experience the irony of seeing a major solution in one period become a major problem in a later period*'.[22]

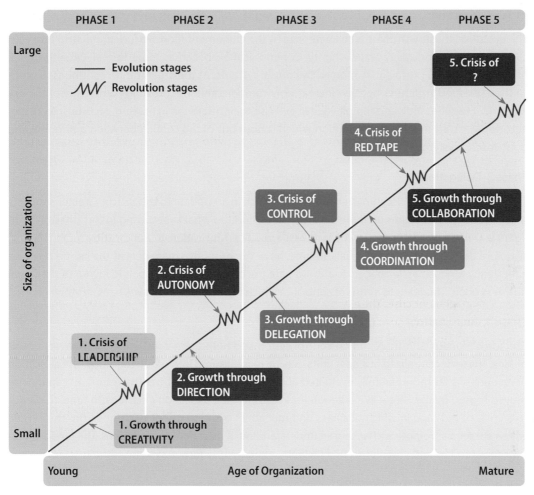

Figure 9.7   The five phases of growth.

Source: 'Exhibit II: The five phases of growth', in L. E. Greiner, 'Growing organizations', *Harvard Business Review*, vol. 50, no. 4 (1972). Copyright © 1972 by the Harvard Business School Publishing Corporation. Reprinted by permission of Harvard Business Review. All rights reserved.

9.4.1 The Five Phases of Growth

The five phases of growth identified by Greiner are: (1) **creativity**; (2) **direction**; (3) **delegation**; (4) **coordination**; and (5) **collaboration**. These are shown in **Figure 9.7**.

Phase 1: Creativity

This is characterized by product development and market growth. Communication between individuals in the organization is informal, and tasks are less clearly defined. The founders of the organization spend their time on the product or service and neglect managerial functions. As the organization grows the founders are unable to keep pace with the increased managerial functions, such as finance, marketing, and manufacturing. At this point a crisis of leadership occurs, which is the basis for the first revolutionary change. A manager is needed to lead the business who has knowledge and experience of managing these different functions. Success in Phase 1 leads the company to Phase 2.

Phase 2: Direction

The evolutionary growth phase is characterized by the implementation of a functional structure with clear lines of responsibility and authority. Communication becomes more formal. Organizational hierarchy becomes prevalent, reinforced by control systems. As the organization continues to grow, so these existing structures become increasingly cumbersome. The growing complexity of the environment requires individual employees to exercise their discretion in making decisions. A crisis of autonomy results in a second revolution which is born out of the conflict between autonomy and tight control systems.

Phase 3: Delegation

This is epitomized by a decentralized structure. In fact, in an update to this article, Greiner suggests that decentralization sums up more clearly than delegation what is occurring in this phase.[23] Managers experience greater autonomy and responsibility. Motivation is achieved through a bonus structure that rewards business goals. In time, however, executive managers at the centre perceive a tendency for business managers to subordinate the overall corporate goals in favour of their own business goals. This leads to a crisis of control, in which top management seek to assert their control.

Phase 4: Coordination

Executive managers institute formal control systems to help them coordinate these diverse businesses. These decentralized business units may be reconfigured into product groups. The allocation of resources is far more carefully evaluated and controlled at the centre. The return on capital employed is used by the centre as a criterion for justifying their allocation decisions. In time, this leads to a crisis of red tape in which business unit managers come to resent decisions from the centre, which are seen as remote and lacking an understanding of local market conditions. The organization becomes too big and complex to be efficiently managed by formal systems—the next revolution begins.

Phase 5: Collaboration

Self-discipline and working towards agreed organizational objectives replace formal control systems. Teamwork, flexible working, and networking are common practices characterizing this evolutionary growth phase. The question for leaders of organizations is what kind of revolution change will supplant this evolutionary growth phase. A real difficulty for leaders is to understand where they are in this development process and consciously act to learn from, rather than replicate, the past. Although the rate of change has accelerated since Greiner first introduced his model, it does provide an outline of the broad challenges that managers of growing organizations face.[24]

Those who advocate revolutionary change accept that all firms need periods of relative stability, but argue that this can breed rigidities. **Organizational rigidity** is an inability and unwillingness to change even when your competitive environment dictates that change is required, such as Blockbuster's inability to adapt to the online streaming of films. In addressing strategic change, tools such as *business process re-engineering* can help managers to see that change must be integrative across the organization's systems rather than be conducted in isolation (see **Section 9.4.1** on integrative change). A challenge for managers of revolutionary change is to avoid the organization sinking back into old rigidities after the change. As we saw in **Chapters 3** and **6**, companies that compete in disruptive environments are forced to innovate constantly. This leaves little room for complacency and resting on former successes.

Those who advocate evolutionary change see revolutionary change as perpetual; another similar-size change will eventually be required after the company sinks back to its old ways. They also point out that such revolutionary change is difficult to sustain and simply awaits another business issue to grab the organization's attention. In contrast, evolutionary change focuses on the organization's long-term goals and moves towards this. Individuals are still expected to learn, share ideas, and engage in innovation. Evolutionary change should embrace all members of an organization. The role of management is to support and facilitate this learning and continuous improvement (see **Strategy in Focus 9.2**).

 STRATEGY IN FOCUS 9.2 Can John Lewis Reinvent Itself?

Social housing ventures to compensate for margin decline as chair seeks expansion 'beyond retail'

John Lewis & Partners is to expand its financial services business and venture into housing and horticulture after warning that margins in retail are too thin to sustain the company in the long term. In a letter sent to the group's 80,000 staff or 'partners', chair Sharon White said a strategic review, which she launched in March 2020 shortly after joining, 'should see green shoots in our performance over the next nine to 12 months, and our profits recovering over the next three to five years'.

Dame Sharon has already warned that sales at both the eponymous department stores and the Waitrose supermarket chain are likely to fall this year. She has also announced hundreds of staff cuts at the group's head office and stated that eight of its 50 department stores will not reopen following the UK's pandemic lockdown, threatening more than 1,000 jobs. But in a subsequent letter she went further, saying that retail profit margins were under pressure and that 'for the partnership to be sustainable over the long-term, we need to expand beyond retail'.

'We have the opportunity to offer our customers new services where trust and a strong sense of purpose are important'. These could include using some of the partnership's significant land and property assets—as well as some freehold stores, it owns a 2,800-acre farm in Hertfordshire, four hotels and various logistics facilities—for private rented housing. Sharon White says 'shops will always be crucial to the brand but they will be in support of online' 'We want to put excess space to good social use. We are exploring with third parties the concept of new mixed-use affordable housing,' she said. The group's former store in Southsea, which it closed last year, is being redeveloped into a hotel and cinema complex.

Richard Lim, chief executive of Retail Economics, said the new ventures risked adding complexity despite a pledge to simplify the business. 'But like everybody, they have got too much space and they need to do something else with it.' The financial service business, run by HSBC under a white-label agreement, will be expanded 'significantly' over the next five years. Feedback from staff has also suggested there is an opportunity in horticulture, a highly fragmented sector where the partnership's existing offerings are disparate and under-developed.

Following the experience of COVID-19, Dame Sharon reiterated that the partnership would become a much more digital business, with around 60 per cent of John Lewis sales and a fifth of Waitrose revenue likely to be generated online in future. Before the pandemic, the proportions were 40 per cent and 5 per cent respectively. 'Shops will always be crucial to the brand but they will be in support of online,' she said. 'Over the next five years we expect to rebalance our shop estate so that we have the right space in the right locations.'

Mr Lim said the stores would increasingly be used for WACD 'what Amazon can't do' including experiences, product demonstrations and personal shopping services. As already indicated, the two partnership's brands will work more closely together, with more Waitrose food in the department stores and John Lewis homewares in the supermarkets. There will also be improvements to pricing, especially in areas of John Lewis, and better loyalty offerings across both brands. The famed 'Never Knowingly Undersold' promise, which dates back to the 1920s, is being reviewed 'to ensure we offer fair value for how our customers shop today'.

Source: Jonathan Eley, 'John Lewis looks to private homes to offset high street pain', *The Financial Times*, 30 July 2020.

9.4.2 Integrative Change

Information technology is often introduced by organizations seeking to address deteriorating business performance. **Michael Hammer's** work on business process re-engineering warns against naively using new technology with outdated business practices to boost performance.[25] Instead of seeing technology as a panacea, it should be viewed as a tool to help radically redesign business processes. As he states:

> Reengineering strives to break away from the old rules about how we organize and conduct business . . . reengineering cannot be planned meticulously and accomplished in small and cautious steps. It's an all-or-nothing proposition.[26]

Hammer argues for a revolutionary approach to change in which management are prepared to embrace an uncertain future. Re-engineering calls for senior management to question the assumptions of their existing business processes and change outdated rules. We have seen that specialization in organizations tends to lead to a subculture in which organizational goals are replaced by their department goals. In re-engineering the fundamental processes of the organization need to be addressed from a cross-functional perspective. Otherwise, any attempt to change a poorly performing department in isolation will be prone to failure.

What is required is an understanding of the interactions and interdependencies between departments. This requires a change management team that is drawn from the units involved in the process being re-engineered, as well as the units that depend on them. This is in order to assess which processes add value. Re-engineering involves a shift in thinking about organizational structure in which the people who undertake the work make the decisions. These individuals would then become self-managing and self-controlling, which allows for management layers to be depleted. It also changes the management role from one of control to one of support and facilitation. Given the disruption and discontinuity of this sort of revolutionary change, re-engineering requires leaders who possess vision. Such leaders are not afraid to adopt audacious goals and possess the drive and ability to see them to completion.

Erik Brynjolfsson et al. argue that effective change requires an understanding of complements that exists between strategy, technology, and business practice.[27] They suggest that management would benefit from adopting a matrix of change approach to help them understand the complicated interrelationships that surround change. Their framework draws upon the work of **Paul Milgrom and John Roberts** on complements.[28] This suggests that in implementing complex change, managers needs to take account of the interactions that exist between business practices, rather than trying to implement change in a disaggregated fashion. The matrix allows managers to think through the following change issues before attempting implementation: (a) feasibility—the coherence and stability of any proposed change; (b) sequence—the order in which change should take place; (c) pace—the speed with which change should be undertaken and the magnitude of change; and (d) location—whether a proposed change should take place at an existing or a new site.

The drivers of organizational change, which include information technology and increasing competition, have brought about new organizational forms. Where these forms constitute a discontinuity, or break with old practices, the benefits to organizations can be considerable. For example, Hallmark, which produces greeting cards, gift wrapping, and other personal expression products, was able to reduce the time it takes to introduce new products by 75 per cent. This was achieved by changing their practice of sequential product development to one involving a cross-functional team. A difficulty arises, as we saw earlier, when organizations introduce technology without thinking through the contingent changes in working practices. This is one reason why US firms have failed to obtain the same benefits from introducing technology that comparable Japanese firms achieve.

A matrix of change system involves three matrices: (1) *an organization's current practices*; (2) *its proposed or target practices*; and (3) *a transitional state* that helps an organization move from matrix (1) to matrix (2). In addition, the matrix system includes stakeholder evaluations which provide employees with a forum to state the importance of the practices to their jobs. The matrix of change helps managers to be aware of the assumptions that underlie how their organization works. Its value is in identifying complementary and competing practices.

Complementary practices are reinforcing. This means that undertaking more of one complement increases the return to the other complement. In contrast, doing less of a competing practice actually increases the return to other competing practices. In making complementary and competing practices explicit, managers can immediately see where there is likely to be reinforcement or interference between existing and target practices. This allows managers to select the practices that will be most effective in meeting organizational goals.

Therefore, to achieve superior performance we require an understanding of change that takes into account a complete and coherent system of practices. However, we need to recognize that organizational performance may experience a decline as new complements disrupt the old ways of doing things. In this respect, putting together a coherent set of complements may take a number of years. This is not to say that change must always be evolutionary, since a powerful leader with a strong vision may introduce rapid system-wide change.

9.4.3 **Strategic Drift**

In discussing the challenges surrounding strategic change, **Gerry Johnson** introduces the term strategic drift.[29] This refers to a situation in which the strategy being pursued by an organization becomes less relevant to the environment in which the organization competes. The process may take a number of years and not be perceived by managers until the drift causes company performance to decline. At this point, the situation is likely to require a transformation change in strategy. Strategic drift occurs because managers are wedded to their existing paradigm.

A **paradigm** is a set of beliefs and assumptions managers hold which are relevant to the organization in which they work. It is the culture or 'taken for granted' view that is held by members of the organization about the company and its business environment. The paradigm develops over time and encompasses all aspects of the company, such as its management style and organizational routines. Ironically, it is more likely to be visible to those outside the company than to those immersed in the culture inside the organization. **Peter Drucker** refers to this as a company's 'theory of the business'.[30]

Managers have a tendency to discount evidence contrary to the paradigm and embrace evidence that supports the paradigm. This is often referred to as **cognitive bias**. This is because change within the paradigm is comfortable for managers. Therefore, they will interpret any uncertain event by looking for familiar patterns in which they tackled similar events. As a result, any strategic change will be based upon what the organization has successfully achieved in the past. This will reinforce the belief in the need for incremental change. And, since the organization is making incremental changes, managers can cite this as evidence that some change is taking place within the organization.

If the markets in which the organization competes are changing gradually then gradual changes in strategy will make sense to managers. This is shown in **Figure 9.8** as the incremental change stage. At this stage, there is little misalignment between the organization strategy and the needs of its markets. In the next stage, strategic drift begins to occur. The organization's strategy is gradually moving away from its business environment. This is because the environment is changing more rapidly than the change in the organization strategy. A reason for this may be due to **core rigidities**; these are the capabilities on which the organization's competitive advantage is based and therefore difficult to change. This is because inherent within these capabilities will be emotional capital invested by

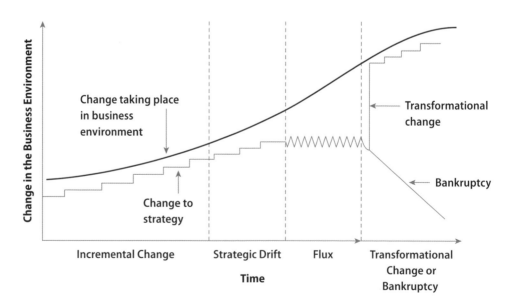

Figure 9.8   Strategic drift.

Source: Adapted from G. Johnson, 'Managing strategic change—strategy, culture, and action', *Long Range Planning*, vol. 25, no. 1 (1992), pp. 28–36, p. 34.

managers throughout the organization. These capabilities are often entwined with the organization's DNA. An example of a core rigidity is Intel's difficulty in moving from memory chips to microprocessors. Another reason will be managers' cognitive bias, mentioned above.

The next phase may manifest itself in deterioration in performance. As this drift becomes apparent the strategy of the organization may enter a period of flux. During a period of flux, there is no clear strategic direction and internal arguments intensify about the strategic direction of the firm. As performance continues to deteriorate, a radical transformation is required to align the organization's strategy with its customers and markets. The final stage is one of **transformational change** or bankruptcy. At this point, the organization's strategy is substantially misaligned with changes in its business environment. Managers are faced with fundamentally rethinking their business model in light of the disruptive changes in the business environment. Organizations infrequently undertake transformational change and usually as a result of substantial losses in market share and profitability. If managers in the organization are unwilling to accept this change, the company will likely cease to trade. Managers may hope for *white knight*: a rescue of the company by another organization.

To avoid strategic drift, it is necessary to surface the assumptions that underlie the dominant paradigms. By making assumptions about business decisions explicit, managers can then openly discuss the barriers to change. These barriers might be political, or part of the control systems, or indeed, any aspect of the organization. The crucial point is that the dominant paradigm cannot be challenged or changed until its assumptions are made explicit.

Gerry Johnson, George Yip, and **Manuel Hensmans** undertook research to ascertain whether companies can undertake strategic change without the advent of a crisis.[31] They researched high-performing companies that successfully transformed themselves in order to find out which management capabilities companies need to develop over time. They found such companies had three fundamental advantages over their peers.

1) **A tradition of creating alternative coalitions**

   Such companies had an ability to maintain their performance while pursuing strategic change. This was possible by creating parallel coalitions of top executives. The first coalition comprised senior executives, who were focused on reinforcing current capabilities, strengths, and successes. The second coalition were younger, but also executives. Their role was to develop new strategies and capabilities. Over time, this parallel behaviour becomes institutionalized within the company. The outlook of the second coalition allowed them to anticipate strategic drift where their strategy was misaligned from their changing business environment.

2) **A tradition of constructively challenging business as usual**

   The companies achieved major transformations with those that were prepared to tolerate a challenge to their existing ways of competing. Disagreements among the alternative coalitions, mentioned above, would over time become less confrontational and more respectful. Therefore, what might have started as open conflict evolves into constructive challenging.

3) **A tradition of exploiting happy accidents**

   Happy accidents are 'unanticipated circumstances or events that ultimately support transformation in the direction favoured by the leaders in waiting'. In effect, executives were able to take advantage of unforeseen events in a way which allowed them to galvanize support for their ideas.

It is important to understand that these capabilities are developed over the long term. In order for such capabilities to be embedded within the organization, managers will have to establish their own traditions.

9.4.4 What Determines a Visionary Organization

What is it that makes an organization the best in its industry and widely admired by its peers? Where does the resilience that allows some companies to overcome adversity come from? Why do some companies make a lasting impact on the world around them? The answers to these questions are part of what determines a visionary organization. Research by **Jim Collins and Jerry Porras** suggests that **visionary organizations** are particularly adept at simultaneously managing continuity and embracing change.[32] Using responses from CEOs, they identified eighteen visionary companies, those with superior long-term performance who have made an impact on society. These were then compared with a control group of companies that had similar products, services, and markets when they were founded. In common with the visionary organizations, the comparison companies were also identified by the CEOs that Collins and Porras surveyed. The difference is that these companies were mentioned less often by CEOs when identifying who they considered to be great companies. The comparison companies had an average founding date of 1892, compared with 1897 for the visionary organizations.

The idea was to identify the factors that distinguish visionary from non-visionary companies. We might add that although the comparison companies did not attain the same performance heights as the visionary companies, nonetheless they outperformed the stock market. The difference is that, whereas the comparison companies outperformed the stock market by a factor of more than two, the visionary companies outperformed it by a factor of more than fifteen. Collins and Porras found that the visionary companies, which include Sony (the only non-US firm in the study), the Walt Disney Company, Merck, 3M, Hewlett-Packard, and Ford, have a **core ideology** that comprises their **core values** and **purpose**.[33]

The core values can be thought of as the principles on which the company was founded. An organization's purpose is the reason why it exists, which transcends merely making money. The core values of an organization do not change; they are the bedrock of the organization. Similarly, visionary organizations pursue their purpose knowing that this is ongoing and will never be fully achieved. John Young, former CEO of Hewlett-Packard, sums up the thinking of visionary companies.

> *We distinguish between core values and practices; the core values don't change, but the practices might. We've also remained clear that profit—as important as it is—is not why the Hewlett-Packard Company exists; it exists for more fundamental reasons.*[34]

Core values and purpose are important for visionary organizations in that they help to guide continuity, but also provide a stimulus for change. In **Chapter 1** we mentioned the importance of Johnson & Johnson's *credo*, a set of core values that guides all members of that organization. The *credo* was applied in helping Johnson & Johnson to make an appropriate decision during the Tylenol issue. Visionary companies are prepared to change everything, except their fundamental core values. Their strategy, structure, practices, resources and capabilities, and systems all need to change at some point to ensure forward momentum or progress. For visionary companies this drive for change comes from within—a constant dissatisfaction with the status quo—rather than a reaction to the external environment.

How do such organizations stimulate change? The answer is that they institute **BHAGs**—big hairy audacious goals. These are clear, stretching goals that can be easily communicated to everyone in the organization. For example, Ratan Tata's idea to produce the Tata Nano, an inexpensive hatchback car which appealed to riders of motorcycles and scooters in India, with its low price of one lakh rupees or US$2,500, was a BHAG. Henry Ford wanted 'to democratize the automobile' by giving the majority of individuals the freedom to buy a car. This was in 1907, when Ford was not the dominant player in the industry. The irony is that Ford failed to replace this BHAG with another to continue to stimulate progress and lost its market dominance to General Motors. Therefore, BHAGs need to be continually updated to avoid organizational complacency.

Gary Hamel and C. K. Prahalad make a similar point using the concept of **strategic intent**.[35] As with BHAGs, strategic intent is more than mere rhetoric. It requires a major level of commitment from the organization to pursue these overarching goals. Although these goals will invariably involve a longer-term time horizon, BHAGs and strategic intent help provide some consistency to short-term actions. The example of Boeing's decision to build the jumbo jet, the 747, when failure would have meant bankruptcy, represents a most audacious goal. Its rival, McDonnell Douglas, tended to adopt a more cautious wait-and-see approach. In short, BHAGs fall outside an organization's comfort zone. They are consistent with its core ideology, and help stimulate progress by maintaining forward momentum.

Visionary companies embrace what Collins and Porras refer to as the genius of the '**AND**', rather than succumb to the tyranny of the '**OR**'. In other words, where rival corporations see paradoxes and conflict, visionary companies succeed in achieving synthesis. For example, visionary companies actively pursue their *ideology and profit*. Being idealistic is not a reason for them to sacrifice the pursuit of profits. Although much is often made of the role of charismatic leaders in shaping organizations, it was found that this was not the case in visionary companies. At various times throughout their history organizations such as 3M, Procter & Gamble, Merck, and Sony have had CEOs who made significant changes, but were not what might be understood as high-profile charismatic leaders. In fact, by setting BHAGs that are independent of management style the succession of charismatic leaders proves far less of a problem. Of course, as was evident with Peters and Waterman's *In Search of Excellence*,[36] the fortunes of such companies can quickly change. The danger of emphasizing specific companies, such as Sony and Hewlett-Packard, is that changes in their environment quickly turn today's darlings into tomorrow's dogs. As such, we need to recognize that being overly prescriptive about visionary organizations can quickly date the relevance of research.

In addition, Collins and Porras also found a *cult-like culture* in visionary organizations. This culture is built around the core values of the organization. It constantly reinforces the core ideology of the organization through socialization. It indoctrinates the employees in the ways of the company and thereby influences their attitude and behaviour. This is manifest in organizations like Walt Disney, Procter & Gamble, and Walmart. Organizational culture can be defined as '*the pattern of basic assumptions that a given group has invented, discovered, or developed in learning to cope with its problems of external adaptation and internal integration*'.[37] It can be thought of as the values and beliefs that members of an organization hold in common. The outward manifestations of organizational culture can include such things as dress code, employee inductions, symbols, and office layout. However, to gain a deeper understanding of culture, it becomes necessary to investigate the assumptions that guide how members of an organization perceive, think, and feel.

A strong sense of culture or shared values, such as exists at Procter & Gamble, can help to coordinate, motivate, and guide individual behaviour. This invariably precludes the need for formal control systems to manage employee behaviour. There are similarities with the *Theory Z* Japanese style of management.[38] A **Theory Z-type-organization** is based on trust. Therefore, it requires a less hierarchical structure which in turn helps to engender greater employee involvement. A key characteristic of a Theory Z organization is its informal control systems reinforced by formal measures.

An organization's culture can be a force for change and innovation, but it may also be an impediment to change. For example, the culture that exists within 3M encourages managers to experiment, to take risks, to try out new ideas, and not be afraid of failure. Within 3M, there is an expectation that managers will spend around ten per cent of their time on projects of their own choosing. These projects are subject to the scrutiny of their peers which provides constructive feedback. Even when an idea seems to fail, there is latitude for employees to enlist the support of like-minded managers (or *product champions*) in an attempt to foster creativity and a breakthrough. The product champion can be thought of as a change agent, someone who takes responsibility for ensuring that change takes place. Without such a culture, the world may never have had Post-it Notes. Its inventor, Art Fry, had been working on developing a strong adhesive for 3M, but failed to achieve this. What he did develop was a weak adhesive, which allows paper to be stuck down, but also easily removed. This resulted in the creation of Post-it Notes.

9.4.5 Good to Great Companies

In subsequent research **Jim Collins** seeks to answer the question: what turns a company from being 'good' into being 'great'? Or, put another way, what strategic change occurs within organizations that allows them to leap from being good to being great?[39] To do this, Collins and his research team identified organizations that had fifteen-year cumulative stock returns at or below the stock market. The companies then experienced a transition point, before going on to achieve cumulative returns at least three times the market over the next fifteen years. The timescale of fifteen years allows the research to filter out those spectacular companies that achieve great results, but which cannot sustain them. The choice of returns three times that of the stock market means that such companies would have to beat the returns achieved by recognized great companies such as Coca-Cola, Motorola, and Intel.

The research team identified eleven companies which met their criteria for great organizations.[40] For comparison they made use of companies that were in the same industry and which had the same opportunities and similar resources at the time of transition, but did not make the transition from good to great, and companies that temporarily went from good to great, but were unable to sustain their performance. A key finding for companies that make the transition from good to great is their use of the **hedgehog concept**.

The hedgehog concept is drawn from Isaiah Berlin's story, 'The Hedgehog and the Fox'. In this story, the hedgehog and the fox are adversaries. The fox is very clever and knows many things. In contrast, the hedgehog knows only one big thing. In their duels, the hedgehog always rolls up into a spiky ball and therefore always beats the fox. Collins draws an analogy between the hedgehog and the leaders of good to great companies. Like the hedgehog, these leaders know and pursue one thing. Their rivals, meanwhile, are trying many different approaches to match the complexity of their world, while the hedgehog-like leaders construct the world into a simple unifying concept, as shown in Collins's book, *Good to Great*, and reproduced here as **Figure 9.9**.

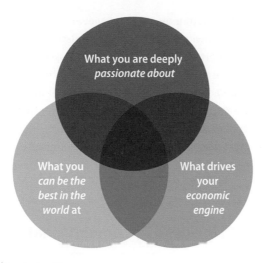

Figure 9.9 The hedgehog concept.
Source: Jim Collins, *Good to Great*, 2001. Copyright © 2001 by Jim Collins. Reprinted with permission.

According to Collins, a route to greatness is defined by an understanding of *three issues*.

1) **'What you can be the best in the world at'**. Collins sees this as going beyond the resource-based view of core competencies, arguing that possessing a core competence does not mean you are the best in the world at it. One might argue that this depends on how you define core competence, since for many organizations their core competence does make them the best in the world at what they do (e.g. Toyota's production system).

2) **'What drives your economic engine'**. This helps managers to understand the single performance measurement that has the greatest impact on their business. For instance, for First Direct it might be overall customer satisfaction.

3) **'What you are deeply passionate about'**. What is it that makes you passionate about the business you are in?

The good to great companies developed their strategies based on an understanding of these three issues. This understanding was then translated into a simple concept—a hedgehog concept. The point for leaders is not to try to be the best, but to understand where you can be the best. We will review leadership in **Chapter 10**.

Summary

The chapter started with a discussion of the trade-off between specialization and coordination and the impact of this on an organization's structure. We evaluated the functional and divisional structures before moving on to more complex matrix and network structures. We discussed Ghoshal and Bartlett's argument for a focus on organizational processes and a more integrative approach. This approach goes beyond the limitations inherent in merely making structural changes.

Goold and Quinn provided three reasons for establishing a strategic control system. They produce a contingency framework highlighting different conditions when strategic control systems might be useful for an organization. We assessed strategic change reviewing Greiner's model, which highlights the challenges facing managers of growing organizations. We also addressed integrative change by showing that change needs to be part of a coherent and stable system that recognizes the role of complements. Strategic drift was discussed, showing that managers need to surface assumptions inherent in their organizational paradigm to facilitate change. We ended the chapter with a discussion of visionary organizations and the use of BHAGs to guide their onward progress, before looking at how so-called 'great' companies deal with strategic change.

In **Chapter 10**, we discuss the role of leadership and assess its impact on strategic change.

CASE STUDY W. L. Gore's Unconventional Success

W. L. Gore is a high-tech manufacturing company best known for its waterproof Gore-Tex fabric. However, its diverse portfolio of products include guitar strings, dental floss, acoustic vents for mobile phones, and medical devices to treat heart defects. The privately owned company has a $3 billion turnover and employs more than 10,000 people worldwide. These employees, referred to as associates, are part owners of the company through its share plan. Gore prefers this private ownership and believes this reinforces a key element of its culture to 'take a long-term view' when assessing

Photo 9.2   Gore-Tex is a waterproof, breathable fabric membrane regularly used in camping and sporting equipment and clothing.
Source: © Cineberg/Shutterstock.com.

business situations. It has offices in more than twenty-five countries, with Shutterstock.com manufacturing operations in the USA, Germany, the UK, China, and Japan.

The company has made a profit every year since its incorporation. It has been granted more than 2,000 patents worldwide in a wide range of fields, including electronics, medical devices and polymer processing.

Company History

W. L. Gore & Associates was founded on 1 January 1958, in Newark, Delaware, by Wilbert L. (Bill) and Genevieve (Vieve) Gore in the basement of their home. In 1969, Bill and Vieve's son, Bob Gore, discovered a remarkably versatile new polymer expanded polytetrafluoroethylene (or ePTFE). This led the company into many new applications in the medical, fabric, aerospace, automotive, mobile electronics, music, and semiconductor industries.

The founders' vision was to build a firm that was truly innovative and move away from the traditional ideas of management. As a result, you will find no rule books or bureaucratic processes. This is because Bill Gore strongly believed that people come to work to do well and do the right thing. Instead of the reward and control systems other companies rely on, Gore uses trust, peer pressure, and the desire to invent great products. Instead of rigid hierarchies there is a unique organization which draws upon the talents of every associate.

Strategic Control Systems

At Gore, there are few employee titles; a major exception is CEO Terri Kelly. Managers are called leaders and they oversee teams and divisions. Any employee's business card will simply have their name and the word 'Associate'. This is irrespective of how much money they earn, how long they've been with the company, or their responsibility. There are no organization charts, no budgets, and no strategic plans like most companies. What Gore does is plan investment and forecast, but without the gamesmanship and inflexibility that comes with traditional budgets. This is because Gore's investments will reach fruition many years ahead and they are keen to avoid short-term decision-making, which is not in the best interests of the company. Therefore, the planning and investment horizons have to match.

Gore is a big, established company which behaves like a small, entrepreneurial organization. One of the keys to its success is the number of employees per plant. Bill Gore found that 'things get clumsy when you reach 150 employees'. Therefore, plant size tends to be no larger than 50,000 square feet, which can accommodate no more than 150 people. As Gore units grow in size, so they simply divide. These small plants are organized in clusters in close proximity with one another. The closeness encourages synergy and a sharing of ideas, while small units encourage ownership and identity. This invariably creates a tension between potential diseconomies of scale and the sharing of ideas through informal relationships.

CEO Terri Kelly has worked at Gore her entire life, after graduating from the University of Delaware with a degree in mechanical engineering. Kelly worked as a product specialist before managing the global fabrics division. She became CEO in 2005, after working for the company for twenty-two years, the fourth CEO in the company's history. Unlike other CEOs, Kelly was not appointed by a board, but as a result of nominations from a wide range of associates. Leadership opportunities at Gore derive from the 'following' an associate has among co-workers. Similarly, peer assessment is used to determine compensation.

The lack of business qualifications and formal business training has been no impediment to the CEO's success. In many respects, her insider understanding of Gore's unique culture allows her to continue the 'Gore' way of doing things in a manner an outsider simply could not.

Without doubt, another reason for Gore's success is its unique culture. Gore doesn't utilize traditional strategic control systems, such as control and rewards to guide behaviour. This is because in small groups, informal relationships are more effective. The use of peer pressure is far more effective than a manager scrutinizing your work. As a result, people strive to achieve what is expected of them. For example, in a Gore plant every part of the process of designing, manufacturing, and marketing becomes subject to this same group scrutiny. In manufacturing firms with larger units, and considerably more people per unit, this kind of functional interrelationship and understanding cannot be achieved.

In effect, everyone at Gore shares a common relationship and unity of purpose. The writer Malcolm Gladwell refers to this relationship as 'transactive memory'. The term was coined by psychologist, Daniel Wegner. It doesn't just refer to ideas and facts stored in our heads; it refers to information we store with other people. Two groups of people were tested with the same statements; one group comprising couples who knew each other, another group comprising couples who did not know each other. The pairs who knew each other remembered more statements than those who did not know each other. Wegner called this a transactive memory system.

What has developed at Gore is a highly effective institutional transactive memory. Every associate in a unit knows other associates well enough to know what they know. And they know them well enough that they can trust them to know their role. At an organizational level, what Gore has achieved with its idiosyncratic culture is the same kind of understanding, knowing, intimacy, and trust that exists within a family. This allows Gore to innovate and rapidly respond to its consumer needs. Knowledge and expertise that reside in one part of the company rapidly disseminate to all parts of the company. This makes for very efficient problem-solving, diffusion of ideas, and speed of execution.

In order to connect with younger associates, Gore has partnered with a Silicon Valley-based company called Institute for the Future. The objective is to utilize technology to help teams move faster and communicate. As with most things at Gore, this approach is careful, incremental, and cautious, benefiting from the approach adopted by the founders.

Sources: 'At W. L. Gore, 57 years of authentic culture', *Fortune*, 5 March 2015;
'Gore-Tex gets made without managers', *The Observer*, 2 November 2008; M. Gladwell,
'*The Tipping Point*', Abacus, 2000; https://www.gore.com (accessed 1 August 2020).

Questions

1. What is the role of culture in helping W. L. Gore to compete successfully?

2. In the absence of overt strategic control systems, how is the behaviour of Gore's associates motivated and guided?

 For more examples and discussion to aid your understanding of this chapter, please visit the online resources and see the Extension Material for this chapter.

 Review Questions

1. Compare and contrast a divisional structure with a matrix structure. In which type of environment might each be best suited?
2. According to Larry Greiner, what is the purpose of the different evolutionary and revolutionary phases an organization experiences, as it grows and develops?
3. How might the 'hedgehog concept' help companies to survive and prosper?

 Discussion Question

'Without a vision, an organization will fail.' ***Discuss***.

 Research Topic

Using company examples from different industries, examine the role of BHAGs in helping companies to produce far-reaching change.

Recommended Reading

For perspectives on the debate between strategy and structure see:

- **T. L. Amburgey** and **T. Dacin**, 'As the left foot follows the right? The dynamics of strategic and structural change', *Academy of Management Journal*, vol. 37, no. 6 (1994), pp. 1427–52.
- **H. Mintzberg**, 'The design school: reconsidering the basic premises of strategic management', *Strategic Management Journal*, vol. 11, no. 3 (1990), pp. 171–95.

For a discussion of how organizations grow and evolve, see:

- **L. E. Greiner**, 'Evolution and revolution as organizations grow', *Harvard Business Review*, vol. 50, no. 4 (1972), pp. 37–46.

For a discussion of strategic control systems and the disadvantages of focusing merely on organizational structure, see:

- **M. Goold** and **J. J. Quinn**, 'The paradox of strategic controls', *Strategic Management Journal*, vol. 11, no. 1 (1990), pp. 43–57.
- **S. Ghoshal** and **C. A. Bartlett**, 'Changing the role of top management: beyond structure to processes', *Harvard Business Review*, vol. 73, no. 1 (1995), pp. 86–96.

For an insightful discussion of visionary organizations, see:

- **J. C. Collins** and **J. I. Porras**, *Built to Last: Successful Habits of Visionary Companies*, Random House, 1994.

www.oup.com/he/henry4e

Visit the online resources that accompany this book for activities and more information on strategy.

Test your knowledge and understanding of this chapter further by trying the multiple-choice questions online.

References and Notes

1. **H. Mintzberg**, *Structures in Fives: Designing Effective Organizations*, Prentice Hall, 1993.
2. **A. Smith**, *The Wealth of Nations*, originally published in 1776.
3. **A. Chandler**, *Strategy and Structure: Chapters in the History of the American Industrial Enterprise*, MIT Press, 1962.
4. **T. L. Amburgey** and **T. Dacin**, 'As the left foot follows the right? The dynamics of strategic and structural change', *Academy of Management Journal*, vol. 37, no. 6 (1994), pp. 1427–52.
5. **Amburgey** and **Dacin**, see n. 4 above, p. 1446.
6. **C. A. Bartlett** and **S. Ghoshal**, 'Matrix management: not a structure, a frame of mind', *Harvard Business Review*, vol. 68, no. 4 (1990), pp. 138–45.
7. **Bartlett** and **Ghoshal**, see n. 6 above, p. 140.
8. **M. Goold** and **A. Campbell**, 'Do you have a well designed organization?', *Harvard Business Review*, vol. 80, no. 3 (2002), pp. 117–24.
9. **S. Ghoshal** and **C. A. Bartlett**, 'Changing the role of top management: beyond structure to processes', *Harvard Business Review*, vol. 73, no. 1 (1995), pp. 86–96.

[10] **R. S. Kaplan** and **D. P. Norton**, 'Using the balanced scorecard as a strategic management system', *Harvard Business Review*, vol. 74, no. 1 (1996), pp. 75–85; **R. S. Kaplan** and **D. P. Norton**, *The Balanced Scorecard*, Harvard Business School Press, 1996.

[11] **M. Goold** and **J. J. Quinn**, 'The paradox of strategic controls', *Strategic Management Journal*, vol. 11, no. 1 (1990), pp. 43–57.

[12] **H. Mintzberg** and **J. A. Waters**, 'Of strategies: deliberate and emergent', *Strategic Management Journal*, vol. 6, no. 3 (1985), pp. 257–72.

[13] **Kaplan** and **Norton**, 'Using the balanced scorecard as a strategic management system', see n. 10 above; **Kaplan** and **Norton**, *The Balanced Scorecard*, see n. 10 above.

[14] **W. G. Ouchi**, 'Markets, bureaucracies, and clans', *Administrative Science Quarterly*, vol. 25, no. 1 (1980), pp. 129–42.

[15] **Goold** and **Quinn**, see n. 11 above, p. 54.

[16] **C. Argyris**, 'Double-loop learning in organizations', *Harvard Business Review*, vol. 55, no. 5 (1977), pp. 15–25.

[17] **J. Lee** and **D. Miller**, 'People matter: commitment to employees, strategy and performance in Korean firms', *Strategic Management Journal*, vol. 20, no. 6 (1999), pp. 579–93.

[18] **Ouchi**, see n. 14 above.

[19] **L. E. Greiner**, 'Evolution and revolution as organizations grow', *Harvard Business Review*, vol. 50, no. 4 (1972), pp. 37–46.

[20] **Greiner**, see n. 19 above, p. 38.

[21] **Greiner**, see n. 19 above, p. 38.

[22] **Greiner**, see n. 19 above, p. 40.

[23] **Greiner**, see n. 19 above, pp. 55–63.

[24] **Greiner**, see n. 19 above, pp. 55–63.

[25] **M. Hammer**, 'Reengineering work: don't automate, obliterate', *Harvard Business Review*, vol. 68, no. 4 (1990), pp. 104–11.

[26] **Hammer**, see n. 25 above, pp. 104–5.

[27] **E. Brynjolfsson**, **A. A. Renshaw**, and **M. van Alstyne**, 'The matrix of change', *Sloan Management Review*, vol. 38, no. 2 (1997), pp. 37–54.

[28] **P. Milgrom** and **J. Roberts**, 'Complementarities and fit: strategy, structure, and organizational change in manufacturing', *Journal of Accounting and Economics*, vol. 19, no. 2 (1993), pp. 179–208.

[29] **G. Johnson**, 'Managing strategic change—strategy, culture and action', *Long-range Planning*, vol. 25, no. 1 (1992), pp. 28–56.

[30] **P. F. Drucker**, *Managing in a Time of Great Change*, Butterworth Heinemann, 1995.

[31] **G. Johnson**, **G. S. Yip**, and **M. Hensmans**, 'Achieving successful strategic transformation', *MIT Sloan Management Review*, vol. 53, no. 3 (2012), pp. 25–32.

[32] **J. C. Collins** and **J. I. Porras**, *Built to Last: Successful Habit of Visionary Companies*, Harper, 1994.

[33] The eighteen visionary companies identified by **Collins** and **Porras** were 3M, American Express, Boeing, Citicorp, Ford, General Electric, Hewlett-Packard, IBM, Johnson & Johnson, Marriott, Merck, Motorola, Nordstrom, Philip Morris, Procter & Gamble, Sony, Walmart, and Walt Disney.

[34] **Collins** and **Porras**, see n. 32 above.

[35] **G. Hamel** and **C. K. Prahalad**, 'Strategic intent', *Harvard Business Review*, vol. 67, no. 3 (1989), pp. 63–76.

[36] **T. Peters** and **R. Waterman**, *In Search of Excellence*, Harper & Row, 1982.

[37] **E. H. Schein**, 'Coming to a new awareness of organizational culture', *Sloan Management Review*, vol. 25, no. 2 (1984), pp. 3–16.

[38] **W. G. Ouchi**, *Theory Z: How American Businesses Can Meet the Japanese Challenge*, Addison-Wesley, 1981.

[39] **J. C. Collins**, *Good to Great*, Random House, 2001.

[40] The eleven 'good to great' companies were Abbott, Circuit City, Fannie Mae, Gillette, Kimberly-Clark, Kroger, Nucor, Philip Morris, Pitney Bowes, Walgreen's, and Wells Fargo; see **Collins**, see n. 38, p. 8 for a list of comparison companies.

CHAPTER 10
STRATEGIC LEADERSHIP

 Learning Objectives

After completing this chapter you should be able to:

- Explain the difference between leadership and management
- Discuss how leaders create a 'learning organization'
- Discuss the links between emotional intelligence and company performance
- Evaluate the benefits and dangers of narcissistic leaders
- Be aware of the importance of understanding different cultures
- Explain the leadership skills necessary for strategic change

Introduction

A key factor in effective *strategy implementation* is the quality of strategic leadership. The ability of leaders to communicate organizational goals clearly and guide employees to focus their attention on achieving these goals is crucial to success. This leadership ability is equally relevant in public, private, and not-for-profit sectors. This is not to imply that individuals lower down in the organization cannot exercise a leadership role. Rather, it is to recognize that without effective leadership at the top of the organization, individuals throughout the organization will be less likely to be empowered and, therefore, less likely to develop their own leadership skills.

The best-formulated strategy in the world will fail if it is poorly communicated and ineffectively implemented. Although the leader of an organization is ultimately responsible for a strategy's success or failure, their role should be to encourage and create an organizational culture that empowers individuals to respond to opportunities. We saw in **Chapter 9** how appropriate reward and control mechanisms help to guide employee behaviour and signpost the important goals of the organization. Systems, structures, procedures, and policies may aid the implementation of a strategy, but ultimately it is individuals who implement strategy. Therefore, it is individuals and groups, within and outside the organization, who must accept the rationale for strategic change.

In this chapter, we address the role that *leadership* plays in strategy implementation. The chapter begins with a discussion of the differences between leadership and management. We discuss the role of leaders in creating a learning organization. We evaluate the impact of emotional intelligence on effective leaders and the links between emotional intelligence and company performance. We assess the advantages and the dangers of narcissistic leaders, noting that this personality type may actually be beneficial in dynamic markets. We discuss the role of leaders in shaping the values of an organization to guide employee behaviour. The effects of national culture on individuals' beliefs and behaviour will also be identified, and the importance of culture on different leadership styles. Given the complexity and uncertainty that surrounds most organizations, we identify some of the leadership skills necessary to achieve strategic change.

10.1 Leadership vs. Management

A great deal of early work on leadership was taken up with discussions on nature and nurture. That is, are leaders born or can leadership abilities be learned? Interesting as this debate might be, we will take it as read that all companies are capable of becoming learning organizations in the right environment. We will focus instead on the role of leaders in helping organizations develop a competitive advantage. We might start by addressing the question: what is leadership and how does it differ from management? We should make it clear that some scholars in the field of strategic management use the term 'management' when it might be more appropriate to refer to 'leadership'. Therefore, readers should be mindful of this as they work through the chapter.

   Peter Northouse defines **leadership** as 'a process whereby an individual influences a group of individuals to achieve a common goal'.[1] This view of leadership is made up of the following components: (a) *process*; (b) *influence*; (c) *groups*; and (d) *common goals*. By defining leadership as a process this avoids issues of specific traits or characteristics that reside in the leader. Instead, leadership is seen as a transactional event that occurs between the leader and the followers. It is about the mutual interaction between a leader and followers. By defining leadership as part of a process Northouse democratizes it, making it available to everyone. Leadership is also about influence which describes how the leader affects the behaviour of followers. Influence is the fundamental characteristic of leadership, since without the ability to influence followers there can be no leadership.[2] Groups are important for leadership because, in most instances, a leader will influence a group to achieve common goals. A group may take many forms such as a community group, an orchestra, or an organization. As before, without groups to lead there can be no leadership.

   A fourth component of leadership is common goals. A common goal implies that leaders and followers share a mutual interest. The pursuit of common goals provides leadership with an ethical dimensional because it emphasizes the need for leaders to work with followers to achieve mutual goals. Leaders and followers are mutually co-dependent; they need each other. However, it is usually the leader who initiates and maintains the relationship. That said, we are moving away from the leader as 'the great man' and instead, understand leaders and followers in relation to each other. The leader is neither above nor superior to the followers. In distinguishing between leadership and management **John Kotter** argues that **management** is all about coping with complexity, whereas leadership is about dealing with change.[3] The complexity arises out of the proliferation of large corporations that occurred in the twentieth century. In order to operate effectively within these corporations managers use a range of practices and procedures (see **Chapter 9** for a discussion of strategic control systems). According to Kotter, a key function of management which helps it to deal with complexity is planning and budgeting. The setting of targets or goals for the next quarter or year, designing detailed steps for achieving those goals, and allocating resources as they are needed. The purpose of planning then is to produce *orderly results*, not change.

In contrast, leadership is concerned with setting the direction for organizational change. It is about producing a vision and developing strategies to realize that vision. The vision does not need to be overly complex or innovative; in fact, it should be clear and readily understood by all within the organization. In their research into visionary organization, **Jim Collins and Jerry Porras** found that successful organizations use **BHAGs**—big hairy audacious goals—to motivate and inspire individuals, thereby creating a *unifying focal point of effort*.[4] They use the example of President Kennedy's challenge for the USA to land a man on the moon and return him safely to earth. BHAGs also have the benefit of providing continued momentum within an organization after the leader has gone (see **Section 9.4.3**, 'What Determines a Visionary Organization'). A key point for any vision is how well it serves the organization's stakeholders and how easy it is to translate into a competitive strategy. The planning of management and the direction setting of leadership works best when they are used to complement rather than substitute for each other. On that basis, a vision can be used to guide the planning process by providing a direction for its efforts and placing boundaries on its activities.

Richard Rumelt argues that an important function of leadership is to absorb the complexity and ambiguity individuals encounter as they try to solve organizational problems.[5] All organizations face some situations which are characterized by complexity and ambiguity. The leader's role is to reframe an ambiguous and complex problem into a simpler problem that can be passed to managers to solve. For Rumelt, the reason many leaders fail is because they promote ambitious goals, but without resolving the ambiguity around specific obstacles that need to be overcome. Leadership is more than a willingness to accept the blame when something goes wrong. It is about setting proximate objectives and providing managers with problems that can be solved. A **proximate objective** refers to a goal that is close enough at hand to be feasible.[6]

In contrast with Collins and Porras, Rumelt argues for proximate goals. The example Collins and Porras provide of a BHAG, Rumelt contends, was actually a carefully chosen proximate goal and readily achievable. Furthermore, when faced with a dynamic environment it is illogical to suggest that a leader must look further ahead. This is because the more dynamic the environment is, the less able a leader is to perceive what is actually going on. Michael Porter argues that the leader's role is to develop strategy and to make the choices and trade-offs within the organization clear. This need to make choices reflects the fact that not all activities an individual may pursue will fit with the organization's strategy. Trade-offs occur when activities are incompatible, implying that more of one activity means less of another. A key role of the leader is to teach managers about strategy and help them to acquire the discipline to make choices in their day-to-day activities.[7]

In modern organizations, as we saw in **Chapter 9**, organizational systems are interdependent. These include such things as structure, reward and control mechanisms, and processes. Therefore, trying to adjust one part of the system in isolation can have no effect, or worse, a negative effect on the organization.[8] The role of management is to develop coherent systems which will allow plans to be efficiently implemented. This means communicating plans to individuals within the organization, making sure that the right people are in place to carry it forward, and providing appropriate incentives. As part of this organizing function, management must also have systems in place to monitor the outcomes of human action. This allows corrective action to be taken to ensure that plans are properly implemented.

The respective leadership role is one of *aligning*. The aim is to get key stakeholders inside and outside the organization to move in the same direction. Alignment can be thought of as an orchestral ensemble which includes everyone who can help implement the leader's vision or who may be able to impede it. Members of the organization, shareholders, suppliers, customers, and regulatory bodies are a few of the cast members who might need to be aligned if change is to occur successfully. It includes communicating the vision clearly, as well as getting individuals to accept the vision. The trust and integrity of the leader are paramount here, as is the perception that a leader's actions reflect their words. This helps to empower people in the organization as they can use their initiative to take decisions that reflect the communicated vision without fear of reprisals. A relatively new field of research into leadership is **authentic leadership**. Authentic leaders have a clear understanding of their own values and behave towards others based on these values. When tested by difficult situations, rather than compromising their values, authentic leaders use those situations to strengthen their values.[9] Johnson & Johnson's handling of the Tylenol scandal is an example of authentic leadership.

Management is also about *controlling* and *problem-solving*. The purpose of control mechanisms is to ensure that people's behaviour conforms to the needs of the plan and that any variance can be quickly identified and corrected. This means that management is about pushing people in a given direction. As Kotter states, *'the whole purpose of systems and structures is to help normal people who behave in normal ways to complete routine jobs successfully, day after day. It's not exciting or glamorous. But that's management.'*[10] In contrast, leadership is about change, and change requires an adjustment in people's behaviour. Unlike the control mechanisms of management, leadership motivates by satisfying our human needs for *achievement, recognition, and a sense of belonging.* An effective and authentic leader will ensure that the organization's vision is in line with its employees' own value system. As such, employees will derive intrinsic satisfaction from working towards its achievement. This satisfaction is likely to increase where individuals are also actively involved in discussions of how the vision can be achieved and are rewarded for their efforts. **Table 10.1** provides a summary of leadership and management activities.

The role of leadership is to create a shared vision of where the organization is trying to get to, and to formulate strategies to bring about the changes needed to achieve the vision. Effective leaders encourage leadership throughout the organization by empowering participants to make decisions without fear of reprisals. This dissemination of leadership allows organizations to deal effectively

Leadership Activities	Management Activities
Dealing with change	Coping with organizational complexity
Developing a vision and setting a direction for the organization	Planning and budgeting
Formulating strategy	Implementing strategy
Aligning stakeholders with the organization's vision	Organizing and staffing to achieve strategy
Motivating and inspiring employees	Controlling behaviour and problem-solving to ensure strategy is implemented
Recognizing and rewarding success	

Table 10.1 Leadership and management activities.

with increasing change in their competitive environments. A challenge is to blend the distinct actions of leadership and management so that they complement each other within the organization.

There is general agreement that management and leadership involve different functions. **Richard Cyert** contends that most people in leadership positions would be better characterized as managers rather than leaders.[11] He argues that leaders perform three broad functions: *organizational*; *interpersonal*; and *decision-making*.

1. The **organizational function** requires the leader to try to get participants in the organization to behave in a way that they feel is desirable. A leader can do this by influencing the process for setting goals in an organization. This is because what will be desirable for a leader will be the achievement of agreed goals, which in turn will derive from the leader's vision. According to Cyert, the leader's role is to steer the organization by setting a vision and being actively involved in the goal structure.

2. The **interpersonal function** requires the leader to ensure that the morale of participants is maintained. This is more of an empathetic role, which requires the leader to be aware of the concerns of members of the organization.

3. The **decision function** compels the leader to take decisions which allow the organization to achieve its goals.

However, we should not forget that organizations are collections of individuals. Regardless of the strategies that are put forward to achieve a vision, it is these individuals who will ultimately determine whether the strategy succeeds or fails. The question then arises as to how leaders ensure that participants in an organization behave in a way that they would like. Cyert claims leaders accomplish this by controlling the *allocation of attention* of members of an organization. The attention of individuals in an organization will be drawn to many different things. The leader's role will be to focus their attention on the achievement of the vision. Organizations operate in dynamic environments. Therefore, if a vision is modified, the leader must ensure that participants' attention, and therefore their behaviour, is also changed to reflect these changing issues. In the same way a leader must ensure that all participants buy into a single goal structure such that any goal conflicts between different parts of the organization are quickly resolved. This ensures that everyone in the organization is working towards the same outcome.

All leaders seek to improve the performance of their organization. A solution is often thought to be a change in the organizational structure. However, as we have seen, the key point to bear in mind is whether this change in structure will have an impact on the attention focus of participants. Any change in organizational structure should only be undertaken with a view to its impact on the attention focus of participants. As Cyert states, '*attention focus is central to the organizational function of leadership*'. Similarly, if we look at the interpersonal function, the style adopted by a leader in their interaction with members of the organization is also important.

However, the issue is not one of whether the leader's style is open or friendly per se, but rather whether the style allows members to focus their attention on issues that the leader feels are important. The same is true for the third function of leadership, the decision function. A leader takes decisions with a view to making the priorities for participants' attention clear. In this way leadership decisions guide and modify individuals' behaviour by focusing on the areas where they want individuals to apply their attention (see **Strategy in Focus 10.1**). This presupposes that the leader possesses sufficient industry-specific knowledge to allow them to identify and translate changes in their environment into the correct attention focus for participants of the organization.

STRATEGY IN FOCUS 10.1 What About Bob?

I have been thinking a lot about 'Bob'. He was a US software developer who worked from home for a large company. In 2013, it emerged Bob had been outsourcing his own job to China. He sent a chunk of his own salary to a Chinese consulting firm to do his work so he could surf Reddit, trade on eBay, update Facebook, and watch cat videos, according to a blog post by Andrew Valentine of Verizon, who investigated the case.

Bob's cunning solution to the work-life balance conundrum is on my mind because of the troubling suggestion that if you work remotely, your employer could eventually realize you are eminently replaceable by someone else doing your task more cheaply on the other side of the world. Out of sight, out of mind, out of work. An AlphaWise survey for Morgan Stanley last month showed only just over a third of UK office staff had returned to their usual workplace, compared with 83 per cent in France and 76 per cent in Italy. In a more recent YouGov poll of British adults, only 13 per cent firmly believed workers who could do their job from home should return to the office.

Helena Morrissey, the campaigner and former fund manager, railed in the *Daily Mail* against the 'persistent atmosphere of exaggerated fear' she believes lies behind those figures. She also raised the spectre of outsourcing. 'Those who opt not to return to the office through fear or complacency may be in for rude awakening,' she wrote. I dispute the implication staff are the crude sum of their marketable skills and the wider suggestion workers have an economic duty to return to their offices. But Dame Helena's point contains a core truth. In the uncertain phase before reliable COVID-19 vaccines and therapies are found, companies will have to use workers more flexibly. They may need to outsource work to cope with any recovery in demand, or offset a prolonged downturn. And they already have the tools to do so.

Not that they always use them. Even in Silicon Valley, recruiters used to ask candidates for programming jobs to write code on whiteboards during face to face interviews. They would tend to hire within a 20-mile radius of their California offices, according to Vivek Ravisankar, co-founder of HackerRank. He says companies are now finally asking 'why can't we open up our applications to anyone in the world?' Mr Ravisankar would say that. HackerRank is a platform to facilitate remote assessment and recruitment, which conducted 100,000 interviews for clients in a thirty-day period earlier this summer.

Nicholas Bloom of Stanford University, who has examined the productivity of remote workers (and reminded me about the Curious Case of the Man Who Outsourced Himself) also foresees a future of hybrid work. Companies will use outsourcing as one of a mix of strategies to cushion themselves against volatility. White-collar employees higher in the traditional office hierarchy may come under threat, he suggests. Prof Bloom's pre-pandemic research shows the greatest productivity gains occur when staff have a choice of where and how to work, so the correct answer to the YouGov question of whether workers should return is the one 36 per cent of respondents gave: it should be up to them.

Even so, simply being in your manager's eye line offers little protection against your job being outsourced. Coercing or scaring people back into offices is bound to backfire, leaving behind a noxious whiff of presenteeism. After Marissa Mayer, then Yahoo's chief executive, ordered employees back to the tech company's mother-ship in 2013, the prescient guru of flexible work Charles Handy told me companies should 'lure staff in, not command them'. In increasingly tough times, staff will, though, have to perform and produce, whether from a muggy front-room or an air-conditioned, COVID-proofed cubicle, and they will have to be well managed.

As Ms Mayer explained in an interview with *MIT Technology Review* last year: 'I wasn't trying to make a big political statement about the way that people want to work in the future . . . I was just trying to say, look, if we're going to try and turn this company around, something like 10 to 20 per cent of the people are a bit out to lunch.' Trusting people to work well from home is one skill managers now have to learn. Verifying that they are not 'out to lunch' is another. It is harder than you might think.

When Verizon's investigators looked into Bob's situation, they examined his record: 'His code was clean, well-written, and submitted in a timely fashion,' they observed. 'Quarter after quarter, his performance review noted him as the best developer in the building.' Except he wasn't in the building, and he wasn't even the developer writing the code.

Source: Andrew Hill, 'If you can do your job anywhere, can anyone do your job?', *The Financial Times*, 17 August 2020, https://www.ft.com/content/fe5a7907-14b9-4e61-9938-ec3dd9d06831 (accessed 6 October 2020).

10.2 **The Learning Organization**

It is said that the only sustainable competitive advantage is the speed and ability of an organization to learn.[12] In the past there were great leaders who 'thought' and 'learned' for the organization. These included Thomas J. Watson of IBM, Alfred Sloan of General Motors, and the eponymous Henry Ford and Walt Disney. The role of everyone else within the organization was assumed to be to carry out the leader's vision and earn their approval. The problem with this is the traditional hierarchical structures that ensure the command and control of individuals are not conducive to competing in dynamic environments or for generating organizational learning.

The shift is away from the leader as a panacea and towards a solution that requires all levels of the organization to participate actively. **Peter Senge** believes that '*the old model, the top thinks and the local acts, must now give way to integrating thinking and acting at all levels*'.[13] Senge sees the learning organization as comprising both *adaptive* and *generative learning*. **Adaptive learning** is the ability to cope with changes in one's environment, while **generative learning** is about creating change by being prepared to question the way we look at the world. A transition from adaptive learning to generative learning can be seen in the total quality movement (TQM) in Japan.

Initially the focus was on making consumer products that were fit for purpose; that is, the product would perform according to its specification. This evolved into understanding and reliably meeting customer needs. Now the focus has shifted to creating what customers want, but may not have yet realized. This requires organizations to be prepared to view the competitive environment differently. A major reason for the success of Japanese automobile companies such as Toyota and Honda is their ability to view issues in manufacture in a systemic way. They adopt a way of thinking that does not focus on one aspect of manufacture as *the problem*,

Henry Ford was the original founder of Ford Motor Company. Source: © aradaphotography/Shutterstock.com.

but see any problem as part of an integrated system. As a result, they avoid being stuck in a cycle of adaptive learning.

10.2.1 **Building the Learning Organization**

The leadership role in a learning organization is one of *designer*, *teacher*, and *steward*. These new roles require the leader to develop a shared vision of where the organization wants to be. But the leader also needs to make explicit and challenge the assumptions on which decisions are made—in other words, to challenge the mental models of how we view the world and to encourage a more systemic pattern of thinking. Senge asserts that the leader's role is to help bring about learning in the organization. This requires the leader to develop a vision of where the organization wants to be and to compare this with the current reality of where the organization actually is.

The difference between 'where we are' and 'where we want to be' generates what Senge refers to as a '*creative tension*'. Creative tension uses the difference between current reality and the vision of where we want to be, to generate change. But, it is not the undesirability of the current situation which generates the creative tension. It is for leaders in organizations to make explicit a vision for their organization which galvanizes people to want to create change. This is very different from problem-solving, which merely seeks to get away from an undesirable current position. The disadvantage with problem-solving is that as soon as the problem is resolved or reduced, the momentum for change decelerates. With creative change, as we saw with visionary companies in **Chapter 9**, the motivation for change is intrinsic, not extrinsic.

10.2.2 **Leadership Roles**

We can address the three distinct leadership roles that Senge identifies. These are *the leader as designer*, *the leader as teacher*, and *the leader as steward*. See **Figure 10.1**.

1. **The leader as designer**

    The leader's role as designer can be seen in the building of the core values and purpose of the organization. This is the quiet behind the scenes work of leadership, which will have an enduring impact into the future. This includes the *credo* of Johnson & Johnson that guided the behaviour of people in the company during the tampering with Tylenol in 1982 and 1989. It includes the decision of American pharmaceutical Merck to give away a drug to cure river blindness—a decision guided by their core values. The other aspects of the leader as designer include developing the strategies and structures that help to convert organizational values and purposes into business decisions.

2. **The leader as teacher**

    The leader as teacher requires leaders to assist individuals in the organization to be aware of their mental models and the assumptions on which these are based. This allows managers to continually challenge their view of reality and overcome their cognitive bias. The intention is for managers to see beyond merely superficial issues and discern the underlying causes of problems. Leaders in learning organizations influence individuals' perceptions of reality at three levels: *events*; *patterns of behaviour*; and *systemic structure*.

    i) **Events** are primarily short term and often dramatic, for example an increase in interest rates as a result of a rise in inflation.

    ii) **Patterns of behaviour** view current events in the light of the historical changes which have an impact in bringing them about. Here, managers would be focusing on extrapolation or trend analysis.

    iii) **Systemic structures** deal with the underlying causes of behaviour. Therefore, the leader's focus is predominately on systemic change. As we saw with Richard Cyert's work on leadership, if we want to engender change it is important to focus attention on what really matters. The example the leader sets will be more likely to be replicated in the focused attention

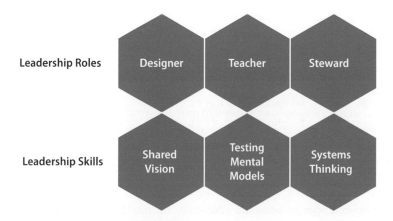

Figure 10.1   Attributes of a learning organization.

of organizational members. Therefore, it is crucial that a leader's behaviour matches their rhetoric. In other words, the leader must be authentic.

3. **The leader as steward**

The concerns of the leader as steward involve stewardship for all the people in the organization whom the leader directs. It also involves stewardship for the purpose and core values on which the organization is based. A leader in a learning organization actively seeks to change how managers view their environment. The intention is to create a more successful organization with more satisfied workers than could be achieved in a traditional organization.

For example, at W. L. Gore, the CEO doesn't utilize traditional strategic control systems such as management control and rewards to guide behaviour. Instead, informal relationships are allowed to develop as employees work in small groups. The use of peer pressure has proven to be more effective than a manager scrutinizing your work. As a result, people strive to achieve what is expected of them.

10.2.3 Leadership Skills

In conjunction with the leadership roles, there is a need for the development of new leadership skills. These leadership skills need to be disseminated throughout the entire organization; they are not the preserve of a few key individuals. They are *building a shared vision, surfacing and testing mental models, and systems thinking*.

1. **Building a shared vision**

Creating a shared vision is an ongoing process, which involves the leader sharing their vision with members of the organization to ensure that it accords with their own personal values. In this way, the shared vision is more likely to be accepted by everyone. Effective leaders create a vision that allows them and others in the organization to see clearly the steps to take to reach their goals. They might build on their present capabilities to work towards the shared vision.[14] It is recognizing that developing a vision is a continuous process.

2. **Surfacing and testing mental models**

If the leader is to attract new and innovative ideas, another leadership skill which needs to be disseminated throughout the organization is surfacing and testing mental models. The leader needs to ensure that members of an organization can differentiate between generalizations and the observable facts on which they are based. In challenging our mental models, we need to be aware of when we are generalizing and when what we say is actually based on fact.

3. **Systems thinking**

To engage in systems thinking leaders need to move beyond a blame culture. They need to discern the interrelationships between actions. They should recognize that small, well-focused actions can have magnified results, if they occur in the right places.[15] This is commonly referred to as a tipping point.[16] A visionary leader who deals only in *events* or *patterns of behaviour* will disseminate a reactive or responsive culture rather than a generative one.

The US mobile phone company Motorola is a firm that one might consider is not a learning organization.[17] Founded in 1928, it developed its own microprocessor in the 1970s, becoming the primary supplier to Apple. In the 1980s Motorola was the world's leading mobile phone supplier. In 1994, it achieved 60 per cent of the US mobile phone market using its analogue technology. Around this time, digital technology, which could support around ten times more subscribers than analogue for a given slice of radio spectrum, allowed companies to spread fixed costs over a broader user base.

Motorola held several digital patents which it licensed to its competitors Nokia and Ericsson, but did not utilize itself. It possessed the capability to make digital mobile phones and had data indicating the market was demanding digital phones, but ignored this. If an organization is unwilling, yet perfectly capable, of coping with change and satisfying consumer demand, this indicates a breakdown in leadership. By the time Motorola launched its own digital mobile phone in 1997, the competition was already far ahead. Undoubtedly, one of the reasons this company failed to meet the challenge in the digital mobile phone market was its strong corporate culture. It was known to focus on engineering first, and the market and its customers second. In the past, its culture had brought the company great success. But it was Motorola's strong culture which was resistant to new ways of thinking and changes in behaviour. Somewhere along the way, Motorola forgot to be 'paranoid', but relied instead on established ideas which defined their managerial thinking. The top executive team was unable to disassociate themselves from their insular thinking of technology before customer mindset.

Criticisms of the Learning Organization

Senge's work, although widely disseminated, is not without its critics. Rumelt, in particular, is critical of the idea of a shared vision as propagated by Senge. He argues that ascribing the success of companies like Ford and Apple to a vision which is shared at all levels of the organization is a 'distortion of history'.[18] Rumelt contends a more likely interpretation of Apple's success is down to the outstanding technical competence of co-founder Steve Wozniak and a certain amount of serendipity.

Furthermore, he argues that this type of thinking can lead to 'template-style strategy' in which you simply fill in the blanks with vision, values, mission, and strategy, rather than undertaking the hard work of analysis. The end result is a one size fits all. Rumelt's concern is that what he refers to as 'New Age' ideas, based on positive thinking, should not replace the difficulty of choice, critical thinking, and coordinated action which is essential for good strategy.

10.2.4 Why Organizations Don't Learn—Problems with Bias

All leaders accept that to stay competitive their companies must learn and improve upon what they do. But the challenge is—how do companies ensure they *continue to learn*? If we look at Toyota, a company famed for continuous improvement, we will see the difficulty it faced in trying to remain a learning organization. In 2009, Toyota had to recall more than 9 million of its cars worldwide. In reflecting on what went wrong, Toyota's leaders admitted that their desire to become the world's largest automobile manufacturer had compromised their commitment to learning.

The Japanese company also announced a recall of more than 2.4 million hybrid (Prius and Auris) vehicles worldwide in 2018 because of a fault in their systems that could cause them to lose power. Toyota said the cars affected had already been recalled previously for other reasons in 2014 and 2015.[19] Based on their research across a wide range of industries, **Francesca Gino and Bradley Staats** came to the conclusion that human biases cause managers to focus too much on the following factors: **(i) success; (ii) take action too quickly; (iii) try too hard to fit in;** and **(iv) depend too much on experts**. We can look at each of these biases, in turn, and how they might be overcome.[20]

(i)   A bias towards success

An organization's focus on success is not surprising but it can stifle learning. Four challenges need to be overcome as a result of this bias. Firstly, there is the *fear of failure*. Leaders often structure projects in a way that allows no time or resources for experimentation, and promote only those who deliver results according to the project plan. This leaves little room to develop new capabilities, or tolerate the failure that comes from a freedom to take risks. Secondly, there is *a fixed mindset*. Managers with a fixed mindset focus on performing well and see failure as something to be avoided, believing it makes them look incompetent. In contrast, managers with a growth mindset seek challenges and learning opportunities.

Thirdly, there is *over-reliance on past performance*. When hiring or promoting employees, leaders place too much emphasis on performance and tend to neglect the potential to learn. Fourthly, there is the *attribution bias*. People tend to credit their success to hard work and skill. However, they tend to blame their failure on things such as chance. This is called attribution bias. The problem is that unless people recognize that failure resulted from their actions, they all unable to learn from their mistakes. To overcome these challenges leaders can destigmatize failure and emphasize that mistakes are learning opportunities rather than something to be punished, and embrace and teach a growth mindset which allows people to embrace challenges and confront obstacles.

(ii)   A bias towards action

Managers feel more productive when they are undertaking tasks rather than simply planning them. When managers have a deadline to meet, planning is particularly seen as a waste of time. In short, managers are more comfortable trying to solve a problem by working harder, putting in longer hours, and putting themselves under stress. This bias prevents continuous improvement because managers become too tired to learn new things or apply what they already know. Furthermore, this bias towards action prevents managers from having time to reflect on what they did well and what did not work well. The researchers suggest that managers need to build downtime or breaks into their working schedule which will allow them time to reflect.

(iii) A bias towards fitting in

The problem with trying to fit in when you join an organization is you develop a belief that you need to conform. And when you conform, you limit what you bring to the organization. As Steve Jobs said, 'It doesn't make sense to hire smart people and tell them what to do; we hire smart people so they can tell us what to do.' In fact, nonconformist behaviours may raise other managers' estimation of your competence and status. Furthermore, when employees conform to how they think they should behave at work, they are less likely to be themselves and less likely to draw upon their individual strengths. The solution is to encourage people to cultivate their strengths by, for example, spending part of their time working on individual projects of their own choosing.

(iv)   A bias towards experts

In many companies there exists a bias that outside experts are the best source of ideas for improvement. This can lead to inadequate employee involvement, where frontline employees who deal directly with customers and who can identify and solve problems, are not empowered to do so. A solution to this is to encourage employees to own problems that affect them. This should prevent leaders from relying too much on consultants and providing frontline workers with autonomy to allow them to come up with solutions.

10.3 Emotional Intelligence and Leadership Performance

A great deal of research has been undertaken to ascertain whether there are certain attributes or capabilities that can distinguish effective leaders. **Daniel Goleman** undertook research into large global companies to determine the personal capabilities that drive outstanding performance.[21] Goleman grouped capabilities into three categories:

(1) **purely technical skills**, such as accounting and business planning;

(2) **cognitive abilities**, such as analytical reasoning; and

(3) **emotional intelligence**, which manifests itself in an ability to work with others.

His findings suggest that an organization's success is linked to the **emotional intelligence** of its leaders. Emotional intelligence appeared to be the key ingredient for outstanding leaders; it was also linked to better performance in organizations.

The traditional attributes of leaders have usually included such factors as technical skills and IQ. Goleman does not dismiss these attributes, but argues that they should be seen as threshold capabilities or entry-level requirements for executive positions. They may be necessary for senior positions, but they are not sufficient criteria for effective performance in leaders. As Goleman states, *'When I calculated the ratio of technical skills, IQ, and emotional intelligence as ingredients of excellent performance, emotional intelligence proved to be twice as important as the others for jobs at all levels.'*[22] This would suggest that effective leaders require more than an analytical mind or a stream of good ideas; they need emotional intelligence.

Goleman identified five components of emotional intelligence; the first three are personal and the last two are social capabilities. They are: ***self-awareness***; ***self-regulation***; ***motivation***; ***empathy***; and ***social skills***.

1. Self-awareness

Self-awareness is the first component of emotional intelligence. Individuals who possess a degree of self-awareness are capable of speaking candidly about their own emotions and the impact of their emotions on their work. Self-aware people can be recognized by their self-confidence. According to Goleman, they play to their strengths, are aware of their limitations, and are not afraid to ask for help if it is needed. It is this emotional capability of self-awareness that also allows these leaders to assess honestly the organization they work for.

2. Self-regulation

Self-regulation is a recognition that as human beings we are driven by our emotions, but we can also manage them and channel them for productive purposes. Leaders who are in control of their feelings and emotions can create an environment characterized by trust and fairness. Self-regulation is helpful in dealing with changes in the environment. This is because a self-regulated individual can consciously listen to new ideas and approaches rather than immediately reacting to what is being said. They are comfortable with change and ambiguity, and are not easily panicked by a change in the competitive landscape. Goleman goes further and argues that self-regulation enhances integrity. In other words, the abuse of corporate power tends to occur where individuals have low impulse control.

3. **Motivation**

A trait found in almost all effective leaders is motivation—a desire to achieve for the sake of achievement. People who are motivated will be passionate about their work and actively seek ways to improve what they are doing. They constantly seek to measure their individual performance and that of their organization. They are committed to their organization and will not be readily swayed to move jobs for mere financial gain. In seeking to stretch themselves, such individuals will also be looking to improve their organization.

4. **Empathy**

Empathy implies that leaders will consciously consider employees' feelings as well as other factors when they are making decisions. For example, when leading a team, a leader must be capable of sensing and understanding the different points of view that each individual in the team holds. In a globalized economy, the need for empathy is required to interpret accurately what people from different regions and cultures may be saying. For example, being empathetic allows a leader to read accurately the body language of an individual, as well as listening to their spoken words. Empathy is also important for leaders who wish to retain people with important tacit knowledge.

5. **Social skills**

Whereas self-awareness, self-regulation, and motivation are emotional capabilities that we self-manage, empathy and social skills concern our capabilities for managing relationships with others. Social skills involve moving people in a desired direction. Cyert refers to this as an organizational function of leadership: getting participants in the organization to behave in a way that the leader feels is desirable.[23] Social skills are the culmination of the other emotional intelligence capabilities. In other words, leaders will be socially skilled when they have honesty in evaluating

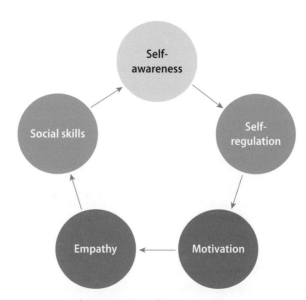

Figure 10.2   The five components of emotional intelligence.

their abilities, have mastered their own emotions, are motivated, and can empathize with others. Therefore, social skills will manifest themselves through the working out of any of the previous four capabilities. It is social skills that enable leaders to put their emotional intelligence to work.

Thus, the question arises: can emotional intelligence be learned? Goleman believes that it can, and furthermore that one's emotional intelligence increases with age. That said, emotional intelligence is not automatic. It requires clearly directed effort and resources if individuals are to learn to enhance their emotional intelligence. The pay-off is more effective leaders throughout the organization and improved company performance.

10.4 Narcissistic Leaders and Leadership Capabilities

We have seen that leaders who possess emotional intelligence are more effective and capable of managing change in organizations. In contrast with these leaders, **Michael Maccoby** identifies a different type of leader who is equally effective in dealing with dynamic change, but also has the potential for creating destruction.[24] Today's leaders who are transforming industries are different from their predecessors, and Maccoby attributes this to a change in their personality. Today's leaders, he argues, exhibit a personality type that Freud termed *narcissistic*. Freud identified three main personality types: *erotic*; *obsessive*; and **narcissistic**.

(1) **Erotic personality types** should not be confused with a sexual personality, but rather one for whom loving and being loved are important. Typically, these are teachers, nurses, and social workers.

(2) **Obsessive personalities** are self-reliant and conscientious. They are always looking for ways to help people, listen better, and find win-win situations.

(3) **Narcissists** are independent, aggressive, and innovative; they want to be admired.

Narcissistic leaders have always existed in the past and tend to emerge in times of political and social upheaval. As business began to dominate the social agenda, so narcissistic leaders such as Henry Ford and John D. Rockefeller emerged. The problem is that the very leaders who may be required for certain epochs can become obsessed with their own grandiose ideas, emotionally isolated, and distrustful of alternative viewpoints. In many respects, a narcissistic leader represents the antithesis of a leader who possesses emotional intelligence. Thus, the key is to differentiate between productive and unproductive narcissism.

Productive narcissistic leaders, such as Jack Welch of GE, are risk-takers who are capable of seeing the big picture. They possess vision and an ability to communicate this vision through oratory. They have a desire to leave a legacy behind. They are able to attract followers through their skilled oratory and charisma, and generate enthusiasm throughout their organization, which helps galvanize change. However, narcissistic leaders need adulation and the affirmation provided by their followers. And herein lies a danger—the very adulation that a narcissist demands brings self-assurance, but also allows them to ignore those who disagree with their views. Narcissistic leaders can become destructive when they lack self-knowledge and restraint, and pursue unrealistic and grandiose dreams.

10

The weaknesses of a narcissistic leader can be seen as they become more successful. They are over-sensitive to criticism and become increasingly poor listeners. They cannot handle dissent and will tend to be hard on employees who question their views. They do not want to change, and their success simply reinforces the need not to. For example, Jan Carlzon, the former CEO of the Scandinavian airline SAS, originally turned around the airline's fortunes and garnered for himself much public adulation. In the 1990s he continued to expand the business with expensive acquisitions, while paying too little attention to spiralling costs. As the organization expanded and losses increased, this brilliant narcissist was eventually fired.

The disgraced CEO of the Royal Bank of Scotland, Fred Goodwin, was known to have a boundless capacity to grind down his opponents. He insisted on RBS acquiring a second-hard car dealership, which was eventually sold back to the original owners at a huge loss. He refused to listen to senior executives who queried why a global bank would want to own a car dealership. He viewed the questioning of his decisions as dissent, which led to a culture of subdued discussions in the boardroom. Goodwin refused to take the advice of his mentor, the Deputy Group Chief Executive, who was concerned with his treatment of subordinates.[25] In 2008, the British taxpayer was forced to acquire a 70 per cent ownership of the collapsed bank.[26]

A narcissistic leader can avoid potentially self-destructive behaviour by forming a close partnership with someone he trusts. At Microsoft, Bill Gates was able to engage in blue-sky thinking because he had Steve Ballmer as chief executive, to run the business. The problem was that both were seen as narcissistic. Another approach is to indoctrinate the organization with your views. Jack Welch did this when he articulated his views that GE should become number one or two in its markets or exit them. Those who disagreed with Welch's approach and the culture it engendered did not last long in GE. The dilemma is that a dynamic environment characterized by discontinuities needs narcissistic leaders. People like former Apple CEO, Steve Jobs, and Tesla's Elon Musk. who possessed intellect, vision, flair, and innovation, to *shape* the future. Another example would be Amazon's Jeff Bezos. The challenge is to get such luminaries to listen to, respect, and internalize the ideas that other members of the organization can contribute. See **Case Study: What Makes a Successful Leader?**

CASE STUDY What Makes a Successful Leader?

Leadership is a quality that is difficult to define, but as a Supreme Court justice remarked about obesity, you know it when you see it. A mistake often made is to equate leadership with charisma. Billy McFarlane was only twenty-five when he set up Fyre Festival. This promised a luxury experience on a desert island in Bahamas. He was able to convince investors he was a visionary entrepreneur and he attracted talented people to work for him. It turns out that McFarlane's idea of luxury was cheese sandwiches, as customers found out when they showed up at the Bahamas. Instead of luxury villas they were put in tents left over from a hurricane relief scheme. According to a book by occupational psychologist Tomas Chamorro-Premuzic, *Why Do So Many Incompetent Men Become Leaders? (And How to Fix It)*, we tend to assume people who are confident are also competent. And although there is no evidence to confirm this relationship, confident people tend to get promoted in organizations.

A similar situation is found with narcissism. According to Sigmund Freud, people with a narcissistic personality type are especially suited 'to take on the role of leaders and to give a fresh stimulus to cultural developments, or to damage the established state of affairs'. This applies to visionary leaders. Researchers have found the rate of narcissism is 40 per cent higher in men than in women. Competence, it would appear, is more important than charisma. But leaders need to be empathetic as well as competent since employees are more likely to be engaged if they receive regular feedback from their bosses, and if they are involved in setting their own goals. Moreover, a large part of leadership success stems from authenticity—a leader's ability to set a good example which members of the organization can agree with and follow. This was borne out by research by Jim Collins in his book *Good to Great* which identified that the most successful bosses were not narcissistic but self-effacing and reflective. This begs the question: do narcissists make the best leaders or the worst?

Technology entrepreneur, Elon Musk. Source: © Wikimedia Commons.

In times of crisis, such as the coronavirus pandemic which grabbed the global economy in 2020 by the throat and gave it a mighty shake, what sort of leaders do corporations require? The unexpected onslaught of COVID-19 meant that CEOs suddenly faced the prospect of repatriating offshored activity and redesigning their supply chain. CEOs were already experimenting with new management styles. Reed Hastings at Netflix adopts a 'radical autonomy' which allows staff to decide their own expenses and to do without formal performance reviews. Satya Nadella is the opposite of his predecessor at Microsoft, Steve Ballmer. Ballmer was, loud, brash, and overconfident. Nadella adopts an 'empathetic leadership' style which has helped him to rebuild Microsoft into a highly successful company as he refocused the company's energies on cloud computing with Azure.

Are leaders able to lead and inspire employees without adopting a purpose beyond making as much money as possible for the shareholders? Of late, many leaders have confessed their support for stakeholder capitalism, which ensures the long-term preservation and resilience of the company, and embeds the company in society. Leaders are expected to understand and weight the risks of economic, social, and governance (ESG) factors. Others argue that eventually there must be a trade-off between different corporate objectives and stakeholders, leading to winners and losers. Nadella, a former engineer who has spent most of his working life at Microsoft, has focused the company around a concept he calls 'equitable growth'. 'It's not just the surplus you have created for your company. What's the state of the world around you?' He clearly believes that happy employees, customers, and partners have to do well for Microsoft's business to flourish. And for him adopting a wider sense of purpose makes Microsoft the best company it can be. The Dutch business leader and former head of Unilever, Paul Polman believes in a multi-stakeholder approach to business. Polman candidly points out that business is not there for the benefit of shareholders; it exists to find longer-term solutions to society's problems. When he launched the company's Sustainable Living Plan in November 2010 the target was to double sales and halve the environmental impact of its products. Now, more than ten years later, Unilever continues to pursue challenging environmental targets with its Sustainable Living Plan.

In contrast to empathetic leaders, narcissistic leaders tend to lack the ability to relate to others. Many managers recruited to top jobs suffer from a narcissistic personality disorder. As such they are full of self-confidence, dynamic, and prepared to take tough decisions. Research from the

BI Norwegian business school involved a study of all 3,200 candidates applying for leadership training at Norwegian air forces officer schools. The study found that candidates with a high degree of narcissistic traits do better in the interview and are more likely to be admitted. Michael Maccoby, in his most quoted *Harvard Business Review* article argues that productive narcissists can be charismatic and inspiring but also highly destructive. A more reassuring leader would be Freud's cautious, careful and disciplined obsessive. These 'disciplined obsessive' leaders can also make improvements to organizations but unlike narcissistic personality types they will not take big risks, such as betting an entire company's fortunes on one product. The established companies tend to stick with productive obsessives as their primary choice of leader. This leaves the visionary entrepreneurs, supported by a venture capitalists, to become the great business leaders of the future. Of course, a business will flourish if it has strong leadership and one way to harness the strengths of a productive narcissist is for them to have an entrusted deputy, a productive obsessive, which allows a narcissist to perform at their best. The danger for employees is that they may start to 'idealize' their boss, seeing them as the ideal type of leader.

A few years ago, a leading UK charity for disadvantaged children, Kids Company, collapsed amid allegations of gross financial misconduct. Its flamboyant founder and CEO, Camila Batmanghelidjh, was elevated to such great heights by her staff, donors, and board of trustees, the government, and the media that her decisions were left unchallenged. During her tenure, Government ministers approved grant payments to the charity totalling £42 million but her charisma and media fame led to her being so 'idealized' that she avoided the levels of scrutiny applied to other organizations. Manfred Kets de Vries, psychoanalyst and professor at INSEAD Business School, says: 'It's a totally reinforcing dance in which, because of a general feeling of helplessness, you idealize the leader and say quickly what the leader likes and wants to hear, and that reinforces the leader's narcissism and vice versa. Unfortunately, the moment the leader accepts this, he is surrounded by liars.' Heaping such admiration and trust on people in power sustains a fantasy that those at the head of corporations are all-knowing, or we believe that being close to great people enables us to feel better about ourselves.

All leaders have a degree of narcissism and therefore are at risk of encouraging this dynamic, but those on the extreme end of the continuum are more likely to be seduced by its allure. The more narcissistic the leader, the greater their need to attain admiration and the security they crave. The gifted South African entrepreneur Elon Musk attended university in both Canada and the USA before dropping out of graduate school at Stanford after only a few days. He made his first fortune as one of the founders of PayPal, the payments company, and then launched both SpaceX, his rocket company, and Tesla in the early 2000s. His dogged persistence, unique visions, and confrontational nature have won him numerous fans and many detractors. 'Often, in personalities this gifted, there is an offsetting, manifest, almost incomprehensible eccentricity and willingness to defy convention,' says Bob Lutz, a former GM executive who worked with Musk on a documentary. 'Musk will fight anyone, or any institution, regardless of size or power, or political orientation, if he perceives a real threat to the company's viability.' Musk tweeted in March 2020 that 'the coronavirus is dumb' predicting that new cases of COVID-19 in the USA would 'fall to close to zero' by late April 2020. The reality was considerably different. Yet Musk has almost single-handedly created the electric vehicle industry with its cleaner battery power.

Clearly, leadership is a most difficult quality to define.

Sources: 'The skills leaders need', *The Economist*, 28 May 2019; 'What it takes to be a CEO in the 2020s', *The Economist*, 6 February 2020; 'The brand of me', *The Economist*, 10 August 2006; 'Covid-19 is a litmus test for stakeholder capitalism', *The Financial Times*, 25 March 2020; 'Exclusive CEO interview: Satya Nadella reviews how Microsoft got its grove back', *Forbes*, 31 December 2018; 'Vain boss? Narcissists more likely to end up in charge, study finds', *The Telegraph*, 1 July 2014; 'We still need visionary leaders', *The Washington Post*, 21 August 2009; M. Maccoby, 'Narcissistic leaders: incredible pros, and inevitable cons', *Harvard Business Review*, vol. 78, no. 1 (2000), pp. 69–77; 'Strengths become weaknesses', *The Financial Times*, 21 September 2009; 'How not to worship your boss', *The Financial Times*, 26 July 2016; 'Elon Musk, Tesla's mad genius defies US lockdown', *The Financial Times*, 15 May 2020.

Questions

1. Why do you think employees, the media, and even government officials tend to idolize and 'idealize' certain business leaders?

2. Why might a narcissistic personality type be needed to lead an organization through a particular business crisis?

3. How does a 'compulsive obsessive' deputy help to keep a narcissist leader focused?

4. Which leadership qualities would you expect to see in your business leaders?

10.4.1 Leadership Capabilities

We have seen that effective leadership is associated with emotional intelligence and a narcissistic personality, particularly in dynamic markets. We might expect leaders who exhibit these qualities, especially emotional intelligence, to be equally effective in different industry environments. **Groysberg, McLean, and Nohria** studied twenty former GE executives who became chairman, CEO, or CEO designate at different companies between 1989 and 2001. Their choice of GE reflects its wide recognition as the premier training ground for top executives. They wanted to see if the skills these leaders possessed were portable; that is, does the fact that such leaders performed well at GE mean that they could also perform as well at another organization?[27] We might also infer that as these executives were successful leaders at GE, they possessed a fair degree of emotional intelligence.

A massive seventeen of the twenty appointments all saw an increase in the market capitalization of the companies to which they were moving. This represents a belief by the stock market that such individuals possess skills that can easily transfer to different settings. For instance, in 2000 when James McNerney and Robert Nardelli were passed over to replace Jack Welch, they moved to 3M and Home Depot, respectively. The value of 3M and Home Depot increased substantially. However, it is not perception but leadership skills that deliver results. Groysberg et al. found that what is important is *context*, or the fit between the executives' strategic skills and the needs and the strategy of the organization. A given executive will possess general management skills such as the ability to develop a vision, motivate employees, and monitor performance. These skills are readily transferable to new environments. Other management skills, such as knowledge of a particular company's processes and management systems, do not transfer as well. Therefore, the reaction of the stock market was simply a signal that it believes these General Electric executives had transferable general management skills.

Their research found that company-specific skills may also be valuable in a new job. Furthermore, they found that other skills and experience which shape performance in one job can have an impact when transferred to a new job. These skills include: *strategic human capital*, which manifests itself in an individual's expertise in cost-cutting and pursuing growth; *industry human capital*, such as technical or regulatory knowledge of a specific industry; and *relationship human capital*, which comprises an executive's effectiveness as a result of the relationships they develop when working as part of a team. The outcome of their research is that human capital can be thought of as part of a portfolio of skills. At one end of the portfolio are skills likely to be portable, while at the other end are skills which are less portable. Thus, at one extreme we find *general management human capital*, which is highly portable. At the other extreme is *company-specific human capital*, which is rarely portable. In between these two fall the three skills mentioned above—that is, *strategic*, *industry*, and *relationship human capital*. Of these, the researchers found strategic human capital to be the most portable and relationship human capital the least portable.

This research tells us that the companies that hired these twenty GE executives performed well relative to the stock market, *depending* on whether there existed a good fit between the executives' human capital and the needs of the companies they went to. If not, they performed poorly against the market. Therefore, the closer the match between an executive's new and old environment, the more likely it is that they will succeed in their new role. When executives enter a new industry, their existing industry human capital will not transfer to the new industry. Their company-specific skills will also not be relevant to a new job and will need to be unlearned. What this research means for companies thinking of hiring such high-profile star executives is that where they come from should not be the deciding factor in hiring them. The deciding factor should be an understanding of the portfolio of human capital that each CEO candidate possesses, and whether their skills will transfer and meet the needs of their new organization's strategy and their new situation. This is particularly important when we remember that such high-profile executives come at a premium.

10.5 The Impact of Leadership on Values and Culture

We can address the role of leaders in relation to an organization's shared values and its culture. We can also identify the effect of national cultures on the beliefs and behaviour of individuals within organizations. An understanding of national cultures and their impact on behaviour is particularly important for leaders of multinational corporations.

10.5.1 Leadership and Values

In looking at how executives spend their time, **Tom Peters** noted that although their time and attention are fragmented this can work to their advantage.[28] For example, when assessing work, top executives tend to be given a single option to review rather than competing options. Their decision on this single option does not say anything about the proposal's optimality, but rather sends a clear signal back to organizational members as to whether the organization is moving in the desired direction or not. Their input is a check on the vision of the organization. It also signals to middle managers, for example, what the next proposal should look like. If senior executives had more time, they would not be inclined to fine-tune proposals, but would be engaged in a more fundamental overhaul. The downside to this fragmentation of time is that the constant flow of information multiplies the opportunity for inconsistent signals to the organization.

Peters' approach portrays top executives as coping with the reality of disorder and non-linear events. This resonates with **Henry Mintzberg's** approach to strategic management in which leaders craft strategy rather than deliberately planning it.[29] Amidst this relative chaos what leaders can do is shape their organization's values and lead by example. In this untidy world '*the effective leader is primarily an expert in the promotion and protection of values*', and dealing with '*the shaping of values becomes pre-eminently the mission of the chief executive*'.[30] The leader's role is to build consensus throughout the organization. Their actions, over time, are part of a '*guiding, directing and signalling process that are necessary to shape values in the near chaos of day-to-day operations*'.[31] How a leader behaves is crucial for sending the right signals to the rest of the organization.

10.5.2 Leadership and Culture

Geert Hofstede studied the culturally determined values of people in more than fifty countries.[32] They all worked in the local subsidiaries of a large multinational corporation (IBM). The benefit of looking at people who work for a multinational corporation is that they are similar in all respects except their nationality. Hofstede was initially able to devise a model of culture based on four separate dimensions. A *dimension* is simply an aspect of culture which can be measured in relation to other cultures. The four dimensions are (1) ***power distance***; (2) ***collectivism versus individualism***; (3) ***femininity versus masculinity***; and (4) ***uncertainty avoidance***. The model is a way of measuring differences between national cultures. A country will attain a score on each of the dimensions according to its nearness to each dimension. Over time a fifth dimension was identified: (5) ***long-term orientation*** to life. Interestingly, Hofstede attributes the fact that this dimension was not identified before was because of the *bias* that existed in the minds of researchers studying culture. That is, even researchers studying culture have their own mental models determined by their own national cultural frames of reference.

Although the use of a dimension is not without its methodological limitations, it does have the benefit of allowing clusters of countries with similar scores to emerge. We might also note that research into national cultures and their dimensions provides only part of the picture of our understanding of corporate culture. We can evaluate each of the five dimensions to determine, to some extent, their impact on organizational behaviour.

1. **Power distance index (PDI)**

   Power distance is defined as the extent to which the less powerful members of institutions and organizations within a country expect and accept that power is distributed unequally.[33] What it shows us is the extent to which employees in IBM's subsidiary in one country answer the same questions differently from IBM employees in another country. Or, put another way, it helps to explain the impact of national cultures on leadership styles. The study showed a high power distance for Latin American countries such as Mexico and Guatemala, and for India, France, and Hong Kong. Lower power distances exist in the UK, the USA, and Scandinavian countries such as Finland, Norway, and Sweden.

   This informs us about dependence relationships in a country. What it tells us is that, other things being equal, employees in high power distance countries have a preference for leadership that involves an autocratic style. There is likely to be much more dependence of subordinate employees on their leaders. In contrast, employees in low power distance countries prefer leadership that involves consultation and much less dependence on their leaders. This helps to explain why certain Western leadership styles which bring success in the UK or USA may flounder when used in Mexico, for example.

2. Individualism versus collectivism

Individualism refers to societies in which there are fewer ties between individuals and where everyone is expected to look after themselves and their own immediate family. At the other end of the spectrum is *collectivism*; this involves societies where people are integrated into strong cohesive groups, and the interests of the individual are subordinate to those of the group.

The extent to which countries scored as individualistic or collectivist was based on respondents' answers to questions about what they would consider as their ideal job. Individualistic employees believe that a job which leaves quality personal time for family is important. In contrast, collectivist individuals saw training opportunities to improve learning as more important. The USA, Australia, and the UK scored highest on this index as the most individualistic nations, and Guatemala, Ecuador, and Panama were the most collectivist. Individualism, such as the pursuit of personal time, emphasizes the individual's freedom from the organization. Training and development, in contrast, is something the organization does for the employees. The extent of a nation's individualism versus collectivism may also go some way to explaining why Japanese leadership practices seem to experience difficulties when transposed verbatim to the USA.

UK, US, and Australian organizations competing abroad need to remember that in collectivist societies, such as Saudi Arabia, the personal relationship between individuals takes precedence over any task and needs to be established first. This takes time and patience.

3. Masculinity and femininity

This concerns *the desirability of assertive behaviour against the desirability of modest behaviour*; Hofstede refers to the former as masculinity, and to the latter as femininity. *Masculinity* refers to societies in which gender roles are clearly defined: men are expected to be assertive and tough. *Femininity* refers to societies in which gender roles are less clearly defined: both men and women are expected to be modest and caring.

This was the only dimension in which male and female IBM employees scored consistently differently. It shows that, among other things, men attach greater importance to earnings and job recognition, whereas women attach more importance to good working relationships with their immediate supervisor and their colleagues. The former is associated with masculine competitive roles, and the latter with more caring feminine roles.

Japan, Austria, and Venezuela scored highest as the most masculine countries, with clearly defined roles for men and women, while Sweden, Norway, and the Netherlands scored highest as the most feminine countries. Therefore, we can deduce that Japan's masculine culture and work practices, which invariably translate into few female management positions, would be difficult to implement in Scandinavian countries.

4. Uncertainty avoidance

Uncertainty avoidance is the extent to which people feel threatened by uncertain or unknown situations. This manifests itself in the need for predictability, and clearly defined rules. Countries that experience high uncertainty avoidance are seeking to reduce ambiguity. People from these countries are looking for structure and stability. Greece, Portugal, and Guatemala scored highest on this index, with Belgium and Japan not far behind. Denmark, Singapore, and Jamaica scored lowest on uncertainty avoidance, closely followed by the UK and the USA. We should be careful not to confuse uncertainty avoidance with risk avoidance. A country that experiences high uncertainty avoidance is still able to take risks.

5. **Long-term orientation**

Nations with a long-term orientation value thrift, persistence, and hard work. In contrast, nations with a short-term orientation tend to be less persistent and expect quick results. If we 'map' a long-term orientation for different countries, we find China, Hong Kong, Taiwan, and South Korea score highest in having a long-term orientation, while Pakistan, Nigeria, and the Philippines scored lowest, followed by Canada, the UK, and the USA.

An understanding of national cultures is clearly important for leaders who manage multinational organizations. For example, when IKEA entered the US market, its executives were surprised at the number of vases they were selling. Eventually, it dawned on staff that Americans were buying them not to put flowers in, but to drink from. The glasses that IKEA stocked were just too small for American tastes. The benefits of an appreciation of national cultures, for instance by leaders involved in international mergers and takeovers, should not be underestimated. An understanding of culture and its effect on employees' behaviour will, among other things, help leaders to develop appropriate reward and control systems. An appreciation of cultures can also help leaders implement strategic change and avoid wasting resources through avoidable cultural errors.

This said, the needs of the competitive environment may force counter-cultural changes. For example, the Japanese investment bank Nomura bought the collapsed Lehman Brothers' European, Middle Eastern, and Asian businesses in order to expand internationally. The former Lehman traders working for Nomura in Japan now face Nomura executives who are much more hands-on than the executives in their former firm. More importantly, Nomura expects that hiring former Lehman employees may help to facilitate a change in the corporate culture in its Japanese operation. For instance, Nomura now offers employees in Japan the prospect of higher pay and bonuses in return for accepting that they can be fired more easily if they fail to

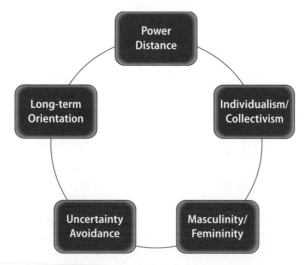

Figure 10.3 Five dimensions of culture.

meet performance targets. This change links remuneration to personal and departmental performance, largely anathema to Japanese employees, rather than organizational performance, which has always been the norm.

10.5.3 **Rethinking Culture, Leadership, and Change**

Edgar Schein and Peter Schein argue that it is time for a new way of thinking about culture, change, and leadership—one that is built upon close professional relationships, openness, and trust.[34] They make a distinction between different levels of relationships. For example, most of our relationships at work are distant and transactional; Schein and Schein refer to these as *Level 1 relationships*.

In **Level 1 relationships**, employees are hired for their skills to undertake clearly defined roles. They are expected to maintain proper social and professional distance from their peers, as well as people higher up or lower down in the hierarchy. But the fundamental weakness of Level 1 relationships is the distance they create between employees. These relationships allow people to avoid open communication and can lead to feelings of distrust among colleagues, especially when they are in competition for career advancement. As a result, the organization may be unaware of issues around quality and customer satisfaction, and is less capable of engaging in innovation.

What is needed is what they refer to as **Level 2 relationships**. In these relationships, people treat each other as whole human beings which has the effect of collapsing the psychological distance in hierarchical organizations. Level 2 relationships are based on personal relationships and open communication which allows leaders to find out what is really going on in the organization. This requires managers being prepared to get to know their employees in order to build open communication channels and two-way levels of trust (see **Strategy in Focus 10.2**). The benefit of Level 2 relationships is that employees feel psychologically safe to speak up when things are not working properly and, importantly, they will exercise leadership when they see a new and better way of getting something done. Some outstanding managers may already be doing this but it has never been a part of traditional managerial culture.

There is a clear link between leadership and culture. As founders and entrepreneurs develop new companies so they create culture from the outset. A relatively new organization may draw upon a wide variety of talents to achieve its objectives. However, as the company grows older, it develops strong beliefs about the kinds of talent it requires and uses its job description to recruit only those types of people. Management of talent in mature organizations then becomes little more than a process in which the existing culture is just recreating itself by employing people who 'fit in' to the organization, both technically and socially. The danger here is that as the external environment changes organizations find themselves needing to innovate but unable to get their own people to do it.

On that basis, if leaders had a clearer understanding of culture they would be more able to implement change. Instead many of the models surrounding leadership, change, and culture are still based on the belief that Level 1 relationships can succeed, when they cannot. In Schein and Schein's model, *'Trust happens through vital information exchange and open sharing as we build relationships that allow us to…[count on each other] to be supportive and collaborative rather than competitive and self-seeking. Building that trust helps us work positively towards mutually defined goals. It's self-reinforcing, and to get there, we need Level 2 relationships.'*[35]

STRATEGY IN FOCUS 10.2 Transparency, Performance, and Remote Work

Netflix founder Reed Hastings was eight when he moved to a new school in Washington DC, where a bigger boy, called Calvin, used to organize fist-fights in the playground. We probably all know, or have known, a Calvin: the work colleague whose bad attitude infects the behaviour of those around them. Netflix applied this lesson when it laid off staff in 2001. In his new book *No Rules Rules*, Mr Hastings writes that the company realized it 'had a handful of people who had created an undesirable work climate. Many weren't great at their jobs in myriad little ways, which suggested to others that mediocre performance was acceptable, and brought down the performance of everyone in the office.'

Such workplace contagion can be hard to detect. It can also be obvious. Anyone who was once identified as the school swot has at some point heard the lazy bully's muttered warning not to dazzle in class. Netflix's solution was to hire and keep the most talented team members, which encouraged laggards to raise their game. On to this 'talent density', the group layered radical candour—'only say about someone what you will say to their face'—and transparency, sharing even sensitive financial information with all staff.

It gradually extended these principles from traditional anonymous written 360-degree performance feedback, via signed feedback, to the frankly terrifying idea of 'live 360s'. These are small, carefully moderated team sessions, lasting up to five hours, where staff are encouraged to air their frank assessments of each other. The Netflix approach fits the growing consensus that transparency is bracingly positive. It helps discourage bad behaviour ('Sunlight is the best disinfectant', in US Supreme Court judge Louis Brandeis's famous dictum). It aligns people with the corporate culture. It encourages trust and responsibility.

But as academic Erin Meyer, Hastings' co-author, points out, transparency 'isn't without its risks'. That is particularly true for staff who do not work at successful, high-octane, high-trust companies such as Netflix. When most of your staff are working remotely, deciding how much information to share, and with whom, becomes even harder. Simply revealing the performance of members of a close-knit team could have an impact on their behaviour, according to peer-reviewed research by Ruidi Shang of Tilburg University and colleagues from the University of Melbourne, published in *The Accounting Review*.

They studied three workgroups from a Chinese state-owned electrical power plant, two of which shared individual monthly performance data with all team members. The manager of the third group handed each employee their own performance score. In the high-transparency groups, the lower performers worked harder, but the ablest workers slacked off, meeting the laggards in the mediocre middle. In the more secretive group, the top workers continued to improve their performance, while the least able members held steady. These Chinese workers were long time employees, for whom group identity was all-important and the prospect of bonuses or promotion low. In such teams, 'the more transparent the information, the more likely you are to conform to it', Prof Shang told me. In a group made up mostly of high performers, transparency should drag the lower-performers upwards, as Netflix's Mr Hastings predicted.

For managers used to encouraging team spirit and raised on the virtues of openness, these findings add to the burdens of an already difficult job. The pandemic, rolling lockdowns and hybrid working, all beyond the remit of the latest study, complicate the management task still further. The crisis may have reduced the risks of workplace contagion—but also its potential rewards. You no longer work next to Calvin so the temptation to mimic his bad behaviour is reduced. Yet with more virtuous colleagues out of sight, you are thrown back on self-motivation, which might lead to ennui or, at the other extreme, paranoid overwork.

Transparency looks like a solution. Some companies are using 'open' video calls for colleagues who want to replicate virtually the experience of working quietly side by side. Sharing more performance data would be an easy next step for managers overseeing digitally connected teams. But 'if someone works really hard because she doesn't know what others are doing, and the manager releases information showing they aren't working as hard, that might affect her behaviour', warns Prof Shang.

Somewhere between bore-out and burnout lies a happy medium for remote workers. I don't envy managers who have to try to help them find it.

Source: Andrew Hill, 'The contagious risks and rewards of remote working', *The Financial Times*, 21 September 2020. https://www.ft.com/content/7515a7f4-33f4-43e7-87b9-fd4c3c765731 (accessed 6 October 2020).

10.6 Leading Strategic Change

In **Chapter 9** we looked in detail at how organizations can undertake strategic change. Here we will address the specific role of business leaders in directing strategic change. We will identify the relationship between the acceptance of ideas for change and an organization's existing culture. We will also look at the leadership skills necessary to implement change effectively and barriers that need to be overcome.

The values of an organization will inevitably manifest themselves in its core or dominant culture. The culture may have existed for generations and will take time to change in a desired direction. Therefore, an organization's culture is a powerful instrument for exhibiting or inhibiting change. Even good ideas that conflict with the existing culture may be difficult to implement. **William Schneider** argues that good ideas will fail unless they are aligned with the organization's business strategy, leadership, and dominant culture. Schneider suggests four reasons why good management ideas may not be adopted within the organization.[36]

1. **All organizations are living social organisms.**

    All organizations have their own idiosyncratic culture. They are communities of people and not machines, although they may have some machine-like characteristics. All living systems grow and develop from the inside out. They start from their core and develop outwards. We can draw a parallel between biological systems and organizations. In the same way, people, organizations, and societies exist in relation to each other. They have their unique patterns, which are non-linear, but their development occurs from the core to the periphery. The point is that for any ideas to work they must be based on the non-linear nature of the organization.

2. **Culture is more powerful than anything else in the organization.**

An organization can have a brilliant strategy, but if it does not align with the organization's culture it will inevitably fail. To succeed, any change must align with one of four different types of culture: *control*, *collaboration*, *competence*, and *cultivation*.[37] Therefore, regardless of the validity of any given idea, it must also fit with the particular type of culture prevalent in an organization if it is to succeed. As Peter Drucker famously said, 'Culture eats strategy for breakfast.'

3. **System-focused interventions work, while component-focused interventions do not.**

We have seen in the previous chapter that a systems approach that emphasizes alignment between different parts of the organization is more likely to succeed in implementing change. This is simply a recognition that 'one size fits all' does not apply.

4. **Interventions that are clearly linked to an organization's business strategy work.**

It is strategy that adds value to an organization. Therefore, all management ideas have to be clearly aligned with the organization's strategy otherwise there is a danger of pushing the organization off course. It is the alignment of new ideas with an organization's value-creating strategy that is important in trying to instigate change.

10.6.1 Transformational Leadership

Transformational leadership is concerned with improving the performance of individuals and developing individuals to their fullest extent.[38] Transformational leaders tend to exert influence, which encourages individuals to accomplish more than what is usually expected of them. They are often assumed to be effective at motivating individuals to work towards some greater good. It is often associated with charismatic and visionary leadership. It can be usefully compared with transactional leadership. **Transactional leaders** exchange things of value to advance their own interests as well as the interests of their followers—for example, a manager who promises an employee promotion if they meet a certain sales target. In contrast, transformational leaders interact with others in a way that raises the level of motivation in both the leader and the individuals.

The paradox of strategic change is that all organizations compete in changing environments, but the individuals who make up these organizations are resistant to change. Organizations face pressures for change from competitors, suppliers, and customers, as well as internally from poor leadership, high labour turnover, and other such factors. These factors will eventually begin to coalesce into an urgency to do something. However, it is often as the need for change becomes increasingly apparent that employees' resistance to change becomes greatest. If the nature of individuals is to avoid change, then the first challenge for leaders is to manage employee resistance. According to **Manfred Kets de Vries** this requires an effective change agent, ideally the CEO, who has power and authority to drive change initiatives.[39] The change agent will be a visionary who combines charismatic qualities with an architectural role. For example, in an effort to restore Sony to profitability its first non-Japanese chief executive, Sir Howard Stringer, implemented an efficiency drive that closed 20 per cent of the consumer electronics company's manufacturing and shed 20,000 jobs. In an effort to gain a creative momentum he persuaded Sony's engineers, amidst much resistance, to embrace the networked era.[40]

Charismatic leaders can be effective change agents because they seek to change the status quo and are gifted at building alliances and making individuals feel valued. This is important because if people are inspired and empowered to act they will produce greater efforts and take risks in pursuit of a shared vision. However, as we saw in **Chapter 9**, trust, rewards, and communication are essential if individuals are to engage in change.[41] Kets de Vries interviewed two leaders who epitomize the ability to sustain change and innovation in their organization: Richard Branson of the Virgin Group, and Percy Barnevik, previously CEO of ABB.

Both leaders combine charismatic leadership with architectural skills to bring about change in their organizations. Richard Branson's Virgin Group is famous for taking on established industries. The Virgin Group's core businesses include megastore retail outlets, hotels, communications, and an airline. The company's business maxim is similar to the *credo* of Johnson & Johnson. Where Johnson & Johnson put customers first, Branson has staff first, customers second, and shareholders third. Branson clearly believes that looking after his people comes first. It is this commitment to staff which helps facilitate change. In addition to charismatic qualities, Richard Branson's architectural skill allows him to design the Virgin Group's structure in a way which encourages a creative entrepreneurial atmosphere.

His divested record company provides a blueprint. When his record company grew to around fifty employees, Branson recalls that he went to see the deputy managing director, the deputy sales manager, and the deputy marketing manager, and said: 'You are now the managing director, the sales manager, and the marketing manager' and put them into a new building, and 'when that company got to a certain size, say fifty people, I would do the same thing again'.[42] The culture that Branson has created is one of speed of decision-making, devoid of formal board meetings and committees. He is accessible to anyone who wants to discuss an idea, but prefers that they just go ahead and do it. His passion is for shaking things up, remoulding established industries. Indeed, his legacy to the Virgin Group will no doubt be this.

Another transformational leader is Percy Barnevik who merged ASEA, a Swedish engineering group, with Brown Boveri, a Swiss competitor, to create ABB. ABB competes in global markets for

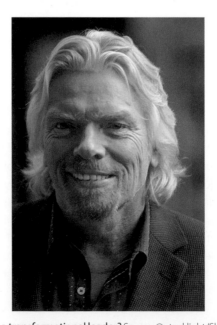

Do you consider Richard Branson a transformational leader? Source: © stocklight/Shutterstock.com.

electric power generation and transmission equipment, robotics, and high-speed trains. Barnevik's vision was one of exploiting the organization's core competences and global economies of scale while maintaining and encouraging a local market presence. Barnevik's architecture involved the introduction of a matrix structure which simultaneously allows managers around the globe to make decisions about product strategy without having to think about their impact on national markets. At the same time, national companies within the group had the freedom to remain focused on their local markets.

As Barnevik stated, 'What I have tried to do is recreate small company dynamism and creativity by building 5,000 profit centres. The advantages lie in communication and feedback. An environment where you can have creative, entrepreneurial people.'[43] Barnevik recognized that to get the best out of people requires more than architecture; it requires tapping into the values of employees and aligning the organizational vision with those values. The vision needs to inspire people and bring out the best in them. The mission statement should make people feel proud of what the organization is trying to achieve. Importantly, the leader must be authentic and live up to the values they set for the organization. Like Branson, Barnevik was passionate about change, breaking into new industries, and galvanizing employees to break new ground.

The charismatic and architectural skill of Richard Branson and Percy Barnevik is not simply building organizational structures, but creating an environment in which employees feel free to make decisions, take risks, and even fail. This requires a focus on the customer as the driving force for change. A key success factor for the Virgin Group is its ability to move fast. As Branson says, '*I can have an idea in the morning in the bath tub, and have it implemented in the evening.*'[44] The need for strategic control systems or transactional leadership is reduced when employees internalize shared corporate values. These values go beyond an increase in the bottom line—which fail to motivate anyone. In directing change, both Branson and Barnevik motivate their employees to embrace the dynamic of change and actively promote environments that mitigate resistance to change. Unlike the narcissistic leader, there is a confidence and security that employees can try ideas that have not emanated from the CEO. There is also a clear recognition that people need more than financial rewards and financial targets to motivate them. As Branson puts it, '*I think fun should be a motivator for all businesses.*'

In contrast with Kets de Vries, Collins and Porras argue that a little too much is often made of the role of charismatic leaders in shaping organizations. Their research (discussed in **Chapter 9**) suggests that charismatic leaders are not of paramount importance in visionary companies.[45] They cite organizations such as 3M, Procter & Gamble, Merck, and Sony, which have at various times throughout their history had leaders who made significant changes, but were not what might be understood as high-profile charismatic leaders. Instead, Collins and Porras argue for the setting of BHAGs that are independent of management style, thereby ensuring that the succession of a charismatic leader becomes less of a problem.

10.6.2 **Theory E and Theory O Leaders**

Michael Beer and Nitin Nohria suggest two theories of change which are based on different assumptions about why and how change should be made.[46] These are **Theory E** and **Theory O**. A Theory E change strategy is based on achieving economic value for shareholders and is characterized by downsizing and restructuring. This type of change is frequently found in the USA, particularly in turnaround situations. Theory O adopts a *softer* approach which recognizes that if change is to be constructive and endure, it must affect the corporate culture and the way in which employees work. This type of theory is more likely to be found in European and Asian businesses. Both theories are useful for organizations, and both have their costs. The challenge is how to build competitive advantage while managing the inherent tensions between Theory E and Theory O.

To do this, leaders must engage in corporate transformations which do not simply institute Theory E and Theory O strategies in sequence, that is, one after the other, but rather combine the two strategies in a more holistic manner. Jack Welch used a sequenced approach to change. He started with a Theory E type strategy by setting a goal for managers to be the first or second in their industry, or else exit. It was only once the *hard* issues of widespread redundancies and restructuring had taken place that Welch turned his attention to organizational changes which affected the culture within GE. The problem with sequencing is the time it takes; at GE the timescale was almost twenty years. Also, unlike Welch, once a leader engages in a Theory E approach they lose the trust and confidence of employees, which is necessary to change the corporate culture.

Few employees would be willing to listen attentively to a CEO who wields a corporate axe in one instance, and then wants to talk about trust and commitment. However, the research by Beer and Nohria suggests that it is possible to increase economic value quickly while also nurturing a trusting corporate culture. This was done by the UK retailer Asda under the stewardship of Archie Norman and his deputy CEO, Allan Leighton. When Archie Norman took over as CEO of Asda, he and Allan Leighton successfully improved economic value and were widely credited with bringing about a change in the behaviour and attitudes of employees. Similarly, when Archie Norman joined the British broadcaster ITV, he encouraged everyone within the corporation to email him about his strategic review, appending his personal email address. At the same time, he was forensically dissecting the company to see where value could be added.

Beer and Nohria argue that all corporate transformations can be compared according to six dimensions of change. These are **goals**, **leadership**, **focus**, **process**, **reward system**, and the ***use of consultants***. Given the different assumptions on which the two theories are based, they will manage change on these six dimensions differently. If we look at each of these in turn, we can see how Norman and Leighton successfully combined the Theory E and Theory O approaches to bring about effective change at Asda.

1. **Goals—confront the tension between Theory E and Theory O.**

   Archie Norman made it clear at the outset that he would be applying E and O strategies of change. He said, 'Our number one objective is to secure value for shareholders', but went on to say 'I intend to spend the next few weeks listening . . . we need a culture built around common ideas and goals that include listening, learning, and speed of response.'[47] In effect, he was saying that without an increase in shareholder value, Asda would fail to exist over the long term. But he was also saying that he wants all employees to participate and be emotionally committed to improving Asda's performance.

2. **Leadership—set the direction from the top and engage people below.**

   Although Norman was clearly the architect of Asda's strategy, he set up programmes such as 'Tell Archie' to encourage employee participation. We saw earlier that a narcissistic leader can often benefit from having a trusted significant other. The same is true for a leader pursuing a strategy of change that involves Theory E. Archie Norman recognized the benefit of employing an opposing leadership style, hence the early recruitment of Allan Leighton who adopted a more employee-focused approach which contrasted with Norman's analytical style.

3. **Focus—address the hard and soft sides of the organization at the same time.**

Norman removed unproductive senior management layers and instigated a wage freeze which affected everyone in the organization—Theory E. At the same time, he was committed to making Asda an enjoyable place to work by removing hierarchies, and making it fairer and more transparent—Theory O.

4. **Process—plan for spontaneity.**

Store managers were encouraged to experiment with their store layout, change employee roles, change the product ranges, and generally use their initiative to make changes that they believed would benefit the consumer. Asda set up some experimental stores to help develop a learning environment. The culture within these experimental stores was 'risk-free'; that is, no negative sanctions were applied for trying things that failed.

5. **Reward system—incentives should reinforce change, not drive it.**

Asda has a share-ownership plan which covers all employees. Financial incentives, an E type incentive, were used to reward employees who were already motivated and committed to change.

6. **Use of consultants—as expert resources who empower employees.**

Consultancy firms were used by Asda, but their role was deliberately cut short by Norman to avoid building up a dependency on their expertise. Consultants were used to reinforce what Norman and Leighton were already planning to do.

Asda is an example of an organization which successfully combined Theory E and Theory O change patterns. This was achieved through its willingness to develop and change in the long term without sacrificing the need to generate acceptable shareholder returns. Asda was bought by Walmart, and Archie Norman stepped down as CEO, having accomplished the changes he set out to achieve.

10.6.3 Can Leaders Deal With Chaos?

In a rational world in which events in the external environment are repetitive or subject to some form of knowable pattern, strategic management as espoused so far has a key role to play. However, if the world is also non-rational and periods of stability sit alongside periods of instability, then this may require leaders to adopt a different mental model when developing strategy. When we see an organization as part of a dynamic system we are concerned with how it changes over time and the patterns of change that subsequently develop. We want to know whether these patterns display properties that are stable or unstable, predictable or unpredictable.

Ralph Stacey defines *chaos* as an irregular pattern of behaviour generated by well-defined non-linear feedback rules commonly found in nature and human society.[48] As systems move away from their equilibrium state they are prone to small changes in their environment which can cause major changes in the behaviour of the system itself. In the business world, a leader may attach great importance to small differences in customer requirements and develop hugely differentiated products. Under conditions of chaos the long-term future of an organization is assumed to be unknowable. If leaders cannot know what the future holds, then chaos theory holds little place for long-term plans and visions of future states.

However, this may be slightly overstating the case since the future may be unpredictable at a specific level, but at a general level there are recognizable patterns. For example, no one can predict the shape of individual snowflakes as they fall to the ground, but we can still recognize them as snowflakes. It is this ability to recognize patterns at a general level that allows leaders to cope with chaos. Indeed, we might argue that this gift is much more highly developed in some than in others. For example, although Bill Gates and Steve Jobs were unable to state specifics, they did correctly envision that a time would come when we would all have computers in the home. It is these boundaries around instability that allow us to make sense of our world. The use of reasoning, intuition, and experience helps us to cope with change and, therefore, chaos.

Chaos Theory and Innovation

Stacey suggests eight steps to help leaders encourage innovation and create a new strategic direction.

1. **Develop new perspectives on the meaning of control.**

   Innovation may be more likely to come about if leaders allow self-organizing processes and learning groups to develop. This means rethinking their traditional ideas about control of individuals' behaviour and letting the group itself exercise that function.

2. **Design the use of power.**

   The group dynamic that is conducive to complex learning occurs when the leader's power is used to create an environment in which the assumptions that are the basis for decisions can be challenged, and there is open questioning of the status quo. In contrast, when power is wielded through force and authority, the group dynamic will be one of submission, rebellion, or suspension of critical faculties. In these cases, complex learning among individual members of the group will not take place.

3. **Encourage self-organizing groups.**

   In common with networks, which we discussed in **Chapter 9**, a self-organizing group is free to make decisions within the context of the boundaries of its work together. A self-organizing group works best if it is allowed to form spontaneously and set its own aims and objectives. The output may conflict with the views of senior management, but this is to be expected when ideas are allowed free rein. In 3M, managers are allowed time to pursue their own 'pet' projects with other managers.

4. **Provoke multiple cultures.**

   This allows new perspectives to proliferate across the organization by moving people from different business units and functions to create a more culturally diverse organization.

5. **Present ambiguous challenges instead of clear long-term objectives or visions.**

   Top management can encourage individuals to think about new ways of doing things by giving them ambiguous challenges and partially developed issues to consider. This conflicts with Rumelt's contention that the leader's role is to reduce ambiguity.[49] Senior management should also be open to having their own ideas challenged by subordinates.

6. **Expose the business to challenging situations.**

   Leaders should not be afraid to expose their organization to demanding situations. We saw in **Chapter 9** how organizations in home markets which have the world's most challenging customers and innovative competitors will learn far more than other organizations, and there-fore will be more likely to build a sustainable competitive advantage.[50]

7. **Devote explicit attention to improving group learning skills.**

   Senior managers encourage new strategic directions to emerge when they allow the dominant mental models that are held within the organization to be challenged. This is a prime role for leaders if learning is to take place.

8. **Create resource slack.**

   New strategic directions and innovations in the organization will only occur when top manage-ment invests sufficient time, effort, and organizational resources.

Chaos theory, then, sees that a traditional planning approach to strategic management may benefit the organization over the short term. Over time, however, the lack of a causal link between organiza-tional actions and outputs means that the role of leadership should be to shun visions and long term plans, and to create instead an environment characterized by spontaneity and self-organization. Chaos theory does not make traditional approaches to strategic management obsolete; rather, it places them in a much more constrained time horizon. As we have seen in preceding chapters, the choice is seldom *either/or*, but more one of *and*.

Summary

We started the chapter with a discussion of the differences between management and leadership in order to distinguish their different roles. We noted that *management* is about coping with com-plexity, whereas *leadership* is about dealing with change. We discussed the role of leaders in build-ing a learning organization. We noted the importance of allowing individuals to challenge mental models that exist within the organization if we desire complex learning to take place. We assessed the impact of emotional intelligence on effective leadership and company performance. We noted that emotional intelligence appears to be a better predictor of success for a leader than either IQ or technical skills.

The benefits and dangers of narcissistic leaders were evaluated and suggestions put forward to help narcissists remain productive. We discussed the impact of leaders on an organization's value and culture. The impact of national cultures on domestic organizations was also considered. We identified the leadership skills necessary for directing strategic change and looked at some of the obstacles to change. Theory E and Theory O strategic changes were introduced as we discussed the importance of successfully combining them to achieve simultaneously lasting change and an increase in shareholder value. The chapter ended with a discussion of chaos theory and its implica-tion for leaders.

 For more examples and discussion to aid your understanding of this chapter, please visit the online resources and see the Extension Material for this chapter.

Review Questions

1. What are the key differences between management and leadership?
2. What is a 'learning organization' and how does this help an organization achieve competitive advantage?
3. Why is emotional intelligence important for managers to achieve better performance?
4. What does 'culture eats strategy for breakfast' mean?

 Discussion Question

'Unless a leader is authentic as a CEO no one will follow them.' **Discuss**.

 Research Topic

Identify an organization where its corporate culture enabled a successful transformational change in strategy. How did their culture help the change to take place?

 Recommended Reading

For a discussion of the respective roles of management and leadership, see:

- **J. P. Kotter**, 'What leaders really do', *Harvard Business Review*, vol. 68, no. 3 (1990), pp. 103–11.

The learning organization is covered in:

- **P. M. Senge**, 'The leader's new work: building learning organizations', *Sloan Management Review*, vol. 32, no. 1 (1990), pp. 7–23.

For an assessment of emotional intelligence on company performance, see:

- **D. Goleman**, 'What makes a leader?', *Harvard Business Review*, vol. 76, no. 6 (1998), pp. 93–102.

For research on the importance of culture for leaders, see:

- **G. Hofstede**, *Cultures and Organizations: Software of the Mind*, McGraw-Hill, 1997.

 www.oup.com/he/henry4e
Visit the online resources that accompany this book for activities and more information on strategy.

Test your knowledge and understanding of this chapter further by trying the multiple-choice questions online.

References and Notes

1. **P. Northouse**, *Leadership: Theory and Practice*, Sage, 2016, p. 6.

2. For a discussion of influence and power, see **Northouse**, see n. 1 above, p. 10.

3. **J. P. Kotter**, *A Force for Change: How Leadership Differs from Management*, Free Press, 1990; **J. P. Kotter**, 'What leaders really do', *Harvard Business Review*, vol. 68, no. 3 (1990), pp. 103–11.

4. **J. C. Collins** and **J. I. Porras**, *Built to Last: Successful Habit of Visionary Companies*, Harper, 1994.

5. **R. Rumelt**, *Good Strategy Bad Strategy: The Difference and Why It Matters*, Crown Business, 2011.

6. **Rumelt**, see n. 5, chapter 7.

7. **M. E. Porter**, 'What is strategy?', *Harvard Business Review*, vol. 74, no. 6 (1996), pp. 61–78.

8. **E. Brynjolfsson**, **A. A. Renshaw**, and **M. van Alstyne**, 'The matrix of change', *Sloan Management Review*, vol. 38, no. 2 (1997), pp. 37–54.

9. **B. George**, *Authentic Leadership: Rediscovering the Secrets to Create Lasting Value*, Jossey-Bass, 2003.

10. **J. P. Kotter**, *A Force for Change: How Leadership Differs from Management*, Free Press 1990; **J. P. Kotter**, 'What leaders really do', *Harvard Business Review*, vol. 68, no. 3 (1990), p. 107.

11. **R. M. Cyert**, 'Defining leadership and explicating the process', *Nonprofit Management and Leadership*, vol. 1, no. 1 (1990), pp. 29–38.

12. **G. Stalk**, 'Time—the next source of competitive advantage', *Harvard Business Review*, vol. 66, no. 4 (1988), pp. 41–51.

13. **P. M. Senge**, *The Fifth Discipline*, Century, 1990; **P. M. Senge**, 'The leader's new work: building learning organizations', *Sloan Management Review*, vol. 32, no. 1 (1990), pp. 7–23.

14. **R. M. Kanter**, *The Change Masters*, Simon & Schuster, 1983.

15. **Brynjolfsson et al.**, see n. 8 above.

16. **M. Gladwell**, *The Tipping Point*, Abacus, 2000.

17. **S. Finklestein**, 'Why smart executive fail: four case histories of how people learn the wrong lessons from history', *Business History*, vol. 48, no. 2 (2006), pp. 153–70.

18. **Rumelt**, see n. 5, chapter 4.

19. https://www.bbc.co.uk/news/business-45756676 (accessed 5 October 2020).

20. **F. Gino** and **B. Staats**, 'Why organisations don't learn: our traditional obsessions—success taking action, fitting in, and relying on experts—undermine continuous improvement', *Harvard Business Review*, vol. 93, no. 11 (2015), pp. 110–18.

21. **D. Goleman**, 'What makes a leader?', *Harvard Business Review*, vol. 76, no. 6 (1998), pp. 93–102.

22. **Rumelt**, see n. 5 above, p. 94.

23. **Cyert**, see n. 11 above.

24. **M. Maccoby**, 'Narcissistic leaders: incredible pros, and inevitable cons', *Harvard Business Review*, vol. 78, no. 1 (2000), pp. 69–77.

25. **I. Martin**, *Making It Happen, Fred Goodwin, RBS, and the Men Who Built the British Economy*, Simon & Schuster, 2014.

26. **Martin**, see n. 25 above.

27. **B. Groysberg**, **A. N. McLean**, and **N. Nohria**, 'Are Leaders Portable?', *Harvard Business Review*, vol. 84, no. 5 (2006), pp. 92–100.

28. **T. J. Peters**, 'Leadership: sad facts and silver linings', *Harvard Business Review*, vol. 57, no. 6 (1979), pp. 164–72.

29. **H. Mintzberg**, 'Crafting strategy', *Harvard Business Review*, vol. 65, no. 4 (1987), pp. 66–75.

30. **Peters**, see n. 28 above, p. 170.

31. **Peters**, see n. 28 above, p. 171.

32   **G. Hofstede**, *Cultures and Organizations: Software of the Mind*, McGraw-Hill, 1997.

33   **Hofstede**, see n. 32 above, p. 28.

34   **E. H. Schein and P. A. Schein**, 'A new era for culture, change, and leadership', *MIT Sloan Management Review*, Summer 2019, pp. 52–8.

35   **Schein** and **Schein**, p. 58.

36   **W. E. Schneider**, 'Why good management ideas fail', *Strategy and Leadership*, vol. 28, no. 1 (2000), pp. 24–9.

37   **Schneider**, see n. 36 above.

38   This section draws upon **P. Northouse**, see n. 1, p. 6.

39   **M. F. R. Kets de Vries**, 'Charisma in action: the transformational abilities of Virgin's Richard Branson and ABB's Percy Barnevik', *Organizational Dynamics*, vol. 26, no. 3 (1998), pp. 7–21.

40   **Leo Lewis**, 'Stringer gives up song and dance act as Sony pulls itself together', *The Times*, 5 February 2010.

41   **J. Lee** and **D. Miller**, 'People matter: commitment to employees, strategy and performance in Korean firms', *Strategic Management Journal*, vol. 20, no. 6 (1999), pp. 579–93; **J. P. Kotter**, 'What leaders really do', *Harvard Business Review*, vol. 68, no. 3 (1990), pp. 103–11.

42   **Kets de Vries**, see n. 39 above, p. 10.

43   **Kets de Vries**, see n. 39 above, p. 13.

44   **Kets de Vries**, see n. 39 above, p. 19.

45   **Collins** and **Porras**, see n. 4 above.

46   **M. Beer** and **N. Nohria**, 'Cracking the code of change', *Harvard Business Review*, vol.78, no. 3 (2000), pp. 133–41.

47   **Beer** and **Nohria**, see n. 46 above, p. 139.

48   **R. Stacey**, 'Strategy as order emerging from chaos', *Long Range Planning*, vol. 26, no. 1 (1993), pp. 10–17; **R. D. Stacey**, *Strategic Management and Organizational Dynamics: The Challenge of Complexity*, 4th edn, Prentice Hall, 2003; **R. D. Stacey** and **C. Mowles**, *Strategic Management and Organizational Dynamics: The Challenge of Complexity to Ways of Thinking about the Organisation*, 7th edn, Pearson, 2016.

49   **Rumelt**, see n. 5, chapter 7.

50   **M. E. Porter**, *The Competitive Advantage of Nations*, Free Press, 1990, chapter 3; **M. E. Porter**, 'The competitive advantage of nations', *Harvard Business Review*, vol. 68, no. 2 (1990), pp. 73–9.

CHAPTER 11
CORPORATE GOVERNANCE AND CORPORATE SOCIAL RESPONSIBILITY

Learning Objectives

After completing this chapter you should be able to:

- Explain the issues surrounding corporate governance
- Evaluate whether the purpose of corporations is to serve shareholders or stakeholders
- Discuss corporate social responsibility (CSR) and its benefit to organizations
- Identify and explain different corporate governance codes
- Assess the issue of excessive executive remuneration
- Be aware of corporate governance reform

Introduction

Corporate governance is inextricably bound up with one's views of the purpose of corporations and, indeed, how one defines a corporation or business. Although different definitions of corporate governance exist, these only really make sense when we place them in the context of the purpose of corporations. We start our discussion of corporate governance with a review of the origins of corporate governance and a discussion of the corporate form. We explain the reasons for the growth of modern corporations, which in turn has led to an increase in the separation of ownership and control. We then evaluate the different perspectives that exist on the role of corporations.

This is important because a divide exists between those who advocate a shareholder approach to corporate governance and those who adopt a stakeholder approach. The collapse of major corporations more than anything else has put corporate governance on the boardroom agenda. We review corporate collapses and regulatory codes to determine if lessons can be learned to avoid further failures. We also discuss whether executive pay should represent some multiple of the average worker's salary. We end the chapter with a discussion of corporate governance reform, asking whether anything has really changed. Although we evaluate corporate governance in this chapter, it may be more properly thought of as permeating all business decisions. As such, it should be an integral part of the strategy of all organizations.

11.1 What is Corporate Governance?

'Governance' means either the action or method of governing, and it is in the latter sense in which it is applied to companies. **Corporate governance** can be defined as *'the system by which companies are directed and controlled'.*[1] Governance issues are about 'power and accountability. They involve where power lies in the corporate system and what degree of accountability there is for its exercise.'[2] **Shleifer and Vishny** state that corporate governance *'deals with the way in which suppliers of finance to corporations assure themselves of getting a return on their investment'.*[3] Their view of corporate governance is concerned with ensuring that the suppliers of finance (investors) receive something back from the managers to whom they entrust their funds.

A broader definition is supplied by **Demb and Neubauer**, *'the process by which corporations are made responsive to the rights and wishes of stakeholders'.*[4] By using the term 'process', the authors emphasize the changing expectations which boards of directors have to meet, while also including stakeholders. The question for boards is who are their stakeholders and what are their rights? In 2004 the **Organisation for Economic Co-operation and Development (OECD)** produced a set of guidelines entitled the *OECD Principles of Corporate Governance*. It stated that corporate governance involves a set of relationships between a company's management, board, shareholders, and other stakeholders.[5] In 2015, these principles were revised to adapt corporate governance to changes in the corporate and financial landscape. It stated: *'The Principles recognise the interests of employees and other stakeholders and their important role in contributing to the long-term success and performance of the company'.*[6]

According to **Ron Baukol** the fundamental basis of corporate governance and responsibility is the value system of the organization. In contrast to others, Baukol argues that corporate governance is necessary to counteract a tendency for corporations to be selfish and myopic. He suggests that the role of corporate governance is to guide corporations to achieve corporate and societal responsibilities.[7] The use of the term 'corporate governance' gained prominence in the UK following the publication of the *Report of the Committee on the Financial Aspects of Corporate Governance* in 1992.[8] This is commonly referred to as the Cadbury Report after its chairman, **Sir Adrian Cadbury**.

The collapse of major corporations in the UK, such as Polly Peck, Coloroll, Bank of Credit and Commerce International (BCCI), and the Mirror Group, highlighted a rift between the annual report and accounts and reality. For example, Polly Peck went from a market capitalization of £1.75 billion to a deficit of almost £400 million in under four weeks.[9] Their annual report and accounts, signed off by external auditors, showed little signs of their true financial state. At the same time, there was growing controversy over directors' pay which effectively widened the remit of the Cadbury Report. Since then, we have experienced corporate failures which make Polly Peck look like pocket change as global corporations such as Enron and Lehman Brothers have collapsed, threatening instability across global financial markets. Beyond the USA, accounting scandals continue to proliferate, for example, the ongoing law suit brought by investors against South African conglomerate, Steinhoff.

Following the collapse of Lehman Brothers in 2008, policy makers around the globe seek to ensure that those in positions of corporate power behave responsibly and with accountability. Terms such as 'ethics', 'transparency', and 'corporate social responsibility' that were previously implicit in boardrooms now have a more explicit resonance. To understand corporate governance we need to go back to the origins of corporations.

11.2 **The Origins of Corporate Governance**

The origins of corporate governance date back at least as far as 1600, when a Royal Charter was granted to The Company of Merchants of London trading into the East Indies.[10] The governance structure of the East India Company consisted of a *Court of Proprietors* and a *Court of Directors*. The **Court of Proprietors** comprised individuals with voting rights, which they received as a result of contributing a sum of money of around £200. The Court of Proprietors seldom met because it comprised hundreds of individuals, but it had ultimate authority. Its authority was required to raise funds and to appoint directors. The **Court of Directors** was the executive body which was responsible for the running of the company, appointing a chief executive, and setting the strategy direction, although each policy decision required agreement by the Court of Proprietors. The Court of Directors consisted of a governor, a deputy-governor, and twenty-four directors who met frequently.

The structure of the East India Company has clear antecedents with modern companies today. The Court of Proprietors were the shareholders, the Court of Directors was the board, and the Royal Charter laid down the framework in which the company operated. Similarly, the issues faced by their board will resonate with modern companies. Some investors adopted a short-term horizon, requesting a return on their money after each sea voyage, while others adopted a longer view. The Court of Directors had the added problem of controlling appointees such as sea captains for the voyage to the East Indies. These individuals were acting not only for the company but also often for themselves. We can, therefore, see that corporate governance issues are rooted in the development of the corporation.

The corporate structure has continued to develop in response to needs that were not being met by earlier corporate forms. In 1932, US Supreme Court Justice **Louis Brandeis** argued *'the privilege of engaging in such commerce in corporate form is one in which the state may confer or may withhold as it sees fit'.*[11] It is interesting to reflect that, for Brandeis, the conferring of corporate status went hand in hand with the needs of public policy and welfare. His concern was that a corporation was used to benefit the public. He went on to state that even when the value of the corporation in commerce and industry was fully recognized, *'incorporation for business was commonly denied long after it had been freely granted for religious, educational, and charitable purposes'.*[12]

The reason incorporation for business was denied was because of a fear that the corporation may use its power to subvert the needs of employees to the needs of investors. With insight, he noted that there was *'a sense of some insidious menace inherent in large aggregation of capital, particularly when held by corporations'.* As a result, incorporation was granted sparingly; usually when it was necessary to procure for the community some specific benefit that would otherwise be unattainable. That incorporation became more common did not signify to him that concerns about corporate domination had been overcome.

While few would deny the enormous benefits and affluence that modern corporations have brought, Brandeis, like the economist **John Kenneth Galbraith** after him, was wary of the influence of overarching powerful corporations. In the 21st century legislative bodies find themselves trying to constrain the power and influence of technology companies such as Facebook, Alphabet (owner of Google), Amazon, and Apple. See **Strategy in Focus 11.1**.

STRATEGY IN FOCUS 11.1 How to Constrain Big Tech Companies

The growing momentum towards curbing Big Tech

Landmark report provides a road map for future legislative action

Jeff Bezos, Tim Cook, Sundar Pichai and Mark Zuckerberg: the big four tech groups have grown into the 'kinds of monopolies we last saw in the era of oil barons and railroad tycoons', according to the report © AP.

For America's big technology companies, 2020 has been the best and worst of times. The coronavirus pandemic has played to their strengths, as millions have relied on them for online shopping, entertainment and business and social contact. Their ability to prosper through lockdown has propelled their market values to new highs. But this year may also go down as the moment when momentum towards US legislative action to curb their power became unstoppable.

A landmark, 449-page report from the House antitrust subcommittee into Amazon, Apple, Google, and Facebook is uncompromising. All four, it alleges, wield monopoly or substantial power, and have abused it. Since each serves as a gatekeeper over a particular distribution channel, they can 'pick winners and losers' throughout the economy. They can charge excessive fees, impose onerous contract terms, and hoard data. The big four have gone from 'scrappy, underdog start-ups', the report says, to the 'kinds of monopolies we last saw in the era of oil barons and railroad tycoons'.

The report's impact is diluted by the refusal of Republican subcommittee members to sign on to it as a whole. They issued a separate 28-page response that backed strong antitrust enforcement but stopped short of the report's toughest recommendations. Still, the findings provide a detailed road map and trove of evidence which could potentially be used by a new Congress to support legislative moves. They could also bolster existing regulatory actions. The justice department is expected to file a new lawsuit within weeks focusing on Google's dominance in search—the biggest since the Microsoft case in the late 1990s. Amazon, Apple, and Facebook are already the subject of antitrust probes by federal regulators and state attorneys-general.

Lawmakers and regulators must tread a fine line. While this has come at a price, the report notes the big four have 'delivered clear benefits to society'. Surveys show consumers fret about data privacy—and, indeed, about whether the tech giants are too powerful—but enjoy the innovations, free-to-use services, and often lower prices they provide. The best way to police them is to reinvent a US antitrust model still based on the concept of consumer harm, or whether prices are being driven up. The focus should be broadened to the impact of corporate power on market structure, competition, innovation, and quality. Regulators also need adequate resources.

Far deeper scrutiny of tech acquisitions is also required, to ensure they are not aimed at neutralizing or killing off competitive threats. Since 1998, the report notes, the four groups have purchased more than 500 companies between them. Antitrust agencies did not block a single one. Reviewing whether some of those acquisitions should be unwound has merit—notably Facebook's 2012 purchase of Instagram. It is less clear, however, whether outright break-ups or the 'structural separations' the report suggests between companies' dominant platforms and other business lines are, for now, the right path.

The USA and the EU could also benefit from closer co-ordination. Though not always a perfect model, Brussels has blazed a trail in tech regulation, and is now preparing in its Digital Services Act to force Big Tech companies to share their vast data reservoirs with smaller rivals. Washington may yet start closing the gap much more quickly.

Source: https://www.ft.com/content/54078f25-b9d7-40d4-a44c-e2acbae32336 (accessed 11 October 2020).

11.3 The Growth of Modern Corporations

The spread and acceptance of the modern corporation is owed to four characteristics: (1) *limited liability of investors*; (2) *free transferability of investor interest*; (3) *legal personality*; and (4) *centralized management*.[13]

11.3.1 Limited Liability

Limited liability involves a separation between the corporation and its owners and employees. This ensures that what is owed to the corporation is not owed to the individuals who are employed by the corporation. Also, whatever debts the corporation owes are not owed by individuals employed by the company. Thus, if a corporation becomes bankrupt and is pursued by its creditors for recovery of debts, the individual members of the corporation are not individually liable. The corporate form provides certainty for investors as to the extent of their loss; it will only ever be the amount of capital they have invested in the company. However, limited liability is accompanied by limited authority to influence the direction of the corporation. It is the shareholders' low level of risk derived from having limited liability that makes their low level of control acceptable.

11.3.2 Transferability

Transferability or an ability to transfer one's holdings freely provides the shareholder with an acceptable level of risk. A shareholder who is concerned that their shares may be losing value can sell almost immediately. However, this does imply some timely information that would prevent the shareholder incurring further losses. Often, by the time this information is disseminated to individual shareholders their holdings may have substantially fallen in value. Transferability is a function of limited authority. The shareholders agree to put their capital at risk. They have little authority to control the corporation, but they have the assurance that they can have some control over their risk by selling their investment when they want to.

11.3.3 Legal Personality

Whereas a partnership dissolves with the death of its partners, a corporation lives for as long as it has capital. A legal personality ensures that actions that would result in a negative sanction for an individual have no such consequences when the individual commits them as part of a corporation. As corporations are defined as legal persons, they may own property, including copyrights.

11.3.4 Centralized Management

The board of directors determines the setting of a company's aims and objectives, and therefore its strategy; managers control its day-to-day operational issues. For the board to drive the company purposefully into the future, it needs to be aware of the opportunities that exist in the marketplace and how best to exploit these. Cadbury argues that it is insufficient for the board simply to determine aims and objectives without also considering the manner of their achievement. Thus, although the board is responsible for devising strategy it needs to undertake these decisions in consultation with management, who have the task of achieving the results. As corporations grew in size and age, their ownership became more dispersed and markets developed to provide for far greater liquidity. At the same time, directors acting on behalf of shareholders are expected to invoke the same sense of duty and care they exercise with their own affairs.

11.4 The Purpose of Corporations

The purpose of the corporation is far from unambiguous. Different perspectives abound that are rooted in ideology and dogma. The growing concern within corporations for the needs of stakeholders and society has had the effect of polarizing these perspectives. To understand *corporate governance*, *corporate social responsibility*, and *business ethics*, we need to address the fundamental question: why do businesses exist?[14]

Before we do so, we can define what we mean by a corporation. **Robert Monks and Nell Minow** argue that definitions of the term *corporation* invariably reflect the perspectives and biases of those writing the definition. They state that *'a corporation is a mechanism established to allow different parties to contribute capital, expertise, and labour, for the maximum benefit of all of them'.*[15] They argue that a corporation has to relate to a wide variety of constituents including directors, managers, employees, shareholders, customers, and suppliers, as well as society and the government, and that each of these relationships has the ability to affect the direction and focus of the corporation. It is generally agreed that a *corporation* is an organization owned by its shareholders, but managed by agents on their behalf.

Baukol contends that corporations exist because, unlike other institutions such as government, the corporation provides economic sustainability. The corporation is unique in allowing individuals to practise their skills in a group setting that creates employment and value which others are prepared to pay for. The corporation generates wealth for society and for its own members. **Mary O'Sullivan** asserts that an understanding of corporate governance needs to first address what the objectives of the corporation are or what a company is in business to do.[16] Once the objectives are established, discussions of corporate governance focus on the mechanisms that will ensure goal achievement. If a company wants to maximize shareholder value, the relevant governance mechanisms are those influencing the relationship between shareholders and corporate managers.

Elaine Sternberg also argues that it is necessary to first understand what business is (and is not) by disaggregating it from other forms of activity. Sternberg argues that the defining purpose of business (a corporation) is 'maximizing owner value over the long term by selling goods and services'.[17] Few would argue with Baukol's assertion that the corporate entity is the major institution for wealth creation. The arguments surround the role and responsibilities of corporations. As Brandeis noted, the corporation will not necessarily pursue the interests of the society of which it is a part.

11.4.1 The Principal–Agent problem

If we take corporations, there is an assumption that these organizations are in business to create value and that the profit they produce is to be distributed among the owners of the business, the shareholders. We saw in **Chapter 4** that there is a presumption that the objective of corporations is to maximize profits. This is standard neoclassical economic theory. In the 1930s, **Berle and Means** cast doubt on profit-maximizing theories. They were not proposing a shift away from profit-maximizing, but rather questioning whether this actually occurs.[18]

Their concerns were around the **principal–agent problem**. This problem refers to the separation of ownership from control within corporations. The owners are the principal, but control of the organization is by salaried managers who act as the agent. There is a tendency for an *asymmetry of information* to exist when managers are running companies which are owned by numerous dispersed shareholders. This *asymmetry of information* between the principal (owners) and the agent (managers) occurs when managers have access to corporate information which the owners do not. This is explained in greater detail in **Section 11.4.3**. That said, the profit-maximizing assumption is contested by behavioural psychologists who claim organizations consist of shifting coalitions and how they behave is dependent on the interests and beliefs of the dominant coalition(s).[19]

It is apparent that the purpose of corporations is by no means clear cut. Many of the arguments are rooted in ideology. With this in mind, we can evaluate the two main perspectives based on shareholders and stakeholders.

11.4.2   Is the Purpose of Corporations to Maximize Shareholder Value?

The Nobel Prize-winning economist **Milton Friedman** argues, *'there is one and only one social respon-sibility of business—to use its resources and engage in activities designed to increase its profits so long as it stays within the rules of the game, which is to say, engages in open and free competition without deception or fraud.'*[20]

Friedman's argument is that corporate executives are agents and, therefore, to engage in forms of corporate social responsibility is using their position to spend someone else's money for a gen-eral social interest.[21] As we observed in **Chapter 4**, the effect of such activities is to impose a tax on the owners by ensuring that they receive lower returns from their investment than they otherwise would. If the effect of such actions by corporate executives raises prices for consumers, then this places a tax on consumers. Likewise, if the effect of such actions lowers the payments some em-ployees receive, they are effectively taxed. Indeed, Sternberg would argue that in the case of corpo-rations, organizations owned by shareholders, the use of an organization's resources by managers for anything other than business purposes is tantamount to theft.[22] The fact that managers may be involved in the pursuit of socially responsible aims does not mitigate their actions and they are still diluting shareholders' wealth.

Friedman's concern was that the blurring of corporate executives' boundaries of responsibilities which resulted from intrusions into social responsibilities may lead to an erosion of free enterprise. This is because if executives are involved in decisions that are in the political domain then such ex-ecutives become public employees and civil servants; though they remain employees of a private enterprise. And public servants should be elected through a political process and not chosen by shareholders. Friedman does concede that actions he terms 'social responsibility' may be in a corpo-ration's self-interest and, therefore, justified to some limited extent.

The American Business Model (ABM) or Washington Consensus

The context for Friedman's ideas is the **American Business Model (ABM)**, often referred to as the Washington consensus. This has been the dominant economic and political philosophy for the past four decades. The ABM is based on four claims.[23]

(1) **Self-interest**: it is self-interested materialism of individuals that govern their lives.

(2) **Market fundamentalism**: markets must be allowed to operate freely without any political inter-ference. This is based on the belief that the regulation of markets is invariably inefficient.

(3) **A minimal role for the state**: the economic role of the government should be largely limited to the enforcement of contracts and private property rights. It should not be to provide goods and services, or to own productive assets.

(4) **Low taxation**: The use of taxation is to finance the activities of a minimal state. And as a result, taxation should be as low as possible. The tax system should not be used to redistribute income and wealth within society.

The belief in the free market draws upon the work of Italian economist, **Vilfredo Pareto**. He devised what is called a *Pareto efficient state*. **A Pareto efficient state** describes an economic situation in which you cannot make the circumstances of one person better off without making another person worse off. The de facto assumption of the ABM is that markets are *Pareto efficient*. Therefore, if the

Government were to intervene in the allocation of resources it would simply result in a Pareto inefficient state: it would make things worse. Indeed, the only reason for the state to intervene in the allocation of resources would be if it could achieve a *Pareto improvement*. **A Pareto improvement** describes an economic situation in which you can make someone better off, but without making anyone else worse off. It goes without saying that advocates of the ABM do not see this as a role for government.

John Kay offers an incisive critique of the ABM.[24] Kay argues that allowing maximum freedom in a framework of rules is bound to fail, and does fail. This is because playing within 'the rules of the game' does not so much exclude unacceptable behaviour as define the limits of what is permissible. Ultimately, the integrity of an organization does not result from its governance structure; it reflects the values of those who work within it. Thus, the central tenet of the ABM, that business activity can be successfully organized around self-regarding individuals constrained by externally imposed rules, is misplaced. Kay argues the account of the market economy proposed by the ABM is not an accurate description of how even the US economy functions.[25] For example, property rights are not fixed, but are part of social constructs. Furthermore, markets operate in a social context which is not separate from our economic lives, but integral to it. The reason why market economies have, for example, outperformed planned societies is not as a result of the ubiquity of greed or self-regarding materialism. It comes from an understanding of the power of disciplined pluralism. In other words, the primary strength of the market economies is that they provide freedom to experiment and opportunity to imitate successful innovation. At the same time, market economies will quickly terminate unsuccessful experiments. In planned economies, this is not the case; innovations tend to be slow and they are allowed to continue when they fail.

The Body Shop is known for its social activism, including an alliance with the charity Greenpeace and campaigns to end cosmetics testing on animals. Source: © Nils Versemann/iStockphoto.

Anita Roddick, the founder of the Body Shop, openly advocated the pursuit of social causes as a legitimate business practice.[26] Given the values of its founder, which clearly permeated the organization, it was somewhat surprising to see the Body Shop acquired by the French multinational L'Oréal. In 2017, the Body Shop was sold to the Brazilian make-up company Natura Cosmeticos for €1 billion (£880 million). The former Chairman of Cadbury Schweppes, Sir Adrian Cadbury, maintains the fact that companies like the Body Shop pursue wider objectives demonstrates that not all shareholders are concerned with maximizing profits.[27] The issue for Cadbury is not whether an organization is pursuing social objectives per se, but whether this is transparent. *Transparency* allows shareholders to make informed decisions about whether to invest in these companies.

Jack Welch, former CEO of GE, believed that managers and investors should not have share price increases as their overall goal. Welch maintains that any short-term profits should be allied with an increase in the long-term value of a company. As he states, *'On the face of it, shareholder value is the dumbest idea in the world.'* He went on to add: *'The idea that shareholder value is a strategy is insane. It is the product of your combined efforts—from the management to the employees.'*[28] For Welch, shareholder value is a result, not a strategy to be pursued. Ironically, the shareholder value movement is commonly traced to a speech given by Welch at New York's Pierre hotel in 1981, shortly after becoming CEO of GE.

11.4.3 The Agency Problem

The principal–agent framework has occupied economists since the time of the Scottish economist **Adam Smith**. In the eighteenth century, Smith documented what is now known as the **agency problem**. This problem arises because of the separation between ownership of an organization and its control. It is inherent in the relationship between the providers of capital, referred to as the principal, and those who employ that capital, referred to as the agents. Smith's concern was that any given person will simply not watch over another person's money in the same way as they would watch over their own money. As the directors of companies are managers of other people's money, Smith asserts it cannot be expected that *'they should watch over it with the same anxious vigilance which the partners in private co-partnery frequently watch over their own . . . negligence and profusion, therefore, must always prevail in the management of the affairs of such a company.'*[29]

We saw in **Chapter 4** that **Jensen and Meckling** argued that an agency relationship exists when one party, the principal, contracts work from another party, the agent, to perform on their behalf. However, this agency relationship can give rise to a number of agency problems.[30] These occur because no contract, however precisely drawn, can possibly take account of every conceivable action that an agent may engage in. The question arises as to how to ensure that the agent will always act in the best interest of the principal. The spread of modern corporations has brought about a separation between the owners of corporations and those who manage those corporations on their behalf. *Agency costs* occur when there is a divergence between these interests. Thus, agency costs are the costs associated with monitoring agents to prevent them acting in their own interests.

There is increasing pressure on institutional shareholders to take a more active role in the corporations in which they invest. This has been driven by corporate scandals which revealed a lack of non-executive director effectiveness, and a tendency, widely reported in the media, for boards of directors to be remunerated for poor performance. This has prompted a call for greater transparency and disclosure in an attempt to rebalance the information asymmetry between principal and agent and to provide investors with more timely information about their company's activities. The agency problem continues to be important in governance terms because it has an influence on the structure and composition of boards. It also affects the requirements for disclosure, and the balance of power between shareholders and directors.[31]

Berle and Means argue that the separation of ownership from management has resulted in shareholders being unable to exercise any form of effective control over boards of directors. However, Cadbury argues that issues of accountability did not arise simply because ownership was divorced from management, but more so because ownership was increasingly dispersed. As he states, 'It was the fragmentation of ownership that neutered the power of shareholders.'[32] This dispersal of ownership is a double-edged sword. The fact that many holdings are small means that shareholders have no difficulty in selling their shares if they lose confidence in the management of their corporation. However, when the majority of shareholdings are small, shareholders are less able to hold the board of directors to account. As we shall see, small shareholdings in the UK and the USA have since given rise to majority holdings by powerful institutional investors.

11.4.4 Is the Purpose of Corporations to Meet the Needs of Stakeholders?

We have seen that where the focus is on shareholders there is a presumption that shareholder value is the dominant objective of the organization. An alternative approach, which is seen to have acquired greater legitimacy following the collapse of Enron[33] and subsequent financial scandals, is a view of the organization that serves the interest of stakeholders. **R. Edward Freeman** defines stakeholders as *'those individuals or groups which affect or are affected by the achievement of an organization's objectives'*.[34] They may include customers, suppliers, employees, government, competitors, the local community, and, of course, shareholders. The primary role of corporations as a vehicle to create shareholder value is contested by those who advocate a stakeholder approach.

Stakeholders may be separated into internal and external stakeholders. Internal stakeholders are those whose impact is felt inside the organization, such as employees; external stakeholders have their impact outside the organization, such as shareholders. This distinction is somewhat arbitrary, since some stakeholders—for example employees—may also be shareholders and, therefore, occupy both internal and external categories. Those who suggest that the corporation should serve stakeholders accept that shareholders are the owners of the organization, but reject the notion that this somehow makes them of greater importance in the organization's decisions. In fact, they would argue that without the involvement of employees, suppliers, and customers there would be no business activity. Of course, the same argument can be said of shareholders as the providers of finance—without which there would be no organization.

Stakeholder theorists argue that many different stakeholders are affected by an organization's decisions and, therefore, the role of management is to balance the needs of each stakeholder rather than focus upon shareholders only. For example, the collapse of the Lehman Brothers in the USA was felt far beyond the capital loss to shareholders. Employees who had invested in the corporation's pension fund found themselves out of work, suppliers suffered the loss of major contracts, and national and international economies experienced instability. The sheer size of some corporations requires an explicit recognition by board executives that their actions have a direct impact on these stakeholders. A narrow definition of shareholder supremacy quickly comes into conflict with the realities of corporate responsibility.

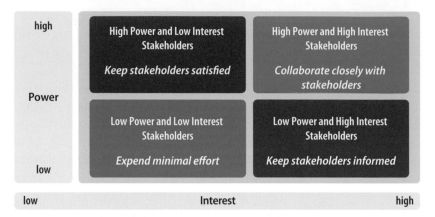

Figure 11.1   The stakeholder power-interest matrix (adapted from Mendelow, 1991).

The problem is that stakeholders may exhibit conflicting needs, which makes the task of management in balancing these different interests very difficult. In an ideal world, it would be great if managers first considered the impact of their strategic decisions upon different stakeholder groups. In reality, this is seldom possible. It is precisely because stakeholders themselves may have different objectives that managers are faced with trying to achieve multiple objectives. One way of trying to prioritize the different interests of stakeholders is to assess the influence they exert on an organization's objectives. See **Figure 11.1**. For example, governments may have a benign interest in the activities of organizations, but be forced to exercise their legislative powers when organizations behave in an unacceptable manner.

An example of government intervention was apparent during BP's disastrous oil rig explosion, which resulted in eleven deaths and unleashed oil from a well head one mile down into the Gulf of Mexico in 2010. This unprecedented threat to marine life and coastal livelihoods led to a personal reprimand of BP's chief executive Tony Hayward and his company by US President Barack Obama. As well as the tens of billions of pounds wiped off BP's share price during the incident, the organization faced a major loss to its corporate reputation. As events unfolded, the British CEO's position became increasingly untenable and he was replaced by an American.

A former Chancellor of the Exchequer, Nigel Lawson, stated emphatically that 'the business of government is not the government of business'. This was a signal to financial markets and the business community that the Conservative government did not expect to regulate the business community. It was assumed that self-regulation would ensure that organizations behaved responsibly. In the USA, the enactment of Sarbanes–Oxley signalled a move away from reliance solely on self-regulation, and marks a recognition of the responsibilities of corporations in the globalized economy. In the UK, following the financial collapse, there has been much debate about the efficacy of 'light-touch' or self-regulation of corporations. When Nike's operations abroad did not conform to US health and safety standards for their overseas workers, including minimum age restrictions on employees, this caused an outcry and was reported worldwide. Although the decision to employ workers abroad was to enhance profitability, the result was a damaged reputation and an initial fall in sales. This illustrates that even where an organization's priority is to create value for its shareholders, it cannot afford to do so without some understanding of the expectations of stakeholders and society.

	Maximize shareholder value/ agency theory	Stakeholder theory
Main players	Principal (owners/shareholders), agent (manager)	Employees, customers, suppliers, shareholders, local community, government
Key objectives	Value maximization, i.e. maximize shareholders' interests	Multiple objectives to try to benefit all stakeholders
Strengths	Clear and achievable	Recognizes that long-term success of the organization depends on the participation of all stakeholders
Weaknesses	Maximizing shareholder wealth fails to motivate employees	Pursuit of multiple objectives is deemed unrealistic and too difficult for managers to achieve
Key protagonists	Milton Friedman (1962, 1970)	R. E. Freeman (1984)

Table 11.1   A comparison of agency theory and stakeholder theory.

Those who adopt a stakeholder perspective expect that organizations will actively pursue measures which result in a net welfare gain to the environment and society. As such, their criteria for successful performance will differ markedly from shareholder maximization. An organization cannot afford to ignore the expectations of stakeholders, and many firms have started to move away from simply paying lip service to important environment issues. The oil industry, arguably one of the worst polluters, has begun to engage stakeholders in debate about renewable sources of energy. This is not altruism, but a realization that their interests are inextricably tied to the interests of their wider stakeholders. **Table 11.1** summarizes the key elements of maximizing shareholder value and stakeholder theory.

The Japanese concept of **kyosei**, loosely translated as 'living and working for the common good' has become a philosophy of doing business for some Japanese corporations.[35] From the perspective of *kyosei*, a corporation is not a self-sufficient organism set apart from society, but is outward looking, aware of its duty to people outside its organization such as customers, suppliers, and the community. By taking account of this wider network of relationships, the corporation can be profitable and sustainable over the long run. For example, Panasonic donates solar lanterns to India to meet the lighting needs of local rural areas.[36] Baukol argues that business leadership is not just about financial success, but that business leaders should also be working to improve their societies, ensuring social, economic, and environmental sustainability.

From this perspective, the proper course of corporate governance is to manage the relationship of the corporation with its stakeholders. Although Baukol acknowledges that corporations will continue to create much of the wealth of society, he sees this is only possible because a corporation is a set of relationships among stakeholders. And each stakeholder plays a role in the success of the corporation. **Corporate social responsibility** occurs when an organization takes into account the impact of its strategic decisions on society. Marks & Spencer announced a £200 million five-year plan to make the company carbon neutral. Its CEO at the time, Stuart Rose, said that 'we believe responsible business can be profitable business'.

We can see that without each stakeholder the corporation cannot function efficiently or cannot function at all. But without capital and shareholders there is no corporate entity. Without banks and other debt investors, the corporation cannot maximize its ability to earn a return on its capital. And without customers there will be no business for the corporation to do. Similarly, without employees, the corporation will be unable to do business. And if the community loses confidence in a corporation it may quickly lose its business legitimacy, resulting in collapse. It is only by aligning and attending to the needs of different stakeholders that the corporation fulfils its duty to society which is to promote prosperity in a sustainable manner.

Stakeholder theory asserts a corporation has duties and responsibilities to different constituents; this presents a number of problems. Sternberg maintains that trying to balance stakeholder needs is unworkable because it leads to an infinite number of stakeholder needs.[37] And stakeholder analysis does not offer guidance as to which stakeholders should be selected. Also, it does not explain what counts as a bona fide need. And finally, it does not provide guidance as to what weighting each stakeholder group should have vis-à-vis other stakeholders. For Sternberg, corporate governance is quite simply corporate actions that ensure that the objectives of the shareholders are adhered to.

11.4.5 Enlightened Value Maximization

Can the divide between shareholder value maximization and stakeholder theory be bridged? **Jensen** proposes *enlightened value maximization* as a way in which organizations might achieve a trade-off between the competing needs of stakeholders.[38] This is accomplished by accepting the maximization of the long-run value of the organization as the criterion for trade-offs between competing stakeholders. This single long-term objective, it is argued, solves the dilemmas managers are faced with when they try to achieve the multiple objectives inherent in stakeholder theory. It is arguable whether proponents of stakeholder theory would accept this as a dispassionate assessment of the corporation's activities or simply another way of saying that shareholders' needs predominate, albeit over the *long term*.

It is clear that the role of corporations is changing. Cadbury states: *'society's expectations of the role of companies in the community are changing and . . . Companies need to engage with those groups which can affect their ability to conduct their businesses'.* He goes on to say that *'companies should stand their ground for what they believe to be in their and society's interests, even if this may lead at times to confrontation'.*[39]

11.5 Corporate Social Responsibility (CSR)

What is *corporate social responsibility* or, as it is commonly known, CSR? **Carroll and Buchholtz** state that *'corporate social responsibility encompasses the economic, legal, ethical and philanthropic expectations placed on organizations by society at a given point in time'.*[40] We can view CSR graphically by using Carroll's four-part model of corporate social responsibility.[41] For Carroll, the four responsibilities identified in his definition, economic, legal, ethical, and philanthropic are interrelated. As such, for a company to be considered socially responsive it must meet the four components identified in **Figure 11.2**.

Figure 11.2 A framework for corporate social responsibility. Source: adapted from A.B. Carroll (1991).

Economic responsibilities are viewed as the cornerstone of corporate social responsibility. This is because the business organization was seen as the basic unit in society designed to provide goods and services to members of society. And, not only did businesses exist to produce goods and services that customers want, they were expected to operate efficiently and make a profit. *Legal responsibilities* are to do with companies performing their activities in a manner consistent with current legislation and regulations. In order to attain this component of corporate social responsibility, companies must provide their goods and services in a way that at least meets their legal minimum requirements.

Ethical responsibilities deal with activities and behaviour that are expected by society even when these activities are not codified into law. Therefore, ethical responsibilities embrace values that society expects organizations to meet, even when those values reflect a higher standard of performance than that currently required by law.

The final component of Carroll's framework corporate social responsibility is what he calls philanthropic responsibilities. *Philanthropic responsibilities* involve organizations engaging in 'corporate actions that are in response to society's expectations that businesses be good corporate citizens'. This includes engaging in activities that promote human welfare. In many corporations philanthropy is seen as discretionary even though there is often the expectation from society that organizations provide it. Although each component of CSR can be discussed separately, they are not to be seen as mutually exclusive but considered as a whole. In Carroll's framework, we can see that CSR involves the simultaneous achievement of a company's economic, legal, ethical, and philanthropic responsibilities.

For a company's board of directors, CSR means they 'should strive to make a profit, obey the law, be ethical, and a good corporate citizen'.[42] Cadbury states that a way to define social responsibility is to say that *'the continued existence of companies is based on an implied agreement between business and society . . . the essence of the contract between society and business is that companies shall not pursue their immediate profit objectives at the expense of the longer term interests of the community'.*[43]

He argues that organizations can distinguish *three* levels of company responsibility. The first level comprises the company's responsibilities to meet its obligations to shareholders, employees, customers, suppliers, to pay taxes and to fulfil its statutory duties. A second level of responsibility is to do with the results of the actions of companies as they carry out these primary responsibilities. This includes making use of society's human resources and avoiding damage to the environment.

For Cadbury, it is not sufficient for a company to say that its carbon emissions or noise levels meet legal requirements. What is required is that companies should be actively seeking to minimize the harmful effects of their actions, rather than seeking to meet the lowest acceptable legal standard.

These two levels of CSR are relatively straightforward as a company's board of directors can make broad estimates about the costs which will be incurred and the benefits which will accrue, from their activities. As we move beyond these two levels of CSR to the third level of corporate social responsibility, what is expected of the company becomes less clearly defined. This is because at this level the question becomes: how far should business reflect society's priorities in addition to its own commercial priorities? Companies now have to look outside of themselves at the changing terms on which society will allow them to carry out their activities, rather than internally at their own performance, which is implied by the other two levels of CSR. It is this third level of corporate social responsibility which occupies most companies in the twenty-first century. Companies are expected to take account of the wider consequences of their decisions on society and to build that awareness into their decision-making processes.

It's fair to say that companies have never been short on advice concerning their responsibilities to society. For example, Milton Friedman measures social responsibility in terms of earnings per share. *'Few trends could so thoroughly undermine the foundation of our free society as the acceptance by corporate officials of a social responsibility other than to make as much money for their stockholders as possible.'*[44] Others, such as former Unilever CEO, Paul Polman, sees corporate social responsibility differently. *'I don't think our fiduciary duty is to put shareholders first. I say the opposite. What we firmly believe is that if we focus our company on improving the lives of the world's citizens and come up with genuine sustainable solutions, we are more in synch with consumers and society and ultimately this will result in good shareholder returns.'*[45] See **Case Study: Stakeholder Capitalism at Unilever**.

We saw in **Chapter 4** that companies that rank highly on corporate social responsibility measures may more likely to be the target of hedge fund activism, according to academic research conducted by Pennsylvania State University's, Erasmus University, and HEC Paris Business School.[46] The research looked at 506 US-based activist campaigns between 2000 and 2016 and found that companies whose CSR ratings were above the industry average had a 5 per cent chance of being subject to hedge fund activism. That compares with a 3 per cent likelihood for the industry average. Why? A focus on ethically oriented practices was seen as a sign of wasteful spending, which 'prevent[s] firms from maximising shareholder value in the short term', wrote the academics, who also interviewed a range of hedge fund managers for their research.

There has been a surge of interest in environmental, social and governance (ESG) investing in recent years. As a result, companies are keen to improve their reputations for ethical behaviour in order to attract investors. Paul Polman, is among business leaders who defends using broader ESG mandates when challenged by outside investors. After he fended off an unsolicited $143bn takeover approach from Kraft Heinz and its private equity investors in 2017, he described the abortive bid for Unilever as 'a clash between people who think about billions of people in the world and some people that think about a few billionaires'.

11.5.1 Environmental, Social, and Governance (ESG)

How do investors, especially institutional investors, know which companies have identified and managed risks arising from **environmental, social, and governance (ESG)** issues which have the potential to reduce, or enhance, long-term shareholder value? The Association of British Insurers (ABI) issues

Guidelines on Responsible Investment Disclosure which is beneficial for companies and investors.[47] The Guidelines provide guidance to companies as to what disclosures an institutional investor might expect to see in the company's annual report.

It allows investors to see the ESG risks in the context of all the risks and opportunities that exist within the company, and what the board is doing to mitigate these risks. For their part, institutional investors should consider ESG risks and opportunities within their overall objective of enhancing shareholder value and not as some additional burden or 'tick box'. Also, when considering remuneration for senior managers the company's Remuneration Committee should ensure the incentives offered to executives does not raise ESG risks, by motivating irresponsible behaviour.

As corporations focus increasingly on their CSR credentials this has attracted major hedge funds such as Man Group and Caxton Associates which look for reliable ways of identifying companies with strong or improving ESG characteristics which could out-perform the stock market.[48] An issue for hedge fund managers is that their clients are increasingly concerned about the type of companies they want to invest in. On that basis, what is needed is companies which can generate above average performance while simultaneously delivering on social, environmental and governance measures. Fund managers, therefore, are keen to try to find a so-called 'ESG factor' which would allow them to identify such stocks in a way which rivals might find hard to copy. The difficulty, of course, is the degree of correlation. How can you be sure that an increase in the value of a company's shares has come about as a result of ESG attributes?

In the past, investors who wanted to invest in **'socially responsible investments'** (SRIs) or **'ethical investments'**, that is investments which consider the ethical, social, and environmental performance of companies, often had to accept lower returns as the price of their convictions. The reason being that SRI tended to exclude stocks seen as harmful to the environment or society, such as oil stocks or arms manufacturers, giving fund managers a limited range of stocks to choose from. This highlights a further difficulty with choosing ESG shares. Consider an electric car manufacturer. Most people would agree this could be considered an ESG stock because its cars are environmentally friendly. However a main component of electric cars is the battery which uses cobalt mined unethically in the Democratic Republic of Congo. This would suggest it is a non-ESG stock and highlights some of the complexities of ESG investing.

11.5.2 Business ethics

Business ethics is about looking at the decisions of corporations and their ultimate outcomes, and the values on which these decisions are based, to understand whether these actions are morally right or wrong. This may involve a company's policies, procedures, and systems but ultimately these internal structures will be determined by the company's own values. It is about the interaction between business and society. Business ethics concerns the changing terms on which society will license corporations to continue to carry on with their activities.

As the former chairman of Cadbury Schweppes succinctly put it *'Business decisions are like stones thrown into a pool, which represents society, and companies are asked to take account of the ripples they cause as they move outwards to the shore. This requires companies to envisage the wider consequences of their decisions and to build that awareness into their decision making processes.'*[49]

One way in which organizations have internalized business ethics is in their use of the term *sustainability*. Sustainability quickly moved beyond environmental considerations as companies

STRATEGY IN FOCUS 11.2 Business and Society: ESG Reports are Not Enough

In the face of coronavirus, companies must now adapt and show they can walk the talk

Governments have blown the dust off the playbook for dealing with financial and economic meltdowns. State support will need to go further than a few rate cuts. That will give business a reciprocal obligation to help the society it depends on. Chief executives fond of polishing their credentials for corporate responsibility must show they can walk the talk. There are some eye-catching examples already. Luxury giant LVMH is repurposing its perfume factories to make hand sanitizer. The gel will go to French hospitals free. Chinese tech companies have dug deep. Alibaba co-founder Jack Ma is sending surgical masks to the USA.

A generous response makes sense. Reputations are at stake. Profiteering will be noticed and remembered. Businesses well-placed to help, notably store chains with their huge distribution networks, can work with government to spread essential supplies. Companies in the front line of fighting the disease face dilemmas. Pharmaceutical groups lost money developing vaccines in response to past epidemics. Now they are reluctant to shoulder risk without public or charitable funding. Pooling resources is one way to overcome a collective action problem. The UK's GSK is offering rivals free use of its immune response-boosting agent, for example.

There are also tricky choices for financially strong businesses. State-approved rescues have toxic form. The decision of Lloyds in 2008 to acquire HBOS, a struggling rival bank, was a disastrous mistake. But there are happier precedents. The fashion industry reveres Chanel's Karl Lagerfeld for preserving craft skills by saving ateliers from collapse.

Business must adapt in ways rarely seen outside wartime. The UK government, for example, wants carmakers to produce medical ventilators. Ministers elsewhere are appealing to patriotism. 'This is a Team Australia moment,' says Prime Minister Scott Morrison. Banks are exhorted to pass on rate cuts; employers to treat workers well; big companies to pay suppliers promptly. Many businesses claim to serve society, as well as shareholders. This is their chance to prove it.

https://www.ft.com/content/44d39d27-64e9-473f-9e54-efb32cd77638 (accessed 14 Oct 2020)

became aware of the difficulty of addressing the natural environment without also considering their impact on the economic and social aspects of communities.[50] **Sustainability** can be defined as *'the long-term maintenance of systems according to environmental, economic and social considerations.'*[51] From an environmental perspective, sustainability is concerned with the conservation of our physical resources for future generations. From an economic perspective, sustainability focuses on both the economic performance of the organization and also how it behaves as a corporate citizen. For example, is it trying to avoid paying its fair share of corporation tax? And, from a social perspective on sustainability the issue is one of social justice and how to improve global inequalities. Sustainability thus becomes an important part of business ethics.[52]

From the point of view of a board of directors, such terms as society may need to be clearly defined for them if they are to be fully aware of the consequences of their decision. For example, if a local factory is dirtying the neighbours' washing by belching out smut from its chimney, local residents may want the company to recognize its responsibility to society and stop polluting their neighbourhood. Let's say the company decides to build a bigger chimney and discharges the smut higher up in the atmosphere. This meets the needs of local 'society' but 'society' in the form of the factory's consumers will end up contributing to the cost of the chimney. And 'society' in the form of some country outside Britain will now receive the factory's discharge.

What this shows is that companies, specifically their board of directors, have to weigh up the consequences of their actions on the different sectors of society which will be affected by their action, before they can decide which is the best way to solve its pollution problem.[53] And, when the company in question is a multinational corporation operating across national borders with supply chains in countries which may not have the same health and safety standards as the home country. And this information can be shared 24/7 with consumers of your products, we begin to see the importance of business ethics for organizations.

11.6 **Corporate Governance Codes**

There is a presumption that corporate managers can be left to act in the best interests of shareholders. This thinking is based on the belief that a poorly performing company will be the subject of takeovers, the threat of which is sufficient to discipline managers to act in the shareholders' interests. However, the reality does not always bear this out. Instead of this threat galvanizing boards of directors to improve their performance, it often leads to them erecting myriad defences. The evidence suggests the market for corporate control is not a very effective way to discipline management. The reason is that if target shareholders win, bidder shareholders invariably break even or lose value. Aligned to this, efficiency gains from takeovers are quite low.[54]

In this respect, takeovers are a costly and inefficient way to change the board of directors. A more efficient way to encourage better corporate performance might be for institutional investors to engage in dialogue with boards of directors. Cadbury suggests that this change in the pattern of share ownership in favour of investing institutions has encouraged the institutions to use their influence with boards. Therefore, rather than simply selling their shareholdings, *exit* is giving way to *voice*, as shareholders seek to improve their returns. Hermes is a UK-based institutional investor that is proactive in its dealings with the companies in which it invests. It published the *Hermes Responsible Ownership Principles*, which detail what they expect of listed companies and what listed companies can expect from Hermes.[55] The intention is to create a common understanding between boards, managers, and owners of the proper goals of a listed company. It sets out a number of expectations which Hermes believe should exist between owners, boards, and managers. By being explicit about their expectations of listed companies, it seeks to create a better framework for communication and dialogue between boards and management on the one hand, and shareholders on the other hand. This aim is to contribute to better management of companies and the sustainable creation of value for their shareholders.

Corporate governance came to prominence following a number of high-profile corporate collapses. At the same time, there was growing controversy over what was seen as excessive directors' pay and rewarding of poorly performing directors. Over the past decades the UK has initiated a series of investigations into ways to improve corporate governance of UK listed companies. These investigations have been high profile, led by experienced individuals who have given their name to the final report. They include the Cadbury Report, the Greenbury Report, and the Hampel Report. The recommendations of these three reports were later embodied into a Combined Code.[56] In addition, there have been specialist reviews dealing with institutional investment, Company Law, the governance of banks and financial institutions, and board diversity. We can address the response to corporate failures by looking at the Cadbury Committee Report and subsequent reports.

11.6.1 The Cadbury Committee

The Committee on the Financial Aspects of Corporate Governance, commonly referred to as the Cadbury Committee, reported its findings in 1992. It was appointed in the aftermath of the collapse of prominent UK listed companies such as Polly Peck. However, its remit was widened to include illegal behaviour at Bank of Credit and Commerce International (BCCI), and Maxwell Communications Corporation. The Committee's sponsors were concerned that the lack of public confidence in financial reporting and the ability of auditors to provide the safeguards sought and expected by users of company reports would undermine London as a major financial centre. The voluntary codes of conduct contained in the report have since gained international currency, although they are not without their critics. Some argue that the focus on the control and reporting functions of boards and the role of auditors is narrow, omitting as it does a substantive role for stakeholders.

At the heart of the Committee's recommendations is a **Code of Best Practice**. All listed companies registered in the UK should comply with the Code and explain reasons for any areas of non-compliance. The Committee acknowledged that '*no system of control can eliminate risk of fraud without so shackling companies as to impede their ability to compete in the marketplace*'. Nevertheless, the Report contained a veiled threat which implied that if companies were to fail to adopt its Code then legislation was a real possibility. '*We recognize, however, that if companies do not back our recommendations, it is probable that legislation and external regulation will be sought to deal with some of the underlying problems which the report identifies*.'[57]

Some of the main recommendations of the Cadbury Report are as follows:

- The board of directors should meet regularly, retain full and effective control over the company, and monitor the executive management.

- There should be a division of responsibilities at the head of the company to ensure that no one individual has unfettered powers of decision.

- Directors' contracts should not exceed three years without shareholders' approval.

A division of responsibilities at the head of the company was to separate the positions of CEO and chairman such that no one individual had *unfettered powers of decision making*. It was a recognition that the role of the chairman and the CEO are distinct. Greater emphasis was placed on non-executive directors' independence from executive board members. The Report recommended their fee be tied to the amount of time they devoted to the company. All listed companies had to **'comply'** or **'explain'**; that is, they either comply with the code or explain in their annual report and accounts *why* they are unable to do so. This puts the emphasis on the board of directors and gives shareholders an opportunity to see which corporations are adhering to the code. It is widely accepted that of all the codes addressing corporate governance issues, the Cadbury Report has had the greatest impact on corporate governance development around the world. Many corporate governance reports, including the King Report I and King Report II of South Africa, acknowledge their debt to Cadbury. These and other reports tend to use the Cadbury Report as a blueprint, but tailor the specifics to suit their individual country's needs.

11.6.2 The Hampel Committee

The Hampel Committee was set up to review the Cadbury Report and the Greenbury Report on directors' remuneration. The Hampel Committee saw no inconsistency in not following some Cadbury Report guidelines, such as the separation of the roles of chairman and chief executive officer, arguing that guidelines will be appropriate in most cases, but not all. In such cases, the Hampel Committee argued, it would be damaging to a company's reputation if its explanation for non-compliance were rejected out of hand. The Hampel Report confirmed the enhancement over time of shareholder investment as the overriding objective of companies, but it did so iterating that business prosperity involved many economic actors working together. Thus, directors can meet their obligations to shareholders and obtain long-term shareholder value only by developing and sustaining stakeholder relationships. Companies need to be mindful of their responsibilities, but this needs to be couched within structures and principles that allow businesses to grow and prosper. The Hampel Report argued that previous reports had placed too great a burden on what it referred to as 'box-ticking' at the expense of wealth creation, although it endorsed the majority of the findings of both committees.

11.6.3 Other Corporate Governance Codes

There has been a plethora of corporate governance codes since the Cadbury Report.[58] The Combined Code, published in 1998, brought together the recommendations of the Cadbury, Greenbury, and Hampel Reports.[59] It functions on the 'comply or explain' formula instituted by Cadbury. Its focus is on companies and institutional investors. Directors are expected to conduct an annual review of the effectiveness of the organization's system of internal control and report to shareholders that they have done so. The Myners Report, published in 2001 and updated in 2008, focused on institutional investment. The Report expects institutional investors to engage in greater shareholder activism, particularly when dealing with underperforming companies. Following the financial crisis there was the Walker Review in 2009. Sir David Walker recommended extensive reforms to strengthen governance in UK banks and increase disclosure on pay.[60]

In 2008, the Financial Reporting Council (FRC) published an updated Combined Code which removed the restriction on an individual chairing more than one FTSE 100 company.[61] The Combined Code became the UK Corporate Governance Code in 2010. This was a review of the Combined Code and retains the central governance feature of 'comply or explain'. In 2014 the UK Corporate Governance Code underwent another revision. This time the focus was on balancing the information needs of investors against the appropriate reporting requirements for companies.

There has been some concern about the lack of diversity in the boardroom, particularly the under representation of women. Lord Davies was asked to identify the barriers that might be preventing women from reaching the boardroom. His initial report was published in 2011, with a review in 2012 and subsequent annual reports.[62] A key recommendation of the Davies Report is that FTSE 100 companies should aim for a minimum of 25 per cent of women in the boardroom by 2015. In February 2011, there were 12.5 per cent of women sitting on FTSE 100 boards. By 2015, this figure had risen to 26.1 per cent.[63]

11.6.4 **The Role of Non-Executive Directors**

The collapse of Enron, a former energy trading giant, was felt far beyond the owners of the corporation. It wiped out shareholders' investments and employees' retirement savings, and led to 21,000 people losing their employment. Enron, once the seventh-largest company in the USA, filed for bankruptcy in December 2001 with debts of £18 billion. It had hidden these mounting debts through a series of complex financial dealings. Its collapse wiped out more than $60 billion in market value. At the time Enron was praised by analysts as a new business model; it had been voted the US's most admired, innovative company. The CEO's use of market-to-market accounting allowed Enron to book potential future profits on the day a deal was signed, irrespective of how much money was actually realized. For example, Enron lost $1 billion on a power plant in India, but the company executives were paid multi-million dollar bonuses on the basis of profits which never materialized. It is clear that the demise of Enron owed much to inadequate checks by its external auditors Arthur Andersen and weak controls within the company. Amanda Martin-Brock, a former Enron executive, has said that the fatal flaw at Enron was 'pride, then arrogance, intolerance and greed'.

In the UK, this lack of accountability led to the Higgs Report, whose remit was to look at the *role and effectiveness of non-executive directors*. A decade earlier the Cadbury Committee had said that non-executive directors required independence of judgement if they were to perform their role effectively. The collapse of Enron cast doubt on the model of effective non-executive directors challenging the decisions of executive board directors. Too often non-executive directors were seen as merely *rubber-stamping* decisions taken by executive directors.

The recommendations of the Higgs Report included the following:

- Non-executive directors should meet as a group at least once a year without executive directors being present.

- The board should inform shareholders why they believe an individual should be appointed as a non-executive director and how they meet the requirements of the role.

- A full-time executive director should not hold more than one non-executive directorship or become chairman of a major corporation.

These and other recommendations sought to tighten the role of non-executive directors in their accountability to shareholders. Although the UK stopped short of legislation, the USA was less reticent; it enacted sweeping legislation in the form of the Sarbanes–Oxley Act. The collapse of Enron is particularly disturbing given the wealth of experience of non-executive directors that sat on the board. These included a British former cabinet minister and Energy Secretary, Lord Wakeham. The implosion of Enron and WorldCom suggested to the US government that the self-regulatory regime in the USA was not working properly. It was quite apparent that it proved incapable of dealing with the largesse of corporate greed. The role of non-executive directors at Enron is interesting. Their high salaries (each was paid a minimum of $350,000), long tenures (they had an average of seventeen years' service), and lack of a nominating committee to ensure transparency should have raised concerns earlier.[64]

The collapse of a major US investment bank, Lehman Brothers, was a result of the same arrogance and greed which brought down Enron. We might ask: what lessons were learned from Enron and where were the checks and balances in the system to prevent such a collapse? A former Chancellor of the Exchequer, **Alistair Darling**, has queried why increasingly reckless lending was never checked by the boards of directors of the banks. He recognizes this is difficult when profits are soaring and you have to challenge someone you know and like, but ultimately that is what boards are there to do.[65]

11.6.5 The Sarbanes–Oxley Act

The Sarbanes–Oxley Act has been called a number of things—a knee-jerk reaction, a piece of poorly drafted legislation, perhaps even tick-boxing ad infinitum. A deeper question that Sarbanes–Oxley does not address is whether we can (or indeed should) legislate for human greed. Sarbanes–Oxley was enacted in July 2002 by the US Congress. It was proposed by Republican Congressman Michael G. Oxley and Democratic Senator Paul Sarbanes. It seeks to correct market imperfections by introducing financial disclosure rules and enhancements to statutory enforcements.

The main recommendations of Sarbanes–Oxley include the following:

- chief executives now have to attest personally for the accuracy of company accounts—this is a concern for corporations wishing to list in New York and may explain the flight of funds to London;
- a higher standard for board members who sit on the audit committee;
- the prevention of loans to executives;
- further criminal and civil penalties for securities violations.

A former US Treasury Secretary, **Henry Paulson**, stated that if the US capital markets are not to be disadvantaged, its regulatory regime must be more responsive to changes in the marketplace. The concern of US corporations is that they are now embroiled in far too much regulation. However, the financial crisis that was precipitated by the collapse of major financial institutions may actually suggest that such institutions require more robust regulation.

11.7 Excessive Executive Pay

A concern with excessive executive pay is a perennial issue. However, the issue is not one of high salaries per se, but the difference between fair and excessive compensation. In the UK, the **Greenbury Report** looked at investor concerns over excessive directors' pay.[66] This followed the huge pay increases awarded to the heads of the recently privatized UK public utilities. At the time, these chief executive officers were referred to as *fat cats*. Their role and responsibilities remained the same post privatization as it had pre privatization; the only discernible difference was their substantial increase in pay. Shareholders and institutional investors have become increasingly vocal about what is seen as compensation for poor performance and the setting of easy bonus targets. There is evidence that the views of shareholders are being taking into account. In 2016, almost 60 per cent of shareholders voted against a £14 million pay package for the chief executive of BP in a year in which the company reported record losses, cut thousands of jobs, and froze its employees' pay.[67]

The question is not always one of easy targets, but sometimes the question is simply: how much is enough? For example, in 2016, Sir Martin Sorrell, CEO of global marketing group WPP, received £48.1 million in total pay, bonuses, and incentive scheme pay-outs. The remuneration, the last to be awarded under WPP's controversial Leap scheme, means Sorrell has received around £210 million in total remuneration since 2012. In 2015, he received £70.4 million, which was opposed by a third of shareholders at the annual general meeting (AGM).[68] Sorrell was subject to a number of shareholder voting revolts at WPP AGMs before retiring in April 2018. However, unlike many CEOs Martin Sorrell built WPP from the ground up into a successful company.

Sorrell founded WPP in 1985, when he borrowed £250,000 to buy a stake in shopping basket maker Wire & Plastic Products. Through a series of well-conceived acquisitions, it became the world's largest marketing and advertising group. In fact, shareholders who have stayed with the group since its inception have seen a substantial increase in their investment. Not surprisingly, Sorrell defended his pay awards pointing out that he has put three decades of his life into turning WPP from a maker of wire baskets into a global marketing business worth billions of pounds. *'I'm not a Johnny-come-lately who picked a company up and turned it round [for a big payday]',* he said. *'Over those 31 years . . . I have taken a significant degree of risk. [WPP] is where my wealth is. It is a long effort over a long period of time.'* We might also note that compared to his US counterparts, his salary could be seen as modest.

As organizations around the world try to cope with the global coronavirus pandemic we can look at whether the pandemic has had any impact on moderating CEO pay. If we look at FT-SE 100 companies we find that only 36 out of the UK's 100 biggest companies reduced their chief executive's pay in order to help their company navigate the coronavirus pandemic and economic crisis. See **Strategy in Focus 11.3**. Research by the Economic Policy Institute found top chief executives earn more than 300 times what an average worker makes.[69] This differential has increased substantially over time. In the USA, CEOs of major companies earned twenty times more than an average worker in 1965. In 1978, this differential had grown to twenty-nine times. By 1989, it had doubled to fifty-eight times more than an average worker, before accelerating in the 1990s to 376 times the average worker's salary. The financial crisis in 2008 resulted in a fall in CEO compensation, which meant that the CEO-to-worker compensation ratio also fell. In 2014 the CEO-to-worker compensation ratio recovered to 303 to 1.

In 2019, the ratio of CEO-to typical-worker compensation was 320-to-1 under the realized measure of CEO pay; up from 293-to-1 in 2018 and a big increase from 21-to-1 in 1965. The Economic Policy Institute uses a 'realized' measure of CEO pay that counts stock awards when vested and stock options when cashed in rather than when granted.[70] Share vesting is the process by which a CEO is rewarded with shares or stock options but receives the full rights to them over a set period of time.

The question the researchers seek to answer is whether the high compensation for chief executive officers is a result of their talent or their ability to earn *economic rent*. **Economic rent** is the difference between the minimum price a seller would accept and the market price. Economic rent for CEOs is the difference between the minimum remuneration they would except and what the market actually pays. It implies a payment above what a CEO would require to stay in that position. The researchers conclude that *'high CEO pay reflects rents, concessions CEOs can draw from the economy not by virtue of their contribution to economic output but by virtue of their position'.* As a result, CEO pay could be reduced without the economy suffering any loss of output. A further implication of rising executive pay is that it reflects income that otherwise would have accrued to others. In other words, the excessive amount chief executives earn means money is not available for salary increases for other employees.[71]

The concern over CEOs' pay is not limited to shareholders. The former CEO and chairman of GE, Jeffrey Immelt, urges business leaders to ensure their pay does not substantially outstrip that of their

STRATEGY IN FOCUS 11.3 Fat Cats and Starving Dogs

Ocado's Tim Steiner is the UK's highest paid CEO. 'It would take an average full-time worker approximately eight years to earn what Steiner could earn in one day,' the report noted. Photograph: David Sillitoe/*The Guardian*.

Just 36 out of the UK's 100 biggest companies reduced their chief executive's pay in order to help their firm navigate the coronavirus pandemic and economic crisis, according to an analysis of executive pay that found FTSE-100 CEOs are now handed, on average, the same as nearly 120 full-time workers.

Research by the Chartered Institute of Personnel and Development (CIPD) and the High Pay Centre published on Wednesday shows that the majority of FTSE 100 companies did not cut top executive pay, despite many of the firms turning to the taxpayer to pay the wages of furloughed workers. The report found that of the 36 companies that did cut CEO pay, the measures taken were 'superficial or short-term'. It found that 14 companies cut bosses' salaries by 20 per cent, but pointed out that 'salaries typically only make up a small part of a FTSE 100 CEO's total pay package'. This is because most CEOs make far more money from bonuses and long-term share schemes than they receive in basic pay.

'None of the 36 companies have chosen to reduce their CEO's long-term incentive plan (LTIP), which typically makes up half of a CEO's total pay package,' the report said. It added that 11 FTSE 100 companies cancelled bonuses for their chief executive. Peter Cheese, chief executive of the CIPD, the professional body for HR and people development, said: 'It doesn't look like the pandemic has proven to be an inflection point for executive pay yet. The bulk of cuts made so far appear to be short-term and don't signify meaningful, long-term change.' Cheese said there was 'a disconnect' between the huge pay packages awarded to CEOs 'and their actual contribution to long-term company performance. Too big a share of CEO payments depends on the fluctuating fortunes of the stock market and not enough on whether they are a responsible custodian of the business for all stakeholders, including, of course, the workers who drive long-term value,' he said.

11

The report warned that sky high CEO pay was likely to prove 'particularly controversial in the case of companies that have drawn on government support'. It found that 19 FTSE 100 companies have taken advantage of the job retention scheme (JRS) or coronavirus corporate financing facility (CCFF) loan scheme. Tim Steiner, the chief executive of supermarket delivery firm Ocado—which did not receive government support—was named as the UK's highest paid CEO, collecting £58.7 million in the year to the end of March 2019 (the latest available).

Steiner, who collected most of the money from an LTIP share deal, was paid 1,935 times that of the median salary of a full-time UK worker (£24,897). 'It would take an average full-time worker approximately eight years to earn what Tim Steiner could earn in one day,' the annual high pay report noted. An additional five companies—AstraZeneca, Diageo, Anglo American, BP, and Experian—paid their CEOs more than £10m. On average FTSE 100 CEOs took home a pay package worth £3.61m—that is 119-times the median earnings of a UK full-time worker. The median FTSE 100 CEO pay was down slightly (0.5 per cent) on the £3.63m collected in 2018.

Luke Hildyard, director of the High Pay Centre think tank, said: 'Very high CEO pay undermines the spirit of solidarity that many companies are trying to project as they battle against the impact of the coronavirus. More pragmatically, multimillion-pound pay awards worth over a hundred times the salary of a typical worker seems like an unnecessary extravagance during a period of such economic uncertainty. If we want to protect as many jobs as possible and give the lower paid workers who have got the country through this crisis the pay rise they deserve, we will need to rethink the balance of pay between those at the top and everybody else.'

The report called for pay to be set in 'a more democratic fashion' with a worker representative appointed to the committees that set CEOs' pay.

Source: https://www.theguardian.com/business/2020/aug/05/uks-largest-firms-fail-to-cut-ceo-pay-to-navigate-covid-19-crisis (accessed 14 October 2020).

senior managers. Immelt believes that if staff are to remain motivated and excessive remuneration is to be avoided, then CEOs' pay should be a small multiple of that of their twenty-five most senior managers. He argues that a multiple that represents up to five times what senior managers make is up for discussion. However, a multiple of twenty times he regards as madness. His own pay was in the range of two to three times that of his top twenty managers.

11.8   Is Reform to Corporate Governance the Answer?

O'Sullivan proposes three different perspectives on corporate governance reform.[72] The first is that the existing system of corporate governance may need some revision, but only around the edges. Second, the system of corporate governance that assumes shareholder primacy needs to be changed, albeit leaving shareholders at the centre. Third, the primacy of shareholders is itself open to question.

The proponents of minor revisions to the existing system argue a debate about the purpose of the corporation is not required. They see the proper role of the corporations as being the maximization of shareholder value.[73] From this perspective corporate governance in the real world is not without faults, but corporate failures such as Enron, Lehman Brothers, and Royal Bank of Scotland (RBS) are presented as statistical outliers rather than a systemic problem. However, the refusal of the USA and UK governments not to allow banking institutions to fail can be seen not as a solution, but a symptom of a deeply dysfunctional financial system. Wall Street firms which scorned the need for government regulation during the boom years were most insistent on being rescued by the government during the financial collapse. Success was seen as an individual achievement, but failure a social problem.[74]

The second perspective argues that reforms need to be more radical. While these reformers apportion some blame to the auditors and regulators, they point out it was the governance mechanisms themselves which failed. This perspective does not, however, question shareholder primacy. A third perspective asks whose interest corporations should be run in. It does not take it as self-evident that corporations should be run in shareholders' interests. **Andrew and Nada Kakabadse** argue that the pursuit of shareholders' interests leads to ever-widening social inequalities.[75] They suggest the governance debate would benefit from being pursued more at a societal or political level, rather than the corporate level. This view stems from their belief that the key issues surrounding governance are ones of social inequality, not economic performance.

In the UK and USA, discussions of corporate governance have invariably put shareholders above stakeholders, such as employees and suppliers. **John Armour et al** note that both the Sarbanes–Oxley Act in the USA and the Higgs Report in the UK completely ignore stakeholder claims in favour of further entrenching accountability to shareholders. They undertook a study of corporate governance institutions in the UK and found that *certain core institutions—takeover regulations, corporate governance codes and the law relating to directors' fiduciary duties are indeed highly shareholder orientated.*[76] On the basis of their analyses of UK institutions, they reject the claim made by some writers that the fundamental issues of corporate ownership have been settled in favour of the shareholder value model.[77]

Those who adopt the stakeholder model of corporate governance recognize a central role for the corporation in wealth creation, but see this in the wider context of meeting differing stakeholders' needs. Whilst accepting the corporation as a force for economic prosperity and social well-being, they argue that this wealth creation requires all stakeholders to actively participate. Therefore, all stakeholders, including society, must be taken account of in the corporation's strategic decisions, including its distribution of the wealth which stakeholders have helped generate. Those who adopt a model of corporate governance that enshrines the primacy of shareholders believe that corporations are the main engines for growth in industrialized societies, that a focus on stakeholders, many of which have conflicting needs, leads to a misallocation of resources and ultimately less help for those members of society who may need it most. The outcome of this might be to raise prices for consumers and/or lower the returns that shareholders could have earned.[78]

11.9 **The Pursuit of Greed**

The UK government was forced to use tax payers' money to bail out failing British banks Royal Bank of Scotland and Lloyds Banking Group to prevent their collapse. What went wrong with these and similar financial institutions? Kay, points to the change in ownership as contributing to the financial crisis.[79] In the past, we had partnerships and owner-managed businesses. The ownership and control of the business lay in the hands of senior employees. The success and loss from business activities was borne by these individuals, whose personal finances were at stake. In this structure, partners would monitor each other's activities, which effectively limited the risks the company incurred. As it was their own money at stake, they were careful to engage in business activities they understood. The capital available to them was limited to the company's profits and their individual contribution to the partnership.

But with the growth of limited liability companies and dispersed shareholding came the negligent management, speculation, and risk-taking that Adam Smith warned against. Instead of long-term commitment to institutions, there was short-term opportunism in pursuit of personal gain. For example, the chief executive of Lehman Brothers, Dick Fuld, continues to be a very rich man after the collapse of the company he presided over. Many of the executives of US financial institutions bailed out by the US government did not even lose their job. Fred Goodwin, who facilitated the collapse of RBS with his ill-conceived takeover of the Dutch bank ABN AMRO, was sacked and stripped of his knighthood. Goodwin's pension was thought to be £400,000 per year, but it was actually double that amount. This amount had been agreed when he was recruited by the then RBS top management. Despite government ministers' protests, and the failure of RBS board, Goodwin insisted on his contractual rights to his full pension.[80] The co-chairman of Berkshire Hathaway, **Charlie Munger**, once gave a speech at Harvard Law School called 'The Psychology of Human Misjudgement'. In his speech he said if you wanted to predict how people would behave, you only needed to look at their incentives. See **Strategy in Focus 11.4** on Kenya Airways.

In common with the US investment bank Lehman Brothers, RBS exemplified management arrogance by engaging in activities which were peripheral to their core activities. It is argued that it is not bad regulation of these institutions that caused the financial crisis, but 'greedy and inept bank executives who failed to control activities which they did not understand'.[81] The Financial Services Authority's report into the collapse of RBS stated it overreached itself, engaging in risks the board of directors did not understand. It is clear that, given the risks it was taking, RBS was massively undercapitalized in the event of failure.

11.9.1 Moral Hazard: Are Some Companies Too Big to Fail?

The argument that banks cannot be allowed to remain 'too big to fail' has found support from the former Governor of the Bank of England, **Mervyn King**. He argues that there is merit in dividing retail and investment banking operations into separate, smaller businesses. That way, problems that arise in these individual elements do not jeopardize the whole corporation. King contended that if the Bank of England were to bail out the banking sector, this would introduce **moral hazard**. This occurs when people become indifferent to the consequences of their actions because they do not have to meet the costs. If there is an expectation of government assistance for failing financial businesses, the individuals who run these businesses will behave in ways that make the need for such assistance more likely.[82]

Others have argued that what is required is better regulation that is fully coordinated across international boundaries to prevent such failures in the future. This coordination will protect consumers and the financial economy, preventing the need for government assistance. However, this approach is seen by some to be little more than wishful thinking. They accept that what is needed if we are to safeguard the economy and protect public finances is to ensure that the

STRATEGY IN FOCUS 11.4 Kenya Airways CEO and Staff Share the Pain of Pay Cuts

Kenya Airways Plc. will cut salaries of executives and staff starting next month to combat a slump in revenue amid the coronavirus pandemic. Chief Executive Officer Allan Kilavuka will take an 80 per cent pay cut, to be reviewed on a monthly basis, while senior management including board members will have their salaries reduced by 75 per cent, according to an internal memo seen by Bloomberg News and verified by the airline. All staff face some reduction in wages, Kilavuka said in the note to all employees dated Friday.

Kenya Airways has suspended about 65 per cent of flights due to reduced demand for air travel 'and this is changing by the hour,' the CEO said in the memo. 'Our passenger numbers are also reducing exponentially and have greatly impacted our revenues.'

The decision to ground planes and place about half the fleet in long-term storage is in line with moves taken by carriers around the world. The industry is among the worst hit so far by the coronavirus, which has killed more than 11,000 people globally and is spreading rapidly. Several governments have banned flights from high-risk countries, while all travel is being discouraged to try and contain the pandemic.

Cash Strapped

The coronavirus crisis comes at a time that Kenya Airways was already strapped for cash, and the airline last month agreed to borrow about $50 million from the country's government, its biggest shareholder. The carrier has made an annual loss since 2013. Senior management will work one paid week for every three without wages, while lower level staff will get two weeks salary for every two without pay. The airline is not firing employees at this point.

'Should this trend continue—and current indications show that it will—we will have to make the difficult decision to temporarily suspend our operations,' Kilavuka said. 'We are in unfamiliar territory and are constantly and carefully evaluating our options.'

Source: 'Kenya Airways CEO, Staff to Take Pay Cut as Virus Batters Sales', Bloomberg, https://www.bloomberg.com/news/articles/2020-03-21/kenya-airways-ceo-staff-to-take-pay-cut-as-virus-batters-sales (accessed 14 October 2020).

financial services needed by individuals and businesses are regulated. At the same time, they argue the government should refuse to underwrite risk-taking. As long as banking groups know their activities will be underwritten by an implicit government guarantee, for them it becomes 'business as usual'.

It is difficult to escape the conclusion; if we have learned anything, it is that we haven't learned anything. When the next financial crisis happens Kay argues that a frustrated public may ultimately turn not only on politicians who have been profligate with public funds, and bankers. They may also begin to question the legitimacy of the market economy and capitalism.[83]

Summary

Corporate governance as a discipline is in a state of flux. A debate within corporate governance concerns whether corporations should be run for the benefit of shareholders or stakeholders. Those who argue that corporations should be run for shareholders cite the fact that shareholders are the owners of the corporation and it is their money that is at stake. Those who argue the case for stakeholders are not convinced that stakeholders are simply a means to an end. They argue that suppliers, customers, employees, and, yes, shareholders must all be able to participate in determining the strategic direction of the corporation.

Following the collapse of major organizations, a number of codes of conduct have been implemented in the UK; these all seek to tighten accountability to shareholders. Sarbanes–Oxley has been implemented in the USA following the collapse of the energy trading multinational corporation Enron. The collapse of major financial institutions such as Lehman Brothers spread unrest throughout global financial markets. One could be forgiven for expecting that this cycle will simply repeat itself if nothing is learned. The thinking that major banks are *too big to fail* and must be propped up by state intervention fails to factor in that this encourages unsustainable risk-taking. It will be interesting to watch corporate governance develop and monitor the direction that corporations take. It will also be interesting to see whether regulation and codes of conduct can ever be effective against the pursuit of greed.

CASE STUDY Stakeholder Capitalism at Unilever

When Paul Polman was made chief executive of Unilever in 2009, he was regarded as a safe pair of hands to lead the maker of Hellmann's mayonnaise, Dove soap and Berry and Jerry's ice cream. A veteran executive from Nestle, and Procter and Gamble, he was known for his fiscal discipline and international experience. But Polman, who resigned as CEO at the end of 2018, quickly set about making dramatic changes when he took over.

Paul Polman (former CEO Unilever).
Source: © Wikimedia Commons.

He stopped issuing quarterly guidance, signalling to investors that he was not going to make decisions to improve the short-term share price. He rolled out a long-term strategy to make Unilever a better steward of the environment and a more socially responsible business, known as the Sustainable Living Plan. The immediate impact of not reporting quarterly earnings was an 8 per cent fall in the share price which put Polman under pressure to reverse the decision. Instead of backtracking on the decision he went on the offensive explaining to investors in Unilever you cannot solve the world's problems based on short termism and quarterly returns. He began acquiring brands known for their ecological authenticity, like Seventh Generation and Tazo tea.

Purpose, Values, and Vision

Unilever's purpose states that to succeed requires 'the highest standards of corporate behaviour towards everyone we work with, the communities we touch, and the environment on which we have an impact.' Their values define how they undertake business and interact with their colleagues, partners, customers, and consumers. Their four core values are integrity, responsibility, respect, and pioneering. As we saw with Johnson & Johnson (see Chapter 1), Unilever's values direct their staff in the decisions and actions they take every day as they expand into new markets, recruit new talent, and face new challenges. Their purpose is about 'making sustainable living commonplace'. Their vision is to be the global leader in sustainable business. In seeking to achieve this vision Unilever adopts their purpose-led business model to drive superior performance. Their aim is to deliver financial results consistently in the top third of our industry.

In the 1890s, William Hesketh Lever, founder of Lever Brothers, wrote down his ideas for Sunlight Soap—his revolutionary new product that helped popularize cleanliness and hygiene in Victorian England. It was 'to make cleanliness commonplace; to lessen work for women; to foster health and contribute to personal attractiveness, that life may be more enjoyable and rewarding for the people who use our products'. That sense of purpose and mission has always been part of Unilever's culture and continues unabated in the twenty-first century. On many occasions Polman has had to remind his audience that businesses have to put long term sustainability as the true fiduciary duty of boards. On that basis, he saw off speculative hedge funds by taking the unusual step of actively courting long-term investment funds to buy the company's shares. Within three years as CEO, aided by his ban on quarterly reporting to the City, he managed to reduce the holding of Unilever shares by hedge funds from 15 per cent to less than 5 per cent. This, in turn, reduced fluctuations in the company's share price. At the time he said that 'historically, too many CEOs have just responded to shareholders instead of actively seeking out the right shareholders'. 'Most CEOs go to visit their existing shareholders; we go to visit the ones we don't yet have.'

The Reason for Sustainability

In explaining his beliefs, Polman candidly pointed out that business is not there for the benefit of shareholders; it exists to find longer-term solutions to society's problems. When he launched the company's Sustainable Living Plan in November 2010 the target was to double sales and halve the environmental impact of its products. There was also a commitment to improve the nutritional quality of Unilever food products by reducing the amount of salt, saturated fats, sugar and calories, and link more than 500,000 smallholder farmers and distributors in developing countries to its supply chain. Substantive progress has been made on all these targets. But the target of sourcing all agricultural raw materials sustainable by 2020 was not met. Targets that are more difficult to achieve are those which require a change in consumer behaviour, such as reducing the use of heat of water in showering and washing clothes, encouraging people to eat foods with lower salt levels.

Nonetheless executives at Unilever believe that companies which operate in a more responsible way on environment, social and governance (ESG) are more successful long term. Their mantra is if you publish more and increase transparency within the corporation, take into account climate change or water scarcity, if your plans are more robust, so you reduce risks for your investors. This, in turn, ensures your cost of capital will be lower. In seeking to protect the environment and society Unilever has introduced 'Sustainable Living' brands across the company. These brands have a clear purpose which, over time, helps to tackle a social or environmental concern. For example, the detergent Domestos is aligned with the purpose of building twenty-five million toilets. In addition, the product itself must also contribute to one or more of the targets set in the Unilever Sustainable Living Plan (USLP), which, in turn contribute to the seventeen UN Sustainable Development Goals. The company believe it has to be purpose-led and future-fit—and that it has to drive superior performance.

To help them on their journey they adopt their Compass strategy. This is a single sustainable business strategy based on three core beliefs: (1) brands with purpose grow (2) companies with purpose last, and (3) people with purpose thrive. An example of a purposeful product in action is Unilever's Hellmann's Red and Green Tomato Ketchup. Its purpose is to reduce food waste which occurs when Unilever manufactures its products. Hellmann's Red and Green Tomato Ketchup, launched in April 2017 which uses green and red tomatoes whereas, traditionally only red tomatoes would be used. By only using red tomatoes, 10 per cent of the total harvest was being discarded so, Unilever developed a new recipe to include both. Hellmann's Red and Green Ketchup has potentially saved 2.5 million tomatoes from going to waste every year and customer feedback shows there's no compromise on taste. A win-win for all its stakeholders.

Multi-stakeholder capitalism

Unilever adopts a 'responsible business model' which they argue makes their brand stronger and improves corporate reputation, which in turn improves the share price. The board's conviction to their business model was tested during the failed bid by Kraft Heinz. Even though the bid offered shareholders an 18 per cent premium, the board stuck to their responsible business model successfully arguing that a rejection of the bid will release greater long-term value for shareholders. Unlike many companies which pay lip service to corporate social responsibility (CSR) Unilever has this embedded in its business model and linked to the success of the brands. As part of his approach to business Polman created systems which are more agile enabling Unilever to respond to events that happen outside their control such as new competitors, a natural disaster, or new legislation. As the world gets increasingly volatile companies must have a quick feedback loop from the market that picks up these signals, and a structure that is very agile and externally focussed. Part of the reason for a purpose is it allows Unilever to be much more connected with what's going on in local markets, which is often a challenge for a big company. And when you're connected, if the environment changes you get a quicker signal and can respond faster.

Unlike many businesses, Polman openly speaks of the need for capitalism to be dynamic. On that basis, if society doesn't function properly then leaders need to do business differently and even try a different form of capitalism. One of the most outspoken and principled business leaders, he is scathing about companies that claim their hands are tied by a fiduciary duty to maximize profits for shareholders in the short-term. He points out that this is:

too narrow a model of Milton Friedman's old thinking. The world has moved on and these people need to broaden their education with the reality of today's world. I don't think our fiduciary duty is to put shareholders first. I say the opposite. What we firmly believe is that if we focus our company on improving the lives of the world's citizens and come up with genuine sustainable solutions, we are more in synch with consumers and society and ultimately this will result in good shareholder returns.

When he was asked to chair a food security task force and co-opt other business leaders he refused. Why? He believed the recommendations from business would have defended first generation biofuels, no one would have thought about land rights, and the issue of women's rights would not have been considered; all factors he is passionate about. Instead he asked Oxfam, the Food and Agriculture Organization of the UN (FAO), the World Food Programme (WFP), and Greenpeace to partner with him. Only then did he invite business companies. 'I would not do anything in Unilever without a multi-stakeholder approach. We have to work with government and civil society. You have to be systemic thinkers, able to work in partnership with national governments. I don't want to work with just businesses anymore'.

Leadership

In an interview about leadership, Polman stated 'Leaders bring a morality, that it is not about yourself, and that is shown through respect for others. The faith in big men is misplaced. Rosa Parks was a true leader—she didn't have a private jet.' Rosa Parks was a black woman who refused to give up her seat on a bus when asked to by the bus driver, for a white man who had just boarded the bus, and move to the back of the bus. This was Montgomery, Alabama in December 1955. In a quiet, calm, dignified manner Mrs Parks refused to move and was arrested. The result was a mass movement boycotting public transport which led to the out lawing of segregation on public transport. Polman laments what he called a chronic lack of leaders. Finding good leaders in times of crisis is perhaps particularly difficult but not insurmountable. Unilever is not unique in this area. For example, during the global pandemic the Dutch shipping giant Maersk was offering its ships and cargo space to get emergency supplies to wherever they were needed, maintaining or creating shipping routes which were not necessarily commercially viable.

In 2009, financial analysts were sceptical of his vision and new direction. During his first few months, which happened to coincide with the financial crisis, Unilever shares fell more than 27 per cent. Since those early days, Unilever's share price has more than doubled and easily surpassed the gains by the FTSE 100 during Polman's tenure. The company had been transparent about its progress, issuing annual reports which include environment, social and governance (ESG), which show improving working conditions in its supply chain and the creation of healthier products.

In order to prove to the markets that rejecting the Kraft Heinz bid was 'the right thing to do' Polman had to set ambitious targets of 3–5 per cent for sales growth and increasing margin growth to 20 per cent. To achieve this the company has had to slash costs while simultaneously increasing demand for new products. He delayered the organization and decentralized management to the countries. Inevitably, there has been a number of setbacks. To improve profits and streamline the company Polman tried to do away with the dual listing structure that includes having two headquarters in London and Rotterdam. Some investors felt that the company was moving to the Netherlands in order to make hostile takeovers, like that attempted by Kraft Heinz, impossible. The plan was rejected and Polman announced his intention to resign.

The Future

Alan Jope, a lifetime employee at Unilever who has been running its largest division, the beauty and personal care business, replaced Polman as CEO in 2018. Since 2009, Polman's vision, integrity, and sheer doggedness has brought Unilever sustained growth and profitability based on its business model of stakeholder capitalism. Adherence to this business model was a key criterion for choosing a successor. In 2020, during the global pandemic, Polman remained busy sharing his message that businesses need to be a force for good, not just profit. He argued that now is the time for asset managers and asset owners who have been talking about ESG and stakeholders, to hold companies they invest in to a higher moral standard. 'You have to call them out,' said Mr Polman. 'Now is a moment for humanity. We need to give up things and sacrifice . . .'

Sources: 'Paul Polman, a crucial voice for corporate responsibility, steps down as Unilever C.E.O', *New York Times*, 29 November 2018, https://www.nytimes.com/2018/11/29/business/unilever-ceo-paul-polman.html; 'Paul Polman on capitalism, leadership and sustainability', Oxfam blogs, 13 December 2018, https://oxfamblogs.org/fp2p/paul-polman-on-capitalism-leadership-sustainability; 'Paul Polman's harsh words for financial services', *The Financial Times*, 25 March 2020, https://www.ft.com/content/39047667-4204-4915-8e19-6b3a193c071b; 'Covid-19 is a litmus test for stakeholder capitalism', *The Financial Times*, 25 March 2020, https://www.ft.com/content/234d8fd6-6e29-11ea-89df-41bea055720b; 'Unilever chief Paul Polman to step down', *The Financial Times*, 29 November 2018, https://www.ft.com/content/4fd75572-f3a6-11e8-9623-d7f9881e729f; 'Unilever's Paul Polman: challenging the corporate status quo', *The Guardian*, 24 April 2012, https://www.theguardian.com/sustainable-business/paul-polman-unilever-sustainable-living-plan; C. Carson, 'The autobiography of Martin Luther King Jr', Abacus 2000; Unilever.com.

Questions

1. How is Unilever able to offer superior performance to shareholders while simultaneously pursuing a strategy of sustainable brands?

2. Why do you think other companies and business leaders are reluctant to adopt stakeholder capitalism?

3. What does Paul Polman's choice of civil rights activist, Rosa Parks, reveal to you about his beliefs concerning the role of leadership?

4. Explain what might attract (or repel) you from working for a company like Unilever.

 **For more examples and discussion to aid your understanding of this chapter, please visit the online resources and see the Extension Material for this chapter.**

 ## Review Questions

1. Why is an understanding of the purpose of corporations helpful for understanding corporate governance?
2. Explain how the separation of ownership and control in organizations has led to an *agency problem* and *agency costs*.
3. Why is a concern for ESG (environment, social, and governance) becoming more prominent in organizations?

 ## Discussion Question

'There is one and only one social responsibility of business—to use its resources and engage in activities designed to increase its profits' (Friedman, 1970). ***Discuss***.

Research Topic

Identify the differences in the approach to shareholder value of Unilever and 3G Capital, a Brazilian-led private equity firm. Why do you think these differences may have led to the failed takeover of Unilever by 3G Capital, and Warren Buffett?

Recommended Reading

For a practical discussion of corporate governance see:

- **A. Cadbury**, *Corporate Governance and Chairmanship: A Personal View*, Oxford University Press, 2002.
- **R. A. G. Monks** and **N. Minow**, *Corporate Governance*, 3rd edn, Blackwell, 2004.

A robust defence of shareholder primacy is provided by:

- **M. Friedman**, 'The social responsibility of business is to increase its profits', *New York Times Magazine*, 13 September 1970.
- **E. Sternberg**, *Just Business: Business Ethics in Action*, 2nd edn, Oxford University Press, 2000.

The case for stakeholder theory is made by:

- **R. E. Freeman**, *Strategic Management: A Stakeholder Approach*, Pitman, 1984.

For a discussion of agency theory, see:

- **M. C. Jensen** and **W. H. Meckling**, 'The theory of the firm: managerial behaviour, agency costs and ownership structure', *Journal of Financial Economics*, vol. 3, no. 3 (1976), pp. 305–60.
- **E. F. Fama** and **M. C. Jensen**, 'The separation of ownership and control', *Journal of Law and Economics*, vol. 88, no. 2 (1983), pp. 301–25.

www.oup.com/he/henry4e

Visit the online resources that accompany this book for activities and more information on strategy.

Test your knowledge and understanding of this chapter further by trying the multiple-choice questions online.

References and Notes

1 **A. Cadbury**, *Corporate Governance and Chairmanship: A Personal View*, Oxford University Press, 2002, p. 1.
2 **Cadbury**, see n. 1 above, p. 3.
3 **A. Shleifer** and **R. Vishny**, 'A survey of corporate governance', *Journal of Finance*, vol. 52, no. 2 (1997), pp. 737–83.

11

[4]   **A. Demb** and **F. F. Neubauer**, *The Corporate Board: Confronting the Paradoxes*, Oxford University Press, 1992.

[5]   *OECD Principles of Corporate Governance*, OECD Publications, 2004.

[6]   *G20/OECD Principles of Corporate Governance*, OECD Publications, 2015.

[7]   **R. Baukol**, 'Corporate governance and social responsibility', 2002; http://www.cauxroundtable.org.

[8]   **A. Cadbury**, *Report of the Committee on the Financial Aspects of Corporate Governance*, Gee & Co. Ltd, 1992.

[9]   **A. Cadbury**, *Corporate Governance and Chairmanship: A Personal View*, Oxford University Press, 2002.

[10] This section draws upon **Cadbury**, see n. 8, chapter 1.

[11] **R. A. G. Monks** and **N. Minow**, *Corporate Governance*, 3rd edn, Blackwell, 2004, p. 10; see also **R. A. G. Monks** and **N. Minow**, *Corporate Governance*, 5th edn, Wiley, 2011.

[12] **R. A. G. Monks** and **N. Minow**, see n. 11 above, p. 11.

[13] **R. C. Clark**, *Corporate Law*, Little, Brown, 1986.

[14] These fundamental questions are discussed by the Caux Round Table, an organization of business leaders who seek to include moral responsibility within business decisions (http://www.cauxroundtable.org); see also **E. Sternberg**, *Just Business: Business Ethics in Action*, 2nd edn. Oxford University Press (2000) for an agency theory perspective.

[15] **Monks** and **Minow**, see n. 11 above, pp. 8–9.

[16] **M. O'Sullivan**, 'Corporate governance: scandals, scoundrels, scapegoats and systems', *INSEAD Quarterly*, vol. 4 (2003), pp. 6–8.

[17] **Sternberg**, see n. 14 above.

[18] **A. A. Berle** and **G. C. Means**, '*The Modern Corporation and Private Property*', Macmillan, 1932.

[19] **R. M. Cyert** and **J. G. March**, *A Behavioural Theory of the Firm*, Prentice-Hall, 1963.

[20] **M. Friedman,** *Capitalism and Freedom*, University of Chicago Press, 1962, p. 133.

[21] **M. Friedman**, 'The social responsibility of business is to increase its profits', *New York Times Magazine*, 13 September 1970.

[22] **Sternberg**, see n. 14 above, p. 41.

[23] **J. Kay**, *The Truth about Markets*, Penguin, 2004.

[24] For a comprehensive discussion of the American Business Model, see **Kay**, see n. 23, chapters 26, 27, and 28.

[25] **J. Kay**, 'Putting the "American business model" in its place', 22 November 2010, https://www.opendemocracy.net/openeconomy/john-kay/putting-american-business-model-in-its-place.

[26] **A. Roddick**, *Business as Unusual*, Thorsons, 2000.

[27] **Cadbury**, see n. 1.

[28] **F. Guerrera**, 'Welch condemns share price focus', *The Financial Times*, 12 March 2009.

[29] **A. Smith**, *The Wealth of Nations*, quoted in Cadbury, see n. 1, p. 4.

[30] **M. C. Jensen** and **W. H. Meckling**, 'The theory of the firm: managerial behaviour, agency costs and ownership structure', *Journal of Financial Economics*, vol. 3, no. 3 (1976), pp. 305–60; **E. F. Fama** and **M. C. Jensen**, 'The separation of ownership and control', *Journal of Law and Economics*, vol. 88, no. 2 (1983), pp. 301–25.

[31] **Cadbury**, see n. 1.

[32] **Cadbury**, see n. 1, p. 4.

[33] For background on the collapse of the Enron corporation, see, **B. McLean** and **P. Elkind**, *The Smartest Guys in the Room*, Penguin, 2004; **G. Zandstra**, 'Enron: board governance and moral failings', *Corporate Governance*, vol. 2, no. 2 (2002), pp. 16–19.

[34] **R. E. Freeman**, *Strategic Management: A Stakeholder Approach*, Pitman, 1984, p. 46.

[35] **R. Baukol**, 'Corporate governance and social responsibility', 2002; http://www.cauxroundtable.org.

[36] Panasonic.com, http://panasonic.net/sustainability/en/lantern/2015/04/donate-india.html.

[37] **E. Sternberg**, 'The defects of stakeholder theory', *Corporate Governance: International Review*, vol. 5, no. 1 (1997), pp. 3–10.

[38] **M. Jensen**, 'Value maximization, stakeholder theory and the corporate objective function', pp. 7–20; **D. H. Chew** and **S. L. Gillan**, *Corporate Governance at the Crossroads: A Book of Readings*, McGraw-Hill Irwin, 2005.

[39] **Cadbury**, see n. 1, p. 217.

[40] **A. B. Carroll** and **A. K. Buchholtz**, *Business and Society: Ethics and Stakeholder Management*, 4th edn, Thomson Learning, 2000, p. 35.

[41] **A. B. Carroll**, 'The pyramid of corporate social responsibility: towards the moral management of organisational stakeholders', *Business Horizons*, July–August (1991), pp. 39–48.

[42] **Carroll**, see n. 41 above, p. 43.

[43] **Cadbury**, see n. 1, p. 160.

[44] **Friedman**, see n. 20, p. 133.

[45] **Jo Confino**, 'Unilever's Paul Polman: challenging the corporate status quo', *The Guardian*, 24 April 2012.

[46] **Laurence Fletcher**, 'Ethical CSR focus triggers hostile investor activism, study finds', *The Financial Times*, 3 August 2020.

[47] **C. A. Mallin**, '*Corporate Governance*', Oxford University Press, 2019.

[48] **Laurence Fletcher**, 'Hedge funds join the hunt for the ESG "factor"', *The Financial Times*, 25 September 2019.

[49] **Cadbury**, see n. 1, p. 162.

[50] **A. Crane** and **D. Matten**, *Business Ethics*, Oxford University Press, 2007.

[51] **Crane** and **Matten**, see n. 50, p. 23.

[52] **Crane** and **Matten**, see n. 50 above.

[53] **Cadbury**, see n. 1, p. 164.

[54] **K. Gugler**, *Corporate Governance and Economic Performance*, Oxford University Press, 2001.

[55] Hermes Responsible Ownership Principles, www.hermes.com.

[56] **Cadbury**, see n. 8; **R. Greenbury**, *Directors' Remuneration*, Gee & Co. Ltd, 1995; **R. Hampel**, *Final Report: Committee on Corporate Governance*; *Combined Code, Principles of Corporate Governance*, Gee & Co. Ltd, 1998.

[57] **Cadbury**, see n. 8, para. 1.10.

[58] For discussion of corporate governance codes, see **C. Mallin**, *Corporate Governance*, 5th edn, Oxford University Press, 2016, chapter 3.

[59] **Hampel**, see n. 56 above.

[60] **D. Walker**, *A Review of Corporate Governance in UK Banks and other Financial Industry Entities, Final Recommendations*, HM Treasury, 2009.

[61] *The Combined Code on Corporate Governance*, FRC, 2008; see also *Developments in Corporate Governance and Stewardship 2016*, FRC, 2017.

[62] **E. M. Davies**, *Women on Boards*, BIS, 2011; **E. M. Davies**, *Women on Boards, One Year On*, BIS, 2012.

[63] *Women on Boards: 5 Year Summary* (Davies Review), BIS, October 2015.

[64] **Monks** and **Minow**, see n. 11, p. 10.

[65] **A. Darling**, *Back from the Brink*, Atlantic Books, 2012, p. 317.

[66] **R. Greenbury**, *Directors' Remuneration*, Gee & Co. Ltd, 1995.

[67] **T. Macalister**, **J. Treanorand**, and **S. Farrell**, 'BP shareholders revolt against CEO's £14m pay package', *The Guardian*, 14 April 2016.

[68] **M. Sweney**, 'Sir Martin Sorrell's pay package plunges from £70m to £48m', *The Guardian*, 28 April 2017.

[69] **L. Mishel** and **A. Davis**, 'Top CEOs make 300 times more than typical workers', *Economic Policy Institute*, 21 June 2015.

[70] https://www.epi.org/publication/ceo-compensation-surged-14-in-2019-to-21-3-million-ceos-now-earn-320-times-as-much-as-a-typical-worker (accessed 14 October 2020).

[71] **J. Bivens** and **M. Lawrence**, 'The pay of corporate executives and financial professionals as evidence of rents in top 1 percent incomes', *Economic Policy Institute*, Working Paper no. 296, 2013; **O'Sullivan**, see n. 16.

[72] **Friedman,** see n. 20.

[73] **M. Lewis**, *The Big Short*, Norton, 2011.

[74] **A. Kakabadse** and **N. Kakabadse**, *The Geopolitics of Governance: The Impact of Contrasting Philosophies*, Palgrave, 2001.

[75] **J. Armour**, **S. Deakin**, and **S. J. Konzelmann**, 'Shareholder primacy and the trajectory of UK corporate governance', *British Journal of Industrial Relations*, vol. 41, no. 3 (2003), pp. 531–55.

[76] **H. Hansmann** and **R. H. Kraakman**, 'The end of history for corporate law', *Georgetown Law Journal*, vol. 89, no. 2 (2001), pp. 439–68.

[77] **Friedman**, see n. 21; **Shleifer** and **Vishny**, see n. 3; **Hansmann** and **Kraakman**, see n. 76 above.

[78] **J. Kay**, *'Other People's Money'*, Profile Books, 2015.

[79] **Darling**, n. 65.

[80] **Kay**, see n. 78.

[81] **Kay**, see n. 78.

[82] **J. Kay**, '"Too big to fail" is too dumb an idea to keep', *The Financial Times*, 28 October 2009.

[83] **Kay**, see n. 82 above.

Glossary

A

Acceptability – relates to the response of stakeholders to the proposed strategy.

Acquisition – when one organization seeks to acquire another, often smaller, organization.

Adaptive learning – the ability to cope with changes in one's environment.

Agency costs – the costs resulting from managers abusing their position as agent, and the associated costs of monitoring them to try to prevent this abuse

Artificial intelligence – any technology that aims to emulate cognitive human behaviour such as learning and problem solving.

Asymmetry of information – exists when the agents (managers) running a corporation have greater access to information than the principal (shareholders) by virtue of their position.

Authentic leadership – authentic leaders have a clear understanding of their own values and behave towards others based on these values.

B

Balanced scorecard – provides managers with a more comprehensive assessment of the state of their organization. It enables managers to provide consistency between the aims of the organization and the strategies undertaken to achieve those aims.

Benchmarking – a continuous process of measuring products, services, and business practices against those companies recognized as industry leaders.

BHAGs – big hairy audacious goals: goals that stretch the organization and are readily communicated to all its members.

Big bang disruption – a change in industry dynamics in which not only the least profitable customers are lured away, but consumers in every segment defect simultaneously.

Big data – extremely large data sets that may be analysed computationally by the use of algorithms.

Big Hairy Audacious Goals *see* **BHAGs**

Blue ocean strategy – allows a company to achieve a leap in value for both the company and its buyers, by driving costs down while simultaneously driving value up for buyers.

Blue oceans – represents a strategic position by competitors that has the potential for demand creation and highly profitable growth.

Business ethics – looking at the decisions of corporations and their ultimate outcomes, and the values on which these decisions are based, to understand whether these actions are morally right or wrong.

Business model – answers questions, such as, who is the customer? And, what does the customer value? It answers a crucial question for managers concerned with how to make money from the business.

Business strategy – deals with how an organization is going to compete within a particular industry or market.

C

Cash cow – a business which has a high market share in low growth or mature industries.

Causal ambiguity – exists when the link between the resources controlled by an organization and its sustainable competitive advantage is not understood or only partially understood.

Chaos – an irregular pattern of behaviour generated by well-defined non-linear feedback rules commonly found in nature and human society.

Cloud computing – the practice of using a network of remote servers hosted on the Internet to store, manage, and process data, rather than a local server or a personal computer.

Cognitive bias – leads managers to rely heavily upon their own intuition and judgements which are based on past experiences.

Competencies – can be defined as the attributes that organisations require in order to be able to compete in the marketplace.

Competitive advantage – occurs when an organization is implementing a value creating strategy that is not being implemented by competitors.

Competitive environment – deals with the industry in which the organization competes.

Competitive strategy *see* **business strategy**

Complementor – a player is a complementor if customers value your product more when they have that player's product than when they have your product alone.

Conglomerate diversification *see* **unrelated or conglomerate diversification**

Consonance – can include an assessment of why the organization exists, the economic foundation which supports the business, and the implications of changes.

Co-opetition – competitive behaviour that combines competition and cooperation.

Core competence *see* **core competencies**

Core competencies – the collective learning of individual members within an organization and their ability to work across organizational boundaries.

Core ideology – this is made up of core values and purpose.

Core rigidity – an organization's way of working that stifles the need to change when its environment changes.

Core values – an organization's essential and enduring tenets which will not be compromised for financial expediency and short-term gains.

Corporate governance – two definitions are provided: (1) the way in which organizations are directed and controlled; or (2) the process by which corporations are made responsive to the rights and wishes of stakeholders.

Corporate parent – refers to all those levels of management that are not part of customer-facing and profit-run business units in multi-business companies.

Corporate parenting – concerned with how a parent company adds value across the businesses that make up the organization.

Corporate social responsibility – is a recognition that organizations need to take account of the social and ethical impact of their business decisions on the wider environment in which they compete.

Corporate strategy – is concerned with what industries the organization wants to compete in.

Cost leadership *see* **cost leadership strategy**

Cost-leadership strategy – is where an organization seeks to achieve the lowest-cost position in the industry without sacrificing its poduct quality.

Critical success factors – the factors in an industry that are necessary for a business to gain competitive advantage.

D

Differential firm performance – refers to the observation that firms which possess similar resources and operate within the same industry experience different levels of profitability.

Differentiation strategy – involves the organization competing on the basis of a unique or different product which is sufficiently valued by consumers for them to pay a premium price.

Diseconomies of scale – occur when an increase in a firm's output causes a more than proportionate increase in its cost.

Disruption (disruptive innovation) – describes a process in which a smaller company with fewer resources is able to successfully challenge established incumbent businesses. When mainstream customers start adopting the new entrant's offerings in volume, disruption has occurred.

Distinctive capabilities – a prerequisite for a distinctive capability is that it must be highly valued by the consumer and difficult for your competitors to imitate.

Diversification – occurs when an organization seeks to broaden its scope of activities by moving into new products and new markets.

Divisional structure – comprises individual business units that include their own functional specialisms and have direct responsibility for their own performance.

Dog – a business which has a low market share within a low-growth industry.

Double-loop learning – the assumptions on which objectives are based are continually challenged and monitored.

Durability – refers to the rate at which an organization's resources and capabilities depreciate or become obsolete.

Dynamic capabilities – the firm's ability to integrate, build, and reconfigure internal and external competences to address rapidly changing environments.

E

Economies of scale – as a firm increases its volume of production so its average cost of production falls.

Emergent strategy – where managers use their experience and learning to develop a strategy that meets the needs of the external environment.

Emotional intelligence – an ability to recognize your own emotions and the emotions of others.

Emotional intelligence is manifest in self-awareness, self- regulation, motivation, empathy, and social skills.

Entrepreneurial process – seeks to motivate employees to manage their operations as if they belonged to them.

Entry mode strategy – the different types of strategy that organizations can use to enter international markets.

Experience curve – suggests that as output doubles the unit cost of production falls by 20–30 per cent. The actual percentage reduction in costs will vary between different industries.

Explicit knowledge – is objective and rational and can be easily communicated and shared, for example, in product specifications, scientific formulas, and manuals.

F

Feasibility – concerns whether a strategy will work in practice.

First-mover advantages – refers to organizations which benefit from the learning and experience they acquire as a result of being first in the marketplace.

Five forces framework – tool of analysis to assess the attractiveness of an industry based on the strengths of five competitive forces.

Focus business strategy *see* **focus strategy**

Focus strategy – occurs when an organization undertakes either a cost or differentiation strategy but within only a narrow segment of the market.

Franchising – a form of licensing that is employed by many international companies such as McDonald's, Benetton, and Pizza Hut.

G

General Electric-McKinsey matrix – this uses a nine-cell matrix to broaden the criteria for assessing the performance of business units.

Generative learning – about creating change by being prepared to question the way we look at the world.

Global strategy – the organization seeks to provide standardized products for its international markets which are produced in a few centralized locations.

Globalization – refers to the linkages between markets that exist across national borders. This implies that what happens in one country has an impact on occurrences in other countries.

Globally integrated enterprise – a company that fashions its strategy, its management, and its operations in pursuit of a new goal: the integration of production and value delivery worldwide.

H

Horizontal integration – occurs when an organization takes over a competitor or offers complementary products at the same stage within its value chain.

Hostile takeover – where an acquisition is unwelcome and contested.

Hybrid strategy – this is where an organization is able to combine being a low cost producer with some form of differentiation.

Hypercompetition – where organizations aggressively position themselves against each other and create new competitive advantages which make opponents' advantages obsolete.

Icarus Paradox – the very capabilities that create a company's success can also be its downfall.

Incumbent firm – an organization already operating in the industry.

Industry   this is determined by supply conditions and based on production processes that allows companies to produce similar products.

Industry life cycle – suggests that industries go through four stages of development which comprise: introduction, growth, maturity, and decline.

Intangible resources – may be embedded in routines and practices that have developed over time within the organization. These include an organization's reputation, culture, knowledge, and brands.

Intended strategy – the strategy that the organization has deliberately chosen to pursue.

International strategy – is based upon an organization exploiting its core competencies and distinctive capabilities in foreign markets.

Internet of Things – refers to a network of physical objects—'things'—embedded with sensors which allow them to interact with other devices over the Internet.

Joint ventures – when two organizations form a separate independent company in which they own shares equally.

Key success factors – elements in the industry that keep customers loyal and allow the organization to compete successfully.

Knowledge management – the recognition that different types of knowledge have different characteristics.

Knowledge-based view of the organization – the most important source of an organization's sustainable competitive advantage is the ability to create and utilize knowledge.

Leadership – is concerned with creating a shared vision of where the organization is trying to get to, and formulating strategies to bring about the changes needed to achieve this vision.

Licensing – can be seen as another way of gaining entry into overseas markets without large resource commitments.

Linkages – the relationships between the way one value activity is performed and the cost or performance of another activity.

Localization – implies that national differences between countries are important and that organizations must take account of these differences in their product offerings, distributions, and product promotions if they are to be successful.

Locational advantages – the activities that go to make up an organization's value chain may be located in different countries to take account of differential costs and other locational advantages that a country may possess.

Macro-environment – consists of factors which that may not have an immediate impact on the organization, but have the capacity to change the industry in which it competes, and even to create new industries.

Make or buy decision *see* **transaction cost analysis.**

Management – is about coping with complexity to produce orderly and consistent results.

Marketing mix – is a set of marketing tools commonly referred to as the 4Ps: product, price, place, and promotion.

Matrix structure – an attempt to increase organizational flexibility to meet the needs of a rapidly changing environment.

Merger – occurs when two organizations join together to share their combined resources.

Mission – seeks to answer the question; what is the purpose of an organization, or, why does an organization exist?

Mission statement – the way in which an organization communicates the business it is in to the outside world.

Mobility barriers – factors that prevent the movement of organizations from one strategic group to another.

Moral hazard – when people become indifferent to the consequences of their actions because they do not have to meet the costs.

Multidomestic strategy – is aimed at adapting a product or service for use in national markets and thereby responding more effectively to the changes in local demand conditions.

Multinational enterprise or multinational corporation (MNE or MNC) – an organization that has productive activities in two or more countries.

Noncustomers – buyers who only minimally purchase an industry's offering, buyers who refuse to use the industry's offerings, and buyers who have never even thought of the industry's offering as an option for them.

Organizational capabilities – a capability is the capacity for a team of resources to perform some task or activity.

Organizational culture – the values and beliefs that members of an organization hold in common.

Organizational rigidity – an inability and unwillingness to change even when your competitive environment dictates that change is required.

Organizational routines – are regular, predictable, and sequential patterns of work activity undertaken by members of an organization.

Organizational structure – the division of labour into specialized tasks and coordination between these tasks.

P

Paradigm – a set of beliefs and assumptions managers hold which are relevant to the organization in which they work.

Parenting advantage – occurs when an organization creates more value than any of its competitors could if they owned the same businesses.

Pareto efficient state – an economic situation in which you cannot make one person better off without making another person worse off.

Pareto improvement – an economic situation in which you can make someone better off, but without making anyone else worse off.

Path dependency – the unique experiences a firm has acquired to date as a result of its tenure in business.

PESTLE analysis – analysis of political, economic, social, technological, legal, and environmental factors.

Porter's diamond of national advantage – seeks to explain why nations achieve competitive advantage in their industries by using four attributes that exist in their home market. These are factor conditions, demand conditions, related and supporting industries, and firm strategy, structure, and rivalry.

Positioning – a view that strategy is about how an organization positions itself to mitigate the prevailing industry structure (five forces) that exists.

Primary activities – are activities which are directly involved in the creation of a product or service.

Principal–agent problem – refers to the separation of ownership from control within corporations. The owners are the principal who provides the capital but control is in the hands of managers who act as agent on the principal's behalf.

Product life cycles – is a concept which states that products follow a pattern during which they are introduced to the market, grow, reach a maturity stage, and eventually decline.

Purpose – the reasons an organization exists beyond making a profit.

Question mark – (also known as 'problem child') a business which competes in high growth industries but has low market share.

Realized strategy – the strategy that the organization actually carries out.

Red oceans – all the industries that currently exist today; the known market space.

Related diversification – movement into an industry in which there are some links with the organization's value chain.

Replicability – is the use of internal investments to copy the resources and capabilities of competitors.

Resource heterogeneity – different organizations competing in the same industry may possess different resources and capabilities.

Resource immobility – the resource and capability differences that exist between organizations may continue over time.

Resource-based view – emphasizes the internal capabilities of the organization in formulating strategy to achieve a sustainable competitive advantage in its markets and industries.

Resources – can be thought of as inputs that enable an organization to carry out its activities.

Ricardian rents – the surplus that is left over when the inputs to a productive process, which includes the cost of capital being employed, have been covered.

Role ambiguity – occurs when the different expectations of managers make it highly unlikely that individuals can meet the expectations of both managers.

S

Scenario – a challenging, plausible, and internally consistent view of what the future might turn out to be.

Scenario planning – allows managers to produce different, internally consistent views of what the future might turn out to be.

Shareholders – individuals or groups who have invested their capital within an organization, and are therefore deemed to be the owners.

Single-loop learning – occurs when firm performance is measured against agreed goals.

Social complexity – an organization's resources may be difficult to imitate because they may be based on complex social interactions. These may exist between managers in the organization, a firm's culture, and a firm's reputation with its suppliers and customers.

Stakeholder theory – a view of corporations which argues that corporations should be run in the interests of all stakeholders.

Stakeholders – are these individuals or groups which affect or are affected by the achievement of an organization's objectives.

Star – a business unit that is characterized by high growth and high market share.

Strategic alliances – when two or more separate organizations share some of their resources and capabilities but stop short of forming a separate organization.

Strategic business unit – is a distinct part of an organization which focuses upon a particular market or markets for its products and services.

Strategic change – the fit between an organization's resources and capabilities and its changing competitive environment.

Strategic drift – a situation in which the strategy being pursued by an organization becomes less relevant to the environment in which the organization competes.

Strategic group – a group of firms in an industry following the same or a similar strategy.

Strategic group analysis – identifying organizations within an industry that possess similar resource capabilities and are pursuing similar strategies.

Strategic inflection point – major changes in the way a company competes, such that simply adopting a new technology or competing in the same old way will be insufficient.

Strategy – the taking of decisions which allow an organisation to achieve a sustainable competitive advantage over the long term.

Strategy canvas – this captures the range of factors which the industry competes on and invests in; the critical success factors.

Structural uncertainties – where no probable pattern of outcomes can be derived from previous experience.

Support activities – are activities which ensure that the primary activities are carried out efficiently and effectively.

Sustainable competitive advantage – occurs when an organization is implementing a value-creating strategy that is not being implemented by competitors and when these competitors are unable to duplicate the benefits of this strategy.

Sustaining innovation – allows an organization to enhance the performance of its existing technology.

SWOT – refers to strengths, weaknesses, opportunities, and threats. Strengths are areas where the organization excels in comparison with its competitors. Weaknesses are areas where the organization may be at a comparative disadvantage. Opportunities and threats refer to the organization's external environment, over which the organization has much less control.

SWOT analysis – analysis of an organisation's strengths, weaknesses, opportunities, and threats.

Synergy – occurs when the total output from combining businesses is greater than the output of the businesses operating individually. It is often described mathematically as $2 + 2 = 5$.

T

Tacit knowledge – is defined as knowledge which is highly personal, hard to formalize and, therefore, difficult to communicate to others.

Tangible resources – refer to the physical assets that an organization possesses and include plant and machinery, finance, and human capital.

Theory E – assumes that organizational change should be based on enhancing shareholder value.

Theory O – assumes that change should help develop corporate culture and improve organizational capabilities.

Theory of the business – the assumptions that affect an organization's behaviour, the decisions about what and what not to do, which determine what an organization thinks are meaningful results.

Threshold capability – is the capability necessary for an organisation to be able to compete in the marketplace. In this respect, all competing organisations possess threshold capabilities; it is a prerequisite for competing in the industry.

Tipping point – an unexpected and unpredictable event that has a major impact on an organization's environment.

Transaction-cost analysis – implies that organizations should produce goods and services internally where the transaction costs of doing so is less than purchasing these on the open market.

Transferability – refers to the ease with which a competitor can access the resources and capabilities necessary to duplicate an incumbent's strategy.

Transformational leadership – is concerned with improving the performance of individuals and developing individuals to their fullest extent.

Transnational strategy – seeks to simultaneously achieve global efficiency, national responsiveness, and a worldwide leveraging of its innovations and learning.

U

Unknowables – where we cannot even imagine the event.

Unrelated or conglomerate diversification – a situation where an organization moves into a totally unrelated industry.

Valuable and rare – resources providing a means of competitive advantage. However, if the organization is to achieve sustainable competitive advantage, it is necessary that competing organizations cannot copy these resources.

Value chain – the activities within an organization that go to make up a product or service.

Value chain analysis – looks at the activities that go to make up a product or service with a view to ascertaining how much value each activity adds.

Value chain system – the relationship between the value chain activities of the organization and its suppliers, distributors, and consumers.

Value curve – a graphic representation of a company's relative performance across its industry's factors of competition.

Value innovation – occurs when organizations shift their focus from beating the competition to making the competition irrelevant by placing equal emphasis on both value and innovation.

Value net – a map of the competitive game, the players in the game, and their relationship to each other.

Value – the difference between the total value received by the organisation from the consumer for its product or service and the total cost of creating the product or service.

Vertical integration – occurs when an organization goes upstream, i.e. moves towards its inputs, or downstream, i.e. moves closer to its ultimate consumer.

Vision – is often associated with the founder of an organization and represents a desired state that the organization aspires to achieve in the future.

VRIO framework – *comprises valuable; rare; imitability;* and *organization*. The framework explains the extent to which these four attributes allow an organization's capabilities to achieve competitive or sustained competitive advantage.

Weak signals – barely perceptible changes in the external environment whose impact has yet to be felt.

Wholly owned subsidiary – where an organization seeks to have total control over its operations abroad.

Zero-sum game – competitors can only succeed at the expense of other players in the industry.

Name Index

Subject Index

W

Y

Z